CONSUMER REPORTS

COMPLETE GUIDE TO

HEALTH SERVICES

FOR SENIORS

Other books by Trudy Lieberman

Slanting the Story—The Forces That Shape the News
How to Plan for a Secure Retirement

Other books by CONSUMER REPORTS

The Consumer Reports Money Book
Consumer Reports Guide to Baby Products
Best Travel Deals
Best Buys for Your Home
Consumer Reports New Car Buying Guide
  and Other Buying Guides

CONSUMER REPORTS

COMPLETE GUIDE TO HEALTH SERVICES FOR SENIORS

WHAT YOUR FAMILY NEEDS TO KNOW ABOUT FINDING AND FINANCING

• MEDICARE • ASSISTED LIVING • NURSING HOMES •

HOME CARE • ADULT DAY CARE

WITH RATINGS OF MEDICARE HMOS AND SUPPLEMENTAL POLICIES

TRUDY LIEBERMAN

AND THE EDITORS OF

Consumer Reports

THREE RIVERS PRESS • NEW YORK

Published by Three Rivers Press, New York, New York.
Member of the Crown Publishing Group.

Random House, Inc. New York, Toronto, London, Sydney, Auckland
www.randomhouse.com

THREE RIVERS PRESS is a registered trademark and the Three Rivers Press
colophon is a trademark of Random House, Inc.

Consumer Reports is a registered trademark of Consumers Union of U.S., Inc.

Printed in the United States of America
Design by Robert Bull Design

Library of Congress Cataloging-in-Publication Data
Consumer reports complete guide to health services for seniors : what your
family needs to know about finding and financing *Medicare *asssisted living
*nursing homes *home care *adult day care *with ratings of Medicare HMOs
and supplemental policies / Trudy Lieberman and the editors of Consumer
Reports—1st ed.
p. cm.
1. Aged—Long-term care—United States. 2. Consumer education. I. Title:
Complete guide to health services for seniors. II. Lieberman, Trudy.
III. Consumer reports.
RA644.6 .C665 2000
362.1'6'0973—dc21   00-023453

ISBN 0-8129-3147-5

10 9 8 7 6 5 4 3 2 1

First Edition

For Beth, with deep gratitude and appreciation

—*Trudy Lieberman*

CONTENTS

APPENDICES

LIST OF WORKSHEETS AND TABLES

WORKSHEETS

TABLES

Consumers Union and CONSUMER REPORTS gratefully acknowledge the support of the Robert Wood Johnson Foundation and The Commonwealth Fund, philanthropic organizations interested in health care, for the development of this book.

This book began to take shape a decade ago when CONSUMER REPORTS started reporting on and rating health care services for the elderly. It is the culmination of many different survey and investigative reporting projects, each one building on the other to present the best information for seniors. Over the years, many people have contributed to the task of informing our elders and their families about the complicated and, at times, inscrutable options they face. Their help and insights are reflected in this book.

I am indebted to Irwin Landau, former editorial director of CONSUMER REPORTS and editor extraordinaire, who taught me how to handle complex material in a straightforward way without condescension or gimmickry; to actuaries John M. Bragg and Gordon R. Trapnell for their pioneering work in rating insurance products for the elderly; to Donna Yee of the National Asian Pacific Center on Aging; John Capitman of Brandeis University; Lisa McGiffert of Consumers Union's Southwest Regional Office; Bob Nichols of the California Health Insurance Counseling and Advocacy Program; Jane Basey of the Austin Grey Panthers; Virginia Fraser, Colorado's long-term-care ombudsman; Anne Hart, Washington, D.C.'s, long-term-care ombudsman; Karen Saliman, Fatima Haskell, and Jeanne Finberg, who spent many hours with me trudging through nursing homes and assisted-living facilities to learn what really goes on inside. To Trish Nemore of the National Senior Citizens Law Center, Jeanette Takamura, assistant secretary for aging, Department of Health and Human Services; Helene Fredeking of the Health Care Financing Administration; and Deborah Cloud of the American Association of Homes and Services for the Aging—who were always ready to help when I needed a question answered or required perspective on the big picture. To Mary Ann Larkin of Consumers Union's Information Center and Jana Abrams Karam for their assistance in compiling the tables on the various services available to seniors in the states; to

Roberta Tracy and Lennis Lyon of the California Health Insurance Counseling and Advocacy Program for their assistance in locating Medicare beneficiaries over the years from whom I learned so much.

A special thank-you goes to Bonnie Burns of the California Health Insurance Counseling and Advocacy Program for her many years of assistance to me and to Consumers Union—her help with several chapters in this book was invaluable. To Marge Frohne, my longtime secretary, who kept many pieces of this project on track; to Joan Daviet, my current secretary, who did the same; to Amy Wolfcale, formerly of Consumers Union's office of public information and now of the Markle Foundation, for her constant moral support; to Rosemary Gibson of the Robert Wood Johnson Foundation and Karen Davis, president of The Commonwealth Fund, for their faith in me, and to both foundations for their financial support for the ratings in this book and their belief that academic research could be translated for a lay audience; and especially to my husband and daughter, Andrew and Kirsten Eiler, for their willingness to live with boxes and boxes of research materials and for giving up precious family time so this book could be completed.

Above all, my deepest appreciation goes to my assistant Beth Peppe, who spent countless hours devising ratings, reading copy, traveling with me to so many long-term-care facilities, supplying hundreds of good ideas, and counseling me on the many tangled issues that are part and parcel of long-term care. She helped me skirt every obstacle that was thrown in our way. This book is for her.

—*Trudy Lieberman*

FOREWORD

Modern old age is a triumph of the twentieth century. As the new century unfolds, an older population is changing the face of the United States. The added years of life will have lasting effects on society, touching everything from family and community life to productivity, public resource allocation, and health.

People are living longer and are healthier than ever. Many are able to stay active well into their later years. In the span of one century, the average life expectancy in the United States jumped from forty-seven to seventy-six years. By 2030, one-fifth of the population will be sixty-five and older. Approximately 70,000 centenarians are alive today. By the end of the twenty-first century, about five million people will be one hundred years of age and older.

We have only to look at the last three hundred years of our country's history to see just how far we've come. Around the time of the American Revolution (1775–1783), colonists could expect to live to age thirty-five, and only 2 percent of the population lived to sixty-five. In 1900 the life expectancy for most Americans was forty-seven. By 1999 the average life expectancy at birth had jumped to 76.5, and a full 80 percent of all deaths occurred after age sixty-five.

An expanded life expectancy is the result of many factors. Progress in medical care in the past fifty years and advances in nutrition have contributed to lengthening life expectancy, as have decreased maternal, childhood, and infant mortality rates and a reduction in late-life mortality. In the future, gene-based medicine will utilize the human genome project to counter both genetic diseases and other diseases in which genes, through their protein products, play a pathogenic role. Scientists may find ways to slow the aging process itself.

We have many reasons to celebrate. Here are a few:

- In a recent study sponsored by the International Longevity Center and the National Council on the Aging, conducted by Harris-Interactive, nearly half of Americans age sixty-five and older described their lives as "the best years of my life," and 84 percent said they would be happy if they lived to be ninety.

- Statistics show that disability rates are decreasing despite the aging of the population.
- Four-generation families are becoming common for the first time in history.
- People expect to live longer. As a consequence, they are becoming more attentive to both health habits and financial planning that will sustain them over a longer period of time.
- A number of industries, among them health care, pharmaceutical, financial planning, tourist, and recreation, are reaping enormous financial rewards from the new markets that have arisen as a result of the increasing numbers of older persons.
- Finally, increased longevity is inspiring consideration of such philosophical questions as to what end and purpose longevity, and what are the responsibilities that go along with old age?

However, as we all know, growing old in America today is cause for some concern. Society as a whole is unprepared for the major economic, social, medical, and legal implications of an older population.

Older people continue to suffer because of social prejudice, loneliness, lack of purpose, and financial worries. Social and emotional turmoil cause depression and despair, which, in turn, compound the effects of physical illness.

The aging population highlights society's dread of growing old, becoming dependent, and of dying and death. Our anxiety creates prejudice against older persons so we may distance ourselves from certain realities of late life. In 1968 I coined the term *ageism*, and, unfortunately, the word has not yet become obsolete.

As people live longer, incidences of disease and disability increase. According to the Administration on Aging, in 1997, older people accounted for 36 percent of all hospital stays and 49 percent of all days of care in hospitals. Many conditions, such as heart disease, cancer, stroke, diabetes, and Alzheimer's disease, occur more frequently in the population of old people.

Persons over eighty-five represent the fastest-growing population. Many are frail and suffer from multiple, chronic conditions. In fact, the average annual health bill for persons over eighty-five is nearly six times as high as that for persons ages nineteen to sixty-four. They are most likely to need a variety of specialized medical care. This population also manifests the highest rates of Alzheimer's disease and other forms of senile dementia.

In recent years the costs of nursing home care have risen more dramatically than any other component of health care. They are the result, in large measure, of care for patients with Alzheimer's disease and other forms of dementia. Few diseases have as great a personal, social, and economic impact. They rob the mind, devastate the family, and increase the claims made upon the health and social care systems.

By age seventy-five most adults have three or more medical conditions, both chronic and acute. Diseases present differently in the old from the way they present in younger adults. Unfortunately, American doctors, nurses, social workers, and other health care providers currently lack the training they need to provide appropriate care to the older population.

Of the 2.56 million registered nurses in the United States, less than 1 percent are certified in geriatrics. Only 3,900 out of 111,000 advanced practice nurses (3.5 percent) are certified geriatric nurse practitioners.

It is estimated that we need 13,000 doctors with sufficient training in geriatrics. The Alliance for Aging Research estimates that currently there are less than six hundred physicians who have the combination of medical, academic, and scientific training to teach geriatrics to medical students and residents. This shortage is a critical issue in health care.

Health care costs will continue to escalate unless new paths are forged in appropriate prevention, diagnosis, and treatment. Research is needed that will focus on developing more effective and affordable treatment modalities. We need to know more about the basic biological changes that occur with aging, and the diseases associated with the aging process. This information will contribute to the development of more effective and affordable care. Such research should include molecular and cellular factors most responsible for aging in human beings; the role of the environment and diet in how people age; the role of genetics in aging; hormonal, metabolic, and immune factors in aging; why diseases such as diabetes and Alzheimer's disease occur with greater frequency in the older population. Health service research also needs to be conducted.

It has been said that a society can be judged by the way it treats its children and its old people. One of the myths in America is that the family does not care for its aging family members. In fact, studies show that the family is the number-one caregiver of older persons. Older people and their children need access to information so that informed decisions can be made.

Trudy Lieberman and the editors of CONSUMER REPORTS provide an extremely valuable guide for everyone who is attempting to navigate through the maze of decisions that need to be made regarding Medicare and insurance options, chronic care, assisted living, continuing-care retirement communities, home care, nursing home care, and end-of-life hospice services.

By 2030 and thereafter, one of five Americans will be over sixty-five. Clearly, a great deal of work needs to be done if we and the generations that follow us in the twenty-first century and beyond are to enjoy the fruits of longevity.

—Robert N. Butler, M.D., president
of the International Longevity Center
and professor of geriatrics at the
Mount Sinai Medical Center

The United States has no national policy on aging. We have no policy on how we will pay for our elders' care; we have few standards for the quality of care that is currently delivered; we feel no collective urgency to treat our oldest citizens with compassion and dignity. We don't, for example, have a national holiday like Japan's Respect for the Aging Day. Says author Mary Pipher, whose book *Another Country: the Emotional Terrain of Aging* explores the psychological dimensions of growing old: "In America we are xenophobic toward our old people."

The cover of an issue of the *Harvard Political Review* pictures an old man with the words *The Enemy?* written in big red letters across his chest. A prominent academic writes a paper called "Can America Afford Its Elderly Citizens?" A story in a think tank publication carries the headline "Geezer Boom." Such sentiments reflect the low regard we have for our elders, which is unheard of elsewhere in the world.

In the United States we revere a culture of youth; we fail to celebrate the longevity of life that technology has made possible. We applaud the snazziest machine and hype the latest "wonder" drug that enables us to live longer, yet at the same time we ignore the basics of food and transportation that make it possible for the elderly to enjoy that extended life. What can loosely be construed as a policy on aging means impoverishing and institutionalizing our elders if they are to receive any kind of public support. It means shifting the burden of care to families, which really means to women. "Public policy in long-term care is not strategic," says Eddie Rivas, formerly director of home- and community-based services at the American Association of Homes and Services for the Aging. "It's always in emergency mode."

In 1963, President John F. Kennedy, quoting the historian Arnold Toynbee, noted in a special message to Congress that "a society's quality and durability can best be measured 'by the respect and care given its elderly citizens.'" Yet only a generation later we tolerate abuse of the elderly residing in the nation's nursing homes; we accept food rationing for seniors on waiting lists for home-delivered meals; we condone the lack of adequate support systems so older people can stay in their communities. And as many adult children know, we put up with the fragmented, inhumane system of care that is a nightmare to navigate when trying to find services for an aged parent who is slipping away. We postpone thinking and planning for our later life as if long-term care and death were options we could pick and choose like a vacation spot or a car.

In the absence of a national policy, resources are directed almost by default to nursing homes—the most expensive place seniors end up living. The payment mechanism, in reality a patchwork of financial options from the federal government, states, and municipalities, drives the system and determines what kind of care seniors receive. Matching services can be like putting a square peg in a round hole. Too often people get services based not on what they need but on who will pay the bill. Elders reside in nursing homes in order to receive public funds from Medicaid when, in fact, they would be better off at home or in day care. But if they can't pay for home or day care, and the county where they live has no program that pays for the kinds of services they need, a nursing home becomes the only option. "It's all about money, not health care," says Paula Wilson, associate professor of the practice of public policy at Columbia University.

The American system of long-term care lacks a "single entry point"—a central place in local communities where someone who needs care can be evaluated objectively and directed to the right services. We don't even have a coordinated system of multiple entry points to determine the various types of care needed and to then channel people quickly to the appropriate agencies for help. These serious flaws in our social fabric produce disastrous consequences. In New York City, two elderly malnourished women both in their late eighties called agency after agency looking for someone to bring them food. It took nearly six months of searching the Yellow Pages, getting referrals, and getting nowhere before they connected to Citymeals-on-Wheels. When food finally arrived, one woman weighed eighty pounds; the other ninety. Their story is not uncommon.

No less a figure in the business of long-term care than Eli Feldman, president of the Metropolitan Jewish Health System in New York City, had trouble finding end-of-life care for his ailing mother who was living in Florida. "I was as blind as everyone else," said

Feldman. "Here I was, a person with thirty years of experience in the field. Even the selection of a hospice wasn't what I would have liked." His story too is common.

For those of us baby boomers seeking care for our parents, the task is daunting. "I'm amazed at how totally helpless people feel when they enter the long-term-care system," says Trish Nemore, a lawyer with the National Senior Citizens Law Center. "People are looking for a process as much as information. They want to know 'How do I go about this?'"

This book tells how to go about the business of finding long-term care for a loved one, made all the more urgent because people live longer with chronic illnesses and their children are often far away. It will answer such commonly asked questions as:

- How much does it cost to be in a nursing home?
- How much money can my parent keep and still qualify for Medicaid?
- What's the difference between a nursing home and assisted living?
- How much does home care cost?
- How do I find a good home care worker?
- Will Medicare pay for a nursing home?
- Can I buy long-term-care insurance for my father who has Alzheimer's disease?
- How does day care work?

I hope this book will be a kind of substitute for what our national leaders have so far failed to give us—a coordinated passageway into long-term care and a simple health care system that addresses our everyday medical concerns. Chapters offer a process and a strategy for negotiating the health care system, as well as support for caregivers and potential caregivers who are lost in a tangle of bureaucracy. The long-term-care section guides readers through the steps of entering the system and offers specifics on home care, care in the community, nursing homes, assisted living, and hospice care. They give practical advice and explain where and how people can obtain services as their medical needs change with advancing age.

Our system of paying for acute care—the medical services people need for everyday illnesses—is just as difficult to negotiate. In Santa Clara, California, sixty-seven-year-old Bob Harrington referred to his wife's kidney transplant as his "insurance adventure." But the process of finding and paying for care was no joke as he parried denials from managed-care companies, agonized over how to pay for the drugs his wife needed after the transplant, and scrambled for new coverage after their HMO pulled out of the county. There are thousands of Bob Harringtons across the country.

Medicare beneficiaries have never understood the program that has paid for most of their care since 1965. Sellers of insurance products exploiting the system have sometimes victimized the elderly, selling too much supplemental insurance or the wrong kind. Now, as Congress has heaped even more complexity onto beneficiaries through the provisions of the 1997 Balanced Budget Act, the task of covering their health care needs has become far more difficult—and likewise, the task of their children who are called on to help. It is indeed paradoxical that at a time in their lives when seniors need the most help and support, they are asked to make difficult choices about the most important thing to them—their health.

In focus groups conducted for the Health Care Financing Administration, which runs the Medicare program, one participant noted: "I think at this time it's kind of scary to have to figure out how to make these decisions. As we get older, we get short-circuited. It's very complicated to figure out what to do for your own self. With the complicated system that we have, it's not easy to make these decisions." Another participant observed: "I'm foggy enough when I'm well; where would I be under the kinds of conditions where I might not even be functioning?" Chapters on Medicare and covering the gaps in Medicare are intended to lift some of the fog and guide people through the process of obtaining and paying for insurance for their acute health care needs.

Brand-name Ratings—CONSUMER REPORTS's stock-in-trade for more than sixty years—are a unique aspect of this book. In the appendices we note which are the best options in thirty cities for covering the gaps in Medicare, evaluating both HMOs and traditional Medicare-supplement policies. And if you don't live in one of those cities, we tell you how to devise your own strategy for selecting supplemental insurance coverage or an HMO. There's a "watch list" for your state that tells which nursing homes have the most problems. We also offer a guide to how well your state detects problems in nursing homes. If you live in a state with weak detection, you must be extra vigilant if you have a relative in a facility. And if you or your parents are thinking about buying long-term-care insurance, the guide to long-term-care policies should be helpful. If you or your relative already have such a policy, we tell you how to use it to pay for care.

This book is designed as a one-stop shopping compendium for adult children to use in planning for the health care needs of their parents or for seniors themselves to use in preparing for their last years. It draws on my experience over the last decade covering issues important to the elderly, and on the lessons I have learned as a journalist who has presented information to consumers for more than thirty years. The long-term-care system in the United States is incredibly complex. I hope this book alleviates some of the difficulty of the task of finding good care and makes the journey over the terrain somewhat less bumpy.

PART 1

PAYING FOR HEALTH CARE SERVICES

Medicare pays the doctor and hospital bills for some 39 million elderly and disabled Americans. There is nothing simple about the system, from the way doctors are paid to the choices beneficiaries have for supplementing their coverage. Beneficiaries have never understood Medicare, and sellers of insurance coverage have made the program more complicated with myriad policies they have sold through the years to cover the gaps in Medicare's coverage.

Anyone trying to help an elderly relative with health care must understand what Medicare does and does not pay for as well as the various options for filling in Medicare's gaps. Seniors who are trying to understand their options will also find this section helpful.

ONE

When Your Loved One Needs Care— Starting the Process

Paula G. understands the financial burden of caring for an aging parent. She currently pays $4,000 a month to keep her eighty-eight-year-old mother in an independent living unit at a continuing care retirement community (CCRC) where she has lived for the past nine years. "I'm using all my savings to pay it," says Paula, the president of a large nonprofit organization. "It's an amazing financial drain."

Her mother didn't start out needing help. She and her husband moved into the community when the monthly payment was only $3,000, which they could comfortably afford on his retirement income—a pension plus Social Security. A few years after they moved in, her husband became ill and needed to go to a nursing home, where he stayed for twenty-eight months until he died. He started out paying the $5,000-a-month nursing home bill with his savings. But within a year, the money was gone, and he turned to Medicaid to pay the bills. Before Medicaid stepped in, Paula's parents were spending $8,000 a month for living arrangements and care.

After her father died, Paula's mother was left with only a small Social Security check—$600 a month—to live on, hardly enough to stay in the CCRC. Paula had to supplement her mother's income so she could continue living in the retirement community where the monthly fees have been increasing at an annual rate of 10 to 12 percent. Her mother, who has severe arthritis, now requires a home health aide two or three hours each day to help her bathe, dress, shop, and go outside. Paula was paying $500 a month for these services until someone told her about the limited number of Medicaid home care slots available in the county where her mother lives. After three months on a waiting list, Paula's mother was eligible for Medicaid funds to pay for the home aides she needed.

When her parents traveled down the path of CCRC living, Paula says, they didn't think ahead to the financial "what ifs"—who pays when one spouse needs a nursing home and the other lives at home with a chronic illness that requires daily care; what kind of income will the surviving spouse have when the partner in the nursing home dies; who pays for his or her care? "I should have thought a lot more about these things," Paula says.

Paula spends a lot of money to care for her mother, and her mother is lucky Paula can pay for the care and housing that she needs. Many older adults are not so fortunate. Yet they need help, too. Unfortunately, a gap often exists between the kind of help children think they are providing and the assistance their parents need. A survey by the American Association of Retired Persons (AARP) found that more than one-third of elderly adults say that their grown children failed to help them. At the same time, only 16 percent of adult children agreed that they did not offer any help; most said they did. Although some 20 percent of grown children report that they "are there for their parents," 89 percent of aging parents surveyed disagreed.

It may be hard for adult children to understand when their mothers and fathers need assistance. How can you know, for example, if your parents are having trouble paying for prescription drugs, or if your mother can no longer shop and cook? You won't know unless they tell you, and odds are they won't. All too often parents are not forthcoming about the help they need. Few older people ask for assistance, especially when they sense their ability to function is declining and the prospect of losing independence looms ahead.

The reality is that more and more people will need care in old age, and their children are likely to be their caregivers. Most people can expect to live a long time with chronic illness. Nearly 100 million Americans suffer from a chronic illness, and for more than 40 million people these illnesses limit their daily activities. A study by the Robert Wood Johnson Foundation (one of the funders of this book) noted that millions of those with chronic illnesses also had health and social needs that were unfilled.

4

It's not uncommon to live twenty years with Parkinson's disease or twelve to fifteen years with Alzheimer's disease, and during that time, care needs change. In the early stages of dementia, for instance, a person may need help at home with activities of daily living, such as bathing, dressing, and using the bathroom; in the middle stages, when severe behavioral changes occur, there may be a need for caretakers who can manage difficult behaviors; in the later stages, when a person loses weight and can't eat, nursing home care may be a certainty.

During the years of chronic illness or after a sudden illness, millions of adult children will be called on to act in some capacity as caregivers. Some 25 percent of adults over forty are already juggling home, their own children, and acting as caregivers for their parents. The number of family caregivers has tripled in the past ten years, with two-thirds of them in the workforce balancing jobs as well. Twenty-two million, or nearly one-quarter of all households in the United States, have at least one person who is performing caregiving tasks, and most of them are women. (The typical caregiver is a forty-six-year-old woman who spends eighteen hours a week caring for her mother.) The health system depends on family caregiving, says Dr. Carroll Estes, a professor at the Institute for Health and Aging at the University of California at San Francisco. "It saves the government money and solves a problem, at the expense of women."

Caregiving is difficult no matter who does it. Often spouses who care for their husbands or wives don't even recognize that they are giving care. "Spouses tend to get worn out tremendously," says Stacey Guthrie, health services administrator at Collington Episcopal Life Care Community in Mitchellville, Maryland. "They tend to hang in there forever and just wear down." It's an understatement to say that caregiving brings on health problems, deteriorating family life, and mounting expenses. In 1997, CONSUMER REPORTS surveyed its readers who were responsible for the long-term care of a family member and found that 17 percent of them paid more than $5,000 between 1992 and 1997 for a relative's care. The magazine also found that about half of the relatives who needed care had annual incomes of less than $12,000. Only 7 percent had incomes of $50,000 or more. Although the survey was not a representative national sample, those figures underscore how little money most seniors have to pay for their care. Carol Levine, director of the families and health care project at the United Hospital Fund in New York City, told the Senate Select Committee on Aging: "Middle-class families who thought they had comprehensive insurance are being impoverished by caregiving, since much of what they need at home is not deemed 'medically necessary' by insurers or falls under the unreimbursable category of 'custodial care.'"

DEFINING LONG-TERM CARE

"When you say long-term care to people, they haven't a clue what it is," says Bonnie Burns, an insurance consultant with the California Health Insurance Counseling and Advocacy Program. "If they have any recognition at all, a nursing home comes to mind." But long-term care encompasses far more than nursing homes. It can be as simple as helping an elder balance a checkbook and installing handrails in the bathtub, or it can be as complex as feeding a nursing home resident through a special tube. No two people start the journey through the long-term-care system in quite the same place. Where families start depends on the kind of frailty your relative has experienced.

Some people experience physical or functional frailty—that is, they cannot perform some of the activities of daily living, such as eating, bathing, or dressing. Others have cognitive impairments caused by dementia or Alzheimer's disease. Still others suffer from medical frailty; they may be in the late stages of a chronic illness such as congestive heart failure or diabetes. These people can still live at home but need substantial help. Some people suffer multiple kinds of frailty that require different kinds of care.

Although families start from different places, sooner or later they all meet at the intersection of Medicare, the system that pays for health care for the elderly, and the myriad payment arrangements for long-term care that literally differ from county to county.

At that juncture, the realization sets in that Medicare may stop paying the bills and that long-term care is not covered. To understand how the two systems work, suppose, for example, that your father suffers a stroke and is left paralyzed on one side. He stays in the hospital for a couple of weeks, and Medicare pays for the care and all pharmaceuticals used while he is there. Afterward, he goes to a rehabilitation center for a month, and Medicare pays for the skilled-nursing care and for the physical and speech therapy he requires. When he goes home, the payments stop, but his need for care continues. He needs help dressing, bathing, and cutting food, and he requires new drugs to help prevent more strokes. Medicare does not pay for the drugs, though it will pay for a personal care aide as long as your father continues to need skilled-nursing care. After he no longer needs skilled care, he is on his own for personal care and will either have to pay out of pocket or find some kind of public assistance to pay for the care he needs.

STICKER SHOCK

The gaps in understanding the cost of health care for their parents are as wide as the gulf between the needs parents have and their children's perceptions of them. "Most people don't think about the money it will take to pay for health care in retirement," says Jeanette Takamura, assistant secretary for aging at the Department of Health and Human Services. Ask the typical person what long-term care costs, and most likely they will underestimate the amount. Ask the typical person what Medicare covers, and they'll say everything, not realizing that Medicare pays only 55 percent of an elderly person's health care expenses. "It takes a long time for a family to realize that Medicare isn't going to help them," says Jean Marx, director of the Alzheimer's Association in New York City.

Sooner or later families experience health care sticker shock. Long-term care can cost far more than $1,000 a month. The average nursing home costs upwards of $3,000 a month. Day care can run $3,000 to $4,000 each month, and assisted-living facilities can cost even more, especially if a person needs a lot of help with daily activities. Even home care, often touted as being cheaper than institutional care, is not always so cheap. As the family profiled at the beginning of Chapter 7 learned, home care can be more expensive than nursing home care. For families who can't pay the price, getting care may mean relying on the public system and impoverishing your relative and his or her spouse. It may mean getting the wrong kind of help, or it could mean draining your own bank account as Paula G. was doing.

PLANNING IN ADVANCE

Caregivers can't change the going price of care. But they can better understand the system and its limitations, and make choices and trade-offs within it. The first step in assisting an older adult is to know what he or she is spending for health care, arguably the largest budget item for many seniors. To start the process of finding care, it is essential to understand your parents' financial situation long before they need any kind of care, and to understand what will happen to the family income when one parent dies. Nineteen percent of all elderly widows live in poverty, and most became poor when their husbands died.

Statistics paint a pretty grim picture of what elders are up against when it comes to covering their health care needs. Fifty-four percent of Medicare beneficiaries have annual incomes of less than $15,000; 67 percent have incomes less than $21,000. On average, elders spend about $2,600 a year on copayments, deductibles, premiums, and prescription drugs. It's not uncommon for many seniors to spend one-half to one-third of their income on prescription drugs.

Income declines as people age, and health expenses increase, leaving elders between the proverbial rock and a hard place. The percentage of Medicare beneficiaries who can afford a Medicare-supplement policy shows how hard it is for some elders to keep up with increases in health care expenses. Among "younger" beneficiaries—those sixty-five to sixty-nine—some 24 percent did not own a Medigap policy to supplement the government's insurance program. Among those eighty-five and older, 33 percent had no additional coverage, most likely because they couldn't afford it.

TALKING ABOUT MONEY

Advance planning, however, involves talking about money, a discussion many older adults prefer to avoid. Look for opportune moments to bring up the subject. For example, if you are buying long-term-care insurance, you might ask if your parents have bought a policy, or if they have thought about how they will cover those expenses. If it's tax time, ask the person who prepares their tax returns if they need help. Sometimes the death of a relative or close friend prompts a family discussion about money matters in later life.

You can also use the worksheet on page 9. Help your relative fill it out. You will learn how much they are spending to cover Medicare's gaps and whether you should be looking at less expensive options, which are explained in Chapter 4. If your mother is spending $1,200

WORKSHEET 1: Figuring Your Parents' Health Care Expenses

Use the following worksheet to inventory what your parents are now spending for health care. This information can help you plan for their eventual long-term care.

Annual Income

Social Security	$ _____
Employer-provided pension	_____
Investment income	_____
Income from current employment	_____
TOTAL	_____

Annual Health Care Expenses

Medicare Part B premium	$546 (for everyone in 2000)
Medicare-supplement premium	_____
or HMO premium	_____
or premium for retiree health coverage from employer	_____
Out-of-pocket prescription drugs	_____
Other expenses	
Part B deductible	$100 (for everyone in 2000)[1]
Balance bills from non-participating doctors	_____
Part A deductible	$776 (for everyone in 2000)[2]
Other	_____
Long-term-care policy premium	_____
Length of benefit	_____ years
Inflation protection	yes/no, what kind
Assisted-living coverage	yes/no
Home care coverage	yes/no
Amount of benefit	_____
TOTAL	_____
Health expenses as a percentage of income	_____ %

[1]May be covered by HMO or Medicare-supplement policy.

[2]May be covered by HMO or Medicare-supplement policy.

a year for a Medicare-supplement policy that does not pay for prescription drugs, and she is having trouble paying for her medications, maybe she should consider an HMO that covers part of those expenses.

The worksheet will also show you whether your parents have purchased a long-term-care policy. If they have, the policy is the first place you should look for payment when the need for care arises. (Chapter 14 tells you how to use the policy.) If your parents don't have such a policy, you can figure out whether they have enough income to purchase one and whether they can afford the rate increases that are likely to come in later years. Many elderly people living on fixed incomes cannot pay those increases. If they have a health condition that's likely to land them in a nursing home in the near future, it's probably too late to buy one anyway. If there is no long-term-care policy in place, you would first look to their savings to pay for services, and then finally to Medicaid.

The worksheet will also show what they are spending for prescription drugs. If they are having trouble paying for them, look to sources of assistance outlined in Appendices C and D.

Knowing your parents' income will also help you in discussing their situation with social workers and other agency personnel who might be in a position to help you find services. As the following chapters point out, eligibility for many public services is related to income. Being fully knowledgeable will enable you to use the chapters that follow more effectively, since so much of the care elders receive depends on what they are able to pay.

KEY DECISION POINTS

1. Consider how much health care your mother or father can afford when your other parent dies. Will there be enough income for prescription drugs and to pay insurance premiums, or will the potential decrease in income mean your parent will have to choose between food and medicine or between the electric bill and medicine?

2. You must understand your parents' finances in order to help them. To that end, find out the names and phone numbers of the health care providers who treat them—doctors,

dentists, pharmacists, psychologists, and so forth. You should also know which managed-care plan they belong to or who the carrier is for their Medicare-supplement insurance or long-term-care policy. Find out what medications they are taking—dosages, prices, the names of pharmacies that dispense the drugs they use, and which alternative or generic drugs might be cheaper.

TWO

Understanding Medicare

When Norman Burns, who runs a small machine-tool business in California, turned sixty-five, he found that his expenses for health insurance dropped dramatically. Burns, as a self-employed person, had carried an individual health insurance policy from Blue Cross. He paid $328 a month for coverage through a Blue Cross–preferred provider organization, a type of managed care. The policy came with a $500 deductible for outpatient care, a $500 deductible for each hospitalization, and 20 percent coinsurance for each visit he made to the doctor. "Everywhere you looked there was a deductible," Burns said. "In a normal year Blue Cross rarely paid anything."

Until he turned sixty-five, Burns could not switch carriers to get a cheaper policy; his diabetes made him persona non grata at other insurance companies. As soon as he signed up for Medicare, his out-of-pocket costs for health insurance dropped to $149 a month—$45.50 for the Part B premium and $103.50 for the premium for his Medicare-supplement policy. "Medicare lowered my stress level," says his wife. "The potential for being impoverished by medical costs has now been reduced."

Like millions of seniors, Burns is far better off under Medicare than he was paying for health insurance out of his own pocket. Yet while he knows the program is indisputably a very good financial deal for him, he has only the vaguest sense of how it works. Indeed, ask any senior how he or she gets health care, and the answer inevitably will be "Medicare." But ask how it works, and the answers will be vague or perhaps elicit an "I don't really know" response. The program, which began in 1965, has always been hard for beneficiaries to understand. Little about the program is straightforward, from the way doctors are paid to the amounts beneficiaries must pay. Benefits are similarly difficult to comprehend.

Medicare was never intended to cover the entire cost of an elderly person's health care. Beneficiaries pay their share of the costs through premiums, deductibles, coinsurance, and excess charges. The Balanced Budget Act passed by Congress in 1997 has not made things any easier. The 39 million beneficiaries now face more choices in supplementing their Medicare coverage, which makes it all the more important that people receiving or about to receive Medicare understand how the system works.

The Balanced Budget Act will also slow the growth in Medicare spending over time, although program expenditures will continue to grow perhaps faster than the rate of inflation. The Act limits the rate of increase in payments to medical providers, sharply increases the premiums beneficiaries must pay, and authorizes a number of options that will begin to shift more of the financial burden to those receiving care.

It's not inconceivable that beneficiaries, who already pay on average $2,600 for deductibles, coinsurance, and premiums, will have to pay even more as the years go by. This chapter focuses on how Medicare currently works; Chapter 3 discusses how to navigate the Medicare system in the future.

MEDICARE BASICS

Medicare is composed of two parts: Part A, which covers hospital services, and Part B, which covers outpatient hospital services, physicians' services, laboratory charges, and medical equipment such as hospital beds and wheelchairs. Each part has its own rules and cost-sharing arrangements. Under Part A, Medicare's prospective payments for hospital inpatient care are designed to cover all of the costs for medically necessary services with the exception of a deductible. Under Part B, Medicare pays 80 percent of what it determines to be the "allowable charge" for most physicians' services, outpatient hospital services, and supplies.

The portion of the allowed charge not paid by Medicare is called "coinsurance" and is paid by the beneficiary. Beneficiaries also pay "deductibles," amounts they must pay before Medicare benefits begin. Coinsurance and deductibles are adjusted each year to account for rising costs. If a physician does not "accept Medicare," beneficiaries may also pay "excess charges"—that is, an amount above Medicare's *allowable charge* that physicians may bill to beneficiaries—a practice called "balance billing." Congress has limited excess charges to 15 percent more than the allowable charge. As a practical matter, most doctors don't find it worth their while to balance bill for excess charges anymore. The following sections explain in more depth the particulars of Parts A and B.

Part A Coverage: Hospital Services

Acute care For the first sixty days you are in a hospital in each benefit period, Medicare pays your entire bill except for a deductible, which in 2000 is $776. A "benefit period" begins when you enter the hospital and ends when you've not used any Part A benefits for sixty consecutive days. If you are hospitalized for, say, fifteen days, discharged, then readmitted twenty days later, you are still in the same benefit period and don't have to pay the deductible again.

If you are hospitalized longer, you pay coinsurance for each of the next thirty days you are in the hospital. In 2000, that amount is $194 per day. If your stay exceeds ninety days, you can use your lifetime reserve days—each beneficiary gets sixty additional lifetime reserve days to use for long hospitalizations—and pay a daily copayment, $388 in 2000. Once you have used your reserve days, however, they are gone forever. And if you're unfortunate enough to have a very long hospitalization, and have used up those reserve days, you'll be responsible for the charges. The hospital automatically uses your reserve days for extended stays unless you request in writing that they not be used. Medicare pays nothing if you are hospitalized longer than 150 days in any benefit period. These days most people don't use their lifetime reserve days. However, sometimes patients on ventilators do.

For Medicare to pay your hospital bills, a doctor must prescribe the care, and the care must be given in a hospital that participates in Medicare (almost all do).

Medicare picks up the tab for most hospital expenses, including the cost of a semiprivate room, lab tests, X-rays, nursing services, meals, drugs provided by the hospital, medical supplies, appliances, and the cost of operating and recovery rooms. Telephones and televisions are not covered, neither is the cost of private-duty nurses or private rooms unless they are medically necessary.

If you need blood, Medicare pays the entire cost of replacing the blood, but only after you have used three pints. The blood deductible applies for each benefit period (you must pay for the first three pints).

Skilled-nursing care Medicare imposes strict eligibility requirements for these benefits. It pays only if care is provided in a Medicare-approved facility, a doctor certifies that such care is needed daily, and you have been in a hospital for at least three days prior to needing skilled-nursing care. For the first twenty days in a skilled-nursing facility, Medicare picks up 100 percent of the cost of a semiprivate room, meals, nursing services, medical supplies, and appliances. For stays lasting longer, you must pay coinsurance for days twenty-one to one hundred. In 2000, that amount is $97 per day. If you require skilled-nursing care for longer than one hundred days, you must pay out of your own pocket or with the proceeds from a long-term-care policy (see Chapter 14). Don't count on Medicare paying much of your bill for skilled-nursing care, especially if you need it for a long time.

Home health care There are strict eligibility rules for home health benefits, and they may get even stricter. Medicare pays if care is provided by a Medicare-certified home health care agency, you require intermittent skilled-nursing care or physical or speech therapy, a doctor orders and regularly reviews such care, and you are homebound. Medicare, however, does not consider a hospital or a nursing facility to be a beneficiary's home, and will not pay home health benefits if someone is confined in those places. It is not clear whether Medicare will pay for home health care if your relative lives in an assisted-living facility.

As long as you need what are considered "skilled" nursing services, you may qualify for Medicare home health benefits. Chapter 7 discusses home care and how to receive Medicare home health benefits. To qualify for that benefit, the needed service must be so complex that it can only be safely and effectively performed under the supervision of professional or technical personnel. If you qualify for this kind of care, Medicare will pay for physical, occupational, or speech therapy; medical social services; home health aides; medical supplies; and durable medical equipment, such as hospital beds and oxygen tanks.

Contrary to what you may have heard, in some circumstances Medicare *does* cover some services provided by home health aides that are considered to be personal or custodial in nature, such as help with bathing, dressing, or getting in and out of bed when you receive skilled care. Note, however, that Medicare *does not* cover home-delivered meals, transportation, housekeeping, and personal-chore services. If you need that kind of help, you should contact the area agency on aging in your locality. Appendix B can tell you how to find the State Unit on Aging, which will tell you how to locate the agency in your area. You may be eligible for those services under the federal Older Americans Act (see Appendix K).

The Balanced Budget Act of 1997 also limits the amount of home health care you can receive. The law restricts skilled-nursing and home health aide services to a combination of less than eight hours per day and a maximum of twenty-eight hours a week. Furthermore, each agency providing these services will be reimbursed a set amount for each patient regardless of medical need. It's hard to say what these restrictions will mean for care in the long run.

Hospice care A hospice is a facility that provides inpatient, outpatient, and home care for the terminally ill. Unlike hospitals, hospices do not try to cure patients but instead focus on counseling, symptom control, and pain reduction. To qualify, you must have Part A, your doctor and the hospice must agree that you have less than six months to live, and you must agree in writing that you are giving up standard Medicare benefits for your terminal illness and treatments for curing the illness.

Hospice benefits last 210 days. Medicare usually does not pay for round-the-clock care, and the amount it covers will depend on how sick you are. When Medicare pays, it covers all expenses for nursing and doctor services, supplies, appliances, social services, counseling, and home health and homemaker services in Medicare-approved hospices. As part of the hospice benefit, Medicare also pays 5 percent of the cost of outpatient drugs or $5 toward each prescription, whichever is less. Chapter 12 explains more about hospice care.

Inpatient psychiatric care Medicare pays the entire cost for inpatient care, less the yearly hospital deductible. Coverage is limited to 190 days for your lifetime.

Part B Coverage: Medical Services

For most Part B services, Medicare pays 80 percent of the allowable charge. You pay the remaining 20 percent. You are also responsible for paying the annual deductible—the first $100 of your medical bills each year—before Medicare starts paying for Part B services. Be aware that this amount is likely to increase over the years. You can meet the deductible requirement in one doctor's visit or by using a combination of services.

The allowable charge Understanding how Medicare figures allowable charges is central to understanding your coverage under Part B. When a doctor submits a Medicare claim, the claim goes to an insurance company under contract to Medicare to process claims. This company, known as the carrier, determines the allowable charge for the service you need. The allowable charge is whatever is smaller: the doctor's actual charge or a set fee determined by Medicare. In 1992, Medicare began paying doctors according to a national fee schedule based on the relative value of the services performed. The effect of this fee schedule has been to compensate general practitioners more fairly and to reduce fees to more highly paid specialists, such as radiologists and ophthalmologists. (Medicare determines the value of each service by calculating the amount of work, overhead costs, and malpractice insurance expenses needed to provide the service.)

Excess charges Medicare gives doctors the option of accepting the allowable charge based on the fee schedule as payment in full or requiring you to pay the difference between the allowable and the actual charge. That gap, as noted on page 14, is called an excess charge, and the doctor who requires patients to pay it is said to engage in balanced billing. However, doctors can charge no more than 15 percent above the allowable charge. The following example shows how this works:

1. Medicare's allowable charge: $100
2. Federal limit is 115 percent of allowable charge
3. Multiply 115 percent × $100 (1.15 × $100): $115
4. Total doctor can charge: $115

Medicare pays 80 percent of the allowable charge—in this example, $80. You pay 20 percent as coinsurance—in this example, $20. If the doctor balance bills, you will also pay $15 on top of the $20, making your total out-of-pocket expense $35.

A few states limit the excess charge even further. In New York and Minnesota, a doctor can charge only 5 percent more than Medicare's allowable charge. Doctors in Massachusetts, Pennsylvania, Ohio, and Rhode Island can't charge anything above the allowable charge.

A doctor who signs an annual contract with Medicare and agrees to accept the allowable charge in all cases is called a "participating" physician. In Medicare parlance, such a physician "accepts assignment." (Doctors who don't accept assignment are "nonparticipating.") Some doctors accept assignment from some people, but don't sign a contract with Medicare. About 80 percent of the doctors serving Medicare beneficiaries are participating physicians. The rest may accept assignment only if they believe you cannot pay the extra charges. In effect, doctors are free to provide their own "means test," accepting the allowed fee for some patients and billing others a higher fee. The likelihood of your doctor accepting assignment depends on where you live, the doctor's specialty, and your age.

Medicare's charge limits also apply to covered services of audiologists, chiropractors, dentists, optometrists, podiatrists, and physical therapists. If you use the services of any of these practitioners, be sure to check your bills carefully and do not pay any amount greater than what the law allows doctors to charge.

Doctors who do not take assignment for elective surgery must give you a written estimate of your out-of-pocket costs if the charge is likely to total more than $500 and there is a chance Medicare will not cover the procedure. If a doctor fails to give you this estimate, you are entitled to a refund of any amount paid that exceeds Medicare's allowable charge.

To find a participating doctor, consult the *Medicare—Participating Physician/Supplier Directory,* which you can find at your local Social Security Administration office. You can also obtain the directory free of charge from the insurance company that handles Medicare claims for your area. Your local Social Security office or area agency on aging can give you the name of your carrier. The carrier is also listed in *The Medicare Handbook* you receive when you sign up for the program. The insurance counseling program in your state might also be able to help you find participating doctors. See Appendix A for a list of state insurance counseling programs.

Part B Benefits

Doctors' fees Part B benefits cover services furnished in a doctor's office or in your home as well as those provided to you as an inpatient or outpatient in a hospital. Services include anesthesia, radiology, pathology, surgery, some podiatric treatment, second-opinion consultations, dental care if it involves jaw surgery or setting broken facial bones, and chiropractic treatment to correct an out-of-place vertebra shown on an X-ray or by other diagnostic tests.

Outpatient hospital coverage These benefits cover outpatient hospital services, including those required in an emergency room or outpatient clinic. In recent years, hospitals have been using outpatient services as an escape hatch from restrictions on amounts Medicare will pay for inpatient services. As they've tried to recoup their costs, the price of outpatient services has risen. If you don't have a Medigap policy, the 20 percent coinsurance can become a huge expense. In some cases, you may pay as much as 50 percent of the allowable charge. New legislation will eventually limit this amount, but the phase-in period will go on for several years.

Blood transfusions are also covered under Part B, but the deductible is different from the one under Part A. If you use three pints and have paid the $100 annual deductible, Medicare picks up 80 percent of the allowable charge for the blood. You pay the 20 percent coinsurance plus replacement costs for the first three pints you use.

Physical and occupational therapy For you to be eligible for this coverage, your doctor must prescribe a treatment plan for you and periodically review it. If therapy is provided in an outpatient hospital facility or skilled-nursing facility or by a home health care agency, clinic, or Medicare-approved rehabilitation agency, the usual cost-sharing arrangement applies.

Psychiatric care Medicare pays for care in either a doctor's office or outpatient hospital facility, but benefits are different depending on where the service is performed. If care is given in an outpatient facility, Medicare pays 80 percent and you pay 20 percent, but if it's given in a doctor's office, Medicare pays only about 50 percent of the allowable charge.

Laboratory fees Medicare pays 100 percent of the allowed charge for clinical diagnostic tests (such as blood and urine) performed in independent laboratories certified by Medicare. If tests are done in a non-certified lab, you must pay for them yourself. Neither laboratories nor doctors who perform clinical lab tests in their offices can bill you for coinsurance or excess charges. Doctors can also charge a small amount for drawing blood. For other diagnostic tests—such as X-rays, EKGs, and tissue biopsies—Medicare's usual cost-sharing applies and nonparticipating physicians can bill more than the allowable charge.

Ambulance services If the following conditions are met, Medicare pays 80 percent of the allowable charge: There is a medical need for an ambulance; the ambulance and its equipment must meet Medicare's standards; and the use of an alternative vehicle could endanger your life. Ambulance services are often subject to claims disputes, and if you think you're entitled to payment, you may have to use the appeal rights that are described later in this chapter.

Drugs Medicare does not cover prescription drugs you purchase from a pharmacy. This is probably the biggest shortcoming of the program. There is, however, an exception for immunosuppressive drugs that are taken within one year after an organ transplant that Medicare has covered and for certain oral cancer medications. Medicare does pay for drugs while you are in a hospital or skilled-nursing facility if Medicare is paying for your care. It also covers certain injections in physicians' offices.

Durable medical equipment Medicare pays 80 percent of the approved amount for things like oxygen, hospital beds, wheelchairs, and walkers. Durable medical equipment has been the subject of considerable fraud and abuse, so don't be surprised if it is difficult to get coverage for certain items. If you use these items, be on the alert for fraud and abuse and charges that seem out of the ordinary or if you receive telephone calls offering to send you equipment or supplies. It may be comforting to get lots of equipment and have someone else pay for it, but if you are overcharged or don't need the equipment, those expenses are simply added to the cost of the health care system. Unnecessary costs ultimately jeopardize the program for everyone.

Preventive services Medicare now pays for some preventive services, including yearly mammograms, Pap smears and pelvic exams, diabetes glucose monitoring, diabetes education, colorectal cancer screening, bone mass measurement, and flu and pneumococcal pneumonia shots. Medicare covers the entire cost of the shots. Mammograms, Pap smears, and pelvic exams are not subject to the Part B deductible.

WHAT MEDICARE DOES NOT COVER

Medicare does not pay for in-hospital private-duty nurses or for private rooms in hospitals or skilled-nursing facilities unless a doctor says your condition is so serious that you need such services. Nor does it pay for televisions, telephones, and personal items such as hearing aids, eyeglasses, or orthopedic shoes.

In general, Medicare pays only for services that are reasonable and medically necessary to help you recover from an illness. You can't submit a claim for setting a broken arm and then bill Medicare for a routine chest X-ray, too. Nor does the program pay for preventive care, such as routine annual physicals (with the exception of screening tests already discussed). It does not pay for insulin injections that patients can administer themselves, nor does it cover ordinary foot or dental care, almost all chiropractic services, or cosmetic surgery.

There are no benefits beyond one hundred days for skilled care in nursing homes. Nor are there benefits for meals delivered to your home through local meals-on-wheels programs. If you become sick while visiting a foreign country or on a cruise ship, Medicare won't cover your expenses. The program pays for treatment only in some Canadian and Mexican hospitals and then only in certain situations.

FILING A CLAIM

The federal government does not pay your medical bills directly. It contracts with private insurance companies to process claims and pay health care providers. The companies that pay claims for Part A coverage are called "intermediaries"; those that pay Part B claims are called "carriers." After you are dismissed from a hospital, the facility bills Medicare directly. You receive a Medicare Summary Notice

(MSN) that tells you what services were covered and paid. For services covered under Part B, your doctor or medical supply company must submit your claim to the carrier even if they don't accept assignment. Neither a doctor nor a medical supply company can charge extra for preparing your claim form.

If your doctor refuses to prepare the claim form, contact the carrier or submit the claim yourself by sending a copy of your Medicare card and the bill to the carrier. The carrier will contact the doctor. If the doctor or supplier accepts Medicare's payment as payment in full, the carrier pays the doctor directly; if the doctor does not accept assignment, Medicare pays you, and you pay the doctor. Medicare will send you a Medicare Summary Notice (MSN) that shows the services that were covered, the charges Medicare approved, how much was credited toward your $100 deductible, and the amount Medicare paid. This notice explains what Medicare paid for both Part A and Part B services.

HOW TO APPEAL UNDER MEDICARE

If you disagree with the amount Medicare pays, or dispute coverage for certain services, you can appeal the decision. Three out of four Part B claims that are appealed result in higher payments for beneficiaries. So it doesn't hurt to try. Consider filing an appeal under the following circumstances:

1. Your Medicare carrier denies payment because it says a service was not medically necessary or was experimental.
2. The carrier denies payment because a provider fails to supply enough information to process the claim.
3. The carrier denies payment because a service is given too often; in other words, too many times that seem reasonable for your particular health condition.
4. The approved charge is significantly lower than the provider's charge.

Before going through the appeals process, check with your carrier to make sure it did not make a mistake. (Your carrier is listed in the Medicare handbook.) If the carrier tells you a mistake was made, it will resubmit the claim. However, if it says a mistake was not made and you think you deserve payment, you or your provider can file an appeal.

To begin the appeals process, send the carrier a copy of your Medicare Summary Notice (be sure to keep one for yourself), a letter requesting a review (include your Medicare number and the claim control number noted on the MSN), and any documents that support your request for higher payment. This documentation may include medical records and a letter from your doctor.

Send the information to the address that appears at the bottom of the MSN and do so by the date listed at the bottom. You should hear from your carrier within six to eight weeks.

If you don't like the decision, your next step is to request a fair hearing before a hearings officer employed by your carrier. The amount of the dispute must be greater than $100, and you must ask for a hearing within six months of receiving Medicare's determination of your appeal. You can appear before a hearings officer, make your case by telephone, or simply have the officer review your papers. An attorney can represent you, or you can represent yourself. You can also ask one of the Medicare advocacy groups listed on page 104 to help you. You can also call Medicare's hot line: 1-800-638-6833.

If the hearings officer rules against you, you can ask for a hearing before an administrative law judge. For this step, the dispute must involve at least $500, and you must ask for a hearing within sixty days after receiving a determination of a fair hearing. The Social Security Administration employs the administrative law judge. It may take a year or more to get a hearing date.

If your dispute involves an HMO, different rules apply—see Chapter 5.

WHAT YOU PAY FOR MEDICARE

Part A is financed through Social Security taxes. Most beneficiaries pay no additional premiums for their Part A coverage. However, some people must pay monthly premiums for hospital coverage, including disabled persons who have gone back to work but are still disabled and people who have not worked the required ten years to obtain Social Security benefits. If you do not have the required work history, you may still be eligible for Part A benefits based on your spouse's work record. But if you and your spouse divorce before your tenth anniversary, you have to pay the Part A premiums to continue your coverage. The Part A premium in 2000 was $301 per month if you worked less than 30 quarters and $166 if you worked more than 30 quarters.

Part B, which is optional, is financed through general tax revenues and premiums paid by beneficiaries. The U.S. Treasury subsidizes about 75 percent of the cost of the program; beneficiaries pay the rest. In 2000, beneficiaries pay $546 a year; in 2001, premiums are estimated to be $707; in 2002, $778, and in 2003, $858. Premiums are deducted from your Social Security checks. If you don't sign up for Part B during the initial enrollment period, you will pay more later; plus, you can't sign up until the following January, when a new enrollment period opens. Benefits won't begin until the following July.

SIGNING UP FOR MEDICARE

If you elect early retirement benefits from Social Security, you automatically receive a Medicare card in the mail when you turn sixty-five. If you sign up for Social Security benefits when you are sixty-five, you receive your Medicare card at the same time. However, if you have turned sixty-five and want to delay your Social Security benefits, you have to apply for Medicare. In that case, do so during the first three months of your initial enrollment period, which is the seven-month period that begins three months before the month you are first eligible for Medicare. For example: You turn sixty-five on October 1, 2000, and become eligible for Medicare on that date. Your initial enrollment period begins on July 1, 2000, and lasts through January 2001 of the following year. If you don't enroll during the three months before your eligibility date, your benefits may be delayed from one to three months. If you don't enroll during the seven-month initial enrollment period, the delay could be as long as sixteen months.

If you worked for a business with twenty or more employees, the Consolidated Omnibus Budget Reconciliation Act of 1985 (COBRA) entitles you and your dependents to continued coverage for at least eighteen months under your former employer's plan. If you are on

Medicare when you trigger COBRA benefits, you can continue on your employer's policy with COBRA, but you will pay all the premium. If you elect COBRA, Medicare becomes the primary carrier. Because you have to pay all the premium with COBRA, staying in your employer's plan may be unwise. Yet if the employer's plan offers drug benefits, it may be worth it to you to pay for the coverage. It is your responsibility to notify the employer's insurance carrier that you are also on Medicare.

If you do not enroll in Part B during your initial enrollment period, but decide later you want benefits, you can sign up during the general enrollment period held each year from January 1 through March 31. If you delay enrolling, your monthly premium goes up by 10 percent for each twelve-month period you are not enrolled in the program. If you continue to work after age sixty-five, you can delay enrollment in Part B without any penalty.

VETERANS' BENEFITS

If you have served in the armed forces, you may be eligible for a variety of veterans' benefits. The ones of most interest to retirees are usually medical, prescription drugs, and burial. Some veterans' homes also offer long-term-care services that may be more desirable than nursing home care.

Medical Most veterans can receive care for a non-service-related medical condition in a Department of Veterans Affairs facility. Admittance depends on your income level and available space in the veterans' hospital. Medical benefits are sometimes extended to spouses as well. If you or your relative is a veteran and you or your relative is having trouble paying for Medicare-supplement policies and prescription drugs, be sure to check out VA care.

Burial Any person who has completed the required period of service and has been discharged under other than dishonorable conditions can be buried in any of the 113 national cemeteries operated by the Veterans Department.

For more information about benefits or the location of the nearest VA facility, contact the regional VA office in your state.

IF YOU ARE DISABLED

Medicare pays the health care bills for disabled persons under age sixty-five who qualify for Social Security disability benefits and have been disabled for at least two years. However, if you have been receiving Medicare benefits as a disabled person and then go back to work before you turn sixty-five, you can continue to receive Medicare benefits only if you are still disabled. After you start working, Part A benefits continue for at least forty-eight months and Part B benefits continue for the same time as long as you pay the Part B premium. Once your hospital benefits run out, you can continue buying both Part A and Part B benefits as long as you are disabled. Different rules apply if you have end-stage renal disease.

FILLING THE GAPS IN MEDICARE

Medicare will not pay all of your health care bills. There are gaps, sometimes substantial ones. The chapters that follow discuss different ways of filling those holes.

Medicare is likely to change in the next few years, and you or your relative could pay an even larger percentage of the total cost for health care. See pages 45–46 for a discussion on what to expect in the future.

KEY DECISION POINTS

1. Choose doctors who take assignment from Medicare (most do). It's cheaper and easier to deal with physicians who accept Medicare's payment as payment in full than to keep track of additional bills.

2. Realize that Medicare does not pay for prescription drugs, although this may change in the near future. Consider looking for discount prescription arrangements that will help reduce out-of-pocket expenses for medicines.

3. Don't look to Medicare to pay for much long-term care. The benefit is not designed for nursing home stays or for much

home care. And it certainly doesn't pay for room and board at an assisted-living facility.

4. Seek help from your state insurance counseling program if you think Medicare has unfairly denied a claim or you are confused about what you should receive.

5. Take advantage of the screening tests Medicare pays for.

THREE

Covering the Gaps in Medicare

Betsy and Bill Hamilton are heading for retirement. Betsy continued to work long after her husband left the workforce, and both had generous health insurance provided by her employer. But when she planned to retire, they faced difficult questions: Should they remain on her employer's coverage, buy a Medicare-supplement policy, or join one of the HMOs in the new town where they moved?

When they started to investigate their options, both realized there were no simple answers. Every answer seemed to come with a trade-off, and some questions had no answers. For example, if Congress enacted a law providing for prescription drug coverage, would that mean premiums for her employer-provided coverage would decrease? There's no way, of course, to answer that question.

"We gathered a lot of information on Medicare supplements," Betsy said. "But when it got down to choosing, they were all similar. So how do you choose?" They wondered if an insurer's past track record for premium increases would predict future rate hikes. When it came to considering coverage from an HMO, the Hamiltons had the same fear others have: Will they have trouble getting to see a specialist if they get sick, and what happens if they're eighty-two and the HMO stops serving elderly people?

They mistakenly signed up for Medicare Part B without considering all their options and long before they needed to apply for that coverage. "I was confused," Bill says. "I was sixty-five and had heard you could not get into a policy if you had a preexisting condition unless I applied within the

28

six-month window of my sixty-fifth year. It seemed like you had to do something quickly. There were a lot of things thrown at us at one time."

The Hamiltons should continue with their employer-provided coverage. They can well afford the $270 a month that it would currently cost. However, ten or fifteen years from now, their options will look very different, and they need to realize that the choice they make today may well be obsolete in a few years.

The Hamiltons are like millions of other couples facing retirement, unsure of what they should do to cover their health insurance needs. Instead of simplifying the choices for the nation's 39 million Medicare beneficiaries, Congress has made their decisions far more difficult by authorizing a variety of options never envisioned when Medicare was established. Furthermore, the long-term uncertainty of the current Medicare program makes planning a nightmarish exercise.

WHERE TO START

As I note in Chapter 2, Medicare was never meant to cover all the health care expenses of an elderly person, and over the years the gaps have grown. While Medicare provides a floor of insurance protection, you will also need to consider how you will cover the expenses that Medicare doesn't. Chapters 4 and 5 provide in-depth information on the various insurance options and the managed-care arrangements that are now available to Medicare beneficiaries. But before deciding how to fill the gaps, you will have to make some decisions regarding work, your income, and any retiree health coverage offered by your employer. If you are advising an elderly relative, consider the decisions you will have to make in the order presented in the following pages. By the time you have answered the questions, you should arrive at the solution that's best for you.

THE FIRST DECISIONS

Will You Continue to Work?

If you continue working after you turn sixty-five, you may want to retain health insurance coverage from your employer. If your employer is paying a good chunk of the premium and the coverage includes prescription drugs, you would be crazy to venture into the confusing world of Medicare supplements and HMOs. In this case, it's best to delay signing up for Medicare Parts A and B. The important thing to remember is that you will still be able to retain your "six-month window" during which you can sign up for any Medicare supplement regardless of your health status. You can be on your deathbed and still get the policy of your choice. Once you sign up for Part B, your six-month window begins. So you don't want to sign up for Medicare until you are sure you are ready to use it. That was the mistake the Hamiltons made.

If for some reason you decide to sign up for Medicare Part B and are still working, and if you work for a company with more than twenty employees, Medicare will be the secondary payer—that is, it will pay after your employer's insurance does. Medicare will not pay more than the difference between what your employer's insurance carrier approves and what the carrier ultimately pays, up to the amount Medicare would have paid if it were primary. For example, your doctor charges $100, and your employer's insurance company approves $80 for the doctor's fee and pays $64, or 80 percent of the allowable charge. Medicare would approve $60 for the doctor's fee and then pay the difference between what the employer's insurance approved ($80) and what it finally paid ($64): $16. Most of the time, Medicare will be paying small amounts, so it may not be worth the trouble to sign up for Part B. That's especially true if you are in your employer's managed-care plan where the copayments are likely to be small. If you do sign up, you will have to exercise your options under the six-month window, and you may prematurely exhaust your ability to buy any supplemental policy you want.

The bottom line: If you know you are going to be working for a few more years after you reach age sixty-five, stay on your employer's insurance plan and see how the Medicare market shakes out. In a few years, your options might be clearer. The same advice applies if you are covered under a spouse's plan provided by his or her employer.

Different rules apply if you continue to work and your company employs fewer than twenty people. If your employer offers insurance coverage, and you elect to stay on the policy, Medicare becomes the primary payer, and you'll have to sign up for Parts A and B. It's possible that some employers may provide a Medicare supplement. Others may not. If your employer will not provide this coverage, you'll have to select an insurance or a managed-care option for covering the gaps.

When you or your spouse quit working and the employer's coverage stops, it's time to visit your local Social Security office and sign up for Medicare. You will have a special eight-month period in which to sign up and avoid penalties. At this time, you'll have to decide whether to purchase a Medicare-supplement policy or enroll in a Medicare HMO to cover Medicare's gaps.

Is Your Income Low?

If your income or your relative's income is low, consider the special programs that help low-income Medicare beneficiaries cover some of their health care costs. Many of these programs are underused either because families don't know about them, or because they smack of welfare that many elders want to avoid. Nevertheless, don't overlook them if you are trying to help a family member pay for health care. Also read Chapter 9. If you live in a state that has special programs for people eligible for both Medicare and Medicaid, consider them as well. Many are simpler and afford more coverage than the programs discussed below. Along with the options discussed in Chapter 9, consider the following:

• **Qualified Medicare Beneficiary Program (QMB)** Under this program, people with incomes around $8,244 in 2000 for an individual and $11,000 for a family don't have to pay Medicare deductibles, coinsurance, and premiums. The state picks up those costs through its Medicaid program, but you do not have to be on Medicaid in order to qualify for this plan. You will, however, have to use physicians who accept Medicaid's payment rate in order for the program to cover the deductibles and coinsurance. If you choose a doctor who does not want to accept payment from Medicaid, you'll pay these amounts yourself.

• **Specified Low-Income Medicare Beneficiary Program (SLMB)** Under this arrangement, which has higher income limits, the state will pay your Medicare Part B premium ($45.50 in 2000). Although the monthly Part B premium will not be deducted from your Social Security checks, you will still need to cover the gaps in coverage through a Medicare supplement or by joining a managed-care plan. Most likely, the managed-care option will be best since the monthly premiums are lower and you will probably get some coverage for prescription drugs.

• **Qualified Individual Program-1 (QI-1)** The state also pays your Part B premium under this program, but income limits are higher than for the

SLMB program. As with SLMB, you will still need a way to cover Medicare's gaps. Some states have capped the amount they will spend on the program, and there may be a waiting list to obtain coverage. This program will end in 2002.

- **Qualified Individual Program-2 (QI-2)** The income limits are higher for this program, which pays only $2.32 of the monthly Part B premium—the cost of Medicare's home health benefit. It's obviously not much of a benefit, and along with the QI-1 program, it will go out of existence in 2002. As with QI-1, there may be a waiting list.

Medicaid If you or a relative qualifies for Medicaid, it may be a better option than the programs just described. The major advantage of Medicaid is that the state provides a full range of health care services, including prescription drugs and home health care. But if you want support from Medicaid, you will have to use doctors who are willing to accept Medicaid payment. Many doctors don't, so the choice of providers may be severely limited. To qualify for Medicaid, your relative must be poor enough or in danger of making him- or herself poor by spending down (see Chapter 13 for more details).

To qualify for any of these programs, states require that you have very few assets. For QMB, SLMB, QI-1, and QI-2, a single individual can have no more than $4,000 in assets, a couple $6,000, not including a house or car. (See table 23 in Chapter 13 for each state's Medicaid requirements.)

To find out more about these programs or to apply, contact your state's Department of Social Services. You can also call the Medicare hot line at 1-800-Medicare or your local area agency on aging (see Appendix B).

If your relative's income is low, he or she might also qualify for some of the programs that offer free prescription drugs. A number of pharmaceutical companies say they will give drugs to people who have trouble paying for them. Several states also have programs that give away prescription drugs at no or low cost. Qualifying for these programs is difficult; companies and states don't make it easy for people to use them. Appendices C and D give a flavor of the requirements and restrictions imposed by both state and pharmaceutical company programs.

Will Your Employer Provide Health Insurance Coverage?

If you continue to work and remain covered by your employer's insurance, don't sign up for Medicare. But if you will stop working after you turn sixty-five and your income doesn't qualify for any of the special programs, the next step is to investigate the kinds of coverage your employer provides to retirees. Increasingly, companies are getting out of the business of retiree health coverage, and the ones that are still providing it may place restrictions on what they will offer.

First, find out what the employer will offer and for how long. Also note what effect the employer's coverage will have on your spouse, if any. When you lose coverage from your employer, and your spouse is much younger, he or she may lose coverage, too, and have few options. The same applies if your spouse is disabled. Employers are mandating that retirees share in more of the cost, imposing spending caps (see page 34), and tightening eligibility for coverage. Many are dropping coverage altogether. If you learn, for example, that your company is planning to terminate its coverage for retirees in the next year or two, then it's best to move to other options right away rather than take employer coverage for a short time.

Understand how your employer figures benefits. Doing this will help you determine how generous your employer's coverage will be and whether you want to take it or choose another arrangement. Most likely your employer will use one of these arrangements:

Carve-out coordination of benefits This is the most common approach. You receive the same benefits as active employees. The insurer calculates the portion of the claim the policy covers if Medicare were not in the picture. It then adds the amount the active employee would pay under this arrangement to the amount Medicare would pay. The insurer subtracts this total from the amount of the claim and pays the difference. The important thing about a carve-out is that the total benefit from your employer and Medicare is the same as it would be before you retired, assuming, of course, the plan remains the same. Employers can change the plan at any time, leaving you with less coverage than you expected.

Standard coordination of benefits with Medicare This method provides the most generous method but fewer employers are using it. The insurer determines the portion of your expenses eligible for payment, subtracts the deductible, then pays 80 percent of the remainder. However, if that amount plus Medicare's payment is greater than the total claim, the insurance company reduces the amount it pays.

Exclusion coordination of benefits This method recognizes only the part of the claim that Medicare does not reimburse. The deductible, if it has not been paid, is subtracted from the portion of the claim Medicare does not cover. The insurer pays 80 percent of what's left.

Vouchers Some employers simply set aside a sum of money for workers to spend on health care. These accounts can range in size from a few hundred dollars to $20,000, depending on whether your employer intends for the account to supplement other health insurance or provide major coverage. If you are offered such an account, you should also buy a good supplemental policy unless your employer sets up a very large account, which is not likely for most people. Some companies may offer their retirees a regular Medicare-supplement policy similar to those you can buy on your own. Still others offer policies with very limited coverage that pay only for hospital-related charges.

Managed-care options Many employers now offer their retirees an HMO or a PPO arrangement instead of traditional indemnity insurance. While only 7 percent of employers offered HMO coverage to retirees in 1991, some 40 percent do today, and that percentage is sure to grow.

Many employers offer prescription drug coverage if retirees use a managed-care program. Drug benefits may be subject to the same deductible, coinsurance, and out-of-pocket limits as the medical plan, or they may be offered through a separate drug-card program with no deductibles—in these you may pay $5 for generic drugs and $10 to $15 for brand-name drugs. You may have to use a mail-order pharmacy and send away for prescription drugs. Chapter 5 discusses the rules and limitations of these programs. If you don't have to use a mail-order arrangement, you probably will have to fill your prescriptions at pharmacies that offer discounts to both employers and employees.

Drug benefits are often the deciding factor in choosing one option over another. Even though you don't use a lot of prescription drugs now, you have no way of knowing whether you'll need more five or ten years from now. If the drug benefit is reasonably generous and the premium relatively low, the benefit, although "managed" in some way, may tip the balance in favor of your employer's coverage.

Spending caps Increasingly, employers are capping the amount they'll spend for retiree health insurance. There are several ways they do this. For example, an employer may decide to spend no more than twice what was spent in 1990. Some may say that their subsidies will not exceed a set amount, such as $2,000. Others may relate the amount of the cap to years of service. No matter the method, the bottom line is the same: Once the cap is reached, you will pay more out of pocket. For example, your employer may pay 90 percent of the cost until a cap of $1,800 is reached. If the cost of providing health care coverage increases to $2,500 in ten years, you may pay 25 percent of the cost instead of 10 percent. If it rises to $4,400 in twenty years, your share could increase to 58 percent.

It's important to know if your employer has imposed a cap and how it works. Remember that income in retirement usually shrinks as you age. If you find that twenty years from now you'll be assuming a large share of the cost, you may want to consider other options. In many cases, retiree plans have not yet triggered spending caps, but sometime in the future they are likely to kick in. If you are already retired, and there's a cap in your plan, be mindful that your health care costs could increase in the future.

Comparing your employer's plan with other options Whether you choose your employer's coverage or another option depends on the generosity of the benefit and the premium you will pay. Your out-of-pocket medical expenses are lowest if your former employer uses the standard coordination-of-benefits approach; they are highest under a carve-out arrangement. Typically, retiree coverage comes with a $300 deductible, 20 percent employee coinsurance, and an out-of-pocket limit of $1,750.

If your employer uses the standard coordination-of-benefits approach and pays the entire premium for your coverage, an additional Medicare-supplement policy is a waste of money. The same is true if your employer uses the carve-out or the exclusion approach and pays the entire premium. Under these plans, you will have some out-of-pocket expenses but pay nothing for the insurance. A supplemental policy can cost close to $2,000 a year, and plans with limited prescription drug coverage can cost even more.

If you still want a supplement as a backup to cover the out-of-pocket costs, consider a less-expensive barebones policy that covers only the 20 percent Medicare coinsurance. Look for Medicare-supplement Plan A when you do your shopping. If your employer uses the carve-out or exclusion approach and requires that you pay most of the premiums, you may be better off buying a supplement that pays most of your bills and forgoing your employer's coverage. The premium may be less than your employer would charge.

If your employer's plan is generally inferior but covers prescription drugs that you must take on a regular basis, you may want to keep the plan and buy a supplemental policy that covers only the Medicare 20 percent coinsurance like Plan A. If you have a preexisting health condition for which you might need immediate coverage, you are probably better off staying with your employer's coverage.

In sum, if you have good coverage from your employer and can pay the premium, stay with it. Do not sign up for Medicare while you are still working until you are ready to give up employer coverage.

COBRA AND MEDICARE

If you are already receiving COBRA benefits when you become eligible for Medicare, your COBRA benefits will end. However, if you are already on Medicare when you become eligible for COBRA, you can have both at the same time. You will need to sign up for Part B because Medicare will become the primary coverage whether you take the COBRA benefits or reject them and buy a supplemental policy.

COBRA benefits are an extension of your employer group benefits and may provide more coverage than a supplement would, such as prescription drugs. If you are a heavy user of medical services, you may want to consider keeping both, even though you will have to pay the group premium plus two percent for administrative expenses. If you decide to keep both, you must notify your employer and the insurance company that you have Medicare which will be your primary coverage. If you don't do this, you could be liable for any expenses the group plan pays that Medicare should have paid. If you fail to sign up for Part B after your employment ends, you can only sign up in January of the next year and you will pay a penalty for each twelve months you didn't have Part B after you stopped working. These rules apply to employees eligible for Medicare as well as to their spouses or dependents who are on Medicare.

THE NEXT DECISIONS

Once you have decided whether to stay in the workforce and continue with your employer's health insurance, determined whether your income is low enough to qualify for special programs, and decided whether to take retiree coverage from your employer, the next step is to consider whether you need a way to cover Medicare's gaps. If you are not going to work, if you are not going to take retiree coverage, or if you are not applying for one of the low-income programs, your choice boils down to one of the insurance options discussed in Chapter 4 or one of the managed-care options discussed in Chapter 5.

Traditional Medicare or Managed Care

For virtually everyone, the choice right now is between selecting traditional Medicare benefits and buying a supplemental policy. (Although the Balanced Budget Act authorized a number of new alternatives, such as medical savings accounts, these options have yet to materialize in the marketplace.)

If your income is low, but not low enough to qualify for one of the special programs described on pages 31–32, a Medicare HMO may be the best choice. CONSUMER REPORTS surveyed the sellers of supplemental policies and Medicare HMOs and has found that, on average, HMO arrangements are substantially cheaper, and many offer some benefits for prescription drugs. While the drug benefits vary widely among plans, even a small benefit is more helpful than no benefit at all.

In return for a lower premium and the drug benefit, you give up the freedom of going to just any physician, particularly specialists. With an HMO, you are restricted to using the doctors in the plan's network; however, many physicians now belong to several plans in an area so chances are the doctors you want to use are in one HMO or another. Specialists are a different matter, and you'll have to weigh the advantage of being able to see any specialist (as you can with the traditional Medicare program) against the disadvantage of seeing the specialists to which your HMO sends you. It may come down to a choice between the freedom to see specialists or a way to pay for prescription drugs and lower out-of-pocket expenses possible with an HMO.

Choosing the traditional Medicare program and covering the cost sharing with a supplemental policy is likely to be more expensive than joining an HMO. Premiums are much higher and the biggest shortcoming is lack of coverage for prescription drugs on most policies. Unless Congress changes Medicare and adds a drug benefit, this will remain a serious gap in health coverage for the elderly. As Chapter 4 points out, the few Medicare-supplement policies that cover prescription drugs offer a very limited benefit, and high premiums for these plans puts them out of reach for many beneficiaries. Traditional Medicare and a supplemental policy allow you to receive care from any physician you choose. Remember, though, HMOs can change their benefits, raise premiums, or drop their Medicare plans. Doctors and hospitals can withdraw from an HMO, or HMOs can drop doctors and hospitals from their lists of providers. So joining an HMO can be risky.

In late 1999, CONSUMER REPORTS evaluated both HMOs that contract with Medicare as well as traditional Medicare-supplement policies. Although cuts in payments by Medicare to HMOs caused many to increase premiums, decrease benefits, or drop coverage in some areas, in 2000, HMOs still provide good value to price-conscious consumers. In many areas it is still possible to sign up for a plan without paying any additional premium, although you might not get prescription drug coverage (one of the main advantages of an HMO). In most cases, HMOs still offer the average consumer more in benefits than the premium charged should theoretically buy (see the Value Index in our Ratings of Medicare HMOs in Appendix G).

Just how good a deal you can get with an HMO varies from area to area. For example, in Miami, all the plans we rated in 2000 offered at least some prescription drug coverage, yet none charged a premium. In Portland, all plans charged a premium, and the plan with the highest-rated drug coverage costs more than $2,000 per year.

Medicare-supplement policies are less attractive financially. Purchasers receive on average fewer benefits than the premium should buy. The trade-off: Consumers can go to any physician they choose, without restrictions on the number of visits or enduring other constraints of managed care.

A CONSUMER REPORTS survey of readers also found that Medicare beneficiaries who enrolled in HMOs were about as satisfied as those staying in the traditional Medicare program and buying a supplemental policy.

If you choose a traditional supplement, be mindful of the six-month window that lets you buy any of the ten standardized supplemental policies even if you have a serious health condition. The six-month window begins as soon as you sign up for Medicare Part B. After the six months are up, however, insurance companies can turn you down for coverage if you have some health condition they don't want to insure. HMOs, on the other hand, must take everyone, even those people who are ill. The exception to this rule is people with end-stage renal disease.

THE MEDICARE + CHOICE OPTIONS

With the passage of the Balanced Budget Act of 1997, Congress tried to inject more private market options into the Medicare marketplace. Many of those options were enacted to satisfy one constituent group or another that wanted a piece of the financial action from Medicare beneficiaries. But many have yet to materialize. Either sponsors have yet to find a way to make them profitable, or they have not figured out how to make them appealing to consumers. Indeed, many are not.

Nevertheless, in planning how you or a relative will pay for health care within the next several years, it's important to understand how these options work and what CONSUMER REPORTS recommends. What follows are sketches of options created by the Balanced Budget Act. The first two are the major options most people will see. There were only four provider-sponsored organizations and one private fee-for-service plan available when we went to press.

Traditional Medicare and Medicare-Supplement Policies

With these, you go to a doctor of your choice. The doctor bills Medicare. Medicare pays the doctor and sends you an explanation of benefits detailing what it paid. The supplemental policy pays some of what Medicare doesn't; you pay the remaining charges.

As Chapter 4 points out, Plan C is best for most people. Plans H, I, and J offer prescription drug coverage with annual deductibles of $250 and limits on how much the plan will pay. There are also two new plans, high-deductible F and high-deductible J, which require you to pay $1,500 before the policies will pay any benefits.

Out-of-pocket expenses:	Premiums: Variable, often increasing with age, as little as $500 for Plan A to $6,000 for plans with prescription drug coverage.
	Coinsurance: None—usually paid by supplemental policy.
	Deductibles: Usually none—paid by supplemental policy. High for F and J variations.
Physician oversight:	None.

Approval for services:	None. Can use any physician or hospital, but a Medicare Select policy requires the use of network hospitals.
Medicare billing protections:	Yes—doctors who do not accept Medicare assignment can charge you no more than 15 percent above Medicare's allowable charge.
Biggest advantage:	Freedom to choose doctors and hospitals.
Biggest disadvantages:	Lack of prescription drug coverage on most supplemental policies. Policies with drug coverage may not be available to sick people. Premiums rise rapidly. Large out-of-pocket costs for new high-deductible plans.
Recommendation:	The best choice for those who put a high value on choosing any doctor or hospital they want and who can afford premiums for a good supplement.

HMOs

You enroll in a managed-care organization that contracts with Medicare, which in turn pays the plan a set amount each month to provide all of your Medicare benefits. Sometimes the money is enough to provide extra benefits not provided by Medicare. You must use providers in the HMO network unless your HMO offers a point-of-service option (POS) that you have elected. If you go outside the network, the HMO is not required to pay for your care.

Out-of-pocket expenses:	Premiums: Low—usually between $0 and $1,000 per year.
	Copayments: Low—between $0 and $20 for most physician services.
	Deductibles: None.
Physician oversight:	Required oversight of care by HMO but no assurance you are getting the correct treatment. You may appeal decisions.
Approval for services:	Usually must go through primary-care physician unless POS option chosen.
Billing protections:	Yes—with the exception of small copayments per visit or service, HMO doctors are not allowed to charge extra for Medicare services.
Biggest advantages:	Low monthly premiums and coverage for prescription drugs.
Biggest disadvantages:	Extra coverage and free prescription drug coverage may disappear, and premiums could rise. Many services, including

skilled nursing and home care, may be tightly controlled. You may experience treatment delays. Some plans leave the market, others enter, providing for a constantly changing mix of plans in any given area. Some counties, particularly rural ones, have no HMOs.

Recommendation: HMOs are good for people who need prescription drug coverage or who can't afford the premiums for a Medicare supplement policy.

Provider-Sponsored Organizations (PSO)

Known as PSOs, provider-sponsored organizations are a group of doctors or hospitals that form a legal entity and contract with Medicare to provide Part A and Part B services. The organization, which operates under a state license or a waiver from the federal government, bears all the risk for your care. As in an HMO, you must receive care from network providers or those the organization may contract with. If you go outside the network, the PSO is not required to pay for your care unless it offers a point-of-service option, and you take it.

Out-of-pocket expenses: Premiums: Low—likely to be similar to HMOs.

Coinsurance: Low—likely to be similar to HMOs.

Deductibles: None.

Physician oversight: Required oversight of care by PSO but no assurance that you're getting the correct treatment or diagnosis. You may appeal decisions, same as in an HMO.

Approval for services: Usually must go through primary-care physician.

Billing protections: Yes—with the exception of copayments for visits and services, doctors can't charge extra for services provided by the PSO.

Biggest advantages: Premiums and copayments may be low. May offer coverage for prescription drugs. If your doctor becomes part of a PSO, you will have continuity of care.

Biggest disadvantages: Some services may be tightly controlled; may have limited number of network providers. May be hard to access certain specialists. Regulations may be weak, leading to problems with solvency or capitalization. Disruptions in care could occur if plan is sold.

Note: In 2000, only four PSO plans are available:
Sun Health MediSun in Arizona, St. Joseph Healthcare PSO in New Mexico, SCHP in Georgia, and Clear Choice Health Plans in Oregon.

Private Fee-for-Service Plans

With these, you buy a policy from an insurance company that has contracted with Medicare to cover all the basic Medicare services. The insurance company can add extra benefits and charge what it wants for them. You have no Medicare benefits other than those paid for by the insurance company; in other words, Medicare won't pay for your care separately. These policies are not the same as Medicare-supplement insurance.

You can easily be confused by these policies. When this book went to press, the only private fee-for-service plan on the market was one sold by Sterling Life Insurance Co., primarily in rural areas. While the plan offers a low premium compared to most Medicare-supplement policies—$55—policyholders could find themselves having to pay high hospital bills if they had several admissions during the year. The Sterling policy requires that policyholders pay a $300 copayment each time they go to the hospital.

While copayments for physicians' visits are similar to those charged by HMOs, the Sterling policy offers no coverage for prescription drugs, eye exams, hearing aids, or glasses. Many HMOs still offer these extras.

If you are trying to decide between a private fee-for-service option and other alternatives such as an HMO or a Medicare-supplement policy, my recommendation is: buyer beware.

Out-of-pocket expenses: Premiums: Could be very high, depends on the company.

Coinsurance: Could be very high. The plan sets copayments subject to Medicare limits; they may be more or less than Medicare's for any specific service. Plan may impose copayments for extra benefits.

Deductibles: Could be very high. The plan may set deductibles subject to Medicare's limits. Plan may impose deductibles for extra benefits.

Physician oversight:	None.
Approval for services:	Can go to any doctor or hospital.
Billing protections:	Very few—providers who contract with the insurance company (or are deemed by Medicare to have a contract) can charge 15 percent more than the insurer's fee schedule. Providers who don't contract can charge no more than the deductible and coinsurance amounts. You must pay whatever the plan doesn't cover but are entitled to a determination in advance on whether the plan covers a particular treatment.
Biggest advantage:	Freedom to roam the health care system.
Biggest disadvantages:	Potentially high premiums and very high out-of-pocket expenses. May be hard to understand what insurer is really offering.
Recommendation:	Only the wealthy who can pay high out-of-pocket costs should consider this option.

Note: In 2000, one private fee-for-service plan was available, sold by Sterling Life Insurance Co.

Private Contracting with Physicians

If the doctor you choose has opted out of Medicare, you can contract directly with that doctor to provide Medicare-covered services. If you do, no Medicare payment will be made for those services, and they will not be covered by supplemental insurance. You sign a private contract which discloses that the services are covered by Medicare and would be paid if you used another doctor, and you agree to pay all charges in full. You still may have Medicare payments to cover Medicare services provided by other doctors who have not opted out of Medicare. You can't be forced to sign a contract when you are facing an emergency or an urgent health problem.

Out-of-pocket expenses:	Premiums: Not applicable.
	Coinsurance: Not applicable.
	Deductibles: Not applicable— expenses could be exorbitant depending on what the doctor charges.
Physician oversight:	None.
Approval for services:	None.
Billing protections:	None—doctors can charge whatever they want.

Biggest advantage:	Freedom to roam the health care system.
Biggest disadvantages:	Potentially very high out-of-pocket expenses. Doctors must opt out of Medicare for at least two years and sign private contracts with any beneficiary they treat during the two-year period. If you sign a contract with one of these physicians, you will not receive Medicare payment for the services of that doctor as long as he or she is out of Medicare. Arrangements may be subject to billing abuse.
Recommendation:	Only the wealthy who can pay the full cost of their care should consider this option.

Note: To date, there has been little interest in this option. It is more likely that high-priced specialists would opt out rather than family practitioners.

Medical Savings Accounts (MSAs)

With MSAs, you buy an insurance policy with a high annual deductible (at least $1,500 but no more than $6,000) that covers the basic Medicare services and possibly extra benefits. You may count toward the deductible only expenses for Medicare-covered services that would have been paid had you stayed in traditional Medicare as well as any extra services covered by the plan. After the deductible is met, the insurance company will pay Part A and Part B benefits and other services the policy covers. Medicare makes a monthly payment to the insurance company to provide the standard coverage. The difference between the premium it charges and the payment Medicare makes is the amount that consumers can deposit into their tax-deferred medical savings accounts each year.

Savings can be used tax-free to pay for tax-qualified medical expenses, which are defined by the IRS. Funds locked in the MSA may accrue from year to year. If the account balance falls below a certain amount because of withdrawals for nonmedical expenses, you're subject to a tax penalty. If you are healthy and never use the money, you can spend it on anything you like at the end of the year, but if you use it for nonmedical purposes, the money withdrawn will be taxed as income.

Out-of-pocket expenses:	Can be high, low, or moderate—depends on marketing strategy of company and Medicare payment rates.
	Coinsurance: Doesn't apply until deductible is met. Then it can be low, high, or moderate.

Deductibles: Very high.

Taxes: Withdrawals for nonmedical expenses are subject to income taxes.

Physician oversight:	None.
Approval for services:	MSAs may be indemnity policies or managed-care arrangements. If indemnity, no requirements to go through a primary-care doctor. If managed care, must usually use primary-care physician and get approvals for referrals to specialists. Insurer may have tough "usual, customary, and reasonable" rules for paying bills.
	Medicare billing protections: None.
Biggest advantage:	If MSA is an indemnity policy, you have freedom to roam the health care system.
Biggest disadvantages:	Potentially very high out-of-pocket expenses and no protections against billing abuses by physicians. Savings account will be of limited value if you get sick. Services could be tightly controlled in managed-care arrangements.
Recommendation:	Not recommended—this is a $6,000 gamble against an insurance company that you will stay healthy.

Note: When this book went to press, no MSAs were available.

LOOKING TO THE FUTURE

The main thing to remember when helping an elderly relative choose health care coverage is that ever-increasing out-of-pocket costs may become onerous, perhaps even jeopardizing his or her ability to get health care. Beneficiaries also face an unstable market for insurance coverage. An option chosen today can evaporate tomorrow. For example, an HMO that offers a good prescription drug benefit now may scale it back next year because the government reduces its reimbursement to the HMO or because its claims from sick beneficiaries exceed what it expected to pay. A Medicare-supplement insurer may offer an affordable premium right now but may raise rates so high in the future that the policy becomes unaffordable.

Another certainty is that premiums for Medicare will rise, too. In 1999, the annual premium for Part B services (physicians and outpatient services) was $546. By 2009, that premium will rise to $1,084;

in 2025, the premium is projected to hit $1,400. The hospital, or Part A deductible, will also rise from $768 to $1,092. Add these to increases in premiums a managed-care organization or a Medicare-supplement insurer imposes and beneficiaries face increased out-of-pocket costs that many won't be able to pay.

The Commonwealth Fund, one of the funders of this book, has estimated that beneficiaries' out-of-pocket medical expenses on average now account for some 19 percent of their income. In twenty-five years, the fund estimates that those expenses will consume around 29 percent. Out-of-pocket costs that average about $2,500 now are expected to rise to close to $4,900 in 2025.

Some members of Congress, however, are proposing to turn Medicare into a defined contribution or a voucher plan in which the government will give each beneficiary a set amount of money to buy all coverage and ultimately cap the amount each beneficiary receives. If that happens, The Commonwealth Fund estimates that beneficiaries' out-of-pocket spending will rise even more. The fund calculates that anywhere from 30 to 37 percent of a beneficiary's income will go for health care, not including expenses for long-term care. Out-of-pocket expenses could exceed $6,000 a year. Prescription drugs are also likely to get more expensive. Currently, 48 percent of Medicare beneficiaries have no way to pay for their medications. Beneficiaries are the only group paying retail prices for their drugs. Most employed people buy their medication at a reduced price, because they have drug benefits as part of their insurance coverage.

Since income often declines as a person ages, considering how you or your family member will accommodate the increasing out-of-pocket costs for health care is essential. Strategies for accommodating these costs might include taking community-rated Medicare-supplement policies (see page 57) or setting aside a portion of your current income each year to pay future health care expenses. This may be a prudent step to protect you in very old age.

KEY DECISION POINTS

1. If you or a relative you are helping has very low income—low enough to qualify for Medicaid—that should be the first place you look for coverage. Depending on your state, you may receive fuller coverage, especially for prescription

drugs, than you would struggling to pay the premiums for a Medicare-supplement policy.

2. Seriously consider taking health coverage offered by your employer. Those arrangements often carry coverage for prescription drugs that could be valuable in the long run.

3. Decide how you are going to pay for health care costs far into the future. Health care expenses are bound to consume an ever-increasing share of your income. The solution may depend on saving as much as you can now, or bowing to the fact you may have to rely on your children for help.

4. Decide how important it is to remain with physicians and specialists who may not be in the network of an HMO you are considering. If you are willing to use other doctors, you can significantly reduce your out-of-pocket expenses.

5. If you plan to work after turning sixty-five, stay on your employer's health insurance plan as long as possible to preserve your open window, the period when you can choose any Medicare-supplement policy you want even if your health is poor. The longer you stay on an employer's insurance plan, the more time will pass for the Medicare market to stabilize, giving a clearer picture of the options you have.

6. If you are still working, don't sign up for Medicare until you are certain you are ready for that coverage.

FOUR

The Insurance Options

Dan and Laura Sites faced an increasingly common problem encountered by thousands of Medicare beneficiaries—the loss of coverage from an HMO and no way to pay for the medications they need. When the HMO that had been providing their care dropped its program for Medicare beneficiaries in California's Monterey County, the Sites had to scramble to find a way to pay for coverage that filled the gaps in Medicare.

Since Dan was a Korean War veteran, he could get treatment through the Veterans Administration medical system and receive care at a clinic at nearby Fort Ord. His wife was not so lucky. A few years ago she suffered a slight stroke and had recently undergone treatment for breast cancer. Her only option was a traditional Medicare-supplement policy that covered the most gaps at a price the family could afford on their tiny income. She settled on Plan C, the most popular of the Medicare supplements. For that coverage, they paid $63 each month.

Laura got Plan C from California Blue Cross. The insurance company sold her a "guaranteed issue" policy, meaning that she could get coverage in spite of her health problems. At first, the Sites had considered a Plan C policy from AARP, but the monthly premium was $110 for identical coverage. It was much too high.

The big shortcoming of Plan C is the lack of coverage for prescription drugs, no small matter for Laura. She must pay $114 each month for tamoxifin, the anticancer medication that her doctors have prescribed for the next few years. It's hard coming up with that money on a monthly income of about $860. Laura worries. "It's the fear of not being able to pay for it," she says.

The Sites learned some hard lessons about the current market for Medicare-supplement insurance—one of the two major ways beneficiaries fill the holes in Medicare. They quickly learned that premiums vary substantially for the same standardized benefits offered by all insurers and that sick people like Laura cannot buy Medicare-supplement policies that include coverage for prescription drugs.

Although the market for Medicare-supplement policies has numerous shortcomings and presents serious problems for beneficiaries, especially those with low and moderate incomes, some 33 million elderly choose to get their benefits through the traditional Medicare program and buy a supplemental policy rather than get their Medicare benefits through an HMO. Still, beneficiaries and their families are at a loss for which policy to choose.

Even though Medicare-supplement insurance is the major insurance option available to Medicare beneficiaries, sellers dangle other insurance products in front of them. Some of these other products even use the word *supplement* in their names, so it's easy to get confused. I discuss these "other" policies at the end of this chapter.

THE TEN STANDARDIZED PLANS

Serious abuse in the sale of Medicare-supplement insurance, or Medigap policies as they are often called, led Congress to standardize these policies in 1992. Before standardization, insurers could add all kinds of bells and whistles to their policies, making it impossible for elders to judge the best value for their money. In some ways, it is still hard.

The Benefits

The following ten standardized plans are mandated in all but three states. Massachusetts, Minnesota, and Wisconsin have different requirements passed before standardization took effect. The standard plans are:

Plan A Every insurer must offer Plan A, which provides core or basic benefits. These include:

- Coverage for Part A coinsurance—the daily amount you must pay for a hospital stay if you are hospitalized from sixty-one to ninety days. In 2000, Part A coinsurance is $194 per day.
- Coverage for Part A coinsurance—the daily amount you must pay for a hospital stay that lasts from 91 to 150 days. In 2000, that amount is $388 per day.
- Coverage for an extra 365 days of hospital care after you have exhausted all of your Medicare benefits.
- Coverage for the cost of the first three pints of blood you may need as an inpatient in a hospital. (In other words, policies will cover the Part A blood deductible.)
- Coverage for Part B coinsurance—20 percent of Medicare's allowable charge.

Plan B Includes all the benefits of Plan A plus:

- Part A hospital deductible.

Plan C Includes all the benefits of Plan A plus:

- Coinsurance coverage for a stay in a skilled-nursing facility. Medicare requires beneficiaries needing skilled-nursing care to pay coinsurance for stays that last from twenty-one to one hundred days. In 2000, the amount of the coinsurance was $197. After one hundred days, neither Medicare nor supplemental insurance pays any part of the bill.
- Part A hospital deductible.
- Emergency medical care in foreign countries.
- Part B deductible—$100 in 2000.

Plan D Includes all the benefits of Plan A plus:

- Coinsurance coverage for a stay in a skilled-nursing facility.
- Part A hospital deductible.
- Emergency medical care in foreign countries.
- Coverage for at-home care following an injury, illness, or surgery. This benefit covers assistance with activities of daily living, such as eating, bathing, and dressing. This benefit is limited to $1,600 a year, and a physician must certify that visits by

a licensed home health aide, homemaker, or personal-care worker are required because of a condition for which Medicare has already approved a home health treatment plan. The benefit can be used for up to eight weeks after Medicare's home health benefit ends.

Plan E Includes all the benefits of Plan A plus:

- Coinsurance coverage for a stay in a skilled-nursing facility.
- Emergency medical care in foreign countries.
- Preventive medical care not covered by Medicare. This benefit covers the cost of an annual physical, thyroid and diabetes screening, a pure-tone hearing test, and cholesterol screening.
- Part A hospital deductible.

Plan F Includes all the benefits of Plan A plus:

- Coinsurance coverage for a stay in a skilled-nursing facility.
- Part A hospital deductible.
- Part B deductible.
- Emergency medical care in foreign countries.
- One hundred percent of Medicare Part B excess charges. (An excess charge is the difference between Medicare's allowable charge and the amount your physician actually bills.)

Plan F offers a high-deductible option. You must pay the first $1,500 of your medical expenses yourself before the policy pays any benefits.

Plan G Includes all the benefits of Plan A plus:

- Coinsurance coverage for a stay in a skilled-nursing facility.
- Part A hospital deductible.
- Emergency medical care in foreign countries.
- Coverage for at-home care following an injury, illness, or surgery.
- Eighty percent of Medicare Part B excess charges.

Plan H Includes all the benefits of Plan A plus:

- Coinsurance coverage for a stay in a skilled-nursing facility.
- Part A hospital deductible.
- Emergency medical care in foreign countries.

- Fifty percent of the cost of prescription drugs up to an annual maximum benefit of $1,250 after the policyholder satisfies a $250 annual deductible. This is the basic prescription drug benefit.

Plan I Includes all the benefits of Plan A plus:

- Coinsurance coverage for a stay in a skilled-nursing facility.
- Part A hospital deductible.
- Emergency medical care in foreign countries.
- Coverage for at-home care following an injury, illness, or surgery.
- One hundred percent of Part B excess charges.
- The basic prescription drug benefit.

Plan J Includes all the benefits of Plan A plus:

- Coinsurance coverage for a stay in a skilled-nursing facility.
- Part A hospital deductible.
- Part B deductible.
- Emergency medical care in foreign countries.
- Coverage for at-home care following an injury, illness, or surgery.
- Preventive medical care.
- One hundred percent of Part B excess charges.
- Fifty percent of the cost of prescription drugs up to an annual maximum benefit of $3,000 after the policyholder meets an annual $250 deductible. This is the extended drug benefit.

Plan J offers a high-deductible option. You pay the first $1,500 of your medical expenses before the plan pays any benefits. The prescription drug deductible must be met as well.

The table on page 53 tells at a glance what coverage each plan includes.

WHICH PLAN SHOULD YOU BUY?

As a practical matter, you won't have to choose from among all ten plans. Some may not be available in your area, or the insurance companies that solicit you may be interested in selling only one or two of them. The American Association of Retired Persons sells all ten plans, so if you want to consider all of them, contact AARP.

TABLE 1: The Ten Standardized Plans—What They Cover

	A	B	C	D	E	F	G	H	I	J
Part A hospital coinsurance, days 61–90 $194 per day, 2000	•	•	•	•	•	•	•	•	•	•
Part A hospital coinsurance, days 91–150 $388 per day, 2000	•	•	•	•	•	•	•	•	•	•
All charges for extra 365 days in hospital	•	•	•	•	•	•	•	•	•	•
Part A blood deductible, 3 pints	•	•	•	•	•	•	•	•	•	•
Part B blood deductible, 3 pints	•	•	•	•	•	•	•	•	•	•
Part B coinsurance 20% of allowable charges	•	•	•	•	•	•	•	•	•	•
Skilled-nursing facility coinsurance, days 21–100 $97, 2000	—	—	•	•	•	•	•	•	•	•
Part A deductible $776 per year, 2000	—	•	•	•	•	•	•	•	•	•
Emergency care in foreign countries	—	—	•	•	•	•	•	•	•	•
Part B deductible $100 per year	—	—	•	—	—	•	—	—	—	•
Part B excess charges	—	—	—	—	—	1	2	—	1	1
At-home care needed after an injury, illness, or surgery	—	—	—	•	—	—	•	—	•	•
Prescription drugs	—	—	—	—	—	—	—	3	3	4
Preventive medical care	—	—	—	—	•	—	—	—	—	•

[1] Pays 100 percent of difference between doctor's bill and amount Medicare pays.

[2] Pays 80 percent of difference between doctor's bill and amount Medicare pays.

[3] $1,250 maximum yearly benefit; $250 deductible; 50 percent coinsurance.

[4] $3,000 maximum yearly benefit; $250 deductible; 50 percent coinsurance.

Certain plans, however, may be more appropriate for some people than others. Think about which of the following scenarios most applies to you.

If paying the premium is difficult Plans A and B are likely to be the least expensive plans, but they afford minimal protection, covering basically the Medicare Part A coinsurance as well as the Part B coinsurance. Remember, this is 20 percent of Medicare's allowable charge (see page 14). These plans cover neither the Part A nor Part B deductibles, nor the coinsurance required for a stay in a skilled-nursing facility. Paying these deductibles out of pocket can total nearly $1,000 if you require a hospital stay during the year. You will have to weigh the extra $1,000 of expenses against the additional premium charged for a supplement that covers the deductibles.

If you continue on your employer's policy and feel you still need a supplement I don't recommend buying a supplement until you leave the workforce or until your employer terminates coverage for its retirees. But if you do buy one, Plan A should be sufficient to supplement your employer's coverage.

If your doctors take assignment As I note on page 18, most doctors these days take assignment—that is, they accept Medicare's payment as payment in full and do not balance bill their patients. If all the doctors you use or are likely to use take assignment, then Plan C is your best bet. There's no sense paying for a plan that covers excess charges billed by physicians if your doctors don't bill them anyway.

If your doctors do not take assignment Plan F is the best choice if you are being billed for excess charges, or if you contemplate using specialists who will (that's one thing you need to check if you are shopping for a specialist). If you are in this situation, consider the price difference between Plan F, which covers 100 percent of the excess charges, and Plan G, which covers only 80 percent. In preparing the Ratings for this book, we found vast differences in pricing. Some companies charge $500 to $600 more for Plan F. In some areas, companies will actually sell Plan F for less than Plan G. Here's where comparison shopping will do you some good. Plans I and J also cover 100 percent of excess charges, but they carry hefty premiums because they cover prescription drugs. They may not be good buys for most people. We found premiums for Plan I ranging from $1,200 to $5,700 in 1999 for a buyer age sixty-five. For a buyer age seventy-five, one company's Plan I was $8,225, an absurdly high amount for almost all but the wealthiest beneficiaries.

If you plan to travel much outside the United States Any of the policies except Plans A and B cover some emergency care in a foreign country. Make your choice among Plans C through J based on your other needs.

If you need coverage for prescription drugs Plans H, I, and J offer coverage for pharmaceuticals, although premiums are high and coverage limited. You still have to pay a $250 deductible and half the price for each prescription, and the total benefit is limited to either $1,250 or $3,000.

The best way to see if the drug plans are worth the high premiums is to add up what you spend each year on prescription drugs and compare that total to what you would pay if you bought a supplement with prescription drug coverage. Table 2 on this page can help.

If you decide that the cost of the various drug plans is too high, you will have to pay for your prescriptions out of your own pocket. Prescriptions are no small item in a senior's budget. Another option would be to join an HMO if one in your area offers drug coverage (see Chapter 5).

TABLE 2: Is a Drug Plan Worth It?

Step 1: How much coverage will you get?

a. Add up the annual cost of your prescriptions		$1,000
b. Subtract the deductible	$250	−$250
		$750
c. Subtract the coinsurance	50% × $750 =	−$375
benefit amount:		$375
d. Compare the result to the overall prescription limit for the plan	$1,250	
The policy will reimburse you for the lesser of the limit or the benefit amount		$375

Step 2: How much extra does drug coverage cost?

a. Enter the annual premium for the drug plan (H, I, or J)		$1,368
b. Subtract the annual premium for a non-drug-plan alternative (Plans A–G)	$900	−$900
Approximate extra cost of drug plan:		$468

Step 3: Compare what you expect to receive from what you expect to pay

a. Enter what you expect to receive (from Step 1)	$375
b. Compare what you expect to pay (from Step 2)	$468
Will you pay out more than you expect to receive?	yes

What about buying drug coverage when you are first eligible for Medicare as a sort of insurance policy against the time when you might need more medications? If you have the funds to pay the high premiums, and feel you might need drugs in the future, then consider buying Plan H, I, or J during the six-month period when insurers have to accept you. Most seniors, however, don't have extra cash to put into a supplemental policy.

It is possible that Congress will add a drug benefit to the Medicare benefit package. But the pharmaceutical companies and others have mounted strong opposition to such a benefit, fearing federal price controls. As this book went to press, Congress had taken no action.

Frills to consider lightly Benefits for at-home recovery care and preventive care are small potatoes when it comes to buying a supplement. Don't base your decision on whether those benefits are available on a Medicare-supplement policy, and don't let a salesperson sell you a policy just because it has these benefits. Both benefits are very limited.

The most popular policies are Plans C and F. Both come with coverage for the $100 Part B deductible. Buying coverage that pays the first $100 of any physician or hospital outpatient charge is simply dollar trading, since you could easily pay $100 in extra premiums for the coverage. In reality, though, you may not have much choice.

WHAT YOU PAY FOR A POLICY

You will have a choice of a policy that comes with "attained age" pricing, "issue age" pricing, or one that is "community rated." It's important to understand those distinctions because they will influence what you or your relative will pay now and in the future. The kind of pricing will ultimately determine whether the policy will be affordable in the long run.

Attained-age policies These offer the best rates to younger beneficiaries at the expense of the oldest and sickest. Insurers offer low rates to those turning sixty-five in an attempt to hook them to the company. In states that allow attained-age pricing, most insurers have chosen to use it. The catch with attained-age policies is that premiums increase each year just because a beneficiary gets older. (Premiums can also increase because of medical inflation.) By the time a policyholder reaches age seventy-five or eighty, yearly rate hikes may mean the policy is out of reach for someone on a fixed or a declining income. For example, one attained-age policy sold in Cincinnati costs only $1,094 for someone age sixty-five, but for someone age seventy-five, the policy costs $1,566, almost $500 more.

Community-rated policies With a community-rated policy, the insurance company charges all policyholders the same rate. A sixty-five-year-old pays the same premium as a seventy-five-year-old for identical benefits. Older policyholders fare better under this arrangement since they won't face steep premiums in their later years. However, it's hard to find community-rated policies these days. The AARP sells them, and so do a few Blue Cross plans. Six states—Connecticut, Maine, Massachusetts, Minnesota, New York, and Washington—require sellers to offer them.

Issue-age policies These policies are a hybrid. Premiums depend on a buyer's age when the policy is purchased, but unlike attained-age policies, premiums don't increase merely because the policyholder ages. Thus they offer some price stability for older beneficiaries, but can and do increase almost every year because the price of medical care continues to rise. Florida and Georgia require insurers to sell only issue-age policies.

Many insurance companies try to gain a competitive advantage by selling attained-age-rated policies. Look out for sales agents who try to persuade you or your relative to switch carriers on the basis of a lower attained-age premium. Seventy-five-year-old Dorothy Starr, who lives near Chicago, got an unexpected call one day from an insurance agent who said she wanted to help Dorothy get a lower premium than the one she was paying for her Medicare-supplement policy from Illinois Blue Cross Blue Shield. The agent pitched policies from Mutual of Omaha and from Pioneer Life, both of which sell attained-age-rated policies. But Dorothy was better off keeping her Blue Cross policy, which would protect her from steep premium increases as she gets older.

If you have a community-rated policy, and an agent tries to persuade you to drop it for an attained-age policy, understand that you will pay much more later. Also, if you have a community-rated policy with prescription drug benefits, it is not wise to switch just because some agent comes along promising a low first-year premium. If you are tempted to switch carriers for a lower premium, ask about the pricing method the insurance carrier uses. Paying more at younger ages may be worth the trade-off of having an affordable premium when you are older. It boils down to paying now or paying later, and which gamble you choose to take.

PREMIUMS USUALLY GO UP

If ever there were a truism in the business of Medicare-supplement policies, it is that premiums will rise every year. If health care costs go up and the costs of Medicare services rise, price increases for Medigap insurance are sure to follow. A sample of premiums for Medicare-supplement policies sold by AARP/UnitedHealthcare, Bankers Life and Casualty, and United American, three of the largest carriers, are up 13 percent over the past year. Some years the increases are smaller, in some years larger.

CONSUMER REPORTS also discovered that there is wide variation in premiums among sellers even within the same geographic area. The ratings in Appendix E give you an idea of the range in premiums across the country.

THE 20 PERCENT TRAP

One of the big reasons for the increase in premiums has been the shift in many hospital procedures to outpatient settings and the inclination of hospitals to increase their billings to Medicare-supplement carriers. When this happens the Medigap insurers simply pass those costs on to policyholders in the form of higher premiums. The mechanics of how the hospital bills are too complex to discuss here, but the result is the carrier ends up paying more than the 20 percent coinsurance amount. If you don't have a Medigap policy, you pay the higher coinsurance amount. For some 5.5 million beneficiaries who don't have a policy, this can result in whopping out-of-pocket expenses. If you are advising an elderly relative who does not have a Medicare supplement or any other kind of insurance to fill in Medicare's gaps, beware of this loophole.

This loophole has resulted in the government paying less than its 80 percent share of the Part B outpatient charges while beneficiaries, through their Medigap carriers, have been paying more than their 20 percent share. (Remember, all Medicare supplements pay the 20 percent Part B coinsurance for doctors' visits and hospital outpatient procedures.) The 1997 Balanced Budget Act took steps to close the loophole, but it will take from twenty to forty years before beneficiaries will really be paying 20 percent of the allowable charges. In the meantime, the 20 percent Part B trap will continue to push up premiums for seniors as hospitals push up their charges for outpatient services.

HOW YOUR HEALTH AFFECTS WHAT YOU CAN BUY

Retirees new to the Medicare-supplement market often wonder whether they will be able to get a policy if they already have certain medical conditions; they also ask if a policy will cover those preexisting conditions. With Medigap insurance, the answers are pretty straightforward.

Looking at Your Health

Some Medigap carriers do "underwrite" this kind of coverage—that is, they carefully look at the health problems you have, and decide if they want to insure you. They may ask if you have ever been diagnosed with internal cancer, cardiovascular problems, Alzheimer's disease, and the like. If you say yes, they may reject you. People facing surgery or those with cataracts may also be rejected since insurers don't want to "buy a claim," as they say.

If you apply for a plan offering drug coverage, the company almost certainly will underwrite you, but it may be very picky about the health conditions you have. If you are already taking medications, the company will probably turn you down. Even the AARP, which issues a policy to everyone who applies for Plans A through G, carefully looks at applicants' health status if they apply for the plans with drug coverage. When a policy is available regardless of a person's health, it is called a "guaranteed issue" policy. Some Blue Cross Blue Shield plans may also sell guaranteed-issue policies.

The Six-Month Rule

During the first six months after you sign up for Medicare Part B, you can buy any Medicare supplement no matter how sick you are. A federal law prohibits insurers from using your health status to deny coverage for applicants sixty-five and older when they first sign up for Medicare. In other words, if you have a chronic health condition, this rule allows you to get any supplement you want, even those with drug coverage. If you are sick, take a lot of drugs, and can afford the premium, then consider Plan H, I, or J.

A word of caution: The six-month window opens once you sign up for Part B, so be sure that you really want Medicare coverage before you sign up. Don't make the mistake of signing up for Medicare, continuing to work, staying on your employer's policy, and losing your six-month window.

Preexisting Conditions Clauses

These impose a waiting period before the policy covers you for medical conditions you have at the time the policy is written. If you have been diagnosed or treated for a particular condition within the last three to six months, the policy will offer no coverage for that condition for a stated number of months, usually three or six. The waiting period can be no longer than six months, but it may be shorter. Most companies must count the months of prior coverage against the preexisting conditions period. A few carriers offer coverage from day one for any health condition. If you have been covered by one Medicare-supplement policy and switch to a new one, the new carrier cannot make you satisfy another preexisting condition requirement. However, the federal Health Insurance Portability and Accountability Act requires that you sign up for new coverage within sixty-three days after your previous coverage ends and under certain circumstances such as when your HMO terminates your coverage. If you don't, you lose the protections of the act and must satisfy the preexisting conditions requirements imposed by the new carrier.

THE RIGHT TO A GUARANTEED-ISSUE MEDICARE-SUPPLEMENT POLICY

The Balanced Budget Act sets up an annual enrollment period for selecting a way to cover gaps in Medicare. Chapter 5 tells when the new rules are to be phased in. The idea was to push as many beneficiaries as possible into various managed-care options. The law also set out rules governing beneficiaries who return to traditional Medicare and Medicare-supplement insurance, making it possible to get a guaranteed-issue policy—that is, a policy you can get without regard to your health status.

The law listed a number of triggering events that affect what you can buy. In all circumstances, you are eligible for Plans A, B, C, and F. But in some cases, such as when an HMO to which you belong stops offering Medicare benefits, you are not allowed to buy any of the plans offering drug coverage. This puts many beneficiaries in a jam. They lose drug benefits from their HMO but can't buy a Medicare-supplement policy plan that offers them.

If you are advising an elderly relative who loses HMO coverage and are unsure of your options, contact your state insurance counseling program (see Appendix A). You can also call your state insurance department to see if there are special protections that apply in your state. (See Appendix F for a list of state insurance departments.)

MEDICARE SELECT POLICIES

Medicare Select policies are a hybrid—they contain elements of both managed-care and traditional Medicare-supplement policies. Companies choose at least one of the ten standardized plans as their Medicare Select option. The AARP, for example, uses only Plan C, but other companies may offer other plans.

If you choose a Select option, you will get all the benefits the policy provides, but if you need care in a hospital, you will have to use one that is part of a network sponsored by the insurer. The hospitals in the network agree to provide care at some discount, which in turn allows the insurance carrier to offer somewhat lower premiums. In this way, they are like Medicare HMOs. If you go outside the network, you may have different benefits, and you may pay more of the cost. Select plans, though, usually do not have networks of doctors. You can see any physician you like. In that way, Medicare Select policies give beneficiaries the same options they would have with a traditional Medicare supplement.

If you don't use network hospitals, you will incur out-of-pocket hospital expenses, but unlike an HMO, Medicare will still pay its share. For example, if you choose AARP's Select plan, and don't use a network hospital, you'll have to pay the Part A deductible, $776 (for each benefit period) in 2000, and the Part A coinsurance as well. With AARP's policy, though, there are two exceptions. You won't have to pay those costs if you receive emergency care in a nonnetwork hospital or if the treatment you need cannot be given in a network hospital.

The biggest reason for choosing a Select option is a lower premium. The 1999 CONSUMER REPORTS study found that premiums for Select policies were on average 20 percent lower than comparable non-Select plans. Savings from Select plans can vary a lot by plan. In Georgia, AARP discounts its Plan C policy by 13 percent, but Pioneer Life discounts its Plan C by 23 percent, and Bankers Life and Casualty discounts its Select offering by 35 percent.

Before opting for the lower premium of a Medicare Select policy, you need to consider the following:

1. Are the network hospitals near your home and do you want to use them? If they are, then a Select plan is a good choice. If network hospitals are thirty miles away, a Select plan is not a good option despite its lower premium.

2. Consider what happens if you need hospital care away from home—say you spend winters in Florida but live in Ohio. Will you have to pay out of your pocket if you use out-of-network hospitals? Or will the insurer pay a percentage of your out-of-pocket costs? AARP says it pays 75 percent of the costs if policyholders use out-of-network hospitals while traveling.

4. Ask in what situations the insurance carrier will not make you pay the Part A deductible or the Part A coinsurance.

5. Find out whether the doctors, including specialists, you use or plan to use have admitting privileges at the network hospitals. If they don't, it's pointless to take a Select plan.

MEDICARE-SUPPLEMENT POLICIES FOR THE DISABLED

Medicare provides benefits for certain disabled people under age sixty-five if they are receiving Social Security disability benefits and have been disabled for twenty-four months. If you are helping a disabled relative who is not yet sixty-five, it's important to keep a few things in mind about Medigap policies. These policies are not available to the disabled in every state, and if a state requires companies to sell policies to this group, it may rule that insurance carriers only have to sell certain plans, which severely limits the choices available to disabled people. Some companies offer only Plan A; others provide additional choices. (In 1999, CONSUMER REPORTS found a wide range in premiums for policies sold to the disabled; for Plan C, for example, premiums ranged from under $800 to more than $3,000.)

The following companies told us they sell policies to disabled people:

Alliance Blue Cross Blue Shield
Bankers Life and Casualty
Blue Cross Blue Shield of Colorado
Blue Cross Blue Shield of New Hampshire
Blue Cross Blue Shield of Indiana
Blue Cross Blue Shield of Kansas City
Blue Cross Blue Shield of Massachusetts
Blue Cross Blue Shield of Michigan
Blue Cross Blue Shield of Minnesota
Blue Cross Blue Shield of Nevada
Blue Cross Blue Shield of North Carolina
Blue Cross Blue Shield United of Wisconsin
Blue Shield of California
Central States Health & Life of Omaha
Combined Insurance Company of America
Conseco Direct Life Insurance Co.
Equitable Life and Casualty
Guarantee Trust Life
Golden Rule Insurance
Standard Life
Trigon Blue Cross Blue Shield
United American Insurance
UnitedHealthcare Insurance Co./AARP

HMOs must accept people with disabilities, so if there is an HMO in your area that offers Medicare benefits, that may be the best option for someone who is disabled (see Chapter 5).

OTHER INSURANCE OPTIONS

It is very important to distinguish between traditional Medicare-supplement insurance and various other health insurance products that an agent may try to sell you over the kitchen table or through a mail solicitation. These products are not Medicare-supplement policies and may even duplicate the coverage provided by Medicare. Carefully consider all the pros and cons before you buy one, even if the premiums sound cheap. Mostly, there are cons.

Hospital Indemnity Policies

These policies are among the worst buys in health insurance, often costing you more in premiums than you'll ever get back in benefits. You don't get very much, and you don't pay very much. Some of these policies have "loss ratios" of 30 and 40 percent; that means policyholders will get back in benefits only thirty to forty cents on the dollar.

How does a hospital indemnity policy work? You simply sign up for a specific benefit that the insurer advertises, and you receive that amount if you are hospitalized. These policies pay a fixed amount for each day you are in the hospital. The benefits are low, usually around $100 to $120, but could be even lower depending on the policy.

With some policies, such as the one sold by AARP, you get a larger benefit if you are in the hospital a long time. For example, with that policy, a policyholder age sixty-five and older would receive $69 a day for each day up to sixty days of hospitalization. The policyholder would receive $120 for sixty-one to ninety days in the hospital, and $192 after that. Collecting the larger amounts is unlikely because the average hospital stay today is only about seven days.

Furthermore, Medicare pays for almost the entire hospital stay, so this benefit is really superfluous. Sellers of this type of coverage try to make a case for their product, arguing that the benefit provides pocket money when someone is sick. The benefit pays for extra expenses that often accompany a serious illness—parking fees, meals, hotel bills, and so forth. In other words, people are using this insurance to pay for non-health-related incidentals. You may want a policy for that reason, but it is an inefficient way to buy health insurance.

Even though the premium is low relative to other kinds of health coverage—annual premiums for AARP's policy, for instance, range from $372 to $186—that money might be more wisely spent on a better long-term-care insurance policy or a more comprehensive Medicare supplement. If you have $300 of extra money in your health insurance budget, that money could go toward buying inflation coverage on a long-term-care policy. Or you could simply save it and build up a health insurance cushion to absorb inevitable increases in prescription drug costs and other out-of-pocket health care expenses (see Chapter 3).

Dread Disease Policies

These policies are similarly poor buys. They pay a fixed amount of money for each day you are in the hospital for treatment for a specific disease, usually cancer. We have the same criticisms of these policies as we do for hospital-indemnity coverage.

THE NEW INSURANCE OPTIONS ALLOWED BY THE BALANCED BUDGET ACT

When this book went to press, only one insurance carrier had come forward to market the private-fee-for-service insurance plans authorized by the Balanced Budget Act of 1997. There were no sellers of MSAs. That is not to say that some of the new options won't show up in the next few years as sellers figure out how to make money from them.

The important thing to keep in mind is "buyer beware" when it comes to the new options, and they should not be confused with traditional Medicare-supplement insurance. As Chapter 3 points out, the insurance company can charge or offer whatever it wants with few or no restrictions. Premiums may be high, especially if the carrier offers drug coverage. Benefits are not standardized, and coinsurance and deductibles are unregulated.

Some sellers may try to lure you in with a generous prescription drug benefit, and indeed that may sound attractive. If you are presented with one of the new options or you are not sure what to do, take these precautions:

1. Ask if the policy is one of the standardized Medicare-supplement plans. If it is not, ask what it is. Make the agent explain what it is and how it fits into the Medicare + Choice program discussed in Chapter 3. Specifically, ask if it is the private-fee-for-service option. If it is, look at the warnings discussed on pages 42–43.

2. Look carefully at the premium, coinsurance, and deductibles, and see how much you would have to pay if you have a serious illness. Can you afford that kind of out-of-pocket expense?

3. If there is a drug benefit, how good is it? What would you still have to pay for prescriptions after the policy pays its share? Is the drug benefit worth the potential risk of high coinsurance and high deductibles (if the policy has these) and potentially high out-of-pocket expenses?

SELECTING A MEDICARE-SUPPLEMENT POLICY

Even though our ratings in Appendix E are based on prices current in 1999, you can still use the ratings to judge which companies have lower premiums in relation to others. A company whose premiums are significantly less than another's will most likely continue to be competitive. The ratings also flag companies that use attained-age pricing, issue-age pricing, or community rates. As I've noted on page 56, attained-age pricing, even though it may offer a lower initial rate, can give you an expensive surprise ten or fifteen years from now. Other than in states that require issue-age or community rating, most companies use attained-age pricing.

You can also use the ratings to determine if you can afford a Medicare-supplement policy. If the premiums are well beyond your budget, you should head straight to an HMO, providing that there is one in your area offering Medicare benefits.

SHOULD YOU SWITCH POLICIES?

If you have an existing policy that predates the law that standardized Medicare-supplement policies—that is, a policy you bought before 1992—you should compare the benefits and premiums to what is now available. For example, one eighty-three-year-old woman in Maryland had an old policy that provided good hospital and surgical coverage, but not much coverage for physician visits. It was still cheaper than the standardized plans, and much cheaper than one with similar hospital coverage. Her old supplement will cover her needs so she did not switch.

If the policy you have now is more expensive than other policies an agent may try to sell you, check to see whether the company has used attained-age pricing, issue-age pricing, or is community rated. If the policy is issue-age rated or community rated, it is probably best to keep it rather than cash it in for a lower premium that will surely rise as the years go on.

If you have a traditional Medicare-supplement policy, should you cash it in and go to an HMO, especially one that offers prescription drug benefits? It is tempting to do that, particularly if you are having trouble paying for your prescriptions. However, there are no guarantees that the plan will continue to offer prescription drug benefits, or that the premiums will remain low, or that the HMO will even continue to offer coverage in future years.

KEY DECISION POINTS

1. If you are continuing to work past age sixty-five and will continue on your employer's policy, don't sign up for Medicare Part B. In fact, don't sign up until you are ready for Medicare so that you don't lose the six-month window during which you can buy any supplement without regard to your health status.

2. Use Table 2 on page 55 as a worksheet to determine if it's worthwhile to buy one of the plans with prescription drug coverage.

3. Think carefully before buying an attained-age policy. The price can rise steeply, perhaps making the policy unaffordable in your later years.

4. If you take many prescription drugs, and can afford the premium, consider buying one of the three drug plans when you are eligible for your six-month open window.

5. Before signing up for a Medicare Select option, be sure you understand the consequences of using an out-of-network hospital. If you do use one, you could be on the hook for thousands of dollars.

6. Do not buy hospital indemnity and dread-disease policies. These are poor insurance buys. If you purchased one when you were younger, consider cashing it in when you reach age sixty-five and putting the premium toward a better supplement policy or long-term-care insurance.

FIVE

The Managed-Care Options

Eighty-four-year-old Mrs. T. fell near her home in Albuquerque, New Mexico, and broke her right arm and right leg. Two weeks later, after she was discharged from the hospital, she still could not walk or care for herself. She needed skilled-nursing care.

Mrs. T. had joined an Albuquerque HMO because the monthly premium of $37 was so much cheaper than she would pay for a Medicare-supplement policy. When the hospital discharged her, the HMO refused to pay for an ambulance but instead sent her in a private car to a skilled-nursing facility, which would provide the follow-up care she needed. There she stayed about two months, receiving the care and therapy her doctor said she required. The HMO refused to pay and Mrs. T. had to deplete her modest savings, paying the bill that totaled nearly $7,000. Her son contacted an attorney specializing in legal problems of the elderly and asked for help.

The attorney asked the HMO to reconsider its denial of benefits. The HMO refused. After a second request and some hard negotiations, the HMO relented, and reimbursed Mrs. T. for her out-of-pocket expenses.

Mrs. T. had chosen to receive her Medicare benefits from an HMO. The $37 monthly premium the HMO was charging was a huge savings over what she would have had to pay for a Medicare-supplement policy. The plan also offered an added bonus:

prescription drug coverage. However, when Mrs. T. fell, she experienced the dark side of managed care: tighter control over medical services, especially skilled-nursing care.

As many seniors soon learn, managed care is neither black nor white. Some seniors love the care they get from HMOs, others detest it. Some have had good experiences in so-called bad plans, others have had bad experiences in "good" plans. The federal government and others have spent millions of dollars trying to figure out the best way to help seniors choose a managed-care plan. Lots of groups think they have the answers. CONSUMER REPORTS has evaluated many of the so-called report cards, including those available for Medicare beneficiaries, and found them difficult to use and not very informative or helpful.

There are many unknowns when it comes to choosing a managed-care option. We do know there are differences among HMOs. The HMOs in your area may contract with different doctors and hospitals, and they may provide both good and bad care; rules for getting approvals for services and referrals to specialists vary among plans—and so does consumer satisfaction. It may be possible to learn some of these things before making your decision but not all of them.

If you or a relative you are advising are thinking about signing up for a managed-care plan, it's important to understand how a plan works, how joining one is different from receiving your benefits from traditional Medicare, what you gain, and what you potentially lose.

HOW MEDICARE MANAGED CARE WORKS

HMOs that want to enroll Medicare beneficiaries contract with the Health Care Financing Administration, the government agency that administers the Medicare program. HMOs agree to provide beneficiaries who enroll all of the benefits that Medicare provides—coverage for hospital care, outpatient services, doctor visits, laboratory services, skilled-nursing services, skilled care at home, prescription drugs needed in the hospital, and so on. In return for providing all Medicare benefits, the government pays the plan what is called a "capitation" rate—a monthly payment intended to cover all the services the average beneficiary might need. The plan is at risk for all services any senior requires. If it can provide them for less than the government pays, the health plan makes money. If it cannot, the HMO may lose money. These arrangements are called "risk" contracts. A few HMOs have a payment arrangement known as a cost contract. With these, the government pays the plan based on the actual cost of treating a beneficiary. Cost contracts will be phased out by 2002, but in the meantime, a few plans still offer them (see page 94).

The Lock-In Feature

Beneficiaries agree to receive all their care through the HMO. This means they have to use the doctors, hospitals, labs, home care agencies, and skilled-nursing facilities that are part of a plan's network. If someone wants to see a specialist for a particular condition, that specialist must be in the network in order for the plan to cover the doctor's services. To get a referral to a specialist, you must first see your primary-care doctor, who acts as a gatekeeper to the specialty care you may need. The primary-care doctor then decides on the referral.

If you go out of network for any reason except emergency care, you will have no Medicare benefits. In other words, you won't be able to go to your favorite heart specialist if he's not in your HMO's network and then send the bill to Medicare. This is called the lock-in feature, and many HMO salespeople gloss over this important provision.

If you are interested in joining a Medicare managed-care plan, call your state insurance department (see Appendix F) and ask which plans operate in your county. You can also call the national Medicare hot line at 1-800-638-6833, or log on to Medicare's website *www.medicare.gov.*

Emergency Care

The rules are somewhat different if you need emergency care. The HMO must pay for emergency care given by out-of-network providers if you need immediate services because of a sudden illness or if your health will be permanently damaged if you do not get immediate care. You do not need preauthorization from the plan for emergency care, and the HMO must pay even if the emergency condition turns out to be a nonemergency; for example, you go to the hospital because you had chest pains, but the diagnosis was really angina instead of a heart attack.

Urgent Care

HMOs must cover urgent-care services—that is, treatment that cannot be delayed because of an unforeseen illness or injury that occurs during a temporary absence from the HMO's service area. The HMO must pay if your illness or injury is unexpected and the illness requires medical attention that cannot be delayed until you return to the plan's service area. However, if you are in the HMO's service area, the HMO won't cover urgent care delivered by out-of-network providers.

If you are in the HMO's service area when an unexpected illness occurs, you must get care from in-network providers or you will have to pay out of pocket for the services you need. HMOs generally do not cover nonurgent care received outside the HMO's service area. So if you plan to do a lot of traveling, an HMO may not be the best option.

WHAT YOU GAIN WITH AN HMO

Lower out-of-pocket expenses Even though many HMOs are not the financial attractions they were a few years ago, they are still better deals than taking a Medicare-supplement policy and receiving benefits through traditional Medicare. On average, almost 50 percent of the plans we rated in 2000 charge no premium. The average monthly premium for the HMOs charging premiums in the thirty cities we examined for this book was almost $55. In comparison, premiums for the Plan C Medicare-supplement policies in our study average around $1,250 a year for a person age sixty-five. So even with premium increases, HMOs still afford considerable savings. Keep in mind that you must continue to pay the Part B premium, which will be deducted from your Social Security check.

With an HMO, cost sharing is likely to be lower as well. You won't be responsible for the hospital coinsurance amounts or the 20 percent Part B coinsurance. All Medicare supplements cover this coinsurance, but for people who can't afford a supplement, this is a significant out-of-pocket expense. For them, joining an HMO relieves them of paying Medicare's coinsurance. However, the HMO may impose its own coinsurance, usually a small amount, when you use the services.

Extra benefits In addition to the usual Medicare benefits (see Chapter 2), many HMOs offer a package of extras, most notably prescription drug coverage. This can be very valuable to seniors struggling to pay for their medicines. The drug benefit is discussed more fully on pages 78–80. Plans may also offer some coverage for eyeglasses, dental care, and chiropractic services.

Wellness and health monitoring programs Some HMOs offer a variety of wellness programs. These may take the form of health and exercise clubs, or they may simply consist of handouts that give nutrition and exercise tips. While these may be helpful, they should not be the reason you choose an HMO, even though some plans may heavily promote such programs. Of more value are special monitoring programs for people who have particular diseases such as diabetes or congestive heart failure. Only 23 percent of plans that responded to a CONSUMER REPORTS study a few years ago said they had implemented programs to assess how well their Medicare members functioned both physically and cognitively—something all plans should do. Very few of them indicated they had established programs to intervene when members were at risk, and virtually none measured the effectiveness of their interventions. Identifying problems and correcting them—in other words, channeling their older members to appropriate services to improve the quality of their lives—is what good managed care should be doing. If you find a plan that can help you or your relative function better, you should strongly consider signing up. Those plans, however, are rare.

WHAT YOU LOSE WITH AN HMO

The ability to see any doctor or specialist or go to any provider You must receive all your care from doctors in the HMO's network. Discounts obtained from providers by the health plan are a major reason why an HMO is able to offer lower monthly premiums. So, of course, the HMO wants you to stay in the plan when you need care. Using plan doctors may be okay for people who are relatively healthy, who don't mind switching physicians (see page 86 for advice on selecting a new doctor), or who really need to save money by going to an HMO.

But for those who have relationships with specialists whom they trust, switching to HMO doctors may be traumatic and unwise. If the hospitals you want to use are near your home and your relatives can easily get to them, but they are not in the network, switching to an HMO and using other hospitals may not be a good idea either.

Slow approvals and referrals to specialists Managed care uses a concept called utilization review, which means the plan may carefully review the care that you need, including tests, referrals to specialists, and treatments. Sometimes you have to wait several days, and occasionally several weeks, for a test or treatment. The wait to diagnose or treat an illness may be agonizingly slow and nerve-racking. This can be a real downside to managed care.

Not all plans make beneficiaries jump through such hoops, but it's difficult to determine which ones control services more tightly than others. The website of the Health Care Financing Administration *(www.medicare.gov)* attempts to tell beneficiaries which plans are easier to get referrals from. However, this measure, "Ease of Getting Referrals to a Specialist," displays the percentage of plan members who said it was not a problem to get a referral to a specialist. There is an underlying caveat to consider when using this measure to judge an HMO. Although individual members may be unhappy if they cannot see specialists when they want to, the savings that managed care is supposed to generate (savings that fund the additional benefits offered by these plans) must come from managing how many services people use. This may require appropriately limiting access to specialists for some patients.

Your access to specialists may also depend more upon the practice style of your primary-care physician than on corporate policy, so keep these caveats in mind when you evaluate this measure on HCFA's website.

Fewer visits for home health aides and fewer days approved for skilled-nursing services Some research indicates that Medicare beneficiaries who join a managed-care plan may get fewer visits for home health services or less skilled-nursing care. (Keep in mind that both benefits are limited anyway.) As Mrs. T., whose story is related at the beginning of this chapter, learned, some plans can be downright chintzy when it comes to providing these services. But as with referrals to specialists, there is little reliable information around to guide you to the more generous plans.

If you think a relative will be needing these services in the near future, you may decide against joining managed care. Of course, you will have to weigh the immediate benefit of lower premiums and other lower out-of-pocket expenses against the possibility of needing such care in the future. Also weigh the issue of continuity of care, higher premiums, and changing benefits. HMOs can throw providers out of their networks, raise premiums, and increase coinsurance. An HMO that offers a good deal today may offer a terrible one next year. Keep in mind that everything can change.

CHOOSING AN HMO

If you have read all the material in the previous pages and decide that an HMO is for you, it's time to choose a plan. Depending on where you live, you may have several plans available to you, only one or two, or maybe none. If you have none, the choice is easy: Pick the lowest-cost Medicare supplement and stay with traditional Medicare. Many counties or areas in the United States are not served by any HMO. Many of these are in rural locations where provider-sponsored organizations, one of the new Medicare + Choice options, may take root. (See pages 41–42 for a discussion of the problems with provider-sponsored organizations.)

If several HMOs serve Medicare beneficiaries in your area, which will be the case in large cities, the choice is more complicated. The Medicare Compare database published by the Health Care Financing Administration (HCFA) on its website (*www.medicare.gov*) provides a good starting point, listing all the plans that offer coverage in your county.

Many organizations make information available to beneficiaries to help them select a plan. Although there is a lot of information, in reality, there is not a lot of good information—much of it is bland and not very helpful. In 1998, CONSUMER REPORTS pioneered a unique methodology for rating both Medicare HMOs and Medicare-supplement policies to determine which options gave beneficiaries the best value for their premiums. We also evaluated the prescription drug benefits for each Medicare HMO. We have updated those ratings for 2000 in Appendix G.

Some of the information made available by various groups purports to tell beneficiaries something about the quality of medical care, but we really know very little about the kind of care that is delivered through HMOs (see pages 84–86).

What follows is CONSUMER REPORTS' guide to finding the best HMO for you.

CONSUMER REPORTS' GUIDE TO CHOOSING AN HMO

Choice 1: Selecting the Network

If you select an HMO, you may find your choice of doctors and hospitals limited. Check the plan's directories to see whether the providers you use already belong to the network. Network directories, though, are often out-of-date. Call the doctors you want to use and ask if they are taking new patients from the HMO you are considering. Sometimes the doctors may take new patients but not from an HMO. If the doctor is still taking new patients from the plan, ask if he or she intends to continue as part of the plan's network.

If the providers are in none of the managed-care networks, you bump into the first trade-off: Is giving up doctors and perhaps specialists you like worth the prospect of lower out-of-pocket costs and a prescription drug benefit?

If your providers are in one or two plans, but not in others, the second trade-off arises: Do you consider HMOs that will make you change providers in return for lower costs and the drug benefit, or do you want to look only at the plans where your doctors are part of the network?

Consider where you will have to go for lab tests. Will a technician come to your home, or will you have to go to the lab? In some parts of the country, plans require frail and infirm beneficiaries to make their way to a lab to have tests done. Presumably to save money, they no longer send technicians to members' homes. If you can't make it to the lab, or your relative can't, don't join an HMO.

Choice 2: Getting Value for Your Money

After you have chosen several plans to investigate further, the next step is to look at what you have to pay and what you get for your money. We have made such an analysis for the HMOs offered in thirty cities. (Cities include: Atlanta, Boston, Chicago, Cincinnati, Cleveland, Dallas, Denver, Detroit, Houston, Jacksonville, Kansas City, Las Vegas, Los Angeles, Louisville, Manchester, N.H., Miami, Milwaukee, Minneapolis, New York, New Orleans, Philadelphia, Phoenix,

Pittsburgh, Portland, Raleigh, Saint Louis, San Francisco, Seattle, Tampa, and Washington, D.C.)

Our unique value calculation shows which plans offer the most benefits for the premium you will pay. We estimated the value of significant benefits offered by the plan in each of the thirty cities and compared that with the value of Medicare benefits plus the premium the plan charged. The results are shown in Appendix G. Most HMOs offer good value for your money. You can see this from the number of HMOs whose value index is greater than 100. The higher the number the better the value.

Within a metropolitan area, an HMO may offer different packages of benefits with different premiums for each. The plan offering the best value may operate in only one county in a metropolitan area. The Ratings show the cheapest premiums charged in that area. Depending on where you live in the area, you may pay more. Such variations result because the government pays HMOs based on the price of medical care in the county where you live. In some counties the payment is more generous because the cost of care is higher. In those counties, plans may have more money to offer a better package of benefits. Nothing in the HMO business is set in concrete. Keep in mind, as I have noted, that benefit packages do change, and a plan offering a good deal this year may offer a poor one next year.

From the tables, pick two or three plans that give you the best value for your money and then proceed to Choice 3 to examine the features in more depth.

If you live in a city whose HMOs we have not analyzed, refer to the website of the Health Care Financing Administration (www.medicare.gov). Your options are likely to be limited (the thirty cities we looked at included most areas where a lot of HMOs operate). Consider the premium, the doctor, the copayment, and the prescription drug benefit. Does it seem to cover your needs? Make sure you are not paying too much for your coverage. Nashville, Tennessee, is not one of the cities we looked at, but the following analysis tells how to use the information you may get from HCFA's website. Beneficiaries have the choice of five HMO options. All the plans cover inpatient hospitalization fully, so you don't need to dwell on that issue. One plan charges a $14-per-month premium but has no prescription drug coverage. The main benefit of that plan appears to be a $5 savings in copayments to doctors; you would need to make thirty-four doctor visits each year just to break even. The other plans offer coverage for no premiums, and two of these have prescription drug coverage. If either of these plans is still on your list, get in touch with the plans to get accurate information concerning their benefits, especially the drug benefit. Find out if your particular prescriptions are on their formulary and calculate how much you will save annually. One plan requires 50 percent coinsurance per brand-name prescription, but has a $2,500 annual cap. This might be a good choice for someone with high prescription drug expenses. The other plan requires a $10 copayment per prescription, but only covers up to $500 per year.

Choice 3: Understanding the Prescription Drug Benefit

The availability of this benefit is a major reason to choose an HMO, but those benefits vary widely among plans. Fewer than 10 percent of the plans we rated in 2000 offered an unlimited prescription drug benefit; a few limit annual expenditures to $250. HMOs say that prices of prescriptions are increasing some 10 to 15 percent a year, and those increases have caused many plans to reduce the benefit or drop it entirely. About 22 percent of the plans we rated had no prescription coverage in 2000. Many plans now use a tiered-pricing arrangement, requiring a lower copayment for generic drugs, a somewhat higher copayment for preferred brand-name drugs, and a much higher copayment for very expensive brand-name drugs or those for which there is a generic therapeutic equivalent. For example, while the copayment might be $5 for a generic and $15 for a preferred brand, a brand-name drug not on the formulary could cost $30.

Our Ratings evaluate the quality of the drug benefit. We considered both the annual cap and the average proportion of drug costs covered. If you have high prescription drug costs, and one of the plans among those you are considering offers a much better drug benefit, then choose that plan. Remember, though, a good benefit now might disappear next year. If a plan believes it is losing money on the benefit and the cost of prescription drugs continues to rise, an HMO may well reduce its benefit next year, perhaps causing you to yet again go through the process of selecting a plan.

If you are considering a plan whose drug benefit we have not evaluated, the worksheet "Paying for Your Medications" (see page 81) will help you decide whether the plan's benefit is worthwhile. Consider the following as you go through the worksheet:

The cap The cap, or limit, is the maximum the plan will pay each year. Some plans have no cap, but most have one that ranges from $250 to $4,000. Some plans limit only brand-name drugs or cover generic drugs even after the cap has been reached; these are slightly less restrictive than the same cap with a combined limit.

Copayment This is the amount the HMO asks you to pay toward the cost of a drug. The amount varies depending on whether the drug is a brand name or a generic and on whether you buy through the mail or go to a pharmacy. Some plans may also require different payments for drugs on their formulary—the list of drugs they will cover.

How the drug price is applied to the cap HMOs deduct the price of the drugs from the cap. The more a drug costs, the faster you'll use up the benefit. Usually plans negotiate significant discounts from the "average wholesale price" (AWP) assigned by the manufacturer—often 15 to 20 percent. Ideally, the plan uses the amount actually paid to determine how much to reduce the cap, but plans may use the retail price of the drug or the average wholesale price, which will eat up your benefit faster. Only a handful of plans we surveyed were willing to talk about their pricing arrangements, but we received enough information to see that there is great variation. Be aware of this variation, and try to get as much information as you can, but be prepared to come up against a blank wall in your quest for details.

The formulary: open, closed, or in between Most plans use a formulary to control which drugs you can get. This helps them keep their costs low yet assures that you get medications that are effective for your condition. Formularies have gotten bad press in recent years because some patients have said they can't get the drugs they need. This may be true in some cases, but on balance, formularies do more good than harm because they do hold down costs and help doctors choose efficacious drugs. Typically, HMOs classify their formularies as open, closed, or tiered. With an open formulary, the plan pays for almost any drug. In a closed formulary, the plan will pay only for drugs on its approved list. However, "open" and "closed" are slippery terms. An open formulary may still have some restrictions. A closed formulary may still offer beneficiaries some leeway. Sometimes doctors can get approval for drugs not on the formulary. Plans with closed formularies told us they grant such approvals anywhere from 10 percent to 99 percent of the time. Some of the more frequently contested drugs are Celebrex, Prilosec, Fosamax, and Vioxx. Does the formulary include the medications you currently take? Just because they are on the list today does not mean they will be tomorrow or next year. Drug prices continue to rise, and HMOs will always try to reduce their costs. This usually means you will pay more. If a drug is not on the formulary, some plans will pay for a portion of the drug's cost, asking you to pay the difference. Or they may allow your doctor to appeal their decision not to pay for a particular drug. Find out how easily a doctor can override the formulary restrictions. Ask your doctor what his or her experience has been getting approval to use nonformulary drugs. Consider whether tiered-formulary pricing will allow you the flexibility you need.

Choice 4: Investigating How Elders View the Plan

What others think of the health plan is important. After you have selected one or two plans based on the premium, benefits, and the drug benefit, look at available data on consumer satisfaction. If a lot of people are unhappy, it usually means there are problems with the plan and it is not satisfying a portion of its members. However, most satisfaction data currently available is very limited. Most respondents are usually in relatively good health and have not had extensive experience trying to get care. Also, consumer satisfaction measures the kind of service people have received in their health plan rather than the actual quality of medical care. Service issues, such as waiting times for appointments, ease of referrals, and whether members got their complaints and problems handled easily and quickly are important and much easier to measure than the quality of medical care delivered by a plan's physicians. Consumer satisfaction also correlates highly with how plan members view their doctors.

Bottom-line advice: Use satisfaction data to temper your initial decisions that are based on price and benefits. If your top plan offers exceptional value, has a good prescription drug benefit, but has terrible satisfaction scores, you may want to go with your second or third choice, which offers somewhat lower value but has higher satisfaction among its members. If low satisfaction scores reported on HCFA's website or reported in CONSUMER REPORTS suggest that the plan may be doing something its members really don't like, you may want to avoid that HMO. Still, even plans that most people like will

WORKSHEET 2: Paying for Your Medications

Prescription drug benefits may tempt you to join an HMO. But that coverage may be less than you think. You must evaluate the benefit and compare it to your current costs for prescriptions. This example shows a calculation for a hypothetical beneficiary who takes three medications.

Step 1: Figure current monthly costs

Calculate your monthly prescription drug costs.

MEDICATIONS	MONTHLY COST
Zocor	$56
Zoloft	59
Allegra	27
Total monthly prescription cost	142
Total current annual cost ($142 × 12)	$1,704

Step 2: Size up the HMO's cap

For each HMO you are considering, find out its maximum annual benefit, called the cap. In this example, the HMO has a cap of $1,000.

Step 3: Determine the copayment

For each HMO, list all the copayments for the drugs you are taking. The example below shows typical copayments you might find; pick the arrangement you're most likely to use.

MEDICATIONS	MAIL ORDER OR PHARMACY	BRAND OR GENERIC	COVERED IN FORMULARY	CO-PAYMENT
Zocor	Mail order	Brand	Yes	$15/quarter
Zoloft	Pharmacy	Brand	Yes	$10/month
Allegra	Pharmacy	Brand	Yes	$10/month

Totals

Zocor (4 quarters × $15 per quarter)	$60
Zoloft (12 months × $10 per month)	120
Allegra (12 months × $10 per month)	120
Total annual copayments	$300

Step 4: Calculate the saving

List the annual copayments, any expenses over the cap, and the premium you'll pay. Compare this to your current costs.

Annual Rx cost (from step 1)	$1,704
Minus total annual copayments	−300
Eligible Rx cost (after copayments)	$1,404
Minus HMO maximum annual benefit (from step 2)	−1,000
Uncovered Rx cost	$404
Monthly HMO premium	$50
Multiply by 12	× 12
Annual premium	$600

Total saving

Eligible Rx cost (after copayments)	$1,404
Minus uncovered cost	−404
Minus annual premium	−600
SAVING	$400

have some disappointed customers, and conversely, even the lowest-rated plans have some highly satisfied beneficiaries. You may be willing to join a plan offering great value knowing that you may have to work harder to fight for referrals or have your complaints addressed.

Choice 5: Considering Preventive Care Measures

The Health Care Financing Administration promotes a set of measures that purports to tell beneficiaries something about the quality of care they will receive in HMOs. These measures, known as HEDIS, for Health Employer Data and Information Set, were developed by the National Committee for Quality Assurance (NCQA), a nonprofit organization that also accredits HMOs. HMOs that serve Medicare beneficiaries collect these data and report them to the Health Care Financing Administration.

HEDIS captures such information as the number of health plan members who have received mammograms, the proportion of women who have had Pap smears, the number of diabetic members who received retinal examinations to help prevent blindness, and the number of members who had heart attacks and received beta-blocker treatment after the attack.

For the most part, HEDIS measures evaluate preventive care. Although important, most people should be able to judge for themselves when they should have mammograms, Pap smears, and so forth, and schedule their appointments accordingly. Most women, for example, know they should have a mammogram each year. The fact that an HMO sends reminder cards or implements other programs to increase the proportion of women who have these screenings is laudable and even demonstrates some commitment to improving medical care, but it should not be the major reason you pick one HMO over another. Just because a plan has high HEDIS scores on one or several measures does not mean that the HMO will deliver high-quality medical care for your particular illnesses all the time. It is also hard to generalize from the HEDIS scores. A plan may have two very good scores and two very poor ones. It's difficult to say what, if anything, that means.

Look at the HEDIS scores presented on HCFA's website and in the Ratings. If, after considering the network, the value for the premium, the drug benefit, and the satisfaction scores, you are still undecided between two health plans, good HEDIS scores might tip the balance in favor of one plan over the other.

Choice 6: Finding Out If the Plan Evaluates Members' Functional Abilities

Specifically, ask what the plan does to assess how well their Medicare members function and what programs they have begun to protect seniors from harmful drug interactions. What do they do to screen their members and what do they do as a follow-up? What kind of drug intervention programs do they have and do they evaluate the results? Make them give you numbers and facts. To test what kind of answers you are getting, ask for particular examples of people who have been helped by various follow-up interventions. If the plan has no answers, then going into that particular HMO for special help and special programs might be a waste of time. Base your decision on other factors.

If a plan seems to pay attention to members' functional status, and has good programs for evaluating and intervening when someone needs help, consider that a plus after looking at all the other parameters previously discussed.

The Health Care Financing Administration (HCFA) has posted the Medicare Compare database on its website *(www.medicare.gov)* to help guide Medicare beneficiaries in choosing an HMO. Beneficiaries can search for the HMOs offering Medicare coverage in their county and compare premiums, benefit highlights, and measures of quality. As of January 2000, the "quality" information on the site displayed eleven measures, a mix of HEDIS data provided directly by the HMO and summary statistics from an HCFA survey of Medicare beneficiaries.

This information does not provide a compelling argument in favor of one health plan over another. As I've noted, the preventive care measures (mammography, beta-blockers, and eye exams for diabetics) focus only on one aspect of care, and other measures also have flaws. For example, the measure "Plan Members Seen by a Provider in the Past Year" implies the plan can make a person come in for care. However, the individual makes that decision, not the plan. A high percentage of board-certified doctors is also no guarantee of quality care. Just because a doctor may have passed exams years ago does not mean he is current on today's techniques and treatments. "Providers Who Stayed in the Managed Care Plan at Least 1 Year," a measure that potentially measures doctor turnover, yielded no useful information for the thirty metropolitan areas we investigated. All plans scored 99 or 100 percent, making the numbers virtually meaningless.

The most useful measure on the HCFA website is the "Overall Rating of Managed Care Plan," and we have included it in our Ratings of Medicare HMOs in Appendix G. Yet even this measure has limitations. It gives the percentage of members surveyed who ranked their plan as the best possible plan; they gave it a "10" on a scale of

0 to 10. This presentation, however, overlooks plan members who gave their plans an 8 or a 9 and are still very satisfied. The bottom line: Don't put too much weight on a low rating for this measure. In fact, our analysis of the underlying data suggests that very few people are seriously dissatisfied with any of the plans, and even some of the highest-ranking plans had some disgruntled members.

HEALTH CARE QUALITY IN MANAGED CARE

Many organizations like to say or imply that HMOs that have good or excellent HEDIS scores are delivering good-quality medical care. In truth, we really don't know if they are or not. We know relatively little about the impact of managed care on health care quality and little about the kind of medical quality Medicare beneficaries receive from their health plans. HEDIS measures provide only a glimpse of one aspect of quality. They measure the degree of underuse of a few medical services. If doctors in a health plan are not prescribing beta-blockers for patients who have had heart attacks, that is considered underuse of a necessary medical service. And indeed one study reported in the *New England Journal of Medicine* found that beta-blockers were "an underused therapy."

Medical quality also means avoiding procedures and treatments that are unnecessary and can cause undue risk and harm to a patient—the so-called overuse problem. Quality also means misuse—when doctors do the right thing but do it badly. Medication errors, which occur in hospitals with alarming frequency, are an example of misuse. HEDIS scores do not measure overuse or misuse. Nor do they measure or evaluate whether a woman, for instance, gets proper treatment if an abnormality is found on a mammogram. They don't address adequacy of treatment.

Unfortunately, neither seniors nor those under age sixty-five can choose an HMO whose doctors always make correct and timely diagnoses, prescribe the right treatment, and avoid mistakes. There are no measures that reflect those aspects of care. Neither are there measures to help people choose quality care in fee-for-service practices. Studies show that the problems of health care quality are pervasive throughout the health care delivery system, and problems occur with about the same frequency in managed care as they do in fee-for-service practices.

In 1998, CONSUMER REPORTS and researchers at the Mount Sinai School of Medicine in New York City conducted a study to see if HMOs that served Medicare beneficiaries were doing a good job of measuring quality and devising programs to improve it. The magazine studied the activities of forty-eight HMOs, and found that most of them had implemented programs to measure the potential underuse of some services such as mammography and beta-blockers. They were following the HEDIS measurement procedures, but in many cases, they went no further. Most were not evaluating whether their interventions were effective, and most were doing little to detect overuse and misuse of services. Only 17 percent of plans reported using criteria that were specific to a particular procedure in order to determine the appropriateness of its use. In other words, HMOs, which are often criticized for withholding services, appeared to allow treatments even when they were unnecessary and perhaps harmful.

CONSUMER REPORTS and the researchers also asked the health plans about what they do to evaluate and promote better functioning among their elderly members. Again, some plans were doing a better job than others. Only 23 percent of the plans conducted screenings to assess functional status. They did this by mail, phone, or in person, and then followed up with an outreach program to help those needing particular services. One should expect all HMOs serving seniors and disabled people to conduct such programs, since HMOs are in a unique position to improve health. The way an HMO treats its elderly and disabled members may be an indicator of how it will treat you when you need services.

When it came to looking for harmful drug interactions, the results were much the same. About one-third of the plans had no programs in place to detect harmful drug interactions, and many of those that did failed to evaluate how effective they were.

So where does this leave Medicare beneficiaries and those advising them? It would appear that at many HMOs, members are no better off than they would be in fee-for-service practices when it comes to helping them function better.

HOW MUCH OF A PROBLEM IS UNDERUSE?

As I've noted, some evidence exists that Medicare beneficaries who join a managed-care plan receive fewer home care visits and fewer days of care in a skilled-nursing facility. Fewer visits and fewer hospital days may be good or bad. If you need more services and the HMO cuts you off, then your relatives must scramble to find other care. If you receive unnecessary services, that wastes money for the entire health care system. There is no objective way to judge the quality of care you get with these services (see Chapter 7).

On the other hand, some studies show that beneficiaries in managed care get more preventive care services. For example, the *Dartmouth Atlas of Health Care* found that 28 percent of women aged sixty-five to sixty-nine had mammograms during the study period compared to 80 percent of women enrolled in not-for-profit and provider-based health plans. A study reported in the *Journal of the American Medical Association* found that Medicare beneficiaries on average were more likely to receive early diagnosis of breast cancer, breast conservation surgery, and radiation when such treatments were appropriate.

Again, there is no easy way to tell which plans are going to give you or your relative a hard time about skilled-nursing or home care. If you are interested in preventive measures, then look at plans that seem to have particularly high HEDIS scores, though, as I've pointed out, these hardly give a complete picture of the medical care you will need or receive. There's no way to tell in advance whether a plan will shortchange you when it comes to providing services.

CHOOSING A NEW DOCTOR

After weighing the various trade-offs discussed earlier in this chapter and in Chapter 3, you may decide that an HMO is a better option than staying with traditional Medicare and buying a Medigap policy. But joining a plan may mean changing doctors. The Ohio Senior Health Insurance Program (OSHIP) offers some excellent suggestions for seniors who are about to switch doctors. They include:

Learning the office routines Find out which days are busiest and when is the best time to reach someone on the phone. Learn the office emergency procedures. Whom do you call, what doctors are on call, and where do you go when the office is closed?

Sharing your medical history This is not the time to be shy about your medical condition. Be honest with your doctor. Tell him or her about your past illnesses, operations, and the health conditions that run in your family. You may want a copy of your records from your old doctor. If the new doctor asks for your records, you may have to sign a release. Tell the new doctor about all other providers who have treated you.

Sharing information about medications This is very important since it will alert the new doctor to any potential problems and drug interactions with new medications. Tell your doctor about every medication you take, including over-the-counter drugs. If you can't remember all the names of the drugs, put all your pill bottles in a paper bag and bring them to the doctor. Include vitamins, laxatives, eye medications, and so on. Some HMOs have paper bag programs for seniors to encourage them to share their medications with their doctors. It's a way to help prevent adverse drug reactions, which can cause serious health complications, even death. If you have allergies, be sure to tell the doctor so he or she will know which prescriptions to avoid. Also mention side effects you have had.

Being honest about your habits Tell the doctor if you have trouble sleeping, if you smoke, exercise, enjoy sex, and so forth. Discuss what you eat and how you get your food. Most physicians are not schooled in nutrition, but as Chapter 8 points out, nutritional problems among the elderly are significant. Many elders suffer from malnutrition and have trouble getting appropriate nutrition services in their community. If you are having trouble shopping, cooking, or preparing food, or you have a relative with those problems, sometimes a physician can make a referral to a community agency. Knowing that food is a problem can help doctors diagnose and treat you.

The Doctor's Office

When selecting a new doctor, it's important to look at some seemingly basic issues. While such points may seem trivial when you are well, when you are sick or unable to walk very far, whether there is an elevator in the building where your doctor is located becomes very important. Consider the following:

How close is the office?
Can you get there on public transportation?
Does the building have an elevator or ramps for wheelchairs?
Is the lighting adequate?

ENROLLING IN AN HMO

Signing up for a plan is pretty straightforward. After you have gone through the choices outlined earlier in this chapter, and have decided on a particular plan, ask the HMO for an enrollment form. Unless you have end-stage renal disease, all HMOs must accept you. Unlike traditional insurance companies, in particular sellers of Medicare-supplement policies, HMOs cannot reject you if you are in poor health.

Most HMOs let you join only at certain times of the year. A few have what's called continuous open enrollment; you can sign up at any time, although that practice is disappearing. Check with your plan to see what the effective date of coverage is. If you submit an application for enrollment or disenrollment between the first and tenth of the month, the effective date of your change will be the first day of the following month. Submitting an application after the tenth means your effective date begins a month later. After your coverage is in effect, you won't need your Medigap policy, but it's a good idea to keep the policy for a few months just in case you don't like the HMO and want to quit. You may have a hard time getting your old coverage back if you become ill in the meantime.

LEAVING AN HMO

It may turn out that medical care from an HMO is not what you bargained for, and you want to leave. If you disenroll from the plan before the tenth of the month, you can return to traditional Medicare the next month or go into another managed-care plan if one is available. If you disenroll after the tenth of the month, you will not be able to return to traditional Medicare until the second month. If you want to disenroll, you must fill out Form 566, available at your local Social Security office, or from the plan. Keep a copy of this form and the date you submitted it. Until you are officially disenrolled, you must continue to use the plan and the doctors in its network.

Starting in 2002, beneficiaries will have to be more certain of their choices. They won't be able to switch as often as they have been doing. In 2002, they can make a change during the first six months. In 2003, they can make a choice only during the first three months. After that they are stuck for the rest of the year. So if you aren't sure that you will like an HMO, it's best not to join, since it won't be so easy to move back and forth between a plan and traditional Medicare. If you don't like the HMO, you'll have to wait until next year to change.

Sometimes an HMO leaves Medicare—that is, it decides it no longer can make enough money serving beneficiaries in your county. The plan simply notifies the Health Care Financing Administration that it is dropping its contract with HCFA at the end of the year. Beneficiaries must find other coverage and must follow the rules for obtaining new coverage. Pay close attention to the letter your HMO sends notifying you it is terminating its plan in your area. Pay close attention to enrollment deadlines.

YOUR RIGHT TO A MEDICARE-SUPPLEMENT POLICY

If you choose to disenroll from the HMO, you face the dilemma of getting a new Medicare-supplement policy or finding another HMO. It may not be easy to get a supplemental policy if you are in poor health. Some states require insurers to accept everyone, even those whose health is bad. Check with your insurance department to see if you live in one. But if you don't live in one of these states, your choices will boil down to AARP's policies or those from a handful of Blue Cross Blue Shield plans that still offer policies regardless of an applicant's health. You may hear these policies referred to as *guaranteed-issue policies*. See Chapter 4 for a discussion of this kind of coverage.

The rules are different if an HMO leaves Medicare. In that case, you have the right to buy Plans A, B, C, or F even if you have a pre-existing health condition. Wisconsin, Minnesota, and Massachusetts have their own plans with similar benefits but different names. When you receive notice that the plan is terminating your coverage, you must remain in the HMO until the end of the year; if you leave before then, you lose your right to a guaranteed-issue policy. There are special rules if you are under age sixty-five and disabled, have kidney disease, are in a nursing home, are on Medicaid, have retiree coverage from a union or former employer, or if your current plan is your first experience with managed care and you have been enrolled for less than one year. The counseling program in your state can help you sort through these rules. See Appendix A.

You can apply for one of the four Medigap policies when you receive written notice from the plan. To avoid any gaps in coverage, make sure your new Medigap coverage begins the same day your

HMO coverage ends and traditional Medicare begins. That may not be until the HMO terminates coverage at the end of the year. Remember, if you use services outside the HMO before you are back in traditional Medicare, neither the HMO nor Medicare will pay for your care.

RETROACTIVE DISENROLLMENTS

Retroactive disenrollment is a technical term for getting out of an HMO if you believe you have been misled by an HMO's salesperson or you did not understand the provisions of the lock-in and other managed-care features, or you moved and did not file Form 556. To obtain such a disenrollment, contact your local Social Security office and be prepared to explain what you did not understand, particularly the network restrictions. Even though the law allows for disenrollments, it might be hard to do.

If you obtain a retroactive disenrollment, the services you received in the HMO are covered as if you had been in traditional Medicare rather than in the HMO. This means you must submit Medicare bills from doctors and hospitals that were not in the HMO, and you will pay any coinsurance and deductibles that you incurred because you will not have any Medigap coverage.

BEWARE OF HMO SALESPERSONS

Through the years, managed-care plans have been very aggressive about signing up new beneficiaries; their Medicare business has been a lucrative one. The Secure Horizons plan for PacifiCare's Medicare beneficiaries has accounted for about half the company's revenue in some years. HMOs that wanted to grab a large share of the Medicare market often engaged in misleading and deceptive sales activities. I have heard many presentations throughout the United States, and more often than not have found them misleading, deceptive, and skirting the real issues surrounding managed care. Sales presentations that I have heard at coffee shops and restaurants usually start off with a soft sell. The plan provides refreshments and gently moves to a discussion of why the assembled group should give up traditional Medicare and join an HMO. Sometimes the HMO strategically places seniors who are plan members in the audience to give testimonials. At one presentation in San Antonio, Texas, the HMO called those helpers its "ambassadors."

Salespeople, however, often sidestep crucial questions. They sometimes avoid mentioning the lock-in provision and overlook other downsides as well. A few years ago, a representative from Oxford Health Plan in New York City told seniors that one reason they should give up Medicare and join was for the emergency benefit. When someone asked how an emergency was defined, the plan official replied "We leave that up to the person who is having an emergency." The plan's literature noted that the plan, not the member, decides what is an emergency.

One salesman in Florida told a beneficiary to lie when the plan representatives later called to see if she understood all the ins and outs of Medicare HMOs. "When the girls call to verify, don't ask any questions," the salesperson warned. "That means you don't understand the program and we'll have to come back and explain it."

While some plans have sought seniors as members, others have been picky about whom they want. One sales representative from PCA Health Plans of Texas, which has since merged into Humana, said candidly at a public meeting that if their representatives found people who were taking too many medications, they would counsel them to stay in traditional Medicare. The plan apparently did not want members who were likely to run up big bills for prescriptions.

Plans can't require preenrollment health screenings or ask any questions about your health. Nor do you have to answer any questions about your health.

In early 1999, the General Accounting Office announced that it had looked at sales materials from sixteen HMOs and found "significant errors and omissions," and that information about benefits and coverage was often "not accurate, timely, or complete." This parallels what I have found witnessing sales presentations and looking at sales literature.

What should you take away from a sales presentation? The answer is very little. The best course is to:

- Carefully read Chapters 3, 4, and 5 in this book and go through the decision trade-offs that are presented.
- Look at the Ratings and see if a plan you are considering is among them.

- Look at the sales literature, but don't consider it the last word on what you need to know.
- Look skeptically at what the salespeople tell you. They won't tell you everything you need to know.
- Do not answer any questions about your health. You do not have to tell plan representatives about the drugs you take, what your health conditions are, or submit to any screenings or diagnostic tests that a plan may offer at a health fair or marketing presentation.

MANAGED CARE AND NURSING HOMES

If you belong to a managed-care organization and need skilled-nursing care, the HMO can send you to any facility it contracts with and is part of its network. This might mean that you cannot return to the nursing home or other facility where you are already living and receive your skilled-nursing care there.

Some states, including Florida, Illinois, Maryland, North Carolina, Ohio, and Virginia, have passed what are called return-to-home laws that permit residents of retirement communities and nursing homes to return to their homes and receive skilled care at that facility.

If you are considering whether to obtain HMO benefits for an elderly relative who may already be in a nursing home, return-to-home protections are an important consideration.

WHAT HAPPENS WHEN SOMETHING GOES WRONG?

Each HMO has a procedure for handling grievances and appeals. A grievance is a complaint about the quality of services the HMO offers, including physicians' services, adequacy of facilities, or the timeliness of treatments and tests. An appeal is a request for services or reimbursement that have been denied. If you do not want reimbursement but merely want to raise an objection about the plan's service, file a grievance. If you want reimbursement or your claim was denied, you must file an appeal. Some HMOs treat appeals as a grievance.

Filing a grievance To file a grievance you must follow your HMO's procedure, which is usually spelled out in the enrollment information. The grievance procedure takes place solely within the HMO.

Filing an appeal The appeals process, on the other hand, takes place both inside and outside the HMO, and there may be several steps and levels of appeal involved before a case is resolved. Filing an appeal can be time-consuming, but is often worth it. You can file an expedited appeal, which speeds up the process. The Medicare Rights Center, a New York City advocacy group, suggests that an appeal might be warranted in the following situations:

- Your doctor fails to prescribe covered treatments and tests, or fails to refer you to a specialist or hospital for treatment.
- The HMO refuses to approve referrals recommended by your primary-care physician.
- Either the HMO or doctor decides to terminate or reduce services you are receiving—for example, home health care.
- There's an unreasonable delay in arranging for surgery.
- The HMO refuses to pay claims for emergency care or out-of-area urgent care that you received from a non-HMO doctor or hospital.
- The hospital wants to discharge you before you think you are ready to go home. You must file this kind of appeal with the hospital peer-review organization. Chapter 6 explains how to do that.

Levels of Appeal

The first step, of course, is to file an appeal with the HMO following the procedures outlined in the plan literature. The HMO must give you a full explanation of your appeal rights. If you don't get it, seek help from an elder law attorney or from one of the Medicare advocacy organizations listed in Table 5 (see page 104).

There are several additional steps in the appeals process. They are:

Reconsideration within the HMO Ask in writing for a reconsideration of your HMO's denial within sixty days of the date the HMO first turns you down. Send your request to the HMO and to the local Social Security office. If the HMO agrees with you, the case is closed. You've won. If it doesn't, it's on to the next step.

Reconsideration at the Center for Health Dispute Resolution This independent organization, which subcontracts with the Health Care

Financing Administration, may uphold the HMO's decision, partially overturn it, fully overturn it, or suggest a retroactive disenrollment. About half the time the center decides in favor of the HMO; about half the time decisions favor beneficiaries.

The center must decide your case within thirty days if the denial is for a service you have yet to receive. Appeals for payments must be decided within sixty days.

Appeals to administrative law judges If the Center for Health Dispute Resolution decides against you and more than $500 is in dispute, you can appeal to an administrative law judge within sixty days of receiving a decision. A hearing can take a long time to schedule.

Appeals to the U.S. Department of Health and Human Services Departmental Appeals Board If appeals to this board are unsuccessful, the last step is to take your case to federal district court.

OTHER MANAGED-CARE OPTIONS

While HMOs are the dominant form of managed care for Medicare beneficiaries, you may come across others.

Cost contracts The HMOs described in this chapter represent the major type of arrangement plans have with the federal government. You may, however, encounter another form of HMO, one that has a cost contract with HCFA. These plans can have cost contracts until 2002.

According to the 2000 Medicare Compare database, the following plans have cost contracts:

Colorado	Rocky Mountain HMO
Florida	Capital Group Health Services of Florida
Hawaii	Hawaii Medical Service Association
Idaho	Regence BlueShield of Idaho
Illinois	John Deer Health Plan
Illinois	Rush Prudential Health Plans
Indiana	The MPlan
New York	Excellus Health Plan
Ohio	The Health Plan

Oregon	Regence HMO Oregon
Texas	Scott and White Health Plan
Wisconsin	Dean Health Plan

If you join an HMO that has a cost contract, the HMO will cover all costs for your care, except for small copayments, for as long as you stay in the network. If you use providers outside the network, Medicare will cover 80 percent of the cost of care. Beneficiaries, coinsurance, deductibles, and premiums are likely to be higher than at regular HMOs. Plans in our survey said the premiums ranged from $0 to $150 per month.

Point-of-service plans Approximately 14 percent of the plans listed in Medicare Compare for 2000 offer some point-of-service (POS) benefits. For Medicare plans, this usually means you can go to doctors outside the plan's network and pay coinsurance of 20 percent for those services. The out-of-network coverage may be part of the base plan or may be optional at additional cost. The amount of out-of-network coverage may be limited, such as a maximum of $2,000 in payments to non-plan doctors during the year, and so the value of this benefit may be pretty minimal.

Some plans say they limit your out-of-pocket financial expenses, but you may still end up with a significant balance bill. If you are considering a plan with POS benefits, be sure to get the plan documents and read them carefully, because there are too many details for Medicare Compare to accurately display.

Preferred provider organizations (PPOs) In 2000, Medicare Compare lists only three preferred provider organizations (PPOs) for the whole country; these are offered by Independence Blue Cross Blue Shield in Philadelphia. In a typical PPO, you do not need a referral from your primary-care physician to see a specialist, and this may be a useful feature. Always check the plan documents to learn the limitations of this benefit.

KEY DECISION POINTS

1. If you have trouble paying for prescription drugs, consider an HMO that offers a reasonably good drug benefit.

2. The value of the benefits in relation to the premium you will pay is the most important aspect of choosing a Medicare HMO after determining if you want to use the doctors in a plan's network.

3. Measures of consumer satisfaction are more important than how well the plan performs on certain indicators of preventive care. Do not choose a plan based on the latter.

4. Realize that no person or organization can guarantee that one HMO instead of another will give you high-quality medical care every time you need treatment.

5. If your relative will likely need skilled-nursing care or home care, then an HMO may not be the best choice. There may be more of these services available if your relative receives benefits under the traditional Medicare program.

6. If you choose an HMO, and later come to dislike managed care, it may be difficult to obtain a new Medicare-supplement policy. So you must be quite certain that managed care is what you want.

7. Nothing is permanent in managed care. Realize that a good deal today can evaporate tomorrow.

PART 2

FINDING LONG-TERM CARE

Not too many years ago, nursing homes and sometimes rest homes were the only places people went when they could no longer care for themselves, or their families were unable or unwilling to assume the burden. Elders, of course, still go to nursing homes, perhaps even when they don't need to be in one. But now there are other choices available for families who must care for an aging relative. Assisted-living facilities, adult day care centers, and special chronic care programs were practically unheard of fifteen or twenty years ago.

This section is intended to acquaint caregivers with all the options currently available for long-term care. Each chapter describes how a particular option works, what to be aware of, and how to select the best possible arrangement.

SIX

Entering the System

Carol Ann Young, like so many middle-aged women, was not prepared for her role as caregiver. She was thrust into the job in the early 1990s when her mother began to show signs of Alzheimer's disease. As her mother gradually lost independence, she grew fearful, suspicious, and confused. Young had to spend more and more time with her, taking her to doctors' appointments, writing checks, handling her personal and financial affairs. "When they start asking for help paying bills, you get nervous," Young said.

That work was a snap compared to what Young was called on to do as her mother's disease progressed. As her mother became irrational, incoherent, and began pacing the floor, she needed help to bathe, dress, and eat, and she needed companionship. Young spent nights with her and looked for home care workers, interviewing potential candidates about their experience with Alzheimer's patients. Most of them, she found, had virtually none. "People who came to work with my mother didn't know what I knew."

Over an eighteen-month period, Young's mother adjusted to thirty different home health aides and attendants. Some played the TV and radio too loudly, creating an unsuitable atmosphere for an Alzheimer's patient sensitive to loud noises. Others didn't show up.

Paying for care was almost as difficult as hiring competent aides. At first, the New York Medicaid bureaucracy rejected her mother's claim for home care services. Medicaid officials changed their minds after Young pursued the matter to a hearing. Then the Medicaid agency allowed only a few hours of care each day. The family paid privately for more hours until Medicaid determined that Young's mother was sick enough to warrant more. "It's not like you apply for Medicaid and they take care of everything. You have to do the work. You can't come into the system and get twelve hours of care."

She began attending support groups, and her mother began attending a day care program where she thrived, stimulated by activities appropriate for her condition. Eventually, though, the disease got worse, and psychiatrists recommended a nursing home that would provide more structure. Even though Young knew this step was coming, the decision to put her mother in a facility was tough.

Young's experiences were far from ideal. Much of the available information she found was not very useful. Sometimes she got misinformation or telephone numbers that led nowhere. She rejected the services of a geriatric case manager who wanted to charge $100 for a phone call. "I lacked information and a process of how to go about things," she says. "I eventually got it because I sought it out." But the stress was incredible, and her graphic arts business ran aground because she had little time to pursue new clients. "Caregiving is the long good-bye," Young says. "You see a person lose the ability to do things all along the way and you cry every time you see it."

Young's odyssey through the long-term-care system was far from unusual. Most adult children who must find care for aging parents experience Young's travails to some degree. "People ask whom do I call, where do I turn, what am I entitled to," says Janet Rothman, communications director at the Metropolitan Jewish Health System in New York City. All too often they turn to the wrong person or place.

In 1997, Consumer Reports asked its subscribers who had some experience with long-term care how they learned about their various options. More than half said they talked to a doctor; one-third said they consulted a hospital discharge planner. A survey by the National Alliance for Caregiving also found that almost two-thirds of those who select long-term-care services sought guidance from a health professional, such as a doctor or a nurse.

Thoughtful decision making is sometimes not part of selecting long-term care. Often there's no time. When a relative suffers an acute

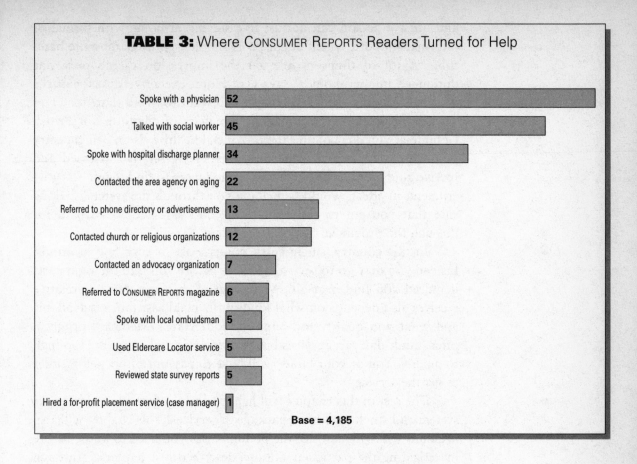

TABLE 3: Where CONSUMER REPORTS Readers Turned for Help

Spoke with a physician	52
Talked with social worker	45
Spoke with hospital discharge planner	34
Contacted the area agency on aging	22
Referred to phone directory or advertisements	13
Contacted church or religious organizations	12
Contacted an advocacy organization	7
Referred to CONSUMER REPORTS magazine	6
Spoke with local ombudsman	5
Used Eldercare Locator service	5
Reviewed state survey reports	5
Hired a for-profit placement service (case manager)	1

Base = 4,185

illness, families need to find care right away. No wonder they turn to doctors and hospital discharge planners.

But neither of those sources may lead you to the best options. Doctors who specialize in treating disease and acute illness are not necessarily conversant with long-term-care alternatives. Most likely they don't know the requirements for Medicaid; they may not know a lot about options for care in the community; and what doctor really does a good assessment on a chronically ill patient?

Hospital discharge planners have an inherent conflict of interest. Their objective is to get you or your relative out of the hospital as fast as they can. So they often recommend a facility or a course of action that may not be in your best interests. In their haste, they may refer you to the first available nursing home instead of trying to find an adult day care program coupled with home care, which might be a better solution. Moving someone out of the family home is disruptive, and often a person can do just fine staying at home with formal or informal support, which might be as simple as grab bars in the bathtub. "A lot of times people get the impression there's only one option—a nursing home," says Gail Hunt, executive director of the National Alliance for Caregiving. "You want to avoid that."

If you lived in the Canadian provinces of Manitoba or British Columbia, you'd encounter the provincial health system's single entry point, an office where you could have your relative assessed and receive guidance on the best options and where to find them. The government, in effect, would be helping you through the system, making sure that you got to the right place, and care would be paid for through the provincial health care system.

In this country, single entry points exist in very few locations. Instead you may go to several agencies before you find the right care, if indeed you find it at all. What kind of care you or your relative receives also depends on what kind of financial assistance is available and what you qualify for. Suppose your state's Medicaid program offers adult day care services but your income and assets are too high to qualify. You or your family will have to pay out of pocket in order to get the service.

The rest of this chapter will help you navigate the long-term-care system and stitch together a package of services. This chapter will also acquaint you with some of the preliminaries you need to know before investigating the particular options described in Chapters 7 through 11. You will need time to explore and evaluate services, and as Carol Ann Young found, there may be obstacles every step of the way.

Your first objective is to buy time to do the legwork and the paperwork. If your relative is experiencing a slow, steady decline in function, you can anticipate his or her needs in advance and will have the luxury of investigating several options. If you need to make choices quickly after a hospital stay, the task is more difficult.

"BUYING" MORE TIME IN THE HOSPITAL

If you or your relative needs long-term care after hospitalization, your primary concern should be to "buy" more time—that is, stay longer in the hospital—which is not easy to do in this era of short stays and prospective payments, where Medicare pays a set amount for a prescribed number of days and no more. Yet "there are alternatives to coming home to chaos," says Carol Levine, director of the families and caregiver project at the United Hospital Fund, a philanthropic organization in New York City.

One of them is to use your appeal rights under Medicare to stay an extra two days, during which time your relative can be scouting long-term-care options. (You can't be charged for those two days.)

Here's how to move through the appeals process:

• You can appeal the decision to discharge as soon as the hospital gives you what's called a Hospital-Issued Notice of Noncoverage, HINN. This explains whether the discharge was approved by your doctor or the Peer Review Organization (PRO). A PRO is a group of doctors and other professionals who review hospital appeals and oversee the quality of care delivered to Medicare beneficiaries. Every state has a PRO that is not part of any hospital or managed-care plan.

You can find the name and phone number of your state's PRO by looking in the Medicare handbook or by looking at a document called "An Important Message from Medicare," which the hospital must give you upon admission. Sally Hart, a Medicare advocacy lawyer in Tucson, Arizona, says families are often intimidated when a hospital or managed-care company asks the patient to leave. "My advice is to stay. They cannot discharge you until you get the notice."

• If your doctor agrees you should be discharged, act quickly to appeal by contacting the PRO by noon of the first working day after you receive the notice of noncoverage. If you make this request on time, you will not be responsible for any hospital charges incurred before the PRO decides your case. The PRO will make a decision by the end of the next business day. If the PRO says you should go home, you are responsible for all charges beginning at noon the day *after* you receive the PRO's decision. In other words, you will have to pay for all charges incurred beginning on the third day after you receive the notice of discharge.

• If your doctor does not agree that you should go home, the hospital must ask the PRO before it can issue a discharge notice. If the PRO disagrees with the doctor and says you should leave, the hospital will issue the notice of noncoverage within two days. Request a reconsideration at once. The PRO can take up to one working day from the time it receives your request to review your case. If the PRO still says you should leave, you'll have to pay any hospital charges

TABLE 4: Appeals at a Glance

	When to Appeal	Liability Starts
Doctor agrees	Before noon of next business day	Noon the day after PRO makes decision
Doctor disagrees	Immediately	2 days after receipt of HINN

Source: Medicare Rights Center

beginning on the third day after you receive the notice of noncoverage.

Medicare gives you sixty days to ask for a hearing before an administrative law judge, but as a practical matter, your relative will probably be settled by then.

Medicare beneficiaries in HMOs receive the same discharge notice and have the same right to an expedited appeal as people with traditional Medicare. So if your HMO says you must leave the hospital, activate an appeal at once.

If you need skilled-nursing care, and the hospital cannot find a facility that's suitable—for example, your family has to drive too far to reach it, or you need a type of care a nearby facility can't provide—

TABLE 5: The Medicare Advocacy Groups

Center for Health Care Rights
Joseph Cislowski, Executive Director
520 S. Lafayette Park Place, Suite 214
Los Angeles, CA 90057
213-383-4519

National Senior Citizens Law Center
1101 4th Street, N.W., Suite 400
Washington, DC 20005
202-289-6976
www.nsclc.org

Center for Medicare Advocacy
Judith Stein
P.O. Box 171
South Windham, CT 06266
860-456-7790
Washington Office
202-216-0028

Medicare Rights Center
Diane Archer
1460 Broadway, 11th Floor
New York, NY 10036
Tel. 212-869-3850 ext. 23
Fax: 212-869-3532

the hospital cannot make you leave. One of the tricks to getting what you need is forceful advocacy, either from family members or your doctor. It often helps to have your doctor write a letter to the PRO. The Medicare advocacy groups listed on page 104 can also help.

THE DISCHARGE PLAN

When you go home, hospitals have a legal obligation under Medicare rules to provide you with a discharge plan if you need one or if you ask for one. The plan typically sets out the care you need and where you will receive it. Too often, though, the plans are skimpy and give too little information. And the law is murky about who is responsible for making sure the plan is carried out. Hospitals don't have to see that your relative gets care that is needed after a hospital discharge, so implementation usually falls to the family. "Hospital discharge planning is a disaster," says Rosalie Kane, a professor of geriatrics at the University of Minnesota. "We provide people with either no choice or poor choices, and no capacity to engage in rational decision making."

Make sure the discharge plan is complete and that you understand it. For instance, a plan that says "watch him carefully" is not helpful. What are the signs to watch for—high fever, convulsions? If you are supposed to change bandages and care for surgical wounds, are you told how to do it? Ask the hospital how to administer any medicines or medical treatments. If hospital personnel can't help, ask the hospital social worker and insist that she tell you whom to contact for help. One source of help is the local Visiting Nurse Association.

If the services provided by a home health agency are part of the discharge plan, the hospital is supposed to give you a list of agencies from which to choose. Often they don't. Many hospitals have their own home health agencies, and steer you to the one they control. That may be convenient, and the hospital's agency may send good workers and supervise them well—or it may not. Choosing good home care is difficult, largely because there are no good ways to measure the quality of care patients receive (see Chapter 7).

Once you have a plan in place and your relative comes home, think of the arrangements as temporary, and reassess your needs every few months or so. During that time, you can look for other types of care.

If your relative is experiencing a long-term decline, you can anticipate and plan for eventual care. The signs of decline in physical or mental function will be unmistakable—poor hygiene, poor housekeeping, depression, forgetfulness, weight loss, falling, irritability, a change in sleeping patterns or eating habits. And often those needing help begin to withdraw from the world around them; they become less venturesome, for instance, going grocery shopping early in the morning when few people are around, or driving only short distances or not taking trips anymore.

Many families muddle along avoiding action until an acute episode, such as a hip fracture, forces them to think about long-term care. Watching a relative decline and failing to act accordingly may deprive him or her of a better quality of life that, say, an intervention like home-delivered meals, friendly visitors, home modifications, or services of a home care aide may offer. Taking action beforehand may also prevent more serious illnesses.

All too typically the person needing help resists. The loss of independence and autonomy is difficult for even the most adaptable person. Sixty-nine-year-old Cliff DeBlasio, who helps other seniors with household chores so they can stay in their homes, knows that only too well. "Independence is one of the most important words to a senior," he says.

Try to remain empathic when dealing with your relative and realize how many losses they might be coping with. The inability to drive is usually the first major loss, followed by the death of friends, relatives, a spouse, even the family doctor. When your parents sense that you want to move them out of the family home, they face yet another loss, so it's understandable there is resistance.

Here are a few techniques to help begin a discussion of long-term care:

• Find out what the older person wants and how that meshes with what the family wants. Mom might want to stay at home, the daughter might want Mom to live with her, and the son-in-law might prefer that Mom lives in a nearby retirement community. A family conference, which includes all the siblings, is usually a good idea at this point.

• Are the older person's desires practical? Mom may want to live at home, but if she suffers from cognitive impairment it may not be the best solution.

• In suggesting the need for a more formal assessment of your relative's function, you might tell your relative that it's important to have such an evaluation done so that if a crisis does arise, you'll know what to do. Social workers say this approach often works.

• Ask what your relative enjoys doing. If she enjoys cooking but hates doing housework, and you think doing housework presents a risk—say, for falls—suggest getting assistance for household chores. Let your relative continue cooking for as long as she can.

Table 6 can help you sort through the various needs your relative may have. Check what services are appropriate and then determine how you will obtain them. Note whether there are income restrictions and whether there are waiting lists. Many services provided under the federal Older Americans Act and under some state Medicaid programs have waiting lists. The trick is to assemble a package of services, public or private, that will help keep your relative independent for as long as possible.

WHERE TO TURN FOR HELP

The Public Entry System

A number of organizations in the public arena are pathways into the long-term-care system, and they usually do not charge for their services. They range from government agencies, such as area agencies on aging and state Medicaid offices, to religious organizations, such as the Jewish Family Services, and groups that advocate for patients with particular diseases.

It is not likely you will get everything you need with one phone call. Expect to make several calls before you arrange care. About half of all caregivers responding to a survey by the National Alliance for Caregiving said they made three or more phone calls before they got necessary services. Keep a separate notebook to record the calls and telephone numbers you have reached and the names of the people to whom you spoke. Note who referred you and what kinds of services might be available. It's important to record how the services you need will be paid for.

The following are some of the major public entry points you might find helpful:

TABLE 6: What Services Do You Need?

The following table will help you decide the services you or your relative needs help with. It's unlikely you'll require all of these services, at least initially. Only when you become very frail and cannot perform any of the so-called activities of daily living will you need most of them.

To use this table, note which services you need and where you can obtain them. This chapter and others in the book will help you fill in this piece of information. Many services paid for by public funds have income eligibility limits and waiting lists. Noting those restrictions on this table will help you focus on other options.

Here are some examples of how to use this table:

1. Suppose your relative needs home-delivered meals and the service is available from your local agency on aging but there is a waiting list. You could investigate whether your local hospital or a private meals-on-wheels organization can deliver food right away. Or you may need a friend or neighbor to bring in food.

2. Suppose your relative needs help getting out of bed and also with bathing and dressing. Your state Medicaid program offers this service but your relative has too much income to qualify. Home health agencies can also provide those services. There's no waiting list, no income limitations, but you have to pay out of pocket for the care.

SERVICE	DOES RELATIVE NEED IT?	WHERE TO OBTAIN IT	INCOME LIMITS	WAITING LIST	COST
Food					
Home-delivered meals					
Congregate meals					
Shopping assistance					
Free groceries					
Care Services					
Personal care					
Bathing					
Dressing					
Toileting					
Continence					
Eating					
Transferring					
Homemaker services					
Laundry					
Cooking					
Cleaning					
Home repairs					
Caregiver respite					

SERVICE	DOES RELATIVE NEED IT?	WHERE TO OBTAIN IT	INCOME LIMITS	WAITING LIST	COST
Help with medications	_____	_____	_____	___	___
Nursing services	_____	_____	_____	___	___
Wound care	_____	_____	_____	___	___
Tube feeding	_____	_____	_____	___	___
Catheter changing	_____	_____	_____	___	___
Injections	_____	_____	_____	___	___
Other	_____	_____	_____	___	___

Financial Management

Banking	_____	_____	_____	___	___
Bill paying	_____	_____	_____	___	___
Insurance policy management/ counseling	_____	_____	_____	___	___
Post office chores	_____	_____	_____	___	___
Tax help	_____	_____	_____	___	___
Legal help	_____	_____	_____	___	___

Social Needs

Friendly visitors	_____	_____	_____	___	___
Telephone reassurance	_____	_____	_____	___	___
Postal alert program	_____	_____	_____	___	___
Escort/transport to doctor	_____	_____	_____	___	___

Physical Activities

Massage	_____	_____	_____	___	___
Walking	_____	_____	_____	___	___
Light exercise	_____	_____	_____	___	___

General Health Needs

Medical alert system	_____	_____	_____	___	___
Transportation to doctors	_____	_____	_____	___	___
Care management	_____	_____	_____	___	___

Social Stimulation

Cards	_____	_____	_____	___	___
Board games	_____	_____	_____	___	___
Puzzles	_____	_____	_____	___	___
Reading	_____	_____	_____	___	___
Movies	_____	_____	_____	___	___

Area agencies on aging In 1965, Congress enacted the Older Americans Act, which established the "aging network." Each state has what's called a "state unit on aging" that channels money from the federal government to various Older Americans Act programs in the state. The state units sometimes go by the designation departments or offices on aging, and they are listed in Appendix B. Each state has one or more area agencies on aging—or, as they are often called, Triple A's—that provide various programs and services. Some six hundred agencies in the country offer services, but there is no uniformity in the services. In one location, the Triple A may offer lots of services; in another, it may offer very few.

The aging network was supposed to act as a place where people could learn about long-term-care services; in other words, it was intended as a kind of one-stop shopping center. In practice, though, lack of money, staff, and other resources have hampered the kinds and quality of services the Triple A's offer. Nonetheless, they provide a starting point for your search. You can call your state unit on aging to obtain the number for your local agency on aging. You can also call the Eldercare Locator (800-677-1116), which will put you in touch with your local Triple A or, in some cases, a local office on aging where you can begin your search. The agency should tell you about publicly funded services—programs provided under the Older Americans Act, state-funded programs, and of course, Medicaid. The Triple A may send you brochures or booklets listing nursing homes and assisted-living facilities. If that's all the agency does, that's not terribly helpful, and you'll have to seek other assistance.

Dealing with the Triple A Most people seeking help from the Triple A's don't know what they need. They know that a relative needs help now or in the future, or they'll call and have one kind of service in mind. Table 6 on pages 108–109 will help you focus on the kinds of services you need. Typically, an adult child will describe a problem hoping that the person at the other end of the phone will have all the answers. However, if your relative is not eating, the underlying problem could be dementia, drug interactions, or the result of disease. A good social worker at the Triple A will ask a lot of questions about your relative's situation—home environment, symptoms, underlying health problems, medications, and nearby family support. If the social worker or intake person does not ask questions, you may not get much help, and the task of finding care will be more difficult.

In describing needed services, be specific. For example, it's not enough to say "I think she needs help with transportation." Specify what kind of transportation—to the doctor, to a senior center, or to the supermarket. Transportation services vary by county and even by neighborhoods within a county; one county might provide taxi vouchers for visits to the doctor while another may offer more comprehensive services.

Ask the Triple A official to describe all the public services available and the financial criteria for qualifying. A particular county, for instance, might have a transportation service but only for people with low incomes. Be prepared to discuss the assets and income of the person needing care. That will help the Triple A determine what programs your relative qualifies for. If your relative's income is too high for some of the programs, there may be a provision to pay based on a sliding scale—that is, your relative may have to pay some portion of the cost. Chapter 1 offers guidance in determining your relative's resources.

State Medicaid offices Dealing with the state Medicaid office is like living through a nightmare. Be prepared for referrals and lots of red tape. However, if your relative will need Medicaid funds to pay for long-term care, it's better to become acquainted with Medicaid in your state sooner rather than later. Appendices I and J list the different programs available in the states. Use them as a starting point to determine the kinds of services you would like Medicaid to pay for. But be aware that the agency may simply refer you to another source for help.

I can't stress enough that you must understand your relatives' financial situation before you begin your foray into the Medicaid bureaucracy. You must know what their income and assets are, whether they are eligible for any of the available programs, or whether they must spend down all their assets. Understanding their finances will help you ask the right questions, such as what forms to obtain and what documentation (bank accounts, insurance policies, and so forth) you must provide.

Disease-specific organizations In a survey conducted in the spring of 1998 by the National Alliance for Caregiving, respondents said the information they found most valuable was related to the diseases their relatives had. Caregivers wanted to know what to expect, how a disease progressed, and how to administer medical treatments. Organizations that advocate for people with specific diseases are listed in Appendix H. They can supply you with information about the disease and how to care for someone who has it.

Help in rural areas People in rural areas have special problems. Many rural communities have large numbers of elderly people; in some counties across the Midwest, as many as 30 percent of the residents are old, and a large number of them are frail. There is often a small tax base in those communities that is used to provide support services to elderly people and a small labor pool from which to draw home health aides and others who can help. It is not uncommon for the old to take care of the old, and respite care is hard to find when caregivers need a break.

Start with the local area agency on aging, which can direct you to such services as transportation, personal care, home-delivered meals, and meals provided at senior centers, often an important place for social contact in rural areas. Nursing homes and rural hospitals are also good sources of information about special programs and services. "Rural nursing facilities don't carry the stigma urban ones do," says Linda Redford, director of the resource and policy center on rural long-term care at the University of Kansas Center on Aging. Nursing homes and hospitals might be able to steer you to people in the community who are willing to act as home care workers. In some rural areas, home health agencies have closed, making it more difficult for families to find aides. Rural hospitals might also offer home-delivered meals, and there may not be waiting lists for them as there could be with meals provided under Older Americans Act programs.

Don't overlook the churches. They are not only a source for spiritual support, but they also offer social contact in rural areas. Place a notice on a church bulletin board to let the community know you are looking for home helpers.

Another good source is the Cooperative Extension Service. Call your county agricultural extension office and ask to speak to the home agent. She will know of services and resources in the community. You can also call the Extension Service at your state's land-grant university. Ask to talk with the specialist in family and consumer sciences. He or she should also be able to direct you.

The Private-Entry System

Sometimes you may find a way into the long-term-care system that requires spending money to find the services you need. Geriatric care managers, a relatively new profession, provide one pathway into the system. Brokers who help arrange housing for seniors also charge for their services. Another private pathway is an employee assistance plan you may have at work.

Geriatric care managers In the last few years a new profession—geriatric care management—has sprung up in response to the growing number of baby boomers who need help finding care for aging parents. People doing this kind of work may be psychologists, nurses, social workers, nurse-practitioners, gerontologists, even financial planners. It's also possible to run into people who think they know something about the field but have little training to do the job. Avoid doing business with them.

What they do Depending on their training, care managers offer a variety of services. Not only do they help find services, but they can provide emotional relief to everyone in the caregiver relationship. The care manager can bridge the different parts of the health care delivery system to the professional services you or your relative needs. Some families look to the managers to validate choices they have already made; others want more hands-on involvement. Their services might be required once, or you may want them for many years. Specifically, care managers can:

- Offer crisis intervention—your mother breaks a hip and needs immediate help; a care manager can help find a rehabilitation center when she is discharged from the hospital.
- Conduct assessments to ascertain your relative's problems with cognitive functioning or activities of daily living and suggest courses of action—your mother exhibits early stages of Alzheimer's disease and you need to know what help she needs.
- Help you select and monitor home health aides and other services—you live in another town and need someone to find a suitable home attendant for your father and keep an eye on the attendant who cares for him. Some geriatric care managers also run registries or placement services for home care workers. While this may be a simple way to find a worker, it pays to follow the guidelines for selecting a worker noted in Chapter 7.
- Provide bereavement counseling.
- Help a relative adjust to a move from the family home—you move Mom out of her house to an assisted-living facility and she has problems connecting to people and a new way of living.

- Refer your relative to geriatric specialists who can diagnose specific conditions—your mom has experienced a change in behavior, and you want to know whether it's caused by a simple drug interaction or a more serious underlying disease.
- Offer information about community resources.

Geriatric care managers can refer you to nursing homes. "We refer to places we know and like," says Barbara Kane, who owns Aging Network Services in Bethesda, Maryland. Recommendations from geriatric care managers may be fine, but I still suggest you do your own shopping, using Chapter 11 as a guide. If their recommendations mesh with your own on-site visits to the facilities as well as other information you gather, chances are you are making a good choice. But if the recommendation from a care manager differs from your own impressions, follow your instincts. You can never be sure if the care manager is receiving a kickback to steer people to particular facilities.

How to find a good manager States have yet to regulate geriatric care managers, and there are no requirements for state licensing. In many ways, the development of this profession parallels others that have gained in stature and respectability over the years. States don't get involved until the horror stories show up. In the meantime, the more conscientious factions of the profession try to regulate themselves. About three hundred care managers have received a certification from the National Academy of Certified Care Managers. (The industry's trade association, the National Association of Geriatric Care Managers, has some twelve hundred members.) Certification means that managers have taken and passed an exam that demonstrates they understand the process of care management and tests their competence in such areas as assessment, care planning, care implementation, monitoring and reassessment, and professional and legal issues.

The mix of a relatively new profession and stressed-out families desperate for help can be lethal. When searching for a manager, caveat emptor is in order. Just because someone has passed a certifying exam doesn't mean he or she will be an outstanding manager for your loved one, and just because someone has hung out a shingle doesn't mean he or she is qualified. Visit two or three potential managers. Ask for a half hour or so of their time and present your situation, outlining your relative's health problems and discussing the kinds of help you need. Ask how they would help solve your problems. If you like the answers they give, and you feel you have good rapport, then you should ask more detailed questions. If you are not comfortable with this person, consider another candidate.

Rona Bartelstone of Rona Bartelstone Associates, a care management firm in Fort Lauderdale, Florida, suggests you get answers to these basic questions as you begin your search:

• What is their training? Some members of the National Association of Geriatric Care Managers have backgrounds that might seem a bit off track for a care manager. You need some assurance the person you hire has worked in human services. If someone is trained as an accountant, what does he or she know about disease management, psychology, or behavior problems of Alzheimer's patients?

• Have they had supervised experience? The person you hire should have worked with others who have guided and evaluated their work. If they have had none, or there is no ongoing supervision, choose another manager.

• What backup is in place? Good managers and the agencies they work for have a backup system in place that comes into play if you or your relative has an emergency and they are not available. Who will cover for the person you hire if he or she is busy and your relative suffers a second stroke?

• How do you reach someone if there is a crisis? Crises with older adults don't always happen during business hours. Look for an agency that offers something more than an answering service. How fast does the agency respond?

A word of caution to adult children: Be sure you understand what is a real emergency and what isn't. Mom falling and breaking a hip is a real emergency. Vague or generalized complaints are not. The latter may require attention, but not in the middle of the night. A good care manager can help you understand when there is a real emergency, and help you deal with it in less anxiety-producing ways.

• What are their fees and what tasks do you want the manager to perform? Not all give written agreements, or understand their importance. I strongly recommend them as a way to protect yourself. The written agreement should spell out just what the care manager is to do if your relative is in a hospital, rehabilitation center, or nursing home. If the care manager is to arrange home care, you should agree on exactly what he or she will do and what you will do. The agreement should also specify when the manager will send bills—weekly or monthly?

• Is the care manager able to customize and individualize a care plan for your relative? This is not a "one size fits all" business. No two families will need exactly the same kinds of services. "Matching people with resources is the easy part," says Karen Knudsen, president of Open Care, a care management service in Charlotte, North Carolina. "Dealing with underlying family issues is much harder." Good geriatric care managers look at both in trying to find care for an elderly person, and sometimes they will come up with very different solutions for people who present the same kinds of problems.

Take, for example, two cases Knudsen handled. In one, a woman had dementia but was functioning fairly well in her own home. She enjoyed gardening, had friends, and her daughter lived in the community. Knudsen recommended a live-in companion, who was paid by the family, as well as modifications to the home—bath benches and grab bars in the bathroom. In the other case, a man with dementia was having a hard time staying at home, which was becoming a hostile environment. The washer and dryer were in the basement, the neighborhood was changing; he was feeling socially isolated. He also needed twenty-four-hour supervision and standby assistance. Knudsen recommended an assisted-living facility.

Spotting problems Once you decide to get help from a care manager, it's a good idea to monitor the quality of the services they are giving. Here are some things to watch for:

- The care manager dictates a care plan without the input of the family and other medical professionals involved in your relative's care.
- The care manager appears to work in isolation and doesn't know how to involve other medical professionals.
- The care manager does not understand the eligibility requirements for public programs, or is vague about what you or your relative must do to qualify.
- The care manager can't handle the emotional dynamics of the family. You don't want someone who yells at you or your mother.

What care management costs Price structures used by care managers vary considerably. Some charge by the hour, some on a per-visit basis, some on a per-function basis—a fee for an assessment, a fee for a home visit, a fee for a call to the physician, and so forth. Some managers bill separately for travel expenses while others fold travel costs into their per-visit or hourly charges. Charging by the hour is the most common arrangement, with the going rates currently ranging from $70 to $170 an hour depending on geographic location.

Because of such variations, comparing prices is difficult. Someone who charges $80 an hour may not include travel costs. Someone charging $95 may include them, making it less clear that the $80 charge is really cheaper in the long run.

When trying to calculate what a geriatric care manager will cost your family, know what services you want using Table 6. This way you'll be prepared to tell prospective care managers exactly what you want them to do for you. Then ask them to be specific about how much they'll charge for the particular service.

Brokers In some states, you may find organizations that act as brokers who can help find long-term-care services for a relative. They are usually paid a finder's fee by the assisted-living facility, board-and-care home, or residential care facility. Since they may be working for the facility and not for you, they may not have your relative's best interests in mind. Be very careful dealing with these organizations.

Employee assistance plans A few employers offer help to their employees who must find long-term-care services for aging parents. The company's elder-care benefit usually consists of a referral service for employees to call to get information about long-term-care options in the community. Sometimes the benefit will provide telephone assistance and counseling. One vendor of these benefits services, Ceridian Performance Partners, employs researchers who customize a packet of information for an employee seeking help. The packet often contains tip sheets on such topics as making homes safer and choosing a nursing home.

Most of these referral services help you get the names of people or places to call, but usually you have to do the legwork yourself. It is rare for an employee assistance plan to actually screen home care workers or help determine your relative's eligibility for Medicaid.

Check with your benefits administrator at work to see if your employer offers help with elder care.

Whether you enter the long-term-care system through a public agency or hire a geriatric care manager, sooner or later your relative will need a formal assessment. If you're looking for Medicaid to pay for nursing home services or for home and other care in the community, the agency most certainly will want an evaluation of your relative's condition to determine medical eligibility for payment. If you enter the long-term-care system by hiring a geriatric care manager, he or she will most likely suggest an assessment to determine appropriate services. Family members need to know whether their relative is capable of making decisions. Many geriatric care managers report that more than half of the people they assist suffer some type of cognitive impairment.

The social worker who visits will probably do a mental status screening test that assesses whether your relative has lost the ability to make decisions and perform some of the activities of daily living. If he or she scores poorly on the screening test, the social worker will probably suggest a full medical workup for dementia, which could include a visit to a neurologist, thyroid tests, blood tests, and a CT scan.

The assessment may also include an evaluation for depression and subsequent referral to a psychiatrist for treatment. It's not uncommon for depression to coexist with Alzheimer's disease and other kinds of dementia. A thorough assessment might also include vision and hearing tests since sensory impairments can also cause confusion in the elderly.

Drug interactions may be a culprit, and a good assessment should include an evaluation of all the drugs your relative is taking. It's not uncommon for elderly people to take as many as seven or eight medications. That's called polypharmacy, and you may hear a professional use that term. The more taken, the greater the chance for adverse reactions. A good social worker can look at the prescriptions and eyeball them for the correct dosage and possible harmful reactions. One case manager says, "We often see older adults on higher doses, and we will make recommendations that they talk to their doctor." Good managers sometimes call the doctor.

The social worker will also evaluate how well your relative moves about, looking at balance and gait to see if he or she has a tendency to fall. The social worker will also ask about continence and assess whether bathrooms are accessible. This may help determine whether your relative can continue to live at home.

Evaluating the home and community are also part of an assessment. If the home is no longer safe—for example, there are too many steps to climb to reach the bathroom or the lighting is poor, or the neighborhood is problematic—the person conducting the assessment might recommend moving a relative, perhaps to a personal care home or to an assisted-living facility.

Moving is traumatic for most older adults, and you should consider it very carefully before coaxing a relative out of the home he or she has lived in for thirty or forty years. "We see a lot of falls and illness around the time a person moves," says Barbara Kane. "It's a very fragile time."

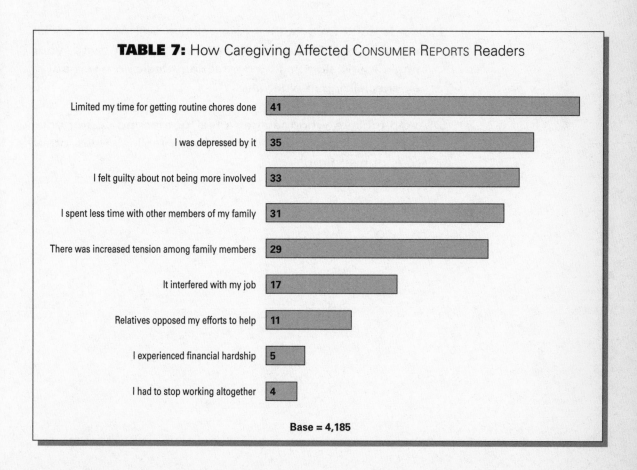

TABLE 7: How Caregiving Affected CONSUMER REPORTS Readers

Limited my time for getting routine chores done	41
I was depressed by it	35
I felt guilty about not being more involved	33
I spent less time with other members of my family	31
There was increased tension among family members	29
It interfered with my job	17
Relatives opposed my efforts to help	11
I experienced financial hardship	5
I had to stop working altogether	4

Base = 4,185

1. If you need more time to shop for long-term-care services, try to keep your relative in the hospital longer by using Medicare's appeal procedures.

2. Know exactly what your relative needs help with and be prepared to discuss those requirements with agency social workers.

3. Prepare your relative for an assessment. Tell him or her that you need to know how to help if there is a crisis.

4. If you have money, hiring a professional geriatric care manager might be a smart idea, but beware of charlatans.

5. Decide early on whether your relative will need financial support from Medicaid. Familiarize yourself with your state's Medicaid rules by contacting Medicaid or an attorney specializing in elder law.

6. Avoid brokers who may get a fee for steering you or your relative to a particular kind of living facility. Seek other types of help first.

SEVEN

Care at Home

When Sally B. turned eighty-five, she began to need more help. She was afraid of falling and could no longer drive or keep appointments. Soon she needed someone to prepare meals. She became disoriented. Her daughter, who lived nearby, arranged for home care, for a housekeeper, and for a driver twice a week.

A year later an aide was coming to fix supper and stay through the night. There were weekend cooks and daily housekeepers who helped Sally dress and get around. At the start, the family was paying helpers $1,325 a month. But as time passed and more assistance became necessary, the cost climbed to $8,300 a month. Yet Sally's family resisted placement in a nursing home even as she needed more and more care.

Eventually fiscal reality set in, and the family succumbed to the inevitable. Sally went to a nursing home where she gets the round-the-clock supervision she needs. By that time, her family had accumulated bills of more than $34,000 for the most recent six months of home care. If she had stayed at home for a full year, the cost would easily have exceeded $70,000—some $19,000 more than the annual cost of her nursing home.

Sally carried long-term-care insurance, which she had bought years ago through AARP. She wanted to pay her own way in old age. However, the policy's home care benefit paid $25 a day. Her family collected only $1,603 toward the $34,000 cost for her last six months of care at home.

Sally's family came to realize that staying at home, no matter how desirable, was not the best option. Few elders elect to go to a nursing home. The desire to remain at home is so strong that families often stretch their budgets and those of the person needing care in order to provide the necessary services at home. One baby boomer interviewed for a story in *Money* magazine said that he wanted his father to be cared for at home. The boomer had purchased a long-term-care insurance policy and told the magazine that "with the insurance I'm much more confident that I will be able to afford to keep him out of a nursing home." His flawed logic and cocky tone exuded an air of certainty and conviction that is just not realistic when it comes to long-term care.

Despite his best intentions and careful financial planning, there is no way to predict whether this man's father will suffer a debilitating illness eventually requiring nursing home care. And there's no way to say for sure that he and his siblings or the insurance policy he bought will cover the escalating costs of home care ten years from now, when his father is likely to need assistance. Like Sally B.'s family, too many people make the mistake of thinking they can handle twenty-four-hour home care. Most can't. Full, round-the-clock home care is just "not reasonable," says Ann Morris, executive director of IVNA Home Health Care in Richmond, Virginia.

Furthermore, home care may be a lonely solution. For many elders who have a place to go at night, day care options in the community either through PACE programs or through day care centers (see Chapters 8 and 9) may offer better care and more social interaction than isolated care given by an untrained home health aide. This is not to say you should avoid the home care option as you begin to plan for the needs of an elderly parent or other relative. For many families, home care works for a while, particularly after a hospital stay for an acute illness. It may even work for a long time with an aide providing personal care services, and it may work in combination with day care. But it's important to be realistic about its usefulness and for how long, and to know when another option is more appropriate.

Your ability to use home care may also depend on whether there is public financing available for the services you need in the community where your relative lives. Seventy-eight percent of public money spent on long-term care goes to nursing homes; only 22 percent is spent on home care. So chances are you may not find much public money available, and if you do, there are likely to be waiting lists for many home care services. Use Table 6 (pages 108–109) to determine what kinds of services your relative needs. Then turn to Appendices I, J, and K, which point out which home care services are available under Medicaid in your state, under non-Medicaid state-funded programs, and under programs available through the federal Older Americans Act. Use these as a starting point to learn what funding your relative is eligible for.

If no public money is available, you may have no choice but to pay out of pocket for care. If your relative gets on a waiting list, you may have to pay during the waiting period. If you have a long-term-care policy that pays for home care, Chapter 14 tells how to access benefits. Be careful that you don't squander all the benefits on home care, exhausting the policy so there's nothing left to pay for nursing home care when the time comes for more intensive supervision. Forty percent of CONSUMER REPORTS readers who had used home care said their relative eventually went to a nursing home; sixteen percent said they went to an assisted-living facility.

Finding good home care is like staring into a big black box; it's not unlike finding good day care for a child. The rest of this chapter will help you find your way through the different types of home care, understand how to protect yourself, learn how to find good care, and how managed care and home care fit together.

The term *home care* covers a wide range of services. It can mean personal care like helping an elder eat, bathe, dress, and use the toilet. It can mean help with simple tasks like grocery shopping and preparing meals, or it can mean help with complex medical procedures such as changing catheters and inserting feeding tubes and breathing devices. Home care has also come to mean services and equipment supplied by companies known as "durable medical equipment" firms.

Traditionally, home care services have been provided by not-for-profit organizations like the Visiting Nurse Association, which has branches in most major cities. But in recent years for-profit entrepreneurs have entered the market, capitalizing on Medicare's willingness to pay the bills and on hospital protocols that send people home quicker and sicker. With the passage of the Balanced Budget Act of 1997, however, Congress has required the Health Care Financing Administration to lower payments to home health agencies to reduce spending for Medicare. In some areas, you may find these restrictions affecting your ability to obtain home care services covered by Medicare.

There's little regulation of the more routine homemaker services, and even the few requirements that do exist for other kinds of services don't demand much in the way of quality. Indeed, it's difficult to judge quality because care delivered in someone's home is less visible than care in a nursing home.

What you get and what you pay for home care depend on the kind of agency you use.

THE HOME CARE FOOD CHAIN

Certified home health agencies Medicare certifies some 8,000 home health agencies that are authorized to provide skilled nursing care at home for Medicare beneficiaries eligible to receive those services. A social worker or a discharge planner at a hospital can tell you about Medicare's home health benefit. If your relative has not been in the hospital, but you think he or she might qualify for the Medicare home health benefit, you can call one of the certified home health agencies listed in the Yellow Pages. (They usually advertise the fact that they are certified by Medicare.) You can also ask your local Social Security office about the benefit and which agencies are certified to provide it.

Certified home health agencies may be for-profit or not-for-profit appendages of hospitals, or they might be run by local governments. Aides sent out by these agencies must have completed a training program, a competency evaluation program, or both. To see if your relative qualifies for the Medicare benefit, the agency will do an assessment (see Chapter 6). Once your relative is eligible for the service, the agency bills Medicare directly the same as doctors bill Medicare for their services.

Eligibility requirements for this benefit are stiff. To receive Medicare home health care, a person must require intermittent skilled-nursing care, which means specific medical services provided or supervised by RNs and by physical, occupational, or speech therapists. A doctor must order and review the care, and your relative must be homebound. In Medicare parlance, homebound means a person is confined to his or her home and cannot leave except for very short absences or trips for medical reasons. Many families find that restriction burdensome since they can't take their relatives anyplace, but it's the price for having Medicare pay the bill. (Agencies that don't take the homebound restriction seriously are sometimes targeted in the crackdown on fraud and abuse.)

As long as your relative requires skilled care, he or she may also be eligible for personal care services such as help with bathing and dressing. But as Chapter 2 points out, Medicare does not pay for transportation, home-delivered meals, or chore services. If no skilled care is needed, Medicare does not pay for any personal care services, and you'll have to find other sources of public funding.

There's no limit on how long your relative can receive home health care, but after one hundred days of care, Medicare shifts its payment from a hospital or Part A service to a medical or Part B service. In 1997, Congress began to restrict this benefit, which was originally designed for short-term care needed by beneficiaries while recovering from acute illnesses such as surgeries or hip fractures. Through the years, however, more and more people with chronic illnesses have come to rely on the benefit, largely because they have no other way to pay for the home care they need. In effect, Congress is now telling those people to find another way to pay for their care and is limiting the skilled-nursing benefit and the services of home health aides to a combination of less than eight hours a day up to a maximum of twenty-eight hours a week. Whether your relative qualifies for this benefit will depend on how Medicare's payment intermediary, most likely the Blue Cross plan in your area, will interpret your relative's condition. It's a good bet that intermediaries will judge your relative's needs in the narrowest way. If you're turned down and think your relative qualifies, file an appeal. Chapter 2 tells how to do that.

Congress is also changing the way home health agencies are paid. Instead of paying them for each service they provide, which has resulted in too many and sometimes unnecessary services, payment is now based on a flat rate for each beneficiary no matter how many services the agency provides. (This payment system is similar to the one Medicare uses for hospitals—the DRG system—which reimburses hospitals based on the diagnosis of their patients.)

It may now be harder to find a certified home health agency to care for your relative, especially if he or she has a progressive chronic disease or complex needs that will require a lot of care. For example, home health agencies may no longer consider diabetics who need help every day or people who need daily care to change dressings on surgical wounds as desirable clients, says Maxine Hochhauser, executive vice president for the Metropolitan Jewish Health System in New York City. "This service will be harder to access. People will be getting fewer services, but the outcomes may not be any worse."

Certified home health agencies can't terminate services as long as the person is not in the hospital. But once a person goes to the hospital and is discharged, it might be hard to get the same services from the same agency again. If you find that an agency is cutting off services for your relative—in other words, abandoning him or her—call the adult protective services agency in your area. Abandonment is not legal in most areas.

If Medicare refuses to pay for the skilled-nursing services your relative needs at home, you may have to pay privately to get the service. Don't be surprised to pay close to $20 an hour for a skilled-nursing aide, although the median hourly rate for a home care worker is about $9 an hour.

Licensed home health agencies There are more than 20,000 licensed home health care agencies across the country that usually provide aides who provide personal care and do household chores. Those agencies are not certified by Medicare, although some of them are hybrids—they have a Medicare-certified business and a noncertified business. Sometimes those agencies subcontract their services to other organizations, which makes it difficult to figure out who is responsible for the aide who comes to the house.

The noncertified part of the agency may operate with little oversight except for perhaps minimal state licensing laws or some kind of private accreditation from the Joint Commission on Accreditation of Healthcare Organizations or the Community Health Accreditation Program. Certification programs don't guarantee the quality of care your relative receives. Aides they send may or may not have much formal training, and they may have no training to care for people with your relative's condition. Families whose relatives have Alzheimer's disease, for example, sometimes complain that home health aides don't know how to handle the problems associated with the illness. One woman said that a support group taught her how to deal with her mother's behavioral problems. She said she knew more than the home aide Medicaid sent to care for her mother.

Many agencies require that a family use at least four hours of care each day. That may be more care than your relative needs. Or if your relative requires, say, six hours of care, you may end up paying for extra hours you don't need. If you need twenty-four hours of care, the agency may give you a break, charging only for sixteen hours, or sometimes even less. Families often make the mistake of thinking that home care may be less expensive than a nursing home. It may not be.

Registries These are basically matching and referral services that maintain a roster of available personnel. When your relative needs a helper, the registry sends someone out, but they do not employ the person who comes to assist your relative. Registries are usually not licensed or certified, and whether they do any screening, training, or supervising of their personnel is questionable. Good registries may do some or all three, but others may be more interested in signing up clients than in checking references.

There's not much difference between using a registry to find a home health aide and looking for someone in your neighborhood who is willing to work off the books. Those interested in directing their own home health aides (see page 129) are more apt to use the services of a registry.

Often you'll have to pay a referral fee to the registry based on a formula related to the wages you pay the helper. Take, for example, At Home Care, a registry in Charlotte, North Carolina. This registry charges a fee equal to 20 percent of the worker's gross wages for an eight-week period. There's a minimum fee of $170 regardless of how many hours the aide works. If you're not happy with the aide, some registries will send a replacement without charging an additional referral fee if the change occurs within a certain time period. After that, they may charge either a full or prorated fee to send a new aide to your relative's home.

If you use a registry, be sure you understand the fee structure. The biggest advantage of a registry over aides from a licensed home health agency is cost; registries charge $1 to $4 less than a licensed home health care agency. To get an idea of the relative price difference, review Table 8 on page 128, which shows what At Home Care Services would charge for three services versus what a traditional home health service in Charlotte would charge.

Paying for Home Care

If your relative needs skilled-nursing services, chances are Medicare will pay for some of the care. If he or she requires nonskilled services, choices boil down to hiring an aide from a licensed home care agency, from a registry, or finding someone who agrees to work for you for the fees you are willing to pay. Whether your relative is eligible for public funds depends on his or her income, the willingness to use that income to pay for home care aides, and what your state offers in the way of

TABLE 8: A Comparison of Home Care Costs: At Home Care Services versus Traditional Home Health Agency Services

Service	At Home Care	Traditional home health	Savings using At Home Care
Live-in companion (first 8 weeks)	$3,360/mo.	$4,463/mo.	$1,103/mo.
Live-in companion after initial 8 weeks of placement (cost of future 1-month intervals)	$2,800/mo.	$4,463/mo.	$1,663/mo.
One 12-hour shift for first 8 weeks (7 days/week)	$3,629/mo.	$4,234/mo.	$605/mo.
One 12-hour shift after initial 8 weeks of placement (monthly cost)	$3,024/mo.	$4,234/mo.	$1,210/mo.
One 8-hour shift for first 8 weeks (7 days/week)	$2,419/mo.	$2,822/mo.	$403/mo.
One 8-hour shift after initial 8 weeks of placement (monthly cost)	$2,016/mo.	$2,822/mo.	$806/mo.

funds for different services. You may find some home care services covered by Medicaid, some by Medicaid waivers, some by non-Medicaid state programs, and some by the Older Americans Act. Sometimes a person may be eligible for both Medicaid and state-funded home care services. But in some states, if a person qualifies for Medicaid, he or she can't receive services under state-funded programs.

To learn what's available in your state, use Appendices I, J, K, and L as a starting point in your search for services.

First check whether Medicaid will pay for the home care services your relative needs—all states provide home care services, though they may be limited. New York has the most generous home care available under Medicaid, and the state program covers many personal care services. Other states offer far more limited services, if they offer any at all.

Medicaid waivers for home care All states offer what are called waivered services. This means they can pay for certain kinds of home care without following guidelines established by the federal government. The federal government allows states to substitute home care for nursing home services. Needless to say, a person receiving care under a waiver must have the same level of impairment as someone who would otherwise be in a nursing home.

Under a waiver, Medicaid pays for a range of services, including personal care, respite care, homemaker and chore services, skilled-nursing care, and transportation. But the services may be limited. Some states also cap the amount they'll pay. The state of Washington pays an amount that cannot exceed 90 percent of what nursing homes in the state cost, or about $115. Arkansas will pay for emergency response systems under its waiver program, but it will cover only one installation. If the device is lost, the state won't pay for a replacement. In New York, where a lot of Medicaid money is available for home care, each county determines how many hours of care a person can receive based on need.

As the appendices show, many states have waiting lists for waivered services. In planning care for aged relatives, consider the waiting lists, what resources he or she has, and how much you and other siblings are able to contribute for care until they reach the top of the list.

With both Medicaid waiver and nonwaivered services, your local (state) office determines which home health agency it will use, and the agency in turn chooses the aide who is sent out. Clients usually have little say about who cares for them.

Client-Directed Contracting

Some states allow Medicaid recipients to select their own home health attendants. Under programs that are loosely called client-directed contracting, those needing home health care or their families select their own aides and Medicaid pays the bills. "These programs offer maximum levels of independence," says Ira Holland, president of Concepts of Independence, a nonprofit consumer-directed personal assistance program in New York City. "You can hire, train, and develop a relationship with your workers."

To participate in a client-directed program, either you or your relative recruits, interviews, hires, trains, supervises, and schedules the home health aide who will come to your home. You will also have to arrange backup care for times when your attendant is unavailable.

You also assume full responsibility for personal injury or loss of property that may result from hiring a personal attendant. You may be required to distribute paychecks to your aide and process the required paperwork—time sheets, enrollment documents, health assessments, and other employment documents.

Organizations like Concepts of Independence act as fiscal intermediaries. They receive Medicaid payments from the state, handle the paperwork for tax withholding and payment of benefits, and process the payroll, paying the prevailing rate for workers within the guidelines set by state Medicaid programs.

Programs similar to Concepts are available in other states, although there may be waiting lists. In Kentucky, for example, there's a five-year waiting list in Louisville for payment for this service under the state-funded program. There are variations in how they work. Some are available mostly for disabled people under age sixty-five, but increasingly seniors are able to use them. In some states, it may be hard to find out about such programs. If a state has a strong interest in making people use Medicare dollars as much as possible for home care, "you may never know the option exists," says Sue Flanagan, a consultant who has studied these programs.

Spending Down

As with nursing home services, your relative must be poor or become poor in order to qualify for Medicaid home care.

If you want Medicaid to pay for home care and your relative has income and assets above your state's threshold, your family will have to decide whether to pay for the services out of pocket or have your relative spend down. As I note in Chapter 13, spending down means that people requesting support from Medicaid must spend virtually all their assets and almost all of their income on care.

If you think your relative will eventually need a nursing home with Medicaid support to pay the bills, is it better to spend down now for home care services or later when nursing home care becomes necessary? If you pay privately for home care, you may have a wider choice of services. If Medicaid pays, your relative will get whatever services Medicaid funds in your state; those services may not be the ones most appropriate for your relative. If he or she avoids a spend-down at the beginning of a stretch of long-term care and dies before going to a nursing home, your relative's savings may be available as an inheritance instead of going to pay for long-term care. Chapter 13 discusses how a spend-down works.

State-Funded Programs

Many states use their own revenues to pay for services for the elderly. Some pay for these services out of their social service block grant money that comes from the federal government. Appendix L shows the programs the states offer.

State-funded home care services may not be subject to the same income-and-asset restrictions as Medicaid services. Some states ask those receiving services to pay a share of the cost based on their income. If you can get the same service from a state-funded program and pay a portion of the cost, that might be better than facing a Medicaid spend-down right away. But state-funded programs may also be limited. In Rhode Island, for example, housekeeping and chore services are limited to six to ten hours per week. In Kansas, adult day care is available only if there are funds.

Older Americans Act Services

Some states use funds channeled from the federal government through the state units on aging to the local Triple A to pay for home care services. A major service is home-delivered meals that may be of particular interest if your relative is homebound. There is no income limit for eligibility for these services, and anyone who is sixty years or older can get them. These programs, however, have been shortchanged by the federal government, and availability is limited in many parts of the country. Funding hasn't kept pace with need, and in many areas there are long waiting lists for all services. Program directors often have to make choices: do they offer more home-delivered meals to the elderly, or do they fund more slots for homemaker services or transportation.

Older Americans Act services should be your first choice if you can get them. But those with greater resources and more family support often have to wait. This means you'll have to look for other payment sources.

Respite Care

Respite care is a type of home care; it is basically substitute care for caregivers who need a break from their task of caring for an infirm relative. In many areas, however, there are few government programs to pay for this. Some states fund respite care through various programs. Again, Appendices I, J, K, and L can guide you.

SHOPPING FOR A HOME CARE AGENCY

There's no foolproof way to find a good home health agency. There are no official measures of quality. The Health Care Financing Administration has records of inspection reports for the certified home health agencies that administer the Medicare home health benefit, but it does not make such data available in any useable way. The inspections evaluate the agencies against some 150 standards. A few years ago, CONSUMER REPORTS looked at the inspection reports for some 22,000 agencies, and noted some disturbing findings:

- Thirty percent of the agencies were not developing care plans that cover pertinent diagnoses, prognosis, nutritional requirements, medications, and safety measures to protect patients.
- Nearly 30 percent failed to keep clinical records.
- Nearly 30 percent failed to administer drugs and treatments that physicians had ordered.
- Twenty-five percent did not follow written care plans.
- Twenty percent failed to check patients' medications to identify adverse drug reactions.
- Fifteen percent did not tell physicians when there appeared to be a need for a change in the care plan.

Keep those shortcomings in mind as you look for a home health agency. Finding out if they have procedures in place to eliminate some of the problems CONSUMER REPORTS noted may make the difference between a good experience and a bad one.

Most people find an agency through the Yellow Pages or from a hospital social worker or discharge planner. "A lot of times they find it through word of mouth. Someone has a positive experience with an agency," says Terese Acampora, administrative director of patient services for the Metropolitan Jewish Health System in New York City. Whatever method you use to select an agency, keep some basic points in mind:

- Ask the agency to send two or three aides for an interview.
- Ask what kind of backup the agency has if the aide you select does not show up.
- How frequently do they do on-the-spot supervision of the aides they send out? If none, you may want to deal with an agency that provides some hands-on supervision.
- Do they perform criminal background checks?

- Make sure that the aide is bonded and the agency has workers' compensation coverage. A bond protects you in case of theft, and workers' compensation covers any injury to an aide that occurs on your property. If an agency does not have workers' compensation coverage, check to be sure your homeowner's policy is adequate.
- Does the agency do cultural sensitivity training for its workers? While people may be more willing to receive care in a hospital from a person who is from a different cultural or ethnic background, they may suddenly become intolerant when it comes to having such a person care for them in their own home. An aide from the West Indies may not be sensitive to your parent's need to maintain a kosher kitchen.
- Does the agency maintain references on the workers it sends for interviews? If it doesn't, you'll have to ask the worker for them.
- What method does the agency have in place for developing care plans; how do they monitor whether a change in the plan is necessary? Get examples of their monitoring activities.
- What procedures does the agency use to monitor adverse drug reactions and drug interactions resulting from patients taking many drugs?
- How does the agency make sure that its aides are following care plans and notifying physicians when something seems to be wrong?
- Does the agency consult with the family concerning the progress or lack of progress their relative is making? Do they allow the family to inspect the clinical records?
- If the patient is cognitively aware, does the agency consult with him or her concerning care needs and preferences?
- Find out how much subcontracting the agency does. The more subcontracted services you receive, the harder it is to know who is accountable and responsible for the care. If something goes wrong, it may be hard to identify the right person to fix it.
- Find out what training the aides must have, if any. An agency should be willing to describe the training program it uses. In some states, the Department of Social Services may require a minimum amount of training for agencies it contracts with under Medicaid. But even if an agency has some minimal requirements, the training may not give aides the skills they need to care for your family member. New York, for instance, does not require agencies to give training in the care for dementia patients. It's hit or miss if an agency includes the topic in its training programs.

SHOPPING FOR AN AIDE

As with home health agencies, there is no surefire way to choose a good home health aide. Indeed, families often complain about the quality of the aides who care for their relatives. One woman said she knew more about caring for her mother with Alzheimer's disease than her home health attendant. She would come home and find the radio and television turned up full volume. The noise agitated her mother. The aide, the woman said, apparently did not know that Alzheimer's patients prefer quiet and calm surroundings.

Finding a home health aide Home health agencies and registries can provide aides for you to screen. But if you want to bypass these agencies and enter into your own arrangement, you'll have to investigate other sources that might give you some idea of who is available for this kind of work, such as support groups, colleges and universities that have departments of gerontology or schools of nursing, adult day care centers, local departments of aging, or area agencies on aging.

You can also place an ad in a local paper or post your ads on bulletin boards at churches or synagogues, senior centers, or local merchants. According to the Alzheimer's Association of New York City, the ad should describe the person to be cared for, the neighborhood, the days and times needed, and what the job offers, such as a separate room for an aide who lives in.

When people answer the ad, conduct a brief telephone interview to weed out unsuitable candidates. You can ask about their qualifications, find out if they are U.S. citizens or have green cards, and are available for the times you need help.

The personal interview Once you have screened the applicants, either those you have found on your own or those sent by an agency, it's time for a personal interview. The Alzheimer's Association suggests that you look for these characteristics:

- Sensitivity and understanding. These are essential qualities for dealing with difficult patients. If your relative has dementia, find out if the applicant has training in dealing with such patients. If not, keep looking.
- Positive attitude. The aide you choose should find caregiving exciting and challenging.

- Flexibility. The ability to adapt to the behavioral problems that your relative might have is essential for good caregivers.
- Creativity. Describe difficult situations and ask how the applicant would handle them. Use different behaviors that you have observed in your relative. Can the candidates come up with innovative solutions to a problem? Do their answers make sense given how your relative behaves?
- Energy. Caregiving can be physically and emotionally draining. Does the applicant have the stamina to do the job? If the person sees the caregiving job as a sedentary one, you probably want to look elsewhere.

The following questions for your personal interview are adapted from the New York City chapter of the Alzheimer's Association:

- Begin the interview by setting a warm and comfortable tone. You want the applicant to see that this is a good family to work for.
- Have the person tell you about him- or herself. Ask about their work history and experience, what their needs and expectations are.
- Find out why the person entered the field of caregiving. Why do they like it? What are their personal goals?
- Ask about their recent jobs. Why did they leave them? What did they like or dislike?
- Ask about special training in caregiving. For example, what do they know about caring for dementia patients? If wound care is needed, do the applicants know how to change dressings and watch for signs of infection?
- Describe your family member's condition and the family's involvement. Be very clear about the tasks you need help with. It may be a good idea to copy the list of needs you developed in Table 6 and give it to the aide. Is he or she comfortable doing the tasks outlined? If the applicant balks at any task, continue your search.
- Describe the rate of pay, days and hours of employment, days off, and vacations.
- Discuss how you will evaluate the aide's performance and how he or she will communicate with you when they notice a change in your relative's condition or behavior.
- Describe how your family member will be involved in his or her own care. For instance, can your mom dress herself if an

aide gives verbal cues? Can she wash herself but needs help getting in and out of the tub?

- At the end of the interview, summarize your discussion and tell the applicant when you will get back to them. Ask for three references. When you call the references, ask about patterns of lateness. It's unlikely that you will want to hire someone who is always late for work.

The written agreement If you are hiring privately, it's a good idea to draw up a written agreement that spells out the tasks you expect the aide to carry out. In general, the agreement should spell out the caregiver's routine, the patient's behavior patterns, medications, numbers for emergency telephone calls, house rules such as respect for privacy, use of petty cash, use of the telephone, television, and computer. The agreement should also spell out the financial details to which both parties have agreed. Even if your relative is residing in an assisted-living facility and hires a home care worker, you should have a written agreement.

Use as your guide the home health aide assistance contract on page 137, which has been adapted from one used by the Collington Episcopal Life Care Community in Mitchellville, Maryland.

On or off the books Because home care costs so much and the desire to keep a relative at home is so strong, it's tempting to find an aide and pay him or her off the books. This, of course, can be dangerous. The person you hire can later claim that you have not paid Social Security taxes and try to collect them from you. You may also find yourself in the middle of a dispute with the IRS. Before you resort to paying off the books, investigate whether there is a PACE program in your area that your relative might qualify for (see Chapter 9). PACE could offer better and less expensive care than paying privately and risking a potential tax problem.

Any family employing an individual at home to help a family member perform domestic duties must apply to the IRS for an employer identification number and is required to withhold Social Security taxes. Call 1-800-tax-form and ask for the IRS application form SS4. Also ask for IRS publication 926, which gives information on Household Employment Taxes, including federal and state unemployment insurance.

TABLE 9: Sample Contract for Private-Duty Nursing Assistance

This contract, dated _____, is between _____, resident, and _____, private-duty assistant. For the sum of $_____ an hour, _____ hours per day, _____ days per week, the private-duty assistant agrees to perform the following duties:

CHECK ALL THAT APPLY

Personal Care and Hygiene:

_____ Receive and give formal report at beginning and end of shift from/to next assistant

_____ Provide and/or assist resident with personal and grooming hygiene needs

_____ Assist with bathing

_____ Assist with bowel/bladder training and toileting

_____ Assist with eating

_____ Learn habits, routines, and goals of resident to provide appropriate assistance with attaining goals

_____ Assist with therapeutic activities, both physical and social

_____ Assist with functional maintenance/restorative nursing needs (ambulation, eating, toileting, ADL training)

_____ Assure a safe and clean environment

_____ Assist in keeping living area clean and orderly

_____ Keep medical records as necessary

_____ Report to family any change in condition, including eating habits, skin condition, sleeping habits, or behavior

_____ Follow individualized care plan and schedule

_____ Follow restorative care guidelines (position, ambulation, range of motion)

_____ Assist in design and implementation of care plan

_____ Assemble, clean, and store specialized equipment

_____ Notify family immediately of any incident or accident

_____ Perform other duties as directed by the family

Housekeeping:

_____ Light housekeeping (dusting, vacuuming, picking up)

_____ Other_____

_____ Wash dishes and keeping kitchen clean

_____ Wash clothing

_____ Ironing

_____ Put clothing away

_____ Mend clothing

_____ Answer phone and take messages

General:

_____ Accompany person on outings; take person for walks

_____ Call family at least two hours before start of shift if cannot be at work or be on time

_____ Maintain a professional manner

_____ Dress in appropriate uniform (white pants/skirt, lab coat, if you want aide to be dressed that way)

_____ Wear name tag

_____ Respond appropriately to emergencies and offer support, comfort, and safety to family members

_____ Perform other duties as agreed upon with family

_____ Request time off at least two weeks in advance

Qualifications:

_____ (insert state) certification as geriatric nursing assistant

_____ Read, speak, and write understandable English

_____ Maintain a level of physical and mental health that enables appropriate care to be given

_____ Maintain confidentiality in all information regarding family member

_____ Demonstrate observational abilities and manual dexterity for performing certain duties and operating equipment

_____ Is pleasant, tactful, and courteous

Financial:

1. will be paid weekly, biweekly, monthly (circle one)
2. family will/will not withhold taxes, etc. (circle one)
3. is/is not entitled to paid vacations and holidays (circle one)
4. is/is not entitled to receive insurance benefits (circle one)
5. is/is not entitled to paid sick leave (circle one)
6. is/is not entitled to receive meals

If the answer to numbers 3, 4, or 5 is "is," details are:_____
_____

This contract has been agreed to by both parties signing below:

_____   _____
Family Member   Date   Private-Duty Assistant   Date

Introducing a Home Aide to Your Relative

It may be hard for your relative to accept the services of a home helper, for such a step means that independence is fading. A nonthreatening approach works best. Sometimes a social setting such as a lunch or a cup of coffee may help break the ice. The Alzheimer's Association suggests that you could introduce the aide as:

- Someone who can help me
- A housekeeper
- A friend who needs a place to stay
- Someone your relative is in charge of
- A companion who will take your relative to special events
- Someone recommended by the family doctor

The Quality of Care

Little is known about the actual quality of care that is delivered in the home by outside home health aides. Nor is it possible to judge whether the aides employed by one agency give better care than those from another. It is not possible to tell whether care from a licensed agency is better than care from an unlicensed one. Nor is it possible to tell whether the worker employed by an agency is better than one you hired from an ad you placed in the local newspaper.

Furthermore, what may be quality to one person is not quality to another. "A lot of time quality is in the eye of the beholder," says Stacey Guthrie, health services administrator for Collington Episcopal Life Care Community in Mitchellville, Maryland. To some people, quality home care may be an aide who shows up on time every day, watches the same soap operas, talks, and keeps your relative from getting lonely. But that aide may do little to supervise medications or watch for signs that your relative may be suffering from adverse drug reactions. Home health experts may define the latter as quality care, but that may be a secondary consideration for your relative. Indeed the CONSUMER REPORTS survey of its readers found that two-thirds were completely or very satisfied with the home health aide who cared for a relative. The biggest problem, they reported, was aides who didn't show up. To these people, arriving for work on time was an indicator of quality. As for home health agencies, CONSUMER REPORTS readers said the most significant problem was lack of worker supervision. Fourteen percent said workers were not supervised well. That's all the more reason to make sure you know what the agency does to monitor the care its workers give.

Home care is not visible to outsiders the way care in a nursing home is. There is no data available on such quality parameters as frequency of deaths, whether patients experience a decline or an improvement in their ability to perform activities of daily living, or whether they are admitted or readmitted to the hospital.

Because of the lack of data that actually measures quality, the discussion about the meaning of high-quality home care usually boils down to whether more services are better. The bottom line is that most experts really don't know if patients benefit from more services. Home care agencies say more is better and managed-care firms argue that less is. "The vehicles for measuring the need for services are crude to say the least," says Penny Feldman, director of research for the Visiting Nurse Association in New York City. "So you get the focus on fraud and abuse and the anecdotal stories about people getting too many services. We don't have evidence of overuse or inappropriate use in hospital-based agencies."

HMOS AND HOME HEALTH CARE

If your relative belongs to a managed-care plan and needs home care, the plan is responsible for arranging and paying for the care to which your relative is entitled under Medicare. The HMO provides Medicare's home health benefit as described in Chapter 2. It usually does not offer other home health care services.

As Chapter 2 points out, Medicare gives the managed-care firm a "capitation" payment to cover all the care your relative is likely to need for the month. So if, say, your mother breaks her hip, the HMO must stretch the capitation payment to cover all the care she needs in the hospital plus any skilled-nursing or home care she requires after she is discharged. HMOs have an incentive to skimp on services provided under the benefit, and there is some evidence this is happening.

The General Accounting Office looked at services provided by home health agencies that had contracts with Medicare HMOs and those that Medicare paid under the old-fashioned, fee-for-service arrangement. The GAO found that HMOs were more likely to focus on short-term goals to help patients function independently than to foster reliance on home health care for the long term. For instance, if someone needed to climb six stairs to reach the bathroom at home, the therapist would concentrate on having the person learn to climb six stairs. Once the patient reached that goal, the HMO was likely to discontinue the therapy if the patient required no further skilled nursing or skilled therapy. Home health agencies that were not paid under a capitation arrangement, but instead received fees for their services, told GAO investigators that they were more likely to provide services over a longer period to make sure the patient had healed completely and knew about his or her condition.

It's hard to know whether all the extra services are really necessary. If your family member belongs to an HMO and does not appear to be receiving the skilled services you think he or she needs, the best thing to do is disenroll from the Medicare HMO and rejoin traditional Medicare. As Chapter 5 notes, your ability to do that becomes more limited in future years, and you have to consider whether your health will be good enough to buy a Medicare-supplement policy, which you will need if you are in the traditional Medicare program.

FRAUD AND ABUSE

The Health Care Financing Administration, along with the Office of the Inspector General, whose mission it is to ferret out wrongdoing in programs administered by the Department of Health and Human Services, have launched Operation Restore Trust in which Medicare beneficiaries help spot fraud and inform the federal government.

Because Medicare covers an unlimited number of visits for each patient, beneficiaries make no copayment, and there's little supervision of services, home care is ripe for fraud. The Office of the Inspector General found that Medicare has paid for some 25 to 40 percent of home care visits that it should not have paid for.

Because there is so little money available in the states to pay for home and other kinds of community-based care, it's no wonder families are tempted to use Medicare's home health care benefit for as long as possible. In effect, the home care benefit has become a substitute for failure on the part of the states and federal government to expand community-based services.

If your relative is receiving home care, be on the lookout for:

- Claims for visits not made
- Claims for visits to beneficiaries who are not homebound
- Claims for visits not authorized by a physician
- High-pressure sales tactics that involve signing up Medicare beneficiaries for services they might not need
- Pressuring physicians into ordering unnecessary personal care services by telling them that their patients are requesting the services and will switch doctors if they don't get the services they want

To report suspected fraud, call 1-800-HHS-TIPS or write:

Department of Health and Human Services
Office of the Inspector General
P.O. Box 23489
L'Enfant Plaza Station
Washington, DC 20026-3489

WHEN HOME CARE IS NO LONGER ENOUGH

Sooner or later many families realize that despite their best efforts, their relative must move to a nursing home either because twenty-four-hour care is too expensive, the patient simply needs more intensive help, or there's no family member around to supervise the care.

Sometimes dementia patients have trouble relating to multiple care-givers during a day. One woman said that her mother could not recognize the aides who had come the day before and was fearful the aides whom she didn't recognize were going to harm her.

About two-thirds of CONSUMER REPORTS subscribers surveyed said their relative used home care for two years or less, and about half said their relative eventually went to a nursing home or an assisted-living facility.

KEY DECISION POINTS

1. If your relatives feel strongly about supervising the home health aide who comes to their home, consider enrolling in a client-directed care program.

2. Don't become so wedded to keeping a relative at home that you're blind to the need for more intense supervision.

3. Look at all the programs available in your state for different kinds of home care services. If there are some for which your relative can pay a share of the cost, look to those programs before considering a Medicaid spend-down.

4. Be persistent in finding out whether the aide you are considering has experience in taking care of patients with the same health conditions as your relative.

5. More services is not necessarily better. Be on the lookout for home care providers who may be providing unnecessary services as a way to pad their bills.

6. Don't hire a home health aide from an agency unless you are very clear about the procedures it has in place for monitoring and supervising its workers.

7. Don't hire an aide without a written agreement that spells out the tasks you want the person to perform.

EIGHT

Care in the Community

Three days a week Bill Travers arrives by van at the Deerfield Senior Day Center in Columbia, Maryland. Once a scoutmaster and teacher of ninth-grade algebra, Travers is now seventy-two and partly paralyzed from a brain aneurysm he suffered thirteen years ago. His right side doesn't function well, and sometimes he struggles to find the right words to say. Sometimes he moves around in a wheelchair. Otherwise, his mind is sharp, and he is eager to work and feel useful.

The Deerfield Center gives Travers what he needs. He works in the office, doing faxing, copying, filing, sorting medical records, and making sure the paperwork is in order for Deerfield's van drivers. He does whatever administrative tasks the center staff has no time for. He set up the center's recycling program and taught the staff to recycle. "Bill has good processing skills, and we try to home in on his strengths," says Nancy Massaro, director of clinical services and training for Deerfield. "He wants to do things, but if he gets frustrated, it sets him back for a whole day. The staff is very sensitive to that. There are baby steps and there are huge revelations. As a human being he is wonderful."

For his part, Bill says he is lucky. His schoolteacher's pension of around $1,400 a month allows him to pay the $70 daily rate for care and transportation; he has a caregiver at home to help him at night, and the center staff makes him feel good about himself. "I like having something to do," he says.

For Travers, the day care center helps fulfill an important goal. It keeps him out of a nursing home and functioning in his community for as long as possible. With basic services such as food and transportation, adult day care programs, and a variety of assistive technology, elders may be able to function quite well for several years. Bill Travers's experiences at Deerfield represent what good care in the community is all about—making people who are physically or mentally impaired feel good about themselves without patronizing, demeaning, or abusing them. A goal of day care should be to help people gain a sense of self-worth and maintain their optimal level of functioning.

ADULT DAY CARE

Adult day care represents a growing option for many families—one that keeps their loved ones out of nursing homes or assisted-living facilities that demand far more in the way of financial resources and may provide far less in the way of social and emotional stimulation. This is not to say that your relative may not eventually require nursing home care or the twenty-four-hour supervision found in many assisted-living facilities, but for many people, it's a good intermediate option for as long as you can make it work.

There are some four thousand adult day care centers around the country—a number that has doubled over the last decade but still falls short of what is needed to care for a growing elderly population. "We have half as many as we need," says Dr. John Capitman, a professor at Brandeis University. "It's clearly the most cost-effective and cost-efficient model of care and balances the needs of family and the growth of the elder. But it's an unfamiliar concept held back by the lack of reimbursement."

Many centers operate in church basements, but day care can be provided in freestanding buildings like the thirteen centers Deerfield operates on the East Coast. Many of those who go to day care are patients with Alzheimer's disease or other kinds of dementia, but people who are simply physically impaired can also profit from day care. Many families who have relatives in assisted-living facilities look for day care programs to find the social stimulation and activities that are sometimes lacking in those residences (see Chapter 10).

Adult day care can be offered by for-profit entrepreneurs, as Deerfield is, or by not-for-profit organizations like religious groups, hospitals, or even nursing homes. Some large nursing homes operate day care centers on their premises to provide what is sometimes called a continuum of care or a kind of one-stop shopping for elder care services.

Adult day care programs devise care plans for the people who come; offer services such as trips, meals, and activities; and provide medical and therapeutic services. A center may provide some minimal nursing services and therapies, or it may offer a more comprehensive array, perhaps providing the full range of occupational, speech, and physical therapy. It is possible to find some adult day programs that offer only activities; they are often called social model day care (the ones with nursing services are called medical model programs). These programs usually serve dementia patients who have few physical problems that need attention on a daily basis.

Don't confuse social model day care with activities offered to elders at a community senior center, where people come for a meal or to sit and socialize for a while (see page 156 for a discussion of congregate nutrition programs). Senior centers usually don't write care plans for those attending or offer much in the way of direct supervision, and many do not take people who have disabilities.

Who Should Go to Day Care?

"Very few people are inappropriate for day care," says Mary Brugger Murphy, director of the National Adult Day Services Association. Says one day care center director: "There's no one I can't customize a program for." Poor candidates are those who are bedridden, violent, or have little stamina to get to day care or to function throughout the day. To make day care work, there must be substantial family support. Those going to day care must have a place to stay at night and at other times when the center is closed. If there is no one to take care of your relative at night, and he or she needs supervision and assistance, day care is not a good option. Assisted living might be better. Families and caregivers must be able to get the person out of the house in the morning and either provide transportation to the center or arrange for it. That can be stressful, not unlike getting a small child ready for preschool or day care.

The Cost

Families or the person needing the care must be able to pay for day care services out of pocket. There is little public money available for day care, and certainly very little through state Medicaid programs. Some states may provide some financial assistance through their state-funded programs for older adults, but don't count on much support. Appendices I, J, K, and L can give you some guidance on what might be available in your state.

The kind of program you choose may well depend on what reimbursement is available in your state and on what your relative qualifies for. If there is state money, most likely it is available for medical model day care rather than for services provided under the social model. If you need public money to help pay for day care, you may have little choice about the kind of center to which your relative will go. Day care is another example of the reimbursement system driving the care rather than the care fitting an elder's needs.

In short, day care is mostly a private-pay option. You or your family must be able to pay around $50 a day for care. Transportation might run an additional $15 to $20 a day. Some centers charge more for van services the farther away someone lives. Some centers provide no transportation; in that case, you will have to arrange for car services, taxis, or local paratransit. Of course, that's extra; so is after-hours care. Most people using day care attend three days a week, so the out-of-pocket expense can easily run $600 to $700 a month, and possibly more.

Families with limited financial resources might consider day care as caregiver respite, using the services from time to time rather than on a regular basis. This arrangement gives caregivers much-needed breaks while keeping the cost of the service down. Some day care centers have special respite programs that have sleeping facilities and provide round-the-clock supervision for people who attend. Some states have money available to pay for respite care. Again, Appendices I, J, K, and L can guide you to which ones. If a full-time caregiver needs a break, investigate the respite programs at adult day care centers in your area.

Finding a Good Program

Some communities have a large selection of day care centers; others have none. If you live in a community that has few options, you may have to take whatever is available or consider other types of care, such as home care. To find adult day care programs, call the Eldercare Locator and your area agency on aging. You might look in the Yellow Pages under "adult day care," "aging services," or "senior citizens services." Your family doctor or religious organization may also lead you to a center. The National Adult Day Services Association in Washington, D.C. (202-479-1200), might be able to suggest a center in your area.

If you find you have a choice of centers, the next task is to find one that provides a good program. There are good and bad centers, and like so much in the realm of elder care, there are few objective, quantifiable quality measures to guide you to the best arrangements, largely because good care is often hard to translate into numbers, and instead often falls into the "I know it when I see it category." Mary Ellen Peters, the program director for the adult day health center at St. Elizabeth's Medical Center in Boston, summed up the concept of day care quality when she said, "We need staff who care about what they are doing." A caring staff is almost an intangible commodity, something only you can determine during many visits to different centers. In several visits to adult day care centers, I saw people who cared about what they were doing and those who did not. The signs were unmistakable when they cared and similarly obvious when they did not.

Even if you do find a good center, that doesn't mean its program is a good match for you or your relative. Some day care programs are very specialized, perhaps too specialized for your relative. Be mindful of this as you search.

First Impressions

Since the decision to place a relative in day care may evolve over several weeks or months, you will probably have time to look at several facilities in your area and observe them closely. During your first visit, consider the physical space and general ambience. Is there a welcoming lobby or space that separates the center's activities from the outside—a transition space between home and the center? Some proponents of day care believe that a center should look like a home; others believe that it ought to have the look of a special place where people go. The best centers combine both. Rooms where activities take place resemble a home and still let the people who come every day know that something special is going to happen there. Look for adequate space for dementia patients to wander and move about. A space that is too confining will be frustrating for the day care participant.

Colors should be bright; bulletin boards should feature the people who come every day. "You want a place that's visually exciting even for folks with late-stage dementia," says Brandeis's John Capitman. There should be a sense of excitement, activity, and movement. You wouldn't want to place a relative in a center where the major activity was watching television. Indeed, many centers don't even have TV sets around. At the ideal center, the day starts quietly with activity peaking around 11:30, when people are stimulated for lunch. The center should be active in the afternoon so people think it's a happy, engaging place when it's time to go home. A good center should offer particular activities that make people seem less anxious about leaving, a common problem for dementia patients.

Note whether all participants do their activities in the same room. Look for segregation of people who are more mentally impaired. People who function well cognitively but are physically impaired are usually not eager to spend time with those who suffer from memory loss. A good day care center also has space for people to be alone. Sometimes participants need quiet time.

A Closer Look

The staff Perhaps the most important thing to notice is how the staff interacts with the participants as well as other staff members. How do they relate to you when you come for a visit? At one center, the person with whom I was speaking seemed hurried, pressed, and could not focus on my questions because she was not sure where one client was and wondered whether another woman had eaten her lunch before leaving on an outing. Our exchange did not inspire confidence.

In contrast, at another center, a staff member leading dementia patients in a group discussion was able to make them laugh and express amusement when she related a personal story about running for safety and hiding in a closet as a tornado was about to descend. Seeing elders laugh and expressing joy was rare in my visits to various kinds of long-term-care facilities around the country. That one activity told me much about the staff and the attitude of the day care center. "We make people feel good about themselves," said Nancy Whipple, a staff member at the Deerfield Center that Bill Travers attended. "Ego is important, even for a senior citizen. If you tell them they look pretty, they feel good about themselves."

When you are evaluating the staff, ask about turnover rates. Many centers have high staff turnover, which is often disconcerting to participants who may need the reassurance of seeing the same people week after week. Also find out how the center uses its staff during the day. Which activities do they lead? How do they participate with people who come every day? It is a bad sign if the staff is brusque or shows impatience with people's frailties.

Activities The biggest complaints from participants in day care are about activities and food. You'll want to pay very close attention to both. Observe several activities to see if they are appropriate and stimulating for the population they are serving. There should be a good mix of mental and physical activities. Physical activities should engage both small and large motor skills. Always observe an exercise program. Is it vigorous? Are people being pushed? "The army slogan 'Be all that you can be' is what you want," advises John Capitman.

Good programs try to stimulate all the senses. At one center, participants who had various forms of dementia made Waldorf salads, which stimulated the senses of taste and smell. Then the group leader engaged them in a discussion of apples. Participants tried to recall different kinds of apples and then talked about associations with autumn. There was continuity to those activities that were much more appropriate than activities I saw at another center. At the latter, a group leader asked dementia patients to pick Indian names. At the same time, the children's song "I've Been Working on the Railroad" played on the intercom. The song was both distracting and patronizing.

As you tour the centers, ask what is going on and what the staff is trying to accomplish with a particular activity. If the answers don't make sense to you, continue your search. Make sure everyone gets a chance to participate in an activity. If the activity is cooking, you wouldn't want your mother standing around while someone else was stirring the pot. Activities should be varied—not the same bingo game every day. A good center offers five to six activities each day lasting for about forty-five minutes. Activities may be shorter for participants with dementia.

Food The noon meal is important to day care participants. Obviously, you want tasty, appealing meals. Many centers bring in catered food, and sometimes the quality is uneven. It's probably a good idea to check out food sanitation practices as well as the appeal of the food. Look at the menus, which are usually displayed on a bulletin board, and stay for lunch. If you like the food, chances are your relative will, too. What does the center do to stimulate camaraderie during lunch or at snack time?

Zeroing In on the Fine Points

Transportation Obviously, you need a reliable way to transport a relative to and from a day care center. Some centers provide none; others offer a service that is contracted out to a transportation company, and some have their own vans. The latter might be better since the center has direct control over the drivers and their schedules. If the center provides a contracted service, will the van pick up your relative when he or she needs to be picked up? Who will escort the person from the door to the van? Many transportation companies won't assume liability for that. If the center provides its own vans, there may be better control and it may be easier to contact someone if something goes wrong. What procedures does the center have in place if the van is late? Are vans equipped with phones so you can contact a driver who may be on the way, or do you have to call an intermediary, which might be a less direct way to solve your problem.

Acclimating your relative to day care Many elders are understandably reluctant to go to day care, and often feel their children or spouses are kicking them out of the house. They often grumble: My daughter dumped me here. How the center makes new participants feel welcome is crucial to a happy experience. It may take several visits before an elder feels comfortable with the arrangement. See if your relative can try out a center for two or three days, perhaps even a week. If he or she still doesn't like center life, ask the staff for suggestions on making the transition easier. As you go through the process of selecting a day care center, ask staff what they do to make it easier for caregivers and participants to effectively use day care. If staff says something like "We're going to do everything we can to make it work short of jeopardizing the safety of anyone in the facility," consider that a good answer. But if a staff person says "In the first couple of weeks, we are going to evaluate the person to see if she is appropriate for our center," keep looking. That answer implies the center may not be interested in making day care work and may not be attuned to your relative's needs.

Managing incontinence Helping people with incontinence is often a thorny issue. If your relative is incontinent, it's important to know how the staff handles the problem. If the staff says that elders should come dressed with incontinence pads and that the center doesn't deal with incontinence, that's hardly reassuring. But if the staff says they help elders go to the bathroom on a regular schedule, that is a good indicator the center has your relative's most sensitive interests in mind. See if the center has a shower on the premises or a way to help participants clean themselves after accidents.

ASSISTIVE TECHNOLOGY AND DEVICES

Whether you or your relative lives at home, moves to an assisted-living facility, or takes part in a day care program, sooner or later physical decline and the inability to manipulate one's surroundings necessitate the use of assistive devices. Such devices may enable you to stay at home longer and live independently. The ABLEDATA database lists some seventeen thousand devices, some of which are in ordinary use for people who are not physically impaired. You can search the database at *www.abledata.com* for suggestions.

Some common devices elders may find useful include:

Bathtub devices As people age, the first activity of daily living that slips away is the ability to bathe. In such cases, stools, chairs, tub boards, reclining bath seats, and transfer benches may be helpful. These devices are better suited for some people than others. *Stools,* for example, are better for lightweight people. Heavy people should not use them because they may collapse. To use any stool, you must be able to get in and out of the tub. Seats come in different sizes and styles; rectangular shapes give a wider seat surface area, horseshoe shapes make it easier for a person to clean his or her private parts. *Chairs* have backs and may have armrests or rails for added support. The chair back, however, makes it harder to wash their backs. Some chairs have padded seats, but vinyl seats can be a problem. They become slippery when covered with soap and water and are not good for people with poor balance. If your relative is prone to falling, don't set them up for a bathtub fall. *Tub boards* rest on the side of the tub and provide a portable seat. They are easy to remove and store, but offer no back support and may be unstable.

Reachers These devices bring things within easy reach for people who have difficulty bending because of lower-back problems or those who have restricted arm movements. Reachers can be used to open and close hot oven racks, open cabinets, take cans and utensils off high shelves. A reacher can hold a mop or a sponge to clean up floors, or it can be used to assist with dressing. Reachers can help people find clothes in their closets, push them off the hangers, and help with opening and closing zippers.

Canes A person can support up to 25 percent of his or her body weight with a cane, and they come in many sizes and styles. They are relatively inexpensive, costing between $5 and $100, and the handles come in a variety of styles. If the person you are advising has a weak grasp, a pistol handle may be the most suitable. Aluminum canes are lighter than wooden ones and can be adjusted for height. Designer canes come in colorful patterns, making it easier for an elder to accept. Look for special features, such as a tripod seat, cane holders, and wrist straps, that let the user's hands remain free while using the cane.

Walkers These are good for people with weak knees or ankles or with balance problems since a walker can support up to half of a person's body weight. Prices range from about $30 to more than $600. A *rigid walker* is constructed of aluminum, and the widths are sometimes adjustable. Using one of these walkers may take some practice since it must be lifted to move forward. The lifting may strain a person's wrists, shoulders, and arms. *Wheeled walkers* remedy some of these problems. The person using the walker simply pushes it, creating a more natural walking style. Wheeled walkers may have automatic brakes. Three- or four-wheeled walkers require less strength to operate and are more maneuverable over carpeting.

Dressing aids Dressing can be a daunting challenge for many seniors. Painful finger joints make it hard to maneuver buttons; stiff backs make it hard to tie shoes. *Dressing sticks*—sticks with a claw on the end—*button hooks,* and *zipper pulls* can be helpful; so can devices that assist with putting on socks and shoes. With a *sock aid,* the user puts a sock on a thin piece of plastic or cloth that holds the sock open, slips his foot into it, and then pulls on the sock with special pull tabs. *Long-handled brushes* and *combs* help people with limited range of motion and weakness in the shoulders and elbows.

Scooters For people who don't want to use wheelchairs, scooters may be a good solution for getting around, enabling them to remain independent for as long as possible. Scooters come in front-wheel- and rear-wheel-drive models. Front-wheel-drive models may be less powerful but can be managed more easily. For outdoor use, rear-wheel-drive models are better. Both kinds operate with batteries, but the batteries must be recharged frequently to avoid losing power while the scooter is in use. Most models come with padded chairs and armrests, but orthopedic chairs can be added.

How to Find Out About Devices

One of the best ways to learn about assistive technology is to consult the website operated by the Center for Assistive Technology at the University of Buffalo in Buffalo, New York. The website address is *http://wings.buffalo.edu/go?cat*. The site gives sources for various kinds of products. You can also call the center at 716-829-3141.

Another source is your state's Assistive Technology Act project, which is better known in the disability community than in the aging network. Every state has a project that is funded by the National Institute of Disability and Rehabilitation Research, part of the U.S. Department of Education. These projects are a starting point for families searching for assistive devices for an elderly relative. They provide information about what is available, what might be suitable, how much devices cost, and where to find them. The projects also have loan libraries that let elders try out various devices to see if they are useful, and they provide information on low-cost financing, so elders can buy the devices that will keep them independent. Since much of the technology is most helpful if an occupational or a physical therapist helps you learn to use it, the AT Act projects can provide referrals to these professionals in your area.

These projects have different names that might not sound like a place to get help; for example, in New York, the project is called Traid; in California, Cats; in Oklahoma, Infotech. To find out about the AT Act projects, call RESNA Technical Assistance Project at 703-524-6686 for more information.

Helping a Relative Accept a Device

It's not always easy to get a loved one to start using a cane, a hearing aid, a magnifier, a tub device, or a dressing aid even if such devices will make life easier. "People are aging with disabilities, but they don't want to be considered part of the disability community. They think 'If I use a cane, I'll be someone with a disability,'" says Jennifer Weir, information director for the Center for Assistive Technology at the University of Buffalo.

When confronting a relative about the need for such devices, it's best to put yourself in his or her shoes and think about the social impact. Consider the person's feelings and how the device will fit in with his or her lifestyle. Think about how you would feel if you were losing your ability to do everyday tasks.

It's usually best to have an occupational therapist help your loved one learn how to use a device. The therapist can also assess your surroundings and suggest aids that might be helpful. Training is crucial to acceptance.

Here are some suggestions that might make it easier for your relative to accept a device:

- Pick a time to introduce the device when your relative is not preoccupied with personal problems, such as the illness of a spouse.
- Hold the training sessions at the person's home or where the device will be used.
- Focus on the practical application of the device rather than on its technical features.
- Omit irrelevant information.
- Repeated short training sessions are more effective than longer sessions. Be mindful of the stamina of the person who will be using the device.

NUTRITION PROGRAMS

Sometimes it is possible to keep elderly adults out of nursing homes by taking advantage of the nutrition programs authorized under the Older Americans Act. Most of the funding for these programs comes from the federal government, but states and local governments sometimes add funds in an attempt to serve more people. Still, programs in many areas of the country don't have enough resources to supply meals to all the people who need them, and there are long waiting lists for these services in some localities. If there is a waiting list in your area, it's better to put your relative on it sooner rather than later.

The meal programs—congregate meals and home-delivered meals—are not entitlements based on income. They are available to anyone sixty years or older as long as a particular program has room. There may be a few other rules. If you have a relative who might benefit from such programs, he or she may have to live within the geographic boundaries served by the home-delivered meals program, or be homebound.

As good as the meal programs are, most provide only one meal a day five days a week. And there are usually no meals on weekdays or holidays unless a particular locality has raised special funds for these "extra" meals. Some cities, like New York and San Francisco, may offer more than five meals a week and provide a second daily meal or weekend as well as holiday food. Aggressive fund-raising by local programs makes additional food possible. Some programs also try to supplement the one meal with frozen meals the recipients can keep on hand so that they can have more than one meal a day.

Congregate meals There are some sixteen hundred congregate meal sites throughout the country. Local churches, social service agencies, and other nonprofit organizations operate these sites, often in senior or community centers. The centers usually serve a hot meal at lunch and seniors come for the meal, participate in some activities, and socialize. Some programs may also serve breakfast. There are generally no waiting lists for service at congregate meal sites.

Home-delivered meals Home-delivered meals are another matter. Here the need is so great and money so scarce that waiting lists are a problem in many localities. The meals, which supply one-third of the recommended dietary allowances that an older person needs, are delivered at noon, often by volunteers who work for the programs. Sometimes a volunteer provides the only human contact an older person has during the day. The volunteer also checks to make sure the elder is okay and can report when something is amiss.

Elders receiving meals through these programs are not required to pay for them, although three-quarters of the people receiving home-delivered meals and nearly everyone who eats at the congregate sites contribute something. Sometimes they contribute as little as 50 cents toward the $5.30 it costs to provide a meal.

To find out about food programs in your area, call the Eldercare Locator at 1-800-677-1116. They will refer you to the agency on aging in your area. The local Triple A will direct you to the nutrition programs. Or you can call your state unit on aging (see Appendix B). In some areas, a privately funded meals-on-wheels program may provide food which supplements that provided under the Older Americans Act programs. Sometimes a local hospital offers meals delivered to a person's home. The local Triple A can tell you if there is such a program in your area, or you can call hospitals in your area.

For home-delivered meals, the local program will probably send a social worker to your home or your relative's home to do an assessment to make sure the person is truly homebound and in need of the service. The social worker may also do some assessments of the nutrition the person is currently receiving. Assessments are not required for participants in congregate meal programs.

TRANSPORTATION SERVICES

Transportation systems in the various states are not set up to accommodate the increasing frailty of elderly people who are no longer able to drive and often find themselves isolated in communities with few transportation options. Once elders are unable to drive, they often feel like prisoners in their own homes. And it's hard for physically frail people to decipher bus route information, let alone climb on several buses to get anywhere. In general, few government resources go toward solving the transportation problems of the elderly. "Adequate transportation does not exist in every community in the country," says Eddie Rivas, a former transportation expert with the American Association of Homes and Services for the Aging. Nevertheless, many communities are trying various ways of transporting senior citizens, and the trick is to find out what is offered and whether the local services will work for your relative. Many families find that transportation assistance helps their elder maintain independence longer.

Again, the Eldercare Locator can help connect you to the network of the area agencies on aging. You can also call the Transit Hotline at 1-800-527-8279. This hot line is run by the Community Transportation Association of America, a national organization that represents rural and small urban transportation providers. Hot line personnel tell callers what kind of transportation is available in their communities and who can get help.

Transportation options vary widely. Some communities may provide senior citizens with vouchers for taxi rides to medical appointments or for shopping. Some may provide transportation to shopping, but not to medical appointments. Others may operate a van service. Some may use private cars or special station wagons that can accommodate wheelchairs. And some may provide none if your relative's income is too high for a program's guidelines.

In using the transportation available to seniors in your community, a few rules apply:

- Don't expect too much. You may have to take what's available, and that may not be the ideal mode of transportation for you. You may prefer pickup at your door but find that the only carriers available stop several blocks down the street.
- Plan ahead. If a community has few vehicles available, you probably have to plan far in advance of the time you'll be needing a ride.
- Expect to pay for some services. The cost depends on the funding source for the transportation. If transportation is funded under the Older Americans Act, payment is not required, although you may be asked to contribute on a voluntary basis much the same as participants in the congregate and home-delivered meals programs may choose to pay some amount. On the other hand, if services are provided under the Americans with Disabilities Act, the person receiving services can be asked to pay twice what the going rate is. To be eligible for transportation services under this program, you must have a disability and be certified that you are disabled. Transportation services under this law are available in any community where normal transit services are provided. These communities must supply what are called paratransit services—that is, vehicles that can accommodate wheelchairs.

FRIENDLY VISITORS AND TELEPHONE REASSURANCE

Sometimes all your relative may need is a kind word from someone who calls to see if he or she is okay and perhaps to chat a little. Elders are often lonely, and someone to talk to means a lot. Ask your area agency on aging if there is a friendly visitor's program or a telephone reassurance program in your locality. Your church or synogogue may also offer such a service.

1. If your relative has a system of caregivers to help out at night, consider an adult day program.

2. Consider every possible means to keep your relative functioning in the community before considering alternatives that require a move to a different place to live. Moving is traumatic, and most elders would rather live in their own homes for as long as possible.

3. Investigate various assistive devices and suggest that your relative learn to use them as a way of staying independent and at home.

4. Keep tabs on what your relative is eating. Malnutrition among the elderly is a serious problem, and most seniors would rather make do with nonnutritious foods than admit they are hungry.

5. If you suspect that a relative is not eating properly, get him or her on a waiting list for home-delivered meals and gradually introduce the idea of meals delivered to the home. Do this as soon as you believe that such meals might be necessary.

6. Investigate transportation services as soon as you suspect a decline in your relative's ability to function.

NINE

Special Programs for Chronically Ill People

Ninety-eight-year-old Mrs. Song F. Lee has been coming to the On Lok Senior Services Center in San Francisco's Chinatown since 1992. She had been living across the street from the center, but her building had no elevator, and after she suffered a compression fracture she could no longer negotiate the stairs to her apartment. She needed two people to move her in and out.

At On Lok, she has a small apartment, one of fifty-four the center provides to help keep their clients out of nursing homes. But it's not the housing that makes On Lok so special. It is the totally integrated stream of long-term care and medical services that Mrs. Lee receives every day. She suffers from dementia, hypertension, hearing loss, and pressure sores on her feet, and she takes eight medications. At On Lok, she participates in exercise activities and other group programs appropriate for her level of frailty, and she gets all her medical care right on the premises.

Her seventy-one-year-old daughter can't say enough good things about On Lok. When she compares On Lok to nursing homes where other relatives live, she shudders. "It's like a family here," she says. "Coming here is like coming home. The staff is very committed and caring." If it weren't for On Lok, says her daughter, Mrs. Lee "would have died a long time ago."

Mary Berglund, seventy-eight, is a large woman who says she is still waiting for gray hair. She does, however, have severe arthritis, and getting around becomes harder each day. "I haven't been able to go shopping for myself in a long time," she says. Nor can she go to the bank or venture outside her small apartment in a senior housing complex in Brooklyn, New York.

Mary is a member of Elderplan, a social HMO that provides far more benefits and services than a regular HMO. One goal of Elderplan is to keep its members out of nursing homes. To that end, it created a program that allows members to do chores and perform services for other people in the plan who need help. When they, in turn, require help, the HMO's beneficiaries stand ready to pitch in.

Annette Katz, who is sixty-nine, visits Berglund once a month and takes her shopping and to the bank. She also runs other errands and provides needed companionship. "The weekends, I don't like," Berglund says. "They are so lonesome."

In return for the help she gets, Berglund makes needlepoint gifts for Elderplan members who are in nursing homes. "This is what keeps me going," she says. Right now Katz doesn't need help, so she is banking her credits for the time when she won't be able to go out by herself.

Mrs. Lee and Mrs. Berglund participate in some of the best chronic care programs this country offers. PACE sites and social HMOs have much to recommend them, as do other chronic care programs discussed in this chapter. PACE is an acronym that stands for Program of All-inclusive Care for the Elderly, and PACE sites offer a fully integrated system of care. PACE is basically a day care arrangement, and participants receive personal care services and social interaction as well as medical care. PACE sites should be universally available instead of limited geographically, as they are now. New regulations, however, are likely to spur new sites in the next few years.

PACE programs are aimed at getting better services to seniors in an easier and more cost-effective manner, and they work outside the normal way long-term and acute care services are paid for. They illustrate both the fragmentation that characterizes our system of long-term care and the innovation in care for the elderly that could flower if more people knew about these programs, used them, and pressured the government to expand them. If you have a relative who needs care now or in the future, this chapter offers guidance in finding and using these programs.

PACE PROGRAMS

On Lok Senior Services, where Mrs. Lee goes every day, is a PACE site, one of thirty-two PACE programs (including a variation called PrePACE) that exist around the country. On Lok was the first PACE program established twenty years ago by a Swiss woman who saw the need to help frail elders in San Francisco's Chinatown who were homebound and couldn't get services they needed.

PACE sites, which are usually run by hospital or nursing home systems or community organizations, are, in effect, comprehensive adult day care centers. To date, all are not-for-profit. PACE offers a care delivery system that provides medical services; hospital care; occupational, physical, and speech therapies; lifetime nursing home care; pharmaceuticals; emergency care; home care; and transportation to the PACE site and to medical appointments.

PACE arranges for clients to be brought to the site for activities several days a week. Clients usually attend three days, but some come more often. The program provides social interaction, meals, snacks, checkups, and preventive care at each site. If clients need to see physicians or other clinicians, such as podiatrists or psychologists, those practitioners may be available on certain days. Some sites have a physician present every day.

At the end of the day, clients return to their homes. PACE is not responsible for housing, although programs pay a lot of attention to where their clients live. Since the goal of PACE is to provide enough supportive services to keep people out of nursing homes, clients need somewhere to go at night, so some programs offer housing arrangements. The program in Portland, Oregon, for example, offers adult foster care homes where people spend their evenings. On Lok in San Francisco owns apartments subsidized by the Department of Housing and Urban Development. The Beth Abraham PACE site in New York City offers clients a chance to live in a nearby private apartment building that it runs.

In short, PACE offers a full spectrum of services under one umbrella, eliminating the need for families to patch together a program of care on their own. PACE programs have not been well-publicized, and only about three thousand people take advantage of them. (They are expensive programs to run and difficult to start up.) Existing programs can serve more clients, however, and they should be one of the first places you investigate if you think your relative needs nursing home care (provided, of course, there's a PACE site nearby).

Table 10, on pages 164–165, shows the location of PACE sites and gives a telephone number to call. PrePACE sites are noted with an asterisk. To find out if there are new PACE organizations, call the National PACE Association in San Francisco (415-749-2680), the organization that represents PACE sites.

In 1993, the Community Health Accreditation Program (CHAP), which also accredits home care agencies, evaluated five PACE sites and found the quality and coordination of care to be "exceptional." In 1997, the Health Care Financing Administration (HCFA) examined PACE, and found that the programs improved the health and quality of life for enrollees. The HCFA also found that PACE clients had lower death rates, gave clients more choice in how they spent their time, and noted that they had greater confidence in dealing with their health and other problems. "We're stopping the preventable flare-ups of chronic illness. We can intervene in ways that nobody else can," says Susan Aldrich, vice president of the Beth Abraham PACE site in New York City.

Signing up Frailty is the key to qualifying for PACE. Your relative must be so impaired that he or she would otherwise require nursing home care. Typically, clients have seven medical diagnoses. Even though PACE is not a payment program for nursing homes per se, your relative must be sick enough to meet your state's medical eligibility requirements for Medicaid (see Chapter 13).

When you call, an intake official will ask questions about family involvement in your relative's care, the medications he or she is taking, emergency contacts, and so forth. The next step is a home visit by a team of health professionals—a doctor, nurse, occupational therapist, dietician, and social worker—who will do an assessment of your relative's physical, mental, emotional, and social functioning. The assessment helps them develop a customized treatment plan. The plan, however, is not fixed in concrete. It changes as your relative's condition and functional status changes. One day at Beth Abraham, a team of providers was discussing the needs of one of their diabetic clients. Using an overhead projector to show detailed reports on the woman's condition, the group decided that her care plan was still working, and other interventions were not likely to change her condition. So they did not change her treatment plan.

TABLE 10: Where to Find the PACE Organizations

California

AltaMed Senior Buena Care

Christina Marr, Los Angeles, 323-980-4000

Center for Elders Independence

Wendy Peterson, Oakland, 610-433-1150

On Lok Senior Health Services

Violette Karavul, San Francisco, 415-550-2234

Sutter SeniorCare

Chris Nantz, Sacramento, 916-446-3100

Colorado

Total Longterm Care

Ann Olson, Denver, 303-869-4684

Hawaii

PACE at Maluhia*

JoAnn Wasson, Honolulu, 808-832-6131

Illinois

Chicago REACH*

Diane Fountain, Chicago, 773-252-8969

Maryland

Hopkins ElderPlus/Johns Hopkins Bayview Medical*

Frances Ladder, Baltimore, 410-550-7046

Massachusetts

Elder Service Plan—East Boston Neighborhood Health Center

Linda Wasserman, East Boston, 617-539-5382

Elder Service Plan of the Cambridge Hospital*

Liz Agnes, Cambridge, 617-868-6323

Elder Service Plan at Fallon

Madeleine Haling, Worcester, 508-852-2028

Elder Service Plan—Harbor Health Services, Inc.

Kathleen E. O'Shea, Dorchester, 617-296-5100

Elder Service Plan of the North Shore, Inc.*

Linda LeBlanc, Lynn, 617-599-0110, ext. 238

Elder Service Plan of Mutual Health Care/Upham's Corner Health*

David Wood, Dorchester, 617-288-0970

Michigan

Center for Senior Independence

Pamela Halladay, Detroit, 313-579-4648

New Mexico

St. Joseph Senior Care*

Denise Marquez-Padilla, Albuquerque, 505-727-7608

New York

Comprehensive Care Management

Pat Moore, Bronx, 718-515-8600

Eddy SeniorCare*

Melissa Holden, Schenectady, 518-382-3290

Independent Living for Seniors

Kim Cosentino, Rochester, 716-266-9040

Independent Living Services*

Virginia Turley, North Syracuse, 315-452-5800

Ohio

Concordia Care*

Elaine Molis, Cleveland Heights, 216-791-3680

TriHealth SeniorLink*

Marcia Bowling, Cincinnati, 513-531-5110

Oregon

Providence ElderPlace in Portland

Karen Casciato, Portland, 503-215-3473

Pennsylvania

LIFE—St. Agnes Medical Center*

Michelle Tiger, Philadelphia, 215-339-4157

LIFE—University of Pennsylvania School of Nursing*

Jennine Groce-Martin, Philadelphia, 215-273-6691

South Carolina

Palmetto SeniorCare

Catherine Moore, Columbia, 803-931-8175

Tennessee

Alexian Brothers Community Services

Criss Chastain, Chattanooga, 423-698-0802, ext. 14

Texas

Bienvivir Senior Health Services

Melinda Urteaga, El Paso, 915-779-2555

Virginia

Sentara Senior Community Care*

Laura Gadsby, Virginia Beach, 757-456-2700

Washington

Providence ElderPlace in Seattle

Susan Hayashida, Seattle, 206-320-5169

Wisconsin

Community Care for the Elderly

Julie Erdmann, Milwaukee, 414-536-2100

Elder Care Options

Cherie Rhode, Madison, 608-245-3076

What you get:

- All Medicare Part A and B benefits
- Rehabilitation and therapy services
- Adult day care services, including social activities and meals plus snacks. Services are available seven days a week, but clients don't have to attend every day.
- Transportation to the site
- Emergency care
- Services of social workers
- Home modifications
- Relief for family caregivers

What you pay: Medicare and state Medicaid programs pay each site a monthly amount that must cover all the services clients require. If your relative is already eligible for Medicaid, say, he or she is considered "categorically" needy in Medicaid parlance—that is, he or she is eligible because income is low—he or she will automatically qualify for PACE. You will pay nothing for the services your relative receives.

If your relatives qualify for Medicaid payments under your state's "medically needy" program—that is, they spend virtually all of their assets and most of their monthly income to qualify for Medicaid coverage of either nursing home or home care—they can join a PACE program and use their own money to pay for services until they are eligible for Medicaid to pay. (See the spend-down requirements in Chapter 13.)

If your relative would otherwise pay out of pocket for nursing home or home care, he or she can join a PACE program and pay the same amount that the state Medicaid program pays PACE. Those rates are listed in Table 11 (page 167). If your relative joins PACE, he or she will not have to pay any of Medicare's deductibles and coinsurance or any other Medicaid cost-sharing amounts. You may find that it is cheaper to pay for care under PACE than to pay for services separately. You will not have to pay for various home care and other long-term-care services or the Medicare-supplement insurance premiums, and the deductibles and coinsurance required by Medicare.

Table 12 compares the costs an eighty-four-year-old woman living in San Francisco would incur under different care arrangements. If she joined On Lok, her services would cost $24,600 a year and include all her medical and long-term-care needs. If she were eligible for Medicaid, that program would cover the costs. But if she wasn't, she could buy into the On Lok program and pay on her own. As the table shows, she would spend far less doing that than if she chose other alternatives. If she chose traditional Medicare with no supplemental policy and arranged her own long-term-care services, she would pay more than $37,000; if she joined a managed-care plan, her expenses would total some $30,000, and if she bought a Medicare-supplement policy to cover some of Medicare's gaps, her out-of-pocket costs would come to about $35,000. On Lok is her best bet, plus it offers the breadth and depth of services she would have a hard time obtaining on her own.

Advantages The prime advantages of PACE are: unlimited benefit for long-term-care services; continuous and coordinated care management; family support, monitoring of your medical condition, and more expert care. PACE clients get more primary medical care and

TABLE 11: PACE Monthly Capitation Rates

These rates may have changed somewhat, but they still can give you an idea of what you would pay if you bought into PACE rather than struggle on your own to put together a package of services.

JANUARY, 1998

PACE site State–City	Medicare Rate	Medicaid Rate	Total Rate
CA–San Francisco	$1,282	$2,213	$3,495
CA–Sacramento	1,224	1,864	3,088
CA–Oakland	1,365	2,245	3,610
CO–Denver	1,228	1,786	3,014
MA–E. Boston	1,554	2,172	3,726
MI–Detroit	1,560	2,046	3,606
NY–Bronx	1,775	4,301	6,076
NY–Rochester	1,004	2,796	3,800
OR–Portland	943	1,750	2,693
SC–Columbia	877	1,907	2,784
TX–El Paso	1,070	2,085	3,155
WI–Milwaukee	1,060	2,132	3,192

PACE Median	Medicare Rate	Medicaid Rate	Total Rate
	$1,226	$2,109	$3,344

Notes:
- Site collects enrollee share of cost in addition to rates shown in CA–San Francisco, MA, and TX.
- NY–Bronx: Medicaid pays two different rates based on different level of care. Rate shown is weighted average.
- SC–Medicaid rate is net after adjustment to revenue.

see doctors more often for their conditions, and because they are at the site every day, PACE care managers and medical personnel can intervene quickly. PACE professionals are skilled at working with the many physical and mental conditions their clients have, and a family member may well get better care at a PACE site than from home

TABLE 12: A Comparison of Annual Health Care Costs—PACE and Its Alternatives

The table below shows what an eighty-four-year-old woman in San Francisco would pay under different types of financial and care delivery programs.

	Traditional Medicare	Managed Medicare	Medicare+ Medigap	On Lok
Total premiums	$526 (Medicare Part B)	$526 (Medicare Part B)	$1,380 (Medicare Part B & Medigap premium)	$24,634 (Total cost of going to On Lok)
Annual checkup	280	7	160	Included—no charge
Physicians/specialists	833	98	579	Included—no charge
Hospital charges	1,528	0	0	Included—no charge
Skilled-nursing care	955	0	0	Included—no charge
Home health care	18,720	18,720	18,720	Included—no charge
Physical therapy	1,080	1,080	1,080	Included—no charge
Occupational/recreational therapy	—	—	—	Included—no charge
Podiatry care	216	42	216	Included—no charge
Mental health care	0	0	0	Included—no charge
Eyeglasses/exams	1,360	341	1,360	Included—no charge
Hearing aids/exams	150	14	150	Included—no charge
Dental care/dentures	2,320	2,320	2,320	Included—no charge
Pharmacy/prescriptions	2,700	700	2,700	Included—no charge
Delivered meals	6,370	6,370	6,370	Included—no charge
Total out-of-pocket costs	$37,038	$30,217	$35,035	$24,634 (if a person buys in)

Clinical Assumptions:

Annual checkup	1 per year	Occupational/recreational therapy	0 per month
GP visits	12 per year	Podiatry care	6 per year
Specialist visits	2 per year	Mental health care	0 per year
Hospital admissions	2 per year	Eyeglasses/exams	2 glasses/4 visits per year
Skilled-nursing facility days (over 20)	10 days per year	Hearing aids/exams	2 exams (no aids) per year
Home health care	18 hours per week	Prescriptions	5 per month
Physical therapy	2 hours per month	Delivered meals	14 per week

Source: On Lok Senior Services

health aides who may have little experience dealing with an older person's condition.

Disadvantages Your relative must agree to use the health care providers in the program, but this could be a small price to pay for the unlimited benefits and coordinated care. While you may not have a choice of fifteen podiatrists, PACE does give a different kind of choice: coordinated or uncoordinated care. PACE usually involves day care so clients must be willing to participate in such care. This may not be appealing to everyone, especially to those who have been loners all their lives. PACE may not be appropriate for people who have no place to go at night or who have no caregivers to help when they are not at the program.

SOCIAL HMOS

Only four social HMOs operate in the United States, although they can be offered as part of the Medicare + Choice options now available to seniors. In the next few years it's possible that more social HMOs will be available. Table 13 lists the current social HMOs and the person to contact.

TABLE 13: How to Find Social HMOs

Elderplan, Brooklyn, New York
 Eli Feldman, CEO: 718-921-8066
 Dan Kasle, COO: 718-921-7994

Senior Advantage II, Kaiser Permanente Northwest Division, Portland, Oregon
 Lucy Nonnenkamp: 503-400-5794

SCAN Health Plan, Long Beach, California
 Sam Ervin, CEO: 562-989-5100, ext. 3220
 Tim Schwab, M.D.: 562-989-5100, ext. 3497

Sierra Health Plan, Las Vegas, Nevada
 Bonnie Hillegass, VP: 702-242-7248
 Pamela Hough, manager of SHMO: 702-242-7591

In its marketing literature, Elderplan, the Brooklyn-based social HMO described at the beginning of this chapter, says it is "Improving Life Beyond Medicare," and indeed social HMOs offer far more benefits than traditional Medicare HMOs, which are discussed in Chapter 5. In September 1998, CONSUMER REPORTS ranked Elderplan the top HMO for seniors in New York City. The magazine's 2000 analysis of Medicare HMOs also shows Elderplan the top-ranked plan in New York City. SCAN, the social HMO based in southern California, also ranks highly. See Appendix G. CONSUMER REPORTS also cited Elderplan in the October 1998 issue for its efforts to improve the quality of health care for its diabetic members.

Signing up If you or a relative are eligible for Medicare and live in the service area of one of the plans listed above, call the contact number and ask for an enrollment package. If you join, you won't need a Medicare-supplement policy, you won't need to belong to another HMO, and you certainly won't need to consider any of the other Medicare + Choice options discussed in Chapter 3.

When you enroll, the plan will first do an assessment to see if your relative is at high risk for falls, prescription drug interactions, malnutrition, depression, and so on. If he or she is, the plan will assign a care manager who will find appropriate services. If the plan determines the individual is not at immediate risk, then he or she would obtain medical services when needed, the same as in any other HMO. As with other HMOs, only providers in the plan's network can give care.

From time to time, the plan will send health status forms to complete. The idea is to find medical problems early and begin treatment.

What you get Social HMOs provide a complete range of primary, acute, and long-term-care benefits, including:

- All Medicare Parts A and B benefits
- Prescription drugs, eyeglasses, hearing aids, dentures, routine foot care, mental health services, and nutritional assessments and services
- Care management services. While most HMOs simply manage costs, social HMOs actually manage care.
- A long-term-care benefit that can be used in a nursing home, assisted-living facility, adult foster care, or for care in your home. The benefit is limited and may be capped at $1,000 a

month. Elderplan, for instance, limits the benefit to $7,800 per year.

If you use the benefit to pay for a nursing home, you will not have to meet Medicare's requirements for skilled-nursing care, but there must be some expectation that you will be able to return to your home.

To qualify for this benefit, beneficiaries must be very frail—frail enough to need care in a nursing home and meet the eligibility standards for that kind of care set by the client's state Medicaid office. The benefit, in effect, is intended to pay for substitute care to keep you out of a nursing facility. The HMO's care manager will help the family determine if you qualify for the benefit and will suggest alternatives to nursing home care.

Plans toss in other services that make a social HMO especially valuable—transportation to medical visits, nutrition counseling, homemaker services, the member-to-member plan sponsored by Eldercare, for example.

What you pay Like all HMOs serving Medicare beneficiaries, social HMOs receive a monthly payment from the Health Care Financing Administration. Because these plans care for some of the frailest beneficiaries, they receive a higher payment than regular HMOs. If that payment is large enough to cover all of the basic services Medicare requires and there is money left over, they may use the money for extra benefits. Sometimes the surplus means the plan will not charge beneficiaries monthly premiums.

Some social HMOs also charge small copayments for prescription drugs, eyeglasses, and hearing aids.

Advantages Social HMOs have many pluses. Besides payment for extra benefits, they offer flexibility in tailoring care. The long-term-care benefit, for example, can be used to pay for a variety of services, such as day care and home health aides needed at night. Care management available through the social HMO can help family members who will not have to coordinate care themselves. The care manager acts as a shoulder for families to lean on for advice and counsel.

Disadvantages You will have to use providers in the plan's network, but it may be worthwhile to give up choice of many doctors in return for the care management services and the long-term-care benefit, even though that benefit is limited.

SPECIAL STATE PROGRAMS

Some states are exploring programs for their elderly residents who are eligible for both Medicare and Medicaid. The idea is to offer a seamless package of care that allows older people to obtain services from one managed-care organization. These programs aim to reduce the red tape for seniors who sometimes find themselves getting care from two or three different HMOs with different rules, case managers, telephone numbers, and identification cards. Because there is little coordination of services, the needs of seniors sometimes fall between the cracks.

How they work Seniors eligible for Medicare and Medicaid choose one HMO that has a contract with either the state or the federal government to provide services under these special programs. Depending on the program, they usually receive all Medicare Part A and B services, home and other community services, and sometimes nursing home care. Plans usually pay the Medicare deductibles and coinsurance, and for dental care, prescription drugs, and some medical transportation.

The managed-care organization assigns a case manager who is responsible for coordinating all the services enrollees need. The plan also tries to involve families in the care process and in devising treatment plans.

Whom to contact Programs vary from state to state. Table 14 indicates the states that have programs—in place or may have in the near future—for seniors eligible for both Medicare and Medicaid. To find out more, call the telephone number listed.

Advantages Like PACE, these special state programs function as one-stop shopping centers

TABLE 14: State Programs for People Eligible for Medicare and Medicaid

Colorado	303-866-5912
Florida	850-414-2096
Maine	207-780-4237
Maryland	410-455-6759
Massachusetts	617-210-5456
	617-210-5466
Minnesota	612-296-2140
New York	716-325-1991
Vermont	802-241-3989
Washington	360-493-2564
Texas	512-438-5067
	512-438-4297
Wisconsin	608-261-8855

for families searching for long-term-care options. Another bonus is less paperwork, which comes from dealing with one HMO instead of several.

Under these programs, there is little incentive to shift costs from one provider to another. Financial incentives under regular programs often work to institutionalize people rather than to find other suitable care alternatives. Under special state programs, incentives are aligned with matching people to the appropriate services. Because only one agency is responsible for care, it is easier to fix accountability and get help when something goes wrong.

Disadvantages Those who sign up must use providers in the health plan's network. You or a relative may feel that such a requirement limits choice.

SPECIAL CARE PROGRAMS FOR NURSING HOME RESIDENTS

EverCare, a division of United Healthcare, a large managed-care organization that sells Medicare-supplement insurance through AARP, offers a special program for nursing home residents that tries to improve the medical care they receive and keep them out of hospitals. Hospitals can be dangerous for the elderly: 63 percent of the frail elderly who enter hospitals suffer at least one complication as a result of the admission.

Operating under a grant from the Health Care Financing Administration, EverCare tries to ensure that nursing home residents maintain their highest level of functioning. The goal of the program is not to cure a resident's underlying health care problems but to improve the care they receive in the nursing facility both from nursing home personnel and from outside health care providers. EverCare aims to increase the amount of primary care residents receive in order to catch problems early and avoid hospitalizations. If the EverCare team of nurse-practitioners that regularly visits the nursing facility finds that a person shows early signs of pneumonia, or that her behavior has changed, or she has not been eating, or is sleepier than usual, the resident can obtain medical treatment and avoid serious illness or complications. If not, the resident could end up in a hospital, where she may spend several days on bed rest, which will leave her weak and disoriented and prone to falls that could result in serious injuries. The resident might also develop pressure sores during the hospital stay. EverCare reimburses physicians when they hold family conferences and when they visit residents in nursing homes. If an urgent visit to a doctor is needed, EverCare pays for that visit, too, in an effort to avoid transporting the resident to an emergency room or even to a doctor's office.

EverCare receives a monthly payment for every nursing home resident who enrolls in its program, an arrangement similar to the payment managed-care firms receive. For that payment, it agrees to provide all the care a resident needs—all the benefits available under Medicare Parts A and B, rehabilitation therapies, medical equipment and supplies. If EverCare wants to make money, the incentive is to keep residents as healthy as possible and out of hospitals.

EverCare has begun to measure the quality of care its members receive in nursing facilities—that is, it is monitoring the number of its members who have pressure sores, catheters, and use feeding tubes. It then works with nursing facilities to reduce the number of residents with these problems. "Too many times, if someone has a stroke and can't eat, the feeding tube goes in and never comes out—even if they can ultimately swallow," says Marcia Smith, EverCare's president.

Signing up EverCare has more than four hundred contracts with nursing homes in Minneapolis, Boston, Baltimore, Atlanta, Tampa, Phoenix, Tucson, Denver, Colorado Springs, and New York City. In the next few years, there may be more. To learn about other locations, consult Medicare's website (www.Medicare.gov). You should consider EverCare or similar programs in your search for a nursing home. When you visit a nursing home, ask if it participates in the program, and if it does, obtain enrollment information.

What you get As an option under Medicare, EverCare provides all Medicare services, pays the Medicare copayments and deductibles, offers preventive services, and extra services such as family conferences and unlimited physician visits. Currently, people who join EverCare do not have to pay a monthly premium. They do, however, pay the Part B premium.

Advantages Case management is one of the main reasons to sign up for EverCare if your relative is already in a nursing home. The team of geriatricians and nurse-practitioners can be your eyes and ears if you cannot visit the facility as often as you'd like.

As Chapter 11 points out, your relative will probably fare better in a nursing facility the more you are there. But the EverCare coordination team might be the next best solution if you can't visit as often as you would like. Support for the family is another advantage. EverCare programs also offer a way to monitor changes in your relative's conditions. Families often complain that nursing home personnel are not always available to discuss their relative's health status, interests, activities, and so forth. The nurse-practitioner who is part of the EverCare team can help.

Your relative is less likely to be hospitalized since the health team is supposed to spot potential problems early. This, too, can be a plus since, as Chapter 11 also notes, when a nursing home resident leaves the facility to go to a hospital, it may be difficult to get back, especially if the facility wants to move the person out to make room for someone not on Medicaid who brings in more revenue.

Disadvantages EverCare is not available in every nursing home, and you'll have to seek out the homes that offer the program. Right now EverCare is limited only to care in nursing homes. In the future, it may expand to home and community-based care.

We evaluated the EverCare benefits in the Ratings in Appendix G. Policies ranked in the middle for most cities. While EverCare charges no premiums, it also offers no benefits for prescription drugs. You will still need a way to pay for medications when your relative is in the nursing home.

EVERCARE LOOK-ALIKES

In the next few years, you may find some arrangements that appear to be similar to the PACE and EverCare programs. An organization dedicated to providing long-term-care services may receive a capitation payment from the government or from a managed-care plan and agree to provide both Medicare and some long-term-care services. Usually these programs are marketed to people who are eligible for both Medicare and Medicaid. But a regular HMO may also sell these plans.

The advantages and disadvantages are similar to those programs already described in this chapter. If you are looking at one of these programs for a relative, be sure you understand what you'll have to pay each month. Your relative may have to pay a monthly premium in addition to the Part B premium.

Your state Medicaid office should be able to tell you whether such programs exist.

KEY DECISION POINTS

1. If your relative already qualifies for Medicaid, see if there is a PACE program in your city.

2. If your relative is not yet eligible for Medicaid, consider buying into PACE and paying your state's Medicaid capitation rate. This might be a more attractive alternative to patching together your own services and paying a lot more.

3. Ask your state Medicaid office if there is a special program that combines services for people eligible for both Medicare and Medicaid. These programs cut down on the paperwork and provide more efficient care.

4. Giving up choice of health care providers may be worthwhile in exchange for coordinated, seamless care.

TEN

Assisted Living

Outside Brighton Gardens, an assisted-living facility in Austin, Texas, Virginia, age seventy-seven, sat on a bench. She was bitter and unhappy, and talked about life inside the facility where she and her eighty-year-old husband had recently moved. "They're all alike," she complained. "This is the beginning of a different life." It was a life her children had chosen for her. She had little say in the decision.

Virginia described life in assisted living. "If you sit at a table with a bunch of loonies, it's bad. No one to talk to," she said. She said it was a "battle" to get anything done. "You pull the cord and you wait and wait. Some of the staff make you feel like you're imposing on them." Virginia's husband was incontinent and needed a bath every day, and the family had understood that he would get one. "After we got on the program, we found out that they bathe people every other morning and not on Sunday," Virginia said. Virginia considered that outrageous since she and her husband were paying $4,000 a month for their care and living space.

Brighton Gardens is managed by Marriott, a big owner and manager of assisted-living facilities arountd the country. The facility did resemble a hotel with nice carpeting and matching furniture. It was clean and even a bit glitzy compared to the austere surroundings found in most Austin nursing homes.

Like many assisted-living facilities, Brighton Gardens promoted itself using slick colorful brochures showing lots of happy, smiling people. "Every meal is a nice occasion to share good food and conversation with friends," the brochure advertised, and touted its "attentive and friendly" staff.

The advertising brochure for Brighton Gardens hardly matched reality for Virginia and her husband. Nor do similar promotional pitches for other assisted-living facilities always match what many elders actually experience once they become residents.

Yet adult children, lured by clever marketing and the classy appearance of many facilities, are coaxing their often reluctant parents into this relatively new type of care arrangement. The price for that care, as in Virginia's case, can exceed that of a nursing home, where the cost now averages some $40,000 a year. Despite the high price tag, the number of residents in assisted living has increased since 1995. Assisted living is big business. Sunrise Assisted Living, a large chain based in McLean, Virginia, shows just how large. In 1998, the chain realized a 458 percent increase in net income, making it one of the most lucrative corporate enterprises in the Washington, D.C., area.

What their parents think about a move to assisted living is often a secondary consideration for adult children. "Marketing assisted living is less about need than where adult children want their friends to know Mom is living," says Dr. Donna Yee, director of policy and research for the National Asian Pacific Center on Aging and a former associate research professor at Brandeis University. "Most people just settle into these places. Living there is not about happiness. It's about doing the best you can." Speaking at an industry conference, Stephen Wright, of Wright Mature Market Services in Tacoma, Washington, was candid: "Resident satisfaction really means family satisfaction." Indeed, on my visits to facilities, I often encountered residents who would have preferred to be somewhere else. At a Sunrise facility in Virginia, I met Emily, who seemed to speak for many residents I met. "This is not what I intended, but I do the best I can. I'm happy in a way, but I'm homesick in a way. I try not to let it get to me."

While Yee was at Brandeis, she and her colleagues conducted the first national study of residents in assisted-living facilities and found that while many experienced fairly independent and autonomous lives, they also had unmet health and long-term-care needs. Sometimes they were socially isolated, experiencing limited participation in activities or community life. The Brandeis study found that residents at high-priced, for-profit facilities often had negative health outcomes that could have been prevented. Yee and her colleagues also discovered that facilities which offered residents a lot of choice over autonomy and independence had more negative health outcomes than residents who lived in facilities that monitored them more closely. Therein lies the crux of assisted living: autonomy versus supervision. Adult children and their parents must understand those trade-offs and what they mean for quality of life long before they fall for a slick marketing brochure and plunk down thousands of dollars to reserve space in one. "The reality is no one knows how to have people age in place in assisted living with a good balance of choice and safety issues," says Dr. Joanne Lynn, director of the Center to Improve Care of the Dying at George Washington University. "The industry doesn't want to admit the emperor has no clothes on. The only way to make the system perfectly safe is to jail these folks." Of course, Lynn meant the residents, but she had a point.

WHAT IS ASSISTED LIVING?

The theory behind assisted living sounds inviting to families struggling with the care needs of an elderly relative. Assisted living is supposed to enhance the capabilities of frail older persons and make it easier for them to live independently for as long as possible in facilities that offer a homelike atmosphere. In practice, assisted living means group living arrangements with a private room or sometimes a shared room, availability of protective oversight, social and recreational activities, and assistance with activities of daily living, such as eating, bathing, and dressing. Assisted-living facilities do not provide medical care, and sometimes the supervision and oversight they do offer is insufficient. Many residents still need home health aides to see them through their day. But home health plus assisted living is an expensive combination.

Susan Morse, who lives in suburban Washington, D.C., knows just how expensive. Her father is a resident at a local assisted-living facility and pays $1,875 per month for his care. But the facility does not provide him with everything he needs, so the family must shell out another $1,500 a week for home health aides, bringing the monthly total to nearly $8,000. Still, he needs an escort to take him to the dining room so he remembers to eat. But instead of paying the facility another $200 for an escort, the family decided to buy a phone message service from the telephone company for $10 a month. "You could pay top dollar and not come anywhere near meeting their needs," Morse says. "We were slow to catch on that assisted living wasn't the great panacea it is made out to be."

Other types of congregate living arrangements might fall under the umbrella of assisted living, since there is no common definition of what assisted living really is. Some of these arrangements include housing subsidized by the federal government under the Department of Housing and Urban Development's Section 202 program (see page 207) as well as what are known in some states as board-and-care homes or group homes. These may not be as lavishly appointed as the hotel-like arrangements of the facilities run by Hyatt or Marriott, and the care in them may be worse, the same, or it might be better.

The best place I visited was a warm, friendly group living arrangement in an old Philadelphia mansion. It was run by an order of nuns who cared about the people in their charge. The facility offered spacious rooms, cozy sitting areas, attractive meals, and lots of activities to keep residents occupied. What's more, it was less expensive than some of the glitzier, for-profit facilities in the Philadelphia area. "There are very different things you can get for your money," says Virginia Fraser, a long-term-care ombudsman in Colorado. "In some cases, people are paying too much for what they are getting. The critical consideration is the philosophy of the place and how the staff carries it out."

Assisted living offered by many entrepreneurs embraces the concept of the "dignity of risk." This means that residents can make their own decisions about their care and safety, and even choose certain courses of action that others consider risky. For example, if a diabetic wants to eat cake and ice cream once a month, should that be his or her choice, or should the facility step in and say no? Should the facility allow a resident to use a walker even if she falls and hurts herself, or should the facility make the woman stay in a wheelchair? Some facilities may require prospective residents to sign contracts that include provisions for negotiated risk—that is, how much risk the resident is willing to assume and how much risk the facility will take.

Unfortunately, the central concept of what assisted living is all about often gets lost in the rush to put Mom and Dad in a nice place. Assisted living has become synonymous with real estate. As the rest of this chapter shows, much of it is sold as real estate rather than as appropriate care for an elderly person. I have visited more than fifty assisted-living facilities over the last few years, and on virtually every visit, someone who identified herself as a marketing director tried to "sell" an apartment complete with meals, laundry, and housekeeping services. On one visit to a facility in Boston, the marketing director pushed the most expensive units, gave numerous details about price and repeatedly asked if we were interested. Hardly any of the facility "tour guides" I encountered were interested in why my mother needed care. At the facility where Susan Morse's father lived, the marketing official talked about the facility as "the product." "There was no indication he was talking about people and he had all the charm of a used-car salesman," she recalled.

Hotel chains as well as independent entrepreneurs construct facilities that appeal to the aesthetics of adult children. "The first impression is the key to marketability," one speaker told attendees at a meeting of the industry's trade association a few years ago. Facilities try to make a good first impression. At a Sunrise facility in Frederick, Maryland, a dining room is called the "butlery" and the Alzheimer's wing "a reminiscence center." A Hyatt facility at Hilton Head, South Carolina, calls its Alzheimer's unit a "memory support center." Eden Gardens in Gainesville, Florida, calls it a Keepsake Neighborhood. Euphemisms equal marketing cachet. So do features like the old-fashioned ice cream parlors and 1940s-style jukeboxes designed to make the World War II generation feel right at home.

"Appearance is 75 percent of the battle to get families to sign up," explained Patti-Ann Hopkins, assisted-living manager at a Marriott facility in Florida. What sells the family, she said, are safety and security, value for price, the food, and a homelike environment. Hopkins did not dwell on the care and staff interaction that make residents feel good, which are most important to residents. Perhaps families are not interested in those dimensions so proprietors don't bother selling them.

A fancy front room with Georgian-style furniture and an ice cream parlor do not guarantee that a resident needing a bath every day will get one, or that the facility will accommodate a resident's declining eyesight with appropriate help and activities. Assisted-living entrepreneurs emphasize that their facilities are not nursing homes and don't look, feel, or smell like them. Yet some practically offer nursing home care with little or no state and federal oversight, a point families should keep in mind as they shop for this kind of arrangement. At an ordinary-looking ranch-style home in Austin, Texas, I saw the home's owner giving complex care to some of the residents. A visitor came away with the impression that this home might have been giving care normally found in more traditional nursing homes. (This is often the case in smaller homes. Under certain conditions where home health aides may be called in, this arrangement may be appropriate. But families should proceed carefully.)

Nor should families consider assisted-living facilities as substitutes for a nursing home. Placing a relative in assisted living does not foreclose the possibility of a nursing home in the future; at some point, an assisted-living facility may make little sense for a person. Many do not admit or keep residents who need ventilators, catheters, or have continence problems they can't manage. About 40 percent of all residents eventually go to a nursing home because the assisted-living facility cannot accommodate their increasing frailty. For many residents, assisted-living facilities are really "predeath homes." About one-quarter die in the facility, and the rest move on to other retirement homes, other assisted-living arrangements, or they move in with children. As with nursing homes, the average stay for a resident is about two years.

IS YOUR RELATIVE A CANDIDATE FOR ASSISTED LIVING?

Despite the frequent mismatch between the promise and the reality of assisted-living facilities and the high cost of living in one, families might want to consider them along with other options discussed in this book such as home health care and adult day care. But before you take the steps outlined in the rest of this chapter, talk with your relative and determine whether he or she is a good candidate for congregate living. People who have been loners all their lives are unlikely to enjoy the communal nature of assisted living. Assuming they can get along by themselves at night, those people might be better off in adult day care or home care that allows them to stay in their own home with attendants coming to help with daily activities.

At its best, assisted living can help your relative remain in charge of his or her life for as long as possible. At its worst, it can mean a stultifying, sad decline toward death. "You lose a lot when you go to assisted living," says Elizabeth Clemmer, manager of consumer policy research at AARP's Public Policy Institute. "The very decision to move to assisted living may mean giving up independence, especially if adult children make the decision."

If you think that your relative is a good candidate for assisted living and your relative is interested in moving to such a facility and can participate in the decision and the careful shopping required to find a good one, follow the steps outlined in the rest of this chapter. Choosing a satisfactory facility is tricky. The financial arrangements are complicated, and the contracts don't always spell out what you need to know. "The main thing we hear is that when people get into facilities, they don't know about the extra charges," says Elma Holder, director of the National Coalition for Nursing Home Reform. "They are not given enough information about when they can be asked to leave based on the health conditions they have."

CHOOSING A FACILITY

To do a good job of selecting an assisted-living facility requires a lot of time and effort. Several visits may be necessary before everyone is comfortable with a particular facility.

The First Visit

Typically, a family contemplating assisted living for a relative should make initial visits to several facilities in the area where you want your relative to live. What you learn on this visit will tell you whether you want to proceed with the admissions process. Most likely the director of marketing, who may, in effect, be doubling as a real estate agent, will show you around.

You will see the common areas—the parlors, library, dining room, laundry facilities, and patio. Then she (most are women) will show the available apartments. Sometimes they are furnished, but often they are not, and you will have to visualize how your relative's furniture and possessions will fit within the space. Where the apartment is located is very important. In many assisted-living facilities, units closest to the dining room are more desirable and therefore cost more. Likewise, units closest to the elevators are also prized. The theory is that frail people have a hard time walking long distances, and if they have trouble getting around, they should pay more for the privilege of a shorter walk. At Brighton Gardens in Austin, for example, the staff member giving me a tour said that residents near the elevator will pay more for their unit than those living in units farthest away. "The less you walk, the more expensive," he said.

What your guide says or does not say offers clues to the kind of facility you are at. If she keeps repeating the price of the apartment, or emphasizes how quickly your relative can move in, or when an apartment will be available, that facility may be more interested in moving real estate than in meeting your relative's needs. At one Boston facility, the marketing official was clearly impatient with my questions, especially when I tried to pin down the details of its transportation arrangements for residents. "They get one van trip per month," she said brusquely, and added, "They can get taxi rides."

What to watch for on your tour

• Be aware of the guide's rapport with the residents and your rapport with the guide. Some of the guides I met on my tours were not interested in my relative's needs, and gave little information about how the facility cares for its residents. If she doesn't ask any questions about your relative's needs, it may be a sign the facility is more interested in filling space than in the care your relative requires.

Watch how staff relates to the residents. Do they talk to them, know them by name, or do they ignore them? Do they seem genuinely interested in the residents and what they are doing, or do they seem phony, putting on a show for prospective families? After you visit three or four facilities, you'll be able to tell.

At one facility, the staff director paid more attention to Philip, the house bird, than to the two residents sitting next to the birdcage. She talked to the bird—"Are you sleeping, little bird?"—completely ignoring the residents. The worksheet on page 187 will help you evaluate different facilities. It includes a warmth index. Note your impressions of facility personnel and consider them when making your selection.

• Look for signs of life or energy. I've never seen anyone eating ice cream at the ice cream parlors. In most places, residents seem to prefer to stay behind closed doors, and there were few activities going on despite the full activities calendars posted on the walls. At two facilities, one in Denver and one in Savannah, visitors were shown activities rooms with craft materials placed as though they were props for a photo shoot. The staged look conveyed the impression that no one ever came to participate. A Denver facility featured an activities room with T-shirts and paint tubes neatly arrayed. It didn't look messy, and it appeared no one ever used them. At a Savannah facility carefully arranged painted clay masks and paint-by-number coloring books were arranged on a table. The pictures in the coloring books were perfectly filled in, so perfectly that it's hard to imagine an elder with arthritic hands and poor coordination able to complete such a task. Be on the lookout for an arts-and-crafts room that seems too perfect and unused. Such "props" almost fall into the category of a deceptive sales practice.

If you see few residents in the common areas or participating in activities, it may signal that the facility is not full. A half-empty facility could bode poorly for the facility's long-term finances. At one deserted facility in Savannah, I asked where the residents were. The staff member acting as the guide replied that they were on an outing, but she did not know where. "Every day is a surprise," she explained.

If a facility needs residents to fill up its units, you might encounter the hard sell. High-pressure tactics are always a sign to continue shopping. At one facility, the marketing director was so eager to sign up my mother that she began to disparage the competition, a tactic more commonly associated with the insurance industry. She tried to sell us on how good the staff was and explained that a competing facility used universal workers. "They use workers who clean the johnnies and then go into the kitchen," she said. "We call in housekeeping."

When you do see an activity, note whether residents are really engaged and enjoying what they are doing. At a facility in Boston's Back Bay, residents gathered in the parlor on a late-winter afternoon to hear a travel program. They asked questions, talked, and appeared to be truly interested in the presentation. This, however, was unusual in my experience. The activities I often saw were more akin to the one at a facility in Palo Alto, California, where residents were celebrating someone's birthday. They sat stoically eating ice cream and cake— more or less going through the celebratory motions. People didn't talk to each other and didn't relate to the person leading the singing. I have seen seniors more engaged in activities at adult day care centers and at PACE sites than at assisted-living facilities (see Chapters 8 and 9). At one day care center, the director said a client came every day from her home, which was in an assisted-living facility, because the family didn't think she got enough stimulation.

Watching activities and noting how engaged participants are is important, for if you don't see much going on, or if people don't participate, it may be a warning. Taking this step is also important if you are placing a relative in the Alzheimer's unit. Margaret O'Kane, president of the National Committee for Quality Assurance, an organization that accredits HMOs, tells how her mother got no stimulation in an Alzheimer's wing at a Maryland facility. "My mother is still with it to enjoy activities, but there's no stimulation," O'Kane said. "She's in bed most of the time. The facility says it is going to change the situation, but nothing changes."

What questions to ask

• Find out what the facility will do to accommodate your relative's current needs and what it will do as those needs intensify and increase. Be forthright and explain exactly what your relative's functional, physical, and mental deficits are and how they are likely to change. For example, someone with glaucoma or macular degeneration may experience a progressive decline in sight. How will the facility accommodate the decline? When that question was posed to an admissions official at a government-subsidized housing unit in Boston, she referred us to the facility's Opti-Lex system, a device that magnified print so residents with failing eyesight could continue to read their mail and other printed matter. When the admissions director at a competing and somewhat glitzier facility was asked the same question, she told about how wonderful a blind resident was, a patronizing remark that begged the question. The first facility tried to accommodate the needs of its residents; the second apparently offered little help to those with failing eyesight, or was not willing to promote what it did, if anything.

If the answers you get don't make sense, or appear to brush off the problem, look elsewhere.

• Closely question facility personnel about independence versus oversight. For example, what is the policy on nightly bed checks? Many facilities have them; staff members walk into residents' apartments and shine their flashlights to make sure residents are okay. At Savannah Commons in Savannah, Georgia, the admissions director admitted: "Every two hours the resident is checked. We have twenty-four-hour supervision. I don't want them sleeping. That's not good." Will your relative be comfortable with such close scrutiny?

• Ask for a copy of the contract and the house rules. This is a test of the facility's interest in full disclosure. An official at a facility in Cambridge, Massachusetts, said she would not provide a copy of the contract. "It's nineteen pages, and it costs to hand it out to anybody." At a Savannah facility, I was told that the contract "would have to wait for another point in time." If there's reluctance to part with such crucial information even at this early stage, consider it a red flag.

• Ask about the elevators. Do they operate at a pace that residents experience as safe and unhurried? Are there stories of people getting stuck because they were confused by the buttons? Has anyone been hit by the door, or were they afraid the elevator would break down?

• Ask if residents have their own social activities in the evening like cards, pool, or a television group. What are the opportunities for men and women to have activities that encourage and sustain lifetime hobbies and interests?

• Can they kick residents out for bathroom "accidents" or incontinence?

WORKSHEET 3: Judging an Assisted-Living Facility

This worksheet will help you choose an assisted-living facility. There are no inspection reports or objective data sources that measure and quantify how good a facility will be at delivering care and serving your relative's needs. This worksheet can help guide you in your search. Use Table 16 (see page 203) to help figure the price of services at each facility you are considering.

	Facility 1	Facility 2	Facility 3
Price:			
Basic monthly rent	_____	_____	_____
Total of extras	_____	_____	_____
How warm and caring is the staff? Note if you dislike, like, or are neutral about facility personel	_____	_____	_____
Relative's needs: Note if the facility does a good, average, or poor job of meeting them	_____	_____	_____
Staff attitude toward residents: Note if you dislike, like, or are neutral	_____	_____	_____
Physical surroundings: Note if they are good, average, or poor	_____	_____	_____

The Marketing Materials

Assisted-living facilities hand out brochures galore. They tend to focus on the real estate aspects of the arrangement and promote themselves as hotels for the elderly. Typically, the get-acquainted packet contains floor plans, sample menus, an activities calendar, and a newsletter. The packet may contain prices for the units, but it may not reveal prices for various levels of care—crucial information for making a decision. Distinguish between amenities and care. The information also contains lofty statements about the goals and operating principles. One brochure, for example, stated that the facility would "show genuine interest in all residents' needs and concerns," and its staff would "smile and be polite." While that may reassure family members, you won't know whether the facility will practice what it preaches until your relative becomes a resident.

Consider the material in the packet as preliminary information. Don't base a decision on it. Most likely it won't tell you one-tenth of what you need to know. A facility that says it will provide information and does not send it to you may also be one that you want to avoid. A Hyatt facility I visited in South Carolina had no information about fees or anything else the day I visited. It promised to send material but never did. Don't go back to those kinds of places. Unkept promises may be a sign of how the facility will care for your relative. How can you be sure that the staff will give your relative a bath on schedule?

The Admissions Process

The waiting list If you have time to think about your relative's eventual care and are interested in assisted living, consider putting him or her on a waiting list. Facilities vary in how their waiting lists work. At some, if a person does not accept an offer when an apartment becomes available, he or she moves to the bottom of the list. At others, the facility simply calls the next person on the list, and your relative maintains the same position. When the next unit is available, the facility calls your relative again. The latter arrangement affords the most flexibility for decision making.

To keep your relative on a waiting list, you will most likely have to leave a deposit, usually ranging from $300 to $500. This money may be nonrefundable if your relative eventually decides not to move in. But if he or she wants to go through the application process, some facilities allow the deposit to be used as an application fee. At one facility in Denver, the admissions director said "$4,000 gets you on the waiting list," but Mom could decline as many times as she wanted. The fee was fully refundable if she didn't move in.

Keep your relative off a waiting list until you are absolutely sure he or she is ready and comfortable with the idea of assisted living.

Your relative's visit I can't stress enough how important it is for your relatives to visit the facility two or three times while on a waiting list, and preferably before they add their name. Visit at different times of the day to see if your relative likes the routines. Look beyond the meals and well-appointed living rooms. Have them spend the night and attend some activities. Ask them how they would like living in such a facility. If you get negative responses, don't push. Another arrangement might be better. Either you or your relative should inquire about adequate staffing. While the facility may tell you that there is sufficient staff, residents often tell a different story—long waits for help, long waits for dining services, few people to talk to. If residents tell you that they have to wait a long time for services or that the facility has cut back on personnel, keep looking. Some cuts in services can be deadly. Residents can die if it takes too long to answer a distress call when they pull the emergency cord in their unit. Chatting with residents in the lobby or outside is the best way to gather this intelligence.

The application The application is detailed and may ask for financial information about your relative's savings and income. The facility wants to make sure you or your relative can pay the basic price for the unit, the monthly fees, plus the inevitable annual rate increases. But just as important, the application tries to find out whether your relative really "qualifies" for care in the facility. "We don't have wanderers. We are not a facility to provide dementia or Alzheimer's care," the admissions official at Avery Crossings in Needham, Massachusetts, made clear during my visit. "We ask Alzheimer's people to leave. Our activities would become frustrating and they'd become isolated." At Hale House in Boston, residents must be able to get themselves up and dressed and down to the dining room without assistance. If they can't, the facility doesn't want them. At a Denver facility, the admissions official said, "If someone has to push your mom in a wheelchair, she is not a candidate for assisted living. She is a candidate for twenty-four-hour nursing care." In other words, that facility signaled to us it was not interested in residents who need wheelchairs populating its assisted-living wing, but would place them in skilled-nursing care almost immediately. If your relative doesn't otherwise need skilled-nursing care, continue your search.

The application is designed to identify the kind of care your relative needs. It will usually ask about your relative's general overall health, physical disabilities, mental condition, symptoms of confusion, forgetfulness, interest in social activities, functional capabilities, and ambulatory status. (Does your relative use wheelchairs, canes, walkers, or other assistive devices?) The facility may also require a doctor's examination, a TB test, a psychological test, or even a personal interview with the applicant. It may require a doctor's statement before your relative can go on the waiting list.

The application not only weeds out people who are not physically or financially qualified, it also serves as a way for the facility to place your relative in a level of care and to assign a price to that care. Often you have no say in the placement.

The Package of Services

Marketing brochures usually list the services that are provided: meals; emergency response systems; scheduled transportation for shopping and medical appointments; social activities; escort service to the dining rooms; laundry and housekeeping; help with medications, bathing, dressing, and continence care. On the surface, then, it seems pretty straightforward to match what you think your relative needs with what the facility says it offers. But often it's not so easy, and here is where families sometimes sour on assisted-living facilities.

Facility personnel determine the kinds of care and services your relative requires based on the application and possibly the personal interview, and you may have little say in the matter. Brochures sometimes don't distinguish between care services and amenities, or if they do, the information is vague and unuseable. Marketing material from Palo Alto Commons touts its "spectrum of services" and the "choice of gracious studio or one-bedroom apartment," "three delicious meals served daily," and "a full calendar of exciting cultural, educational and social programs." Materials also specify five levels of care. Level 1, for instance, provides "light care services," Level 2 "light-to-moderate services," Level 4 "moderate-to-heavy services." They do not tell a prospective member what constitutes light care and moderate-to-heavy care. The facility will make that decision, and you or your relative will pay its established rate. Level I, for example, costs $265 per month; Level IV, $845. These amounts are added to the monthly apartment fee.

Many assisted-living facilities have complex formulas for determining how much care your relative requires. Brighton Gardens in Austin, Texas, figures out how much time it will take nursing assistants to help residents perform various tasks. If they need between sixty-one and ninety minutes a day, for example, the facility considers that Level III care and charges accordingly. A person needing Level IV assistance needs help for up to two hours a day and will pay more. A tour guide at Brighton Gardens told me that the facility places new residents in a higher level of care and then reassesses them after thirty days, possibly moving them to a lower level.

Does your relative really need a higher level of care or is the facility simply trying to enhance the bottom line? It is sometimes hard to say. "We decrease the level of care for 50 percent of my residents," says Patti-Ann Hopkins, an assisted-living manager for a Marriott facility in Florida. You can't get "too greedy with it. I couldn't raise the level of care to make money."

It's important to know when periodic reassessments take place, since they are crucial to the amount you will pay. If you suspect the facility is trying to jack up its fees, you may have to secure an independent assessment from a geriatric care manager. Chapter 6 tells you how to find one.

Another caveat about services: Know when they will be provided and at whose convenience. If your relative is supposed to receive help with a bath three days a week, make sure you and the relative know when the bath will take place and who will give it. The same goes for transportation services. The facility may provide transportation to doctors and to shopping malls. But there may be limits on the number of trips a month or even a year that your relative is entitled to receive. For instance, a facility may offer a ride to medical appointments only six times a year, and specify that the doctor's office must be within a radius of five to seven miles from the facility. One marketing director said that residents could always get rides "if they can find Joe available." But Joe may not be around when your relative needs a lift. Where will your relative eat? In a communal dining room for people who are cognitively impaired as well as for those who function normally, or will there be segregated dining rooms? At one facility, the admissions official noted that those in assisted living ate in a separate dining room. "It is a different lifestyle," she said.

The Price

Monthly fees for assisted living can easily exceed $3,000 or $4,000 a month, and families sometimes don't know what they will be paying until they sign up. Comparing prices of facilities in a particular area is not like comparing the price of store-brand canned peaches with Del Monte's. It's darn difficult to disentangle different fee arrangements. Since so much of the price depends on what kind of assistance your relative needs, and those needs change, it's tricky to figure out whether one arrangement is financially more attractive than another. Assisted-living facilities generally use one of these ways to charge for their services:

- A flat or a bundled rate. With this arrangement, the facility estimates the average amount of care residents will need. Some need more than the average, some less, but with this approach everyone will pay the same for personal care services that are folded into the basic rent for the living unit. Facilities that use this method don't raise fees as a resident gradually needs more help with activities of daily living. (Fees may increase for general inflation, however. This pricing structure is similar to that used by insurance companies that use community rating for their Medicare-supplement policies.

- A tiered rate. A facility may include four or five tiers, or rate levels, in its pricing structure. Each tier represents different levels of care needed by a resident. The first tier at some facilities may simply include the basic rent, housekeeping services, meals, and little or no personal care services. The fourth or fifth tier represents heavy-duty care, the maximum a facility will provide. Alzheimer's and dementia patients may require this level of care.

- Flat rate with an hourly charge for assistance. With these arrangements, facilities charge a basic rate and then add additional fees based on an hourly rate for various services needed by the residents. Hourly charges add up. At one Boston facility, residents could be charged an extra $6 for every fifteen minutes of personal care they needed beyond what was specified in the base rate. At another facility, the tour guide noted that if someone needs an extra fifteen minutes of care, that adds $135 to the monthly bill. Fees can be as outrageous as charging for tying shoes or opening draperies.

Assisted-living facilities don't work like continuing care retirement communities (CCRCs), which may require an entrance fee ranging in the hundreds of thousands of dollars. But there may be one-time entrance or community fees that can equal a month's rent, though they rarely exceed $5,000. One facility that was charging $2,000 called it a membership fee. "We could have called it anything," the admissions official said. "It's just the cost of doing business."

Many CCRCs have assisted-living units attached to them as part of a continuum of care. When you're shopping, be sure to distinguish between the stand-alone assisted-living facility and the ones that are part of a CCRC. The financial arrangements of the latter may be more complicated.

In either case, you don't have ownership rights to the unit. Most people sell the family home when they move to an assisted-living facility and use the proceeds from the sale to pay the monthly charges. In effect, a spend-down occurs in the assisted-living facility rather than in a nursing home. If this spend-down occurs before a nursing home stay becomes necessary, the residents will most likely be eligible for Medicaid when they enter the nursing facility.

Rate increases Caring for physically and mentally impaired elders is labor intensive and very costly, and most facilities raise their rates 5 to 7 percent each year. But that increase may exceed what some residents can afford. Some run out of money while still in an assisted-living facility, especially if they stay a long time. The case of eighty-seven-year-old Helen Roberts, who lives in a Sunrise facility in northern Virginia, shows what can happen. Roberts moved into the facility in 1990 and paid a monthly fee of $2,432. By 1999, she was paying $3,400. Roberts can still pay the increases, but she says many residents could not, and some moved in with family or went to a nursing home and spent down their assets so Medicaid could pay. Roberts lives in Sunrise units designated for residents who can still live independently. But she is thinking ahead to the time when she will need more services, which will, of course, cost more money. "Five years ago I realized this was taking more than I had planned," she says. At one point, Roberts said Sunrise announced an increase of 5 percent, but Roberts's cost-of-living raise from Social Security that year was only 2.4 percent. Residents, working through their active residents' council, prevailed on Sunrise to limit the increase to 4 percent. "None of this was written in the entrance papers," Roberts said.

If you can't afford to continue living in your unit, the facility may ask you to move to a smaller one or to share a room with someone to reduce monthly expenses. At that point, you may have little choice but to go along with the new arrangement, move in with family, or go to a nursing home and apply for Medicaid. If your relative cannot pay the annual increases, reconsider whether assisted living is a good option.

Sometimes residents require visits from home health aides in addition to the assistance the facility staff provides. If the facility does not permit its staff to give insulin injections, for example (some facilities supervise medications but do not actually allow staff to administer them), you may have to arrange for the services of a home health aide. And this adds to the monthly expense. It may be cheaper in the long run to hire a home health aide instead of paying more to have facility staff handle the increasing care needs of your relative. Figure how much more the facility will charge per month for the care, and then find out what a local home health agency will charge for the same services. Some 40 percent of assisted-living facilities charge extra for administering medications.

A facility can require residents to use certain home health agencies. These tie-ins can be an expensive solution to your care needs. Furthermore, some facilities do not allow residents to access Medicare benefits. They require residents to use designated home health providers, who are not certified by Medicare. Unless you use a Medicare-certified provider, Medicare does not pay. When you make your initial visits, find out whether the facility has special arrangements with home health agencies and whether they are high-cost providers.

You may also find such a requirement pertaining to prescription drugs. One facility switched to a new pharmacy that prepared medications in blister packs for ease of administration with the result that some families paid more for prescriptions. The old pharmacy charged one family $4.44 for twenty-seven Brethine tablets; the new one charged $102.93 for thirty. Using the new pharmacy was the only option if the family wanted the facility to administer their mother's medications.

The Second Visit

Once you have done some financial projections to determine that your relative has enough money to pay for care in an assisted-living facility and can remain there for at least two years, perhaps longer, it's time for a second visit. Said one marketing expert: many families "buy on emotion and later justify with the facts." Placing a relative in assisted living should not be an emotional decision, and the second visit should be regarded as a serious fact-finding mission. Patti-Ann Hopkins of the Florida Marriott facility says that too many families "come in and tell me Mom's needs and say 'Can you take care of them?' One thing families don't ask about is what's the philosophy of care and the training of the staff—how do we screen them, how do we train them?" The second visit is the time to find out.

Staff training How good the staff is depends largely on the facility's commitment to the kind of care it wants to deliver; there may be few requirements for staff training in your state. Regulations vary widely. Only half the states require training to prevent infections, fifteen require a staff knowledgeable about cardiopulmonary resuscitation (CPR), and only ten states require the staff to complete an approved course in providing care for residents.

Call the agency that licenses assisted-living facilities in your state (see Appendix N) and get a copy of the requirements, if there are any. Ask the facility how it meets or exceeds the state minimums. Ask about training in such areas as direct care to patients, safety and emergency care, first aid, CPR, care for dementia patients, sanitation, mental health and emotional needs, residents' rights, and medication administration. Don't settle for answers such as "We give staff training." Get specifics: How many hours in what fields? Do they have continuing education requirements? If your relative will be in the Alzheimer's or dementia wing of the facility, learning about how the staff is trained to interact with difficult residents is very important. It doesn't hurt to inquire about staff turnover. How long do staff members stay? If there is high turnover, something may be wrong, and you probably don't want to place your relative there.

Activities The second visit is the time to study the kinds of activities the facility offers. If your relative is a loner and not interested in social participation, then he or she will probably prefer to be alone, even at the facility. But if your relative likes to be around people, carefully scrutinize the activities calendar. This is one piece of information that facilities eagerly hand out. Is there a good mix of spiritual, physical, and intellectually stimulating things to do? How often do they provide them? One facility in Colorado told me that it shows movies only twice a month. If your relative enjoys movies, is that often enough? If your relative will be going to the dementia wing, pay careful attention to activities provided for people who have cognitive impairments. How many times a day do they provide an activity? Once or twice a week probably isn't enough.

While many facilities say they offer activities, those activities may not be evident when you visit. During my many visits to assisted-living facilities, I often saw no activities going on. Time your visits so that you see how a facility conducts its activities. Are people engaged and does the activities director make an effort to get residents to participate? Do residents enjoy the activities? Ask some of them during your visit.

Inquire about a residents' council and find out how active it is. One resident noted that without the residents' council, the facility "would walk all over us." Does the facility provide an adequate place for the council to meet? A resident at one facility said that the council once met in the activities room, but the facility management turned over part of the room to an outside business that provided health services to residents.

The contract By the time you make a second visit, it's crucial that you understand the contract and the rules that will govern your relative's life in the facility. A few years ago the American Bar Association's Commission on Legal Problems of the Elderly analyzed contracts from assisted-living facilities for CONSUMER REPORTS. The bar association found that even though assisted living is supposed to foster independence, dignity, privacy, and connections to the community, the contracts appeared to be silent on those issues, or they appeared to promote the opposite by limiting residents' autonomy.

Does the facility subscribe to the philosophy of negotiated risk? Some facilities may want families and the resident to engage in a process of care planning that respects a resident's preferences even if those preferences involve risk to the person or to others. For example, if a resident falls using a walker, should he or she be allowed to continue using it even if the fall causes an injury?

The facility, the resident, and the family generally come to some agreement during the care planning process that spells out the services that will be provided to a resident, taking into consideration the resident's preferences. The written agreement may list the needs and desires for a range of services and specific areas of activity provided under each service. Negotiated service agreements reflect a philosophy that stresses consumer choice, autonomy, and independence, but they may also provide a way for the facility to escape liability if the resident suffers harm as a result of certain actions. If you go down the path of negotiated risk, have a lawyer examine your agreement.

Where will the resident live? Contracts should specify where the resident will live, and provide for flexibility when it comes to bringing your own furnishings or modifying the unit, who can come to live or visit, and whether the same unit will be available after a temporary hospital stay. Many contracts are silent on these points. They don't specify the particular room your relative will get nor do they mention adapting or customizing the unit, or providing for changes in the household composition, which can occur if a resident marries or wants to live with someone. Be sure you are clear about what happens when your relative returns after being discharged from the hospital. Unlike with nursing homes, the facility is not required to hold a room. Be sure that yours will. Going to a new facility can be disorienting and confusing to an elder who has just experienced an acute illness.

Are meals included? Contracts usually specify which meals are provided. Some facilities don't offer special diets, something you should find out about if your relative has special dietary needs. You might also want to find out if the facility gives credits for meals not eaten or provides tray service if your relative is ill and confined to the apartment. These charges can add up. One facility charges $6 per meal. Some may charge more or less.

How do you get about? Whether the resident can leave the facility freely to shop, dine out, attend religious services, or visit a doctor is key to quality of life and independence. Contracts should specify who will provide what kinds of transportation and where. Some contracts don't say, or they specify that residents must arrange their own transportation. When they do mention the subject, contracts may impose restrictions and conditions. For example, they may say the facility will provide transportation for medical appointments only on certain days of the week at certain times. Or they may limit transportation to within a certain radius of the facility. Some say the resident must notify the facility one or two days before needing a ride.

What services are provided? Facilities should specify exactly which services—housekeeping, laundry, nursing care, activities, meals— they'll provide, how often, and whether they can stop providing them. Helen Roberts and her fellow residents found that over the years the facility had scaled back services. She complained of waiting twenty minutes to make a dinner reservation for a guest because the receptionist had to help set up the dining room for dinner. It's best if a contract specifies when a service can be eliminated—for example, after a thirty-day notice—but you are more likely to find them saying services will be provided when the facility deems they are appropriate or are required. The vagueness of those provisions is tailor-made for abuse and neglect, and it's possible for a facility to manipulate the services to meet financial objectives rather than the needs of its residents.

Will your privacy be protected? Residents need their privacy, but at the same time, they need assurance that they are safe. Some facilities conduct bed checks during the night, a practice many residents find objectionable. Understand how the facility you are considering keeps tabs on its residents, day and night. A contract may say little about privacy, but it's important to find out just what you'll be allowed to do or not do.

What's the cost? Most contracts spell out the costs of living in the facility, and there are many—entry deposits, cleaning charges, vacating fees, processing fees, and fees that increase as more intensive care is needed. Then there are the optional fees—breakfasts, companion visits, RN/LPN visits, medication administration, help with bathing and dressing. Comparing fees is tricky because of the way facilities bundle their services. Use Table 16 (see page 203) to estimate what you will have to pay and see how many of them the facility is willing to specify in the contract. Bear in mind, however, that most contracts are not negotiable.

Can you see your own doctor? Most residents prefer to see their own doctor, but in some facilities, you may have to use the doctor the facility provides. Contracts may be vague about medical care and fail to explicitly give you the right to choose your own physician. If the contract says you can choose your own, does it then say the doctor must meet standards set by the facility? If a facility requires all residents to use the same doctor, and if you belong to an HMO that requires the use of its own physicians and other providers, you could be caught in the middle, unable to obtain medical care without incurring unnecessary out-of-pocket expenses. Furthermore, these physicians can decide if it is appropriate for you to stay in the facility. Often you or your family have no say in the decision.

Who is in charge of medications? Contracts should specify who is responsible for administering, coordinating, and scheduling medications. Is it the facility, the resident, a family member, or a visiting nurse? In some facilities, you may have to hire a nurse to administer medications because the facility offers only standby assistance—that is, facility personnel simply see that your relative takes the required medication. If the contract uses the word *supervise,* be sure you understand what supervision means. It could mean different things at different facilities.

What if a resident's health fails? Few contracts specify what happens when a resident's physical or mental status declines. What happens, for example, if a resident's eyesight declines or disappears, or if he or she can no longer walk to the dining room? Ideally, contracts should specify that the facility will devise an individual program to accommodate those needs. But instead the contract might say you can hire your own aides and assistants to help with your changing needs. Many facilities are neither licensed nor equipped to deal with the increasing frailty of their residents.

Who decides about transfers? It's not uncommon for residents to live in several units during their stay in assisted living, first in a private unit and then, as money runs low, in a shared room, perhaps in an undesirable wing or floor. Nor is it uncommon for residents to be shipped off to a nursing home or placed in a higher level of care as their physical or mental capacity declines. Knowing who makes the decisions about transfers, the factors they're based on, and whether a resident has any say in the matter is crucial.

Many facilities told me that the staff makes the decision after consulting with family members, but care managers who have had experience placing people in assisted-living facilities and ombudsmen who get complaints say that the facility often makes the decisions unilaterally. Ideally, the facility should provide for a committee composed of facility staff and the resident or the resident's representative to make the tough choices. Residents should have a say when a transfer is recommended in a nonemergency situation. Contracts, however, usually put the decisions in the hands of the facility and sometimes in the hands of one person, the facility's physician, without providing for consultation, as I've noted. Beware of contracts that say decisions are "determined" by the facility.

Can they kick you out? Even though the marketers promise that your relative can "age in place," many contracts are designed to get rid of residents the facility does not want to bother with. They contradict what the sellers say to entice you in. Contracts should allow for a minimum thirty-day notice if the facility wants to end the agreement, something every facility should have the right to do if a resident can't pay the bill or harms others. See if the contract provides for a probationary period during which the resident decides if he or she is suited for assisted living. If no probationary period is allowed, will the facility offer a prorated refund of the fees you have paid if your relative decides to move out after a few weeks? Discharge from the facility is basically an eviction, and you usually have no opportunity to appeal. When does the facility ask you to leave? "Discharge is often arbitrary and not up front," says Pearlbea LaBier, a social worker in Bethesda, Maryland. "It's really consumer beware. It's a mess."

What will the facility do to accommodate increasing frailty? This is a major issue since most people who enter an assisted-living facility eventually experience a decline in physical or mental functioning. Talk candidly about your relative's condition and the likely progression of his or her disease. What will the facility do to accommodate the decline? For example, if your relative has glaucoma that may get worse, how will the facility deal with the gradual loss of sight? Does the facility provide books with large print, assistive devices that help elders read, and training in the use of those devices? An answer like "we show them the handrails in the halls" is not an acceptable answer. But if the facility says it has a machine that enlarges type so a person can read her mail or write a check, that's a good answer.

A more in-depth look at physical surroundings The second visit is the time to take a hard look at the physical surroundings. Look well beyond the matching Georgian-style furniture that seems to be common in many of these places. Instead, focus on how easily your relative can get around. How accessible is the dining room, for example? If it is far from the unit where your relative will reside, will he or she be able to get there without a lot of effort? Look for what are called adjacencies in the assisted-living business. For instance, is the beauty shop near the dining room so your mother can easily have her hair done before or after lunch? This could be an important consideration if she has trouble walking.

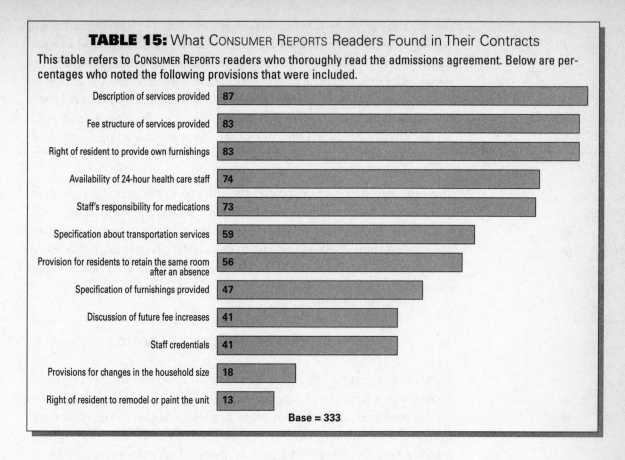

TABLE 15: What CONSUMER REPORTS Readers Found in Their Contracts

This table refers to CONSUMER REPORTS readers who thoroughly read the admissions agreement. Below are percentages who noted the following provisions that were included.

Provision	Percent
Description of services provided	87
Fee structure of services provided	83
Right of resident to provide own furnishings	83
Availability of 24-hour health care staff	74
Staff's responsibility for medications	73
Specification about transportation services	59
Provision for residents to retain the same room after an absence	56
Specification of furnishings provided	47
Discussion of future fee increases	41
Staff credentials	41
Provisions for changes in the household size	18
Right of resident to remodel or paint the unit	13

Base = 333

Focus on the carpeting and grab bars. Can someone with arthritic hands hold on to them easily? One Savannah facility was equipped with handrails that were nothing more than grooves in the wall that would be hard for someone to grasp. A competing facility in the area had discreet handrails that protruded from the wall and were much easier for residents to hold on to. Dizzying patterns that blend together and make it hard for elders with poor eyesight to distinguish between patterns and colors and floors and walls might be unsafe and throw them off balance. Look at things nonelderly people take for granted, like big-screen TVs with the controls near the floor. It may be hard for an older person to stoop down to turn the set on. Or consider cupboards in the kitchens. One resident I visited had all her kitchen paraphernalia stacked on counters because she couldn't reach the high cupboards. Consider the bathrooms in the common areas. At one facility the paper towels were so far away from the sink that a person using a walker would have quite a time moving sideways from the sink to the towels to dry her hands. If your relative has dementia and wanders, what is the wandering space like? Is it sufficient and can residents wander without interfering in whatever other activities are going on? Physical space is very important. One hallway for people to wander in is hardly sufficient. At one Maryland board-and-care home, dementia patients had nowhere to go. They walked back and forth across the tiny living room and up the three steps leading to the bedrooms, and then they walked back down again.

The care plan The second visit is the time to ask about the care plan, who draws it up and how much input the resident and family will have. Both should have a say. If your relative is able to make decisions, the facility should ask about their preferences. A care plan drawn up solely by the staff is likely to be a source of trouble later when things go wrong.

WHO PAYS FOR ASSISTED LIVING?

Eighty-six percent of the one million or so residents in assisted-living facilities pay for care out of their own funds. The rest get help from family and friends and from state agencies. Medicare does not pay unless skilled-nursing care is needed and given in certified skilled-nursing facilities. Assisted-living facilites usually do not meet Medicare's requirements. However, Medicare does pay for some skilled care if your relative meets the requirements for the Medicare home health benefit.

Thirty-two states pay for care in assisted-living facilities through their Medicaid waiver programs. But as Chapter 13 points out, your relative must be poor or become poor by spending down assets in order to qualify. Because states limit the number of people served through waiver arrangements, you may encounter long waiting lists even if your relative qualifies financially.

Long-term-care insurance policies are beginning to cover some care in assisted-living facilities. While this coverage may seem like a useful benefit, it should be used carefully, especially if you have purchased a policy with a "pool of money" approach. It's possible to use up the entire benefit on care in an assisted-living facility and have nothing left when the time comes for nursing home care. About 40 percent of assisted-living residents eventually end up in nursing homes.

TABLE 16: What You Will Pay at Your Facility

Use this worksheet to get a rough idea of the services and what they will cost at the facility you select.

Step 1: Check the type of rate structure

a. Flat daily rate _____

b. Tiered daily rate (varies according to the amount of assistance your relative needs) _____

c. Base rate (plus additional hourly) _____

Step 2: List the community or other one-time charge _____

Step 3: List the monthly fee for the type of unit you select

Studio	$	_____
One bedroom	$	_____
Two bedroom	$	_____
Other	$	_____
Second person fee	$	_____

Step 4: Check other services included in the base rate, and add services that require an extra charge

	INCLUDED IN BASE RATE	ADDITIONAL COST PER MONTH
Meals		
Breakfast	_____	$ _____
Lunch	_____	$ _____
Dinner	_____	$ _____
Snacks		$ _____
Special diets		$ _____
Guest meals		$ _____
Room service		$ _____
Escorts to meals		$ _____
Housekeeping		
Daily	_____	$ _____
Times per week	_____	$ _____

Laundry Services		
Personal (loads per week)	_____	$ _____
Linens	_____	$ _____
Apartment Amenities		
Emergency response system	_____	$ _____
Bathroom (sink, shower/bathtub, toilet)	_____	$ _____
Bathroom (toilet & sink only)	_____	$ _____
Fully furnished unit	_____	$ _____
Carpeting	_____	$ _____
Cable TV hookup	_____	$ _____
Mini-refrigerator	_____	$ _____
Lockable door	_____	$ _____
Gas/electric/water	_____	$ _____
Window treatments	_____	$ _____
Basic cable TV service	_____	$ _____
Microwave oven	_____	$ _____
Stovetop burners	_____	$ _____
Local phone service	_____	$ _____
Transportation		
Scheduled	_____	$ _____
Unscheduled	_____	$ _____
Car	_____	$ _____
Van/minibus with lift	_____	$ _____
Other	_____	$ _____
Social/Recreational Activities	_____	$ _____
Services		
Awake staff on premises 24 hours per day	_____	$ _____
On-site licensed nursing staff (hours per day)	_____	$ _____

Supervision of self-medication (i.e., reminders)	_____ $ _____	
Medication administration by licensed professional	_____ $ _____	
ADL assistance		
Unlimited	_____ $ _____	
Limited	_____ $ _____	
Beauty/barber shop	_____ $ _____	
Wander management system	_____ $ _____	
Shopping assistance	_____ $ _____	
Incontinence supplies	_____ $ _____	
Toiletries	_____ $ _____	

Other personal care services: _____ $ _____

_____ _____ $ _____

_____ _____ $ _____

_____ _____ $ _____

Total Additional Charges: $ _____

Step 6: Estimate your total monthly expenses

Base monthly rate $ _____

Second-person fee
(if applicable) $ _____

Cost of extra services you
must pay for $ _____

Total Monthly Charges $ _____

Source: Adapted from consumer information statement created by the American Seniors Housing Association and the Assisted Living Federation of America

Some people who hold long-term-care insurance policies are beginning to experience trouble tapping their benefits if they live in assisted living. If your relative is considering a long-term-care policy, be sure the policy covers the kind of assisted living you may need.

REGULATION OF ASSISTED LIVING

Regulations vary widely from state to state. Only about half have some kind of licensing requirements. Those states that do address such issues as residents' agreements, who can be admitted, who can be terminated, definitions of allowed or required services, staffing requirements, and medication administration and assistance and whether you can keep control of over-the-counter medications like aspirin. Understand what your state's requirements are as you embark on your quest for a facility. Most likely your relative will need some help with medications, and it's a good idea to know what your state rules are before you start asking the facilities for theirs. In Kansas, for example, the licensing law says that "appropriate staff may assist with self-administration and administer medications." But in Michigan the law does not permit assisted-living staff to administer medications.

TABLE 17: States That Pay for Care in Assisted-Living Facilities

In early 1999, the following states paid for some care in assisted-living facilities either through their regular Medicaid programs or through a federal waiver. If your state is not on this list, check with your state's department of social services (Medicaid office) to see if assisted-living services have been added.

Alaska	Nebraska
Arizona	Nevada
Arkansas	New Hampshire
Colorado	New Jersey
Delaware	New Mexico
Florida	New York
Georgia	North Carolina
Illinois	North Dakota
(demonstration project)	Oregon
Iowa	Rhode Island
Kansas	South Dakota
Maine	Texas
Maryland	Vermont
Massachusetts	Virginia
Minnesota	Washington
Missouri	Wisconsin
Montana	

Unlike for nursing homes, there is no national database that provides information on the quality of care delivered in assisted-living facilities. The Health Care Financing Administration, for instance, does not collect data, and states do not always inspect the facilities as they do with nursing homes. A few states—Florida is one—inspect assisted-living facilities. Ask your state health department whether it has inspection reports on such facilities. If it does, be sure to examine them.

WHERE TO GO FOR HELP

You may find that you need help once your relative becomes a resident in a facility. Many long-term-care ombudsmen also monitor assisted-living facilities in their jurisdiction. Because the ombudsmen in some states are under severe political pressure from the nursing-home and the assisted-living industry, the quality of help you get could varies considerably. In one state, for instance, when the ombudsman criticized a facility for not allowing residents in wheelchairs to eat in the communal dining room, the owners tried to get her fired. Ask the ombudsmen if any facilities have ever denied them access. If a facility has, that's not a place you want to place a relative.

Nevertheless, if you are having a problem, start with the ombudsman. See Appendix O for a list of the state ombudsmen who can put you in touch with the ombudsman in your locality. You might also try contacting the Consumer Consortium on Assisted Living at *www .ccal.org* or 703-533-8121. This organization can provide general information about assisted living, but it does not give specific recommendations.

GROUP AND BOARD-AND-CARE HOMES

These kinds of homes for the elderly have been around for many years. They offered assistance to people long before Marriot, Sunrise, and Hyatt came on the scene with their expensive glitzy offerings designed more to appeal to adult children than to elders. Group homes are found in every state and most states require them to be licensed, regulated, or certified in some way. Sometimes Medicaid pays for care in them.

People who have space in their homes obtain a license and provide care and assistance with daily living to four, five, and sometimes more residents. These homes may not offer much in the way of space, privacy, activities, or help, but the price may be much lower than in the Marriott and Hyatt facilities. The care may be good, or it may be bad. If, for financial reasons, you want to place a relative in a board-and-care home, check out the state licensing requirements. Find out how much experience the staff has and whether they will respond to your relative's care needs. Space is also important. One board-and-care facility I saw in Florida had virtually no place for a woman who needed physical therapy. When the therapist came, she was able to walk the resident only a few feet from the chair to the coffee table. There was no other place to go. The therapist said there was not much more she could do.

You may find small group homes available for Alzheimer's patients, and it may be tempting to place a relative in one, especially if the price is right. However, bear in mind that the supervision could be minimal and what staff is available may be inadequately trained to care for difficult patients. One ombudsman told of a small facility that employed just one staff member to care for six or seven patients twenty-four hours a day. Also, there may be limited activities for patients living in small homes. You don't want to place a relative in one only to find that he or she will not receive appropriate stimulation.

SECTION 202 HOUSING

An alternative to the heavily marketed, expensive assisted-living facilities are the variety of government-subsidized housing units found in communities scattered across the country. There are only about 1.5 million units available, a minuscule amount considering the potential need for such housing. The Department of Housing and Urban Development estimates that at least 1.5 million more units are needed right now to assist elders who have low and moderate incomes, and more will be needed as the population ages. Congressional appropriations for subsidized housing for the elderly have been decreasing over the last twenty years, creating a situation where there are waiting lists for virtually all federally assisted housing units. Sometimes it takes two or three years before a unit is available. In some areas, the shortage is so severe that managers no longer keep waiting lists, and do not accept new applicants. Still, if you are contemplating care for a relative, you should consider this type of housing.

What's available? Most units are available under what is called Section 202 housing (the name comes from the 1959 Housing Act). Because government programs have changed through the years, there's a mix of financial arrangements. In some units, the federal government directly subsidizes tenants; in others, residents are simply given vouchers to help pay the rent. Many of the units are operated by not-for-profit owners such as religious organizations, but some owners operate them to make a profit.

What do you get? Facilities vary considerably in the amenities and the ambience of the buildings. The first units built in the 1960s and 1970s tended to be larger and offered more services. Units built later, when the government embarked on cost-cutting programs, are less attractive. For example, some have no kitchen facilities; perhaps only a hot plate for warming coffee.

If your relative rents an apartment in such a facility, you may have to stitch together your own package of services. Only about one-third of Section 202 projects have coordinators on the premises to help find services for their residents. If you place a relative in a building without a service coordinator, you are on your own just as if your relative were living in his or her own home or apartment. Many facilities have communal dining rooms that serve one or two meals a day. If more food is required, you'll have to arrange for it yourself through the home-delivered meals programs in your area or through some other means. Some have limited or no medical personnel around, although there may be emergency pull cords in the rooms.

Section 202 projects may not be fancy, but on my travels, I saw some of the happiest elders living in them. At Emerson Gardens in Denver, a resident named Jean came up to me and said, "The thing I like best here is the management. It's like family here. After I was here two months, I asked for a fifty-year lease." In turn, the director, who simply exuded warmth and caring, said: "My philosophy is that this is their home. If you work with people, it will work out. We do all we can to make it work." Apparently this facility does it right, down to the houseplants that seemed to be everywhere. No one living there has much money, but they all contribute a dollar or two to support the indoor garden. In Boston, the Golda Meir Home, operated by the Jewish Community Homes for the Elderly, was more appealing than the fancier for-profit assisted-living facilities located nearby. It was the only facility that I visited in Boston where the director asked what kind of services and care my mother needed. She did not try to sell any real estate, but clearly explained how her facility could accommodate my mother's declining eyesight. Not all 202 facilities can do that, and one thing to find out is how they will be able to handle increasing frailty.

What do you pay? Many residents in Section 202 housing have incomes of less than $10,000 a year, and for most units, residents pay a monthly rent based on their income. Typically, most pay 30 percent of their adjusted gross income, or around $200.

How do you learn about 202 housing? Like most aspects of long-term-care services, it's difficult to learn about these options. They are not widely advertised, as are for-profit assisted-living facilities. You can ask your local area agency on aging to direct you to any Section 202 projects in the area where your relative will live. You can also contact your local government aging office, a city planning or health department, or even the mayor or city council. You can also contact the state office of the American Association of Homes and Services for the Aging, a national trade association representing nonprofit operators of senior housing, including nursing homes and assisted-living facilities. Call 202-783-2244 to find out how to contact the state association. You can also visit the association's website at *www.aahsa.org*.

KEY DECISION POINTS

1. Decide if your relative really is a good candidate for assisted living. Many people are not.

2. Take a realistic look at your relative's financial picture. Do some hypothetical financial projections; look ahead at least four years or maybe more to see if he or she can continue in an assisted-living facility. Consider the likely possibility of increasing frailty, increasing needs, increasing expenses and higher monthly charges. Will future income and assets cover those contingencies?

3. Carefully consider the philosophy of care given by the facility. Does the facility seem caring and concerned about your relative, or are personnel more interested in keeping units filled?

4. Be sure you understand what the facility can and cannot do to accommodate your relative's increasing frailty. Will personnel help you make arrangements for care that is needed but that the facility does not provide?

5. Don't be swayed by a facility's fancy interior. Matching furniture and fancy appointments don't guarantee good or even barely adequate care. Is the space functional for residents who may have different kinds of canes, walkers, wheelchairs, and abilities to navigate distances?

6. If your relative's income is low, consider Section 202 housing, and put your relative's name on a waiting list at a facility in your area. It may take two or three years until a unit becomes available.

7. Consider board-and-care homes in your community and make several visits to them. Ask the state or local agency that regulates them if there have been any problems—and if so, what kind.

8. What will assisted living add to the quality of your relative's life? Will it really provide more camaraderie, activity, and support, or is it just providing you with expensive peace of mind knowing he or she is not alone?

ELEVEN

Nursing Homes

Mrs. G., a resident of a Colorado nursing home, knows all too well the indignities that nursing home residents suffer. When the state surveyor came for the facility's annual inspection, Mrs. G. was brutally honest about her care: "First thing in the morning I need to go to the bathroom. I put on the call light. When someone finally comes in, they say they will be right back. Usually half an hour later when they return, I haven't been able to hold it. I'm really embarrassed but I can't help it. It happens every day."

Bath times for Mrs. G. were not much better. They are "sometimes really unpleasant," she told the surveyor. "They don't wash you well, just throw you around as if you were nothing. It doesn't feel good, especially when you are not well. I haven't complained because I don't want to get into trouble. I have to live here."

Mrs. G.'s plight is far from unusual. Such abuse, neglect, and lack of respect occur every day in the nation's nursing homes. Often the problems Mrs. G. revealed go unnoticed by state inspectors, or if they are detected, they are not written down and made part of the state inspection survey as they were in this case. "These very typical basic care issues are harder to document," says Virginia Fraser, Colorado's long-term-care ombudsman. "It's easier to spot bedsores or bruises from falls than it is to see neglect of basic care."

The failure to help someone go to the bathroom, a disregard for personal hygiene, and lack of respect are emblematic of the abuse and patient neglect found in many nursing homes. No wonder nursing homes are the last place on earth most people want their relatives to live, and families often go to extraordinary lengths to keep their relatives out of them. Then there are the families who use such facilities as dumping grounds and take little interest in where their loved ones are "placed." But between those two extremes are thousands of families who have little choice for a relative whose deteriorating physical or mental condition dictates nursing home placement. Those families face the painful task of choosing a facility that will keep their relative both safe and able to function at his or her optimum level.

As distasteful as selecting a nursing facility may be, families who need one have some of the best consumer information available. It is indeed ironic that truly good information exists for selecting a nursing home, a service that most people would rather do without. Unlike much of the "educational" material that is supposed to guide consumer choice, information about nursing homes can be concrete, explicit, and useful. It moves far beyond the empty, simplistic tips that pass for consumer education these days. Unfortunately, few people make use of what is available.

The CONSUMER REPORTS survey asked its readers how they selected long-term-care facilities for their relatives. One-third did not shop for a facility, and 26 percent followed the suggestion of someone else, primarily a physician. When it came to nursing homes, two-thirds of respondents said they selected a facility based on cleanliness, general appearance, and location. About half made their selection based on general reputation.

While these may be important characteristics, relying solely on them deprives you of other benchmarks that yield a fuller picture. Only 5 percent of CONSUMER REPORTS readers said that a recommendation from the long-term-care ombudsman, whose job it is to monitor nursing facilities in nearly every locality in the country, was one of the top three reasons for choosing a particular nursing facility for their relative; only 5 percent said the state inspection survey was a major selection factor; and only 5 percent mentioned a referral from an advocacy group as one of the top reasons for the choice they made. Only one-quarter of CONSUMER REPORTS respondents asked to see the state survey report, one of the best pieces of consumer information that exists anywhere for any product or service (see page 221).

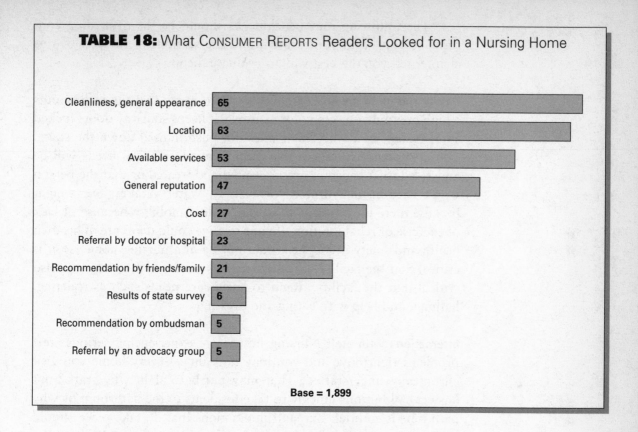

TABLE 18: What CONSUMER REPORTS Readers Looked for in a Nursing Home

Cleanliness, general appearance	65
Location	63
Available services	53
General reputation	47
Cost	27
Referral by doctor or hospital	23
Recommendation by friends/family	21
Results of state survey	6
Recommendation by ombudsman	5
Referral by an advocacy group	5

Base = 1,899

WHAT YOU WANT FROM A FACILITY

A nursing home is a place that provides medical care for very sick people, but it is also a home, and it may be the last place your relative lives. So the choice of a good one must necessarily encompass qualities that relate to both medical care and the comforts of home. Finding a facility that fulfills both functions well all the time is tricky, and it may not always be possible to hit the ideal, resulting in compromises in your final choice.

Bad or mediocre nursing homes always seem to outnumber good ones, or so the media seem to tell us. Weak enforcement of health and safety regulations, difficulty on the part of nursing home operators to find competent staff, changes in reimbursement from the federal government, and changes in corporate ownership all play a role in the questionable care delivered today in the county's nursing homes. "In terms of basic care, it's as bad as I've ever seen it," says Virginia Fraser, who has monitored Colorado nursing homes for the past twenty years.

The following four benchmarks should be the overriding concerns as you begin your search, and the sections in the rest of this chapter tell you the best way to evaluate them.

Safety and good medical care You want to know that the facility puts a high premium on safety; for example, it keeps stairway doors locked so a resident in a wheelchair does not push himself down the stairs. You also want assurances that your relative's medical needs will be addressed, that bedsores are prevented and treated or that the person won't become dehydrated for lack of water intake, lose weight because there is no help with eating, or lose mobility because of lack of exercise or rehabilitation. If your relative could take care of his own health and safety needs, he would not be in a nursing home, so it is critical that the facility be able to do the job for him or her. It is also critical that the facility attend to basic care needs such as toileting, bathing, and help with eating and dressing.

Interactions with staff Nursing homes are experiencing serious staff problems right now, and you may find almost every home you visit chronically understaffed. That may partly explain why staff can't answer call buttons quickly to take residents to the bathroom or why bath time is so brief. But staff interactions that do take place should be pleasant and helpful. It doesn't take much to say "Hello, Mrs. Jones, how are you today?" or "Gee, you look so pretty today." You wouldn't want to see the person serving meals stick a tray under a resident's nose and say nothing. It's far better to hear staff saying "Boy, does this look good!" Research has shown that relationships with staff are one of the most important aspects of life in a nursing home.

Stimulation Even severely demented people need stimulation and can express pleasure. A nursing home needs to provide such stimulation and must do more than tack a list of activities on the bulletin board. Residents should be encouraged to attend activities and make the most of what the facility offers.

Pleasant and safe environment Needless to say, you want the nursing home to be pleasant, bright, clean, and odor-free. It should be a place that you want to visit. If you don't want to be there, your relative probably won't like it either. That doesn't mean, however, that the nursing home must have matching furniture and sport some thematic decor such as Georgian colonial. Plenty of good care goes on at facilities that don't look like they should be featured in a glossy magazine promoting life in a nursing home.

BEGINNING YOUR SEARCH

Even though a sudden illness can require a stay in a nursing home, most families who have aged relatives can plan ahead and investigate their options. Only 10 percent of CONSUMER REPORTS readers said they had to choose a facility in an emergency situation. Sixty percent indicated that they had more time and were able to shop around and compare several choices. Those readers are probably pretty typical of most people who must find a nursing facility. If you think you will need a facility for a relative, one good way to find out about those in your area is to volunteer your services to a nursing home. Residents appreciate visitors from the outside, and it's an excellent way to find out what kind of care is actually delivered.

If you must find a nursing home after a sudden illness, try to bargain for more time in the hospital, using the appeal rights explained in Chapter 6. You want to avoid having the hospital discharge your relative to the first nursing home that has a bed available. In this situation, your shopping may be briefer than if you did not have to act quickly, but you can still investigate the sources discussed in the following pages.

If you are beginning a search for a nursing home that you think you are likely to need at some point in the future, you will obviously have more time to explore all the sources of information about nursing homes. No one source will be the final word on what facility you should choose. If you consider several indicators, including those presented in this chapter, chances are you will have a reasonable shot at finding a good, or at least an acceptable, facility.

Gathering Data

The following are tools that you should use to select a facility.

Lists of facilities where your relative will live The first step is to learn what the universe is—the names and locations of all nursing homes in the area where your relative will live. The Eldercare Locator (1-800-

677-1116) will put you in touch with the local area agency on aging, which can supply such a list. Another source is the long-term-care ombudsman for your locality. Appendix O lists the state ombudsmen who can connect you with the ombudsman for your area. Local or state nursing home watchdog groups such as Citizens for Better Care in Michigan and Friends and Relatives of the Institutionalized Aged in New York City also have directories of nursing facilities. See Appendix P for a list of those groups.

It may be best to place your relative in a facility near your home. That way you can visit frequently. Frequent visits are good not only from the standpoint of providing interaction with the person in a facility, but they are an important way of keeping tabs on the care that is given. If the nursing home staff knows you are a frequent visitor and that you pay attention to the care they give, they are less likely to abuse your relative and be more attentive to his or her needs. Long-distance caregiving can be problematic. If you live far from a relative in a nursing home, you might want to hire a geriatric care manager to periodically look in on your relative. Or you may want to consider placing your relative in a location where there are friends or family nearby.

The ombudsmen Theoretically, one of the best sources of information is the long-term-care ombudsman in your area. The ombudsman program was established in 1975 as part of the Older Americans Act. From the ombudsmen you can learn whether the facility is likely to keep your relative safe and offer good medical care, whether it has adequate staff or chronic staffing problems, and whether there is adequate stimulation. There is a state ombudsman in every state and local ombudsmen stationed in many counties throughout a state.

Ombudsmen know the good, the bad, and the ugly about all the nursing homes in their jurisdictions. They work closely with the agency that surveys nursing homes and usually receive their reports. They resolve complaints on behalf of nursing home residents, make periodic visits to facilities when there are problems and even when there are none. They generally know how well a particular home cares for its residents. Some ombudsmen are willing to say which facilities are particularly good. A few years ago the ombudsman in New Orleans told me that the Maison Hospitalière in the French Quarter was a good home. "It has an excellent program and rarely has deficiencies," she said. A visit to the nursing home confirmed what she said. In preparing this book, I again visited the Maison Hospitalière and found the same good facility I had seen earlier. Someone who relied on that ombudsman's judgment would not have been unhappy with the choice.

Ombudsmen, however, are under tremendous political pressure from nursing home owners who have significant clout in state capitals. An ombudsman who comes down too hard on a facility, publicizing a facility's problems and steering families and potential residents away may find him- or herself in trouble. More than one ombudsman has been fired for speaking out too forcefully. Because there are so many empty nursing home beds these days (there are some 222,000 empty beds, 90,000 more than there were fifteen years ago), ombudsmen might be especially wary of making negative comments. Nevertheless, they can be helpful if you read the signals properly.

Pay attention to comments like "You may want to look further," "They're okay," "I'd put it far down on the list," "Is there any reason you want to put your mother there?" These are tip-offs that the place you are asking about is less than desirable. If you get answers like those, ask the ombudsman if there are any facilities that he or she can more enthusiastically endorse. If there are, you may want to start your search at those homes with both an unannounced and an announced visit. After you have completed your visits, you may want to return to the ombudsman and discuss what you found. See if he or she is more forthcoming with information. The ombudsman may confirm either positively or negatively what you see on your visits.

Local watchdog groups These are local organizations that monitor care in nursing homes. Unlike the ombudsmen, they are usually free from political pressure and may be more candid about the problems in particular homes. Use Appendix P to see if there is an advocacy group in your area. If there is, ask the group about staffing, resident abuse, and what you can do to help monitor the care.

The state survey report This may be one of the most valuable pieces of information you can use in evaluating a nursing home. It is known as Form 2567 from the Health Care Financing Administration. It is also called the state inspection survey. You can ask for it by both names. States, usually through their health departments, are responsible for carrying out and enforcing federal regulations that apply to nursing homes. Nursing homes must adhere to a long list of rules and regulations that are meant to ensure the safety, well-being, and dignity of nursing home residents, monitor the quality of care they get, ensure adequate social and emotional stimulation, and meet their needs. Each possible deficiency is given a number designation called a prefix tag (also called an F-tag). Table 19 (see page 219) gives some examples of serious deficiencies and their F-tag numbers.

As the list shows, nursing homes can receive deficiencies for failure to treat bedsores, failure to provide necessary medical care, failure to respect a resident's dignity, failure to provide activities and stimulation, failure to keep accident hazards to a minimum, and making errors in administering medications. Inspectors have discretion in assigning codes for scope and severity. (Was the problem widespread? Could it cause severe harm?) When certain deficiencies are cited with higher levels of scope and severity, they are considered substandard quality of care violations. Obviously, those are the most serious.

State surveyors make unannounced visits to nursing homes every nine to fifteen months and spend time talking to residents, looking at their charts, observing the care that is given, and checking sanitary conditions. Surveyors also investigate complaints made against nursing homes. When the surveyors are finished with their inspections, including those that are the result of a complaint, they issue a report that sometimes contains a lengthy statement of the deficiencies they find plus a plan of correction that the facility has agreed to.

This report must be posted in the nursing home in a conspicuous place so that residents, family members, and visitors can find it. Too often, though, the survey is not conspicuous. Refusal to post the survey is a violation of federal requirements. In the last four years, 10 percent of all nursing homes have received citations for failing to post their state surveys. A few years ago a CONSUMER REPORTS investigation of nursing homes revealed that some facilities were taking what seemed like extraordinary measures to hide their state surveys. When I looked for the surveys, I found them hidden under piles of magazines in the lobby, posted in hallways where visitors seldom walked, posted upside down so people would have a hard time reading them, and locked in cases that made them hard to get. Sometimes they were out of date and illegible. At a facility in New Orleans, an admissions official explained that the missing survey might have been eaten by a resident whom she said ate everything, including paper.

TABLE 19: Common Problems Found in Nursing Homes

The following shows what deficiencies state surveyors are likely to find in nursing homes. The number at left is the F-tag for each deficiency.

371   The facility must store, prepare, distribute, and serve food under sanitary conditions.

314   The facility must ensure that (1) a resident who enters the facility without pressure sores does not develop pressure sores unless the individual's clinical condition demonstrates that they were unavoidable; and (2) a resident having pressure sores receives necessary treatment and services to promote healing, prevent infections, and prevent new sores from developing.

332   The facility must ensure that it is free of medication error rates of 5 percent or greater.

224   The facility must not use verbal, mental, sexual, or physical abuse, corporal punishment, or involuntary seclusion.

327   The facility must provide each resident with sufficient fluid intake to maintain proper hydration and health.

441   The facility must establish and maintain an infection control program designed to provide a safe, sanitary, and comfortable environment, and to help prevent the development and transmission of disease and infection.

324   The facility must ensure that each resident receives adequate supervision and assistance devices to prevent accidents.

241   The facility must promote care for residents in a manner and in an environment that maintains or enhances each resident's dignity and respect in full recognition of his or her individuality.

309   Each resident must receive and the facility must provide the necessary care and services to attain or maintain the highest practicable physical, mental, and psychosocial well-being, in accordance with the comprehensive assessment and plan of care.

248   The facility must provide for an ongoing program of activities designed to meet, in accordance with the comprehensive assessment, the interests and the physical, mental, and psychosocial well-being of each resident.

Source: State Operations Manual Provider Certification, Health Care Financing Administration, June 1995.

Using the survey report Ideally, you should obtain the two or three most recent state surveys for each nursing home you are considering. Ask the facility for a copy and sit down and read it carefully. If the facility doesn't comply, you may have to get it from the state health department or whatever agency conducted the survey. (A list of those agencies appears in Appendix N.) If the nursing home refuses to give you the survey, that is an immediate trouble sign. You should wonder what the facility is hiding. Unless there is some compelling reason to use that particular nursing home (it may be the only one in town or the one closest to your home), you should quickly look elsewhere.

You can also learn what's on the most current survey for any particular facility by accessing the Nursing Home Compare database on the website of the Health Care Financing Administration (HCFA). (*www.Medicare.gov*). (States may have their own websites, and the local ombudsman can tell you if there is one for your state and how to access it.) The HCFA site provides information about the characteristics of residents living in a particular nursing home. For instance, it lists the number of residents who are bedfast, the number on restraints, the number with urinary incontinence, the number with pressure sores, the number with restricted joint motion, the number with unplanned weight gain or loss, and the number with behavioral symptoms. This data is self-reported by the nursing homes and may not be accurate. Yet it can provide the basis for more detailed questions and more intense observations. For example, if the website reports that a facility has a low number of residents on physical restraints relative to the state average, which is given, it may be a good sign. But if during your visit you observe a lot of residents restrained in their wheelchairs by ties or by tables attached to the chairs, it is a signal that the home could be fudging its numbers. You could ask the administrator about such discrepancies. If you find that a facility has a high number of residents who need help eating, and your relative functions at a fairly high level, you may not want your relative at that facility. Mealtimes might prove especially frustrating.

The website also provides a list of the quality standards that a facility has failed during its latest inspection. But the site does not give the graphic details that make the survey report so telling and useful. The annotated sample survey report in Table 20 (see page 221) shows how richly detailed some of these reports are. They provide a great deal of information to help in your search. While the website can be helpful in pinpointing problems, you need to read the survey to get the details.

TABLE 20: What a State Survey Looks Like and How to Read One

X4) ID PREFIX TAG	SUMMARY STATEMENT OF DEFICIENCIES (EACH DEFICIENCY MUST BE PRECEDED BY FULL REGULATORY OR LSC IDENTIFYING INFORMATION)	ID PREFIX TAG
157	(Continued from Page 5) identify them	
	The facility staff failed to notify the family and physician of the resident's change of condition per regulation and the facility protocol.	
241 S=E	483.15(a) REQUIREMENT: QUALITY OF LIFE[1]	F 241[1]
	The facility must promote care for residents in a manner and in an environment that maintains or enhances each resident's dignity and respect in full recognition of his or her individuality.	
	This REQUIREMENT is not met as evidenced by[2]	
	Based on observation, record review, and staff and resident interviews, the facility failed to promote care for residents in a manner and in an environment that maintained or enhanced each resident's dignity and respect in full recognition of his or	

RM HCFA-2567L[3]

X4) ID PREFIX TAG	SUMMARY STATEMENT OF DEFICIENCIES (EACH DEFICIENCY MUST BE PRECEDED BY FULL REGULATORY OR LSC IDENTIFYING INFORMATION)	ID PREFIX TAG
F 241	(Continued from Page 10) Orientation format revealed that many of the above mentioned issues were covered in the orientation process	
	The following were observations that supported the above stated concerns from the residents:	
	1. On 7/8/99 at approximately 11:20 A.M., a call light was observed to be on at the end of the 1300 hall, room 1307. Halfway down the 1300 hall, loud voices were overheard from room 1307. The surveyor stopped outside room 1307 and heard a nurse talking in a loud, argumentative tone to nonsample resident #34.[4] The	

TABLE 20: (*Continued*)

resident was observed from the hallway sitting on the toilet with the bathroom door and room door opened to the hall. The nurse yelled, "I can't get you up." "I need to put the light on." The resident stated she wanted to get off of the toilet immediately. The nurse stated in a loud voice, "I can't, you sent the other girl away," and continued to say, "You	

FORM HCFA-2567-L

X4) ID PREFIX TAG	SUMMARY STATEMENT OF DEFICIENCIES (EACH DEFICIENCY MUST BE PRECEDED BY FULL REGULATORY OR LSC IDENTIFYING INFORMATION)	ID PREFIX TAG
F 241	(Continued from Page 22) 9. On 7/9/99 at 9:15 A.M. on the Renaissance unit, noninterviewable nonsample resident #44 was observed being wheeled backward by a CNA into the activity room. Two aides then transferred the resident from the wheelchair to the couch. Neither aide explained to the resident what they were going to do. A gait belt was not used to help transfer the resident. Instead, one aide grabbed the seat of the resident's pants, swung the resident around a half circle, and abruptly sat her down. The resident became agitated during the transfer and yelled, "Oh," "Oh help me."[5] The confused resident could not see where she was being wheeled. The aides did not explain the transfer to the resident, which was done in a rough, inappropriate, and undignified manner. 10. Noninterviewable sample resident #25 was admitted 1/20/98. Diagnoses	

FORM HCFA-2567-L

X4) ID PREFIX TAG	PROVIDER'S PLAN OF CORRECTION (EACH CORRECTIVE ACTION SHOULD BE CROSS-REFERENCED TO THE APPROPRIATE DEFICIENCY)[6]	(X5) COMPLETION DATE

If continuation sheet Page 22 of 177[7]

[1] F-tags identify the problems.

[2] Here is where to start looking for details.

[3] Identifies state survey report, which must be posted at every nursing home.

[4] Read the details carefully.

[5] More details that show violations.

[6] Look here to see if the facility plans to correct the problems observed.

[7] The more pages, the more violations.

The survey reports not only identify the F-tag for each deficiency that is given but graphically and completely describes the number of instances in which a violation occurred. Surveys that describe violations of residents' dignity, failure to treat pressure sores, failure to provide necessary medical care, failure to provide adequate food and water so residents maintain proper body weights and protein levels should give anyone pause before placing a relative in such a facility.

Next on the survey, note the plan of correction that the facility says it will carry out. Does the plan seem reasonable? Will it correct the problems? Speak to the administrator about the survey. Ask sharp questions about the violations that are detailed. The administrator may try to cover up for lapses in care, or he or she may say violations have been corrected. If the administrator tells you that the facility has corrected the problems, the only way for you to satisfy yourself that corrections have been made is to spend lots of time at the facility observing what goes on during the day. Also weigh what the administrator says against other information you obtain. Indeed this may seem like a lot to do and a lot of information to absorb, but doing the homework may help you find a better nursing home.

Be forewarned, however. A survey report that shows no deficiencies does not necessarily indicate that the nursing home is wonderful or immune from problems. As good as the survey report may be in pointing out bad practices at many facilities, it is only as good as the inspection process and the surveyors who carry out the inspections. Sometimes, for political reasons and because of pressure from nursing home operators, state surveyors go easy on some facilities in some states. They may avoid citing homes even though there are violations. If you find no deficiencies on the state surveys you examine, you must ask more questions and seek corroborating information. The state detection index that we devised for this book gives an indication of how stringently your state's surveyors enforce the regulations.

Consumers Union's state detection index To determine how well states are detecting problems in nursing homes, we constructed an index using the following components: the percentage of surveys in each state with no deficiencies; the average number of deficiencies per survey in which deficiencies are reported; and the maximum number of deficiencies per survey.

It is a rare nursing home that does not have problems, so a state inspection system that turns up few or no deficiencies may not be finding them, may be ignoring them for political reasons, or simply not citing them. We assumed that problems in nursing homes occur in about the same frequency in all states, and that no one state has a preponderance of bad nursing homes. So if a state has a high percentage of surveys with no deficiencies, that may signal low detection of problems by its inspectors. Our analysis shows wide disparities among states. For example, in Nevada, only 2 percent of the surveys indicated no deficiencies while 45 percent in Kentucky showed none. We also considered a high average number of deficiencies a signal of high detection. Averages ranged from a low of 2.0 per survey in Connecticut to 13.7 percent in Nevada. We also considered a high maximum number of deficiencies a signal of a high level of detection. Inspectors in Michigan cited a facility that received 55 deficiencies in the course of one survey. Alaska cited a maximum number of fourteen.

Using the detection index Table 21 (see page 225) shows how the states stack up when it comes to detecting problems in nursing homes. States with a high detection index tend to find and report deficiencies in many facilities, generally citing several when they do find problems. Inspectors appear willing to cite a large number of deficiencies, if necessary. If you live in a state with a high detection index and are considering a facility that has few deficiencies on its surveys, that facility may indeed be a good one. In all likelihood, state inspectors would have cited problems if there had been any.

On the other hand, if you live in a state that has a low or an average detection index, a facility with no deficiencies may not necessarily be good and a "good" inspection report is not necessarily reassuring. The state index could simply mean that the inspectors were not citing problems very often. If you live in a state with a low detection index and have a relative in a nursing home, you will have to be especially vigilant in your oversight of the care that is given. In these states, it might be very important to choose a facility that is nearby so you can make frequent visits.

Like all tools that can be used to select a nursing home, our state detection index is not foolproof. It does, however, give a good indication of a state's willingness to look for problems and cite facilities. In New York, for instance, which ranks low compared to other states, the Health Department actually returned money to the federal government instead of using its federal funds to hire more inspectors. The index does point out the states where you will have to be extra watchful when you place a relative in a facility.

TABLE 21: State Detection Index

The Detection Index below represents a composite ranking of three factors: (1) the percentage of state inspection surveys resulting in no deficiencies for the facility, (2) the average number of deficiencies per survey in which deficiencies are reported, and (3) the maximum number of deficiencies in a single survey. States that report lots of deficiencies rank high, meaning that the state inspectors are finding and citing many facilities. States that report few deficiencies rank low, meaning that inspectors are either not finding many violations or are not citing facilities.

State	Detection Index	State	Detection Index
Michigan	100	Pennsylvania	54
California	99	Oregon	45
Nevada	93	Wyoming	45
Arkansas	91	North Carolina	43
Indiana	87	Louisiana	43
Illinois	85	Oklahoma	43
Delaware	84	Massachusetts	41
Kansas	82	Wisconsin	41
South Carolina	77	Rhode Island	39
Arizona	74	South Dakota	38
Florida	74	Kentucky	37
West Virginia	74	Virginia	37
Washington	73	Minnesota	34
Idaho	71	New Hampshire	31
Ohio	68	New Jersey	29
Hawaii	67	Maine	26
Alabama	65	Maryland	25
North Dakota	65	Georgia	22
Montana	59	Nebraska	18
Utah	59	Alaska	17
Tennnesee	59	Vermont	17
Mississippi	57	New York	16
District of Columbia	55	Connecticut	13
Iowa	55	New Mexico	11
Texas	55	Colorado	9
Missouri	54		

State enforcement penalties It is easy in some states to learn about the fines and other penalties that the state has assessed against nursing facilities. In others, it is a struggle to get this information. Only about half the states would give us a record of the fines they have assessed against nursing facilities in recent years. It is worth asking your state attorney general's office or state health department for a list of these penalties. The ombudsman's office or local nursing home advocacy group may also have them.

If you find that the state has fined a particular facility, ask why and be especially cautious about choosing that facility. It is possible that the nursing home has cleaned up and is now nearly problem-free; it may have been sold to a new owner who takes the job of caring for the elderly more seriously than previous owners. But what is called yo-yo compliance is too often part of a nursing facility's history. Bad homes clean up, do better on their state surveys, and then become problematic again.

Nursing home watch lists To help you spot nursing facilities that have had problems, we constructed the Consumer Reports Nursing Home Watch List for each state. We looked at the survey reports for some seventeen thousand nursing homes in the database from the Health Care Financing Administration. For each facility, we examined the last four survey reports and looked at patterns of deficiency citations.

Each facility's deficiencies were evaluated on five criteria: (1) the total number of deficiencies in each survey, (2) the number of repeated deficiencies, (3) whether the facility was cited for any substandard quality of care deficiencies, (4) the number of deficiencies with the highest level of severity, and (5) any citations for limiting the availability of the survey report. From this we developed a way to highlight facilities which we judged to have questionable patterns. These are the facilities on the watch lists noted in Appendix M.

Using the watch lists There may be facilities with problems that do not appear on our watch lists, which capture the problems particular nursing homes have had at one point in time. Other facilities may have developed problems after the period we examined. Should you avoid placing a relative in a facility that is on the watch list? That depends on other options you have and on other priorities. If a nursing home on the watch list is the only one in your area, you may have no choice. If the facility is very close to your home and you can easily get to it to keep an eye on your relative, that consideration may outweigh a troublesome history. The facility may have changed ownership or there may be a current survey report showing no deficiencies. In that case, take extra care to investigate the state surveys and the details behind the deficiencies cited. You may want to visit many times to satisfy yourself that the home will provide good care, or that it has improved.

What if your relative already lives in a facility on your state's watch list? Moving is usually not a good idea, since it is traumatic for the resident. Keep in close contact with the local ombudsman or local nursing home advocacy group to spot problems. Visit your relative often and raise questions when the care doesn't seem quite right.

Nursing facility waiting lists Believe it or not, some nursing homes have waiting lists for new residents. While a waiting list may be a way for facilities to hold out for potential residents who can pay privately rather than rely on Medicaid, they can also indicate a demand for good quality care. Ask about waiting lists when you visit the facility and see if the facility will give you names of families who are waiting. Contact them and compare notes on your shopping experiences.

THE UNANNOUNCED VISIT

After you have gathered data on several nursing homes, make an unannounced visit to each. You may want to make more than one visit at different times of the day. Visit in the morning, during a meal, and in the evening and on weekends when fewer staff members are around. Seeing a nursing home at different times will give you a better idea of what goes on there than one visit will. It is pretty easy to walk into nursing homes and look around. But remember, this is the residents' home and take care not to invade anyone's privacy. Sometimes you may be stopped and the facility may require that a staff member accompany you. If that's the case, simply say you are considering placement for your mother and want to see what the facility is like. Good facilities won't object to prospective families making their own visits. "We encourage people to come back without notice," says Joe Warner, president and chief executive officer of Heritage Enterprises, a chain of twenty-nine nursing homes located in central Illinois. What follows is a tour of a nursing home and what to look for along the way. Make notes of things you see using the following information as a guide. Discuss your findings with the facility administrator when you make your official visit. The sales pitch and marketing materials may not match reality.

Touring the Nursing Home

Lobby The lobby gives you your first clue about the facility. The first thing to look for is the state survey report. If you don't see it, ask. As noted, facilities frequently place the report in an inconspicuous place, making it difficult for outsiders (and those on the inside, for that matter) to examine. If the state survey is not readily available, that's a bad sign and you should be wary. It means the facility may have something to hide. Depending on other information you have collected about the place, you may want to move on to another nursing home and not waste time at a facility that hides its state survey.

If the survey is posted, and you continue the tour, look closely at residents sitting in wheelchairs. Are they strapped or tied into their chairs? Restraints are becoming passé in nursing homes, and you don't want to see residents tied down. Research shows that very few residents need restraints, and many facilities have instituted programs to become as restraint-free as possible. If you see many residents tied down or in chairs with trays that act as barriers, that's also a bad sign. In a few cases, a physician or the family may have ordered that the facility use a restraint, but that is rare.

Alternatives to ties, belts, vests, and bed rails require a staff dedicated to understanding residents' behavior and devising more humane ways of accommodating it. That takes time and creativity, and many homes have been unwilling to invest in either. If you see a lot of people restrained, you could ask about programs to eliminate restraints, or you can keep looking. A facility that has not figured out how to eliminate restraints may be one you don't want for your relative. Thirty-three percent of all facilities received a citation for using physical restraints during the period we studied.

The lobby should also be odor-free. If you notice strong urine odors or the thick scent of air fresheners that cover up unpleasant smells, that could be an indication of what you will find on your tour. High-quality homes have no lingering stench.

The lobby is a good place to talk to residents. If you visit in the middle of the day—late morning or in the afternoon—residents should be out and about. If you don't see any, find out where they are. Is everyone too sick to come out? Does the facility encourage them to leave their rooms? When you are chatting with the residents, try to learn if the staff is attentive to their needs. How long does it take to get help when they push the call button or pull the emergency cord? Does the staff take them to the bathroom when they need to go, or do they wait a long time and accidents result? Answers to that question tell much about the care in the facility.

You want the lobby to be attractive and clean, but don't be swayed by matching or fancy furniture. Pay little attention to the decor. Matching furniture, pleasing color schemes, and amenities like libraries and ice cream parlors may make family members comfortable with the idea of placing a relative in a nursing home, but they generally don't reveal much about the quality of care.

Dining room Pay close attention to the dining room. Plan at least one of your visits at mealtime and observe the residents and how they interact with staff. Are there a lot of residents eating together? Mealtime is often the highlight of the day, and you would want to see interaction among the residents as well as with the staff who serves the meals, helps residents cut their food, and in some cases helps them eat. What does the facility do to promote social interaction at mealtime? You wouldn't want to see a nearly empty dining room or a single resident either eating by herself or waiting for a meal. I have seen both. If residents drop or spill food, is it cleaned up quickly to prevent accidents?

Obviously, you should taste the food. Ask residents who can communicate if they like what they are served and if the food is served at the right temperature. Check the menus that are posted. Do they sound appetizing and appealing? How often does the facility rotate its menus so there is sufficient variety? Most facilities post their menus, but they may not always follow them. Eleven percent of all facilities received a deficiency for failing to follow their posted menus. Some skimp on bedtime snacks—a seemingly trivial point but one that is very important to residents who look forward to their snacks. Ten percent of facilities were cited for failing to provide three meals a day and snacks over their last four surveys.

Kitchen Most nursing homes won't let you tour the kitchen. But you certainly want to know whether food is prepared under sanitary conditions. Outbreaks of food-borne illnesses in nursing homes do occur, and sometimes facilities don't do a good job of providing meals.

Eleven percent did not plan and follow menus that meet residents' nutritional needs. Deficiencies related to storage, preparation, distribution, and serving food rank at the top of the ten most frequently cited nursing home deficiencies. Look for deficiencies related to food service that are noted on the state survey. If a facility has a pattern of food-related citations, find out from the administrator why these problems continue.

Patio and other outdoor space Having pleasant outdoor space is important, but if residents can't easily get to it, that's a problem. At one nursing home I saw a resident using a walker struggling to hold the door open to come in from the garden. At one in suburban Maryland, the door leading to the patio appeared much too small to accommodate a wheelchair. Look around and see how residents access the outdoor space. It is a definite minus if they have to wheel themselves through long halls and around many obstacles to get outside.

Activities room Each facility posts an activities calendar listing the activities and the time they are scheduled. Pick two or three you want to observe and come back. Usually they take place late morning or after lunch. It's crucial to observe some activities, for they offer a clue as to the kind of stimulation and social interaction your relative may receive. If after several visits all you see is a bored lineup of residents in front of the television set, you need to ask why the facility is failing to stimulate its residents. Ask them what they do, what works, and what doesn't.

Judge whether the activities appear innovative and interesting. At one Texas facility I saw women clearly enjoying a makeup session. They were having fun choosing and trying various colors of eye shadow and rouge. At a Maryland nursing home, residents gathered around a long table and intently watched a staff member demonstrate how to make crepes. Each resident got to eat one. They were having a good time, chatting with each other as well as the staff who stopped by to see how the activity was going. But at too many homes, activities are ordinary and sometimes not very stimulating or engaging.

When you do observe an activity, watch whether the residents are engaged and participating. Few people participating in a posted activity signals trouble. "When you see so few people, either they aren't encouraged to come, or the activity isn't exciting," says one social work student who has worked in one of New York City's fanciest nursing homes. "Residents should want to come out of their rooms unless they are depressed, and if that's the case, ask why." Talk to some of the residents about the activities. If they don't like what is offered, or say they don't participate, keep that point in mind to explore further with the facility's administrator.

Corridors Corridors are good places to observe life in a nursing home. After you move beyond the obvious—adequate lighting, user-friendly handrails—corridors reveal much about whether the facility provides good care. First of all, are they free of unpleasant odors? A good nursing home doesn't smell of either urine or disinfectant, which many facilities use to mask the odors. I visited one nursing home in New Orleans twice, and never smelled feces, urine, or disinfectant. That facility is a fine home in other aspects of its care as well. If you smell feces, it may indicate that the facility is not cleaning up quickly enough or that residents are not taken to the bathroom or cleaned up after an accident. Accidents happen in every nursing home, but how fast they are cleaned up is key to quality of care. If intense odors waft from rooms at 10 A.M., it could mean that the staff has not changed residents' diapers since the night before. Nursing homes that allow residents to sit in their own wastes for long periods are inviting trouble—skin breakdown that can lead to infection and even death. Look for evidence of this when you read the state survey report. If you find that the facility has been cited for not attending to the personal hygiene of its residents, pay close attention to smells and other evidence that indicates this is still a problem. Many people enter a nursing home continent but lose their ability to use the toilet soon afterward, usually because the staff fails to take them to the bathroom.

While you are inspecting the corridors, look for safety hazards. Mops and brooms propped against the handrails in the corridors, puddles of spilled orange juice, wet towels on the floor, and carts sitting idle are potential safety hazards to old people who have diminished eyesight and use walkers to get around. Such hazards indicate carelessness on the part of the facility and could signal other problems as well. Accidents rank high on the list of the ten most frequently cited deficiencies in nursing homes. Thirty-six percent of all nursing homes received a deficiency for failing to keep accident hazards to a minimum, and 25 percent have been cited for not providing adequate supervision to avoid accidents.

As you walk through the corridors, observe how well the staff treats residents. Corridors are good places to look for violations of residents' dignity. In many ways, maintaining the dignity of their residents is the most important task of a nursing home and one that most fail to do well. Thirty-one percent of the homes in the database we examined were cited for failing to respect the dignity of their residents.

You can observe a lack of respect for resident's dignity when you see staff wheeling people backwards, a fairly common occurrence in nursing homes. When you see people half naked either in their rooms or roaming the hallways, it indicates that staff has paid little attention to them. Poor grooming and dressing also indicate neglect. If residents are wearing soiled or ill-fitting clothes, have greasy hair and dirty fingernails, need a shave, or are inappropriately dressed for the season, don't put your relative among them. If it's winter and residents are wearing summer clothes, the facility may not be looking out for their best interests.

Corridors are also the place to observe how the staff relates to the residents—a crucial indicator of the quality of care. It's a bad sign if the interactions are rude and unpleasant. I have seen staff scream at residents. "Did you move your bowels today? You'd better," one aide shouted. "You can't get out," an aide at another home told a resident. In my many visits to nursing facilities, residents appeared starved for affection and a kind word, stretching out their hands to be touched. One wheelchair-bound resident at a Maryland facility was so grateful we talked to her. She said she had been a resident for a long time and was losing her eyesight and could no longer read. "Reading was such a pleasure," she said sadly. Does the staff take time to give residents like this woman a hug, hold their hands, or say something nice— something as simple as "You sure look pretty today." Or have they provided talking books?

At the excellent facility in New Orleans, staff members said hello to the residents, and the residents responded in kind. One woman struggled to maneuver her walker through the door leading to the patio. Two staff members quickly came to help. In the Alzheimer's unit, three staff members monitored nine or ten residents who were sitting in a room listening to music. One resident had just won a dollar playing bingo. The staff made a big deal about her winnings; in other words, they made her feel special. That's the kind of interaction you want to see. At this facility, the Maison Hospitalière, the supervising nurse volunteered that she had worked at the home for eight years—a remarkable achievement given that staff turnover is high, as much as 100 percent a year for nursing assistants at some facilities. She said that other staff members had also stayed a long time. "We get along," she said, "and we function like a team." That's what you want to see and hear.

Most likely, though, you won't find that kind of longevity or staff interaction. Maintaining staff is a big problem in nursing homes these days, and you will likely find high turnover and lack of continuity in most places. "Staffing problems are absolutely horrendous everywhere," says Virginia Fraser, the long-term-care ombudsman in Colorado. "Everyone across the country is pretty desperate." Nursing homes are having trouble hiring and retaining aides who can get better paying and more pleasant jobs elsewhere. Before this book went to press, the Health Care Financing Administration released a report showing that in three states, 54 percent of the nursing homes do not meet minimal staffing requirements for nurses' aides. The requirements call for a minimum of two hours of care per patient. This means you must pay close attention to the kind of care delivered by whatever staff is around and be extra vigilant once you place a relative in a facility. Look for signs of understaffing: lunch dishes visible at 4 P.M., residents ringing their call buttons repeatedly, residents calling out for an aide to take them to the bathroom, residents calling for help, dirt and debris on the floor.

Don't be bashful about talking to staff. Ask how many residents they care for. Is it too many or too few? Ask how the facility managers treat their workers. Is it a good company to work for? Does the company ask for their opinions? "A lot of times an employee will say a lot of things," says Joe Warner of Heritage Enterprises. If you get negative answers, that is a very bad sign; unhappy workers caring for your relative make for unhappy life in the facility. If they are unhappy, don't count on wonderful care. The aides may do only the minimum required and fail to give your relative any extra attention and care that would make life more pleasant. If top management cares about providing top-quality care, that goal will filter through its staff down to the aides who perform the most menial tasks. If the leaders don't care, neither will the staff.

Rooms As you walk through the corridors, peek inside the rooms. Do they smell? Have the beds been made? Are residents crying out for help? If you hear cries for assistance, hang around and record how long it takes for staff to respond. A long wait might indicate severe staffing problems or plain, old negligence. Be careful, though, about invading residents' privacy. Think before looking and consider what information peering into someone's room will yield.

Look for barriers and signs of abuse. At one facility in California, an aide had placed the bed at an angle in such a way that it prevented the resident from escaping, apparently what the aide had in mind. At a facility in suburban Washington, D.C., I looked into a room and saw a woman with Kleenex stuffed in her mouth. She appeared to be in distress. When an aide saw me look in, she quickly closed the door.

Look for obvious signs of physical abuse—scratches, bruises, cuts, swelling, burns. Sometimes you will see residents with black and blue marks on their faces and bodies. Did they fall because no one was watching, or was their skin fragile? Try to find out. Look for signs of pressure sores—sores on the skin that can be fatal if they are not treated properly. Pressure sores are a big problem in nursing homes, and state inspectors have given repeated deficiencies to some homes for not preventing and treating them. Some 35 percent of all homes received a deficiency from state inspectors for allowing pressure sores to develop, or for failing to give necessary treatment.

You can't peek under the covers or lift up a lap robe to see if a resident has pressure sores that have been left to fester and bleed. You have no way of knowing whether residents are turned or moved frequently enough to prevent sores from forming. But you can look for such signs as residents with foot pads or elbow pads, or residents lying in bed with their feet suspended. These signs could mean that the facility is treating the sores or is taking precautions to prevent them. Also, as you see residents throughout the facility, look for sores on their legs and arms.

If you see evidence of pressure sores, check the survey report to see if the facility has been cited for failing to treat them. You will also want to discuss this with the administrator when you make your announced or official visit to the facility. Some residents already have pressure sores when they enter a facility, and sometimes they are hard to treat. The facility may try to claim it is not responsible for problems people had before they came.

Nevertheless, if you see any evidence of pressure sores, that's a sign to thoroughly investigate the facility. Check the state surveys for deficiencies that might relate to pressure sores—failure to provide adequate nutrition (patients need adequate protein to help sores heal), residents allowed to sit in their own wastes for long periods of time, and failure to treat the sores themselves.

How the rooms look is also important. You want to see evidence that residents have personalized their rooms with touches from their former homes. Look for pictures, furniture, family mementos. If you see these items, it could indicate the facility encourages residents to bring such things from home. At a facility in San Antonio, Texas, room after room was appointed with residents' chairs, dressers, plants, books, curtains, and bedspreads. It was quite a contrast to the hospital-like rooms found in most nursing homes. One resident was so proud of his room, he wanted me to come see it. It was obvious this facility was his home. If on your first unannounced visit you see little evidence of a resident's former life, that is something to probe with the facility administrator.

Look for evidence that the staff is doing what are called range-of-motion exercises with residents. Residents must walk, move their bodies and limbs to function properly and prevent pressure sores. Aides should be walking residents or helping them to move their arms and legs. Again, if you see little of that going on, note it for discussion with the administrator.

Stairs and elevators Make sure residents are unable to push their wheelchairs through stairwells. Doors leading to stairwells should be locked and accessible only to staff. Are elevators large enough to accommodate wheelchairs and are buttons low enough for someone who is wheelchair-bound to reach?

THE ANNOUNCED VISIT

After you make two or three visits to the facility incognito, it's time to ask for an official appointment with the administrator. He or she may give an additional tour. By all means go and question the administrator about what you see. The official visit is also the time to inquire about the findings from your unannounced visits. Ask about:

- Any deficiencies that appeared on the state survey that indicate poor quality of care or any deficiencies that gave you concern.
- The number of residents who are incontinent, and of that number, the proportion who were incontinent when they arrived.

Ask for the number of residents who are involved in a regular program to maintain continence. Consider the answers you get in light of the smells you encounter. Unpleasant odors and no program to take residents to the bathroom equal problems with continence. Similarly, vague answers should make you think twice before placing a relative.

- The number of residents confined with restraints. These days restraints in nursing homes are taboo, and good, enlightened facilities have programs to eliminate their use. One Maryland nursing home I visited proudly displayed on a public bulletin board the results of its campaign to end the use of restraints. If you see a lot of residents in restraints, and the facility has no plan to eliminate them, keep searching.

- Specifically ask about the proportion of residents who have pressure sores and find out how many had them before coming to the facility. What is the facility doing to treat them? As I have noted, pressure sores are extremely serious and the way a facility cares for residents who have them is a strong indicator of the quality of care it delivers. Thirty-five percent of all facilities have been cited for failing to treat pressure sores.

- Probe the administrator's philosophy of care and how he or she respects residents' dignity and communicates that philosophy to the staff. Good care starts at the top, and in my travels it was evident why some nursing homes were better than others—top management cared about the residents. Ask what happens if they see staff whisking someone backwards in a wheelchair. What do they do to show the residents affection? Ask what the administrator is doing to hire and retain competent staff.

- Try to find out something about the facility's finances. Is it part of a large chain? Has it recently been bought or sold? Is it likely to change hands soon? The nursing home business is not static, and changes in ownership are common. Stability may mean that care is better. A facility about to be sold may be a problem nursing home. Likewise one recently purchased may be trying to improve, but it may still have lingering problems.

- Ask about staff turnover, particularly how long the director of nursing has been on the job, how long the staff usually stays, how long the administrator stays. Ask about their predecessors. If there seems to be high turnover, that could indicate problems with the facility or its owners. Also find out if the facility has changed owners. Ask why new owners have taken it over. What were the problems under the old management?

During your visit with the administrator, the issue of care plans and money inevitably arises. Even if you use all the tools I have described and find the best home, the nursing facility may not want to accept your relative depending on how you or your relative will pay for care.

WHO PAYS

Medicaid pays for about half of all stays in nursing homes. Families finance the remainder, paying out of their own pockets. Long-term-care insurance covers a tiny amount—about 2 percent of all stays. Chances are if your relative stays a long time, Medicaid will step in. Among CONSUMER REPORTS readers, 43 percent reported in the 1997 survey that a relative in a nursing home had spent down and required financial support from Medicaid within the first six months they were in the facility. Chapter 13 details how a Medicaid spend-down works.

Medicare pays for some care in nursing homes if a person requires skilled-nursing care. Such care may be required after a hospitalization for an acute illness, say, major surgery or after a stroke. But as other chapters point out, this benefit is limited, and you should never count on it to pay for a long stay. Nevertheless, you may find some nursing facilities that want only residents for whom Medicare will pay the bill. Those facilities are no doubt aiming their services at people who need posthospital care. They operate what are called subacute wings—special floors or areas that are designated for people needing hospital-level care.

Some of these facilities turn away prospective residents who are likely to start out needing support from Medicaid or who will need it in the very near future. You may encounter these facilities as you do your shopping. If your relative is not a candidate for subacute care or will need Medicaid assistance right away, you may have little choice but to look at nursing homes that will take Medicaid recipients at the outset.

Some facilities prefer new residents who can pay privately for a few months, and they make their own rules for selection. Some may require new residents to pay one month, six months, nine months, or even a year out of their own funds before they will accept them.

Others may require that your relative pay privately at least for some period of time in order to get a private room. Still others may take only those who have not used many of their allotted days of skilled-nursing care available from Medicare. As Chapter 2 points out, Medicare pays for only one hundred days of care in a skilled-nursing facility. Most people use on average fifty-seven days. If someone has many unused days, he or she may be more attractive to a facility that will be able to look to Medicare reimbursement, which is often more generous than Medicaid's.

If your relative begins to pay privately or needs skilled-nursing care reimbursed by Medicare, it's a good idea to learn about the facility's payment policy once private funds or Medicare reimbursement runs out. Does the nursing home ask residents to leave, or does it agree to accept Medicaid payment eventually, and when? See if you can pin this point down in writing. In some states, Medicaid reimbursement might be skewed toward residents who need the heaviest care—that is, the facility may prefer residents who need a lot of attention because they will get more money from the state to care for them. If that's the case, you may find some nursing homes will turn you down if your relative needs light care.

EXTRA CHARGES

If you pay privately, you must look beyond the nursing home's stated daily rate to the bundle of extra charges that the facility will bill each month. The daily rate gives no clue about the total cost when a facility loads on the extras. Typically, facilities charge extra (and exorbitantly) for supplies such as diapers, catheter tubes, and rubber gloves, as well as for special services like incontinence care, pressure-sore treatment, hand or tube feeding, even turning and positioning. Doing laundry also generates a separate charge.

Physical, occupational, and speech therapy cost extra, too. Prices are usually quoted as price per unit of treatment, which often lasts fifteen minutes. At those prices, it's not hard to see how therapy is beyond the means of those families who must pay for these services on their own. Families often complain that they are not able to continue therapy after Medicare stops paying. Even if you find cheaper therapy services, a facility might not allow you to bring your own therapist into the nursing home. A few years ago the U.S. General

Accounting Office found "widespread examples of overcharges to Medicare for therapy services" delivered by rehabilitation companies and nursing homes. The GAO noted that "extraordinary markups" for therapy services result when providers exploit ambiguities in the regulatory system and weaknesses in Medicare's payment rules.

Prescription drugs are another profit center at nursing homes. Drugs and other supplies residents need carry high markups, and families are often captives of the nursing homes and pharmaceutical outlets connected with them. Sometimes they charge more than suppliers you could find on your own would charge.

Some facilities even make it difficult to use cheaper suppliers. Instead, they require that you use pharmaceutical outlets with whom they have relationships. If you are shopping for a facility, find out where and how you get supplies. Figure out what you will need—supplies, medications, extra services—and ask the facility what it would charge each month for this bundle of extras. If the facility will not allow you to purchase items from a cheaper place, you may have to factor this into your selection decision. If, for other reasons, you must choose a facility that refuses to let you buy supplies on the outside, consider taking the matter to the family council. Look for allies among other families and demand the right to purchase drugs and other supplies outside the nursing home.

THE NEED FOR MEDICARE AND MEDICARE-SUPPLEMENT INSURANCE

A stay in a nursing home doesn't mean that your relative won't need to have coverage from Medicare either through an HMO or through the traditional program. Even if your relative will be paying for long-term care with private funds, you will still need a way to pay for any acute illnesses that may arise. It's probably best to keep whatever arrangements are already in place rather than look for new insurance policies or a new HMO. That cuts down on the stress associated with moving a loved one to a facility.

As Chapter 9 notes, a relatively new program called EverCare, sponsored by UnitedHealthcare, a managed-care organization based in Minneapolis, tries to keep seniors from going to the hospital. This program provides Medicare benefits to residents in nursing homes. Like many HMOs, it has a strong preventive care component.

EverCare uses a network of nurse-practitioners to regularly visit its members living in nursing homes. They try to spot small health problems before they develop into big serious ones that require hospitalization. Compared to other HMOs serving Medicare beneficiaries, EverCare ranks in the middle of our Ratings in Appendix G, largely because it offers no prescription drug benefits. However, other advantages may be worth the trade-off.

If Medicaid pays for your relative's stay, then Medicaid will pay the bills for most of the health care that's needed. It usually doesn't pay for eyeglasses, hearing aids, and dental care. In that case, you won't need to continue paying premiums for the supplemental policy. Medicaid covers the cost of prescriptions in most states, so once your relative spends down, one big expense is usually taken care of.

See if your state has a program for nursing home residents who are eligible for both Medicare and Medicaid. Such programs can reduce inefficiencies that come with being eligible for two different programs. Use Chapter 9 as a starting point.

THE CARE PLAN

The care plan is vital to the quality of life and care your relative will receive in the nursing home. When someone enters a nursing home, federal law requires the facility to complete an assessment that measures the individual's physical, mental, and social abilities. The facility must also draft a care plan, a blueprint that outlines such things as physical and speech therapy, range-of-motion exercises, appropriate activities, and nutrition required for proper functioning. The care plan sets the goals that should enable a resident to reach the highest practical level of functioning.

"It's not easy to translate the plan into action," says Cynthia Rudder, director of the Nursing Home Community Coalition of New York. "That is something families have to keep watch on." Thirteen percent of all facilities in the Health Care Financing Administration database were cited at least once during their last four surveys for failing to develop sufficient care plans. Two percent, or about three hundred homes, were cited twice. That's a pretty poor track record.

To help prevent the nursing facility from neglecting the care plan for your relative, you must be involved in the planning from the very beginning. Families and residents are supposed to be part of the care planning meeting, but, says Rudder, "Residents often don't have relatives present at the meetings." Make sure you are at the initial meeting along with your relative if he or she is able to participate. Care plans are revised monthly. Try to be at the meetings where the plan is reviewed and revised. That is the time to speak up if your relative is not getting the care specified in the original plan.

If the plan requires your relative to be walked two times a day or taken to the bathroom every two hours, you or your family might have to assume the role of policeman to be sure that it is done. Families must also follow up to make sure that the aides who are supposed to give the care are part of the meetings. Too many times the care plan may say walk the person ten feet down the hall, but the aides don't do it. The aides may not even know it should be done.

If the state survey report notes that the facilities you are considering have failed to devise care plans or have failed to implement them, it is a signal that you will have to be especially watchful over the care your relative receives.

ENSURING GOOD CARE

Frequent visits are crucial to good care. Nursing home personnel know which residents have family members who visit and which ones are neglected. Neglecting your relative could invite the facility to do the same. Good homes have family councils and residents councils. Get involved and have your relative get involved. Through these councils, you can often make your wishes known and monitor the quality of care that is delivered.

Nursing home advocates say that too many times families as well as residents are afraid to speak up when the care is not good. Family members hesitate to complain for fear the facility will retaliate against their relative, and residents are afraid because they don't want to rock the boat and are at the mercy of the staff for care they need. There's no guarantee there won't be retaliation, but without complaints there won't be any changes either.

If the care is not satisfactory, or you suspect your relative is being abused, and the facility won't listen to you or make changes, seek help from the long-term-care ombudsman. Every nursing home is supposed to post the name and the telephone number of the local ombudsman. You can also call your state ombudsman listed in Appendix O and ask who handles problems and complaints in your area.

WHEN YOUR RELATIVE GOES TO THE HOSPITAL

Sometimes nursing home residents must leave their facility and go to an acute-care hospital for illnesses that develop at the nursing home. Obviously, such admissions are difficult for seniors. They may be even more difficult if the hospital stay is for a prolonged period.

Many states require facilities to hold beds for residents for a certain length of time. Bed-holding periods range from zero to fifteen days. If residents stay longer, there may be no bed for them when they're ready to return. Some states are trying to shorten these bed-hold periods as a way to reduce their Medicaid costs. Be sure you know what your nursing home allows. Federal law requires that a nursing home readmit a resident when the next bed becomes available. Of course, that could mean you will have to scramble to find another nursing home in the meantime.

KEY DECISION POINTS

1. Investigate nursing homes long before your relative needs one.

2. Obtain state surveys and read them carefully. They may be your best guide to the quality of care delivered in the facility.

3. Contact the local ombudsman.

4. Use other tools, including the Watch List and State Detection Index developed by CONSUMER REPORTS, to help you select a nursing home.

5. Don't let a hospital discharge planner make your decisions.

6. Tour a nursing home several times at different times of the day, and make notes about what you observe.

7. Have a frank discussion with the administrator. Make him or her explain poor survey results and troublesome areas you find during your unannounced visits.

8. Talk to residents. Ask them what life is like for them. Ask how the facility treats them.

9. If you or your relative pays privately, be sure to find out how much all the extra services, supplies, and medications will cost. Can you buy these from your own suppliers? If not, you may want to consider another facility.

10. Once your relative becomes a resident, involve yourself in the initial care plan and attend all monthly care plan meetings. Speak up when care is poor or even mediocre.

11. Don't be shy about involving the long-term-care ombudsman if you have a problem. Third-party intervention is sometimes helpful.

TWELVE

Care at the End of Life

Eighty-four-year-old Ida Baltimore was dying. An aggressive form of thyroid cancer was wiping out what had been a good retirement from her job as assistant director of nursing at a New York City hospital. Initially, Baltimore took radiation and chemotherapy treatments, but after finishing eighteen of the thirty that were required, she decided to call it quits. Her skin curled up and burned, and she couldn't swallow. "I said *que sera, sera,*" she recalled, and agreed to go to a facility for dying cancer patients.

But as she was packing up her life, a social worker suggested that she stay home and sign up for Medicare's hospice benefit that would provide a variety of support services. She did. Even though the benefit is limited to people who have six months or less to live, Baltimore has been recertified twice. Her condition stabilized, enabling her to stay in her apartment, get out to the grocery store with a walker, which she called her "Cadillac," and live as normal a life as possible.

With the hospice benefit, Baltimore received all her medications, as well as visits from a social worker, a registered nurse, a chaplain, a music therapist, and a home health aide who came five days a week from 9 A.M. to 1 P.M. These professionals tended to all her spiritual, emotional, and physical needs. "I like the team approach and the individual interest shown by the people who come to visit," she said. "I am always pleased and uplifted when they come." At the end of one visit, Baltimore gave her nurse a big hug. "You are my mainstay," she told her.

Baltimore needed to talk about her past. She had been a professional woman, a highly respected African-American nurse at a time when it was difficult for women of her race to move ahead. Baltimore was also fearful—scared of being alone as her disability increased, scared of being unable to eat.

"Part of the hospice process is giving someone space and freedom and a safe place to work through issues at the end of life," said Eileen Diaz, the nurse who supervised Baltimore's care. "Hospice helps people recap their lives."

Perhaps because Baltimore had once been a bedside nurse, she knew the ordeal of a high-tech death in a hospital. Perhaps she knew what it was like to die heavily medicated with all kinds of tubes and equipment needed to keep life going a little longer. In any case, hospice was a good choice for her as it is for thousands of other dying patients who may not be lucky enough to know about the benefit.

Only a small number of people use this benefit. In 1997, 374,723 beneficiaries used the hospice benefit. "The alternative of hospice is not understood. It's a major alternative to a high-tech hospital or Dr. Kevorkian," says Jack Gordon, director of the Hospice Foundation. Dr. Jeffrey Kahn, director of the Center for Bioethics at the University of Minnesota, puts it this way: "If we could make people pain-free and comfortable, there will be less demand for people to kill themselves. People need to know more about hospice and good palliative care." A study funded by the Robert Wood Johnson Foundation revealed that the vast majority of people die alone, hooked up to machines, and in great pain.

WHAT IS HOSPICE?

Hospice is a philosophy of care that prepares people for the ending of life. It embraces the notion that with enough support—social, emotional, and spiritual—people can die in the setting of their choice with enough appropriate pain and symptom management. The goal is to make a patient's last days comfortable enough that he or she can continue to carry on the normal activities of daily living. Hospice care is not curative, and much of what it does is provide support for family members so they can manage the last days of their loved one. It does not try to lengthen life or make death come more quickly, but instead focuses on the quality of life that remains.

The first hospice in the United States began in 1973 in Connecticut, and since then the movement has grown to embrace three thousand hospice programs, one in almost every large community. Contrary to what you may think, a hospice is not necessarily a freestanding building like a hospital or a nursing facility. In fact, only a few programs have buildings attached to them. Rather, hospice is a program that embraces an array of services that are brought into a dying person's home—whether that home is in a nursing facility or an assisted-living facility.

Hospice care is the opposite philosophy of care embraced by most U.S. hospitals. That philosophy makes use of every possible procedure (including those that are experimental) whether or not they are likely to save or prolong life. "It's easier to call in the VNA [Visiting Nurse Association] than face the truth," says Paul Brenner, who directs the Jacob Perlow Hospice at New York's Beth Israel Medical Center. "Doctors haven't been trained to be truth tellers. The patient feels abandoned and the blame goes to the patient for failing the treatment. The medical system doesn't recognize that the treatment failed the patient."

MEDICARE'S HOSPICE BENEFIT

If hospice is a philosophy of care, Medicare's hospice benefit is the reimbursement system that sustains it. Indeed, it is the major reimbursement system for people desiring hospice care at the end of life. While people can pay out of pocket for hospice services, most elderly do not; they turn to Medicare. The Medicare benefit, however, comes with some tough rules—rules that may have hampered more widespread use of the benefit. These days most people are referred to hospice care within seven days of death. This may mean that they have been deprived of supportive care that could have made their last days somewhat easier.

Eligibility To be eligible for the benefit, your doctor and the hospice medical director must certify that you or a relative you are advising have six months or less to live. This requirement makes it difficult to take advantage of hospice services, since it is not always possible to predict exactly how long someone will live. People live many years with chronic, debilitating illnesses. Sometimes beneficiaries don't die "on time," but if they are alive after six months, Medicare allows recertification of the benefit, as in Ida Baltimore's case.

To be eligible for the Medicare benefit, you must also be enrolled in Medicare Part A and certify in writing that you would prefer pain and symptom management rather than curative treatments. In essence, you must agree to give up standard Medicare benefits for your illness and treatments for the disease.

Services With this benefit, you get all the standard Medicare services described in Chapter 2, but Medicare won't pay for services that are considered treatments for your disease. If you need treatments for some other health conditions, Medicare will pay. You can revoke the hospice benefit at any time and return to the regular Medicare program.

A major benefit of Medicare's hospice program is coverage for nearly all the costs for prescription medication needed for pain relief and symptoms of your disease. Beneficiaries pay 5 percent or $5 toward each prescription, whichever is less. This can be a great help to families struggling to cover the cost of prescriptions for very sick relatives. As Chapter 2 points out, Medicare does not cover the cost of outpatient prescription drugs. Indeed, hospice is the only option that affords coverage for drugs people need at the end of life.

Another important part of the hospice benefit is respite care. Medicare pays the bills for stays in hospital and other care facilities so family caregivers can get a rest from the demanding task of looking after someone about to die. States have few programs that cover respite care, so in considering the potential need for this benefit, look at whether your state has programs for respite care (see Appendix L).

Hospice staff and volunteers provide help with activities of daily living, eating, bathing, and dressing. They also administer pain medications, arrange for medical equipment, various therapies, and transportation to medical appointments. They may help with household chores and financial matters, and provide a shoulder for family members to lean on. The hospice may also arrange visits from clergymen, social workers, and even music therapists if they can help a patient live comfortably during the last days.

In sum, hospice takes care of most services and expenses people need at the end of life. One man whose wife was using the hospice benefit said that the greatest gift of hospice was that the bills stopped coming to his house.

Most hospice programs provide up to one year of bereavement counseling and support for families.

What if you're a member of an HMO? The benefit is the same whether you are enrolled in traditional Medicare and have a Medicare-supplement policy or you are a member of an HMO. Managed-care organizations, however, may not be eager to tell you about the benefit. Nor are they eager to advertise that hospice is part of the benefit package it sells to Medicare beneficiaries. "They don't want to have a large number of people who may later need the benefit sign up," says Dr. Kathleen Foley, director of the Project on Death in America sponsored by the Open Society Institute.

If you are in an HMO and later choose the hospice benefit, you do not need approval from the HMO to obtain it. You or your relatives can contact the hospice directly to sign up for the program, and you do not have to use a hospice the HMO recommends. If a person is already receiving hospice care, he or she cannot join an HMO.

CHOOSING A HOSPICE PROGRAM

There are some three thousand hospice programs in the United States. The National Hospice Organization has a list of them. Call 1-800-658-8898 or the Hospice Foundation at 1-800-854-3402 to get one. You can also contact the state hospice association listed in Appendix Q.

Not all the programs are identical. "There's variation in quality and supervision," explains Dr. Joanne Lynn, director of the Center to Improve Care of the Dying at George Washington University. If you live in an area served by more than one, you might want to investigate two or three before making a choice for a relative.

Ask the following questions, and be sure you are comfortable with the answers.

Is the hospice licensed by the state and certified by Medicare to provide care? Most states require hospices to be licensed, and the Health Care Financing Administration requires certification of programs that serve Medicare beneficiaries. Most licensing and certification programs don't speak to the quality of care delivered, so you should not consider this assurance that your relative will be well cared for. It does, however, assure that some outside party has at least looked at the program. The Joint Commission for Accreditation of Health Care Organizations accredits some programs, but like most accreditation programs, it, too, doesn't guarantee that you will get a quality program.

Where is inpatient and respite care provided? Does the hospice use hospitals that are easily accessible to relatives and friends who may want to visit? It does little good to sign up for a program that sends patients to a hospital miles from where you live. Which nursing homes do they use? While you may have every intention of keeping a relative at home, the reality is that at the end of life, home care may not be feasible. If a nursing home is required, which homes does the hospice have contracts with? Are they nearby?

Does the hospice provide extra services, like massage or music therapy? Sometimes these extras can make the difference in quality of life to a dying patient.

What is the program's "on call" policy? In other words, whom do you reach when there is an emergency? Do you reach the staff or an answering service? Obviously, it is better if you can reach a staff person twenty-four hours a day who can direct you to services, send out volunteers, or help obtain medical treatment. If the hospice assumes round-the-clock care, is a doctor always available day or night? Who supervises the emergency calls that come in—a professional staff person or a triage nurse? Where do you get assistance when the office is closed?

What does the hospice expect from you and your caregiver support system? What are its rules, and what kind of services does the family have to provide?

What is the hospice's policy on resuscitation, giving fluids to sustain life, and antibiotics for secondary infections? If you are not comfortable with its positions on these matters, look for another program.

What are the out-of-pocket expenses you are likely to incur? If you or your relative cannot pay for them, does the hospice have a sliding fee schedule or provide services through a charitable-care fund? What happens if you can't pay?

Is there a support program for caregivers? These can be invaluable to those coping with a dying relative. How does the hospice connect with you?

What about keeping doctors and caregivers, such as home care aides, that you already have? Can you keep them even though their fees may be paid by another funding source? For some people, giving up home health aides is traumatic and may be one reason why hospice care may not work for you.

ALTERNATIVES TO HOSPICE

Hospice, of course, is just one alternative to care at the end of life. Others include:

Home care that you pay for or is covered by a state program Many people choose this alternative even though it may not necessarily result in the best quality of life at the end. With home care you may receive nursing services, but nursing care that treats your disease may not be what you want. Nurses' aides may take care of your physical needs, but home care won't supply the supportive services that hospice does.

Home health care is also very expensive, especially if twenty-four-hour care is required. Even if your state has a program that covers some visits by home health aides, you or your relatives may have to pay part of the bill. Do a quick calculation of how much it is likely to cost to employ a home health aide for six months. Add in the cost of prescription drugs that will be needed for pain management. Compare that total to the out-of-pocket expenses you are likely to have with hospice. Remember, hospice includes coverage for prescription drugs.

On the other hand, if your relative has been comfortable with home health aides, joining a hospice could be traumatic. It may mean switching caregivers. You will have to weigh familiarity and comfort with current caregivers against a more humane and supportive approach and a cheaper way to pay for care.

Nursing home placement Nursing homes, too, focus on keeping people alive. State laws require that if patients need feeding tubes or other kinds of life-sustaining interventions, nursing homes must provide them. Such interventions may be contrary to what you or your relative desires at the end of life.

Hospice care can be delivered in a nursing home, and about one-quarter of all nursing homes have a relationship with a hospice program. "A nursing home that enters into a contract with a hospice is an indication of concern for quality care," says Paul Brenner of the Jacob Perlow Hospice. If you are considering a nursing home for a relative, ask about its connections to hospice programs in the area.

Assisted suicide The downsides and legal ramifications of this alternative are obvious. This volume will not delve into them.

Pain management and palliative care Another alternative is to select pain management and palliative care that might be given in a special palliative-care unit at a hospital. Most hospitals don't have these, since there is no official government reimbursement for this kind of care. Palliative treatment can involve medication to relieve pain and other symptoms such as nausea and vomiting. Ask your doctor or hospital about this alternative.

PREPARING FOR THE END OF LIFE

The best time to prepare for the end of life is long before death is imminent. This means that adult children should approach the subject with aged parents and make sure that their wishes are known and spelled out. It also means doing some deep soul-searching to see how you want to live your last days. Taking these steps means staying in control even when you are very ill.

The most important question to ask is what kind of life you want at the end. To answer that, you must confront such issues as where you want to live and who you want to provide care and services. Do you want a life governed by medical treatment schedules, or do you want to set your own priorities? Do you want to maximize your time at the end of life with loved ones? Do you want time to say good-bye? Then ask yourself who are the best providers to accomplish your desires for the end of your life, and put a plan in place to make sure your wishes are carried out.

Planning for the end of life also involves drawing up "advance directives," which are sometimes called health care declarations. These include living wills, health care proxies, and anatomical gifts.

Living Wills

A living will is a declaration that if you should become terminally ill, you do not want any extraordinary measures taken to prolong life. It gives guidance to family members and the health care professionals caring for you. If you don't want them to use expensive, high-tech technology to keep you alive, then the living will is the place to make those desires known.

With a living will, you can specify which medical procedures you want and don't want. For example, if you don't want to be on a respirator or have experimental procedures done to you, you can say that. You can also say what you do want done; for example, do you want food and water or drugs to alleviate pain, or none of them. You may not want antibiotics to treat secondary infections. Withholding food and water is a gray area, but most states allow you to state your wishes regarding feeding.

Just because you have a living will doesn't mean that your wishes will be carried out. You may not be able to participate in the medical decisions that will be made, and doctors and family members may want to keep you alive. I recommend that you write a living will; courts often look upon one as an expression of intent in right-to-die cases.

You can write your own living will on forms provided by Choice in Dying, Inc. (1035 30th Street, N.W., Washington, DC 20007, 202-338-9790, or 475 Riverside Drive, Room 1852, New York, NY 10115, 212-870-2003). The will must be dated and witnessed by two people who are not family members and who do not stand to inherit your estate. In some states, the signatures may have to be notarized. Give copies to your spouse, other family members, and physician. Keep a copy among your personal papers, but not in a safe-deposit box—no one but you can get into it. You can always revoke a living will and change it as time goes on.

Health Care Proxies

A health care proxy gives someone else the authority to make health care decisions for you when you cannot. The powers can be as broad or as limited as you choose. The person you designate as the proxy can tell your doctor not to resuscitate you, or withhold certain treatments or even pain-relieving drugs. You can also instruct your agent to take you home to die, and if you choose to remain on life support machines, the agent can make those wishes known to the medical team that is caring for you.

The person you choose as your proxy is usually legally bound to carry out your wishes, although some states may have rules that can contradict your proxy. In New York, for example, a person acting as an agent can order a doctor not to administer food or drink only if he or she has knowledge of your wishes on the subject that were expressed in a living will.

To execute a health care proxy, obtain forms from Choice in Dying, Inc. You must carefully discuss your wishes with the person you choose as your proxy, and make sure he or she is comfortable with the assignment. Some people you approach may not be up to the task and ask you to pick someone else. You should also contact an attorney who can give advice on your state's rules. For an attorney specializing in elder care, contact the National Academy of Elder Law Attorneys (520-881-4005). Once your document is prepared, have your signature witnessed by two people. The person who will act as your agent should not be among them. Give copies to your agent, your family members, and your physician.

It's best to execute both a living will and a health care proxy. The former is an expression of your wishes at the end of life. The latter directs someone to carry them out.

Anatomical Gifts

If you wish to make a gift of your organs, the easiest way to make that known is to follow the instructions on your driver's license. This usually means signing the card and asking two people to witness the signature. If your state does not use the driver's license procedure, obtain a card from the United Network for Organ Sharing (P.O. Box 13770, Richmond, VA 23225-8770, 1-800-243-6667). Once you have signed the card, carry it with you at all times. Be sure to tell your family members and doctors who will first learn of your death that you have signed such a card.

You can also wear a metal tag engraved with the words *Organ Donor,* or register at any of the several central organ-donor registries that coordinate anatomical gifts and keep records of potential donors. Appendix R lists them.

KEY DECISION POINTS

1. Consider hospice care as an alternative to more conventional home care arrangements. It is likely to be cheaper for you and your family and offer more services.

2. Think about hospice far in advance and investigate two or three programs so you'll know what they offer and the differences among them.

3. Make sure you or your relative has executed a living will and has chosen a health care proxy. Without a living will, your family will not know what your wishes are and neither will the health care providers who will treat you.

4. Carefully consider what you want at the end of life. Define your goals, and take steps to make sure they are implemented.

PART 3

PAYING FOR LONG-TERM CARE

Half of all women and a third of all men who are now sixty-five will spend their last years in a nursing home at an annual cost of $40,000 or more. Currently there is no federal entitlement program similar to Medicare that pays long-term-care expenses for the elderly. Some people pay their entire nursing home bill with their savings. Others begin to pay with their own savings, then turn to Medicaid when the money runs out. Still others rely on Medicaid from the beginning.

Nursing home patients and their families currently pay about half the $80 billion annual tab for nursing home care. Medicare pays for 2 percent of all nursing home stays, and private insurance policies pay for about 1 percent. Medicaid, the federal–state program that pays medical expenses for the poor, covers most of the rest.

If you have a relative who may soon need long-term care, the chapter on Medicaid offers guidance on how the program works and what your relative must do to qualify. If you have time to plan for your own eventual long-term care, the chapter on long-term-care insurance gives advice on picking a policy and what coverages you should buy.

THIRTEEN

How Medicaid Pays for Long-Term Care

During their forty-eight years of marriage, Harold and Dolores M. had managed to save a small nest egg of $150,000, mostly made up of General Electric stock. Harold had worked at GE; his wife, a schoolteacher, gave up her career to raise three children. After Harold retired, they had a total income of $2,395—his Social Security benefit of $1,050, his pension from GE of $820, and her Social Security benefit of $525. With that income, they were able to maintain a modest home valued at about $75,000.

A few years ago Harold suffered a massive stroke and survived, but he needed full-time care in a nursing home. After Medicare paid for one hundred days of skilled-nursing care in the facility, Dolores had to pay the $195 daily charge.

Dolores applied for Medicaid, but was told she first had to spend $75,180 of the family savings on nursing care to reach New York's maximum allowable asset limit, which was then $74,820. The couple's combined income was also over the income limit, then $2,019 a month, so Dolores had to contribute $281 each month to the cost of Harold's care.

She completed the spend-down and became eligible for Medicaid in February 1999. A few weeks later Harold suffered another stroke and died. Dolores is now left with about $69,000 and a Social Security widow's benefit of $1,050 a month. She cannot afford to maintain her home on an annual income of about $12,000.

Her predicament is typical of that faced by families who have had a spouse in a nursing home. In order for Medicaid to pay, Dolores had to practically impoverish herself. Her situation was made worse because of the way New York State interprets the Medicaid rules. Her children stepped in to help. Other widows are not as lucky.

Medicaid is a government program that pays medical bills for people who are poor. It also pays for about half of all nursing home costs in the United States—some $40 billion each year. So unless you or your relative are very wealthy, chances are Medicaid will pay for some part of your long-term care. Most likely that care will be given in a nursing home, but it may also be given at home, and in some states, Medicaid might pay for care in adult day care centers.

Medicaid is an extraordinarily complex program. Ask anyone who has applied, and they'll relate horror stories of long, complicated applications, long waits, and insensitive personnel. This chapter won't help you avoid those problems, but it will provide an overview of the program, how crucial features of it work, and what you need to do to qualify for coverage.

The federal and state governments share the cost for Medicaid. (In a few states, local governments also participate in the cost.) The federal government pays at least 50 percent of each state's Medicaid budget, and states (and local governments) fund the rest, usually out of general tax revenues. States administer the program within broad federal guidelines. In all states, people receiving Aid to Families with Dependent Children (AFDC) or Supplemental Security Income (SSI) from the Social Security Administration are eligible for Medicaid, usually on an automatic basis. These people are considered "categorically" needy. Most states cover "medically needy" people who have some income but are still considered poor. If you are not poor but eventually need Medicaid's help to pay for long-term nursing care, you'll most likely qualify under the medically needy program in your state.

In the nineteen states that don't have a program for the medically needy, in 2000 you cannot qualify for Medicaid nursing home assistance at all if your income exceeds $1,536 a month even if your income doesn't cover the cost of a nursing home. To qualify in those states—known as "income cap" states—people with incomes slightly above the cap can set up a special type of irrevocable trust, sometimes called a Miller trust, to receive and disburse the income. Medicaid

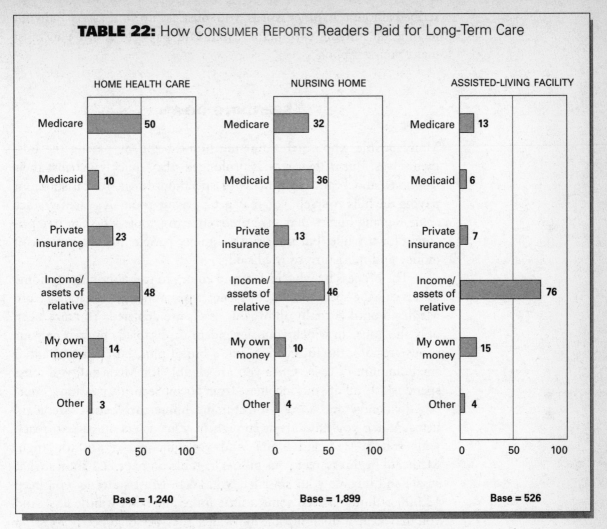

TABLE 22: How CONSUMER REPORTS Readers Paid for Long-Term Care

HOME HEALTH CARE

Medicare	50
Medicaid	10
Private insurance	23
Income/assets of relative	48
My own money	14
Other	3

Base = 1,240

NURSING HOME

Medicare	32
Medicaid	36
Private insurance	13
Income/assets of relative	46
My own money	10
Other	4

Base = 1,899

ASSISTED-LIVING FACILITY

Medicare	13
Medicaid	6
Private insurance	7
Income/assets of relative	76
My own money	15
Other	4

Base = 526

NOTE: Charts show percent who checked sources of payments for the *most recent month* of care. Respondent could have checked more than one source of payment.

ignores the income placed in the trust in figuring your eligibility, but counts it when determining how much you must pay to the nursing home. The trustee then pays out most of your income to the nursing home, and Medicaid pays the remainder of the monthly bill.

Eligibility requirements vary from state to state, and it's more difficult to qualify for benefits in some states than in others. In each state, though, you must meet an income-and-asset or resource test, which means you must have neither income nor assets that exceed a prescribed amount. In other words, you must use up your assets and your income on nursing care before Medicaid pays. In short, you must make yourself poor.

SPENDING DOWN

Many people who enter a nursing home begin by paying the bills themselves. But if their stay is prolonged, they quickly exhaust their resources and begin the process of spending down. If you start out paying the bills yourself, you may get a private room in a facility, since some nursing homes may give preference to people who can pay privately for a while, but the reality is many people quickly run out of money and must turn to Medicaid.

The process by which Medicaid comes to pay your nursing home bills is called a spend-down. In essence, you cannot get assistance from Medicaid until virtually all of your assets are depleted. You may keep only the house in which your dependent or disabled children or your spouse resides, the furniture, a car, a burial plot, burial funds, and a small amount of cash. Once you are eligible for Medicaid, you must spend nearly all of your income—from Social Security, pensions, interest, dividends, and so on—on nursing home care before Medicaid helps. When you have spent enough of your assets on care to reach your state's Medicaid limits, and your income is not too high, Medicaid begins to pay your bills. The table on page 261 shows what assets and income your state lets you keep. Most states let you keep $2,000 of liquid assets, some a little more and some a little less. And you may keep a small income allowance for "personal needs"—$30 a month in many states. The more assets you have, of course, the longer it takes to spend down.

The following example shows how a spend-down works: Imagine you are a widow living alone in New York City. Your annual income is $15,000, or $1,250 a month. You also have $25,000 in certificates of deposit. Nursing home costs in New York City run about $6,000 a month, so your income is insufficient to cover the cost. You must turn to Medicaid for help. But at the time you enter the nursing home, your assets and income exceed New York's Medicaid limits— $600 in annual income and $3,450 in assets for a single person. You enter the nursing home and for a while pay the bills out of your savings. You must spend $20,000 of the $25,000 before Medicaid steps

TABLE 23: What Medicaid Lets You Keep

In 1999, these were the amounts states used to figure eligibility for Medicaid. The numbers change slightly every year. They give you an idea of what you or a relative will be able to keep.

State	Your Asset Allowance	Your Spouse's Minimum Asset Allowance	Your Personal Monthly Needs Allowance	Your Spouse's Monthly Income Allowance
Alabama	$2,000	$25,000	$30.00	$1383.00
Alaska	2,000	81,960	75.00	2049.00
Arizona	2,000	16,392	75.00	1500.00
Arkansas	2,000	16,392	40.00	1382.50
California	2,000	81,960	35.00	2049.00
Colorado	2,000	81,960	55.00	1383.00
Connecticut	1,600	16,392	51.00	1382.50
Delaware	2,000	25,000	42.00	2019.00
District of Columbia	2,600	81,960	70.00	2049.00
Florida	2,000	81,960	35.00	1357.00
Georgia	2,000	81,960	30.00	2049.00
Hawaii	2,000	81,960	30.00	2049.00
Idaho	2,000	16,400	30.00	1383.00
Illinois	2,000	81,960	30.00	2049.00
Indiana	1,500	16,392	50.00	1383.00
Iowa	2,000	24,000	30.00	2049.00
Kansas	2,000	16,392	30.00	1357.00
Kentucky	2,000	81,960	40.00	2049.00
Louisiana	2,000	81,960	38.00	2049.00
Maine	2,000	81,960	40.00	1383.00
Maryland	2,500	16,392	40.00	1383.00
Massachusetts	2,000	81,960	60.00	1383.00
Michigan	2,000	16,392	30.00	2049.00
Minnesota	3,000	23,171	65.00	1383.00

State	Your Asset Allowance	Your Spouse's Minimum Asset Allowance	Your Personal Monthly Needs Allowance	Your Spouse's Monthly Income Allowance
Mississippi	$2,000	$81,960	$44.00	$2049.00
Missouri	1,000	16,392	30.00	1383.00
Montana	2,000	16,392	40.00	1383.00
Nebraska	4,000	16,392	50.00	1383.00
Nevada	2,000	16,392	35.00	1383.00
New Hampshire	2,500	16,392	50.00	1383.00
New Jersey	2,000	16,392	35.00	1383.00
New Mexico	2,000	31,290	30.00	1357.00
New York	3,550	81,960	50.00	2049.00
North Carolina	2,000	16,392	30.00	1383.00
North Dakota	3,000	81,960	40.00	2049.00
Ohio	1,500	16,392	40.00	1383.00
Oklahoma	2,000	25,000	30.00	2049.00
Oregon	2,000	16,392	30.00	1383.00
Pennsylvania	2,400	16,392	30.00	1383.00
Rhode Island	4,000	16,392	50.00	1383.00
South Carolina	2,000	66,480	30.00	1662.00
South Dakota	2,000	20,000	30.00	1383.00
Tennessee	2,000	16,392	30.00	1356.00
Texas	2,000	16,392	30.00	2049.00
Utah	2,000	16,392	45.00	1383.00
Vermont	1,500	81,960	47.25	2049.00
Virginia	2,000	16,392	30.00	1383.00
Washington	2,000	81,960	41.62	1383.00
West Virginia	2,000	16,392	30.00	1383.00
Wisconsin	2,000	50,000	40.00	2049.00
Wyoming	2,000	81,960	30.00	2049.00

in. (In 1999, New York allowed you to keep $4,950: a $3,450 allowance plus $1,500 for burial expenses.) If you turn over *all* of your monthly income to the nursing home (excluding the personal needs allowance), you have to withdraw $4,750 from your savings each month to cover the $6,000 monthly bill. At that rate, you would spend the $20,000 excess assets in a little more than four months. After that, you are eligible for Medicaid. Once you qualify for coverage, Medicaid requires you to spend virtually all your monthly income for your nursing care. You can keep $50 of your $1,250 monthly income for personal needs and deduct medical expenses, including health insurance premiums if there are any. The rest must go to the nursing home. You keep the $50 personal needs allowance and contribute $1,200 toward your care; the state of New York pays the rest—$4,800 a month.

IMPOVERISHING YOUR SPOUSE

For many families, a spend-down once meant poverty for the spouse who remained at home, since all the family's assets went toward nursing home care for the other spouse. However, Congress has made it a little easier for spouses to maintain a more comfortable standard of living. (This also means that a spend-down occurs faster, since more of the family's assets are sheltered.)

Federal law provides a formula to determine how much of a couple's assets the spouse living at home can keep. States can adjust the result upward to favor the applicant up to a federally imposed ceiling. A couple's home, household goods, car, and personal effects are not counted as assets. Both the asset and income limits are adjusted for inflation and change each year. If family members would suffer financial hardship because of the limits, they can petition the state to allow them to keep more money.

Whether the state uses an income-first rule—requiring a family to first tap the income of the spouse in the nursing home instead of assets to come up to the state's allowable limits—is crucial in determining whether the surviving spouse has enough money to live on after the spouse in the nursing home dies. A state that allows the spouse at home to keep assets sufficient to provide income, which, when combined with her own income, bring her up to the spousal allowance, is more generous than one that requires her to use assets to reach the allowable income requirement. The more assets she can keep, the better off she will be after her spouse dies. Assets can be used to generate an income stream on which to live; as Chapter 1 points out, women often suffer a significant decline in income when their husbands die.

Let's see how the spend-down provisions work in New York, a state that has adopted the maximum limits for both income and assets. In 1999, after adjusting for inflation, the asset limit was $80,760 and income limit was $2,019. Suppose a couple's monthly income was $1,000 and their assets totaled $25,000 when the husband entered a nursing home. After deducting the $50 personal allowance for the husband, $950 of their $1,000 monthly income was left. His wife, who remained at home, could keep all of that, since it was less than $2,019. The husband kept $4,950 of the couple's $25,000 of assets ($3,450 for personal needs plus a $1,500 burial allowance), and the wife kept the remaining $20,000, since it was less than the state's $80,760 maximum asset limit. Medicaid then would pay all the nursing home bills, which were about $6,000 a month.

But suppose the couple had a monthly income of $2,500 and $100,000 of assets. After deducting the $50 personal needs allowance, $2,450 remained. The wife could keep only $2,019; $431 went to the nursing home. Medicaid's share of the monthly nursing home bill was $5,569. But before it would pay, Medicaid required the couple to spend down. As in the previous example, the husband kept $5,000, which left $95,000. His wife could retain $80,760, but they had to spend the remaining $14,240 before Medicaid stepped in.

PROTECTING YOUR ASSETS

In states like New York, California, and Florida, which have adopted high income-and-asset limits, middle-income people qualify more quickly for Medicaid than they would in states that have lower limits. In a state that applies the federal formula without any upward adjustment, a couple whose assets, for example, are $100,000 would get to keep one half that amount, or $50,000, for the spouse at home plus $2,000 for the spouse in the nursing home. The couple would have to spend $48,000 before Medicaid would pay.

In determining your eligibility for Medicaid, a state carefully reviews all the assets available to you and your spouse. Your home, your car, personal property, and a limited amount set aside for burial expenses are not counted in determining your eligibility for Medicaid. Putting an asset in your spouse's name does not protect it from Medicaid, and states consider money held in joint bank accounts as an available asset to pay for nursing home care.

If you give away assets within thirty-six months of applying for Medicaid, or set up a trust within five years, you may be ineligible for Medicaid. If you effect a transfer in fewer than thirty-six months, set up a trust in fewer than sixty months, or transfer assets for less than their fair market value, you are usually ineligible for Medicaid coverage for nursing facility services, or for services obtained under a special program providing home care and care in the community for a period equaling the total uncompensated value of your assets divided by the average monthly cost of nursing home care in your area. The period of ineligibility begins the month you transfer assets. There is no period of ineligibility for transferring assets if you receive care in your home. While this provision may sound like an ideal solution—stay at home and have Medicaid pay—keep in mind that few states pay for home care under their Medicaid programs.

Let's say a widow in Florida decides she can get by on Social Security and a small pension without dipping into a $60,000 nest egg she had hoped to leave to her three grandchildren. Fearful that a future stay in a nursing home would consume much of her grandchildren's inheritance, she gives each of them $20,000. A year later, she enters a nursing home. Medicaid would not pay for her care immediately, since she had given away assets that could have been used for her care. Instead, it would divide the $60,000 given away by a factor reflecting the monthly cost of nursing home care in her area ($3,300). The result, eighteen, is the number of months she would be ineligible for Medicaid, counting from the month of the gift. The woman would not receive any benefits until she had been in a nursing home for six months (eighteen minus the twelve months since the date of the gift). She could only hope her grandchildren were willing to ante up some of the $20,000 that six months of care would cost.

You can also make some kinds of transfers regardless of the thirty-six-month limitation and not jeopardize your eligibility for Medicaid benefits. For example, you can transfer your home to your spouse; to a minor, disabled, or blind child; or to a sibling who had an equity interest in your home and who has lived there for at least one year before you need nursing home care. You can also transfer your home to a child who has lived with you for at least the two years before you were institutionalized and who provided care that delayed your nursing home stay. If you, your spouse, or a dependent relative remain in your home, Medicaid cannot count it as an asset in determining your eligibility for benefits.

If you transfer your home to someone other than those named above, the transaction is counted as a transfer that results in a period of ineligibility. If you own your home when you die, Medicaid can put a lien on the property to recover what it paid for your nursing care. However, Medicaid cannot foreclose on the lien until your spouse dies, a disabled child is no longer disabled, or a dependent child turns twenty-one. Transferring your home to a spouse may be a worthwhile move to avoid a Medicaid lien after your death, or if you are too sick to return home.

You can try to set up a trust so long as you do it sixty months before applying for Medicaid. The trust must be written in such a way that neither you nor the trustee can tap the principal for your benefit. You may receive only the income from the assets held in the trust. This requires some careful planning. If you set up a trust and the trustee has the power to invade the principal for your benefit, Medicaid considers that you own the trust even though you have no control over the principal, never receive any benefits, and have named other beneficiaries. And if the income from the trust is greater than your state's Medicaid income limit, a trust isn't much help. Medicaid still requires you to use any income that exceeds the state limit before it pays its share of your nursing home bills.

If you set up a trust, Medicaid asks for a copy of the trust agreement when you apply for benefits. Officials scrutinize it to see whether it complies with the rules and whether the assets you put into the trust should, in fact, be counted in determining your eligibility. When you set up a trust, you are also gambling that you will eventually need nursing home care. If your principal is tied up in the trust, and you live a long time without seeing the inside of a nursing home, you could well find yourself in a financial bind. You'll be unable to tap the trust for more money. If you have substantial assets, buying a good long-term-care insurance policy may be a better strategy.

Another device for protecting your assets is to give them away as gifts at least thirty-six months before you require care in a nursing home. Medicaid usually does not count these assets in determining your eligibility. Obviously, if you give money or property away, you won't have the assets or the income from those assets to live on, and may find yourself in the position of having to go to your children or the other recipients of your assets and asking for money. Taking such a serious step requires careful planning and coordination with all your sources of income. You will need the help of an attorney who specializes in elder law to help you. The National Association of Elder Law Attorneys can help you find one in your area. Call 520-661-4005 for information or visit the association's website at *www.naela.org*. The association has a directory of elder law attorneys that details their experience and shows which ones are certified to practice elder law.

MEDICAID AND HOME CARE

Most states provide Medicaid payments for some kinds of home care services and for care in your community, such as in adult day care centers. Usually these services include nonmedical personal care for such activities as bathing, dressing, preparing meals, or eating. There may also be transportation or case management services available. When personal care is given in your home, the home care agency that provides your home attendant must be licensed or certified by Medicaid in order for Medicaid to pay the bills (see Chapter 7).

All states except New York provide home care and care in the community under a special "waiver" program from the federal government. These waivers allow states to pay for care in your home if you are debilitated enough to require care in a nursing home. The idea behind the waivers was to keep people in their own homes rather than in an institution. Unfortunately, for political reasons, most states have little Medicaid money available to pay for this kind of care. So they set quotas that determine the number of people needing nursing home care who can instead get similar care at home. Some states may have waiting lists, and people often end up in nursing homes anyway simply because that's where Medicaid will pay for their care.

New York offers home care as part of its regular Medicaid program. This program is generous, and if you or your relative needs nursing home care, most likely there will be a period of home care paid by Medicaid before a nursing home stay begins. Appendices I and J show the kinds of Medicaid waivered and nonwaivered services available in your state.

You qualify for home care services the same way you qualify for nursing home care—that is, by spending down. Since most of your income must go for medical care in order to qualify, that often leaves very little for living expenses. So this may be an unattractive option for some families.

The same procedures for protecting your spouse from impoverishment apply if you or your relative are spending down to qualify for Medicaid home care or other covered services.

Applying for Medicaid

When the time comes to apply for Medicaid benefits, the nursing home will help you or your spouse do so. If it turns out that you qualify for benefits, Medicaid pays the nursing home directly. For the portion of the bills you must pay, Medicaid may collect directly from you or from a surrogate, usually a relative who handles your personal business. In some cases, Medicaid helps arrange to have your Social Security check sent directly to the nursing home. You don't have to deposit your personal needs allowance with the nursing facility, but if you do, the nursing home must keep your personal needs allowance in a special account for you.

Because rules governing Medicaid are complicated and change frequently, nursing home personnel may not always be aware of all the requirements. Even state officials may not keep track of changes in the rules. So if you or your family has been told by Medicaid or a nursing home administrator that you are ineligible for benefits because you've set up a trust or transferred assets, seek another opinion.

KEY DECISION POINTS

1. If you want to preserve assets for your spouse or children, consult an attorney specializing in elder law long before you think you will need nursing home care.

2. If you think a nursing home stay is coming, and you will need to spend down, consider converting assets that Medicaid will count toward a spend-down (bank accounts, CDs, and other investments) into assets (such as home improvements) that Medicaid won't count in determining your eligibility.

3. Consider applying for Medicaid home care coverage if your state offers a reasonable package of services. If you don't qualify, or if few services are available, then you'll have to tap your own resources to pay for care.

4. Consider transferring title to your house to your spouse to make sure he or she has a place to live if you go to a nursing home and Medicaid will be paying for your care.

5. If you don't want to spend down, and transferring assets is out of the question, consider buying a long-term-care policy—if you can comfortably pay the premiums now and in the future.

FOURTEEN

Insurance for Long-Term Care

Janet Blau, age sixty-six, and her husband, Larry, age seventy-two, thought they were doing the right thing by purchasing long-term-care insurance and modifying their home to accommodate the potential need for wheelchairs in old age. Both had experienced nursing homes firsthand, having had parents who lived in them for more than five years. "You'd be better off shooting yourself than go to one of them," Larry says. "We didn't want that."

So they asked three insurance companies to make sales presentations. One company's representative gave a high-pressure sales pitch. Another, GE Capital, would sell Larry a policy with only a two-year benefit because he walks with a limp and wears special shoes—the result of childhood polio. But the Blaus wanted a policy to cover all their long-term-care expenses for the rest of their lives, either in a nursing home or for care at home; two years of coverage wouldn't do.

They finally settled on a policy from American Travellers that gave them lifetime benefits, a $100 daily benefit that Janet thought "sounded good," a $25 daily benefit for home care, and a $12.50 daily benefit for homemaker services. They also wanted no elimination period, which meant the policy would pay as soon as they entered a nursing home. The premium for this package of coverage came to about $3,500 a year for two policies. The Blaus did not buy inflation coverage, which would have increased their daily benefit over the years; they felt they couldn't afford it on their $30,000 annual income from Social Security, his pension, and her pocket money from selling Avon products. Like many people the Blaus had already cashed in their 401(k) plans and IRAs to buy other things. "We got what we wanted and what we could afford," Larry said. They did not bargain for premiums that went up.

But a year and a half after they bought the policy in 1997, the Blaus said the company notified them that it was raising the premiums 18 percent. "At no time did the agent tell us this would happen," says Janet. "She knew what we had to live in." For the moment, they are paying the higher premiums.

The Blaus did some of their homework before buying long-term-care insurance, but there was no way they could have learned that American Travellers had a history of raising premiums in several states dating back to at least 1993. Many sellers of long-term-care insurance have begun raising their premiums and causing families like the Blaus to rethink whether they can afford the policies they have already bought. Future rate hikes are the biggest potential trap lurking in long-term-care insurance. There are other traps as well that families must consider before plunking down several thousand dollars a year for a policy that they may be forced to drop long before the need for nursing home care arises. And no matter what your intentions, a long-term-care policy does not guarantee that you will get the care you want or need. Despite what sellers say, long-term-care insurance does not guarantee that you will receive quality care in a nursing home.

Insurance companies say that the sale of long-term-care insurance is an emotional one. And even if people manage to leave emotion out of the decision, do their research, and shop around like the Blaus, there's no guarantee that they will end up with the best policy for them. This chapter is intended to help you decide whether to buy long-term-care insurance, how to go about the process of selecting a policy, and how to access and use the benefits once you or your relative has the coverage.

Long-term-care insurance is the most complex insurance product on the market. There are myriad combinations of benefits, waiting periods, options, and prices, and it's tempting to have an agent make the decision for you. However, that approach may not lead you to the policy you'll need for the long haul. The decision to buy at all is not straightforward like, say, buying auto or homeowner's insurance, where the need for coverage is clear-cut. Policies and coverage are not clear-cut either. Long-term-care policies are far less standardized and much less understood than either auto or homeowner's coverage. With long-term-care insurance, it is often hard to see your need for a policy. But examining need is the first step. Consider your needs long before you call in an agent. Once the agent arrives, he or she may convince you that you need a policy for all the wrong reasons. Perhaps you shouldn't buy one at all.

WHY BUY A POLICY?

Preserving Your Estate

A major reason many people choose long-term-care insurance is to save their estate for their heirs. If you have insurance to cover a large portion of a nursing home stay, then you will not have to spend down or spend down as quickly (see Chapter 13), perhaps leaving money for your spouse or children. Indeed, insurance companies promote long-term-care policies as a protection for assets that are built up over a lifetime. In other words, if you are confined to a nursing home, you won't have to tap into some or all of your savings so long as you have the policy to cover your expenses. For many people, this alone is a good reason to buy the coverage.

Another reason for insurance is to protect assets for your spouse or a dependent member of your family. Or you may simply feel more comfortable having a policy that helps you avoid impoverishment or reliance on government programs for family members in your later years.

But here is one of the gambles you take when you buy. Unless you buy a large enough policy that offers coverage for several years, or you don't stay in the nursing home too long, you still may have to deplete your estate on nursing home care. If you are unlucky enough to stay a long time, or your policy is too small, you may still face a Medicaid spend-down.

If the value of your assets (excluding your house) is $10,000 or less, you probably don't need insurance coverage—in most states you would qualify fairly quickly for Medicaid. If your assets are between $10,000 and $50,000, you probably don't need a policy either. Your need for long-term-care coverage is marginal at best, especially if these assets produce some of the income you are living on. And you probably can't afford current or future premiums.

If your assets are $50,000 or more, and your current income is sufficient to pay the premiums, you might seriously consider buying a policy. If your assets far exceed $50,000, you should contact an attorney specializing in estate planning to find other suitable alternatives. Worksheet 4 (below) will help you decide what assets you have to protect and whether you have sufficient income to buy a policy.

Getting into a Better Nursing Home

In recent years, insurance agents have touted this as a reason for buying. While it's true that some nursing homes prefer to take residents who

---

WORKSHEET 4: Figuring Your Assets

1. Total Assets

Stocks	_____
Bonds	_____
CDs	_____
Treasury securities	_____
Mutual funds	_____
Money market funds	_____
Checking accounts	_____
Other bank accounts	_____
401(k) plan	_____
IRAs	_____
Employer pension plan	_____
Annuities	_____
Market value of home	_____
Car	_____
Household goods	_____
Cash-value life insurance	_____
Burial fund	_____
Value of burial plot	_____
TOTAL	_____

2. Medicaid-Exempt Assets

Market value of home	_____
Car	_____
Household goods	_____
Burial fund	_____
Value of burial plot	_____
TOTAL	_____

3. Countable Assets

(Total 1 minus total 2)   _____

4. Your Asset Allowance

(See Table 23, What Medicaid Lets You Keep, on page 261)   _____

5. Your Assets Subject to Spend-Down

(3 minus 4)   _____

---

can "pay privately"—that is, those who do not have to rely on Medicaid at the beginning of their stay—there is no assurance that those homes are indeed the best nursing facilities or that you will get good care just because you are paying privately. In my experience, some of the glitziest-looking places offered mediocre-to-poor care. Just because one facility looks better than others does not mean it offers the best care.

If you don't need to rely on Medicaid when you first enter, you may, however, have a wider choice of nursing homes. But beware: Some facilities ask residents to leave when they can no longer pay privately and must turn to Medicaid. Eventually many people do. You will also have to weigh a potentially larger selection of facilities against the cost of buying a policy.

Getting into an Assisted-Living Facility

Assisted-living facilities, discussed in Chapter 10, are rapidly becoming the long-term-care option of choice for many families. They are, however, expensive, and usually public benefit programs do not pay for care in them. Many long-term-care policies now promise to pay benefits for services in these facilities, and you may find that an attractive reason to buy. But again, be careful. Many assisted-living facilities do not fit the definition for care in one of these facilities outlined in the policy. Insurance companies define what they mean by assisted living, and the facility selling assisted living may not match that description. It's also easy to use up the policy benefits on assisted living. When you need nursing home care, as many of assisted-living facility residents eventually do, the policy benefits will be depleted, and you may have to spend down anyway. Consider that possibility when you shop for coverage.

Paying for Home Care

Agents also tout the policies as a way to pay for home care, which almost everyone prefers to a nursing home. Here again you must consider the possibility of exhausting the policy benefits before you need a nursing home. You must consider whether you can be cared for at home and whether policy benefits will be used up before you go to a nursing home. Many people who start out with home care need nursing home care in the end. Chapter 7 discusses whether home care is likely to be a realistic alternative for you. Before buying a policy to cover home care or even adult day care, determine whether your relative might be better off participating in a PACE program (see Chapter 9).

The Doing Nothing Option

It is possible that you will decide to take your chances—that you will not need a nursing home or any other type of long-term care. Or you may decide that your income simply will not support the purchase of a policy and allow you to continue paying the premiums and the probable rate increases over the years. If you have to give up the quality of life you have right now to buy a policy, then maybe you should take your chances and not buy. Buying a policy today and dropping it later when you can't afford the premiums is not a good option. Neither is struggling to pay the policy premiums at the expense of food, shelter, and transportation.

You may also decide to buy only one policy—for the spouse who has the greater risk. This is often the best course to follow. Older married women usually have far less income to live on once their husbands die, especially if they have not worked outside the home for most of their adult lives. The Older Women's League estimates that women's incomes decline significantly when their husbands die. Furthermore, it's not uncommon for one-third to one-half of their monthly checks to go for prescription drugs.

But even though a widow may have less income with which to pay expensive insurance premiums, her need for long-term care increases as she gets older, ironically making her a candidate for long-term-care insurance. If a woman is able to afford the premiums after the death of a spouse, she should consider buying a policy and perhaps one with a larger benefit than her husband's. Married men are often cared for at home by their wives, while single women (and men) are more likely to end up in nursing homes because no one is at home to care for them when they are ill or infirm. Even though insurance agents like to push policies for both spouses, and sometimes offer discounts for buying two, the best option may be to buy coverage only for the wife.

THE PRICE

If you have realistically thought about why you want long-term-care coverage and feel you need the insurance, the next step is to consider the price. Ask yourself if you can pay the premium out of your retirement income. For most retirees, the answer is no. The average annual per capita income for someone sixty-five or over is about $17,000. A sixty-five-year-old could pay about $3,057 each year for a long-term-care policy with unlimited benefits and inflation protection. That's 18 percent of annual income. Add another $1,200 or $1,300 or so for Medicare-supplement insurance, and decent health and long-term-care insurance comes to about $4,300 a year, or nearly $9,000 for a couple. Of course, you can tailor your policy and omit certain coverages, which will lower the price. But remember, only unlimited coverage will give you all the protection you need and minimize the risk of spending down. The section on trade-offs (see page 295) tells you how to make those choices.

Based on a study of long-term-care insurance in 1997, CONSUMER REPORTS believes that premiums for many policies are likely to increase over the years. The magazine asked state insurance departments about rate increases or decreases that insurers have requested for their long-term-care policies. States reported numerous increases. Increases of 25 percent were not uncommon, and a few policies had multiple increases totaling 100 percent or more. Another independent study found that thirty-four companies that had sold long-term-care insurance increased their rates in the last few years. While many of those increases were in the neighborhood of 15 to 20 percent, many were much higher, though a few were lower. If you can't afford to pay a premium in the future that is 50 percent higher than the one you pay when you first purchase a policy, it's not a good idea to buy.

State regulators are also becoming concerned that carriers have underpriced their policies to entice buyers. One actuary at the Kansas Insurance Department said there is evidence that "a significant number of companies are marketing products that offer tremendously rich benefits, have low prices, and sloppy underwriting [the process of checking on a person's health]. This is a fraud on consumers."

Companies are unwilling to guarantee rates far into the future. That's because insurers still have too little data to accurately predict how many people will file claims, how large those claims will be, and how many people will drop their policies. (If people do that, the company generally keeps premiums it has already collected, without ever needing to pay future claims from those policyholders.)

The Ratings in Appendices S and T show which companies may have underpriced their policies. Keep them in mind as you shop. A cheap policy today is not necessarily the best policy later on. If the company raises premiums and you can't pay them and must drop the policy, you will have wasted a lot of money.

A few companies may offer an option that lets policyholders make ten yearly payments. The carriers then guarantee that their policies will not be subject to rate increases after that ten-year period. This provides some protection in the later years when your income is likely to decline. But you will pay a higher premium. In a way, these kinds of policies work like mortgages. With a fifteen-year mortgage, you would make a higher monthly payment than you would if you took out a thirty-year mortgage.

Many insurance companies are trying to get out of the long-term-care insurance business and are selling what is called in the insurance business "blocks" of business. A policy you buy may be in one of these blocks. If that happens, your new insurance company may well raise the premiums on all the policies it assumes from your old carrier.

WHEN SHOULD YOU BUY?

Agents, of course, would like to insure everyone at younger ages. The premiums are much lower, and it's easier for them to make a sale. But if you buy a policy now and are likely to use the benefits far into the future, say in twenty, thirty, or even forty years, that coverage may be useless when you actually need care. New kinds of delivery systems for care no doubt will emerge and will not be covered by a policy purchased today. For example, ten years ago, assisted-living facilities were not places where people received long-term care. In fact, few facilities existed and few people had ever heard of the ones that did. Policies did not pay for care in them. Today, however, benefits for care in assisted-living facilities are common.

For that reason, it makes little sense to buy long-term-care insurance before age fifty-five. Between the ages of fifty-five and sixty-five, consider insurance only if you have a medical condition, such as diabetes, that could get worse and eventually put you in a nursing home. But by age sixty, you should begin to assess whether you need this type of coverage.

The later you buy, the more expensive the policy. While a sixty-five-year-old would pay on average $3,200 for a comprehensive policy, a seventy-five-year-old would pay about $7,100. Should adult children buy a policy for their parents? It's a tempting idea, especially if they want to protect their inheritance, but the same caveats apply no matter who is paying the premium. Adult children should ask themselves if they can afford several thousand dollars a year for the coverage, and if they can continue paying the premiums when they inevitably go up.

WHAT POLICIES COVER

After you have carefully thought about the reasons for buying a policy, it's time to learn about the policies themselves. No two long-term-care policies are exactly alike. Some offer comprehensive benefits, paying for services provided in nursing facilities or in various community settings. Others offer coverage only for nursing home services. And some policies pay only for home care. We don't recommend that you buy home care–only policies. If you decide to purchase a long-term-care policy, these are the main points to consider:

- How large a daily benefit amount do you need?
- How long should benefits last?
- How do you qualify for benefits?
- Will benefits increase with inflation protection?
- When should benefits begin?
- What services are covered?
- Should you include home care coverage?

BENEFITS

How Big a Benefit?

The heart of a policy is the daily benefit. Your choice of benefit—somewhere between $20 and $300 a day for nursing home care—governs the premium you'll pay. The daily benefit for home care, if you choose that option, may be half the nursing home benefit, but many companies are now offering home care benefits that equal the coverage for nursing homes. Benefits for care in assisted-living facilities are usually stated as some percentage of the nursing home benefit.

Some policies pay the full daily nursing home benefit you select no matter what the actual charges are. Others pay only the actual charges up to the selected benefit. When selecting a benefit, keep in mind that your actual charges may exceed the nursing home's stated rate. Extra charges for drugs, supplies, and special services could boost the bill several hundred dollars each month (see Chapter 11). So choose a benefit that is at least as high as the average price of nursing homes in your locality. Call several homes to see what their current rates are, and don't buy a policy with a benefit that is less than the current going price of care in your community unless in the future you have sufficient income to pay the difference between the cost of care and your daily benefit.

How Long a Benefit?

Companies offer a selection of benefit periods—one, two, three, four, five, or six years, and lifetime coverage. Not all offer each choice. Because you don't know how long a nursing home stay will last, and because lifetime coverage with an adequate daily benefit is extravagantly expensive, you need to play the odds. The only policy that totally protects you from a spend-down is one with unlimited coverage. But nearly 90 percent of all people who enter a nursing home between the ages of sixty-five and ninety-four stay less than four years. Most stay an average of two and a half years.

If you're willing to play the odds, a four-year benefit may be a reasonable gamble. Even if you are among the small minority who will require nursing home care for a longer period, a four-year benefit will at least give you and your family time to prepare for, and adjust to, the financial consequences of a longer stay.

The Pool-of-Money Option

Most companies now offer a "pool of money" approach. For comprehensive policies that include home care, you choose the daily benefit and a benefit period. Then you multiply the annual value of the benefit by the number of years it is to last. The result is a pool of money available for any type of care covered by the policy. Say you choose a benefit of $120 a day for a four-year comprehensive policy. The policy will pay a total of $175,200 for home care, nursing home services, or both. Theoretically, you could trade benefits for one type of care for another. But in a pool-of-money approach, unlike with a traditional policy, benefits used for one kind of care decrease the amount available for the other. While these policies might sound like the ultimate in flexibility, remember that they do not increase coverage. They simply let you spend the money in another way. The danger in this is that you could use up all the benefits on home care or in an assisted-living facility. When the time comes for a nursing home, there may be no money left.

Keeping Up with Inflation

Between 1985 and 1995, nursing home prices increased an average of 9.7 percent, much higher than the rate of increase in the Consumer Price Index. In 1995, for example, with inflation in the general economy at only 2.8 percent, nursing home prices increased some 8 percent. Because the policy you buy today may be called on to pay benefits twenty or twenty-five years from now, it is vital your benefits increase with the price of nursing home care. If nursing home prices escalate at an annual rate of 8 percent, then a nursing home that costs $120 a day today would cost $559 a day twenty years from now. Without inflation coverage, a $120 daily benefit would then be virtually useless.

Policies are typically offered without inflation coverage. Agents don't like to sell it, because it raises the premium, sometimes to the point you can't afford the policy. Nevertheless, a policy that doesn't increase with inflation is no bargain and could be of limited use down the road. The following are the inflation options agents generally recommend in decreasing order of usefulness.

Five percent compounded option This arrangement, which increases the benefit at a rate of 5 percent a year, compounded, comes closest to ensuring that the policy will still provide a meaningful benefit in the future. If you buy a daily benefit of $120, roughly the average cost of nursing home care today, this option will give you a daily benefit twenty years from now of $318, and thus keep pace with inflation that averages 5 percent a year. This option, of course, still leaves you short if nursing home costs increase at a faster pace, but it's the most generous available. The cost of this protection varies by company and by age of the buyer. At age sixty-five, it increases the premium by some 70 percent on average; at age seventy, by about 60 percent. Inflation protection costs more for buyers who are younger when they purchase a policy.

Five percent simple option With this option, 5 percent of the original benefit, not of the previous year's benefit, is added each year—that is, there is no compounding. A $120 daily benefit would increase to $240 in twenty years, leaving you to pay some $78 a day out of pocket if nursing home rates increased 5 percent a year. This option increases the premium for a sixty-five-year-old by about 50 percent on average.

Extra coverage at the outset Some agents may paint a realistically grim picture of inflation but suggest you prepare for it by starting out with a daily benefit that's larger than the current daily nursing home rate. This helps agents close a deal, because the premium will look relatively low compared with the premium for true inflation protection. The downside is that it's poor coverage. Agents often recommend this option particularly for people in their seventies on the theory that if they enter a nursing facility at all, they are likely to do so in the near future. But a seventy-five-year-old who buys a $140 benefit instead of a $120 benefit will still have a $140 benefit in ten years. At 5 percent annual inflation, the nursing home would cost $195, leaving a gap of $55 a day, or about $1,650 each month, between the cost of the nursing home and the insurance benefit. The gap grows as the years go on, and as nursing homes increase their daily rates.

Increase coverage periodically Some companies guarantee the right to buy additional coverage every two or three years, or sometimes annually, without passing the company's medical requirements. The amount you can buy may be unlimited, it may be restricted to $10 or $20 increases, or it may be based on some formula related to the Consumer Price Index. This option has serious drawbacks. You must remember to take advantage of the offer. If you refuse the offer a certain number of times and sometimes only once, you lose your right to increase your coverage.

The price of increasing your coverage is based not only on the larger benefit but also on your new, higher age, so you will be paying more for those increments over time than you would had you chosen a different option to begin with. One company sells a policy that lets you voluntarily add to the benefit incrementally in a way intended to match the increase in benefits with the "5 percent compounded" option. At the outset, the policy with the incremental option costs someone age sixty-five $770 a year, compared with $1,598 for the same benefit with a clear-cut 5 percent compounded arrangement. Twenty years later, however, the premium for the policy with the "cheaper" incremental inflation protection would be $5,250 a year, while the premium for the "more expensive" 5 percent fully compounded option would still be $1,598.

Insurance companies and their agents argue that older people need not buy inflation coverage since very few years will elapse before they begin to draw on the policy benefits. They advise young people to buy the coverage because it will be a long time before they will use the policy. But their argument falls apart if the "old" people live a long time and need nursing home care.

Consider what happened to one Nebraska woman. The woman bought a policy for herself and her husband ten years ago when she was seventy-three and he was seventy-nine. Both were in good health and chose a policy paying a $50 daily benefit, which was at the time the going rate for nursing homes in their area. The two policies cost $2,364. They did not buy inflation protection.

Ten years later, when nursing home rates more than doubled, the couple realized their $50 daily benefit was insufficient, and they would still have to spend assets in the event one went to a nursing home. They tried to buy another $50 benefit from their insurance carrier, but because both had developed health problems by then, they were turned down. They found another company that would provide the additional coverage, but they had to pay an annual premium of $5,386 for the two new policies. The total for all their long-term-care policies now came to $7,750. Add the $3,277 for two Medicare-supplement policies and their total for health insurance amounts to $11,000 a year. Even though paying for long-term-care insurance is a struggle, the woman has no choice. If her husband were to go to a nursing home, the $100,000 nest egg on which she depends for her monthly income would eventually be depleted, and she would have little to live on except her $160 monthly Social Security benefit. Their story is not atypical.

When Do Benefits Begin?

Like most insurance, long-term-care policies come with deductibles that are known as "elimination" periods—twenty, thirty, sixty, ninety, or one hundred days—during which you must pay for nursing home care out of your own pocket. As with other types of insurance, the larger the deductible (or in this case, the longer the elimination period), the lower the premium.

Don't let a low premium tempt you into choosing an elimination period you can't afford—or may not be able to afford in the future. A policy with a ninety-day elimination period might cost $300 a year less than a policy with a twenty-day elimination period. After twenty years, you would have saved $6,000 in premiums. But with 5 percent inflation, the cost of care for seventy additional days of the elimination period would amount to $22,288.

Qualifying for Benefits

Companies vary in how they determine when you are sufficiently disabled to require long-term care. They measure a disability against a policyholder's ability to perform what industry jargon calls "activities of daily living." There are potentially seven of them—eating, walking, transferring from a bed to a chair, dressing, bathing, using a toilet, and remaining continent. Older people tend to lose the ability to perform their ADLs in the order they acquired them as a baby or toddler. Bathing and walking are usually the first ones that people can no longer perform; eating is the last.

The insurer defines disability by the number of these activities you are unable to perform. Some say you must be unable to perform three out of the seven before you qualify as disabled; others choose six and say you must fail to perform two or three of the six; still others pare the list to five and say policyholders must be unable to perform two of them. However, more and more companies are choosing two of six ADLs.

In general, the longer the list of activities and the fewer you have to fail, the easier it is to get benefits. In reviewing a policy, note particularly if bathing is on the list of activities. A disabled person is more likely to need help with bathing than with any other activity. If it's on the list specified in the policy, a policyholder might be able to qualify more easily than with a policy that doesn't include bathing as an essential activity of daily living. Newer policies require policyholders to fail three out of six ADLs and generally include bathing among them.

Policies also define the inability to perform an activity in different ways. Among the policies we reviewed in 1999, we found that many companies are now more precise in defining what they mean by the inability to perform activities of daily living. Some policies say that you must require "substantial assistance" to perform the activities of daily living, and they include standby assistance in the definition as well. John Hancock, for example, defines substantial assistance as "hands-on physical assistance from another person to perform an activity of daily living more than half of the times that a particular activity is performed." The company now has expanded the definition to mean "standby assistance" as well. Hancock defines standby assistance as "the presence of another person within arm's reach in order to prevent, by physical intervention, injury to the policyholder while they are performing the activity of daily living."

Look for the broadest definitions possible to increase your chances of qualifying for coverage when you become disabled.

A second way to qualify for benefits is to suffer some cognitive impairment. All policies now cover Alzheimer's disease and other types of dementia. But almost all say you must fail certain clinical tests to receive benefits. While companies appear to have liberalized their benefit triggers for qualifying through the ADL route, they have made it harder to qualify if you suffer from reduced mental capacity, often called a cognitive impairment. Companies may say that a policyholder qualifies for benefits if there is a deterioration or loss in intellectual capacity that requires "substantial supervision," which they go on to define as "continual supervision." That definition can be tricky since someone with early-stage Alzheimer's disease or dementia may not need continual supervision. Years from now that definition could result in conflicts over payment.

A third pathway to benefits is "medical necessity." The policy will pay if you have a medical condition—congestive heart failure, say, or coronary artery disease—that makes you too frail to care for yourself even though you may be able to perform all activities when taken individually. Note that certain "tax qualified" policies cannot include medical necessity among the recognized reasons for long-term care (see page 289). If you choose a tax-qualified plan, you may be gaining a minor tax break but giving up an easier pathway to coverage.

WHERE WILL THE POLICY PAY?

All long-term-care policies pay for care in licensed nursing homes. Assisted-living facilities, which provide less client care than a nursing home, are another matter. Some policies explicitly state they will cover stays in such a facility. Others may or may not cover assisted living as part of an "alternative plan of care." Under such a policy, the insurance company will discuss alternatives to a nursing home with the family, but will pay for assisted living only if both parties agree to the alternative. There's no guarantee.

Not all assisted-living facilities that care for elderly people qualify for benefits. Some policies, for example, say that a staff member must be on the premises twenty-four hours a day, a doctor must be on call, and the facility must be able to supervise medications. A policy may also define a facility by the number of residents, refusing to pay for care in very small facilities. Companies may require facilities to serve three meals a day or cater to special dietary needs.

The daily benefit for assisted-living care is commonly 50 or 60 percent of the nursing home coverage, but sometimes it is the same as the nursing home benefit. Occasionally it might also be the same as the benefit for home care. Although the benefit for assisted living is often smaller than for nursing home care, some assisted-living facilities cost $3,000 to $4,000 a month, about the same as nursing homes. A flexible policy should cover you for either type of facility. Look for this flexibility when you shop. Take your long-term-care policy with you to assisted-living facilities when you shop and match what the policy says with the kind of facility you are considering.

WHICH FRILLS ARE USEFUL?

Insurers tack on a number of extraneous benefits, many of them useful more as selling points for insurance agents than as succor for a consumer in need of care. One potentially useful frill is a service offering advice to a policyholder in need of care. Unfortunately, many of the provisions we examined direct you to an insurance company's in-house service or to a service under contract to the company. Those arrangements are restrictive and may lead to care that serves the insurer's interest rather than yours. Another potentially useful frill helps pay for alterations to your home—a stair lift, for example—that might help a policyholder stay at home rather than enter a nursing home.

Other frills are nearly universal. These include: a bed-reservation benefit, which reserves your space in the nursing home should you go to the hospital and return; a respite-care benefit, which pays for a substitute caregiver when yours needs a break; and a waiver of premium benefit, which pays the insurance premiums once you're in a facility. A few companies waive the premium as soon as a policyholder receives the first payment. But waits of between sixty and ninety days are more typical. Most don't waive premiums if the policyholder receives nursing care at home.

IF YOUR POLICY LAPSES

You should never buy a long-term-care policy unless you intend to keep it for the rest of your life. Unfortunately, it's all too easy for elderly people to allow a policy to lapse inadvertently or because they can no longer afford the premiums. Some companies have begun to add safeguards to make sure the people who want to stay insured do. If you miss a premium, some insurers will send a notice of a missed premium to a third party. Others offer an extra-long grace period—sixty-five days instead of the customary thirty-one. Or the company may offer the right to reinstate the policy after five months if it has lapsed because a policyholder was cognitively or functionally impaired. Some policies let policyholders reduce their coverage in return for a lower premium if they can't pay the full premium.

States require companies to offer "nonforfeiture benefits" as an option. This is a promise of a certain value to the policyholder even if the policy lapses. The typical value is the policy's daily benefit provided for a shorter period. If you drop your policy, the company will apply all the premiums you've paid for nursing home care for as long as the money lasts. This type of benefit adds, on average, 20 percent to the premium. Not many people buy this benefit.

You might find a policy that provides a death-benefit refund to the policyholder's estate—the total of any premiums paid minus any benefits the company paid on the policyholder's behalf. This benefit is usually payable only if the policyholder dies before a certain age, typically sixty-five or seventy. It adds to the cost of the policy.

HOW'S YOUR HEALTH?

Insurance companies are strict underwriters. This means that before they issue a policy, they will carefully scrutinize your health in an attempt to weed out people with health conditions likely to send them to a nursing home, including diabetes, signs of Alzheimer's disease, and cardiovascular disorders that might predispose them to strokes. Companies have long lists of conditions and long lists of medications that make people unacceptable—conditions like Parkinson's disease, osteoporosis, and chronic pancreatitis, and medicines like Haldol, which is prescribed for psychotic disorders.

But that doesn't mean that all insurers look at conditions the same way. A condition that's unacceptable to one might be acceptable to another. To gauge this variation, CONSUMER REPORTS asked insurers whether they would cover people with certain health conditions. Almost all said they would not insure a sixty-year-old man who showed signs of confusion and disorientation. Most would accept a sixty-five-year-old woman complaining of blurred vision and diagnosed with glaucoma. What about a sixty-eight-year-old man with hypertension who had undergone carotid-artery surgery? Here there was no consensus. Some would deny coverage, others would cover him at higher rates. And one company would insure him only if he had a healthy spouse who could act as a caregiver.

Several companies now sort applicants into various classes and charge them rates commensurate with the risk they represent. The names companies attach to their underwriting classes often add confusion. One company uses the term *standard* to mean its worst class. Another uses that term to mean the middle of five rate classifications. Watch for these "word games" as you do your shopping.

The underwriting process can take a month or two. Applicants answer questions about their health and sometimes furnish a physician's statement detailing their health history. Companies usually interview older applicants by phone, looking for signs of cognitive impairment. Occasionally they conduct face-to-face interviews. Some companies also look for lifestyle clues that suggest likely candidates for a nursing home. A company may say that anyone needing assistance with housekeeping, shopping, and household finances is not acceptable. You may be asked to describe in your own handwriting and in your own words what you do in a typical day. The theory is that if you are active and get out and about, you're not likely to go to a nursing home any time soon and cost the company a lot of money.

You might hear agents and others talk about preexisting-conditions clauses. These have little practical meaning in long-term-care insurance. The wording in a policy may exclude nursing home payments for six months for conditions you have when the policy is written. But despite the wording, an insurer probably won't sell you the policy if it suspects you might actually enter a nursing home within six months. Some carriers may issue a policy after you have sufficiently recovered from some illness. Or they may limit the amount of coverage you can buy if you have certain health conditions.

COVERAGE FOR HOME CARE

Agents know people fear nursing homes, and not without reason. They play off that fear, often pushing home care coverage as an alternative, knowing full well that the benefit won't help much if someone really needs care twenty-four hours a day, every day. With home health aides costing around $13 an hour, a typical $55 daily benefit would buy only about four hours of care each day. When it comes to qualifying, the factors used to determine eligibility for nursing home care usually apply. Chances are, then, that to qualify one will have to be frail enough to need more than the four hours of care the benefit will buy.

The home care benefits differ from policy to policy. Policies usually will pay home care benefits for skilled-nursing care, therapists, and aides who assist with dressing, bathing, and other activities of daily living. Most will cover adult day care services. A few policies pay for the services of dieticians or for home-delivered meals. A few pay for homemaker services, help with cooking, paying bills, doing the laundry, and cleaning.

Insurance companies generally want you to receive home care from licensed home health agencies that provide the most expensive kind of help. If you use one of these agencies, you may find your benefit won't stretch as far as it might if you had free choice of providers. A few policies offer benefits for informal caregivers, but keep in mind these benefits are not identical from company to company. One might say that informal caregivers are people who already live with you. Another may allow friends and neighbors to assume that role. The daily benefit for informal care may be limited to an hourly rate that is one-half the daily home care benefit. A policy may also limit the hourly amount it will pay. So if your policy paid a $55 daily benefit for home care, informal caregivers would get $27.50.

You may come across a policy that allows you to use an informal caregiver rather than an aide from a licensed agency, but the company may charge more for that flexibility. UNUM, for instance, at one point offered a comprehensive policy with a home care benefit that allowed policyholders to use friends and relatives to care for them. The premium for that benefit could cost more than twice as much as a similar policy requiring policyholders to use aides from licensed home care agencies.

If home care is important to you, carefully read the policy to find out who can provide the service. Many policies specify that family and friends cannot provide care. Home care coverage with a benefit paying half the nursing home benefit adds about 30 percent to the price of a policy. Some carriers offer home care coverage that equals the nursing home benefit. That can boost the price another 20 percent.

Because home care coverage adds substantially to your premium, I recommend that you carefully consider whether you need it. It may make sense to buy home care coverage for a husband who is likely to have a wife around to care for him, but a woman who has no family or friends to keep an eye on her care may not need the coverage. As attractive as home care may sound, consider it only if you have a good support network of family and friends nearby. No matter how good the benefit, you'll need people around to watch the home health aides and chore workers who come in; you may need volunteer help when the professional help has left for the day; and you'll need someone to judge when home care is no longer enough.

TAX-QUALIFIED POLICIES

Under one of the provisions of the 1996 Health Insurance Portability and Accountability Act, up to $2,500 of premiums for a new class of "qualified" long-term-care insurance plans are tax deductible as medical expenses, as are up to $2,500 of premiums for all policies bought before 1997. The deduction may not amount to much in tax savings. Only 29 percent of taxpayers and very few seniors itemize deductions. For those who do, medical expenses are deductible only to the extent that the total of all such expenses exceeds 7.5 percent of adjusted gross income. So a person with, say, $60,000 in adjusted gross income can deduct from income (not from taxes) only those expenses above $4,500 for the year.

If you think counting the premium as a medical expense would result in worthwhile tax savings, you might consider a qualified plan. But they are far more restrictive than many nonqualified plans. Before you can receive benefits, a licensed health care provider must certify that you are chronically ill; the disability must last at least ninety days; and you must be unable to perform at least two of five or six specified "activities of daily living." You can also qualify if you suffer cognitive impairment that requires "substantial supervision." You cannot, however, receive benefits for a nursing home stay resulting from "medical necessity"—a common benefit trigger in nonqualified plans.

The benefits of a qualified plan are not taxable, but it is not clear whether that's true for benefits from a nonqualified plan. The insurance industry lobbied hard for these tax incentives. Not only are they selling points (if not very convincing ones), but the limitations dictated by law will save insurers money in benefits that should have gone to policyholders in need of care. A few companies are continuing to sell nonqualified plans; others have chosen to sell only tax-qualified plans. Consider both kinds.

PARTNERSHIP POLICIES

You may decide to compromise on a policy that will pay benefits for four years, since only 10 percent of nursing home residents stay longer and lifetime benefits are extremely expensive. But your efforts to insure against financial ruin can be thwarted if you stay after your benefits run out and you are forced to go on Medicaid. In four states— California, Connecticut, Indiana, and New York—you can buy a special policy that guarantees to protect some or all of your assets from a Medicaid spend-down, so you don't need lifetime coverage. The policies are sold by private insurers in a partnership with each state's Medicaid program, and are intended to help people with assets of between $30,000 and $100,000—the nonpoor who are the ones most likely to lose everything should they be forced onto Medicaid.

Here's how "partnership" policies work: In California, Connecticut, and Indiana, you buy a policy that pays benefits equal to the amount of assets you want to protect. If you want to shelter, say, $100,000 in assets, you buy a policy that comes close to paying out benefits of $100,000. If you become eligible for Medicaid, you can keep $100,000 of your assets. In New York, asset protection is even more generous. Buy a policy with three years of coverage, and you become eligible for Medicaid after that period (or after six years of home care) without spending down any of your assets.*

Partnership policies protect only assets, not income. To become eligible for Medicaid after benefits are exhausted, you must still meet all of the eligibility requirements and spend all your income on care, apart from any allowance for a spouse or for personal needs. The same is true for nonpartnership policies. Contrary to what agents may tell you, no policy protects your income once benefits are used up and you go on Medicaid.

Some partnership policies are better than the more traditional offerings, and several have features we consider paramount, such as built-in 5 percent compounded inflation coverage, so benefits automatically keep up with inflation. Some also have guaranteed coverage of some types of assisted living, which you may want in a policy. Partnership policies do have one drawback: If you move to another state, you retain the policy's coverage but not the feature that protects your assets from a Medicaid spend-down after the benefits are exhausted, that is, unless you move back to the state where you bought the policy.

Agents don't particularly like to sell partnership policies, and you may hear them disparage the coverage. Keep a lookout for agents who compare the premium for a partnership plan with inflation coverage to the premium for a nonpartnership plan without inflation coverage or without some other important option. They are doing that to make the nonpartnership policy look cheaper.

If you live in one of the four states offering these plans, seriously consider them, unless you know for sure you are planning to retire outside the state.

HOW TO DEAL WITH THE AGENT

While you are doing your shopping, it's important to understand the sales pitch. Most insurance companies train their agents to parry your

---

* Indiana has changed its law to allow protection for all assets if maximum benefits are at least equal to the state-determined dollar amount.

concerns, gloss over objections, and steer you to a policy that most benefits them, not you. If you understand what they are really saying, it will be easier to arrive at the right decision about coverage, benefits, and inflation protection.

What follows is the six-step presentation that most agents follow to some degree, gleaned from watching thirteen sales presentations for long-term-care insurance, and advice on how to interpret what you may hear.

The Warm-up

What agents say Training manuals recommend getting a prospect's attention by "disturbing him or her with the facts about long-term care." "What if you woke up and couldn't get out of bed or dress yourself?" asked one agent. Another expounded on the presumed horrors of nursing homes, especially those with Medicaid patients. "There are those that smell and those that don't," he said flatly.

What to remember The quality of a nursing home has little to do with who pays the bill. The purpose of insurance is to protect your assets. It won't make life in a nursing home any easier. If you have few assets, or if you don't need to preserve your assets for your spouse or your heirs, you don't need long-term-care insurance.

Establishing Need

What agents say Most focus on the likelihood of a nursing home stay rather than on the true reason to buy insurance. They compare the risk of a nursing home stay to the lower risk of a house fire or a traffic accident. "The probability your home will burn down is one in four-teen hundred, but for those over sixty-five, three out of five will use a long-term-care facility," explained one salesman.

Some agents promise that insurance guarantees the quality of care you'll receive in a nursing home. "This insurance makes sure you have good care," one agent asserted. "Facilities are full," said another. "A lot of times plans help get you in. It almost acts like a VIP card."

Other agents get right to the point. "I'm going to establish if you need it," said one. "Nursing homes cost between $50,000 and $2 million. Would you have $2 million to remain self-insured?" When they do mention Medicaid or Medicare, it's to disparage both programs. One agent told of her "dear friend," who died of lung cancer. "I learned too powerfully what Medicare pays. You know Medicare kicks you out."

What to remember Comparative statistics about the risk of fires and auto accidents have no relevance to your need for a long-term-care policy. And private insurance doesn't guarantee good care. Many facilities that accept Medicaid offer fine care, while some that want only those who can pay privately are dreadful places. Even if insurance got you a private room in a facility, it will not guarantee that facility won't eventually make you share a room once the policy benefits are depleted.

Don't confuse Medicare with Medicaid. Medicare does not pay for much long-term care. It never has.

Pitching the Product

What agents say "Most consumers don't understand benefits," says Glen Levit, vice president of Penn Treaty Life. Besides, he says, "an agent can make any policy sound better than another." Or make them sound all the same. "All policies are virtually identical," one agent said. "It's not real important to compare benefits."

Another said that "the better policies are renewable for life. Guaranteed renewability is not in all policies." (In fact, all policies are guaranteed renewable.) He added that "a lot of policies state you must be in the hospital for three days." That's a condition for Medicare skilled-nursing coverage, not a condition now found in insurance policies.

It was a rare agent who explained the crucial points of difference. "The most exciting thing about our policy is that it pays for assisted living," said one enthusiastic saleswoman. How did the policy define assisted living? She didn't know. She admitted that she hadn't really read the policy.

No agent discussed how disabled you must be to qualify for benefits—a major difference among policies. Instead, they harped on frills—"the icing on the cake," as one agent put it. They ticked off provisions for reserving beds, restoring benefits after a short stay, and other such peripheral provisions.

What to remember Ask for a thorough explanation of what degree of disability triggers benefits, and ask the agent to tell you how the policy defines "assisted living." Those are the things that matter, and that's where we found big differences among policies. Get the actual policy, and read it before you buy.

Distrust any agent who talks about three-day hospital stays and guaranteed renewability. State laws long ago wiped out requirements for hospital stays before nursing home coverage begins, and all policies are guaranteed renewable. Agents who mention those things are living in the dark ages of long-term-care insurance. Everything else they tell you is suspect.

Ignore the frills. They are not the reason to buy.

Trashing Inflation Coverage

What agents say Companies and their agents don't like to discuss inflation coverage because it can more than double the premium and scotch a sale. "The only people buying inflation coverage are those who feel a deterioration in their health," said one agent. "People who are not healthy are taking advantage of this." Another agent offered this bit of demographic and economic wisdom: "Older people are less vulnerable to inflation. They are going to die before it doubles. Nursing home costs won't double in ten years."

What to remember Think of a premium quoted for a policy without inflation coverage as a fictitious price. Such coverage is essential. Assuming 5 percent inflation per year, a stay that costs $3,300 a month today will cost $5,375 in ten years and $8,756 in twenty years. Older people are just as vulnerable. Reread what happened to the Nebraska woman (see page 282).

Finding the Right Premium

What agents say Salespeople size you up by looking at your home and neighborhood, and then try to tailor a policy to a premium they think will close the deal. "We're going to look at prices first, and then I'll tell you what is best," said one. If eliminating inflation coverage doesn't hold down the premium, out come other options, such as survivor's benefits or discounts for buying two policies instead of one.

What to remember Don't let the prospect of a lower premium push you into a policy that provides less coverage than you really need. A lower daily benefit brings down the premium; a high deductible, or elimination period, brings down the premium; and less than full inflation coverage brings down the premium. But a premium that leaves you underinsured is no bargain.

The Close

What agents say Agents know how to parry your objections. When you say you'll have to think about it, the agent will tell you, "If you wait too long, the price goes up, and your health could deteriorate."

If you appear concerned about the cost, the agent is likely to play the "quality company" card. One agent was bold enough to say his company had never denied a claim. "The company doesn't review them," he asserted. "You and your doctor are in charge. We had one woman in a facility in Wisconsin because her doctor said she shouldn't be on icy sidewalks." Another agent came up with this: "Making comparisons is hard to do," he said. "It's like comparing oranges and tangerines. You have to go through the same brain damage we've just done." Then he pulled out a chart that illustrated the company's 28 percent share of the market. "What this implies," he said, "is that we must meet our obligations. If we don't keep our ear to the ground, we'd lose our 28 percent share in a heartbeat."

What to remember Don't buy from the first salesperson who comes along. Take your time. It's true that the price depends on your age at the time you buy, but the price won't increase much in the few months it may take to shop carefully. Company strength is important, but you can't judge it by market share or by anything else a salesperson is likely to tell you.

MAKING TRADE-OFFS

Unless you are very wealthy, it's not likely you can buy everything you want in a policy. Here is a guide to narrowing down your choices:

1. Find out what a comprehensive policy with lifetime benefits and full inflation coverage costs. This is the policy that will protect you in

case of all contingencies. Since most people can't afford that coverage, the next step is to begin dropping off what is secondary in importance.

2. Consider whether home care is really necessary. If home care is not feasible for you, don't add this coverage to your policy. If you already have health problems, can you realistically care for a frail spouse? You can save a lot of money by not adding home care coverage. A comprehensive policy with home care coverage costs a sixty-five-year-old $3,057 on average. A nursing home–only policy costs on average $2,299, or about 25 percent less.

3. If you want home care, what benefit level is realistic at what price? Using a home care benefit that is the same as a nursing home benefit probably means you should be in a nursing home anyway, probably at a lower cost. Do you really need a large home care benefit? If you have to pay a lot more for the ability to use informal caregivers like family and friends, the price may not be worth it.

4. Do you want to buy one policy or two, or investigate a shared benefit option offered by some companies? With a shared benefit, the company allows one spouse to use some of the benefits from the other spouse's policy when his or her own coverage has been used up. If you can afford only one policy, buy coverage for the spouse who has the greatest risk. That decision depends on the health of both spouses, their relative ages, and availability of family members to take on caregiving chores.

5. If you want two policies, cutting the benefit period for both may free up enough money for two premiums.

6. Reduce the benefit period instead of forgoing inflation coverage. If you are healthy enough to pass a company's underwriting requirements, chances are you won't be using the policy for a long time. Inflation will devour the policy's purchasing power.

7. If you reach the point of having to cut inflation coverage, you probably should not buy a policy.

USING THE RATINGS

The Ratings in Appendices S and T give information about many policies currently on the market. The guide to the Ratings tells how to use them to pick a policy.

Pay close attention to the value index in the Ratings, which gives an idea of how likely a rate increase might be. A lower index suggests future price increases; a higher one may indicate more stability. While the past does not necessarily predict what a carrier is likely to do in the future, and our Ratings are based on 1997 policies, it may give some indication of which companies may have underpriced their policies. Like the Blaus featured at the beginning of this chapter, most people have a hard time learning about rate increases. States don't make this information readily available, and if they do, it's almost impossible to use. Partly because of the Blaus' experience, the state of California now requires companies to disclose their history of rate increases not only in California but in all states where they have sold long-term-care insurance.

IF YOU HAVE AN OLD POLICY

Policies considered state of the art in the early 1990s are inferior today. An older plan might be very restrictive—it might require a hospital stay before paying benefits for nursing home care, or it might not cover assisted living. Or more likely, the daily benefit may be too low to cover current nursing home costs, let alone costs in the future.

To evaluate an old policy, do the following:

1. Consider how much income you will have to cover nursing home care. Look at your income from Social Security, private pensions, and investments as well as coverage provided by long-term-care insurance. Consider what that income will be when you are eighty or eighty-five. Income usually does not increase at the same rate as nursing home costs, so chances are you will have less income in your later years to cover large nursing home bills.

2. If your income from all those sources is not sufficient, and you don't want to spend down to become eligible for Medicaid, you may have to buy more insurance—that is, if you are healthy enough to qualify for a policy.

3. Next, examine the coverage on your old policy. What types of facilities are covered and how much does the policy pay? Is there inflation protection? Are the benefit triggers too restrictive? If the policy comes up short, you will also need to supplement your coverage.

4. If your current policy is deficient, see if you can update coverage to bring the benefit in line with today's costs and to add inflation protection for the future. If your insurance company offers future purchase options, take them.

5. If you can't add to your existing policy, think about buying a new policy to supplement the one you have, providing, of course, you can pay the premium and your health is good enough to qualify. It's usually unwise to drop a policy on which you have paid premiums for a long time.

USING A LONG-TERM-CARE POLICY

Insurance counselors report that adult children frequently do not know their parents have purchased long-term-care coverage. They don't know until they examine the contents of their parents' safe-deposit box. The worksheet in Chapter 1 will help you figure out if they do. It's a good idea to locate the policy and know what it covers long before your parents must use it. If your parents have purchased one of the newer policies, it may have a provision for notifying a third party, such as an adult child, if the premiums are not being paid.

Once you have located the policy, contact the company to file a claim. Ask what documents the company requires, such as the license for the facility your relative has entered, bills, medical records, and so forth.

If you find that your relative owns a very old policy—one that requires him or her to be hospitalized for three days before entering a nursing home—you could try negotiating with the company to waive the requirement. (Newer policies don't have that restriction.) If that doesn't work, you could contact your state's insurance counseling program or an attorney specializing in elder law.

Consider when you want the benefits to begin. It may not be prudent to use up the benefit quickly on home care and have nothing left over for more intensive types of care. You may want to arrange for family and other informal caregivers rather than paying aides from an agency. That could save the benefit. It may take some creative planning on your part to use the policy benefits wisely.

If you do have a dispute over payment, see if the company will accept an independent assessment of your relative's situation. Your state insurance counseling program might be able to tell you where to get such a review.

Be aware that families have gotten into disputes with insurance companies over these issues:

- The three-day prior hospitalization rule
- Whether the care required is skilled or custodial
- Qualification of caregivers
- The type of facility where the policyholder resides is not covered by the policy

KEY DECISION POINTS

1. Is your income high enough to pay premiums now and in the future and will it accommodate premium increases? If the answer is no, you're not a candidate for long-term-care insurance. If you cannot afford a 50 percent increase in your premium, don't buy.

2. If you're considering buying a policy while you are young, say sixty or sixty-five, and you can't afford to buy full 5 percent inflation coverage, it's best not to buy at all. It's better to save the premiums than to have a policy that will be practically useless in twenty or twenty-five years.

3. Don't buy home care coverage just because an agent recommends it. If you will not have family or friends around to supervise your care, home care coverage is not a good option.

4. Look carefully at the "benefit triggers"—the rules that let you qualify for benefits. Buy the least restrictive policy you can find—that is, one that requires you to fail the fewest number of ADLs, activities of daily living, before benefits kick in. Try to find a policy that lists bathing among the activities you must be unable to perform. Bathing is the easiest ADL to fail.

5. Consider coverage from your employer, but remember there are trade-offs to taking employer coverage. You might be able to get coverage even if you have a health condition that disqualifies you from an individual policy. But when it comes to inflation coverage and other benefits,

your employer gets to choose what to offer, and what is offered may not be what you need.

6. If you have an old policy that still offers sufficient protection against nursing home costs in your area, keep it. If it doesn't, consider adding new increments of coverage from your present carrier or think about buying an additional policy that fills in the gaps.

APPENDIX A: State Insurance Counseling Programs

These programs can help if you have trouble finding a supplemental policy or a Medicare HMO, or if you are having trouble with Medicare.

STATE	ADDRESS	PHONE/FAX
Alabama	Insurance Information Counseling & Assistance Program Alabama Commission on Aging 770 Washington Avenue Montgomery, AL 36130	334-242-5743 334-242-5594 (f)
Alaska	Insurance Counseling & Assistance Program Division of Senior Services 3601 C Street, #310 Anchorage, AK 99503-5209	907-269-3669 907-269-3690 (f)
Arizona	Arizona SHIP Aging & Adult Administration Dept. of Economic Security 1789 W. Jefferson, #950A Phoenix, AZ 85007	602-542-6446 602-542-6575 (f)
Arkansas	Seniors Insurance Network Arkansas State Insurance Dept. 1200 W. 3rd Street Little Rock, AR 72201	501-371-2785 501-371-2618 (f)
California	Health Insurance Counseling & Advocacy Program California Dept. of Aging 1600 K Street Sacramento, CA 95814	916-323-6525 916-327-2081 (f)
	California Health Advocates California HICAP Assoc. P.O. Box 1433 Paradise, CA 95967-1433	530-877-6794 530-877-6790 (f)
Colorado	Senior Health Insurance Assistance Program Colorado Division of Insurance 1560 Broadway, #850 Denver, CO 80202	303-894-7499 x355 303-894-7455 (f)
Connecticut	Connecticut Programs for Health Insurance Assistance Outreach Information & Referral Counseling Eligibility and Screening (CHOICES) Dept. of Social Services Elderly Services Division 25 Sigourney Street, 10th Floor Hartford, CT 06106-5033	860-424-5244 860-424-4966 (f)

District of Columbia	Health Insurance Counseling Project	202-496-6240
	Building A-B, 1st Floor	202-293-4043 (f)
	2136 Pennsylvania Avenue	
	Washington, DC 20052	
	DC Office on Aging	202-724-5626
	441 4th Street, NW, #950	202-724-4979 (f)
	Washington, DC 20001	
Delaware	Elder Information	302-739-6266
	Delaware Insurance Dept.	302-739-5280 (f)
	841 Silver Lake Boulevard	
	Dover, DE 19903	
	Division of Services for Aging & Adults with Physical Disabilities	302-577-4791
	1901 N. DuPont Highway	302-577-4793 (f)
	New Castle, DE 19720	
Florida	Serving Health Insurance Needs of Elders (SHINE)	850-414-2060
	Dept. of Elder Affairs	850-414-2002 (f)
	4040 Esplanade Way, #280 S	
	Tallahassee, FL 32399-7000	
Georgia	Health Insurance Counseling Assistance & Referral for the Elderly	404-657-5347
	Division of Aging Services	404-657-5285 (f)
	#2 Peachtree Street, NE, 36th Floor	
	Atlanta, GA 30303	
Hawaii	SAGE PLUS	808-586-7300
	Executive Office on Aging	808-586-0185 (f)
	250 S. Hotel Street, #109	
	Honolulu, HI 96813-2831	
Idaho	Senior Health Insurance Benefits Advisors	208-334-4350
	Dept. of Insurance	208-334-4389 (f)
	700 W. State, 3rd Floor	
	Boise, ID 83720-0043	
Illinois	Senior Health Insurance Program	217-782-0004
	Dept. of Insurance	217-782-4105 (f)
	320 W. Washington Street	
	Springfield, IL 62767-0001	
Indiana	SHIIP Senior Health Insurance Information Program	317-233-3551
	Indiana Dept. of Insurance	317-232-5251 (f)
	311 W. Washington Street, #300	
	Indianapolis, IN 46204-2787	

Iowa	SHIIP Senior Health Insurance Information Program	515-242-5190
	IA Insurance Division	515-281-8449 (f)
	330 Maple Street	
	Des Moines, IA 50319-0065	
Kansas	Senior Health Insurance Counseling for Kansas (SHICK)	316-337-6010
	Kansas Insurance Dept.	316-337-6018 (f)
	130 S. Market Street, #4030	
	P.O. Box 3850	
	Wichita, KS 67201-3850	
Kentucky	SHIP	502-564-7372
	Office of Aging	502-564-4595 (f)
	Cabinet for Health Services	
	5th Floor West—CCF	
	275 E. Main Street	
	Frankfort, KY 40621	
Louisiana	Senior Health Insurance Information Program	225-342-6334
	Louisiana Dept. of Insurance	225-219-4640 (f)
	P.O. Box 94214	
	Baton Rouge, LA 70804-9214	
Maine	Maine Health Insurance Counseling Program	207-624-5335
	Bureau of Elder & Adult Services	207-624-5361 (f)
	35 Anthony Avenue	
	State House, Station #11	
	Augusta, ME 04333-0011	
Maryland	Senior Health Insurance Assistance Program (SHIP)	410-767-1109
	Dept. of Aging	410-333-7943 (f)
	State Office Building, #1007	
	301 W. Preston Street	
	Baltimore, MD 21201	
Massachusetts	Serving Health Information Needs of Elders (SHINE)	617-222-7435
	Executive Office of Elder Affairs	617-727-9368 (f)
	1 Ashburton Place, 5th Floor	
	Boston, MA 02108	
Michigan	Medicare/Medicaid Assistance Program	517-373-4071
	Michigan Office of Services to the Aging	517-373-4092 (f)
	P.O. Box 30676	
	Lansing, MI 48909-8176	
Minnesota	Minnesota Health Insurance Counseling Program	651-296-3839
	Board on Aging	651-297-7855 (f)
	444 Lafayette Road	
	St. Paul, MN 55155-3843	

Mississippi	Mississippi Insurance Counseling & Assistance Program	601-359-4929
	Dept. of Human Services	601-359-4370 (f)
	Division of Aging & Adult Services	
	750 N. State Street	
	Jackson, MS 39202	
Missouri	Community Leaders Assisting the Insured of Missouri (CLAIM)	573-893-7900 x237
	MPCRF, CLAIM Program	573-893-5827 (f)
	505 Hobbs Road, #100	
	Jefferson City, MO 65109	
Montana	Montana Partnership for Health Insurance Information Counseling &	406-585-0773
	Assistance Program	406-585-0773 (f)
	212 Ridge Trail	
	Bozman, MT 59715	
Nebraska	Nebraska Health Insurance Information, Counseling & Assistance Program	402-471-4506
	Dept. of Insurance	1-800-234-7119
	941 O Street, #400	402-471-6559 (f)
	Lincoln, NE 68508	
Nevada	Division for Aging Services	702-486-3545
	SHIP State Health Insurance Advisory Program	702-486-3572 (f)
	340 N. 11th, #203	
	Las Vegas, NV 89101	
	Nevada State Health Insurance Advisory Program (SHIP)	775-964-1033
	HC65 Box 8	
	Austin, NV 89310	
New Hampshire	HICEAS—Health Insurance Counseling Education Assistance Services	603-862-0092
	325 Nesmith Hall	603-862-0107 (f)
	131 Main Street	
	Durham, NH 03824	
	Division of Elderly & Adult Services	603-271-3944
	State Office Park South	603-271-4643 (f)
	115 Pleasant Street, Annex Bldg., 1	
	Concord, NH 03301-7325	
New Jersey	State Health Insurance Assistance (SHIP)	609-588-3385
	Dept. of Health & Senior Services	609-588-4565 (f)
	Division of Senior Affairs	
	Box 807	
	Trenton, NJ 08625-0807	
New Mexico	Health Insurance Benefits Assistance Corps	505-827-7640
	State Agency on Aging	505-827-7649 (f)
	La Villa Rivera Building	

	228 E. Palace Avenue, Ground Floor Santa Fe, NM 87501	
New York	Health Insurance Information Counseling & Assistance Program (HIICAP) Office for the Aging 2 Empire State Plaza Agency Building 2 Albany, NY 12223-1251	518-473-5108 518-486-2225 (f)
North Carolina	Seniors' Health Insurance Information Program Dept. of Insurance 111 Seaboard Avenue Raleigh, NC 27604	919-733-0111 1-800-443-9354 919-733-3682 (f)
North Dakota	Senior Health Insurance Counseling Insurance Dept. 600 E. Boulevard Department 401 Bismarck, ND 58505	701-328-2977 701-328-4880 (f)
Ohio	Ohio Senior Health Insurance Information Program Office of Consumer Advocate Dept. of Insurance 2100 Stella Court Columbus, OH 43215-1067	614-644-3399 614-752-0740 (f)
Oklahoma	Senior Health Insurance Counseling Program Dept. of Insurance P.O. Box 53408 3814 N. Santa Fe Oklahoma City, OK 73152-3408	405-521-6628 405-522-3761 (f)
Oregon	SHIBA Dept. of Consumer & Business Services Insurance Division 350 Winter Street, NE, #440-2 Salem, OR 97310	503-947-7263 503-378-4351 (f)
Pennsylvania	APPRISE Dept. of Aging Forum Place 555 Walnut Street, 5th Floor Harrisburg, PA 17101-1919	717-783-8975 717-772-2730 (f)
Puerto Rico	ICA Program Governor's Office for Elderly Affairs P.O. Box 50063 Old San Juan Station San Juan, PR 00902	787-721-8590 787-721-6510 (f)

Rhode Island	Senior Health Insurance Program (SHIP)	401-222-2880 x232
	Dept. of Elderly Affairs	401-222-2858 x232
	160 Pine Street	401-222-2130 (f)
	Providence, RI 02903-3708	
South Carolina	Dept. of Health & Human Services	803-898-2850
	Bureau of Senior Services-I-CARE	803-898-4513 (f)
	Division on Aging	
	1801 Main Street	
	Columbia, SC 29202	
South Dakota	SHIINE Program	605-773-3656
	Office of Adult Services & Aging	605-773-6834 (f)
	700 Governors Drive	
	Pierre, SD 57501-2291	
	SHIINE	605-336-2475
	East River Legal Services	605-336-6919 (f)
	335 N. Main Avenue, #300	
	Sioux Falls, SD 57102-0305	
	SHIINE	605-342-3494
	2525 W. Main Street, #203	605-342-7718 (f)
	Rapid City, SD 57702-2439	
Tennessee	Tennessee Association of Legal Services	615-242-0438
	211 Union Street, #833	615-244-4920 (f)
	Nashville, TN 37201	
	TN Commission on Aging	615-741-2056
	500 Deaderick Street, 9th Floor	615-741-3309 (f)
	Nashville, TN 37243-0860	
Texas	Texas Dept. on Aging	512-424-6857
	4900 North Lamar, 4th Floor	512-424-6891 (f)
	Austin, TX 78704	
	Texas Dept. of Insurance	512-322-4340
	P.O. Box 149091	512-305-7463 (f)
	Austin, TX 78714-9091	
Utah	Health Insurance Information	801-538-3910
	Division of Aging & Adult Services	801-538-4395 (f)
	Dept. of Social Services	
	Box 45500	
	120 North—200 West	
	Salt Lake City, UT 84103	

Vermont	Health Information Counseling & Assistance Program	802-241-4425
	Dept. of Aging & Disabilities	802-241-2325 (f)
	103 S. Main Street	
	Waterbury, VT 05671-2371	
	Northeastern Vermont AAA	802-748-5182
	1161 Portland Street	802-748-6622 (f)
	St. Johnsburg, VT 05819	
Virginia	Virginia Insurance Counseling Assistance Project (VICAP)	804-662-7048
	Dept. for the Aging	804-662-9354 (f)
	1600 Forest Avenue	
	Preston Building, #102	
	Richmond, VA 23229	
Virgin Islands	Virgin Islands ICA Program	340-778-6311 x2338
	Governor Juan F. Louis Hospital & Medical Center	340-778-5500 (f)
	Estate Diamond Ruby/Box 18	
	St. Croix, VI 00820-4421	
Washington	Statewide Health Insurance Benefits Advisors (SHIBA)	206-654-1833
	State Office of Insurance Commissioner	360-407-0349 (f)
	P.O. Box 40256	
	Olympia, WA 98504-0256	
West Virginia	West Virginia Senior Health Insurance Network	304-558-3317
	WV Bureau of Senior Services	304-558-0004 (f)
	1900 Kanawha Boulevard, E	
	Charleston, WV 25305-0160	
Wisconsin	Medigap Helpline: Elderly Benefit Specialist Program	608-267-3201
	Bureau of Aging & LTC Resources	608-267-3203 (f)
	Dept. of Health & Family Services	
	217 S. Hamilton Street, #300	
	Madison, WI 53703	
Wyoming	Wyoming Senior Health Insurance Information Program	307-777-7401
	Wyoming Insurance Dept.	307-777-5895 (f)
	122 W. 25th Street	
	Herschler Building, 3-East	
	Cheyenne, WY 82002	
	Wyoming Senior Citizens	307-856-6880
	1130 Major Avenue	307-856-4466 (f)
	P.O. Box BD	
	Riverton, WY 82501	

APPENDIX B: State Units on Aging

Use these agencies to find your local area agency on aging, which in turn can help you find services for your loved one.

Alabama
Commission on Aging
P.O. Box 301851
770 Washington Avenue, #470
Montgomery, AL 36130-1851
334-242-5743
1-800-243-5463
Fax: 334-242-5594

Alaska
Division of Senior Services
Dept. of Administration
P.O. Box 110209
Juneau, AK 99811-0209
907-465-4879
Fax: 907-465-4716

Arizona
Aging & Adult Administration
Dept. of Economic Security
1789 W. Jefferson, #950A
Phoenix, AZ 85007
602-542-4446
Fax: 602-542-6575

Arkansas
Division of Aging & Adult Services
Arkansas Dept. of Human Services
P.O. Box 1437, Slot 1412
7th and Main Streets
Little Rock, AR 72203
501-682-2441
Fax: 501-682-8155

California
Dept. of Aging
1600 K Street
Sacramento, CA 95814
916-322-5290
Fax: 916-324-1903

Colorado
Division of Aging & Adult Services
Dept. of Human Services
110 16th Street, #200
Denver, CO 80202-5202

303-620-4147
Fax: 303-620-4189

Connecticut
Elderly Services Division
Dept. of Social Services
25 Sigourney Street
Hartford, CT 06106
860-424-5277
Fax: 860-424-4966

Delaware
Division of Services for Aging & Adults w/Physical
    Disabilities
Dept. of Health & Social Services
1901 N. DuPont Highway
New Castle, DE 19720
302-577-4791
Fax: 302-577-4793

District of Columbia
Office on Aging
One Judiciary Square
441 4th Street, NW, 9th Floor
Washington, DC 20001
202-724-5622
Fax: 202-724-4979

Florida
Dept. of Elder Affairs
Building B, #152
4040 Esplanade Way
Tallahassee, FL 32399
850-414-2000
Fax: 850-414-2004

Georgia
Division of Aging Services
#2 Peachtree Street NW #36-385
Atlanta, GA 30303
404-657-5258
Fax: 404-657-5285

Guam
Division of Senior Citizens
Dept. of Public Health & Social Services

Government of Guam
P.O. Box 2816
Hagaina, Guam 96932
011-671-475-0263
Fax: 671-477-2930

Hawaii
Executive Office on Aging
No 1 Capitol District
250 S. Hotel Street, #109
Honolulu, HI 96813-2831
808-586-0100
Fax: 808-586-0185

Idaho
Commission on Aging
3380 Americana Terrace, #120
P.O. Box 83720
Boise, ID 83720-0007
208-334-2423
Fax: 208-334-3033

Illinois
Dept. on Aging
421 E. Capitol Avenue
Springfield, IL 62701
217-785-2870
Fax: 217-785-4477

Indiana
Bureau of Aging in Home Services
402 W. Washington Street
P.O. Box 7083
Indianapolis, IN 46207-7083
317-232-7020
Fax: 317-232-7867

Iowa
Dept. of Elder Affairs
Clemens Bldg., 3rd Floor
200 10th Street
Des Moines, IA 50309-3609
515-281-5187
Fax: 515-281-4036

Kansas
Dept. on Aging
New England Building
503 S. Kansas
Topeka, KS 66603-3404
785-296-4986
Fax: 785-296-0256

Kentucky
Office of Aging Services
Cabinet for Health Services
275 E. Main Street, 5 West
Frankfort, KY 40621
502-564-6930
Fax: 502-564-4595

Louisiana
Office of Elderly Affairs
Elderly Protective Services
P.O. Box 80374
412 N. 4th Street
Baton Rouge, LA 70898-0374
225-342-9722
Fax: 225-342-7144

Maine
Bureau of Elder & Adult Services
Dept. of Human Services
#11 State House Station
Augusta, ME 04333-0011
207-624-5335
Fax: 207-624-5361

Maryland
Dept. of Aging
State Office Building, #1007
301 W. Preston Street
Baltimore, MD 21201
410-767-1100
Fax: 410-333-7943

Massachusetts
Executive Office of Elder Affairs
1 Ashburton Place, 5th Floor
Boston, MA 02108
617-222-7470
Fax: 617-727-6944

Michigan
Office of Services to the Aging
P.O. Box 30676
Lansing, MI 48909-8176
517-373-8230
Fax: 517-373-4092

Minnesota
Board on Aging
444 Lafayette Road
St. Paul, MN 55155-3843

651-296-2770
Fax: 651-297-7855

Mississippi
Council on Aging
Division of Aging & Adult Services
750 N. State Street
Jackson, MS 39202
601-359-4929
Fax: 601-359-4370

Missouri
Division of Aging
Dept. of Social Services
P.O. Box 1337
615 Howerton Court
Jefferson City, MO 65102-1337
573-751-3082
Fax: 573-751-8687

Montana
Senior Long-Term-Care Division
111 Sanders Street
P.O. Box 4210
Helena, MT 59604
406-444-7788
Fax: 406-444-7743

Nebraska
Division of Aging Services
Dept. of Health & Human Services
P.O. Box 95044
301 Centennial Mall–South
Lincoln, NE 68509
402-471-2307
Fax: 402-471-4619

Nevada
Division for Aging Services
Dept. of Human Resources
3416 Goni Road, Building D-132
Carson City, NV 89706
775-687-4210
Fax: 775-687-4264

New Hampshire
Division of Elderly & Adult Services
State Office Park South
129 Pleasant Street
Concord, NH 03301-3843
603-271-4394
Fax: 603-271-4643

New Jersey
Division of Senior Affairs
Dept. of Health & Senior Services
P.O. Box 807
Trenton, NJ 08625-0807
609-588-3141
Fax: 609-588-3317

New Mexico
State Agency on Aging
La Villa Rivera Building
228 E. Palace Avenue, Ground Floor
Santa Fe, NM 87501
505-827-7640
Fax: 505-827-7649

New York
Office for the Aging
New York State Plaza
Agency Building #2
Albany, NY 12223
518-474-5731
Fax: 518-474-1398

North Carolina
Division of Aging
CB 29531
693 Palmer Drive
Raleigh, NC 27626-0531
919-733-3983
Fax: 919-733-0443

North Dakota
Aging Services Division
Dept. of Human Services
600 S. 2nd Street, #1C
Bismarck, ND 58504
701-328-8910
Fax: 701-328-8989

Mariana Islands
CNMI Office on Aging, DC&CA
P.O. Box 2178
Saipan, MP 96950
011-671-734-4361
Fax: 011-670-2331327

Ohio
Dept. of Aging
50 W. Broad Street, 9th Floor
Columbus, OH 43215-5928

614-466-5500
Fax: 614-466-5741

Oklahoma
Aging Services Division
Dept. of Human Services
P.O. Box 25352
312 N.E. 28th Street
Oklahoma City, OK 73105
405-521-2327
Fax: 405-521-2086

Oregon
Senior & Disabled Services Division
500 Summer Street, NE, 2nd Floor
Salem, OR 97310-1015
503-945-5811
Fax: 503-373-7823

Pennsylvania
Dept. of Aging
Forum Place
555 Walnut Street, 5th Floor
Harrisburg, PA 17101-1919
717-783-1550
Fax: 717-772-3382

Puerto Rico
Governor's Office for Elderly Affairs
P.O. Box 50063
Old San Juan Station
San Juan, PR 00902
787-721-5710
Fax: 787-721-6510

Rhode Island
Dept. of Elderly Affairs
160 Pine Street
Providence, RI 02903-3708
401-222-2858
Fax: 401-222-1490

(American) Samoa
Territorial Administration on Aging
American Samoa Government
Pago Pago, American Samoa 96799
011-684-633-1251-1252
Fax: 684-633-2533

South Carolina
Dept. of Health & Human Services
P.O. Box 8206

1801 Main Street
Columbia, SC 29202-8206
803-898-2501
Fax: 803-898-4515

South Dakota
Office of Adult Services & Aging
700 Governors Drive
Pierre, SD 57501
605-773-3656
Fax: 605-773-4855

Tennessee
Commission on Aging
Andrew Jackson Building
500 Deaderick Building, 9th Floor
Nashville, TN 37243-0860
615-741-2056
Fax: 615-741-3309

Texas
Dept. on Aging
4900 N. Lamar, 4th Floor
Austin, TX 78751-2316
512-424-6840
Fax: 512-424-6890

Republic of Palau
Agency on Aging
P.O. Box 100
Koror, PW 96940

Utah
Division of Aging & Adult Services
Dept. of Social Services
Box 45500
120 North—200 West
Salt Lake City, UT 84145-0500
801-538-3910
Fax: 801-538-4395

Vermont
Aging & Disabilities
103 S. Main Street
Waterbury, VT 05671-2301
802-241-2400
Fax: 802-241-2325

Virginia
Dept. for the Aging
1600 Forest Avenue
Preston Building, #102

Richmond, VA 23229
804-662-9333
Fax: 804-662-9354

Virgin Islands
Senior Citizen Affairs
Dept. of Human Services
#19 Estate Diamond Fredericksted
St. Croix, VI 00840
340-692-5950
Fax: 340-692-2062

Washington
Aging & Adult Services Administration
Dept. of Social & Health Services
P.O. Box 45050
Olympia, WA 98504-5050
360-902-7797
Fax: 360-902-7848

West Virginia
West Virginia Bureau of Senior Services
1900 Kanawha Boulevard, East

Holly Grove-Building 10
Charleston, WV 25305-0160
304-558-5609
Fax: 304-558-5609

Wisconsin
Bureau of Aging & LTC Resources
Dept. of Health and Family Services
One West Wilson Street
P.O. Box 7851
Madison, WI 53707-7851
608-266-2536
Fax: 608-267-3203

Wyoming
WDH, Division on Aging
Hathaway Building, #139
Cheyenne, WY 82002-0710
307-777-7986
1-800-442-2766
Fax: 307-777-5340

APPENDIX C: State Pharmaceutical Assistance Programs

Some states have programs that help residents obtain pharmaceuticals. Note that there are restrictions and sometimes tough eligibility requirements.

NAME OF PROGRAM AND CONTACT INFORMATION	DESCRIPTION, LIMITATIONS, AND RESTRICTIONS	ELIGIBILITY, COPAYMENTS	ENROLLMENT
CONNECTICUT			
Connecticut Pharmaceutical Assistance Contract to the Elderly & the Disabled Program ConnPACE P.O. Box 5011 Hartford, CT 06102 *www.dss.state.ct.us/elderly/health/htm*	• Supplements the cost of many prescription drugs, insulin, and diabetic supplies • 30-day supply or 120-dose limit, whichever is greater • Excludes antihistamines, contraceptives, cough preparations, diet pills, experimental drugs, multivitamins, smoking cessation gums, drugs deemed ineffective by the FDA, products described for cosmetic purposes, and drugs not made by specific pharmaceutical companies • Generic drugs are mandatory	• Age 65+ or disabled adults 18+ who receive Social Security Disability or SSI benefits • Connecticut residency for at least six months prior to application • Have an adjusted gross income at or below a level that is determined annually • Not enrolled in Medicaid or other insurance program that reimburses for prescription drugs • $12 copayment • $4.10 dispensing cost	• $25 annual fee • Applications available at pharmacies, senior centers, social service and municipal agencies for the elderly • Include proof of age, residency, income; disability if applicable, and any existing insurance cards • Members receive a pharmacy benefit card • Annual reenrollment • Call 1-800-423-5026 or 203-678-1740 for information; 860-832-9265 in the Hartford area

DELAWARE

The Nemours Health Clinic Pharmaceutical Assistance Program

1801 Rockland Road

Wilmington, DE

19803

302-651-4400

- This program is funded by the Alfred I. Du Pont Foundation, not the state of Delaware
- It discounts on prescriptions at specific locations throughout the state and also maintains a senior citizens clinic
- Maximum benefit of $2,000 based on average retail cost
- Excludes injectables, except insulin and most over-the-counter drugs except as prescribed
- 30-day or 100-dose supply

- Age 65 or more
- Delaware resident
- U.S. citizen
- Current income, including Social Security, must not exceed $12,500 single, $17,125 married
- Pay $5.50 copayment
- Pay 20 percent of drug cost
- Pay $4 dispensing fee

- Provide documentation of age, U.S. citizenship, U.S. residency, and all current income
- For information call New Castle County 302-642-4405;

  Kent and Sussex call 1-800-292-9538 or 1-800-763-9326

NEW JERSEY

Pharmaceutical Assistance to the Aged and Disabled (PAAD)

P.O. Box 715

Trenton, NJ 08625

609-588-7049

800-792-9745

- Excludes drugs not approved by the FDA, purchased outside of the state, or those whose manufacturers have declined to participate
- Covers most prescription drugs, diabetic supplies, and injectable drugs for the treatment of multiple sclerosis
- Also offers financial assistance for Lifeline medical emergency communications and hearing aids
- Generic drugs will be used except when physicians prescribe otherwise
- 34-day or 100-dose supplies for initial prescription, 90-day supplies for refills

- Age 65 or older or
- Disabled adults aged 18 and receiving Social Security Disability (documentation required)
- Permanent residency of 30 days or more
- Have a household income at or below specified amount
- Pay $5 copayment per prescription
- Dispensing fee varies between $3.73 and $4.07
- Authorize the state to collect payments on applicant's behalf from assistance, insurance, and retirement programs
- Not have Medicaid or health insurance or retirement benefits equal or better than the state's program offers. People with limited or partial coverage may be eligible.

- Married couples file separately
- Supply social security number and two current proofs of residency
- Complete application PDF 407K and mail to: AAD Lifeline and Special Benefit Programs CN 715, Trenton, NJ 08625-0715
- Call for more info 1-800-792-9745; (TTY) 609-588-7180
- Upon approval, applicants receive a pharmacy ID card, usually within 30 days
- Most beneficiaries must reapply biannually; some reapply annually

NAME OF PROGRAM
AND CONTACT INFORMATION

DESCRIPTION, LIMITATIONS,
AND RESTRICTIONS

ELIGIBILITY, COPAYMENTS

ENROLLMENT

MAINE

Elderly Low-Cost Drug Program

Maine Bureau of Taxation

State House Station 24

Augusta, ME 04332

207-622-8475

1-800-773-7895

TDD: 207-287-4477

Bureau of Medical Services

Augusta, ME

04333-0011

1-800-321-5557 x7-1818

in Augusta

207-287-1818

- Reduces the cost of drugs to $2 or 20 percent of the price permitted by the Human Services Department, whichever is greater
- Limited to those drugs whose manufacturers participate in the plan

- Age 62 or more or live with a household member who is
- Not getting SSI
- Disabled, defined by receipt of federal disability benefits and age 55 or more. If the disabled person is married and below age 62 they can only claim benefits if their spouse is also disabled
- Residents of Maine for at least one year
- Have household incomes at or less that determined by state legislature
- People who spend 40 percent of their household income on prescription drugs may qualify with higher household income limits
- Pay 20 percent of drug costs
- Pay dispensing fee of $3.35

- Applications available at senior centers, health departments, or call 207-624-7895
- Fill out an application and send it to: Maine Revenue Services, 24 State House Station, Augusta, Maine 04333-0024 (the same form used to apply for tax or rent reform)
- A pharmacy card is mailed to qualified applicants in about four weeks
- Local area agencies on aging will help applicants complete forms if necessary
- Applications may be filed at any time
- Annual reapplication is necessary; apply by November 1 to get new card by January 1
- Touch-Tone phone users may call to apply 207-624-7875

MARYLAND

Maryland Pharmacy
Assistance Program

P.O. Box 386

Baltimore, MD 21203

- Reimbursement program for diabetic drugs and supplies, anti-infectives, AZT, and maintenance drugs for persistent conditions such as hypertension, asthma, heart conditions, osteoporosis, lower back pain, substance abuse, and diabetes
- 75 percent utilization prior to refill
- Excludes prisoners

- Age 19–64
- Income and asset levels as determined by program administrators
- Copayments of $5
- Dispensing fee of $4.21
- Prescriptions must be filled within 10 days of date written
- Only two refills permitted, if prescribed, before new prescription is required

Call to prequalify: 410-767-1455

MASSACHUSETTS

NAME OF PROGRAM AND CONTACT INFORMATION	DESCRIPTION, LIMITATIONS, AND RESTRICTIONS	ELIGIBILITY, COPAYMENTS	ENROLLMENT
Senior Pharmacy Program 124 Watertown Street Watertown, MA 02472 1-800-953-3305	• Benefits limited to $750 per year • Includes most drugs except those excluded by Mass-Health (Medicaid)	• Age 65 or more • Have resided in Massachusetts for at least the previous six months • Are not enrolled in MassHealth (Medicaid) or other prescription drug insurance • Have gross annual income of $12,084 or less • Copayments of $3 for generic drugs and diabetic supplies • Copayments of $10 for nongeneric drugs	• Couples apply individually, annual enrollment fee of $15; automatically deducted from $750 benefit • Submit an application to 124 Watertown Street, Watertown, MA 02472 • 1-800-953-3305 • Upon approval, the program sends approval notice and pharmacy ID cards • Home care corporations offer help completing the applications, including assistance for non-English-speaking residents

MICHIGAN

Emergency Pharmaceutical Program for Seniors

P.O. Box 30676

Lansing, MI

48909-8276

517-373-8230

www.mdch.state.mi.us/mass/masshome.html

- Assists low-income residents with $600 to $1,200 of credit for prescription drugs
- The total amount of the state drug refund program is $20 million. If credits claimed exceed the budgeted amount, credits will be prorated

- Age 65 or older
- Michigan residents
- Have household incomes at or less than determined by legislature
- Have not resided in licensed health care facilities for at least six months during the year claimed
- Must have spent 5 percent or more of household income on prescription drugs, excluding those reimbursed by other insurance programs
- Reimbursement checks mailed in August

- Call for information and applications:
  517-335-1356;
  (TDD) 517-373-9419
- Apply for reimbursement between January 1 and June 1 for drug expenses incurred the previous year
- Send applications to Michigan Dept. of Treasury, Office of Communications
- Area agencies on aging can assist with applications, call local offices or 1-800-487-7000

NAME OF PROGRAM
AND CONTACT INFORMATION

DESCRIPTION, LIMITATIONS,
AND RESTRICTIONS

ELIGIBILITY, COPAYMENTS

ENROLLMENT

NEW JERSEY

Pharmaceutical Assistance to the Aged and Disabled (PAAD)

P.O. Box 715

Trenton, NJ 08625

609-588-7049

1-800-792-9745

- Excludes drugs not approved by the FDA, purchased outside the state, or those whose manufacturers have declined to participate
- Covers most prescription drugs, diabetic supplies, and injectable drugs for the treatment of multiple sclerosis
- Also offers financial assistance for Lifeline medical emergency communications and hearing aids
- Generic drugs will be used except when physicians prescribe otherwise
- 34-day or 100-dose supplies for initial prescription, 90-day supplies for refills

- Age 65 or older or
- Disabled adults aged 18 and receiving Social Security Disability (documentation required)
- Permanent residency of 30 days or more
- Have a household income at or below specified amount
- Pay $5 copayment per prescription
- Dispensing fee varies between $3.73 and $4.07
- Authorize the state to collect payments on applicant's behalf from assistance, insurance, and retirement programs
- Not have Medicaid or health insurance or retirement benefits equal or better than the state's program offers. People with limited or partial coverage may be eligible.

- Married couples file separately
- Supply social security number and two current proofs of residency
- Complete application PDF 407K and mail to: AAD Lifeline and Special Benefit Programs, CN 715, Trenton, NJ 08625-0715
- Call for more info: 1-800-792-9745; (TTY) 609-588-7180
- Upon approval, applicants receive a pharmacy ID card, usually within 30 days
- Most beneficiaries must reapply biannually; some reapply annually

NEW YORK

The Elderly Pharmaceutical Insurance Program (EPIC)

P.O. Box 15018

Albany, NY

12212-5018

1-800-332-3742, also an information hot line, or write to EPIC or go online to:

www.health.state.ny.us /nydoh/epic/epicform.htm

- EPIC has two types of plans; one is fee-based, the other has a deductible
- Most prescription medications are covered, including insulin and diabetic supplies
- 100 tablets or 30-day supply available at any one time
- Prescriptions only available at participating pharmacies

- New York State residents
- Age 65 or older
- Low to moderate annual incomes
- Without Medicaid or other prescription insurance that is equal or better than EPIC
- Seniors with incomes ($0 to $24,400) qualify for the fee plan, which charges annual fees from $8 to $280 per person qualify for the EPIC deductible plan pay full prescription fees until they have established a deductible, after which they save 50 percent on prescriptions for the remaining portion of the year
- Seniors with incomes $10,801 to $24,400 pay deductibles of $438 to $638 per person
- After paying required fees and establishing deductibles, enrollees pay copayments of $3 to $23
- Pay dispensing fee of $2.75 to $3.00

- For applications contact EPIC at the address listed in column 1
- Proof of age is required
- Do not send payment with application; the state bills enrollees

PENNSYLVANIA

Pennsylvania Pharmaceutical Assistance Contract for the Elderly (PACE) and Needs Enhancement Tier (PACENET)	• All prescription drugs and diabetic supplies are covered except for
	
	  • medicines whose manufacturers have declined to participate
	
	  • experimental drugs and medicines for baldness and wrinkles
	
	• With documentation, the program will cover DESI (Drug Efficacy Study Implementation) medicines if documented
		• Pennsylvania residents
		• Age 65 or more
		• Meet a $500 deductible before reimbursement begins
		• PACE copayment is $6 per generic prescription
		• PACENET copayment is $8 per generic prescription; $15 for brand-name medications
		• Dispensing fee of $3.50
			• Call to apply
			1-800-225-7223 or go online to *www.aging.state.pa.us*
			• PACENET sends approved applicants an ID card for presentation to dispensing provider
			• Applicants must file claims *before* filling prescriptions

RHODE ISLAND

Rhode Island Pharmaceutical Assistance to the Elderly Dept. of Elderly Affairs 160 Pine Street Providence, RI 02903	• Drug assistance for persistent conditions such as Alzheimer's, cancer, diabetes, depression, glaucoma, heart problems, high cholesterol, hypertension, incontinence, and Parkinson's disease	• Age 65 or more • Rhode Island resident • Copayment is 40 percent of drug cost • Dispensing fee of $2.50 • Phone bill reduction and reduced installation costs of new line also available	• One-time application • Include proof of age, income, address, and health insurance • Qualified applicants receive pharmacy cards within four to six weeks; call 401-222-3330 or 1-800-322-2880

VERMONT

NAME OF PROGRAM AND CONTACT INFORMATION	DESCRIPTION, LIMITATIONS, AND RESTRICTIONS	ELIGIBILITY, COPAYMENTS	ENROLLMENT
Vscript State Pharmaceutical Assistance Program for Elderly & Disabled 103 South Main Street Waterbury, VT 05671 802-241-2880	Limited • To long-term medical problems • To drugs whose manufacturers participate in the program • By the amount of available monies in the state's health access fund • No experimental or OTC drugs • 30–60-day supply for nonmaintenance drugs, 90 days for maintenance drugs • Available discounts depend on the legislature's appropriation for any given year	• At least 65 years of age or • Receiving Social Security disability benefits or Medicare • Have been Vermont residents for at least 12 months • Copayment is 50 percent of drug cost • Dispensing fee is $4.25	• Enrollment fee of $20 or less • Applications are available in state income tax booklets, at social welfare offices, or through the Central Eligibility Unit, 802-241-3978 • Contact Senior Help Line for assistance with the forms 1-800-642-5119 or write: Champlain Valley Agency on Aging, P.O. Box 158, Winoski, VT 05404-0158
Vermont Health Access Program Pharmacy	• Discount prescription program for low-income residents; limited by the amount of available monies in the state's health access fund	For those • Who are at least 65 years of age or receiving Social Security disability benefits or Medicare • Whose incomes are below a certain amount for their family size • Receive SSI disability or Medicare • Have been Vermont residents for at least 12 months • Have no prescription insurance • Copayment is $1 to $2 • Dispensing fee is $4.25	• Enrollment fee of $20 or less • Applications and income eligibility information is available by calling the Health Access Eligibility Unit at 1-800-250-8427 or the Senior Help Line at 1-800-642-5119 or write: Champlain Valley Agency on Aging, P.O. Box 158, Winoski, VT 05404-0158 • Eligibility determined within 30 days

APPENDIX D: Pharmaceutical Company Assistance Programs

Pharmaceutical companies make their products available to low-income consumers. Note the restrictions and eligibility requirements.

NAME OF PROGRAM	AVAILABLE DRUGS	ELIGIBILITY REQUIREMENTS, RESTRICTIONS, AND LIMITATIONS	APPLICATION PROCESS, TIME, AND FEE
ALZA PHARMACEUTICALS			
Indigent Patient Assistance Program	Bicitra, Ditropan, Elmiron, Mycelex, Neutra-Phos, Neutra-Phos-K, Ocusert, PolyCitra, PolyCitra-K, Progestasert, Testoderm	Eligibility is based on patient's insurance status and income Patients must be ineligible for any other third-party reimbursement or support program	Physicians request Indigent Patient Assistance applications from ALZA: Indigent Patient Assistance Program, c/o Comprehensive Reimbursement Consultants, 8990 Springbrook Drive, #200, Minneapolis, MN 55433; 1-800-577-3788
AMGEN INC.			
SAFETY NET® Program for EPOGEN®	EPOGEN® (Epoetin alfa)	Eligibility is based on • medical indigence • being uninsured or underinsured Dialysis patients only Amgen's SAFETY NET®	Amgen's program follows a 12-month patient year, not a calendar year Providers apply on behalf of the patient Any dialysis center, physician, hospital, or home-dialysis supplier may sponsor a patient by applying to the program on his or her behalf Phone-in or written applications are acceptable. Providers and physicians can call: Amgen SAFETY NET® Program for EPOGEN® 1-800-272-9376

NAME OF PROGRAM	AVAILABLE DRUGS	ELIGIBILITY REQUIREMENTS, RESTRICTIONS, AND LIMITATIONS	APPLICATION PROCESS, TIME, AND FEE
AMGEN INC. *(continued)*			
SAFETY NET® Program for INFERGEN®	INFERGEN® (Interferon alfacon-1)	Chronic hepatitis C patients only	Providers may enroll a patient or the patient may enroll him or herself. Any administering physician, hospital, community pharmacy, or home health company may sponsor a patient by applying to the program on his or her behalf
			Phone-in or written applications are acceptable. Patients or providers can contact the Amgen SAFETY NET® Program by calling 888-508-8088
SAFETY NET® Program for NEUPOGEN®	NEUPOGEN® (Filgrastim)		Phone-in or written applications are acceptable for program enrollment

NAME OF PROGRAM	AVAILABLE DRUGS	ELIGIBILITY REQUIREMENTS, RESTRICTIONS, AND LIMITATIONS	APPLICATION PROCESS, TIME, AND FEE
ASTRA MERCK INC.			
Astra Merck Patient Assistance Program	LexxelTM (enalapril maleate-felodipine ER), Plendil® (felodipine), Prilosec® (omeprazole), and Tonocard® (tocainide HCl)	Astra Merck's Patient Assistance Program is available to patients who • have a medical need • a financial hardship that would prevent the patient from filling his or her prescription • do not have insurance reimbursement for prescriptions • are not eligible for governmental assistance programs (e.g., Medicaid) • have no other means to pay for their medication Up to 90 days' supply of medication is provided at a time	Only physician referrals are accepted Physicians can request applications from the Astra Merck Patient Assistance Program 1-800-355-6044 Astra Merck sends medication to the doctor's office 2 to 4 weeks after its distribution center receives and approves the physician's application

NAME OF PROGRAM	AVAILABLE DRUGS	ELIGIBILITY REQUIREMENTS, RESTRICTIONS, AND LIMITATIONS	APPLICATION PROCESS, TIME, AND FEE
ASTRA USA, INC.			
Foscavir® Assistance and Information on Reimbursement (F.A.I.R.)	Foscavir® (foscarnet sodium) Injection	Astra determines eligibility based on income information provided by the physician If patient is not covered for outpatient prescription drugs under private insurance or a public program, patient's income must fall below level selected by the company Patient may or may not be poor, but retail drug purchase would cause hardship If patient is covered for outpatient prescription drugs, he or she may be eligible for assistance with deductibles or maximum benefit limits	Direct physician requests to: State and Federal Associates, 1101 King Street, Alexandria, VA 22314; 1-800-488-FAIR (3247); (fax) 703-683-2239

NAME OF PROGRAM	AVAILABLE DRUGS	ELIGIBILITY REQUIREMENTS, RESTRICTIONS, AND LIMITATIONS	APPLICATION PROCESS, TIME, AND FEE

ATHENA NEUROSCIENCES, INC.

Athena Indigent Patient Program	Permax® (pergolide mesylate), Zanaflex® (tizanadine [Facts and Figures] hydrochloride), Diastat® (diazepam rectal gel)	Patients: • must be U.S. residents • must have a net worth less than $30,000 • no third-party prescription coverage Athena requires that new requests be filed for additional product	Prescribing physicians and patients must provide • a letter of denial from the state Medicaid program • patient's most recent income tax return • bank or financial statement • physician request and assurance of financial need on physician letterhead and • prescription for 3-month supply Direct physician requests to: Athena Indigent Patient Program, Athena Neurosciences, Inc., 800 Gateway Boulevard, South San Francisco, CA 94080 Athena ships medication for approved applications to physicians by express courier

NAME OF PROGRAM	AVAILABLE DRUGS	ELIGIBILITY REQUIREMENTS, RESTRICTIONS, AND LIMITATIONS	APPLICATION PROCESS, TIME, AND FEE
BAYER CORPORATION PHARMACEUTICAL DIVISION			
Bayer Indigent Program	Most Bayer prescription medications	Bayer offers up to a 3-month supply of medicine at any one time	Patient/physician can qualify over the phone by calling 1-800-998-9180. If all information needed is obtained over the phone, approval or denial is given immediately. If patient is approved, an application is generated and sent to the physician's office for signatures Physicians should direct requests to: Bayer Indigent Program, P.O. Box 20209, Phoenix, AR 85038-9209
BIOGEN, INC.			
Avonex® Access Program	Avonex® (interferon beta-1a)	Eligibility is based on patient's insurance status and income level	Direct physician requests to Avonex® Support Line 1-800-456-2255

NAME OF PROGRAM	AVAILABLE DRUGS	ELIGIBILITY REQUIREMENTS, RESTRICTIONS, AND LIMITATIONS	APPLICATION PROCESS, TIME, AND FEE
BOEHRINGER INGELHEIM PHARMACEUTICALS, INC.			
Partners in Health	Alupent® MDI, Atrovent®, Catapres-TTS®, COMBIVENT®, FLOMAX®, Mexitil®, Serentil® for FDA-approved indications only	All requests are reviewed and approved on a case-by-case basis BIPI determine eligibility. Patient must be a U.S. citizen and ineligible for prescription assistance through Medicaid or private insurance Patient must meet established financial criteria Maximum 3-month supply provided per request	Complete financial reapplication is required annually BIPI requires application form, prescription, and patient's income documentation Renewal requests within the same year require only the application form and a prescription Direct physician requests to: Boehringer Ingelheim Pharmaceuticals, Inc., P.O. Box 368, Ridgefield, CT 06877-0368 1-800-556-8317
BRISTOL-MYERS SQUIBB COMPANY			
Bristol-Myers Squibb Patient Assistance Program	Many Bristol-Myers Squibb pharmaceutical products	This free medicine program provides temporary assistance to patients • with a financial hardship • who are not eligible for prescription drug coverage through Medicaid or any other public or private health program	Physicians and other health care professionals who are interested in enrolling a patient should call the toll-free number to request an application form Direct physician requests to: Bristol-Myers Squibb Health Patient Assistance Program, P.O. Box 4500, Princeton, NJ 08543-4500, Mailcode P25-31; 1-800-332-2056 or 609-897-6859

CIBA GIEGY   (see Novartis)

DUPONT MERCK PHARMACEUTICAL COMPANY

NAME OF PROGRAM	AVAILABLE DRUGS	ELIGIBILITY REQUIREMENTS, RESTRICTIONS, AND LIMITATIONS	APPLICATION PROCESS, TIME, AND FEE
DuPont Merck Pharmaceutical Company Patient Assistance Program	All marketed noncontrolled prescription products	DuPont Merck determines eligibility based on the patient's insurance status and income level/assets Patients • should have exhausted all third-party insurance, Medicaid, Medicare, and all other available programs • must be U.S. residents	The physician should request an application by calling 1-800-474-2762, prompt 5 Patients must complete and sign the patient-designated area of the application. Physicians complete and sign the physician-designated area of the application and include a signed, completed prescription After the company receives an approved application, it delivers the medication to the physician within two weeks Direct physician requests to: Michelle Paoli, DuPont Merck Pharmaceutical Company, P.O. Box 80723, Wilmington, DE 19880-0723; 1-800-474-2762

NAME OF PROGRAM	AVAILABLE DRUGS	ELIGIBILITY REQUIREMENTS, RESTRICTIONS, AND LIMITATIONS	APPLICATION PROCESS, TIME, AND FEE
EISAI INC.			
Aricpet® (donepezil HCl) Patient Assistance Program	Aricept® (donepezil HCl) 5 mg and 10 mg tablets	Patients must be • U.S. residents • without prescription drug coverage through either public or private insurance Eisai provides free Aricept® to patients who • have incomes that fall within a predetermined range • are diagnosed by a physician as having mild to moderate dementia of the Alzheimer's type • have no insurance or other third-party payer prescription drug coverage, including Medicaid coverage or Medicare managed-care coverage • Patient must requalify after 90-day initial supply	Direct physician requests to: The Aricept® Patient Assistance Program 1-800-226-2072

NAME OF PROGRAM	AVAILABLE DRUGS	ELIGIBILITY REQUIREMENTS, RESTRICTIONS, AND LIMITATIONS	APPLICATION PROCESS, TIME, AND FEE
FUJISAWA USA, INC.			
NebuPent® Indigent Patient Program	NebuPent® (pentamidine isethionate)	This program provides NebuPent® (pentamidine isethionate) to AIDS patients who cannot otherwise afford the treatment Approved patients receive two shipments each with a 90-day Prograf™ supply, from an affiliated mail-order pharmacy The pharmacy will bill the patient $20 per shipment for fulfillment expenses	Requests must be written by physician and should include the patient's medical, financial, and insurance information To enroll patients, physicians must register by submitting patient enrollment forms and prescriptions If continued assistance is required after six months, the physician must reapply for the patient Direct physician requests to: Product Manager NebuPent Fujisawa USA, 3 Parkway North Center Deerfield, IL 60015-2548; 847-317-8874, (fax) 847-317-5941 Call Susan Lindsey at 847-317-8874 or Mary Beth McNamara at 847-317-8617 for more information

NAME OF PROGRAM	AVAILABLE DRUGS	ELIGIBILITY REQUIREMENTS, RESTRICTIONS, AND LIMITATIONS	APPLICATION PROCESS, TIME, AND FEE
FUJISAWA USA, INC. *(continued)*			
Prograf™ Patient Assistance Program	Prograf™ capsules (tacrolimus, FK506)	Fujisawa USA, Inc. developed the Prograf™ Patient Assistance Program for patients who • have no health insurance, • limited financial resources, and • meet income and insurance criteria Call the Prograf™ Reimbursement Hotline (1-800-4-PROGRAF) for an application or for information about eligibility	Physicians describe a patient's insurance and financial situation, so hotline staff can determine whether the patient is likely to qualify for the Prograf™ Patient Assistance Program Direct physician requests to Prograf™ Patient Assistance Program, c/o Medical Technology Hotlines SM, P.O. Box 7710, Washington, DC 20044-7710; 1-800-4-PROGRAF, 1-800-477-6472, or 202-393-5563 in the Washington, D.C., area

NAME OF PROGRAM	AVAILABLE DRUGS	ELIGIBILITY REQUIREMENTS, RESTRICTIONS, AND LIMITATIONS	APPLICATION PROCESS, TIME, AND FEE
GILEAD SCIENCES, INC.			
Gilead Sciences Support Services	VISTIDE® (cidofovir injection), for the treatment of cytomegalovirus (CMV) retinitis in patients with AIDS	The program assists insured and uninsured patients in receiving reimbursement for VISTIDE. *It does not offer drugs* The Support Services program offers • insurance claims assistance • referrals for financial support • referrals to AIDS service agencies Support specialists also consult with insured patients and their physicians regarding • prior authorization or third-party insurance claims, • contacting insurance companies on behalf of patients, and • offering appeal procedures	Direct physician requests to: Gilead Sciences Support Services, 1-800-Gilead 5 (445-3235), (fax) 1-713-760-0049 To determine eligibility, physicians or patients may request a VISTIDE Patient Assistance application and mail or fax the completed form to Gilead Sciences Support Services

NAME OF PROGRAM	AVAILABLE DRUGS	ELIGIBILITY REQUIREMENTS, RESTRICTIONS, AND LIMITATIONS	APPLICATION PROCESS, TIME, AND FEE

GLAXO WELLCOME INC.

Glaxo Wellcome Patient Assistance Program	All marketed Glaxo Wellcome prescription products	This is an interim program available to outpatients who meet criteria, including • inability to qualify for drug benefits through private insurance or • government-funded programs, and • income eligibility based upon multiples of the U.S. poverty level, adjusted for household size Enrolled outpatients can qualify for 90 days of medication, provided through pharmacies except for injectable products, Glaxo provides to health care providers via direct shipment Glaxo Wellcome may ask patients and providers to participate in reimbursement case management. It also makes alternative funding suggestions	Direct physician requests to: Glaxo Wellcome Inc. Patient Assistance Program, P.O. Box 52185, Phoenix, AZ 85072-2185; 1-800-722-9294, (fax) 1-800-750-9832 Additional information and program materials are available at *www.Helix.com*

NAME OF PROGRAM	AVAILABLE DRUGS	ELIGIBILITY REQUIREMENTS, RESTRICTIONS, AND LIMITATIONS	APPLICATION PROCESS, TIME, AND FEE
HOECHST MARION ROUSSEL, INC.			
Indigent Patient Program	All prescription products made by Hoechst Marion Roussel, except Rifadin, Rifamate, Rifater, Tenuate		Direct physician requests to: Indigent Patient Program, Hoechst Marion Roussel, Inc., P.O. Box 9950, Kansas City, MO 64134-0950; 1-800-221-4025
1. The Anzement Patient Assistance Program 2. The Anzement Reimbursement Program		The program provides access to products for indigent patients who • fall below the federal poverty level and • have no other means of health care coverage Usually a 3-month supply of product is available at any one time Physicians determine eligibility based on patient's income level and lack of insurance	Physicians obtain application forms from Anzement Patient Assistance Program, c/o Comprehensive Reimbursement Consultants (CRC), 8990 Springbrook Drive, #200, Minneapolis, MN 55433; 888-259-2219

NAME OF PROGRAM	AVAILABLE DRUGS	ELIGIBILITY REQUIREMENTS, RESTRICTIONS, AND LIMITATIONS	APPLICATION PROCESS, TIME, AND FEE

JANSSEN PHARMACEUTICA

Janssen Patient Assistance Program	All of Janssen's prescription products [Duragesic® (fentanyl transdermal), Ergamisol® (levamisole), Hismanal® (astemizole), Imodium® (loperamide), Nizoral® Cream (ketaconazole cream), Nizoral® Shampoo (ketaconazole shampoo), Nizoral® Tablet (ketaconazole tablet), Propulsid® (cisapride), Sporanox® (itraconazole), Vermox® (mebendazole)]	Janssen makes its products available free to people who • meet specific medical criteria and • lack financial resources and third-party insurance necessary to obtain treatment Reimbursement specialists determine eligibility	Direct physician requests to: Janssen Patient Assistance Program, 1800 Robert Fulton Drive, Reston, VA 22091-4346; 1-800-652-6227
• The Risperdal Patient Assistance Program • The Risperdal Reimbursement Support Program	RISPERDAL® (risperidone)	Reimbursement specialists determine patient eligibility Janssen makes the drug free to those who • meet specific medical criteria • lack financial resources, and • lack third-party insurance necessary to obtain treatment One or 2 months' supply available; varies by product	Janssen requests that physicians not charge patients beyond insurance coverage for professional services Direct physician requests to: Janssen Cares, The Risperdal Patient Assistance Program, 4828 Parkway Plaza Boulevard, #120 Charlotte, NC 28217-1969; 1-800-652-6227, (fax) 704-357-0036

NAME OF PROGRAM	AVAILABLE DRUGS	ELIGIBILITY REQUIREMENTS, RESTRICTIONS, AND LIMITATIONS	APPLICATION PROCESS, TIME, AND FEE

KNOLL PHARMACEUTICAL COMPANY

Knoll Indigent Patient Program	Isoptin® SR (verapamil HCl), Mavik (trandolapril), [Rythmol® (propafenone HCl), Collagenase Santyl, [Synthroid® Tablets (levothyroxine sodium, USP), Tarka (trandolapril and verapamil)	It distributes a maximum 3-month supply on any one request	Physician must submit prescriptions and documentation that demonstrates patient indigence Knoll requires for every request. Direct physician requests to: Knoll Indigent Patient Program, Knoll Pharmaceutical Co., 3000 Continental Drive North, Mount Olive, NJ 07828-1234 Attn: Telemarketing

LEDERLE LABORATORIES   See Wyeth-Ayerst Laboratories Indigent Patient Program

Lederle PARTNERS IN
   PATIENT CARE™

NAME OF PROGRAM	AVAILABLE DRUGS	ELIGIBILITY REQUIREMENTS, RESTRICTIONS, AND LIMITATIONS	APPLICATION PROCESS, TIME, AND FEE
ELI LILLY AND COMPANY			
Lilly Cares	Most Lilly prescription products and insulins (except controlled substances) are covered by this program Gemzar® is covered under a separate program described below	Lilly determines eligibility on a case-by-case basis according to: • Patient's inability to pay • Lack of third-party drug payment assistance including insurance, Medicaid, government-subsidized clinics, and other government, community, or private programs • Patients must be U.S. residents • Inpatients and those who can otherwise obtain drug reimbursement are ineligible The quantity supplied depends upon type of product Lilly sends medications directly to the physician Requests for replacement drugs are not honored	Direct physician requests to: Lilly Cares Program Administrator, Eli Lilly and Company, P.O. Box 25768, Alexandria, VA 22313; 1-800-545-6962 Physicians complete patient qualification form, which requires prescription information, including signature and DEA number, and confirmation of patient ineligibility for other outpatient drug coverage Lilly also requires patients provide other "pertinent" information and state their financial need Patients requiring additional assistance must submit new prescriptions and restate their medical and financial need

NAME OF PROGRAM	AVAILABLE DRUGS	ELIGIBILITY REQUIREMENTS, RESTRICTIONS, AND LIMITATIONS	APPLICATION PROCESS, TIME, AND FEE
ELI LILLY AND COMPANY *(continued)*			
Gemzar® Patient Assistance Program	Gemzar® (gemcitabine hydrochloride)	Lilly determines eligibility based on • income • no medical insurance • ineligibility for any programs with a drug benefit provision, including Medicaid, third-party insurance, Medicare • all other programs have denied coverage for Gemzar in writing, and all appeals have been exhausted	Request applications and direct physician requests to Gemzar® Reimbursement Hotline, 888-4-GEMZAR (888-443-6927)

NAME OF PROGRAM	AVAILABLE DRUGS	ELIGIBILITY REQUIREMENTS, RESTRICTIONS, AND LIMITATIONS	APPLICATION PROCESS, TIME, AND FEE

THE LIPOSOME COMPANY, INC.

Financial Assistance Program for ABELCET®	ABELCET® (amphotericin B lipid complex injection)	Patients must • be uninsured (not eligible to receive reimbursement through any other third-party drug reimbursement program, i.e., Medicaid, local or federal agencies, Blue Cross/Blue Shield, private insurance programs, and private foundations) • be unable to pay for the product out of pocket, and • receive ABELCET® from a hospital, physician, or home health care company The company also uses medical and financial information provided on behalf of the patient by the hospital or physician	Providers may enroll patients by submitting physician-signed enrollment forms, which they can get by calling 1-800-335-5476 or by contacting a Liposome area sales manager Direct physician requests to: Financial Assistance Program for ABELCET®, The Liposome Company, Inc., One Research Way Princeton, NJ 08540-6619; 1-800-335-5476

NAME OF PROGRAM	AVAILABLE DRUGS	ELIGIBILITY REQUIREMENTS, RESTRICTIONS, AND LIMITATIONS	APPLICATION PROCESS, TIME, AND FEE
MERCK & CO., INC.			
The Merck Patient Assistance Program	Most Merck products Requests for vaccines and injectables are not accepted, with the exception of requests for anticancer injectable products	Patients must reside in the U.S. and have a U.S. treating physician This is temporary assistance to patients who have no access to any insurance coverage for prescription medications and are unable to afford prescription medications The patient must have exhausted all options for prescription benefits and coverage, including: private insurance, HMOs, Medicaid, Medicare, state pharmacy assistance programs, Veterans Assistance, and any other social service agency support Once eligibility has been verified, up to a 3-month supply of the prescribed medication(s) is sent directly to the prescriber's office for distribution to the patient	Each application must be signed by both the prescriber and the patient Applications must be mailed with an original, signed, dated prescription with the prescriber's name, address, professional designation, and a DEA or state license number Health care professionals with prescribing privileges may call 1-800-994-2111

NAME OF PROGRAM	AVAILABLE DRUGS	ELIGIBILITY REQUIREMENTS, RESTRICTIONS, AND LIMITATIONS	APPLICATION PROCESS, TIME, AND FEE
MERCK & CO., INC. *(continued)*			
SUPPORT™ Reimbursement Support and Patient Assistance Services for Crixivan®	Crixivan® (indinavir sulfate)	The SUPPORT™ program assists patients • for whom Crixivan® is prescribed • who are uncertain of their insurance coverage in locating payment sources for the medicine • who reside in the U.S., and • have a U.S. physician Product is shipped to the prescriber's office	Health care professionals or patients may call 1-800-850-3430

NAME OF PROGRAM	AVAILABLE DRUGS	ELIGIBILITY REQUIREMENTS, RESTRICTIONS, AND LIMITATIONS	APPLICATION PROCESS, TIME, AND FEE
NOVARTIS PHARMACEUTICALS			
Novartis Patient Assistance Program	Certain single-source and/or life-sustaining products, excluding controlled substances	This is a temporary assistance program for patients experiencing financial hardship and without prescription drug insurance, until alternative sources of funding are obtained	Patients are required to complete an application along with their physician's and return it for evaluation Direct physician requests to: Novartis Pharmaceuticals Patient Assistance Program, P.O. Box 52052, Phoenix, AZ 85072-9170; 1-800-257-3273
ORTHO BIOTECH INC.			
Financial Assistance Program (FAPTM) for PROCRIT® (Epoetin alfa) and LEUSTATIN® (cladribine) Injection	PROCRIT® (Epoetin alfa) for nondialysis use LEUSTATIN® (cladribine) Injection	The program issues free PROCRIT® and/or LEUSTATIN® available to patients who • meet specific medical criteria, and • lack the financial resources and third-party insurance necessary to obtain treatment	Application forms are available by calling 1-800-553-3851 Reimbursement specialists can help determine eligibility or whether an alternative program is appropriate Direct physician requests to: The Ortho Biotech FAPTM Program, 1800 Robert Fulton Drive, #300, Reston, VA 20191-4346; 1-800-553-3851

NAME OF PROGRAM	AVAILABLE DRUGS	ELIGIBILITY REQUIREMENTS, RESTRICTIONS, AND LIMITATIONS	APPLICATION PROCESS, TIME, AND FEE

ORTHO DERMATOLOGICAL AND ORTHO-MCNEIL PHARMACEUTICAL, INC.

Ortho Dermatological Patient Assistance Program Ortho-McNeil Patient Assistance Program	Prescription products prescribed according to approved labeled indications and dosage regimens	Patients should • not have insurance coverage for prescription medication • not be eligible for other sources of drug coverage, • have applied to public sector programs and been denied, and • have income that falls below poverty level and suffer hardship as a result of retail purchase Medication will be sent to the practitioner	Health care practitioners should request application forms, complete them, and send them accompanied by a signed and dated prescription to: Ortho Dermatological Patient Assistance Program, Ortho-McNeil Patient Assistance Program, 1800 Robert Fulton Drive, #300, Reston, VA 20191-4346; 1-800-797-7737

PARKE-DAVIS, A DIVISION OF WARNER-LAMBERT COMPANY

Parke-Davis Patient Assistance Program	Accupril, Cognex, Dilantin, Loestrin, Neurontin, Rezulin, and Zarontin	Patients must • not be eligible for other sources of drug coverage • be deemed financially eligible based on company guidelines and physician certification The company sends up to 3-month supply of medicine to the physician	Physicians can get application forms from their Parke-Davis sales representative and send them, accompanied by a signed and dated prescription, to: The Parke-Davis Patient Assistance Program, P.O. Box 1058, Somerville, NJ 08876; 908-725-1247

NAME OF PROGRAM	AVAILABLE DRUGS	ELIGIBILITY REQUIREMENTS, RESTRICTIONS, AND LIMITATIONS	APPLICATION PROCESS, TIME, AND FEE
PARKE-DAVIS, A DIVISION OF WARNER-LAMBERT COMPANY *(continued)*			
Lipitor Patient Assistance Program	Lipitor (atorvastin calcium)	Patients must • not be eligible for other sources of drug coverage, and • be deemed financially eligible based on company guidelines and physician certification Up to a 3-month supply will be delivered	Physicians should request an application form from their Parke-Davis or Pfizer sales representative and then send them, accompanied by a signed and dated prescription, to: Lipitor Patient Assistance Program, P.O. Box 1058, Somerville, NJ 08876; 908-218-0120
PASTEUR MERIEUX CONNAUGHT			
Indigent Patient Program	IMOVAX® Rabies, rabies vaccine; IMOGAM® Rabies-HT, rabies immune globulin (human); TheraCys® BCG live intravesical (*Note:* IMOVAX® and IMOGAM® Rabies-HT are provided on a postexposure basis)	Determined on a case-by-case basis and limited to those individuals who have been identified as indigent, uninsured, and ineligible for Medicare and Medicaid TheraCys®—6 doses are provided for one course of therapy. Connaught does provide for a full 11-dose course of therapy—induction and maintenance—at the physician's discretion	Rabies: The physician needs to specify the quantity of IMOGAM® Rabies needed for patient (in mL) as well as the number of doses of IMOVAX® Rabies Direct physician requests to: Customer Account Management, Pasteur Merieux Connaught, Route 611, P.O. Box 187, Swiftwater, PA 18370-0187; 1-800-822-2463

NAME OF PROGRAM	AVAILABLE DRUGS	ELIGIBILITY REQUIREMENTS, RESTRICTIONS, AND LIMITATIONS	APPLICATION PROCESS, TIME, AND FEE
PFIZER INC.			
Pfizer Prescription Assistance	Most Pfizer outpatient products with chronic indications are covered by this program Diflucan® and Zithromax® are covered by a separate program, described below	Pfizer reserves the right to limit enrollment of patients Patients must • have incomes below $12,000 (single) or $15,000 (family) • not be receiving or be eligible for third-party or Medicaid reimbursements for medications No copayment or cost-sharing is required by the patient Pfizer ships products to the physician	The physician must write and sign a letter on his or her letterhead to Pfizer stating that the patient meets income criteria and is uninsured for pharmaceuticals and enclose a prescription for the desired product Direct physician requests to: Pfizer Prescription Assistance, P.O. Box 25457, Alexandria, VA 22313-5457; 1-800-646-4455 It may take up to 4 weeks to receive the product Physicians can get refills by resubmitting requests
Diflucan® and Zithromax® Patient Assistance Program	Diflucan® (fluconazole) and Zithromax® (azithromycin)	Pfizer reserves the right to limit enrollment of patients Patient must • not have insurance or other third-party coverage, including Medicaid • not be eligible for a state's AIDS drug assistance program • have an income of less than $25,000 a year without dependents, or less than $40,000 a year with dependents	On behalf of their patients, physicians should call the Diflucan® and Zithromax® Patient Assistance Program and explain the patient's situation to the Patient Assistance Specialist Pfizer then sends a qualifying form requesting insurance status, income information, and the amount of Diflucan® or Zithromax® needed Upon receipt of the completed form, the Program

PFIZER INC. *(continued)*

			staff determines patient eligibility and sends a letter notifying the physician of the patient's eligibility or ineligibility
			It may take 3 weeks from the first call to the product delivery
			Direct physician requests to: Diflucan® and Zithromax® Patient Assistance Program 1-800-869-9979
Sharing the Care is a joint effort of Pfizer, the National Governors' Association, and the National Association of Community Health Centers. It works through community, migrant, and homeless health centers funded under Section 330 of the Public Health Service Act and that have in-house pharmacies	Certain Pfizer single-source products	Product is dispensed to patient at health center pharmacy Pfizer reserves the right to limit enrollment of patients and health centers. To be eligible, patients must • be registered at a participating health center • not be covered by any private insurance or public assistance covering pharmaceuticals • not be Medicaid-enrolled • must have a family income that is equal to or below the federal poverty level	Direct physician requests to: Sharing the Care Pfizer Inc., 235 E. 42nd Street, New York, NY 10017-5755; 1-800-984-1500

NAME OF PROGRAM	AVAILABLE DRUGS	ELIGIBILITY REQUIREMENTS, RESTRICTIONS, AND LIMITATIONS	APPLICATION PROCESS, TIME, AND FEE
PHARMACIA & UPJOHN, INC.			
RxMAP Prescription Medication Assistance Program	Numerous products	Eligibility is based on federal poverty level and no prescription drug coverage	All inquiries should go to RxMAP at 1-800-242-7014, or RxMAP, P.O. Box 29043, Phoenix, AZ 85038
PROCTER & GAMBLE PHARMACEUTICALS, INC.			
	Alora, Asacol, Dantrium Capsules, Didronel, Helidac, Macrodantin, Macrobid	To qualify, patients should • not have insurance coverage for prescription medicines or Medicaid reimbursements • have incomes that fall below the federal poverty level • have no other means of health care coverage The quantity supplied depends on diagnosis and need, but a one-month supply is usually provided for a chronic medication P&G sends medication to the physician	Physicians and patients should complete application forms and send them with original prescriptions duly signed by the attending physician to: Procter & Gamble Pharmaceuticals, Inc., P.O. Box 231, Norwich, NY 13815, Attn: Customer Service Department; 1-800-448-4878 To get refills, physicians must submit new applications and prescription forms

NAME OF PROGRAM	AVAILABLE DRUGS	ELIGIBILITY REQUIREMENTS, RESTRICTIONS, AND LIMITATIONS	APPLICATION PROCESS, TIME, AND FEE

RHONE-POULENC RORER INC.

Rhone-Poulenc Rorer Patient Assistance Program	All products are included, with some limitations	Patients are eligible to apply if • there is a medical and financial need for assistance as identified by a physician, social agent, or agency, and • the effort to obtain help from all third-party payers, Medicaid, Medicare, and other government support has been exhausted The company sends medication to the physician	Physicians fill out forms and send them, along with a valid prescription, to the address below If the same patient requires more medication, the physician must fill out new prescription and new application forms that confirm the patient's financial status are required No photocopies accepted Direct physician requests to Medical Affairs/Patient Assistance Program Rhone-Poulenc Rorer Inc., P.O. Box 5094, 500 Arcola Road, Mailstop #4C29, Collegeville, PA 19426-0998; 610-454-8110, (fax) 610-454-2102

NAME OF PROGRAM	AVAILABLE DRUGS	ELIGIBILITY REQUIREMENTS, RESTRICTIONS, AND LIMITATIONS	APPLICATION PROCESS, TIME, AND FEE

ROCHE LABORATORIES, INC.   A Division of Hoffmann-La Roche Inc. Roche Products Inc.

NAME OF PROGRAM	AVAILABLE DRUGS	ELIGIBILITY REQUIREMENTS, RESTRICTIONS, AND LIMITATIONS	APPLICATION PROCESS, TIME, AND FEE
Roche Medical Needs Program	Roche product line with some exceptions	This is an *interim* program designed for outpatients until alternative funding is determined Eligible patients • lack third-party outpatient prescription drug coverage under private insurance, government-funded programs (Medicaid, Medicare, Veterans Affairs, etc.) • lack private or community sources • are unable to afford to purchase products on their own The company may request patients and providers to participate in reimbursement case management The company ships up to a 3-month supply to the practitioner within 2 to 3 weeks	The program is offered through licensed practitioners and not intended for clinics, hospitals, and/or other institutions Practitioners can get application forms from Roche Medical Needs Program, Roche Laboratories, Inc., 340 Kingsland Street, Nutley, NJ 07110; 1-800-285-4484 Roche requires physician and patient signatures and a DEA number on all applications The company requires new applications to obtain refills
Roche Medical Needs Program for CellCept®	CellCept® (mycophenolate mofetil), CYTOVENE® (ganciclovir capsules), and CYTOVENE®-IV (ganciclovir sodium for injection) CYTOVENE products	For use with transplant patients who meet the above-mentioned eligibility requirements	Direct physician requests to: Roche Transplant Reimbursement Hotline 1-800-772-5790

NAME OF PROGRAM	AVAILABLE DRUGS	ELIGIBILITY REQUIREMENTS, RESTRICTIONS, AND LIMITATIONS	APPLICATION PROCESS, TIME, AND FEE
ROCHE LABORATORIES, INC. *(continued)*			
Roche Medical Needs Program for FORTO-VASETM	FORTOVASETM (saquinavir), INVIRASE® (saquinavir mesylate), CYTOVENE® (ganciclovir capsules), CYTOVENE®-IV (ganci-clovir sodium for injec-tion), and HIVID® (zalcitabine). CYTOVENE products	For use with HIV/AIDS patients	Direct physician requests to: Roche HIV Therapy Assistance Program 1-800-282-7780
Roche Medical Needs Program for Roferon®-A	Roferon®-A (Interferon alpha-2a, recombinant), Vesanoid® (tretinoin), and Fluorouracil Injection		Direct physician requests to Oncoline™/Hepline™ Reimbursement Hotline 1-800-443-6676 (press 2 or 3)

NAME OF PROGRAM	AVAILABLE DRUGS	ELIGIBILITY REQUIREMENTS, RESTRICTIONS, AND LIMITATIONS	APPLICATION PROCESS, TIME, AND FEE

ROXANE LABORATORIES, INC.

Patient Assistance Program	Duraclon; Marinol® (dronabinol) Capsules 2.5 mg; Oramorph SR® (morphine sulfate sustained release) Tablets 15 mg, 30 mg, 60 mg, and 100 mg; Roxanol™ (morphine sulfate concentrated oral solution) 20 mg/mL and 120 mL bottles; Roxanol 100™ (morphine concentrated oral solution) 100 mg/5 mL and 240 mL bottles; Roxicodone (oxycodone) Tablets 5 mg; Oral solution 5 mg/5 mL; Roxicodone Intensol™ 20mg/mL; Viramune® (nevirapine)	Patients who are • uninsured and • meet annual income requirements can get free product through their pharmacies	Physicians should call the toll-free number 1-800-274-8651 and discuss patient eligibility with a program representative. Roxane will send a qualification form if the patient is eligible Direct physician requests to: Nexus Health, 4161 Arlingate Plaza, Columbus, OH 43228

SANDOZ PHARMACEUTICALS CORPORATION   (see Novartis)

NAME OF PROGRAM	AVAILABLE DRUGS	ELIGIBILITY REQUIREMENTS, RESTRICTIONS, AND LIMITATIONS	APPLICATION PROCESS, TIME, AND FEE
SANOFI PHARMACEUTICALS			
Needy Patient Program	Aralen®, Breonesin®, Danocrine®, Drisdol®, Hytakerol®, Mytelase®, NegGram®, pHisoHex® Plaquenil®, Skelid® Primaquine®, Primacor®, Photofrin®	Once it grants eligibility, Sanofi sends medication to the physician's office in 4 to 6 weeks Patients can receive a 3-month supply of medication and one refill option for a total of 6 months medication per year Sanofi allows physicians to enroll 6 patients per year	Physicians can contact the Sanofi Pharmaceuticals Product Information Department to get patient applications, which they complete and return with a signed prescription The physician must contact Sanofi's office for refills Direct physician requests to: Sanofi Pharmaceuticals, Needy Patient Program, c/o Product Information Department, 90 Park Avenue, New York, NY 10016; 1-800-446-6267
SCHERING LABORATORIES / KEY PHARMACEUTICALS			
Commitment to Care	Most Schering/Key prescription drugs	Economic and insurance eligibility criteria are currently being reevaluated and may be subject to change	Physicians and patients complete application forms Repeat requests require a new applications Direct physician requests to: For Intron A/Eulexin: 1-800-521-7157 For Other Products: Schering Laboratories/Key Pharmaceuticals, Patient Assistance Program, P.O. Box 52122, Phoenix, AZ 85072; 1-800-656-9485

NAME OF PROGRAM	AVAILABLE DRUGS	ELIGIBILITY REQUIREMENTS, RESTRICTIONS, AND LIMITATIONS	APPLICATION PROCESS, TIME, AND FEE
SEARLE			
Patients in Need®	Antihypertensives: Aldactazide® (spironolactone with hydrochlorothiazide), Aldactone® (spironolactone), Calan® SR (verapamil HCl) sustained-release, Kerlone® (betaxolol HCl) Antihypertensive/AntiAnginal/Antiarrhythmic: Calan® (verapamil HCl), Covera-HSTM (verapamil HCl) Antiarrhythmics: Norpace® (disopyramide phosphate), Norpace® CR (disopyramide phosphate) extended-release, and prevention of NSAID-induced gastric ulcers: Cytotec® (misoprostol)	Physicians determine eligibility based on their patients' medical and economic need Searle provides guidelines but they are not requirements	Physicians give patients prescriptions for appropriate Searle medications and Patient in Need®, which they redeem at the pharmacy of choice The pharmacist dispenses the prescription to the patient without charge and submits the certificate to Searle for reimbursement Direct physician requests to: Searle Sales Representatives, or Searle Patients in Need® Foundation, 5200 Old Orchard Road, Skokie, IL 60077; 1-800-542-2526, (fax) 847-470-6633
SERONO LABORATORIES, INC.			
Connections for Growth	Saizen® (somatropin [rDNA origin] for injection) for treatment of pediatric growth hormone deficiency		Direct physician requests to: Executive Director, Corporate Communications, Serono Laboratories, Inc., 100 Longwater Circle, Norwell, MA 02061; 1-617-982-9000, (fax) 617-982-1369

NAME OF PROGRAM	AVAILABLE DRUGS	ELIGIBILITY REQUIREMENTS, RESTRICTIONS, AND LIMITATIONS	APPLICATION PROCESS, TIME, AND FEE
SERONO LABORATORIES, INC. *(continued)*			
Serono Laboratories' Helping Hands Program	Fertinex™ (urofollitropin for injection, purified), Gonal-F (follitropin alfa for injection) for treatment of infertility		Direct physician requests to: Helping Hands Program, Serono Laboratories, Inc., 100 Longwater Circle, Norwell, MA 02061; 617-982-9000 ext. 5522, (fax) 617-982-1369
Patient Assistance Program	SerostimTM (human growth hormone [rDNA origin]) for treatment of AIDS wasting		Direct physician requests to: Executive Director, Corporate Communications, Serono Laboratories, Inc., 100 Longwater Circle, Norwell, MA 02061; 617-982-9000, (fax) 617-982-1369

NAME OF PROGRAM	AVAILABLE DRUGS	ELIGIBILITY REQUIREMENTS, RESTRICTIONS, AND LIMITATIONS	APPLICATION PROCESS, TIME, AND FEE

SIGMA-TAU PHARMACEUTICALS, INC.

NORD/Sigma-Tau Carnitor® Drug Assistance (CDA) Program	Carnitor® (levocarnitine)	The company determines eligibility by medical and financial criteria and a cost-share formula. A patient applying must • have a legal prescription for Carnitor® • prove financial need above and beyond the availability of federal and state funds, private insurance, or family resources • be a citizen or permanent resident of the United States If applicants are minors or adult dependents, the company may request financial information of family members or guardians	Patients 18 or older may submit their own applications. If a patient is an adult under guardianship or a minor, the patient and his/her guardian or parents must jointly submit an application One application per patient, per year, will be accepted unless a significant change in a patient's circumstances occurs New applications are required annually Direct physician requests to: Carnitor® Drug Assistance Program, c/o NORD, P.O. Box 8923, New Fairfield, CT 06812-8923; 1-800-999-NORD

NAME OF PROGRAM	AVAILABLE DRUGS	ELIGIBILITY REQUIREMENTS, RESTRICTIONS, AND LIMITATIONS	APPLICATION PROCESS, TIME, AND FEE
SMITHKLINE BEECHAM PHARMACEUTICALS			
SB Access to Care Program	Most SmithKline Beecham outpatient prescription products are covered with the exception of controlled substances and vaccines Kytril, Hycamtin and Paxil are covered under separate Access to Care programs described below	Patients must • have annual household incomes less than $25,000 • have no medical insurance • be ineligible for government (e.g., Medicare) or private programs that cover the cost of prescription pharmaceuticals • be U.S. residents SmithKline requires physicians and patients certify that program guidelines are being observed The quantity shipped depends on the product prescribed SmithKline sends product to physicians who verify receipt by signature	The company requires physicians to initiate requests and submit patient's original SB Access to Care application enrollment forms. No photocopies accepted Periodic reapplication is required Direct physician requests to: Access to Care Program, SmithKline Beecham, One Franklin Plaza—FP1320, Philadelphia, PA 19101; 1-800-546-0420
Oncology Access to Care Program	Kytril (granisetron HCl) and Hycamtin (topotecan HCl)		Direct physician requests to: The Oncology Access to Care Hotline 1-800-699-3806
Access to Care Paxil Certificate Program	Paxil® (paroxetine HCl)		Direct physician requests to: Access to Care Paxil Certificate Hotline 1-800-729-4544

NAME OF PROGRAM	AVAILABLE DRUGS	ELIGIBILITY REQUIREMENTS, RESTRICTIONS, AND LIMITATIONS	APPLICATION PROCESS, TIME, AND FEE

SOLVAY PHARMACEUTICALS, INC.

The Patient Assistance Program	CREON® 5 capsules (Solvay 1205); CREON® 10 Capsules (Solvay 1210); CREON® 20 Capsules (Solvay 1220); [ESTRATAB® (esterified estrogens tablets, USP) 0.3 mg] (Solvay 1014); ESTRATAB® (esterified estrogens tablets, USP) 0.625 mg (Solvay 1022); ESTRATEST® (esterified estrogens and methyl-testosterone) Tablets (Solvay 1026); ESTRATEST® HS (esterified estrogens and methyl-testosterone) Tablets (Solvay 1023); LITHOBID® (lithium carbonate, USP) Tablets 300 mg (Solvay 4492); PROMETRIUM® Capsule SV; ROWASA® Enema (Solvay 1924); ROWASA® Suppository (Solvay 1928); LUVOX® (fluvoxamine maleate) Tablets 25 mg (Solvay 4202); LUVOX® (fluvoxamine maleate) Tablets, 50 mg (Solvay 4205); LUVOX® (fluvoxamine maleate) Tablets, 100 mg (Solvay 4210); Advanced Formula ZENATE® Prenatal Multivitamin/Mineral Supplement Tablets (Solvay 1148)	Eligibility is determined by: • U.S. residency • inability to pay • lack of insurance • ineligibility for Medicaid Ongoing patient participation is available if medical and financial needs continue Solvay sends medication to the physician	Physicians apply on behalf of their patients with written request forms. Forms are available by writing to the company or calling the Patient Assistance Program Message Center at 1-800-788-9277 Direct physician requests to: Solvay Pharmaceuticals, Inc., c/o Phoenix Marketing Group, One Phoenix Drive, Lincoln Park, NJ 07035; 1-800-788-9277

NAME OF PROGRAM	AVAILABLE DRUGS	ELIGIBILITY REQUIREMENTS, RESTRICTIONS, AND LIMITATIONS	APPLICATION PROCESS, TIME, AND FEE
3M PHARMACEUTICALS			
Indigent Patient Pharmaceutical Program	Most drug products sold by 3M Pharmaceuticals in the United States	Patients whose physicians consider 3M pharmaceuticals necessary but whose financial and insurance circumstances prevent them from obtaining the drug products are eligible	Direct physician requests to: Medical Services Department 275-2E-13, 3M Center, P.O. Box 33275, St. Paul, MN 55133-3275; 1-800-328-0255, (fax) 612-733-6068
WYETH-AYERST LABORATORIES			
Norplant Foundation	The Norplant® (levonorgestrel implants) 5-year contraceptive system	Limited to people who • cannot afford the medicine • are ineligible for coverage under private and public sector programs	Direct physician requests to: The Norplant Foundation P.O. Box 25223 Alexandria, VA 22314 (703) 706-5933
Wyeth-Ayerst Laboratories Indigent Patient Program	Various products, excluding schedule II, III, and IV products	Limited to individuals who have been identified by their physicians as "indigent," meaning: low or no income, and not covered by any third-party agency A 3-month supply of specific products is provided directly to the physician	Although access to the program is through physicians, the company requires the patient's signature on application forms Direct physician requests to: John E. James, Professional Services IPP, 555 E. Lancaster Avenue, St. Davids, PA 19087

NAME OF PROGRAM	AVAILABLE DRUGS	ELIGIBILITY REQUIREMENTS, RESTRICTIONS, AND LIMITATIONS	APPLICATION PROCESS, TIME, AND FEE

ZENECA PHARMACEUTICALS

Zeneca Pharmaceuticals Foundation Patient Assistance Program	ACCOLATE® (zafirlukast), ARIMIDEX® (anastrozole), CASODEX® (bicalutamide), KADIANTM (morphine sulfate, sustained release), NOLVADEX® (tamoxifen citrate), SEROQUEL® (quetiapine fumarate), SORBITRATE® (isosorbide dinitrate), SULARTM (nisoldipine), TENORETIC® (atenolol/chlorthiazide), TENORMIN® (atenolol), ZESTRIL® (lisinopril), ZESTORETIC® (lisinopril/hydrochlorthiazide), ZOLADEX® (goserelin acetate implant), ZOMIGTM (zomitriptan)	The foundation determines eligibility based on • income level • assets • absence of outpatient private insurance, third-party coverage, or participation in a public program	Physicians can obtain application forms from the Zeneca Pharmaceuticals Foundation Reapplication is required annually Direct physician requests to: Zeneca Pharmaceuticals Foundation, P.O. Box 15197, Wilmington, DE 19850-5197; 1-800-424-3727

APPENDIX E: Ratings of Medicare-Supplement Insurance Policies

Policies are ranked by Type of Pricing (Community, Issue Age, and Attained Age), and then by Value Index.

GUIDE TO RATINGS: The ratings below evaluate two plans sold by insurance companies throughout most of the United States—Plan C and Plan I. Plan C provides a basic level of coverage (although Plans A and B provide less, see pages 50–52). Plan I provides some prescription drug coverage. The **Annual Premium** is listed for ages sixty-five and seventy-five, and represents the lowest price offered within each metropolitan area. Premiums often vary by county or zip code; be sure to check what is actually available in your area.

The **Value Index** compares the value of significant benefits for each plan to the value of Medicare benefits plus the premium. A value index greater than 100 indicates you are getting a lot of value for your money; an index less than 100 means you are getting less. Variations within five points are not significant.

The **Type of Pricing** affects the premiums a company charges. Attained-age pricing usually offers a good deal to people who are younger, but buyers must pay higher premiums (sometimes much higher) as they get older. With issue-age pricing, buyers lock in their annual premium when they first buy their policies. The premium does not rise as buyers get older, but there will be increases due to the rising cost of medical care. Community rating is the most stable arrangement; buyers of all ages pay the same premium, and the only increases reflect higher health care costs.

SELECT plans are special types of Medicare-supplement policies that resemble managed care. With a SELECT plan, you will have to use hospitals that belong to the insurance company's network.

Atlanta (Georgia)

STATE	COMPANY	TYPE OF PRICING	ANNUAL PREMIUM AGE 65	ANNUAL PREMIUM AGE 75	VALUE INDEX AGE 65
PLAN C SUPPLEMENT					
GA	UnitedHealthcare Ins. Co./AARP*	Community	1404	1404	92
GA	Bankers Life and Casualty	Issue age	1172	1509	96
GA	Standard Life	Issue age	1201	1462	95
GA	Combined Ins. Co. of America	Issue age	1233	1542	95
GA	Blue Cross Blue Shield of GA*	Issue age	1284	1644	94
GA	Conseco Direct Life Ins. Co.	Issue age	1342	1694	93
GA	United American Insurance	Issue age	1612	2024	90
GA	Pioneer Life Insurance	Issue age	1646	1947	89
GA	Guarantee Trust Life	Issue age	1699	2044	89

| STATE | COMPANY | TYPE OF PRICING | ANNUAL PREMIUM | | VALUE INDEX |
			AGE 65	AGE 75	AGE 65
SELECT					
GA	UnitedHealthcare Ins. Co./AARP*	Community	1221	1221	95
GA	Bankers Life and Casualty	Issue Age	763	976	102
GA	Pioneer Life Insurance	Issue Age	1262	1493	94
PLAN I SUPPLEMENT					

Plan I includes Basic Prescription Drug Coverage. This coverage is similar to prescription drug coverage offered by Medicare HMOs that we judged to be "Average," see Appendix G.

GA	UnitedHealthcare Ins. Co./AARP	Community	2004	2004	88
GA	Pioneer Life Insurance	Issue Age	2567	3042	81

Boston (New Hampshire)

STATE	COMPANY	TYPE OF PRICING	AGE 65	AGE 75	AGE 65
PLAN C SUPPLEMENT					
NH	UnitedHealthcare Ins. Co./AARP*	Community	1182	1182	94
NH	Combined Ins. Co. of America	Issue Age	1138	1431	94
NH	United American Insurance	Issue Age	1386	1753	91
NH	Blue Cross Blue Shield of NH*	Attained Age	927	1636	98
NH	Bankers Life and Casualty	Attained Age	988	1405	97
NH	Pioneer Life Insurance	Attained Age	1139	1653	94
PLAN I SUPPLEMENT					

Plan I includes Basic Prescription Drug Coverage. This coverage is similar to prescription drug coverage offered by Medicare HMOs that we judged to be "Average," see Appendix G.

NH	UnitedHealthcare Ins. Co./AARP	Community	1509	1509	92
NH	Pioneer Life Insurance	Attained Age	1904	2746	86

*Guaranteed Issue

Boston (Massachusetts)

CORE SUPPLEMENT

STATE	COMPANY	TYPE OF PRICING	AGE 65	AGE 75	AGE 65
MA	Blue Cross Blue Shield of MA*	Community	708	708	97
MA	UnitedHealthcare Ins. Co./AARP*	Community	834	834	96

SUPP 1 SUPPLEMENT

STATE	COMPANY	TYPE OF PRICING	AGE 65	AGE 75	AGE 65
MA	Blue Cross Blue Shield of MA*	Community	1326	1326	94
MA	UnitedHealthcare Ins. Co./AARP*	Community	1341	1341	94

SUPP 2 SUPPLEMENT

STATE	COMPANY	TYPE OF PRICING	AGE 65	AGE 75	AGE 65
MA	Blue Cross Blue Shield of MA*	Community	3408	3408	79
MA	UnitedHealthcare Ins. Co./AARP*	Community	3408	3408	79

*Guaranteed Issue

Chicago (Illinois)

PLAN C SUPPLEMENT

STATE	COMPANY	TYPE OF PRICING	AGE 65	AGE 75	AGE 65
IL	UnitedHealthcare Ins. Co./AARP*	Community	1437	1437	90
IL	Combined Ins. Co. of America	Issue Age	1486	1865	89
IL	Country Life Insurance	Attained Age	764	1049	101
IL	Pioneer Life Insurance	Attained Age	1015	1474	97
IL	Guarantee Trust Life	Attained Age	1071	1441	96
IL	Central States Health	Attained Age	1099	1550	95
IL	Standard Life	Attained Age	1170	1581	94
IL	Bankers Life and Casualty	Attained Age	1277	1825	92
IL	United American Insurance	Attained Age	1472	1934	90

SELECT

STATE	COMPANY	TYPE OF PRICING	AGE 65	AGE 75	AGE 65
IL	Pioneer Life Insurance	Attained Age	753	1072	101
IL	Bankers Life and Casualty	Attained Age	1012	1416	97
IL	Bankers Life and Casualty	Attained Age	1106	1548	95

STATE	COMPANY	TYPE OF PRICING	ANNUAL PREMIUM AGE 65	ANNUAL PREMIUM AGE 75	VALUE INDEX AGE 65

PLAN I SUPPLEMENT

Plan I includes Basic Prescription Drug Coverage. This coverage is similar to prescription drug coverage offered by Medicare HMOs that we judged to be "Average," see Appendix G.

STATE	COMPANY	TYPE OF PRICING	AGE 65	AGE 75	VALUE INDEX
IL	UnitedHealthcare Ins. Co./AARP	Community	1908	1908	86
IL	Pioneer Life Insurance	Attained Age	1751	2527	89

*Guaranteed Issue

Cincinnati (Indiana)

PLAN C SUPPLEMENT

STATE	COMPANY	TYPE OF PRICING	AGE 65	AGE 75	VALUE INDEX
IN	UnitedHealthcare Ins. Co./AARP*	Community	1287	1287	91
IN	Combined Ins. Co. of America	Issue Age	999	1262	95
IN	United American Insurance	Issue Age	1570	2079	86
IN	Golden Rule Insurance	Attained Age	877	1134	98
IN	Standard Life	Attained Age	957	1294	96
IN	Bankers Life and Casualty	Attained Age	1047	1489	95
IN	Central States Health	Attained Age	1077	1518	94
IN	Guarantee Trust Life	Attained Age	1080	1453	94
IN	Pioneer Life Insurance	Attained Age	1094	1566	94
IN	Anthem Blue Cross of IN	Attained Age	1099	1555	94

SELECT

STATE	COMPANY	TYPE OF PRICING	AGE 65	AGE 75	VALUE INDEX
IN	UnitedHealthcare Ins. Co./AARP*	Community	1032	1032	95
IN	Bankers Life and Casualty	Attained Age	770	1073	100
IN	Pioneer Life Insurance	Attained Age	875	1253	98
IN	Anthem Blue Cross of IN	Attained Age	946	1281	96

PLAN I SUPPLEMENT

Plan I includes Basic Prescription Drug Coverage. This coverage is similar to prescription drug coverage offered by Medicare HMOs that we judged to be "Average," see Appendix G.

STATE	COMPANY	TYPE OF PRICING	AGE 65	AGE 75	VALUE INDEX
IN	UnitedHealthcare Ins. Co./AARP	Community	1689	1689	88
IN	Pioneer Life Insurance	Attained Age	1812	2613	86

*Guaranteed Issue

Cincinnati (Kentucky)

PLAN C SUPPLEMENT

STATE	COMPANY	TYPE OF PRICING	AGE 65	AGE 75	AGE 65
KY	Anthem Blue Cross of IN	Community	1185	1185	93
KY	UnitedHealthcare Ins. Co./AARP*	Community	1254	1254	92
KY	Combined Ins. Co. of America	Issue Age	1392	1744	90
KY	United American Insurance	Issue Age	1535	2026	87
KY	Central States Health	Attained Age	966	1362	97
KY	Standard Life	Attained Age	1064	1438	95
KY	Guarantee Trust Life	Attained Age	1142	1536	94
KY	Pioneer Life Insurance	Attained Age	1166	1693	93
KY	Bankers Life and Casualty	Attained Age	1294	1846	91

SELECT

STATE	COMPANY	TYPE OF PRICING	AGE 65	AGE 75	AGE 65
KY	Anthem Blue Cross of IN	Community	967	967	97
KY	UnitedHealthcare Ins. Co./AARP*	Community	1053	1053	95
KY	Guarantee Trust Life	Attained Age	779	1048	100
KY	Pioneer Life Insurance	Attained Age	932	1354	97
KY	Bankers Life and Casualty	Attained Age	1124	1565	94

PLAN I SUPPLEMENT

Plan I includes Basic Prescription Drug Coverage. This coverage is similar to prescription drug coverage offered by Medicare HMOs that we judged to be "Average," see Appendix G.

STATE	COMPANY	TYPE OF PRICING	AGE 65	AGE 75	AGE 65
KY	UnitedHealthcare Ins. Co./AARP	Community	1812	1812	87
KY	Pioneer Life Insurance	Attained Age	1841	2656	86
KY	Bankers Life and Casualty	Attained Age	4074	5857	64

*Guaranteed Issue

Cincinnati (Ohio)

PLAN C SUPPLEMENT

STATE	COMPANY	TYPE OF PRICING	AGE 65	AGE 75	AGE 65
OH	UnitedHealthcare Ins. Co./AARP*	Community	1380	1380	92
OH	Anthem Blue Cross of IN	Issue Age	1073	1430	96

| STATE | COMPANY | TYPE OF PRICING | ANNUAL PREMIUM | | VALUE INDEX |
			AGE 65	AGE 75	AGE 65
OH	Combined Ins. Co. of America	Issue Age	1265	1587	93
OH	Medical Mutual of Ohio	Issue Age	1369	1853	92
OH	United American Insurance	Issue Age	1667	2117	88
OH	Golden Rule Insurance	Attained Age	877	1134	99
OH	Standard Life	Attained Age	1011	1366	97
OH	Anthem Blue Cross of IN	Attained Age	1081	1475	96
OH	Central States Health	Attained Age	1147	1617	95
OH	Conseco Direct Life Ins. Co.	Attained Age	1166	1661	95
OH	Bankers Life and Casualty	Attained Age	1189	1698	95
OH	Equitable Life and Casualty	Attained Age	1194	1694	94
OH	Guarantee Trust Life	Attained Age	1203	1619	94
OH	Pioneer Life Insurance	Attained Age	1282	1860	93

SELECT

STATE	COMPANY	TYPE OF PRICING	AGE 65	AGE 75	AGE 65
OH	UnitedHealthcare Ins. Co./AARP*	Community	1083	1083	96
OH	Anthem Blue Cross of IN	Attained Age	835	1227	100
OH	Central States Health	Attained Age	930	1311	99
OH	Pioneer Life Insurance	Attained Age	998	1420	97
OH	Bankers Life and Casualty	Attained Age	1019	1421	97

PLAN I SUPPLEMENT

Plan I includes Basic Prescription Drug Coverage. This coverage is similar to prescription drug coverage offered by Medicare HMOs that we judged to be "Average," see Appendix G.

STATE	COMPANY	TYPE OF PRICING	AGE 65	AGE 75	AGE 65
OH	UnitedHealthcare Ins. Co./AARP	Community	1800	1800	89
OH	Anthem Blue Cross of IN	Issue Age	1840	2454	88
OH	Anthem Blue Cross of IN	Attained Age	1846	2358	88
OH	Equitable Life and Casualty	Attained Age	2298	2960	83
OH	Pioneer Life Insurance	Attained Age	2313	3336	83

*Guaranteed Issue

Cleveland (Ohio)

PLAN C SUPPLEMENT

STATE	COMPANY	TYPE OF PRICING	AGE 65	AGE 75	AGE 65
OH	UnitedHealthcare Ins. Co./AARP*	Community	1380	1380	93
OH	Anthem Blue Cross of IN	Issue Age	1073	1430	97
OH	Medical Mutual of Ohio	Issue Age	1369	1853	93
OH	Combined Ins. Co. of America	Issue Age	1391	1746	93
OH	United American Insurance	Issue Age	1667	2117	89
OH	Golden Rule Insurance	Attained Age	877	1134	100
OH	Standard Life	Attained Age	1011	1366	98
OH	Anthem Blue Cross of IN	Attained Age	1081	1475	97
OH	Central States Health	Attained Age	1147	1617	96
OH	Bankers Life and Casualty	Attained Age	1226	1750	95
OH	Conseco Direct Life Ins. Co.	Attained Age	1265	1804	94
OH	Pioneer Life Insurance	Attained Age	1282	1860	94
OH	Guarantee Trust Life	Attained Age	1340	1803	93
OH	Equitable Life and Casualty	Attained Age	1357	1929	93

SELECT

STATE	COMPANY	TYPE OF PRICING	AGE 65	AGE 75	AGE 65
OH	UnitedHealthcare Ins. Co./AARP*	Community	1083	1083	97
OH	Anthem Blue Cross of IN	Attained Age	835	1227	101
OH	Central States Health	Attained Age	930	1311	99
OH	Pioneer Life Insurance	Attained Age	998	1420	98
OH	Bankers Life and Casualty	Attained Age	1019	1421	98

PLAN I SUPPLEMENT

Plan I includes Basic Prescription Drug Coverage. This coverage is similar to prescription drug coverage offered by Medicare HMOs that we judged to be "Average," see Appendix G.

STATE	COMPANY	TYPE OF PRICING	AGE 65	AGE 75	AGE 65
OH	UnitedHealthcare Ins. Co./AARP	Community	1800	1800	90
OH	Anthem Blue Cross of IN	Issue Age	1840	2454	89
OH	Anthem Blue Cross of IN	Attained Age	1846	2358	89
OH	Pioneer Life Insurance	Attained Age	2313	3336	84
OH	Equitable Life and Casualty	Attained Age	2611	3365	81

*Guaranteed Issue

Dallas (Texas)

PLAN C SUPPLEMENT

TX	UnitedHealthcare Ins. Co./AARP*	Community	1614	1614	89
TX	Combined Ins. Co. of America	Issue Age	1242	1562	94
TX	Equitable Life and Casualty	Attained Age	1076	1528	97
TX	Central States Health	Attained Age	1088	1534	96
TX	Standard Life	Attained Age	1223	1653	94
TX	Guarantee Trust Life	Attained Age	1248	1679	94
TX	Pioneer Life Insurance	Attained Age	1383	2008	92
TX	Bankers Life and Casualty	Attained Age	1391	1991	92
TX	United American Insurance	Attained Age	1514	2032	90

SELECT

TX	UnitedHealthcare Ins. Co./AARP*	Community	1359	1359	92
TX	Bankers Life and Casualty*	Attained Age	971	1335	98
TX	Pioneer Life Insurance	Attained Age	1040	1481	97

PLAN I SUPPLEMENT

Plan I includes Basic Prescription Drug Coverage. This coverage is similar to prescription drug coverage offered by Medicare HMOs that we judged to be "Average," see Appendix G.

TX	UnitedHealthcare Ins. Co./AARP	Community	2106	2106	86
TX	Equitable Life and Casualty	Attained Age	1800	2318	89
TX	Pioneer Life Insurance	Attained Age	2313	3336	83

*Guaranteed Issue

Denver (Colorado)

PLAN C SUPPLEMENT

STATE	COMPANY	TYPE OF PRICING	AGE 65	AGE 75	AGE 65
CO	UnitedHealthcare Ins. Co./AARP*	Community	1359	1359	91
CO	Combined Ins. Co. of America	Issue Age	990	1244	97
CO	Equitable Life and Casualty	Issue Age	1003	1278	97
CO	United American Insurance	Issue Age	1639	2099	88
CO	Golden Rule Insurance	Attained Age	975	1260	97
CO	Standard Life	Attained Age	1011	1366	97
CO	Bankers Life and Casualty	Attained Age	1079	1540	96
CO	Guarantee Trust Life	Attained Age	1089	1465	96
CO	Central States Health	Attained Age	1239	1747	93
CO	Pioneer Life Insurance	Attained Age	1401	1829	91

PLAN I SUPPLEMENT

Plan I includes Basic Prescription Drug Coverage. This coverage is similar to prescription drug coverage offered by Medicare HMOs that we judged to be "Average," see Appendix G.

STATE	COMPANY	TYPE OF PRICING	AGE 65	AGE 75	AGE 65
CO	UnitedHealthcare Ins. Co./AARP	Community	1671	1671	90
CO	Equitable Life and Casualty	Issue Age	2290	2633	82
CO	Blue Cross Blue Shield of CO	Attained Age	1597	2175	91
CO	Pioneer Life Insurance	Attained Age	3673	4242	69

*Guaranteed Issue

Detroit (Michigan)

PLAN C SUPPLEMENT

STATE	COMPANY	TYPE OF PRICING	AGE 65	AGE 75	AGE 65
MI	Blue Cross Blue Shield of MI*	Community	1080	1080	99
MI	UnitedHealthcare Ins. Co./AARP*	Community	1503	1503	95
MI	United American Insurance	Issue Age	1685	2146	93
MI	Combined Ins. Co. of America	Issue Age	1704	2143	93
MI	Guarantee Trust Life	Attained Age	1150	1548	99
MI	Pioneer Life Insurance	Attained Age	1172	1677	98

STATE	COMPANY	TYPE OF PRICING	ANNUAL PREMIUM AGE 65	ANNUAL PREMIUM AGE 75	VALUE INDEX AGE 65
MI	Central States Health	Attained Age	1425	2009	96
MI	Bankers Life and Casualty*	Attained Age	1447	2066	95
MI	Conseco Direct Life Ins Co	Attained Age	1694	2409	93

SELECT

STATE	COMPANY	TYPE OF PRICING	AGE 65	AGE 75	AGE 65
MI	Pioneer Life Insurance	Attained Age	939	1363	101
MI	Bankers Life and Casualty	Attained Age	1266	1754	97

PLAN I SUPPLEMENT

Plan I includes Basic Prescription Drug Coverage. This coverage is similar to prescription drug coverage offered by Medicare HMOs that we judged to be "Average," see Appendix G.

STATE	COMPANY	TYPE OF PRICING	AGE 65	AGE 75	AGE 65
MI	UnitedHealthcare Ins. Co./AARP	Community	1878	1878	93
MI	Pioneer Life Insurance	Attained Age	1812	2613	94
MI	Bankers Life and Casualty	Attained Age	5721	8225	65

*Guaranteed Issue

Houston (Texas)

PLAN C SUPPLEMENT

STATE	COMPANY	TYPE OF PRICING	AGE 65	AGE 75	AGE 65
TX	UnitedHealthcare Ins. Co./AARP*	Community	1614	1614	91
TX	Combined Ins. Co. of America	Issue Age	1367	1718	94
TX	Central States Health	Attained Age	1088	1534	98
TX	Equitable Life and Casualty	Attained Age	1188	1690	96
TX	Standard Life	Attained Age	1383	1869	94
TX	Bankers Life and Casualty	Attained Age	1391	1991	94
TX	Pioneer Life Insurance	Attained Age	1452	2108	93
TX	Guarantee Trust Life	Attained Age	1496	2013	92
TX	United American Insurance	Attained Age	1514	2032	92

SELECT

STATE	COMPANY	TYPE OF PRICING	AGE 65	AGE 75	AGE 65
TX	UnitedHealthcare Ins. Co./AARP*	Community	1359	1359	94
TX	Bankers Life and Casualty*	Attained Age	971	1335	99
TX	Pioneer Life Insurance	Attained Age	1204	1715	96

STATE	COMPANY	TYPE OF PRICING	ANNUAL PREMIUM AGE 65	ANNUAL PREMIUM AGE 75	VALUE INDEX AGE 65

PLAN I SUPPLEMENT

Plan I includes Basic Prescription Drug Coverage. This coverage is similar to prescription drug coverage offered by Medicare HMOs that we judged to be "Average," see Appendix G.

STATE	COMPANY	TYPE OF PRICING	AGE 65	AGE 75	AGE 65
TX	UnitedHealthcare Ins. Co./AARP	Community	2106	2106	88
TX	Equitable Life and Casualty	Attained Age	1991	2563	89
TX	Pioneer Life Insurance	Attained Age	2428	3503	85

*Guaranteed Issue

Jacksonville (Florida)

STATE	COMPANY	TYPE OF PRICING	AGE 65	AGE 75	AGE 65
FL	Central States Health	Issue Age	1321	1799	96
FL	UnitedHealthcare Ins. Co./AARP*	Issue Age	1380	1821	95
FL	Standard Life	Issue Age	1513	1890	93
FL	Bankers Life and Casualty	Issue Age	1565	2064	93
FL	Guarantee Trust Life	Issue Age	1586	2011	92
FL	Combined Ins. Co. of America	Issue Age	1671	2094	92
FL	Blue Cross Blue Shield of FL*	Issue Age	1711	2245	91
FL	United American Insurance	Issue Age	1887	2293	89
FL	Pioneer Life Insurance	Issue Age	1894	2360	89

SELECT

STATE	COMPANY	TYPE OF PRICING	AGE 65	AGE 75	AGE 65
FL	UnitedHealthcare Ins. Co./AARP*	Issue Age	1257	1608	96
FL	Bankers Life and Casualty*	Issue Age	1379	1706	95
FL	Pioneer Life Insurance	Issue Age	1457	1643	94

PLAN I SUPPLEMENT

Plan I includes Basic Prescription Drug Coverage. This coverage is similar to prescription drug coverage offered by Medicare HMOs that we judged to be "Average," see Appendix G.

STATE	COMPANY	TYPE OF PRICING	AGE 65	AGE 75	AGE 65
FL	UnitedHealthcare Ins. Co./AARP	Issue Age	2049	2535	90
FL	Pioneer Life Insurance	Issue Age	4358	4850	71

*Guaranteed Issue

STATE	COMPANY	TYPE OF PRICING	ANNUAL PREMIUM AGE 65	ANNUAL PREMIUM AGE 75	VALUE INDEX AGE 65

Kansas City (Kansas)

PLAN C SUPPLEMENT

STATE	COMPANY	TYPE OF PRICING	AGE 65	AGE 75	AGE 65
KS	UnitedHealthcare Ins. Co./AARP*	Community	1527	1527	90
KS	Combined Ins. Co. of America	Issue Age	1159	1456	95
KS	United American Insurance	Issue Age	1681	2116	88
KS	Standard Life	Attained Age	957	1294	98
KS	Central States Health	Attained Age	1115	1572	96
KS	Guarantee Trust Life	Attained Age	1150	1548	95
KS	Pioneer Life Insurance	Attained Age	1195	1735	95
KS	Blue Cross Blue Shield of Kansas City	Attained Age	1236	1980	94
KS	Bankers Life and Casualty	Attained Age	1285	1828	93
KS	Conseco Direct Life Ins. Co.	Attained Age	1353	1925	92
KS	Blue Cross Blue Shield of Kansas City*	Attained Age	2028	2808	84

PLAN I SUPPLEMENT

Plan I includes Basic Prescription Drug Coverage. This coverage is similar to prescription drug coverage offered by Medicare HMOs that we judged to be "Average," see Appendix G.

STATE	COMPANY	TYPE OF PRICING	AGE 65	AGE 75	AGE 65
KS	UnitedHealthcare Ins. Co./AARP	Community	2136	2136	85
KS	Pioneer Life Insurance	Attained Age	1998	2883	87

*Guaranteed Issue

Kansas City (Missouri)

PLAN C SUPPLEMENT

STATE	COMPANY	TYPE OF PRICING	AGE 65	AGE 75	AGE 65
MO	UnitedHealthcare Ins. Co./AARP*	Community	1440	1440	91
MO	Combined Ins. Co. of America	Issue Age	1024	1283	97
MO	Guarantee Trust Life	Issue Age	1100	1323	96
MO	United American Insurance	Issue Age	1355	1751	92
MO	Equitable Life and Casualty	Attained Age	999	1424	98
MO	Central States Health	Attained Age	1072	1511	96
MO	Pioneer Life Insurance	Attained Age	1113	1615	96

| STATE | COMPANY | TYPE OF PRICING | ANNUAL PREMIUM | | VALUE INDEX |
			AGE 65	AGE 75	AGE 65
MO	Standard Life	Attained Age	1117	1510	96
MO	Blue Cross Blue Shield of Kansas City	Attained Age	1188	1896	95
MO	Bankers Life and Casualty	Attained Age	1226	1748	94
MO	Blue Cross Blue Shield of Kansas City*	Attained Age	2052	2844	84

SELECT

MO	Pioneer Life Insurance	Attained Age	625	894	104
MO	Bankers Life and Casualty	Attained Age	916	1289	99
MO	Blue Cross Blue Shield of Kansas City	Attained Age	1068	1668	97
MO	Blue Cross Blue Shield of Kansas City*	Attained Age	1608	2232	89

PLAN I SUPPLEMENT

Plan I includes Basic Prescription Drug Coverage. This coverage is similar to prescription drug coverage offered by Medicare HMOs that we judged to be "Average," see Appendix G.

MO	UnitedHealthcare Ins. Co./AARP	Community	1863	1863	88
MO	Pioneer Life Insurance	Attained Age	1904	2746	88
MO	Equitable Life and Casualty	Attained Age	1929	2481	88

*Guaranteed Issue

Las Vegas (Arizona)

PLAN C SUPPLEMENT

AZ	UnitedHealthcare Ins. Co./AARP*	Community	1392	1392	94
AZ	Combined Ins. Co. of America	Issue Age	1257	1581	95
AZ	United American Insurance	Issue Age	1785	2269	89
AZ	Golden Rule Insurance	Attained Age	1024	1323	99
AZ	Central States Health	Attained Age	1111	1566	97
AZ	Pioneer Life Insurance	Attained Age	1184	1719	96
AZ	Standard Life	Attained Age	1223	1653	96
AZ	Bankers Life and Casualty	Attained Age	1253	1793	95
AZ	Equitable Life and Casualty	Attained Age	1298	1845	95
AZ	Conseco Direct Life Ins. Co.	Attained Age	1353	1925	94
AZ	Guarantee Trust Life	Attained Age	1398	1882	94

STATE	COMPANY	TYPE OF PRICING	ANNUAL PREMIUM AGE 65	AGE 75	VALUE INDEX AGE 65

SELECT

STATE	COMPANY	TYPE OF PRICING	AGE 65	AGE 75	AGE 65
AZ	Pioneer Life Insurance	Attained Age	947	1375	100
AZ	Bankers Life and Casualty	Attained Age	1099	1535	97

PLAN I SUPPLEMENT

Plan I includes Basic Prescription Drug Coverage. This coverage is similar to prescription drug coverage offered by Medicare HMOs that we judged to be "Average," see Appendix G.

STATE	COMPANY	TYPE OF PRICING	AGE 65	AGE 75	AGE 65
AZ	UnitedHealthcare Ins. Co./AARP	Community	1833	1833	91
AZ	Equitable Life and Casualty	Attained Age	2171	2798	87
AZ	Pioneer Life Insurance	Attained Age	2313	3336	86

*Guaranteed Issue

Las Vegas (Nevada)

PLAN C SUPPLEMENT

STATE	COMPANY	TYPE OF PRICING	AGE 65	AGE 75	AGE 65
NV	UnitedHealthcare Ins. Co./AARP*	Community	1311	1311	94
NV	Combined Ins. Co. of America	Issue Age	1010	1263	98
NV	Central States Health	Attained Age	1168	1646	96
NV	Standard Life	Attained Age	1170	1581	96
NV	Bankers Life & Casualty	Attained Age	1238	1772	95
NV	Conseco Direct Life Ins. Co.	Attained Age	1265	1804	95
NV	Guarantee Trust Life	Attained Age	1301	1751	94
NV	Equitable Life and Casualty	Attained Age	1321	1877	94
NV	Pioneer Life Insurance	Attained Age	1452	2108	92
NV	United American Insurance	Attained Age	1512	2007	92

PLAN I SUPPLEMENT

Plan I includes Basic Prescription Drug Coverage. This coverage is similar to prescription drug coverage offered by Medicare HMOs that we judged to be "Average," see Appendix G.

STATE	COMPANY	TYPE OF PRICING	AGE 65	AGE 75	AGE 65
NV	UnitedHealthcare Ins. Co./AARP	Community	1644	1644	92
NV	Blue Cross Blue Shield of NV	Attained Age	1548	1999	94
NV	Equitable Life and Casualty	Attained Age	2211	2847	86
NV	Pioneer Life Insurance	Attained Age	2331	3363	85

*Guaranteed Issue

STATE	COMPANY	TYPE OF PRICING	ANNUAL PREMIUM AGE 65	AGE 75	VALUE INDEX AGE 65

Los Angeles (California)

PLAN C SUPPLEMENT

STATE	COMPANY	TYPE OF PRICING	AGE 65	AGE 75	AGE 65
CA	UnitedHealthcare Ins. Co./AARP*	Community	1665	1665	92
CA	Combined Ins. Co. of America	Issue Age	1364	1715	95
CA	Blue Cross of CA	Attained Age	984	1572	100
CA	Guarantee Trust Life	Attained Age	1062	1429	99
CA	Bankers Life and Casualty	Attained Age	1240	1774	97
CA	Conseco Direct Life Ins. Co.	Attained Age	1265	1804	96
CA	Standard Life	Attained Age	1276	1725	96
CA	Pioneer Life Insurance	Attained Age	1364	1952	95
CA	United American Insurance	Attained Age	1521	1916	93
CA	Central States Health	Attained Age	1815	2558	90

PLAN I SUPPLEMENT

Plan I includes Basic Prescription Drug Coverage. This coverage is similar to prescription drug coverage offered by Medicare HMOs that we judged to be "Average," see Appendix G.

STATE	COMPANY	TYPE OF PRICING	AGE 65	AGE 75	AGE 65
CA	UnitedHealthcare Ins. Co./AARP*	Community	1839	1839	92
CA	Blue Shield of CA*	Attained Age	1920	2652	91
CA	Pioneer Life Insurance	Attained Age	2812	4056	83

*Guaranteed Issue

Louisville (Indiana)

PLAN C SUPPLEMENT

STATE	COMPANY	TYPE OF PRICING	AGE 65	AGE 75	AGE 65
IN	UnitedHealthcare Ins. Co./AARP*	Community	1287	1287	92
IN	Combined Ins. Co. of America	Issue Age	999	1262	96
IN	United American Insurance	Issue Age	1570	2079	88
IN	Golden Rule Insurance	Attained Age	877	1134	99
IN	Standard Life	Attained Age	957	1294	97
IN	Bankers Life and Casualty	Attained Age	1076	1530	95
IN	Central States Health	Attained Age	1077	1518	95

STATE	COMPANY	TYPE OF PRICING	ANNUAL PREMIUM AGE 65	AGE 75	VALUE INDEX AGE 65
IN	Guarantee Trust Life	Attained Age	1080	1453	95
IN	Pioneer Life Insurance	Attained Age	1094	1566	95
IN	Anthem Blue Cross of IN	Attained Age	1099	1555	95

SELECT

STATE	COMPANY	TYPE OF PRICING	AGE 65	AGE 75	AGE 65
IN	UnitedHealthcare Ins. Co./AARP*	Community	1032	1032	96
IN	Bankers Life and Casualty	Attained Age	796	1109	100
IN	Pioneer Life Insurance	Attained Age	875	1253	99
IN	Anthem Blue Cross of IN	Attained Age	946	1281	97

PLAN I SUPPLEMENT

Plan I includes Basic Prescription Drug Coverage. This coverage is similar to prescription drug coverage offered by Medicare HMOs that we judged to be "Average," see Appendix G.

STATE	COMPANY	TYPE OF PRICING	AGE 65	AGE 75	AGE 65
IN	UnitedHealthcare Ins. Co./AARP	Community	1689	1689	89
IN	Pioneer Life Insurance	Attained Age	1812	2613	87

Louisville (Kentucky)

PLAN C SUPPLEMENT

STATE	COMPANY	TYPE OF PRICING	AGE 65	AGE 75	AGE 65
KY	Anthem Blue Cross of IN	Community	1185	1185	95
KY	UnitedHealthcare Ins. Co./AARP*	Community	1254	1254	94
KY	Combined Ins. Co. of America	Issue Age	1392	1744	92
KY	United American Insurance	Issue Age	1535	2026	90
KY	Central States Health	Attained Age	966	1362	98
KY	Standard Life	Attained Age	1064	1438	96
KY	Guarantee Trust Life	Attained Age	1142	1536	95
KY	Pioneer Life Insurance	Attained Age	1166	1693	95
KY	Bankers Life and Casualty	Attained Age	1294	1846	93

SELECT

STATE	COMPANY	TYPE OF PRICING	AGE 65	AGE 75	AGE 65
KY	Anthem Blue Cross of IN	Community	967	967	98
KY	UnitedHealthcare Ins. Co./AARP*	Community	1053	1053	97
KY	Guarantee Trust Life	Attained Age	779	1048	101

STATE	COMPANY	TYPE OF PRICING	ANNUAL PREMIUM AGE 65	AGE 75	VALUE INDEX AGE 65
KY	Pioneer Life Insurance	Attained Age	932	1354	99
KY	Bankers Life and Casualty	Attained Age	1124	1565	96

PLAN I SUPPLEMENT

Plan I includes Basic Prescription Drug Coverage. This coverage is similar to prescription drug coverage offered by Medicare HMOs that we judged to be "Average," see Appendix G.

KY	UnitedHealthcare Ins. Co./AARP	Community	1812	1812	89
KY	Pioneer Life Insurance	Attained Age	1841	2656	88
KY	Bankers Life and Casualty	Attained Age	4074	5857	67

*Guaranteed Issue

Manchester (New Hampshire)

PLAN C SUPPLEMENT

NH	UnitedHealthcare Ins. Co./AARP*	Community	1182	1182	93
NH	Combined Ins. Co. of America	Issue Age	1138	1431	94
NH	United American Insurance	Issue Age	1386	1753	90
NH	Blue Cross Blue Shield of NH*	Attained Age	927	1636	97
NH	Bankers Life and Casualty	Attained Age	988	1405	96
NH	Pioneer Life Insurance	Attained Age	1139	1653	94

PLAN I SUPPLEMENT

Plan I includes Basic Prescription Drug Coverage. This coverage is similar to prescription drug coverage offered by Medicare HMOs that we judged to be "Average," see Appendix G.

NH	UnitedHealthcare Ins. Co./AARP	Community	1509	1509	91
NH	Pioneer Life Insurance	Attained Age	1904	2746	85

*Guaranteed Issue

Miami (Florida)

PLAN C SUPPLEMENT

STATE	COMPANY	TYPE OF PRICING	AGE 65	AGE 75	AGE 65
FL	Combined Ins. Co. of America	Issue Age	1671	2094	98
FL	Bankers Life and Casualty	Issue Age	1780	2351	98
FL	United American Insurance	Issue Age	1887	2293	97
FL	Central States Health	Issue Age	1922	2617	97
FL	UnitedHealthcare Ins. Co./AARP*	Issue Age	1971	2595	96
FL	Guarantee Trust Life	Issue Age	2014	2553	96
FL	Standard Life	Issue Age	2132	2663	95
FL	Blue Cross Blue Shield of FL*	Issue Age	2197	3014	95
FL	Pioneer Life Insurance	Issue Age	2239	2788	95

SELECT

STATE	COMPANY	TYPE OF PRICING	AGE 65	AGE 75	AGE 65
FL	Bankers Life and Casualty*	Issue Age	1564	1938	99
FL	Pioneer Life Insurance	Issue Age	1722	1941	98
FL	UnitedHealthcare Ins. Co./AARP*	Issue Age	1797	2295	98

PLAN I SUPPLEMENT

Plan I includes Basic Prescription Drug Coverage. This coverage is similar to prescription drug coverage offered by Medicare HMOs that we judged to be "Average," see Appendix G.

STATE	COMPANY	TYPE OF PRICING	AGE 65	AGE 75	AGE 65
FL	UnitedHealthcare Ins. Co./AARP	Issue Age	2919	3609	92
FL	Pioneer Life Insurance	Issue Age	5151	5732	80

*Guaranteed Issue

Milwaukee (Wisconsin)

BASIC, PARTS A AND B DEDUCTIBLES SUPPLEMENT

STATE	COMPANY	TYPE OF PRICING	AGE 65	AGE 75	AGE 65
WI	UnitedHealthcare Ins. Co./AARP	Community	N/A	N/A	N/A
WI	Combined Ins. Co. of America	Issue Age	1046	1296	94
WI	United American Insurance	Issue Age	1536	2011	86
WI	Guarantee Trust Life	Attained Age	944	1281	96

| STATE | COMPANY | TYPE OF PRICING | ANNUAL PREMIUM | | VALUE INDEX |
			AGE 65	AGE 75	AGE 65
WI	Blue Cross Blue Shield United of WI	Attained Age	1056	1408	94
WI	Pioneer Life Insurance	Attained Age	1078	1433	94
WI	Central States Health	Attained Age	1114	1628	93
WI	Bankers Life and Casualty	Attained Age	1166	1755	92

BASIC, PART A DEDUCTIBLE, PART B EXCESS CHARGES SUPPLEMENT

WI	Combined Ins Co of America	Issue Age	1060	1335	93
WI	United American Insurance	Issue Age	1472	1947	86
WI	Guarantee Trust Life	Attained Age	965	1342	94
WI	Pioneer Life Insurance	Attained Age	1055	1449	93
WI	Bankers Life and Casualty	Attained Age	1108	1715	92
WI	Blue Cross Blue Shield United of WI	Attained Age	1151	1502	91
WI	Central States Health	Attained Age	1173	1744	91

*Guaranteed Issue

N/A: UnitedHealthcare Ins. Co./AARP offers a different combination of benefits

Minneapolis (Minnesota)

MC1 SUPPLEMENT

MN	Blue Cross Blue Shield of MN	Community	612	612	97
MN	Central States Health	Community	625	625	97
MN	UnitedHealthcare Ins. Co./AARP	Community	648	648	96
MN	Combined Ins. Co. of America	Community	679	679	96
MN	Bankers Life and Casualty*	Community	802	802	93
MN	Guarantee Trust Life	Community	1002	1002	90
MN	United American Insurance	Community	1126	1126	88
MN	Pioneer Life Insurance	Community	1138	1138	87

Minneapolis (Wisconsin)

BASIC, PARTS A AND B DEDUCTIBLES SUPPLEMENT

STATE	COMPANY	TYPE OF PRICING	AGE 65	AGE 75	AGE 65
WI	UnitedHealthcare Ins. Co./AARP	Community	N/A	N/A	N/A
WI	Combined Ins. Co. of America	Issue Age	976	1208	93
WI	United American Insurance	Issue Age	1536	2011	82
WI	Guarantee Trust Life	Attained Age	944	1281	94
WI	Bankers Life and Casualty	Attained Age	1025	1543	92
WI	Pioneer Life Insurance	Attained Age	1025	1363	92
WI	Blue Cross Blue Shield United of WI	Attained Age	1056	1408	91
WI	Central States Health	Attained Age	1114	1628	90

BASIC, PART A DEDUCTIBLE, PART B EXCESS CHARGES SUPPLEMENT

STATE	COMPANY	TYPE OF PRICING	AGE 65	AGE 75	AGE 65
WI	Combined Ins. Co. of America	Issue Age	990	1247	91
WI	United American Insurance	Issue Age	1472	1947	82
WI	Guarantee Trust Life	Attained Age	965	1342	91
WI	Bankers Life and Casualty	Attained Age	970	1496	91
WI	Pioneer Life Insurance	Attained Age	1004	1379	90
WI	Blue Cross Blue Shield United of WI	Attained Age	1151	1502	87
WI	Central States Health	Attained Age	1173	1744	87

*Guaranteed Issue

N/A: UnitedHealthcare Ins. Co./AARP offers a different combination of benefits

New Orleans (Louisiana)

PLAN C SUPPLEMENT

STATE	COMPANY	TYPE OF PRICING	AGE 65	AGE 75	AGE 65
LA	UnitedHealthcare Ins. Co./AARP*	Community	1599	1599	92
LA	Guarantee Trust Life	Attained Age	1115	1501	98
LA	Standard Life	Attained Age	1276	1725	96
LA	Bankers Life and Casualty	Attained Age	1307	1873	95
LA	Equitable Life and Casualty	Attained Age	1354	1928	95
LA	Central States Health	Attained Age	1457	2054	94

| STATE | COMPANY | TYPE OF PRICING | ANNUAL PREMIUM | | VALUE INDEX |
			AGE 65	AGE 75	AGE 65
LA	Pioneer Life Insurance	Attained Age	1626	2336	92
LA	United American Insurance	Attained Age	1655	2186	91

PLAN I SUPPLEMENT

Plan I includes Basic Prescription Drug Coverage. This coverage is similar to prescription drug coverage offered by Medicare HMOs that we judged to be "Average," see Appendix G.

LA	UnitedHealthcare Ins. Co./AARP	Community	2295	2295	87
LA	Equitable Life and Casualty	Attained Age	2273	2925	87
LA	Pioneer Life Insurance	Attained Age	2498	3603	85

*Guaranteed Issue

New York (New York)

PLAN C SUPPLEMENT

NY	UnitedHealthcare Ins. Co./AARP*	Community	1314	1314	96
NY	First United American*	Community	1659	1659	92

PLAN I SUPPLEMENT

Plan I includes Basic Prescription Drug Coverage. This coverage is similar to prescription drug coverage offered by Medicare HMOs that we judged to be "Average," see Appendix G.

NY	UnitedHealthcare Ins. Co./AARP*	Community	2127	2127	89

*Guaranteed Issue

Philadelphia (New Jersey)

PLAN C SUPPLEMENT

NJ	Guarantee Trust Life	Attained Age	841	1131	101
NJ	United American Insurance	Attained Age	871	1218	101
NJ	Bankers Life and Casualty	Attained Age	951	1318	100

STATE	COMPANY	TYPE OF PRICING	ANNUAL PREMIUM AGE 65	ANNUAL PREMIUM AGE 75	VALUE INDEX AGE 65

Philadelphia (Pennsylvania)

PLAN C SUPPLEMENT

PA	UnitedHealthcare Ins. Co./AARP*	Community	1872	1872	90
PA	Combined Ins. Co. of America	Issue Age	1206	1624	97
PA	United American Insurance	Issue Age	1274	1549	96
PA	Guarantee Trust Life	Attained Age	1074	1530	99
PA	Pioneer Life Insurance	Attained Age	1145	1640	98
PA	Central States Health	Attained Age	1157	1631	98
PA	Standard Life	Attained Age	1223	1653	97
PA	Bankers Life and Casualty	Attained Age	1230	1704	97

PLAN I SUPPLEMENT

Plan I includes Basic Prescription Drug Coverage. This coverage is similar to prescription drug coverage offered by Medicare HMOs that we judged to be "Average," see Appendix G.

PA	UnitedHealthcare Ins. Co./AARP	Community	2091	2091	90

*Guaranteed Issue

Phoenix (Arizona)

PLAN C SUPPLEMENT

AZ	UnitedHealthcare Ins. Co./AARP*	Community	1392	1392	94
AZ	Combined Ins. Co. of America	Issue Age	1257	1581	96
AZ	United American Insurance	Issue Age	1785	2269	89
AZ	Golden Rule Insurance	Attained Age	1072	1386	98
AZ	Central States Health	Attained Age	1111	1566	98
AZ	Pioneer Life Insurance	Attained Age	1243	1804	96
AZ	Equitable Life and Casualty	Attained Age	1298	1845	95
AZ	Standard Life	Attained Age	1330	1797	95
AZ	Conseco Direct Life Ins. Co.	Attained Age	1353	1925	95
AZ	Bankers Life and Casualty	Attained Age	1355	1942	94
AZ	Guarantee Trust Life	Attained Age	1398	1882	94

STATE	COMPANY	TYPE OF PRICING	ANNUAL PREMIUM AGE 65	AGE 75	VALUE INDEX AGE 65

SELECT

STATE	COMPANY	TYPE OF PRICING	AGE 65	AGE 75	AGE 65
AZ	Pioneer Life Insurance	Attained Age	994	1444	99
AZ	Bankers Life and Casualty	Attained Age	1189	1664	97

PLAN I SUPPLEMENT

Plan I includes Basic Prescription Drug Coverage. This coverage is similar to prescription drug coverage offered by Medicare HMOs that we judged to be "Average," see Appendix G.

STATE	COMPANY	TYPE OF PRICING	AGE 65	AGE 75	AGE 65
AZ	UnitedHealthcare Ins. Co./AARP	Community	1833	1833	91
AZ	Equitable Life and Casualty	Attained Age	2171	2798	88
AZ	Pioneer Life Insurance	Attained Age	2428	3503	85

*Guaranteed Issue

Pittsburgh (Pennsylvania)

PLAN C SUPPLEMENT

STATE	COMPANY	TYPE OF PRICING	AGE 65	AGE 75	AGE 65
PA	UnitedHealthcare Ins. Co./AARP*	Community	1485	1485	92
PA	Highmark Blue Cross Blue Shield	Community	1587	N/A	90
PA	Combined Ins. Co. of America	Issue Age	1206	1624	95
PA	United American Insurance	Issue Age	1274	1549	94
PA	Guarantee Trust Life	Attained Age	1074	1530	97
PA	Pioneer Life Insurance	Attained Age	1145	1640	96
PA	Central States Health	Attained Age	1157	1631	96
PA	Standard Life	Attained Age	1223	1653	95
PA	Bankers Life and Casualty	Attained Age	1230	1704	95

PLAN I SUPPLEMENT

Plan I includes Basic Prescription Drug Coverage. This coverage is similar to prescription drug coverage offered by Medicare HMOs that we judged to be "Average," see Appendix G.

STATE	COMPANY	TYPE OF PRICING	AGE 65	AGE 75	AGE 65
PA	UnitedHealthcare Ins. Co./AARP	Community	1662	1662	92

*Guaranteed Issue

Portland (Oregon)

PLAN C SUPPLEMENT

STATE	COMPANY	TYPE OF PRICING	AGE 65	AGE 75	AGE 65
OR	UnitedHealthcare Ins. Co./AARP*	Community	1179	1179	92
OR	Combined Ins. Co. of America	Issue Age	1031	1300	94
OR	United American Insurance	Issue Age	1351	1677	89
OR	Equitable Life and Casualty	Attained Age	987	1400	95
OR	Standard Life	Attained Age	1011	1366	95
OR	Bankers Life and Casualty	Attained Age	1032	1475	94
OR	Conseco Direct Life Ins. Co.	Attained Age	1056	1507	94
OR	Pioneer Life Insurance	Attained Age	1154	1675	92
OR	Guarantee Trust Life	Attained Age	1212	1632	91

SELECT

STATE	COMPANY	TYPE OF PRICING	AGE 65	AGE 75	AGE 65
OR	UnitedHealthcare Ins. Co./AARP*	Community	1026	1026	94

PLAN I SUPPLEMENT

Plan I includes Basic Prescription Drug Coverage. This coverage is similar to prescription drug coverage offered by Medicare HMOs that we judged to be "Average," see Appendix G.

STATE	COMPANY	TYPE OF PRICING	AGE 65	AGE 75	AGE 65
OR	UnitedHealthcare Ins. Co./AARP	Community	1623	1623	88
OR	Equitable Life and Casualty	Attained Age	1650	2125	87
OR	Pioneer Life Insurance	Attained Age	2097	3025	81
OR	Bankers Life and Casualty	Attained Age	5501	7909	52

Portland (Washington)

PLAN C SUPPLEMENT

STATE	COMPANY	TYPE OF PRICING	AGE 65	AGE 75	AGE 65
WA	Combined Ins. Co. of America	Community	1068	1068	93
WA	UnitedHealthcare Ins. Co./AARP*	Community	1239	1239	90
WA	Bankers Life and Casualty	Community	1414	1414	87
WA	Standard Life	Community	1417	1417	87
WA	United American Insurance	Community	1451	1451	87
WA	Pioneer Life Insurance	Community	1786	1786	82

STATE	COMPANY	TYPE OF PRICING	ANNUAL PREMIUM		VALUE INDEX
			AGE 65	AGE 75	AGE 65
SELECT					
WA	UnitedHealthcare Ins. Co./AARP*	Community	1107	1107	93
PLAN I SUPPLEMENT					

Plan I includes Basic Prescription Drug Coverage. This coverage is similar to prescription drug coverage offered by Medicare HMOs that we judged to be "Average," see Appendix G.

STATE	COMPANY	TYPE OF PRICING	AGE 65	AGE 75	AGE 65
WA	UnitedHealthcare Ins. Co./AARP	Community	1680	1680	87
WA	Bankers Life and Casualty	Community	4115	4115	61
WA	Pioneer Life Insurance	Community	4165	4165	60

*Guaranteed Issue

Raleigh (North Carolina)

STATE	COMPANY	TYPE OF PRICING	AGE 65	AGE 75	AGE 65
PLAN C SUPPLEMENT					
NC	UnitedHealthcare Ins. Co./AARP*	Community	1194	1194	92
NC	Combined Ins. Co. of America	Issue Age	1103	1408	93
NC	Blue Cross Blue Shield of NC	Issue Age	1146	1575	93
NC	United American Insurance	Issue Age	1307	1687	90
NC	Central States Health	Attained Age	891	1256	97
NC	Guarantee Trust Life	Attained Age	920	1239	97
NC	Standard Life	Attained Age	957	1294	96
NC	Bankers Life and Casualty	Attained Age	977	1392	96
NC	Conseco Direct Life Ins. Co.	Attained Age	979	1397	96
NC	Pioneer Life Insurance	Attained Age	1047	1520	94
SELECT					
NC	UnitedHealthcare Ins. Co./AARP*	Community	1062	1062	94
NC	Bankers Life and Casualty	Attained Age	656	903	102

PLAN I SUPPLEMENT

Plan I includes Basic Prescription Drug Coverage. This coverage is similar to prescription drug coverage offered by Medicare HMOs that we judged to be "Average," see Appendix G.

NC	UnitedHealthcare Ins. Co./AARP	Community	1524	1524	90
NC	Blue Cross Blue Shield of NC	Issue Age	1695	1956	87
NC	Pioneer Life Insurance	Attained Age	1890	2727	84

*Guaranteed Issue

San Francisco (California)

PLAN C SUPPLEMENT

CA	UnitedHealthcare Ins. Co./AARP*	Community	1425	1425	92
CA	Combined Ins. Co. of America	Issue Age	1309	1643	93
CA	Blue Cross of CA	Attained Age	864	1524	100
CA	Conseco Direct Life Ins. Co.	Attained Age	979	1397	98
CA	Guarantee Trust Life	Attained Age	1062	1429	97
CA	Standard Life	Attained Age	1170	1581	95
CA	Pioneer Life Insurance	Attained Age	1178	1686	95
CA	Bankers Life and Casualty	Attained Age	1240	1774	94
CA	United American Insurance	Attained Age	1521	1916	91
CA	Central States Health	Attained Age	1546	2179	90

PLAN I SUPPLEMENT

Plan I includes Basic Prescription Drug Coverage. This coverage is similar to prescription drug coverage offered by Medicare HMOs that we judged to be "Average," see Appendix G.

CA	UnitedHealthcare Ins. Co./AARP	Community	1575	1575	93
CA	Blue Shield of CA*	Attained Age	1680	2256	91
CA	Pioneer Life Insurance	Attained Age	2428	3503	82

*Guaranteed Issue

Seattle (Washington)

PLAN C SUPPLEMENT

WA	Combined Ins. Co. of America	Community	1068	1068	95
WA	UnitedHealthcare Ins. Co./AARP*	Community	1239	1239	92
WA	Bankers Life and Casualty	Community	1414	1414	89
WA	Standard Life	Community	1417	1417	89
WA	United American Insurance	Community	1451	1451	89
WA	Pioneer Life Insurance	Community	1786	1786	84

SELECT

WA	UnitedHealthcare Ins. Co./AARP*	Community	1107	1107	94

PLAN I SUPPLEMENT

Plan I includes Basic Prescription Drug Coverage. This coverage is similar to prescription drug coverage offered by Medicare HMOs that we judged to be "Average," see Appendix G.

WA	UnitedHealthcare Ins. Co./AARP	Community	1680	1680	89
WA	Bankers Life and Casualty	Community	4115	4115	64
WA	Pioneer Life Insurance	Community	4165	4165	63

*Guaranteed Issue

St. Louis (Illinois)

PLAN C SUPPLEMENT

IL	UnitedHealthcare Ins. Co./AARP*	Community	1437	1437	91
IL	Combined Ins. Co. of America	Issue Age	1292	1622	93
IL	Country Life Insurance	Attained Age	764	1049	101
IL	Central States Health	Attained Age	1000	1409	97
IL	Pioneer Life Insurance	Attained Age	1015	1474	97
IL	Standard Life	Attained Age	1064	1438	96
IL	Guarantee Trust Life	Attained Age	1071	1441	96

| STATE | COMPANY | TYPE OF PRICING | ANNUAL PREMIUM | | VALUE INDEX |
			AGE 65	AGE 75	AGE 65
IL	Bankers Life and Casualty	Attained Age	1277	1825	93
IL	United American Insurance	Attained Age	1472	1934	90

SELECT

IL	Pioneer Life Insurance	Attained Age	753	1072	101
IL	Bankers Life and Casualty	Attained Age	1012	1416	97
IL	Bankers Life and Casualty*	Attained Age	1106	1548	96

PLAN I SUPPLEMENT

Plan I includes Basic Prescription Drug Coverage. This coverage is similar to prescription drug coverage offered by Medicare HMOs that we judged to be "Average," see Appendix G.

IL	UnitedHealthcare Ins. Co./AARP	Community	1908	1908	87
IL	Pioneer Life Insurance	Attained Age	1751	2527	89

*Guaranteed Issue

St. Louis (Missouri)

PLAN C SUPPLEMENT

MO	UnitedHealthcare Ins. Co./AARP*	Community	1440	1440	88
MO	Combined Ins. Co. of America	Issue Age	1024	1283	95
MO	Guarantee Trust Life	Issue Age	1100	1323	94
MO	United American Insurance	Issue Age	1355	1751	90
MO	Central States Health	Attained Age	1072	1511	94
MO	Alliance Blue Cross Blue Shield	Attained Age	1073	1712	94
MO	Standard Life	Attained Age	1117	1510	94
MO	Equitable Life and Casualty	Attained Age	1143	1628	93
MO	Pioneer Life Insurance	Attained Age	1225	1779	92
MO	Bankers Life and Casualty	Attained Age	1226	1748	92

SELECT

MO	Pioneer Life Insurance	Attained Age	688	985	102
MO	Bankers Life and Casualty	Attained Age	916	1289	97
MO	Alliance Blue Cross Blue Shield	Attained Age	933	1490	97

STATE	COMPANY	TYPE OF PRICING	ANNUAL PREMIUM AGE 65	ANNUAL PREMIUM AGE 75	VALUE INDEX AGE 65

PLAN I SUPPLEMENT

Plan I includes Basic Prescription Drug Coverage. This coverage is similar to prescription drug coverage offered by Medicare HMOs that we judged to be "Average," see Appendix G.

STATE	COMPANY	TYPE OF PRICING	AGE 65	AGE 75	AGE 65
MO	UnitedHealthcare Ins. Co./AARP	Community	1863	1863	85
MO	Alliance Blue Cross Blue Shield	Attained Age	1664	2662	88
MO	Pioneer Life Insurance	Attained Age	2097	3025	82
MO	Equitable Life and Casualty	Attained Age	2205	2837	81

SELECT

STATE	COMPANY	TYPE OF PRICING	AGE 65	AGE 75	AGE 65
MO	Alliance Blue Cross Blue Shield	Attained Age	1533	2454	90

*Guaranteed Issue

Tampa (Florida)

PLAN C SUPPLEMENT

STATE	COMPANY	TYPE OF PRICING	AGE 65	AGE 75	AGE 65
FL	UnitedHealthcare Ins. Co./AARP*	Issue Age	1380	1821	95
FL	Central States Health	Issue Age	1441	1963	95
FL	Bankers Life and Casualty	Issue Age	1565	2064	93
FL	Guarantee Trust Life	Issue Age	1586	2011	93
FL	Standard Life	Issue Age	1650	2061	92
FL	Combined Ins. Co. of America	Issue Age	1671	2094	92
FL	Blue Cross Blue Shield of FL*	Issue Age	1711	2245	92
FL	United American Insurance	Issue Age	1887	2293	90
FL	Pioneer Life Insurance	Issue Age	1894	2360	90

SELECT

STATE	COMPANY	TYPE OF PRICING	AGE 65	AGE 75	AGE 65
FL	UnitedHealthcare Ins. Co./AARP*	Issue Age	1257	1608	97
FL	Bankers Life and Casualty*	Issue Age	1379	1706	95
FL	Pioneer Life Insurance	Issue Age	1457	1643	94

PLAN I SUPPLEMENT

Plan I includes Basic Prescription Drug Coverage. This coverage is similar to prescription drug coverage offered by Medicare HMOs that we judged to be "Average," see Appendix G.

STATE	COMPANY	TYPE OF PRICING	AGE 65	AGE 75	AGE 65
FL	UnitedHealthcare Ins. Co./AARP	Issue Age	2049	2535	90
FL	Pioneer Life Insurance	Issue Age	4358	4850	71

*Guaranteed Issue

Washington, DC (District of Columbia)

PLAN C SUPPLEMENT

STATE	COMPANY	TYPE OF PRICING	AGE 65	AGE 75	AGE 65
DC	UnitedHealthcare Ins. Co./AARP*	Community	1305	1305	96
DC	United American Insurance	Issue Age	1386	1753	95
DC	Guarantee Trust Life	Attained Age	1089	1465	98
DC	Conseco Direct Life Ins. Co.	Attained Age	1694	2409	91

PLAN I SUPPLEMENT

Plan I includes Basic Prescription Drug Coverage. This coverage is similar to prescription drug coverage offered by Medicare HMOs that we judged to be "Average," see Appendix G.

STATE	COMPANY	TYPE OF PRICING	AGE 65	AGE 75	AGE 65
DC	UnitedHealthcare Ins. Co./AARP	Community	1509	1509	96

*Guaranteed Issue

Washington, DC (Maryland)

PLAN C SUPPLEMENT

STATE	COMPANY	TYPE OF PRICING	AGE 65	AGE 75	AGE 65
MD	UnitedHealthcare Ins. Co./AARP*	Community	1320	1320	95
MD	United American Insurance	Issue Age	934	1195	100
MD	Guarantee Trust Life	Attained Age	921	1239	100
MD	Pioneer Life Insurance	Attained Age	973	1413	99
MD	Bankers Life and Casualty	Attained Age	1065	1520	98

STATE	COMPANY	TYPE OF PRICING	ANNUAL PREMIUM AGE 65	ANNUAL PREMIUM AGE 75	VALUE INDEX AGE 65

PLAN I SUPPLEMENT

Plan I includes Basic Prescription Drug Coverage. This coverage is similar to prescription drug coverage offered by Medicare HMOs that we judged to be "Average," see Appendix G.

STATE	COMPANY	TYPE OF PRICING	AGE 65	AGE 75	AGE 65
MD	Pioneer Life Insurance	Attained Age	1753	2529	92
MD	Bankers Life and Casualty	Attained Age	2829	4068	81

Washington, DC (Virginia)

PLAN C SUPPLEMENT

STATE	COMPANY	TYPE OF PRICING	AGE 65	AGE 75	AGE 65
VA	UnitedHealthcare Ins. Co./AARP*	Community	1347	1347	92
VA	Pioneer Life Insurance**	Issue Age	1061	1385	96
VA	Trigon Blue Cross Blue Shield	Issue Age	1356	1560	92
VA	Golden Rule Insurance	Attained Age	877	1134	99
VA	Standard Life	Attained Age	957	1294	98
VA	Central States Health	Attained Age	994	1402	97
VA	Bankers Life and Casualty	Attained Age	1014	1442	97
VA	United American Insurance	Attained Age	1037	1436	96
VA	Conseco Direct Life Ins. Co.	Attained Age	1166	1661	94
VA	Guarantee Trust Life	Attained Age	1168	1572	94

SELECT

STATE	COMPANY	TYPE OF PRICING	AGE 65	AGE 75	AGE 65
VA	Trigon Blue Cross Blue Shield	Issue Age	888	1068	99

PLAN I SUPPLEMENT

Plan I includes Basic Prescription Drug Coverage. This coverage is similar to prescription drug coverage offered by Medicare HMOs that we judged to be "Average," see Appendix G.

STATE	COMPANY	TYPE OF PRICING	AGE 65	AGE 75	AGE 65
VA	UnitedHealthcare Ins. Co./AARP	Community	1617	1617	91
VA	Trigon Blue Cross Blue Shield	Issue Age	1560	1776	92
VA	Pioneer Life Insurance**	Issue Age	2720	3118	78

SELECT

STATE	COMPANY	TYPE OF PRICING	AGE 65	AGE 75	AGE 65
VA	Trigon Blue Cross Blue Shield	Issue Age	1212	1428	97

Washington, DC (West Virginia)

PLAN C SUPPLEMENT

STATE	COMPANY	TYPE OF PRICING	AGE 65	AGE 75	AGE 65
WV	UnitedHealthcare Ins. Co./AARP*	Community	1218	1218	90
WV	United American Insurance	Issue Age	1556	1987	84
WV	Golden Rule Insurance	Attained Age	975	1260	95
WV	Standard Life	Attained Age	1011	1366	94
WV	Bankers Life and Casualty	Attained Age	1034	1477	93
WV	Central States Health	Attained Age	1042	1469	93
WV	Guarantee Trust Life	Attained Age	1089	1465	92
WV	Pioneer Life Insurance	Attained Age	1111	1613	92

PLAN I SUPPLEMENT

Plan I includes Basic Prescription Drug Coverage. This coverage is similar to prescription drug coverage offered by Medicare HMOs that we judged to be "Average," see Appendix G.

STATE	COMPANY	TYPE OF PRICING	AGE 65	AGE 75	AGE 65
WV	UnitedHealthcare Ins. Co./AARP	Community	1614	1614	87
WV	Pioneer Life Insurance	Attained Age	2204	3179	78

*Guaranteed Issue

**Pioneer Life offers Issue Age premiums in VA for an enrollees' first three years. After this time, premiums increase and are attained-age rated.

APPENDIX F: State Insurance Departments

These agencies can help you learn about insurance policies offered in your state. If you have a problem with an insurance company, you can also file a complaint with these agencies.

STATE	ADDRESS	PHONE/FAX
Alabama	Alabama Dept. of Insurance 201 Monroe Street, #1700 Montgomery, AL 36104	334-269-3550 (fax) 334-241-4192
Alaska	Please use as primary mailing address Alaska Division of Insurance 3601 C Street, #1324 Anchorage, AL 99503-5948	907-465-2515 (fax) 907-465-3422
	Dept. of Commerce & Economic Development P.O. Box 110805 Juneau, AL 99811-0805	907-269-7900 (fax) 907-269-7910
	Federal Express Packages: 333 Willoughby Avenue, 9th Floor Juneau, AL 99801	
American Samoa	Office of the Governor American Samoa Government Pago Pago, American Samoa 96799	011-684-633-4116 (fax) 011-684-633-2269
Arizona	Arizona Dept. of Insurance 2910 N. 44th Street, #210 Phoenix, AZ 85018-7256	602-912-8400 (fax) 602-912-8452
Arkansas	Arkansas Dept. of Insurance 1200 W. 3rd Street Little Rock, AR 72201-1904	501-371-2600 (fax) 501-371-2629
California	California Dept. of Insurance 300 Capitol Mall, #1500 Sacramento, CA 95814	916-492-3500 (fax) 916-445-5280
	State of California 45 Fremont Street, 23rd Floor San Francisco, CA 94102	415-538-4040 (fax) 415-904-5889
	300 S. Spring Street Los Angeles, CA 90013	213-346-6400 (fax) 213-897-6771
Colorado	Colorado Division of Insurance 1560 Broadway, #850 Denver, CO 80202	303-894-7499 (fax) 303-894-7455

STATE	ADDRESS	PHONE/FAX
Connecticut	Connecticut Dept. of Insurance P.O. Box 816 Hartford, CT 06142-0816 Federal Express Packages: 153 Market Street, 11th Floor Hartford, CT 06103	860-297-3802 (fax) 860-566-7410
Delaware	Delaware Dept. of Insurance Rodney Building 841 Silver Lake Boulevard Dover, DE 19904	302-739-4251 (fax) 302-739-5280
District of Columbia	Dept. of Insurance & Securities Reg. Government of the District of Columbia 810 1st Street, NE, #701 Washington, DC 20002	202-727-8000 x3018 (fax) 202-535-1196
Florida	Florida Dept. of Insurance State Capitol Plaza Level Eleven Tallahassee, FL 32399-0300	850-922-3101 (fax) 850-488-3334
Georgia	Georgia Dept. of Insurance 2 Martin L. King, Jr. Drive Floyd Memorial Bldg., 704 West Tower Atlanta, GA 30334	404-656-2056 (fax) 404-657-7493
Guam	Dept. of Revenue & Taxation Insurance Branch Government of Guam Building 13-3, 1st Floor Mariner Avenue Tiyan, Barrigada, Guam 96913 Post Office Box Address: P.O. Box 23607 GMF, Guam 96921	671-475-1843 (fax) 671-472-2643
Hawaii	Hawaii Insurance Division Dept. of Commerce & Consumer Affairs 250 S. King Street, 5th Floor Honolulu, HA 96813 Post Office Box Address: P.O. Box 3614 Honolulu, HA 96811-3614	808-586-2790 (fax) 808-586-2806

STATE	ADDRESS	PHONE/FAX
Idaho	Idaho Dept. of Insurance 700 W. State Street, 3rd Floor Boise, ID 83720-0043	208-334-4250 (fax) 208-334-4398
Illinois	Illinois Dept. of Insurance 320 W. Washington Street, 4th Floor Springfield, IL 62767-0001	217-785-0116 (fax) 217-524-6500
	100 West Randolph Street, #15-100 Chicago, IL 60601-3251	312-814-2420 (fax) 312-814-5435
Indiana	Indiana Dept. of Insurance 311 W. Washington Street, #300 Indianapolis, IN 46204-2787	317-232-2385 (fax) 317-232-5251
Iowa	Division of Insurance State of Iowa 330 E. Maple Street Des Moines, IA 50319	515-281-5705 (fax) 515-281-3059
Kansas	Kansas Dept. of Insurance 420 SW 9th Street Topeka, KS 66612-1678	785-296-7801 (fax) 785-296-2283
Kentucky	Kentucky Dept. of Insurance P.O. Box 517 215 W. Main Street Frankfort, KY 40602-0517	502-564-6027 (fax) 502-564-1453
Louisiana	Louisiana Dept. of Insurance Attn: Craig Johnson 950 N. 5th Street Baton Rouge, LA 70802 Post Office Box Address: P.O. Box 94214 Baton Rouge, LA 70804-9214	225-342-5423 (fax) 225-342-8622
Maine	Maine Bureau of Insurance Dept. of Professional & Financial Reg. State Office Building, Station 34 Augusta, ME 04333-0034 Federal Express Packages: 124 Northern Avenue Gardiner, ME 04345	207-624-8475 (fax) 207-624-8599

STATE	ADDRESS	PHONE/FAX
Maryland	Maryland Insurance Administration 525 St. Paul Place Baltimore, MD 21202-2272	410-468-2090 (fax) 410-468-2020
Massachusetts	Division of Insurance Commonwealth of Massachusetts One South Station, 4th Floor Boston, MA 02110	617-521-7301 (fax) 617-521-7758
Michigan	Michigan Insurance Bureau Dept. of Commerce 611 W. Ottawa Street, 2nd Floor North Lansing, MI 48933-1020	517-373-9273 (fax) 517-335-4978
Minnesota	Minnesota Dept. of Commerce 121 7th Place East, #200 St. Paul, Minnesota 55101-2145	651-296-1643 (fax) 651-282-2568
Mississippi	Mississippi Insurance Dept. 1804 Walter Sillers State Office Building 550 High Street Jackson, MS 39201 Post Office Box Address: P.O. Box 79 Jackson, MS 39205	601-359-3569 (fax) 601-359-2474
Missouri	Missouri Dept. of Insurance 301 W. High Street, 6 North Jefferson City, MO 65102-0690	573-751-4126 (fax) 573-751-1165
Montana	Montana Dept. of Insurance 126 North Sanders 270 Mitchell Building Helena, MT 59601	406-444-2040 (fax) 406-444-3497
Nebraska	Nebraska Dept. of Insurance Terminal Building, #400 941 O Street Lincoln, NE 68508	402-471-2201 (fax) 402-471-4610
New Hampshire	Dept. of Insurance State of New Hampshire 56 Old Suncook Road Concord, NH 03301	603-271-2261 (fax) 603-271-1406
New Jersey	New Jersey Dept. of Insurance 20 W. State Street, CN325 Trenton, NJ 08625	609-292-5360 (fax) 609-984-5273

STATE	ADDRESS	PHONE/FAX
New Mexico	New Mexico Dept. of Insurance P.O. Drawer 1269 Santa Fe, NM 87504-1269 Federal Express Packages: PERA Building 1120 Paseo de Peralta Santa Fe, NM 87501	505-827-4601 (fax) 505-476-0326
Nevada	Nevada Division of Insurance 1665 Hot Springs Road, #152 Carson City, NV 89706-0661	775-687-4270 (fax) 775-687-3937
New York	New York Dept. of Insurance 25 Beaver Street New York, NY 10004-2319 Agency Building One Empire State Plaza Albany, NY 12257	212-480-2289 (fax) 212-480-2310 518-474-6600 (fax) 518-473-6814
North Carolina	North Carolina Dept. of Insurance P.O. Box 26387 Raleigh, NC 27611 Federal Express Packages: Dobbs Building 430 N. Salisbury Street Raleigh, NC 27603	919-733-7349 (fax) 919-733-6495
North Dakota	North Dakota Dept. of Insurance 600 E. Boulevard Bismarck, ND 58505-0320	701-328-2440 (fax) 701-328-4880
Ohio	Ohio Dept. of Insurance 2100 Stella Court Columbus, OH 43215-1067	614-644-2658 (fax) 614-644-3743
Oklahoma	Oklahoma Dept. of Insurance 3814 N. Santa Fe Oklahoma City, OK 73118	405-521-2828 (fax) 405-521-6635
Oregon	Oregon Division of Insurance Dept. of Consumer & Business Services 350 Winter Street NE, #200 Salem, OR 97310-0700	503-947-7980 (fax) 503-378-4351
Pennsylvania	Pennsylvania Insurance Dept. 1326 Strawberry Square, 13th Floor Harrisburg, PA 17120	717-783-0442 (fax) 717-772-1969

STATE	ADDRESS	PHONE/FAX
Puerto Rico	Puerto Rico Dept. of Insurance Cobian's Plaza Building 1607 Ponce de Leon Avenue Santurce, PR 00909 Post Office Box Address: P.O. Box 8330 Fernandez Juncos Station Santurce, PR 00910-8330	787-722-8686 (fax) 787-722-4400
Rhode Island	Rhode Island Insurance Division Dept. of Business Regulation 233 Richmond Street, #233 Providence, RI 02903-4233	401-222-2223 (fax) 401-222-5475
South Carolina	South Carolina Dept. of Insurance 1612 Marion Street Columbia, SC 29201 Post Office Box Address: P.O. Box 100105 Columbia, SC 29202-3105	803-737-6160 (fax) 803-737-6229
South Dakota	South Dakota Division of Insurance Dept. of Commerce & Regulation 118 W. Capitol Avenue Pierre, SD 57501-2000	605-773-3563 (fax) 605-773-5369
Tennessee	Tennessee Dept. of Commerce & Insurance Volunteer Plaza 500 James Robertson Parkway Nashville, TN 37243-0565	615-741-2241 (fax) 615-532-6934
Texas	Texas Dept. of Insurance 333 Guadalupe Street Austin, TX 78701 Post Office Box Address: P.O. Box 149104 Austin, TX 78714-9104	512-463-6464 (fax) 512-475-2005
Utah	Utah Dept. of Insurance 3110 State Office Building Salt Lake City, UT 84114-1201	801-538-3800 (fax) 801-538-3829
Vermont	Vermont Division of Insurance Dept. of Banking, Insurance & Securities 89 Main Street, Drawer 20 Montpelier, VT 05620-3101	802-828-3301 (fax) 802-828-3306

STATE	ADDRESS	PHONE/FAX
Virginia	State Corporation Commission Bureau of Insurance Commonwealth of Virginia P.O. Box 1157 Richmond, VA 23218 Federal Express Packages: Virginia Bureau of Insurance State Corporation Commission 1300 E. Main Street Richmond, VA 23219	804-371-9694 (fax) 804-371-9873
Virgin Islands	Attn.: Marileen Thomas #18 Kongens Gade, Charlotte Amalie, St. Thomas, VI 00802 Division of Banking & Insurance 1131 King Street, #101 Christiansted St. Croix, VI 00820	340-774-7166 (fax) 340-774-9458 or 340-774-6953 340-773-6449 (fax) 340-773-4052
Washington	Washington Office of the Insurance Commissioner 14th Avenue & Water Street P.O. Box 40255 Olympia, WA 98504-0255	360-753-7301 (fax) 360-586-3535
West Virginia	West Virginia Dept. of Insurance P.O. Box 50540 Charleston, WV 25305-0540 Federal Express Packages: State of West Virginia 1124 Smith Street Charleston, WV 25301	304-558-3354 (fax) 304-558-0412
Wisconsin	Office of the Commissioner of Insurance State of Wisconsin 121 E. Wilson Madison, WI 53702 Post Office Box Address: P.O. Box 7873 Madison, WI 53707-7873	608-267-1233 (fax) 608-261-8579
Wyoming	Wyoming Dept. of Insurance Herschler Building 122 W. 25th Street, 3rd East Cheyenne, WY 82002-0440	307-777-7401 (fax) 307-777-5895

APPENDIX G: Ratings of Medicare HMOs

Policies are ranked by Value Index

GUIDE TO THE RATINGS: These ratings evaluate two benefit packages sold by HMOs in each metropolitan area. A "B" following the plan name describes a basic plan, which offers a lower level of benefits. An "E" designates an enhanced plan, which offers a higher level of benefits, often including prescription drug coverage.

The **Annual Premium** describes how much the plan charges for coverage. Premiums and benefits may vary by county; the premium shown is the lowest available in each metropolitan area.

The **Value Index** compares the value of significant benefits for each plan to the value of Medicare benefits plus the premium. A value index greater than 100 indicates you are getting a lot of value for your money; an index less than 100 means you are getting less. Variations within five points are not significant.

The **Prescription Drug Quality Index** measures the value of the drug benefits and the drug limit. A plan with an Excellent rating has essentially unlimited benefits, covering more than 75 percent of average drug costs. A plan with a Good rating has a benefit that is at least as comprehensive as that available in Medicare Supplement Plan J. A Plan with an Average rating has a benefit that is at least as comprehensive as that available in Medicare-Supplement Plans H and I. Plans rated Poor either limit all drugs to less than $625 per year or provide unlimited generic drugs but limit brand-name prescriptions to less than $500 per year. All other plans are rated Fair.

How Elders View the Plan and **Levels of Preventive Care** show data provided by the Health Care Financing Administration (HCFA), the agency that administers Medicare. Satisfaction is the percentage of members surveyed who rated their plan a 10 on a scale of 0 to 10 (10 being the best possible managed-care plan). **Ease of Referrals** is the percentage of members surveyed who said it was not a problem to get a referral to a specialist. **Mammograms** indicate the percentage of women between the ages of fifty-two and sixty-nine who received a mammogram within the prior two years. **Beta-Blockers** refers to the percentage of plan members who were prescribed a beta-blocker following a hospital stay for a heart attack. **Diabetic Eye Exams** refers to the percentage of members with diabetes who received an eye exam, an important aspect of care for diabetics. These three levels of preventive care are widely accepted as common measures of quality, although they measure only one dimension of quality—underuse. Plans should be striving to come as close to 100 percent as possible.

If HCFA did not show any information for the plan, it is marked with a " — ". If a plan shows an "NR," Medicare determined that the percentage was not accurate. If the plan could not report a value because there were too few Medicare members included in the measurement, it is marked "NA."

A Social HMO offers not only the same types of benefits offered by standard Medicare HMOs, but also home- and community-based services such as homemaker services, personal care services, adult day care, respite care, and medical transportation. There are four Social HMOs in our ratings: Health Plan of Nevada, Elderplan in New York City, Kaiser Foundation Health Plan of the Northwest in Portland, Oregon, and SCAN Health Plan in Los Angeles.

A Provider Sponsored Organization (PSO) is a group of doctors, hospitals, and other health care providers who run a managed-care plan by themselves rather than operate through an insurance company. There are two PSOs in our ratings: Sun Health MediSun in Phoenix and SCHP in Atlanta.

State	Plan Name/Product	Annual Premium	Value Index	Rx Index	HOW ELDERS VIEW THE PLAN		LEVELS OF PREVENTIVE CARE		
					Satisfaction	Ease of Referrals	Mammograms	Beta-Blockers	Diabetic Eye Exams
Atlanta, Georgia									
GA	SCHP Medicare Secure Choice (B)	0	117	Fair	—	—	NR	NA	—
GA	Kaiser Foundation HP (1) Kaiser Permanente Senior Advantage (B)	0	113	Poor	52	90	80	NA	—
GA	CIGNA HealthCare CIGNA HealthCare for Seniors (B)	0	112	Fair	—	—	—	—	—
GA	UnitedHealthcare (2) EverCare (B)	0	111	None	—	—	NA	NA	—
GA	BCBS of Georgia Blue Choice Platinum (B)	0	110	Fair	45	85	NA	90	—
GA	Aetna U.S. HealthCare (3) Medicare 10 Enhanced (E)	432	104	Fair	31	78	82	NA	—
GA	Aetna U.S. HealthCare (3) Medicare 10 (B)	120	103	None	31	78	82	NA	—
GA	UnitedHealthcare Medicare Complete (B)	0	102	Poor	51	81	72	91	—
Boston, Massachusetts & New Hampshire									
MA	Harvard Pilgrim (1) (3) First Seniority (B)	0	117	Fair	59	90	85	92	61
MA	Fallon Community HP (1) (3) Fallon Senior Plan (B)	0	116	Fair	67	89	86	95	79
MA	Tufts Associated HMO (1) (3) Secure Horizons (B)	0	116	Poor	62	86	81	95	72
MA	BCBS Mass (3) Blue Care 65 (B)	300	111	Poor	51	86	85	97	54
MA	UnitedHealthcare (2) EverCare (B)	0	111	None	—	—	NA	NA	22

State	Plan Name/Product	Annual Premium	Value Index	Rx Index	HOW ELDERS VIEW THE PLAN		LEVELS OF PREVENTIVE CARE		
					Satisfaction	Ease of Referrals	Mammograms	Beta-Blockers	Diabetic Eye Exams
NH	Tufts Health Plan (1) (3) Secure Horizons (B)	300	104	None	—	—	NA	NA	76
NH	Harvard Pilgrim (1) (3) First Seniority (B)	660	101	Poor	49	87	89	NA	64
MA	UnitedHealthcare Medicare Complete (B)	0	97	None	66	88	83	NA	58

Chicago, Illinois

State	Plan Name/Product	Annual Premium	Value Index	Rx Index	Satisfaction	Ease of Referrals	Mammograms	Beta-Blockers	Diabetic Eye Exams
IL	Humana Health Plan Chicago Value (B)	0	117	Fair	51	80	64	74	50
IL	Humana Health Plan Chicago Premium (E)	468	112	Fair	51	80	64	74	50
IL	United Health Plans Medicare Complete—Prestige (B)	0	106	Poor	52	81	60	87	33
IL	Aetna U.S. HealthCare (3) Medicare 10 (B)	732	101	Fair	—	—	—	—	—
IL	Aetna U.S. HealthCare (3) Medicare 5 (E)	1,044	99	Average	—	—	—	—	—
IL	United Health Plans Medicare Complete—Premier (E)	480	98	None	52	81	60	87	33

Cincinnati, Ohio & Kentucky

State	Plan Name/Product	Annual Premium	Value Index	Rx Index	Satisfaction	Ease of Referrals	Mammograms	Beta-Blockers	Diabetic Eye Exams
OH	Community Insurance Co. Anthem Senior Advantage (B)	0	115	Fair	49	82	65	88	56
KY	Anthem BCBS Anthem Senior Advantage (B)	0	111	Fair	—	—	—	—	—
OH	UnitedHealthcare (2) Medicare Complete (B)	0	110	Poor	50	92	76	92	53
OH	PacifiCare Secure Horizons (B)	288	108	Fair	48	89	66	95	32
OH	Community HP of Ohio CHPO Seniors (B)	780	104	Fair	—	—	—	—	—
OH	Humana Health Plan Humana Gold Plus (B)	708	104	Fair	48	78	62	54	24

State	Plan Name/Product	Annual Premium	Value Index	Rx Index	Satisfaction	Ease of Referrals	Mammograms	Beta-Blockers	Diabetic Eye Exams
KY	PacifiCare Secure Horizons (B)	468	104	Fair	48	89	66	95	32
OH	UnitedHealthcare of Ohio (2) Medicare Complete EverCare (B)	0	104	None	50	92	76	92	53
OH	Aetna U.S. HealthCare (3) Medicare 10 (B)	120	103	None	—	—	NA	NA	59
KY	Aetna U.S. HealthCare (3) Medicare 10 (B)	120	103	None	—	—	NA	NA	59
KY	Humana Health Plan Humana Gold Plus (B)	708	103	Fair	48	78	62	54	24
OH	Aetna U.S. HealthCare (3) Premier (E)	1,020	102	Average	—	—	NA	NA	59
KY	Aetna U.S. Healthcare (3) Premier (E)	1,020	101	Average	—	—	NA	NA	59

Cleveland, Ohio

State	Plan Name/Product	Annual Premium	Value Index	Rx Index	Satisfaction	Ease of Referrals	Mammograms	Beta-Blockers	Diabetic Eye Exams
OH	Home Town Health Plan Home Town SecureCare (B)	0	117	Fair	—	—	NA	NA	1
OH	Community Insurance Co. Anthem Senior Advantage (B)	0	116	Fair	53	83	67	87	53
OH	Emerald HMO Emerald Horizons (B)	0	116	Fair	—	—	NA	NA	33
OH	Prudential HealthCare (4) Prudential HealthCare SeniorCare (B)	0	115	Fair	50	77	71	84	51
OH	Kaiser Foundation HP Kaiser Permanente Medicare Plus (B)	0	114	Poor	44	77	83	98	74
OH	SummaCare Health Plan SummaCare Secure (B)	0	113	Fair	63	87	78	87	55
OH	QualChoice Health Plan Preferred B (E)	0	112	Poor	49	86	72	74	NR
OH	Kaiser Foundation HP Kaiser Permanente Medicare Gold (E)	588	107	Fair	44	77	83	98	74
OH	QualChoice Health Plan Preferred A (B)	0	106	None	49	86	72	74	NR

State	Plan Name/Product	Annual Premium	Value Index	Rx Index	Satisfaction	Ease of Referrals	Mammograms	Beta-Blockers	Diabetic Eye Exams
OH	UnitedHealthcare Medicare Complete (B)	0	105	Poor	54	90	72	84	51
OH	Aetna U.S. HealthCare (3) Medicare 10 (B)	120	103	None	42	83	73	70	55
OH	Aetna U.S. HealthCare (3) Premier (E)	1,284	99	Average	42	83	73	70	55

Dallas, Texas

State	Plan Name/Product	Annual Premium	Value Index	Rx Index	Satisfaction	Ease of Referrals	Mammograms	Beta-Blockers	Diabetic Eye Exams
TX	Texas Health Choice L.D. Golden Choice (B)	0	119	Average	—	—	—	—	—
TX	Harris Methodist Texas HP (1) The Senior Health Plan (B)	0	117	Fair	57	86	74	91	62
TX	NYLCare HP Premier (E)	324	113	Average	53	81	67	NA	48
TX	NYLCare HP Medicare 10 (B)	0	112	Poor	53	81	67	NA	48
TX	PacifiCare Secure Horizons (B)	300	108	Fair	51	80	64	77	40

Denver, Colorado

State	Plan Name/Product	Annual Premium	Value Index	Rx Index	Satisfaction	Ease of Referrals	Mammograms	Beta-Blockers	Diabetic Eye Exams
CO	TRICARE Senior Prime (5) TRICARE Senior Prime (B)	0	127	Excellent	—	—	—	—	—
CO	Kaiser Foundation HP Senior Advantage Silver (B)	0	121	Average	42	88	83	93	79
CO	Antero Healthplans Medicare Preferred (B)	360	112	Average	45	80	27	NA	35
CO	Kaiser Foundation HP Senior Advantage Gold (E)	588	112	Excellent	42	88	83	93	79
CO	UnitedHealthcare EverCare (B)	0	111	None	—	—	NA	NA	19
CO	HMO Colorado Blue Advantage for Seniors (B)	348	110	Fair	34	76	74	89	37
CO	PacifiCare Secure Horizons (B)	1,068	97	Average	40	77	72	74	47

| | | | | | How Elders View the Plan | | Levels of Preventive Care | | |
| | | Annual Premium | Value Index | Rx Index | Satisfaction | Ease of Referrals | Mammograms | Beta-Blockers | Diabetic Eye Exams |
State	Plan Name/Product								
Detroit, Michigan									
MI	Selectcare HMO Selectcare Medicare Gold (B)	0	117	Fair	—	—	86	NA	50
MI	M-CARE Senior Plan (B)	0	116	Fair	54	85	90	NA	65
MI	Mercy Health Plans Care Choices Senior Premier (E)	480	111	Fair	—	—	78	NA	54
MI	Blue Care Network, Southeast Medicare Blue Southeast Basic (B)	0	108	None	—	—	77	NA	48
MI	Blue Care Network, Southeast Medicare Blue Southeast Premier (E)	540	108	Fair	—	—	77	NA	48
MI	M-CARE Senior Plan Prestige (E)	768	108	Average	54	85	90	NA	65
MI	Mercy Health Plans Care Choices Senior Principal (B)	0	108	None	—	—	78	NA	54
MI	Paramount Care Standard Plan (E)	420	108	Poor	66	90	72	85	43
MI	Blue Care Network, East Medicare Blue East Premier (E)	900	103	Fair	—	—	NA	NA	64
MI	Blue Care Network, East Medicare Blue East Basic (B)	420	102	None	—	—	NA	NA	64
MI	Paramount Care Basic Plan (B)	420	101	None	66	90	72	85	43
Houston, Texas									
TX	Texas Health Choice Golden Choice (B)	0	121	Average	52	75	47	NA	39
TX	MethodistCare MethodistCare 65 Plus (B)	0	120	Average	—	—	—	—	—
TX	NYLCare Health Plans Medicare 5 Enhanced (E)	0	120	Average	61	87	72	68	44
TX	Humana HP Humana Gold Plus (B)	0	119	Average	48	65	51	63	53

State	Plan Name/Product	Annual Premium	Value Index	Rx Index	HOW ELDERS VIEW THE PLAN		LEVELS OF PREVENTIVE CARE		
					Satisfaction	Ease of Referrals	Mammograms	Beta-Blockers	Diabetic Eye Exams
TX	CIGNA HealthCare CIGNA HealthCare for Seniors (B)	0	118	Fair	51	82	68	NA	50
TX	Memorial Sisters of Charity CHOICE 65 (B)	0	118	Average	53	76	NA	NA	38
TX	PacifiCare Secure Horizons (B)	0	114	Fair	41	66	52	89	36
TX	Prudential HealthCare (4) Prudential HealthCare SeniorCare (B)	0	113	Fair	52	88	76	93	51
TX	NYLCare Health Plans Medicare 10 (B)	0	107	None	61	87	72	68	44

Jacksonville, Florida

State	Plan Name/Product	Annual Premium	Value Index	Rx Index	Satisfaction	Ease of Referrals	Mammograms	Beta-Blockers	Diabetic Eye Exams
FL	BCBS FL/Health Options Medicare & More (B)	0	106	Poor	46	80	71	NA	47
FL	Humana Medical Plan Humana Gold Plus (B)	468	105	Fair	41	80	70	NA	24
FL	Prudential HealthCare (4) Prudential HealthCare SeniorCare (B)	600	102	Poor	54	87	77	NA	60
FL	AvMed Health Plan AvMed Health Plan (B)	1,176	90	Poor	54	85	72	NA	49

Kansas City, Kansas & Missouri

State	Plan Name/Product	Annual Premium	Value Index	Rx Index	Satisfaction	Ease of Referrals	Mammograms	Beta-Blockers	Diabetic Eye Exams
KS	Kaiser Foundation Health Plan Senior Advantage Silver (B)	0	115	Fair	42	86	73	NA	85
MO	Kaiser Foundation Senior Advantage Silver (B)	0	115	Fair	42	86	73	NA	85
MO	Principal Health Care Advantra-Basic (B)	0	114	Fair	—	—	—	—	—
KS	Principal Health Care Advantra-Basic (B)	0	114	Fair	—	—	—	—	—
KS	Humana Health Plan HMO Gold Plus Value (B)	120	113	Fair	46	81	76	89	65
MO	Humana Health Plan HMO Gold Plus Value (B)	120	113	Fair	46	81	76	89	65

State	Plan Name/Product	Annual Premium	Value Index	Rx Index	HOW ELDERS VIEW THE PLAN		LEVELS OF PREVENTIVE CARE		
					Satisfaction	Ease of Referrals	Mammograms	Beta-Blockers	Diabetic Eye Exams
MO	HealthNet Standard Plan (B)	0	112	None	55	88	79	85	65
MO	HealthNet Premier Plan (E)	0	112	None	55	88	79	85	65
KS	HealthNet Standard Plan (B)	0	112	None	55	88	79	85	65
KS	HealthNet Premier Plan (E)	0	112	None	55	88	79	85	65
KS	Kaiser Foundation Health Plan Senior Advantage Gold (E)	468	110	Fair	42	86	73	NA	85
MO	Kaiser Foundation Senior Advantage Gold (E)	468	110	Fair	42	86	73	NA	85
KS	Humana Health Plan HMO Gold Plus Premium (E)	1,560	95	Fair	46	81	76	89	65
MO	Humana Health Plan HMO Gold Plus Premium (E)	1,560	94	Fair	46	81	76	89	65

Las Vegas, Nevada

State	Plan Name/Product	Annual Premium	Value Index	Rx Index	Satisfaction	Ease of Referrals	Mammograms	Beta-Blockers	Diabetic Eye Exams
NV	PacifiCare Basic Plan (B)	0	121	Average	38	76	63	86	46
NV	PacifiCare Plus Plan (E)	300	119	Good	38	76	63	86	46
NV	Health Plan of Nevada Basic Plan H2961 (B)	0	118	Average	41	71	62	95	30
NV	Health Plan of Nevada Basic Plan H2931 (B)	0	114	Average	42	72	60	86	27
NV	Health Plan of Nevada Optima Plan H2961 (E)	419	113	Good	41	71	62	95	30
NV	Health Plan of Nevada Optima Plan H2931 (E)	419	110	Good	42	72	60	86	27

Los Angeles, California

State	Plan Name/Product	Annual Premium	Value Index	Rx Index	Satisfaction	Ease of Referrals	Mammograms	Beta-Blockers	Diabetic Eye Exams
CA	UHP Healthcare UHP Healthcare for Seniors (B)	0	126	Average	43	69	80	26	79

State	Plan Name/Product	Annual Premium	Value Index	Rx Index	HOW ELDERS VIEW THE PLAN		LEVELS OF PREVENTIVE CARE		
					Satisfaction	Ease of Referrals	Mammograms	Beta-Blockers	Diabetic Eye Exams
CA	Blue Shield of Calif. Blue Shield 65 Plus (B)	0	124	Excellent	—	—	70	NA	46
CA	Inter Valley Health Plan (3) Service to Seniors (B)	0	124	Good	55	85	78	84	61
CA	SCAN Medicare + Choice Benefit Plan (B)	0	124	Excellent	44	70	65	NA	58
CA	Maxicare Max 65 Plus (B)	0	123	Average	45	73	58	NR	33
CA	Aetna U.S. HealthCare (3) Medicare 0 (B)	0	121	Average	45	78	76	NA	61
CA	Blue Cross of Calif. Senior Secure (B)	0	121	Excellent	40	69	74	NA	58
CA	Kaiser Foundation Health Plan Kaiser Permanente Senior Advantage (B)	0	121	Excellent	49	81	82	95	66
CA	PacifiCare Basic Plan (B)	0	120	Average	46	80	70	92	63
CA	CIGNA HealthCare CIGNA HealthCare for Seniors $0 Individual (B)	0	118	Fair	34	78	74	85	63
CA	PacifiCare Plus Plan (E)	144	118	Average	46	80	70	92	63
CA	Aetna U.S. HealthCare (3) Premier (E)	360	117	Average	45	78	76	NA	61
CA	HealthNet Health Net Seniority Plus (B)	0	116	Average	—	—	75	89	56
CA	CIGNA HealthCare CIGNA HealthCare for Seniors Premium Plan (E)	468	111	Fair	34	78	74	85	63
CA	Health Net Health Net Security Plus (B)	900	91	None	—	—	75	89	56

Louisville, Kentucky & Indiana

State	Plan Name/Product	Annual Premium	Value Index	Rx Index	Satisfaction	Ease of Referrals	Mammograms	Beta-Blockers	Diabetic Eye Exams
KY	Anthem BCBS Senior Advantage (B)	300	104	Fair	—	—	—	—	—

RATINGS OF MEDICARE HMOS

State	Plan Name/Product	Annual Premium	Value Index	Rx Index	Satisfaction	Ease of Referrals	Mammograms	Beta-Blockers	Diabetic Eye Exams
IN	Humana Health Plan Humana Gold Plus Value (B)	168	103	None	48	80	71	67	37
KY	Humana Health Plan Humana Gold Plus Value (B)	168	102	None	48	80	71	67	37
KY	Humana Health Plan Humana Gold Plus Premium (E)	1,332	95	Fair	48	80	71	67	37
IN	Humana Health Plan Humana Gold Plus Premium (E)	1,332	93	Fair	48	80	71	67	37

Manchester, New Hampshire

State	Plan Name/Product	Annual Premium	Value Index	Rx Index	Satisfaction	Ease of Referrals	Mammograms	Beta-Blockers	Diabetic Eye Exams
NH	Tufts Health Plan (1) (3) Secure Horizons (B)	300	104	None	—	—	NA	NA	76
NH	Harvard Pilgrim Health Care (1) (3) First Seniority (B)	660	101	Poor	49	87	89	NA	64

Miami, Florida

State	Plan Name/Product	Annual Premium	Value Index	Rx Index	Satisfaction	Ease of Referrals	Mammograms	Beta-Blockers	Diabetic Eye Exams
FL	Foundation Health Senior Value (B)	0	128	Excellent	51	80	73	87	33
FL	AvMed Health Plan AvMed Health Plan (B)	0	127	Excellent	56	83	74	87	59
FL	BCBS FL/Health Options Medicare & More (B)	0	127	Excellent	47	86	73	81	60
FL	Humana Medical Plan Humana Gold Plus Core (B)	0	127	Excellent	48	81	80	88	67
FL	Preferred Medical Plan Preferred Medicare Plus (B)	0	125	Average	—	—	—	—	—
FL	UnitedHealthcare of Florida Medicare Complete (B)	0	125	Excellent	55	64	70	47	56
FL	Beacon Health Plans Beacon Medicare Extra (B)	0	124	Excellent	—	—	—	—	—
FL	Neighborhood Health Partnership Senior Health Choice (B)	0	124	Average	61	79	77	NR	NR
FL	Physicians Healthcare Plans Physicians Care Plus Plan (B)	0	124	Excellent	—	—	—	—	—

State	Plan Name/Product	Annual Premium	Value Index	Rx Index	How Elders View the Plan		Levels of Preventive Care		
					Satisfaction	Ease of Referrals	Mammograms	Beta-Blockers	Diabetic Eye Exams
FL	HIP Health Plan HIP VIP Medicare (B)	0	122	Fair	40	79	77	82	73
FL	Prudential HealthCare (4) SeniorCare (B)	0	118	Fair	48	85	80	90	55
Milwaukee, Wisconsin									
WI	Network Health Plan of Wisc. (1) Community Senior Plan Standard (B)	0	108	None	—	—	—	—	—
WI	BCBS United of Wisc. Medicare Blue (B)	360	105	Fair	—	—	—	—	—
WI	Network Health Plan of Wisc. (1) Community Senior Plan Plus (E)	588	105	Fair	—	—	—	—	—
WI	PrimeCare Health Plan PrimeCare (B)	360	98	None	58	89	77	81	60
Minneapolis, Minnesota									
MN	UCare Minn. Value (B)	600	93	None	—	—	—	—	—
MN	Medica HP/Allina Health System SeniorCare Basic (B)	767	89	None	47	91	76	NR	56
MN	HealthPartners Partners for Seniors (B)	1,137	85	None	39	86	86	100	76
MN	HealthPartners Partners for Seniors (plus Rx) (E)	3,240	71	Excellent	39	86	86	100	76
MN	Medica HP/Allina Health System SeniorCare Complete (E)	3,359	71	Excellent	47	91	76	NR	56
MN	UCare Minn. Ultimate (E)	3,588	70	Excellent	—	—	—	—	—
New Orleans, Louisiana									
LA	SMA HMO SmartPlan 65 (B)	0	120	Fair	59	88	63	90	36
LA	Tenet Choices 65 (3)* Choice 1 (B)	0	119	Fair	—	—	NA	NA	55

State	Plan Name/Product	Annual Premium	Value Index	Rx Index	HOW ELDERS VIEW THE PLAN		LEVELS OF PREVENTIVE CARE		
					Satisfaction	Ease of Referrals	Mammograms	Beta-Blockers	Diabetic Eye Exams
LA	Gulf South Health Plans Option 65 (B)	0	118	Fair	62	81	65	60	46
LA	Ochsner Health Plan Total Health 65 (B)	0	118	Fair	67	85	75	79	51
LA	HMO Louisiana Blue Medicare Plan (B)	0	117	Fair	—	—	—	—	—
LA	Maxicare Health Plans Maxicare (B)	0	116	Fair	—	—	—	—	—
LA	Aetna U.S. HealthCare (3) Medicare Premier (E)	708	110	Average	45	83	NR	NA	58
LA	Aetna U.S. HealthCare (3) Medicare 10 (B)	348	106	Poor	45	83	NR	NA	58

*One of three options.

New York, New York

State	Plan Name/Product	Annual Premium	Value Index	Rx Index	Satisfaction	Ease of Referrals	Mammograms	Beta-Blockers	Diabetic Eye Exams
NY	Elderplan (3) Elderplan (B)	0	125	Excellent	55	80	43	82	49
NY	AmeriChoice AmeriChoice Personal Care Plan (B)	0	115	Fair	—	—	—	—	—
NY	HIP Health Plan (3) HIP VIP Medicare Plan Option A (B)	0	115	Fair	39	81	74	72	64
NY	Physicians Health Services SmartChoice (B)	0	115	Fair	47	80	74	87	58
NY	UnitedHealthcare Medicare Complete (B)	0	115	Fair	—	—	NA	NA	41
NY	Empire BCBS BlueChoice Senior Plan (B)	0	113	Poor	50	83	67	63	43
NY	HIP Health Plan (3) HIP VIP Medicare Plan Option B (E)	372	112	Fair	39	81	74	72	64
NY	UnitedHealthcare of New York (2) EverCare (B)	0	111	None	—	—	NA	NA	41
NY	Managed Health HealthFirst 65 Plus (B)	0	110	Poor	35	85	73	NA	71

State	Plan Name/Product	Annual Premium	Value Index	Rx Index	Satisfaction	Ease of Referrals	Mammograms	Beta-Blockers	Diabetic Eye Exams
NY	Oxford Health Plans Oxford Medicare Advantage (B)	0	110	Poor	46	87	67	91	57
NY	CIGNA HealthCare CIGNA HealthCare for Seniors (B)	0	109	Poor	41	71	45	NA	37
NY	Aetna U.S. HealthCare (3) Medicare Premier (B)	540	108	Fair	46	86	72	74	65
NY	MDNY HealthCare MDSelect65 (B)	0	107	Poor	47	90	63	NA	62
NY	Aetna U.S. HealthCare (3) Medicare 10 Base (B)	120	102	None	46	86	72	74	65
NY	MDNY HealthCare MDClassic65 (E)	540	102	Fair	47	90	63	NA	62
NY	Physicians Health Services SmartChoice Plan 2 (E)	1,068	99	Fair	47	80	74	87	58

Philadelphia, Pennsylvania & New Jersey

State	Plan Name/Product	Annual Premium	Value Index	Rx Index	Satisfaction	Ease of Referrals	Mammograms	Beta-Blockers	Diabetic Eye Exams
PA	Health Partners Senior Partners (B)	0	120	Average	63	79	NA	NA	38
PA	AmeriChoice AmeriChoice Personal Care Plus (B)	0	118	Fair	—	—	—	—	—
NJ	AmeriChoice AmeriChoice Personal Care Plus (B)	0	115	Fair	—	—	—	—	—
PA	QualMed Plans for Health Wise Choice (B)	0	115	Fair	52	80	68	80	27
PA	HealthCentral HealthCentral Senior (B)	0	112	Fair	—	—	—	—	—
PA	Aetna U.S. HealthCare (1) (3) Medicare 10 (B)	360	108	Fair	50	91	79	95	72
PA	Keystone Health Plan East (1) (3) Keystone 65 (High Option IV) (E)	600	108	Fair	60	88	73	97	56
PA	Keystone Health Plan East (1) (3) Keystone 65 (Group Basic) (B)	0	106	None	60	88	73	97	56
PA	Aetna U.S. HealthCare (1) (3) Premier (E)	960	103	Fair	50	91	79	95	72

State	Plan Name/Product	Annual Premium	Value Index	Rx Index	HOW ELDERS VIEW THE PLAN		LEVELS OF PREVENTIVE CARE		
					Satisfaction	Ease of Referrals	Mammograms	Beta-Blockers	Diabetic Eye Exams
NJ	AmeriHealth HMO AmeriHealth 65 (Group Basic) (B)	180	102	None	44	85	72	100	52
NJ	Horizon Healthcare (BCBS of NJ) Horizon Medicare Blue (E)	600	101	Poor	54	83	44	48	29
NJ	Oxford Health Plans Oxford Medicare Advantage (B)	0	101	None	41	84	65	94	50
NJ	AmeriHealth HMO AmeriHealth 65 (High Option III) (E)	1,080	100	Fair	44	85	72	100	52
NJ	Horizon Healthcare (BCBS of NJ) Horizon Medicare Blue (B)	300	98	None	54	83	44	48	29
PA	Independence Blue Cross Personal Choice 65 (High Option II) (E)	1,500	95	Fair	49	90	43	NA	36
PA	Independence Blue Cross Personal Choice 65 (Group Basic) (B)	840	95	None	49	90	43	NA	36
NJ	Aetna U.S. HealthCare (1) (3) Medicare 10 Enhanced (E)	1,320	94	Fair	53	91	75	99	69
NJ	QualMed Plans for Health Wise Choice Plan 2 (E)	1,428	94	Fair	52	80	68	80	27
NJ	QualMed Plans for Health Wise Choice (B)	708	94	None	52	80	68	80	27
NJ	Aetna U.S. HealthCare (1) (3) Medicare 10 (B)	1,020	92	None	53	91	75	99	69

Phoenix, Arizona

State	Plan Name/Product	Annual Premium	Value Index	Rx Index	Satisfaction	Ease of Referrals	Mammograms	Beta-Blockers	Diabetic Eye Exams
AZ	Maricopa County Health Plan Maricopa Senior Select Plan (B)	0	123	Good	48	72	59	13	50
AZ	Sun Health MediSun Basic (B)	0	120	Average	—	—	—	—	—
AZ	Aetna U.S. HealthCare (3) Medicare 5 (B)	0	119	Average	—	—	NA	NA	56
AZ	Humana Health Plan Humana Gold Plus Value (B)	0	119	Average	45	75	61	61	26
AZ	PacifiCare of Arizona (3) Secure Horizons (Basic 1) (B)	0	119	Average	41	75	75	93	50

State	Plan Name/Product	Annual Premium	Value Index	Rx Index	HOW ELDERS VIEW THE PLAN		LEVELS OF PREVENTIVE CARE		
					Satisfaction	Ease of Referrals	Mammograms	Beta-Blockers	Diabetic Eye Exams
AZ	Intergroup of Arizona Standard (B)	0	117	Average	35	71	76	80	45
AZ	CIGNA HealthCare CIGNA HealthCare for Seniors $0 Individual (B)	0	116	Fair	38	82	80	90	70
AZ	Sun Health MediSun Plus (E)	360	115	Good	—	—	—	—	—
AZ	Aetna U.S. HealthCare (3) Premier (E)	360	114	Average	—	—	NA	NA	56
AZ	Intergroup of Arizona High (E)	480	111	Average	35	71	76	80	45
AZ	UnitedHealthcare (2) EverCare (B)	0	111	None	—	—	NA	NA	NA
AZ	PacifiCare of Arizona (3) Preferred Plan (E)	720	110	Good	41	75	75	93	50
AZ	UnitedHealthcare Medicare Complete (B)	0	106	Fair	47	87	80	88	38

Pittsburgh, Pennsylvania

State	Plan Name/Product	Annual Premium	Value Index	Rx Index	Satisfaction	Ease of Referrals	Mammograms	Beta-Blockers	Diabetic Eye Exams
PA	QualMed Plans for Health of PA Wise Choice (B)	0	114	Fair	—	—	—	—	—
PA	HealthAmerica Advantra Advantra (B)	156	113	Fair	46	89	86	73	66
PA	Aetna U.S. HealthCare (3) Premier (E)	720	109	Average	50	85	70	96	62
PA	Highmark BCBS (3) SecurityBlue Deluxe (E)	564	109	Fair	52	86	72	88	57
PA	Aetna U.S. HealthCare (3) Medicare 10 (B)	360	107	Fair	50	85	70	96	62
PA	Highmark BCBS (3) SecurityBlue Basic (B)	0	107	None	52	86	72	88	57

Portland, Oregon

State	Plan Name/Product	Annual Premium	Value Index	Rx Index	Satisfaction	Ease of Referrals	Mammograms	Beta-Blockers	Diabetic Eye Exams
OR	Regence BCBS Oregon First Choice 65 (B)	474	99	None	46	82	64	89	48

RATINGS OF MEDICARE HMOS

State	Plan Name/Product	Annual Premium	Value Index	Rx Index	HOW ELDERS VIEW THE PLAN Satisfaction	Ease of Referrals	LEVELS OF PREVENTIVE CARE Mammograms	Beta-Blockers	Diabetic Eye Exams
WA	Regence Health Maintenance First Choice Sixty Five (B)	474	99	None	38	70	NA	NA	NA
OR	PacifiCare of Oregon Secure Horizons (B)	504	97	None	52	87	—	—	—
WA	Kaiser Foundation Health Plan Senior Advantage (B)	972	96	Average	45	85	82	96	65
OR	Kaiser Foundation Health Plan Senior Advantage I (B)	972	96	Average	45	85	82	96	65
WA	Pacificare of Washington Secure Horizons (B)	696	94	None	48	86	73	93	57
OR	Regence BCBS Oregon First Choice 65 Premier (E)	1,476	88	Poor	46	82	64	89	48
OR	Kaiser Foundation Health Plan Senior Advantage II (E)	2,112	86	Excellent	52	86	84	NA	72
WA	Kaiser Foundation Health Plan Senior Advantage II (B)	2,112	85	Excellent	52	86	84	NA	72

Raleigh, North Carolina

State	Plan Name/Product	Annual Premium	Value Index	Rx Index	Satisfaction	Ease of Referrals	Mammograms	Beta-Blockers	Diabetic Eye Exams
NC	WellPath Select WellPath 65 Medicare Select (B)	0	104	None	—	—	NA	NA	31
NC	UnitedHealthcare Medicare Complete (B)	0	102	None	—	—	—	—	—
NC	WellPath Select WellPath 65 Medicare Select Plus (E)	540	100	Fair	—	—	NA	NA	31
NC	Partners National Health Plans Partners Medicare Choice (B)	600	96	None	59	90	69	41	32

San Francisco, California

State	Plan Name/Product	Annual Premium	Value Index	Rx Index	Satisfaction	Ease of Referrals	Mammograms	Beta-Blockers	Diabetic Eye Exams
CA	Chinese Community HP CCHP Senior Program (B)	0	119	Average	35	65	64	NA	42
CA	PacifiCare Secure Horizons Standard (B)	0	119	Average	—	—	—	—	—
CA	Kaiser Foundation Health Plan Kaiser Permanente Senior Advantage (B)	0	118	Average	48	82	81	93	72

State	Plan Name/Product	Annual Premium	Value Index	Rx Index	HOW ELDERS VIEW THE PLAN		LEVELS OF PREVENTIVE CARE		
					Satisfaction	Ease of Referrals	Mammograms	Beta-Blockers	Diabetic Eye Exams
CA	Blue Cross of Calif. Senior Secure (B)	0	116	Average	41	73	67	NA	65
CA	PacifiCare Secure Horizons Basic (B)	240	115	Average	—	—	67	88	59
CA	Health Net Health Net Seniority Plus (B)	0	114	Fair	41	84	77	92	58
CA	Western Health Advantage Care+ (B)	180	114	Fair	—	—	—	—	—
CA	Health Plan of the Redwoods (1) MediPrime (B)	288	112	Fair	50	81	79	NA	57
CA	National Health Plans SecurityCare (B)	240	112	Fair	51	85	79	NA	46
CA	PacifiCare Secure Horizons Plus Plan (E)	384	112	Average	—	—	67	88	59
CA	Aetna U.S. HealthCare (3) Medicare 10 (B)	120	110	Poor	40	79	80	NA	56
CA	Aetna U.S. HealthCare (3) Medicare Premier (E)	780	107	Fair	40	79	80	NA	56
CA	Blue Shield of Calif. Blue Shield 65 Plus (B)	960	104	Average	—	—	66	NA	56

Seattle, Washington

State	Plan Name/Product	Annual Premium	Value Index	Rx Index	Satisfaction	Ease of Referrals	Mammograms	Beta-Blockers	Diabetic Eye Exams
WA	TRICARE Senior Prime (5) TRICARE Senior Prime (B)	0	127	Excellent	—	—	—	—	—
WA	PacifiCare Secure Horizons (B)	0	109	None	52	80	74	91	49
WA	Aetna U.S. HealthCare (3) Medicare 10 (B)	0	107	None	—	—	—	—	—
WA	Aetna U.S. HealthCare (3) Premier (B)	240	105	None	—	—	—	—	—
WA	First Choice Health Plan SeniorsFirst (B)	348	103	None	—	—	—	—	—
WA	Premera HealthPlus Senior Partners (B)	348	103	None	48	82	77	97	72

State	Plan Name/Product	Annual Premium	Value Index	Rx Index	HOW ELDERS VIEW THE PLAN		LEVELS OF PREVENTIVE CARE		
					Satisfaction	Ease of Referrals	Mammograms	Beta-Blockers	Diabetic Eye Exams
WA	RegenceCare HealthSense (B)	336	103	None	—	—	—	—	—
WA	Group Health Cooperative Group Health Cooperative Standard Plan (B)	348	100	None	48	85	85	91	80
WA	Options Health Care Options Medicare Plan (B)	348	100	None	35	81	77	NA	72

St. Louis, Illinois & Missouri

State	Plan Name/Product	Annual Premium	Value Index	Rx Index	Satisfaction	Ease of Referrals	Mammograms	Beta-Blockers	Diabetic Eye Exams
MO	Group Health Plan Advantra (B)	0	114	Fair	55	84	80	45	44
MO	HMO Missouri Blue Horizons Medicare HMO (B)	0	113	Poor	43	86	66	NA	49
IL	Group Health Plan Advantra (B)	420	108	Fair	55	84	80	45	44
MO	UnitedHealthcare Medicare Complete (B)	0	107	Poor	53	82	74	85	43
IL	UnitedHealthcare Medicare Complete (B)	0	107	Poor	53	82	74	85	43
IL	Mercy Health Plans Basic PremierPlus (B)	468	106	Poor	—	—	—	—	—
MO	Mercy Health Plans Basic Premier Plus (B)	468	105	Poor	—	—	—	—	—
IL	Mercy Health Plans High Option PremierPlus (E)	828	101	Fair	—	—	—	—	—
MO	Mercy Health Plans Premier Plus (E)	828	100	Fair	—	—	—	—	—

Tampa, Florida

State	Plan Name/Product	Annual Premium	Value Index	Rx Index	Satisfaction	Ease of Referrals	Mammograms	Beta-Blockers	Diabetic Eye Exams
FL	CIGNA HealthCare CIGNA HealthCare for Seniors $0 Individual (B)	0	113	Fair	52	88	80	NA	73
FL	Humana Medical Plan Humana Gold Plus Core Premium (E)	228	113	Fair	48	82	81	79	59
FL	UnitedHealthcare (2) EverCare (B)	0	111	None	—	—	NA	NA	37

State	Plan Name/Product	Annual Premium	Value Index	Rx Index	HOW ELDERS VIEW THE PLAN		LEVELS OF PREVENTIVE CARE		
					Satisfaction	Ease of Referrals	Mammograms	Beta-Blockers	Diabetic Eye Exams
FL	BCBS FL/Health Options Medicare & More (B)	420	109	Fair	50	86	61	79	47
FL	Humana Medical Plan Humana Gold Plus Core Value (B)	0	108	Poor	48	82	81	79	59
FL	UnitedHealthcare Medicare Complete (B)	0	108	Poor	—	—	76	90	46
FL	Aetna U.S. HealthCare (3) Medicare 10 Base (B)	300	101	None	—	—	NA	NA	56
FL	Prudential HealthCare (4) Prudential HealthCare SeniorCare (B)	780	101	Fair	49	89	79	88	32
FL	AvMed Health Plan AvMed Medicare (B)	756	98	Fair	58	87	71	91	54
FL	Aetna U.S. HealthCare (3) Medicare 10 (B)	996	97	Fair	—	—	NA	NA	56

Washington D.C., Maryland & Virginia

State	Plan Name/Product	Annual Premium	Value Index	Rx Index	Satisfaction	Ease of Referrals	Mammograms	Beta-Blockers	Diabetic Eye Exams
DC	CIGNA HealthCare CIGNA HealthCare for Seniors $0 Individual (B)	0	113	Poor	—	—	—	—	—
DC	Kaiser Foundation HP Kaiser Permanente Senior Advantage (B)	228	113	Fair	—	—	75	83	59
MD	CIGNA HealthCare CIGNA HealthCare for Seniors $0 Individual (B)	0	112	Poor	—	—	—	—	—
VA	CIGNA CIGNA HealthCare for Seniors $0 Individual (B)	0	112	Poor	—	—	—	—	—
MD	Kaiser Foundation HP Kaiser Permanente Senior Advantage (B)	228	112	Fair	—	—	75	83	59
MD	UnitedHealthcare (2) EverCare (B)	0	111	None	—	—	NA	NA	25
DC	FreeState Health Plan Medi-Care First (B)	600	109	Fair	—	—	73	100	37
MD	FreeState Health Plan Medi-Care First (B)	600	108	Fair	45	85	73	100	37
MD	UnitedHealthcare Medicare Complete (B)	0	107	Poor	51	83	44	89	38

State	Plan Name/Product	Annual Premium	Value Index	Rx Index	HOW ELDERS VIEW THE PLAN		LEVELS OF PREVENTIVE CARE		
					Satisfaction	Ease of Referrals	Mammograms	Beta-Blockers	Diabetic Eye Exams
VA	Kaiser Foundation HP	588	105	Fair	—	—	75	83	59
	Kaiser Permanente Senior Advantage (B)								

[1]Designated as having an "Excellent" Current Accreditation Status by the National Committee for Quality Assurance.

[2]EverCare plans are available only to residents of participating nursing homes.

[3]Designated as having above-average quality-improvement initiatives by CONSUMER REPORTS in October 1998.

[4]Prudential Health Plans were acquired by Aetna U.S. Healthcare.

[5]Tri-Care plans are available only to military retirees.

APPENDIX H: Disease-Specific Organizations

These organizations can help you learn more about the disease your elderly relative has.

Alzheimer's Disease
Alzheimer's Disease Education and Referral Center
P.O. Box 8250
Silver Spring, MD 20907-8250
800-438-4380

Alzheimer's Disease and Related Disorders Association
919 N. Michigan Avenue, #1000
Chicago, IL 60611-1676
800-272-3900 or
312-335-8700

National Institute of Neurological Disorders and Stroke
P.O. Box 5801
Bethesda, MD 20824
800-352-9424 or
301-496-5751

Amyotrophic Lateral Sclerosis
The Amyotrophic Lateral Sclerosis Association
21021 Ventura Boulevard, #321
Woodland Hills, CA 91364-2206
800-782-4747 or
818-340-7500

Les Turner Amyotrophic Lateral Sclerosis Foundation
8142 Lawndale Avenue
Skokie, IL 60076
847-679-3311

National Institute of Neurological Disorders and Stroke
P.O. 5801
Bethesda, MD 20824
800-352-9424 or
301-496-5751

Cancer
American Cancer Society
1599 Clifton Road, NE
Atlanta, GA 30329
800-227-2345 or
404-320-3333

Cancer Information Center
800-422-6327 (800-4-CANCER)
In Oahu, Hawaii: 524-1234; call collect from other Hawaiian
  islands

Brain Cancer
American Brain Tumor Association
2720 River Road
Des Plaines, IL 60018
800-886-2282 (patient line) or
847-827-9910

The Brain Tumor Society
84 Seattle Street
Boston, MA 02134-1245
800-770-8287 or
617-783-0340

National Brain Tumor Foundation
785 Market Street, #1600
San Francisco, CA 94103
800-934-2873 or
415-284-0208

Leukemia, Lymphomas, and Multiple Myeloma
International Myeloma Foundation
2120 Stanley Hills Drive
Los Angeles, CA 90046
800-452-2873 (800-452-CURE) or
213-654-3023

Leukemia Society of America
600 3rd Avenue
New York, NY 10016
800-955-4572 (800-955-4LSA) or
212-573-8484

Lung Cancer
American Lung Association
1740 Broadway
New York, NY 10019-4374
800-586-4872 or
212-315-8700

Skin Cancer
American Academy of Dermatology
930 N. Meacham Road
Schaumburg, IL 60173-4965
847-330-0230

Skin Cancer Foundation
245 5th Avenue, #1403
New York, NY 10016
212-725-5176

Cardiovascular Disease
American Heart Association
7272 Greenville Avenue
Dallas, TX 75231-4596
800-242-8721 or
214-373-6300

National Heart, Lung and Blood Institute Information Center
P.O. Box 30105
Bethesda, MD 20824-0105
302-251-1222

American Association of Cardiovascular and Pulmonary
    Rehabilitation
7611 Elmwood Avenue, #201
Middleton, WI 53562
608-831-6989

Cerebrovascular Stroke
National Stroke Association
96 Inverness Drive, #I
Englewood, CO 80112
800-787-6537 or
303-649-9299

Stroke Connection of the American Heart Association
7272 Greenville Avenue
Dallas, TX 75231-4596
800-553-6321 or
214-706-1777

Chronic Obstructive Pulmonary Disease (Emphysema)
American Lung Association
1740 Broadway
New York, NY 10019-4374
800-586-4872 or
212-315-8700

National Heart, Lung and Blood Institute Information Center
P.O. Box 30105
Bethesda, MD 20824-0105
302-251-1222

American Association of Cardiovascular and Pulmonary
    Rehabilitation
7611 Elmwood Avenue, #201
Middleton, WI 53562
608-831-6989

Diabetes
American Diabetes Association
1660 Duke Street
Alexandria, VA 22314
800-342-2383 (800-DIABETES)

National Diabetes Information Clearinghouse
1 Information Way
Bethesda, MD 20892-3560
301-654-3327

Head Injury
Brain Injury Association
1776 Massachusetts Avenue, NW, #100
Washington, DC 20036
800-444-6443 or
202-296-6443

Kidney Disease
American Association of Kidney Patients
100 S. Ashley Drive, #280
Tampa, FL 33602
800-749-2257

American Kidney Fund
6110 Executive Boulevard, #1010
Rockville, MD 20852
800-638-8299 or
301-881-3051

National Kidney and Urologic Disease Information Clearinghouse
3 Information Way
Bethesda, MD 20892-3580
301-654-4415

The National Kidney Foundation
30 E. 33rd Street, 11th Floor
New York, NY 10016
800-622-9010 or
212-889-2210

Liver Disease

American Liver Foundation
1425 Pompton Avenue
Cedar Grove, NJ 07009
800-223-0179 or
201-256-2550

National Digestive Diseases Information Clearinghouse
2 Information Way
Bethesda, MD 20892-3570
301-654-3810

Parkinson's Disease

The American Parkinson's Disease Association
1250 Hylan Boulvard, #4B
Staten Island, NY 10305
800-223-2732 or
718-981-8001

National Parkinson Foundation
1501 NW 9th Avenue
Bob Hope Road
Miami, FL 33136-1494
800-327-4545 or
305-547-6666

Parkinson's Disease Foundation
William Black Medical Research Building
Columbia-Presbyterian Medical Center
710 W. 168th Street
New York, NY 10032
800-457-6676 or
212-923-4700

United Parkinson Foundation
833 W. Washington Boulevard
Chicago, IL 60607
312-733-1893

Rare Disorders

National Organization for Rare Disorders
P.O. Box 8923
New Fairfield, CT 06812-8923
800-999-6673 or
203-746-6518

APPENDIX I: Medicaid Waivered Services in the States

Be sure to check with your state. Availability of services could have changed.

State	Alabama	Alaska	Arizona	Arkansas
	Commission on Aging 800-243-5463	CHOICES Medicaid Waiver Program 907-269-3666	Arizona Access 602-417-4000	Carelink 501-812-0550
Adult day health	Yes	Yes	Yes	Yes; 184 hours per month
Adult foster care	No	Yes	Yes	Yes
Case management	Yes	Yes	Yes	No
Emergency response system	No	Yes	Yes	Yes
Home adaptation	No	Yes	Yes	No
Home aide (client-directed)	No	No	No	No
Homemaker/chores	Yes	Yes	Yes	Yes; 43 hours per month
Medical equipment	No	Yes	Yes	No
Mental health counseling	No	No	Yes	No
Personal care	Yes	No	Yes	No
Personal care attendant	No	No	Yes	No
Respite	Yes	Yes	Yes	Yes; 25 days a year
Transportation	No	Yes	Yes	No

State	California	Colorado	Connecticut	Delaware
	Department of Aging 916-322-4383	Health Care Policy & Financing 800-221-3943	State of Connecticut Department of Social Services 860-424-5277	Division of Aging 302-453-3825
Adult day health	No	Yes to day care, no to health care	Yes	Yes
Adult foster care	No	No	Yes	No
Case management	Yes	No	Yes	Yes
Emergency response system	No	Yes	Yes	Yes
Home adaptation	No	Yes	No	No
Home aide (client-directed)	No	No	No	No
Homemaker/chores	No	Yes	Yes	Yes
Medical equipment	No	No	No	Yes
Mental health counseling	No	No	Yes	No
Personal care	No	Yes	Yes	Yes
Personal care attendant	No	No	No	Yes
Respite	No	Yes	Yes	Yes
Transportation	No	Yes	Yes	No

State	District of Columbia	Florida	Georgia	Hawaii
	Medicaid Assistance Administration 202-727-9304	Office of LTC Policy 850-414-2000	Division of Aging Services 404-657-5252	Department of Human Services 808-586-0185
Adult day health	No	Yes	Yes	Yes, a waiting list exists
Adult foster care	No	No	No	Yes
Case management	Yes	Yes	Yes	Yes, a waiting list exists
Emergency response system	Yes	Yes	Yes	Yes, a waiting list exists
Home adaptation	Yes	Yes	No	Yes, a waiting list exists
Home aide (client-directed)	No	No	No	No
Homemaker/chores	Yes	Yes	Yes	Yes, a waiting list exists
Medical equipment	No	Yes	No	Yes, a waiting list exists
Mental health counseling	No	Yes	No	No
Personal care	Yes	Yes	Yes	Yes, a waiting list exists
Personal care attendant	No	Yes	Yes	No
Respite	Yes	Yes	Yes	Yes, a waiting list exists
Transportation	No	No	No	Yes, a waiting list exists

State	Idaho	Illinois	Indiana	Iowa
	Department of Health & Welfare 208-334-5795	Department of Aging 800-252-8966 217-524-6837	Area Agencies 800-986-3505	Department of Elder Affairs 515-281-5187
Adult day health	Yes	No	No	No
Adult foster care	Yes	No	No	No
Case management	Yes	Yes	Yes	Yes
Emergency response system	Yes	No	Yes	Yes
Home adaptation	Yes	No	Yes	Yes
Home aide (client-directed)	Yes	No	No	Yes
Homemaker/chores	Yes	Yes	Yes	Yes
Medical equipment	Yes	No	No	Yes
Mental health counseling	No	No	No	Yes
Personal care	Yes	Yes	Yes	Yes
Personal care attendant	Yes	No	Yes	Yes
Respite	Yes	Yes	Yes	Yes
Transportation	Yes	Yes	No	Yes

State	Kansas	Kentucky	Louisiana	Maine
	Department of Aging 785-368-7215	Office of Aging 502-564-6930	Department of Health & Hospitals 225-219-4149	Bureau of Adult Elder Services 800-262-2232
Adult day health	Yes	Yes	Yes	Yes
Adult foster care	No	No	No	No
Case management	Yes	Yes	Yes	Yes
Emergency response system	Yes	No	Yes	Yes
Home adaptation	No	Yes	Yes	Yes
Home aide (client-directed)	Yes	Yes	No	Yes
Homemaker/chores	Yes	Yes homemaking, but no chores	Yes	Yes
Medical equipment	No	No	No	Yes
Mental health	No	No	No	No
Personal care	Yes	Yes	Yes	Yes
Personal care attendant	Yes	Yes	Yes	Yes
Respite	Yes	No	No	Yes
Transportation	No	No	No	Yes

State	Maryland	Massachusetts	Michigan	Minnesota
	Department of Health & Mental Hygiene, Medical Care Policy Administration 410-767-5220	Mass Health Customer Service 800-841-2900; out-of-state 617-422-5870	Department of Community Health 517-241-2112	Board of Aging 651-296-2770; for Senior Linkage 800-333-2433
Adult day health	As medical day care under state plan	Yes	No	No
Adult foster care	No	Yes	No	Yes
Case management	As administrative service	Yes	Yes	Yes
Emergency response system	No	No	Yes	Yes
Home adaptation	Yes	Yes	Yes	Yes
Home aide (client-directed)	No	No	No	No
Homemaker/chores	As part of assisted-living service	Yes	Yes	Yes
Medical equipment	Under state plan	Yes	Yes	Yes
Mental health counseling	No	No	Yes	No
Personal care	No	Yes	Yes	Yes
Personal care attendant	No	Yes	No	Yes
Respite	No	Yes	Yes	Yes
Transportation	No	Yes	Yes	Yes

MEDICAID WAIVERED SERVICES IN THE STATES

State	Mississippi	Missouri	Montana	Nebraska
	Division of Medicaid 601-359-6050	Division of Medical Services 573-751-7988	Home and Community-Based Services 406-444-4150	Division of Aging 402-471-2307
Adult day health	No	No	Yes	Yes
Adult foster care	No	No	Yes	No
Case management	Yes	No	Yes, a waiting list exists	Yes
Emergency response system	No	No	Yes	Yes
Home adaptation	No	No	Yes	Yes
Home aide (client-directed)	No	No	No	No
Homemaker/chores	Yes	Yes	Yes	Yes
Medical equipment	No	No	Yes	No
Mental health counseling	No	No	No	No
Personal care	No	No	Yes	No
Personal care attendant	No	No	Yes	No
Respite	Yes	Yes	No	Yes
Transportation	Yes	No	Yes	Yes

State	Nevada	New Hampshire	New Jersey	New Mexico
	Division of Aging 702-486-3545	Division of Elder Adult Services 800-852-3345	Department of Health & Senior Services Easy Access Single Entry 877-222-3737	Department of Health Long Term Care Division 505-827-2574
Adult day health	No	Yes	Yes	Yes
Adult foster care	No	No	No	No
Case management	Yes, a waiting list exists	Yes	Yes	Yes
Emergency response system	Yes	Yes	No	Yes
Home adaptation	No	No	No	Yes
Home aide (client-directed)	No	No	Yes	No
Homemaker/chores	Yes	Yes	Yes	Yes
Medical equipment	Yes	No	No	No
Mental health counseling	No	No	No	No
Personal care	Yes	Yes	No	Yes
Personal care attendant	Yes	No	No	Yes
Respite	Yes	Yes	Yes	Yes
Transportation	No	No	Yes, for medical, nonemergency purposes	No

State	New York	North Carolina	North Dakota	Ohio
	The Long-Term Health Care Program for the Aged & Disabled 518-474-7354	Division of Medical Assistance 919-857-4021	Department of Human Services, Aging Services Division 800-451-8693	Department of Aging 614-466-1220
Adult day health	No	Yes	No	Yes
Adult foster care	No	No	Yes	No
Case management	Yes	Yes	Yes	Yes
Emergency response system	Yes	Yes	Yes	Yes
Home adaptation	Yes	Yes	Yes	No
Home aide (client-directed)	No	No	Yes	Yes
Homemaker/chores	Yes	No	Yes	Yes
Medical equipment	Yes, for respiratory therapy	No	Yes	Yes
Mental health counseling	No	No	No	Yes
Personal care	Yes	Yes	Yes	Yes
Personal care attendant	Yes	No	Yes	Yes
Respite	Yes	Yes	Yes	Yes
Transportation	No	No	Yes, for nonmedical purposes	Yes

State	Oklahoma	Oregon	Pennsylvania	Rhode Island
	Department of Human Services 405-521-2327	Senior & Disabled 503-945-5811	Department of Aging 717-783-6207	Home & Community Care 401-222-2858
Adult day health	Yes	No	No	Yes
Adult foster care	No	Yes	No	No
Case management	Yes	No	No	Yes
Emergency response system	No	No	Yes	Yes
Home adaptation	Yes	No	Yes	Yes
Home aide (client-directed)	No	No	No	No
Homemaker/chores	Yes	No	Yes	Yes
Medical equipment	Yes	No	Yes	Yes
Mental health counseling	No	No	Yes	No
Personal care	Yes	No	Yes	Yes
Personal care attendant	No	No	Yes	Yes
Respite	Yes	No	Yes	No
Transportation	No	No	Yes	No

State	South Carolina	South Dakota	Tennessee	Texas
	Department of Health & Human Services, Long-Term Care Division 803-253-6142	Office of Adult Services & Aging 605-773-3656	Department of Finance & Administration, Long-Term Care Division 615-741-0218 *Only some counties offer some waivered services*	Client Assistance 512-438-3280
Adult health care	Yes	No	No	No
Adult foster care	No	Yes	No	Yes, a waiting list exists
Case management	Yes	Yes	No	No
Emergency response system	Yes	Yes	No	Yes, a waiting list exists
Home adaptation	Yes	No	No	Yes, a waiting list exists
Home aide (client-directed)	Yes	No	No	No
Homemaker/chores	Yes	Yes	No	Yes, a waiting list exists
Medical equipment	No	Yes	No	Yes, a waiting list exists
Mental health counseling	No	No	No	No
Personal care	Yes	Yes	No	Yes
Personal care attendant	Yes	No	No	Yes
Respite	Yes	Yes	No	Yes, a waiting list exists
Transportation	No	Yes	No	No

State	Utah	Vermont	Virginia	Washington
	Division of Aging & Adult Services 810-538-3910	Senior Helpline 800-642-5119	Department of Aging 804-662-9325	Aging & Adult Services Admin. 360-493-2500 in-state: 800-422-3263
Adult day health	No	No	Yes	No
Adult foster care	No	No	No	Yes
Case management	Yes	Yes, a waiting list exists	Yes	Yes
Emergency response system	Yes	Yes	No	Yes
Home adaptation	No	Yes, but limited financially and to assisting devices and modifications	Yes	Yes
Home aide (client-directed)	No	Yes, as part of personal care	Yes	Yes
Homemaker/chores	yes	Yes, as part of personal care	Yes	Yes
Medical equipment	No	Yes, but limited to $500 annually for assisting devices and modification	Yes	Yes
Mental health counseling	No	No	Yes	Yes
Personal care	Yes	Yes	Yes	Yes, capped at 184 hours per month
Personal care attendant	No	Yes, can be client-directed	Yes	Yes
Respite	Yes	Yes	Yes	No
Transportation	Yes, for non-medical purposes	Yes, as part of personal care	No	Yes

State	West Virginia	Wisconsin	Wyoming
	Bureau of Senior Services 304-558-3317	Bureau of Aging & Long-Term Care Resources 608-267-7285	Division on Aging 800-442-2766
Adult day health	No	Yes	Yes
Adult foster care	No	Yes	No
Case management	Yes, a waiting list exists	Yes	Yes
Emergency response system	No	Yes	Yes
Home adaptation	No	Yes	No
Home aide (client-directed)	No	No	Yes
Homemaker/chores	Yes, a waiting list exists	Yes	No
Medical equipment	No	Yes	No
Mental health counseling	No	Yes	No
Personal care	No	Yes	Yes
Personal care attendant	No	Yes	Yes
Respite	No	Yes	Yes
Transportation	No	Yes	Yes

APPENDIX J: Medicaid Nonwaivered Services in the States

Be sure to check with your state. Availability of services could have changed.

State	Alabama	Alaska	Arizona	Arkansas
	Medicaid Agency 334-242-5009	Division of Senior Services 907-269-3666	No program	Division of Medical Services, Client Assistance 800-482-5431
Adult day care	No	No	No	No
Case management	Yes	No, except for complex cases	No	Yes
Homemaker/chores	No	No	No	No
Hospice care services	Yes	No	No	Yes
Personal care	Yes	In some cases; a waiting list exists	No	Yes
Respite	No	No	No	No
Transportation	Yes	Yes, with authorization	No	Yes

State	California	Colorado	Connecticut	Delaware
	Department of Health Benefits Branch 916-657-1460	Health Care Policy Financing Eligibility & Enrollment 800-221-3943	Department of Social Services 860-424-5177	Department of Social Services 302-577-4900
Adult day care	No	No	No	No
Case management	Yes	No	No	Yes
Homemaker/chores	Yes, with personal care. Capped at 283 hours per month	No	No	No
Hospice care services	Yes, with prior authorization	Yes	No	Yes
Personal care	Yes, with homemaker. Capped at 283 hours per month	No	Yes	No
Respite	Yes, with prior authorization	No	No	No
Transportation	Yes, with prior authorization	Yes, for medical purposes	Yes	Yes

State	District of Columbia	Florida	Georgia	Hawaii
	LTC Services 202-727-2240	Agency for Health Care Administration 888-419-3456	Medicaid Eligibility 404-656-3200 800-282-4536	Mediquest 808-692-8124
Adult day care	Yes	No	No	No
Case management	No	No	Yes, but limited	No
Homemaker/chores	No	No	No	No
Hospice care services	Yes	Yes	Yes	Yes
Personal care	Yes	No	No	No
Respite	No	No	No	No
Transportation	Yes	Yes	Yes	Yes

State	Idaho	Illinois	Indiana	Iowa
	Department of Health & Welfare 208-334-5795	Department on Aging 217-524-6911	Access Network 800-986-3505	Department of Human Services 515-281-5189
Adult day care	No	Yes	No	No
Case management	Yes	No	No	Yes
Homemaker/chores	No	Yes	No	Yes
Hospice care services	Yes	Yes	Yes	Yes
Personal care	Yes	No	No	Yes
Respite	No	Yes	No	No
Transportation	Yes	Yes	Yes, for medical purposes	Yes

State	Kansas	Kentucky	Louisiana	Maine
	Division of Health Care Policy 785-296-3981	Division of Long-Term Care 502-564-3084	Office of Medicaid Director 225-342-5568	Human Services 800-262-2232
Adult day care	No	Yes	No, 225-219-4282	Yes
Case management	Yes	No	No	Yes
Homemaker/chores	No	No	No	Yes, a waiting list exists
Hospice care services	Yes	Yes	No, 225-922-0015	No
Personal care	No	No	No	Yes
Respite	No	No	No	Yes
Transportation	Yes, for medical purposes	Yes	Yes, 225-342-9485	Yes

State	Maryland	Massachusetts	Michigan	Minnesota
	Department of Mental Health & Hygiene 410-767-5220	Massachusetts Health Customer Service In-state: 800-841-2900 Out-of-state: 617-422-5870	Department of Community Health 517-241-2112	Board of Aging 800-333-2433
Adult day care	Yes, under medical day care	Yes	No	No
Case management	Yes, as an administrative service	Yes	Yes	Yes
Homemaker/chores	As part of personal care	Yes	No	No
Hospice care services	Yes	Yes	Yes	Yes
Personal care	Yes	Yes	Yes	Yes
Respite	No	Yes	No	No
Transportation	Yes, for medical purposes	Yes	Yes, for medical purposes	Yes

State	Mississippi	Missouri	Montana	Nebraska
	Division of Medicaid 601-359-6050	Division of Medical Services 573-751-7988	Public Health & Human Services 406-444-5622	Division of Aging 402-471-2307
Adult day care	No	Yes	No	No
Case management	No	Yes	No	No
Homemaker/chores	No	No	No	No
Hospice care services	Yes	No	Yes	Yes
Personal care	No	Yes	Yes	Yes
Respite	No	No	No	No
Transportation	Yes, nonemergency	No	Yes	Yes, for medical purposes

State	Nebraska	Nevada	New Hampshire	New Jersey
	Division of Aging 402-471-2307	Division of Health Care Policy & Financing 775-687-4775	Division of Family Assistance 800-852-3345	Department of Health & Senior Services, Easy Access 877-222-3737
Adult day care	No	No	Yes	No
Case management	No	No	Yes, for some populations	No
Homemaker/chores	No	No	No	No
Hospice care services	Yes	Yes	Yes	Yes
Personal care	Yes	Yes	Plans approved for wheelchair-bound	Yes
Respite	No	No	Yes	Yes
Transportation	Yes, for medical purposes	Yes	Yes, for medical appointments	No

State	New Mexico	New York	North Carolina	North Dakota
	Human Services Medical Assistance 505-827-3100	Division of Health Care Policy & Financing 775-687-4775 *No services under this program*	Division of Medical Assistance 919-857-4021	Medical Services Division, North Dakota Department of Human Services 701-328-2321
Adult day care	No	No	No	No
Case management	Yes	No	No	No
Homemaker/chores	Part of home health, with medical approval based on medical necessity	No	Yes	No
Hospice care services	Yes	No	Yes	Yes
Personal care	No	No	Yes	No
Respite	Yes	No	No	No
Transportation	Yes	No	No	Yes

State	Ohio	Oklahoma	Oregon	Pennsylvania
	Medicaid Consumer Hotline in-state: 800-324-8680 out-of-state: 614-466-6742 TDD: 800-292-3572	Department of Human Services 405-530-3439	No Medicaid program	Medical Assistance 717-772-6323
Adult day care	No	No	No	No
Case management	Yes	Yes	No	No
Homemaker/chores	Yes	No	No	No
Hospice care services	Yes	No	No	No
Personal care	Yes	Yes	No	No
Respite	Yes	No	No	No, except as a component of hospice
Transportation	Yes	Yes, for medical purposes	No	Yes, for medical purposes

State	Rhode Island	South Carolina	South Dakota	Tennessee
	Department of Elderly Affairs 401-222-2858	Department of Health & Human Services 803-253-6119	Medical Services 605-773-3495	No services under this program
Adult day care	Yes	Yes	No	No
Case management	Yes	Yes	Yes	No
Homemaker/chores	Yes	No	No	No
Hospice care services	No	Yes	No	No
Personal care	No	Yes	No	No
Respite	No	Yes	No	No
Transportation	No	Yes	Yes, for medical purposes	No

State	Texas	Utah	Vermont	Virginia
	Department of Human Services 512-438-3195	Division of Health Care Financing 801-538-6636	Office of Vermont Health Access 802-241-3985 800-250-8427	Department for the Aging 800-552-3402
Adult day care	Yes	No	No	No
Case management	No	No	No	No
Homemaker/chores	Yes, limited hours	No	No	No
Hospice care services	Yes, 512-438-3174	Yes	Yes	Yes
Personal care	Yes, limited hours	Yes	No	No
Respite	No	No	No	No
Transportation	No	Yes, for medical purposes	Yes	Yes

State	Washington	West Virginia	Wisconsin	Wyoming
	Aging & Adult Services Admin. 360-493-2500 In-state: 800-422-3263	Bureau of Medical Services 304-926-1700	Department of Work Force Development, Medicaid Payment Eligibility 608-266-9700	Division on Aging 800-442-2766
Adult day care	Yes	Yes	No	No
Case management	Yes	Yes	No	Yes
Homemaker/chores	No	No	No	No
Hospice care services	Yes	Yes	Yes	Yes
Personal care	Yes	Yes	Yes	No
Respite	No	No	No	No
Transportation	Yes	Yes	Yes	Yes, for medical purposes

APPENDIX K: Older Americans Act Services in the States

Be sure to check with your state. Availability of services could have changed.

State Services	Alabama Commission on Aging 334-242-5764	Alaska Commission on Aging 907-465-4876	Arizona Aging Adult Administration 602-542-4446	Arkansas Division of Aging & Adult Services 501-582-8150
Personal care	Yes, possible waiting list	No	Yes, a waiting list exists	No
Homemaker	Yes, possible waiting list	Yes	Yes, a waiting list exists	Limited geographically, based on funding; a waiting list exists
Chores	Yes, possible waiting list	Yes	Yes, a waiting list exists	Limited, a waiting list exists
Home-delivered meals	Yes, a waiting list exists	Yes	Yes, a waiting list exists	Yes, a waiting list exists
Adult day care	Yes, possible waiting list	No	Yes, limited based on funding; possible waiting list	Limited
Case management	Yes	No	Yes	No
Congregate meals	Yes, a waiting list exists	Yes	Yes	Yes
Nutritional counseling	Yes	Yes	Limited in nutrition centers	Limited
Asst. transportation	Yes, possible waiting list	Yes	Limited geographically, based on funding	Yes

State	California	Colorado	Connecticut	Delaware
Services	Department of Aging 916-322-9184	Division of Aging 303-620-4147	Department of Social Services 860-424-5287 800-677-1116	Division of Services for Aging & Adults 302-577-4791
Personal care	Yes	Limited, a possible waiting list exists	Limited	Yes, a waiting list exists
Homemaker	Yes	Yes	Limited	Yes, a waiting list exists
Chores	Yes	Yes	Limited	No, but light housekeeping is available; a waiting list exists
Home-delivered meals	Yes	Yes, office	Yes, possible waiting list	Yes, a waiting list exists
Adult day care	Yes	Limited	Limited	Yes, a waiting list exists
Case management	Yes	No	Yes	Yes
Congregate meals	Yes	Yes	Yes	Yes
Nutritional counseling	Yes	Yes	Yes	Yes
Asst. transportation	Yes	Yes	Limited	Limited to areas with volunteer programs

State Services	District of Columbia Office of Aging 202-727-8368	Florida Department of Elderly Affairs 850-414-2000	Georgia Division of Aging Services 404-657-5317	Hawaii Executive Office on Aging 808-586-0100
Personal care	Yes	Limited geographically, possible waiting list	Yes, possible waiting list	Yes
Homemaker	Yes	Yes, possible waiting list	Yes, possible waiting list	Yes
Chores	Yes	Limited geographically, possible waiting list	No	No
Home-delivered meals	Yes, a waiting list exists	Yes, possible waiting list	Yes, a waiting list exists	Yes
Adult day care	Yes	Limited geographically, possible waiting list	Yes	Yes
Case management	Yes	Limited geographically, possible waiting list	Limited	Yes
Congregate meals	Yes	Yes, possible waiting list	Yes	Yes
Nutritional counseling	Yes	Limited geographically	Yes	Yes
Asst. transportation	Yes	Limited geographically	Yes	Yes

State	Idaho	Illinois	Indiana	Iowa
Services	Commission on Aging 208-334-3833	Department of Aging 217-785-3371	Bureau of Aging and In-Home Services Section 317-232-1734	Department of Elder Affairs 515-281-5187
Personal care	No	Limited	Yes, possible waiting list	Yes, a waiting list exists
Homemaker	No	Limited	Yes, possible waiting list	Yes, a waiting list exists
Chores	No	Yes	No, except as part of homemaking	Yes
Home-delivered meals	Yes	Yes	Yes	Yes
Adult day care	Limited	Yes	Limited	Yes, a waiting list exists
Case management	Yes	Yes	Yes	Yes, a waiting list exists
Congregate meals	Yes	Yes	Yes	Yes
Nutritional counseling	No	No, except that which is offered through congregate meals	Yes	Yes
Asst. transportation	Limited	Yes, although medical needs have priority	Yes	Yes

State	Kansas	Kentucky	Louisiana	Maine
Services	Department on Aging 785-296-4986	Office of Aging Services 502-564-6930	Office of Elderly Affairs 225-342-6545 225-342-6859	Bureau of Elder & Adult Services 207-624-5335
Personal care	Yes, a waiting list exists	Yes, possible waiting list exists	Limited	No
Homemaker	Yes, a waiting list exists	Yes, possible waiting list exists	Limited	No
Chores	Determined by area agencies	Yes, possible waiting list exists	Limited	Limited geographically
Home-delivered meals	Yes, possible waiting list	Yes, possible waiting list exists	Yes	Yes
Adult day care	Limited geographically	Yes, possible waiting list exists	No	Limited geographically
Case management	Yes	Yes, possible waiting list exists	Limited	No
Congregate meals	Yes	Yes, possible waiting list exists	Yes	Yes
Nutritional counseling	Yes	Yes, possible waiting list exists	Limited	No
Asst. transportation	Yes	Yes, possible waiting list exists	Limited	Yes

State	Maryland	Massachusetts	Michigan	Minnesota
Services	Department of Aging 410-767-1112	Office of Elder Affairs 617-727-7750	Office of Services to the Aging 517-373-8230	Board on Aging 800-882-6262
Personal care	Yes, a waiting list exists	Yes, part of home care	Yes, possible waiting list	Yes
Homemaker	Yes	Yes, part of home care	Yes, possible waiting list	Yes
Chores	Yes	Yes, part of home care	Yes	Yes
Home-delivered meals	Yes, a waiting list exists	Yes	Yes, possible waiting list	Yes
Adult day care	Yes	Yes	Yes	Yes
Case management	Yes	Yes	Yes	Yes
Congregate meals	Yes, a waiting list exists	Yes	Yes	Yes
Nutritional counseling	Yes	Yes	Yes	Yes
Asst. transportation	Yes	Yes	Yes	Yes

State	Mississippi	Missouri	Montana	Nebraska
Services	Council on Aging 601-359-4929	Department of Social Services 517-751-3082	Long-Term Care Division 406-444-7788	Division of Aging 402-471-2307
Personal care	Limited	Limited geographically	Limited	Limited geographically
Homemaker	Yes	Limited geographically	Yes	Limited geographically
Chores	Yes, as part of homemaker services; a waiting list exists	Limited, part of homemaker services	Yes	Yes
Home-delivered meals	Yes, a waiting list exists	Yes	Yes, possible waiting list	Yes
Adult day care	Limited	Limited	Limited	Limited geographically
Case management	Limited	Yes	Limited	No
Congregate meals	Yes	Yes	Yes	Yes
Nutritional counseling	Yes	No, however nutritional education is offered	Yes	Limited geographically
Asst. transportation	Yes, a waiting list exists	Yes	Yes	Limited

State	Nevada	New Hampshire	New Jersey	New Mexico
Services	Aging Services 775-688-2964	Division of Elderly & Adult Services 603-271-4683	Office of AAA 609-588-3139	Agency on Aging 505-827-7640
Personal care	No	Yes	Yes, possible waiting list	Limited
Homemaker	Limited geographically, possible waiting list	Yes	Yes, possible waiting list	Yes, possible waiting list
Chores	No	No	Yes	Yes
Home-delivered meals	Yes, possible waiting list	Yes	Yes, possible waiting list	Yes
Adult day care	Limited geographically, possible waiting list	Yes	Yes	Limited
Case management	Limited geographically	No	Yes	Limited
Congregate meals	Yes	Yes	Yes	Yes
Nutritional counseling	Yes	Yes	Yes	Limited
Asst. transportation	Yes	Yes	Yes	Limited

State	New York	North Carolina	North Dakota	Ohio
Services	Office for the Aging 518-474-7158	Division of Aging 919-733-3983	Division of Aging 701-328-8909	Department of Aging 614-466-9927
Personal care	Limited	Yes, a waiting list exists	No	Yes, a waiting list exists
Homemaker	Limited	Yes, a waiting list exists	No	Yes, a waiting list exists
Chores	Limited	Yes	Limited	Yes, a waiting list exists
Home-delivered meals	Yes	Yes, a waiting list exists	Yes	Yes, a waiting list exists
Adult day care	Limited	Yes, a waiting list exists	No	Yes, a waiting list exists
Case management	Limited	No	No	No
Congregate meals	Yes	Yes	Yes	Yes
Nutritional counseling	Limited	No	No	Yes
Asst. transportation	Limited	No, but transportation is offered; a waiting list exists	Yes	Yes

State	Oklahoma	Oregon	Pennsylvania	Rhode Island
Services	Office for the Aging 405-522-3073	Senior & Disabled Services 503-945-6413	Department of Aging 717-783-1550	Department of Elderly Affairs 401-222-6161
Personal care	Limited	Limited geographically	Yes	No
Homemaker	No	Limited geographically, possible waiting list	Limited, consists of home health and home support	No
Chores	Limited	Limited geographically	Limited, consists of home health and home support	Yes
Home-delivered meals	Yes, a waiting list exists	Yes, possible waiting list	Yes	Yes, a waiting list exists
Adult day care	No	Limited geographically	Limited	No
Case management	Limited	Limited geographically	Yes	Yes
Congregate meals	Yes	Yes	Yes	Yes
Nutritional counseling	Yes	Limited geographically	Limited to screening in some counties	Yes
Asst. transportation	Yes	Limited geographically	Limited	No

State	South Carolina	South Dakota	Tennessee	Texas
Services	Bureau of Senior Services 803-898-2850	Office of Adult Services & Aging 605-773-3656	Commission on Aging 615-741-2056	Department on Aging 512-424-6869
Personal care	Limited geographically	No	Limited	Limited
Homemaker	Yes, a waiting list exists	Yes	Limited, a waiting list exists	Limited
Chores	Yes, a waiting list exists	No	Limited	Yes
Home-delivered meals	Yes, a waiting list exists	Yes	Yes, a waiting list exists	Yes
Adult day care	Limited geographically	Yes	Limited	Limited
Case management	No	Yes	Limited	Limited
Congregate meals	Yes, a waiting list exists	Yes	Yes	Yes
Nutritional counseling	Limited geographically	Yes	Yes	Yes
Asst. transportation	Limited geographically	Yes	Limited	Yes

State	Utah	Vermont	Virginia	Washington
Services	Division of Aging & Adult Services 801-538-3910	Department of Aging & Disability 802-241-2400	Department for the Aging 804-662-9325	Aging & Adult Services Administration 360-493-2548
Personal care	No	Limited	Limited geographically, possible waiting list	Limited
Homemaker	No	Limited	Limited geographically	Limited
Chores	Yes	Limited	Limited geographically	Limited
Home-delivered meals	Yes	Yes	Yes, a waiting list exists	Yes, possible waiting list
Adult day care	No	Limited	Limited geographically	Limited
Case management	Yes	Yes	Limited geographically	Yes
Congregate meals	Yes	Yes	Yes, a waiting list exists	Yes
Nutritional counseling	Yes	Limited	Yes, possible waiting list	Limited to nutritional education
Asst. transportation	Limited	Yes	No	Limited

State	West Virginia	Wisconsin	Wyoming
Services	Bureau of Senior Services 304-558-3317	Department of Aging 614-466-9927	Division of Aging 307-777-7988
Personal care	Limited	Yes, a waiting list exists	Yes
Homemaker	Limited	Yes, a waiting list exists	Yes
Chores	Limited	Yes, a waiting list exists	Yes
Home-delivered meals	Yes	Yes, a waiting list exists	Yes
Adult day care	Limited	Yes, a waiting list exists	No
Case management	Limited	No	Yes
Congregate meals	Yes	Yes	Yes
Nutritional counseling	Limited	Yes	Yes
Asst. transportation	Limited	Yes, a waiting list exists	Yes

APPENDIX L: State-Funded Programs by State

Be sure to check with your state. Availability of services may have changed.

State	Alabama	Alaska	Arizona	Arkansas
	Medicaid Agency 334-242-5009	Commission on Aging 907-465-3250	Aging & Adult Administration 602-542-4446	Division of Aging & Adult Services 501-682-2441
Adult day/health care	Yes	Yes, a waiting list exists	Yes, a waiting list exists	No
Case management	Yes	Yes, a waiting list exists	Yes, a waiting list exists	Yes
Friendly visitor or phone reassurance	No	Yes, a waiting list exists	Yes	Yes
Home care aide (client-directed)	Yes	No	Yes, a waiting list exists	Yes
Home-delivered meals	Yes	Yes, a waiting list exists	Yes, a waiting list exists	Yes, but geographically limited
Housekeeping/ chores	Yes	Yes, a waiting list exists	Yes, a waiting list exists	Yes
Personal care	No	No	Yes, a waiting list exists	Yes
Respite	Yes	Yes, a waiting list exists	Yes, a waiting list exists	Yes
Transportation	No	Yes	Yes	No

State	California	Colorado	Connecticut	Delaware
	Department of Aging Information Line 800-510-2020	Health Care Policy 800-221-3943	Department of Social Services, Elderly Services Division 860-424-5277	Division of Aging 302-453-3820
Adult day/health care	Yes	No	Yes	Day care but no health care
Case management	Yes	No	Yes	Yes
Friendly visitor or phone reassurance	Yes	No	Yes	No
Home care aide (client-directed)	No	Yes	Yes	Some
Home-delivered meals	Yes	No	Yes	Yes
Housekeeping/ chores	No	No	Yes	Yes
Personal care	No	No	No	Yes, a waiting list exists
Respite	Yes	No	Yes	Yes
Transportation	No	No	Yes	No

State	District of Columbia	Florida	Georgia	Hawaii
	Office on Aging 202-727-8368	Office of LTC Policy 850-414-2000	Division of Aging Services 404-657-5258	Executive Office on Aging 808-586-0100
Adult day/ health care	Yes	Yes to day care; no to health care	Yes	Yes
Case management	Yes	Yes	Yes, but limited geographically. Primarily in Atlanta metro area	Yes
Friendly visitor or phone reassurance	Yes	Yes	No	No
Home care aide (client-directed)	No	No	No	(Attendant care)
Home-delivered meals	Yes	Yes	Yes, a waiting list exists	Yes
Housekeeping/ chores	Yes	Yes	Yes, a waiting list exists	Yes
Personal care	Yes	Yes	Yes, a waiting list exists	Yes
Respite	Yes	Yes	Yes	No
Transportation	Yes	Yes, for medical purposes	Yes	Yes

State	Idaho	Illinois	Indiana	Iowa
	Commission on Aging 208-334-5795	Department on Aging 217-524-6911	Area Agencies 800-986-3505	Department of Elder Affairs 515-281-5187
Adult day/ health care	No	Yes	Adult day care but not health care	Adult day care but not health care
Case management	Yes	Yes	Yes	Yes
Friendly visitor or phone reassurance	Volunteer program	Yes	No	Yes
Home care aide (client-directed)	No	No	No	No
Home-delivered meals	No	Yes	Yes	Yes
Housekeeping/ chores	Yes, a waiting list exists	Yes	Yes	Yes
Personal care	No	Yes	Yes	Yes
Respite	Yes	Yes	Yes	Yes
Transportation	Yes	Yes	Yes, for medical purposes	Yes

State	Kansas	Kentucky	Louisiana	Maine
	Commission on Aging 800-432-3535	Office of Aging 502-564-6930	Governor's Office of Elderly Affairs 225-342-7100	Bureau of Elder & Adult Services 800-262-2232
Adult day/health care	Yes, but geographically limited	Yes, a waiting list exists	No	No
Case management	Yes	Yes, a waiting list exists	No	Yes
Friendly visitor or phone reassurance	No	No	No	Yes
Home care aide (client-directed)	No	Yes, a waiting list exists	No	Yes
Home-delivered meals	Yes, a waiting list exists	Yes, a waiting list exists	Yes	Yes, a waiting list exists
Housekeeping/ chores	Yes, a waiting list exists	Yes, a waiting list exists	Yes	Yes, a waiting list exists
Personal care	Yes, a waiting list exists	Yes, a waiting list exists	No	Yes, a waiting list exists
Respite	Yes, a waiting list exists	Yes, a waiting list exists	No	Yes, a waiting list exists
Transportation	Yes, for medical purposes	No	No	Yes

State	Maryland	Massachusetts	Michigan	Minnesota
	Department of Aging 410-767-1108	Executive Office of Elderly Affairs 800-882-2003	Services to the Aging	Board of Aging, Senior Linkage 800-333-2433
Adult day/health care	Yes, a waiting list exists	Yes	Yes	Yes
Case management	Yes, a waiting list exists	Yes	Yes	Yes
Friendly visitor or phone reassurance	Yes, a waiting list exists	Yes	Yes	Yes
Home care aide (client-directed)	No	Yes	Yes	No
Home-delivered meals	Yes, a waiting list exists	Yes	Yes	Yes
Housekeeping/ chores	Yes, a waiting list exists	Yes	Yes	Yes
Personal care	Yes, a waiting list exists	Yes	No	Yes
Respite	Yes, a waiting list exists	Yes	Yes	Yes
Transportation	Yes, a waiting list exists	Yes	Yes	Yes

State	Mississippi	Missouri	Montana	Nebraska
	Division of Medicaid 601-359-6050	Division of Aging 573-751-3990	Public Health & Human Services 406-444-5622	Division of Aging 402-471-2307
Adult day/ health care	No	No	No	Yes
Case management	No	Yes, a waiting list exists	No	Yes
Friendly visitor or phone reassurance	No	No	No	Yes
Home care aide (client-directed)	No	No	No	Yes
Home-delivered meals	No	No	No	Yes
Housekeeping/ chores	No	Yes, a waiting list exists	No	Yes
Personal care	No	Yes, a waiting list exists	No	Yes
Respite	No	Yes, a waiting list exists	No	Yes
Transportation	No	No	No	Yes

State	Nevada	New Hampshire	New Jersey	New Mexico
	Division of Aging Services 775-687-4210	Division of Elder & Adult Services 800-852-3345	Department of Health & Senior Services, Easy Access 877-222-3737	Department of Long-Term Health Care 505-827-2574
Adult day/ health care	Yes	No	Yes	Yes
Case management	Yes	No	Yes	Yes
Friendly visitor or phone reassurance	Yes	Yes	Yes	Yes
Home care aide (client-directed)	No	No	Yes	No
Home-delivered meals	No	No	No	Yes
Housekeeping/ chores	Yes	No	No	Yes
Personal care	Yes	No	No	Yes
Respite	Yes	Yes, for Alzheimer's and related disorders	Yes	Yes
Transportation	No	No	Yes	Yes

State	New York	North Carolina	North Dakota	Ohio
	New York State Senior Citizens Hotline 518-474-7158	Division of Aging 919-733-0440	Department of Human Services; Aging Services Division 800-451-8693	Department of Aging 614-466-5500
Adult day/health care	Yes	Yes	Yes	Yes
Case management	Yes	Yes	Yes	Yes
Friendly visitor or phone reassurance	Yes	Yes	No	No
Home care aide (client-directed)	Yes	Yes, but geographically limited	Yes	No
Home-delivered meals	Yes	Yes	No	Yes, a waiting list exists
Housekeeping/chores	Yes	Yes	Yes	Yes
Personal care	Yes	Yes	Yes	Yes
Respite	Yes	Yes	Yes	Yes
Transportation	Yes	Yes	Yes, nonmedical	Yes

State	Oklahoma	Oregon	Pennsylvania	Rhode Island
	Aging Services Division 800-211-2116	Consumer Relations & Community Education 503-945-5812	Department of Aging 717-783-6207	Department of Elderly Affairs 401-222-2858
Adult day/health care	Yes	No	Yes	Yes
Case management	Yes	No	Yes	Yes
Friendly visitor or phone reassurance	Yes	No	Yes, but geographically limited	No
Home care aide (client-directed)	Yes	No	Yes, but geographically limited	No
Home-delivered meals	Yes, but geographically limited	No	Yes	No
Housekeeping/ chores	Yes	Yes	Yes	Yes, limited to 10 hours per week
Personal care	Yes	No	Yes	No
Respite	Yes	No	Yes, but geographically limited	No
Transportation	Yes	No	Yes	No

State	South Carolina	South Dakota	Tennessee	Texas
	Department of Health & Human Services 803-253-6177	No program	No program	Department of Human Services 512-438-3280
Adult day/health care	Yes	No	No	Yes, a waiting list exists
Case management	Yes	No	No	No
Friendly visitor or phone reassurance	Yes	No	No	No
Home care aide (client-directed)	No	No	No	Yes, a waiting list exists
Home-delivered meals	Yes	No	No	Yes, but limited to 5 meals per week; a waiting list exists
Housekeeping/ chores	Yes	No	No	Yes, limited hours and a waiting list exists
Personal care	Yes	No	No	Yes, a waiting list exists
Respite	Yes	No	No	Yes, a waiting list exists
Transportation	Yes	No	No	No

State	Utah	Vermont	Virginia	Washington
	Division of Aging & Adult Services 810-538-3910	Department of Aging & Disabilities 802-241-2400	Aging Services 800-552-3402	Aging & Adult Services Admin. 360-493-2500 In-state: 800-422-3263
Adult day/ health care	Yes	Yes, a waiting list exists	Yes	Yes
Case management	Yes	Yes	Yes	Yes
Friendly visitor or phone reassurance	Yes	Yes	Yes	No
Home care aide (client-directed)	Yes	Yes, a waiting list exists	No	Yes
Housekeeping/ chores	Yes	Yes, a waiting list exists	Yes	Yes, a waiting list exists
Home-delivered meals	Yes	Yes	Yes	Yes
Personal care	Yes	Yes, a waiting list exists	Yes	Yes
Respite	Yes	Yes	Yes	No
Transportation	Yes	No	Yes	Yes

State	West Virginia	Wisconsin	Wyoming
	Bureau of Senior Services 304-558-3317	Bureau of Aging & Long-Term Care Resources 608-267-7285	Division on Aging 800-442-2766
Adult day/ health care	No	Yes	Yes, to day care
Case management	No	Yes	Yes
Friendly visitor or phone reassurance	No	Yes, typically volunteers	Yes
Home care aide (client-directed)	No	Yes	No
Home-delivered meals	No	Yes	Yes
Housekeeping/ chores	No	Yes	Yes
Personal care	Yes	Yes	Yes
Respite	No	Yes	Yes
Transportation	No	Yes	Yes

APPENDIX M: Nursing Home Watch List by State

GUIDE TO THE RATINGS: The following facilities had state inspection surveys during the period from July 1995 to October 1998 that we have judged to raise questions about the quality of care delivered to residents.

To compile our Watch List, the deficiencies shown in the surveys between July 1995 and October 1998 were evaluated on five criteria that we selected: (1) citations for failing to provide adequate access to the survey report, (2) high numbers of repeat deficiencies, (3) high-severity deficiencies, (4) substandard quality-of-care deficiencies, and (5) high numbers of total deficiencies. This list includes the facilities with the most questionable patterns of deficiencies (approximately 10 percent of all facilities in each state).

Since July 1995, each deficiency cited by inspectors is rated according to its scope and severity. There are three levels of scope (how many residents could be or were affected) and four levels of severity (how much harm did or could occur). The highest level of severity is immediate jeopardy to nursing home residents.

Substandard Quality of Care deficiencies are defined by the Health Care Financing Administration to be violations of certain types of deficiencies (such as quality of care and quality of life) that also have more serious combinations of scope and severity.

Because some facilities historically have a "yo-yo" pattern of compliance, meaning that inspectors find no deficiencies one year and many the next, it is possible that a facility listed here now has a current survey showing no deficiencies. If you are using or considering one of these facilities, check surveys reported over a four-year period to assure yourself that prior problems have indeed been corrected.

NOTE: The Facility ID Number is the number used by the Health Care Financing Administration (HCFA) to identify facilities regulated for Medicare or Medicaid funding. The data used in our Watch List is from the OSCAR data reporting system of the Health Care Financing Administration.

STATE	FACILITY ID NUMBER	NAME OF FACILITY	ADDRESS	CITY
AK	025024	Wesley Rehabilitation Care Center	431 First Ave. (P.O. Box 430)	Seward
AK	025018	Providence Extended Care Center	4900 Eagle	Anchorage
AL	015011	Montrose Bay Health Care Center	Highway 98 P.O. Box 256	Montrose
AL	015037	Woodley Manor Living Center	3312 Woodley Rd.	Montgomery
AL	015103	Cogburn Health Center Inc	148 Tuscaloosa St.	Mobile
AL	015120	National Healthcare	2300 Coleman Rd. P.O. Box 1790	Anniston
AL	015174	Coosa Valley Health Care Inc	513 Pineview Ave.	Glencoe

STATE	FACILITY ID NUMBER	NAME OF FACILITY	ADDRESS	CITY
AL	015303	Fairview Nursing & Convalescent Home	1028 Bessemer Rd.	Birmingham
AL	015390	Capitol Hill Health Care Center	520 South Hull St.	Montgomery
AL	015419	Hartford Health Care	Toro Rd. P.O. Box 190	Hartford
AL	015164	Willow Trace Nsg Center and Asst Liv Center	1406 East Pushmataha St.	Butler
AL	015192	Care Center of Opelika	1908½ Pepperell Pkwy.	Opelika
AL	015001	Dalraida Health Center Inc	100 Perry Hill Rd.	Montgomery
AL	015143	Forest Manor Inc	2215 32nd St.	Northport
AL	015196	Lanett Geriatric Center	702 South 13th St.	Lanett
AL	015016	Athens Convalescent Center Inc	611 West Market St.	Athens
AL	015113	Sunrise Care and Rehab for Decatur	1350 Fourteenth Ave. Southeast	Decatur
AL	015144	Integrated Health Svcs at Briarcliff	850 Northwest Ninth St.	Alabaster
AL	015388	Lakeview Nursing Home Inc	8017 Second Ave.	Birmingham
AL	015429	Sea Breeze Health Care Center	550 Congress St.	Mobile
AL	01E354	Alice M. Kidd Intermediate Care Fac	200 University Blvd. P.O. Box 20707	Tuscaloosa
AL	015397	Windsor House	4411 Mcallister Dr.	Huntsville
AL	015127	Westside Health Care Center	4320 Judith Lane	Huntsville
AR	045070	Rogers Rehabilitation and Living Center	1149 W New Hope Rd.	Rogers
AR	045251	Clay Healthcare Inc	806 West Walnut	Corning
AR	045253	Zimmerman Nursing Home Inc	1937 Ark Hwy. 13 So.	Carlisle
AR	045261	Woodland Manor Inc	811 West Elgin St.	Siloam Springs
AR	045311	Sunchase Nursing Center	6811 South Hazel St.	Pine Bluff
AR	04E115	Southwest Homes Inc	2821 W. Dixon Rd.	Little Rock
AR	045193	Beverly Health and Rehab Williamsburg	6301 Lee Ave.	Little Rock
AR	04A232	Robinson Healthcare Inc	519 Donovan Briley Blvd.	North Little Rock
AR	04E058	Keith Acres	112 W Clinton	Blytheville
AR	045018	Beverly Health and Rehab Services Jvil	1320 W Braden St.	Jacksonville
AR	045319	Rose Care Center of Stuttgart	1211 East 22nd St.	Stuttgart
AR	045163	Pine Lane Healthcare	1100 Pine Tree Ln.	Mountain Home
AR	045298	Four Oaks Living Center	2600 Barrow Rd.	Little Rock
AR	04A228	Northwest Nursing and Retirement Center	27 E Appleby Rd.	Fayetteville
AR	04A245	Osceola Healthcare	406 South Broadway	Osceola

STATE	NUMBER	NAME OF FACILITY	ADDRESS	CITY
AR	045098	Beverly Healthcare Golf Links	552 Golflinks Rd.	Hot Springs
AR	045063	Little Rock Healthcare & Rehab Center	5720 W Markham	Little Rock
AR	045231	Clarksville Conv Home	400 Oak Court St.	Clarksville
AR	045237	Rochier Hgts Nursing Center	1001 Rochier St.	Fayetteville
AR	045263	Rosewood Manor	1316 Park Ave.	Hot Springs
AR	04A123	Medi Home of Prairie Grove	621 S Mock St.	Prairie Grove
AR	04A223	Westlake Living Center	245 Indian Bay Dr.	Sherwood
AR	045256	Sheridan Nursing and Rehab Center	113 South Briarwood Dr.	Sheridan
AZ	035092	Desert Sky Healthcare & Rehab Center	5125 N 58th Ave.	Glendale
AZ	035129	Hearthstone of Mesa	215 S Power Rd.	Mesa
AZ	035168	Heather Glen Care Center	5910 W Northern Ave.	Glendale
AZ	035234	Arizona State Veteran Home—Phoenix	4141 North 3rd St.	Phoenix
AZ	035242	Chinle Nursing Home	P.O. Box 910	Chinle
AZ	035086	Hacienda Rehabilitation & Care Center	660 Coronado Dr.	Sierra Vista
AZ	035131	Las Fuentes Care Center	1045 Scott Dr.	Prescott
AZ	035165	Manorcare Health Services	3705 N Swan Rd.	Tucson
AZ	035174	Sunrise Park Villa Care & Rehabilitation	2001 N Park Ave.	Tucson
AZ	035091	Los Arcos Health Care Center	800 W University Ave.	Flagstaff
AZ	035117	Payson Care Center	107 E Lone Pine Dr.	Payson
AZ	035169	Kingman Health Care Center	1081 Kathleen Ave.	Kingman
AZ	035181	Desert Gardens	2502 N Dodge Blvd.	Tucson
AZ	035095	Desert Cove Nursing Center	1750 W Frye Rd.	Chandler
AZ	035216	Gila River Nursing Home	8201 W Baseline Rd.	Laveen
AZ	035139	Pueblo Norte Nursing Center	2401 E Hunt St.	Show Low
CA	055116	Sunrise Care Center for Pacifica	751 San Pedro Terrace Rd.	Pacifica
CA	055223	Cloverleaf Healthcare Center	275 North San Jacinto	Hemet
CA	055276	Parkmont Rehabilitation & Nsg Care Center	2400 Parkside Dr.	Fremont
CA	055292	Shields/Richmond Nursing Center	1919 Cutting Blvd.	Richmond
CA	055298	Fallbrook Hosp District SNF	325 Potter Ave.	Fallbrook
CA	055322	Point Loma Conv Hosp	3202 Duke St.	San Diego
CA	055334	Sunrise Pacific Care Center	2211 Harrison Ave.	Eureka

STATE	FACILITY ID NUMBER	NAME OF FACILITY	ADDRESS	CITY
CA	055474	Magnolia Convalescent Hospital	8133 Magnolia Ave.	Riverside
CA	055674	Knott Avenue Care Center	9021 Knott Ave.	Buena Park
CA	055742	Casa Pacifica	861 S Harbor Blvd.	Anaheim
CA	055861	Acacias Care Center	601 N Montgomery St.	Ojai
CA	055885	Sunrise Care and Rehab for Fremont	2500 Country Dr.	Fremont
CA	056084	Astoria Convalescent Hospital	14040 Astoria St.	Sylmar
CA	056280	Oakridge Conv Center	2919 Fruitvale Ave.	Oakland
CA	056436	Medical Center Convalescent Hospital	467 E Gilbert St.	San Bernardino
CA	056447	Hayward Hills Conv Hosp	1768 B St.	Hayward
CA	05A130	Alice Manor	8448 E Adams Ave.	Fowler
CA	05A357	Napa State Hosp	2100 Napa-Vallejo Hy.	Napa
CA	05E509	Claritas Intermediate Care Hosp	955 23rd St.	Richmond
CA	555020	Laguna Honda Hosp	375 Laguna Honda Blvd.	San Francisco
CA	555093	St Edna Subacute & Rehabilitation Center	1929 N Fairview St.	Santa Ana
CA	555153	Homestead of Fair Oaks, The	11300 Fair Oaks Blvd.	Fair Oaks
CA	555246	Life Care Center of Vista	304 N Melrose Dr.	Vista
CA	555252	Sunrise Care Center for Paradise	8777 Skyway	Paradise
CA	555466	Ashby Care Center	2270 Ashby Ave.	Berkeley
CA	555496	Whispering Hope Care Center	5320 Carrington Circle	Stockton
CA	555517	Kern Valley Hospital D/P SNF	6412 Laurel Ave.	Lake Isabella
CA	555663	Lindsay Gardens	1011 West Tulare Rd.	Lindsay
CA	055108	Sunrise Care Center for Pleasant Hill	550 Patterson Blvd.	Pleasant Hill
CA	055187	Garden View Care Center	14475 Garden View Ln.	Baldwin Park
CA	055676	Community Conv Hospital of Glendora	638 E Colorado Ave.	Glendora
CA	055872	Citrus Nursing Center	9440 Citrus Ave.	Fontana
CA	055874	Eden West Rehab Hosp	1805 West St.	Hayward
CA	056261	Merritt Manor Conv Hosp	604 E Merritt Ave.	Tulare
CA	056300	Sunrise Granada Care & Rehabilitation	2885 Harris St.	Eureka
CA	05E574	Villa Scalabrini Special Care Unit	10631 Vinedale St.	Sun Valley
CA	555010	Skylight Convalescent Hospital	1201 Walnut Ave.	Long Beach
CA	555532	Harbor Health Care	2222 N Harbor Blvd.	Fullerton
CA	055142	Magnolia Gardens Convalescent Hospital	17922 San Fernando Mission Blvd.	Granada Hills

STATE	FACILITY ID NUMBER	NAME OF FACILITY	ADDRESS	CITY
CA	055776	Hilltop Manor Conv Hosp #2	12225 Shale Ridge Ln.	Auburn
CA	055984	Anaheim Healthcare Center	501 South Beach Blvd.	Anaheim
CA	056038	Milpitas Care Center	120 Corning Ave.	Milpitas
CA	056120	Westside Care Center	300 Douglas St.	Petaluma
CA	056287	Moyles Hi-Desert Convalescent Hospital	55475 Santa Fe Tr.	Yucca Valley
CA	056392	Pleasanton Conv Hosp	300 Neal St.	Pleasanton
CA	056476	Sunrise Rosewood Care & Rehabilitation	1911 Oak Park Blvd.	Pleasant Hill
CA	056478	Fountain Gardens Convalescent Hospital	2222 Santa Ana Blvd.	Los Angeles
CA	056483	Sherwood Oaks Health Center	130 Dana St.	Fort Bragg
CA	555046	Providence St Joseph Medical Center	501 South Buena Vista	Burbank
CA	555216	Sharp Chula Vista Medical Center D/P SNF	751 Medical Center Ct.	Chula Vista
CA	555290	Stanford Court Nursing Center of Santee	8778 Cuyumaca St.	Santee
CA	555585	Pleasant Care Nsg/Rehab Center-San Diego	2828 Meadowlark Dr.	San Diego
CA	555652	Willow Creek Healthcare Center	650 West Alluvial	Clovis
CA	555687	Roberts Nursing Home	415 Browns Valley Rd.	Napa
CA	055114	Stanford Court Nursing Center of La Mesa	7800 Parkway Dr.	La Mesa
CA	055222	Springs Road Living Center	1527 Springs Dr.	Vallejo
CA	055534	Home for Jewish Parents	2780 26th Ave.	Oakland
CA	055571	Buena Park Nursing Center	8520 Western Ave.	Buena Park
CA	055798	Guardian Rehabilitation Center	16412 Los Gatos Blvd.	Los Gatos
CA	055876	Willow Tree Nursing and Rehabilitation	2124 57th Ave.	Oakland
CA	056212	Willow Glen Conv Hosp Rest Care Center	1267 Meridian Ave.	San Jose
CA	056382	Pineridge Care Center	14122 Hubbard St.	Sylmar
CA	555095	N M Holderman Memorial Hospital-SNF	Veterans Home of Calif-P.O. Box 1200	Yountville
CA	555161	Napa Nursing Center	3275 Villa Ln.	Napa
CA	555420	Modoc Medical Center	228 McDowell St.	Alturas
CA	555678	Veterans Home of California-Barstow	100 E Veterans Pkwy.	Barstow
CA	055017	Cypress Rehabilitation and Nursing	2605 Paul Minnie Ave.	Santa Cruz
CA	055301	Marlinda Convalescent Hospital	830 Pratt Ave.	Saint Helena
CA	056017	Torrey Pines Convalescent Hospital	2552 Torrey Pines Rd.	La Jolla
CA	056066	Woodland Care Center	7120 Corbin Ave.	Reseda

STATE	FACILITY ID NUMBER	NAME OF FACILITY	ADDRESS	CITY
CA	056207	Pacific Gardens Nursing and Rehab Center	577 South Peach St.	Fresno
CA	056284	Pleasant Care Convalescent of Ukiah	131 Whitmore Ln.	Ukiah
CA	555269	Palomar Continuing Care Center	1817 Avenida del Diablo	Escondido
CA	555412	Village Square Nursing & Rehab Center	1586 W San Marcos Blvd.	San Marcos
CA	555566	Life Care Center of Corona	2600 South Main St.	Corona
CA	055379	Dreier's Sanitarium	1400 W Glenoaks Blvd.	Glendale
CA	055906	Rinaldi Convalescent Hospital	16553 Rinaldi St.	Granada Hills
CA	056322	Verdugo Valley Convalescent Hospital	2635 Honolulu Ave.	Montrose
CA	056363	Grand Valley Health Care Center	13524 Sherman Way	Van Nuys
CA	05A027	Sierra Vista	3455 E Highland Ave.	Highland
CA	555068	Guardian Santa Clara Valley	1990 Fruitdale Ave.	San Jose
CA	555076	El Cajon Valley Convalescent Center	510 E Washington Ave.	El Cajon
CA	555334	Alvarado Convalescent & Rehab Hospital	6599 Alvarado Rd.	San Diego
CA	055064	Madison Care Center	1391 E Madison Ave.	El Cajon
CA	055987	Sonoma Care and Rehabilitation	1250 Broadway	Sonoma
CA	056488	Sunnyside Rehabilitation & Nursing Center	22617 S Vermont Ave.	Torrance
CA	555308	Lake Forest Nursing Center	25652 Old Trabuco Rd.	Lake Forest
CA	555318	Villa Rancho Bernardo Care Center	15720 Bernardo Center Dr.	San Diego
CA	555427	Life Care Center of Escondido	1980 Felicita Rd.	Escondido
CA	555431	Country Hills Hlth Care Center	1580 Broadway	El Cajon
CA	055150	Valley Manor Rehabilitation Center	3806 Clayton Rd.	Concord
CA	055335	Sunrise Care & Rehab for Oceanside	3232 Thunder Dr.	Oceanside
CA	055645	Mission Skilled Nursing & Subacute Center	410 N Winchester Blvd.	Santa Clara
CA	056298	Sunrise Care Center Park Central	2100 Parkside Dr.	Fremont
CA	056323	Emmanuel Convalescent-San Joaquin	1611 Height St.	Bakersfield
CA	555487	Mission de la Casa Nursing & Rehab Center	2501 Alvin Ave.	San Jose
CA	055003	Sunrise Care and Rehab for Eureka	2353 Twenty-third St.	Eureka
CA	056105	Bayside Rehabilitation and Care Center	3520 4th Ave.	San Diego
CA	056351	Chatsworth Park Convalescent Hosp	10610 Owensmouth Ave.	Chatsworth
CA	555478	Victoria Care Center	5445 Everglades St.	Ventura
CA	055034	Motion Picture & Television Hospital	23388 Mulholland Dr.	Woodland Hills

STATE	FACILITY ID NUMBER	NAME OF FACILITY	ADDRESS	CITY
CA	055249	Merced Living Care Center	510 West 26th St.	Merced
CA	056334	Oceanview Convalescent Hospital	1340 15th St.	Santa Monica
CA	056431	Sunrise Care & Rehab-Palomares	250 W Artesia St.	Pomona
CA	555098	Greenhaven Country Place	455 Florin Rd.	Sacramento
CA	555574	Golden State Care Center	21820 Craggy View St.	Chatsworth
CA	055099	Creekside Healthcare Center	1900 Church Ln.	San Pablo
CA	055614	Vallejo Conv Hosp	900 Sereno Dr.	Vallejo
CA	055208	Sunrise Seaview Care Center	8400 Purdue Dr.	Eureka
CA	055337	Sunrise Care and Rehab-Escondido-East	1260 E Ohio St.	Escondido
CA	056292	Camarillo Convalescent Hospital	205 Granada St.	Camarillo
CA	555398	Vintage Estates of Hayward	25919 Gading Rd.	Hayward
CA	555371	Pacific Care Center	1405 Teresa Dr.	Morro Bay
CA	055782	Quail Ridge Health Care Center	1440 168th Ave.	San Leandro
CA	555138	St Erne Sanitarium	527 West Regent St.	Inglewood
CA	555366	Sacred Heart Convalescent Hospital	18949 Redwood Rd.	Castro Valley
CA	555659	Chase Care Center	1201 S Orange Ave.	El Cajon
CA	555640	Moyle's Indio Convalescent Hospital	47763 Monroe Ave.	Indio
CA	056005	Canoga Care Center	22029 Saticoy St.	Canoga Park
CA	055604	Visalia Nursing and Rehabilitation Center	1925 E Houston Ave.	Visalia
CO	065100	Westwind Village	2515 Pitman Pl.	Pueblo
CO	065147	Integrated Health Svcs at Cheyenne Mtn	835 Tenderfoot Hill Rd.	Colorado Springs
CO	065203	Cherrelyn Manor Health Care Center	5555 S Elati St.	Littleton
CO	065216	Conejos County Hospital LTC	19021 S H 285 P.O. Box 639	La Jara
CO	065240	Brighton Care Center	2025 Egbert St.	Brighton
CO	065249	Integrated Health Services at Delta	2050 S Main St.	Delta
CO	065282	Life Care Center of Longmont	2451 Pratt St.	Longmont
CO	065297	Allison Care Center Inc	1660 Allison St.	Lakewood
CO	065317	Exempla Healthcare St Joseph Hosp TCU	1835 Franklin St.	Denver
CO	06A172	Park Forest Care Center Inc	7045 Stuart St.	Westminster
CO	06A190	Colo State Veterans Nursing Home	23500 U S Hwy. 160	Walsenburg
CO	065242	Brookshire House	4660 E Asbury Cir.	Denver

STATE	FACILITY ID NUMBER	NAME OF FACILITY	ADDRESS	CITY
CO	065337	Sable Care Center Inc.	656 Dillon Way	Aurora
CO	065253	Integrated Hlth Svcs at La Villa Grande	2501 Little Bookcliff Dr.	Grand Junction
CO	065298	Lakeridge Village Care Center	1655 Yarrow St.	Lakewood
CO	06A042	Arkansas Valley Reg Med Center NH	514 W 10th St.	La Junta
CO	06A148	Evergreen Terrace Care Center	1625 Simms St.	Lakewood
CO	065034	Amberwood Court Care Center	4686 E Asbury Cir.	Denver
CO	065238	Elms Haven Care Center	12080 Bellaire Way	Thornton
CO	065272	Cornerstone Care Center	1432 Depew St.	Lakewood
CO	065274	Arkansas Manor Care Center	3185 W Arkansas Ave.	Denver
CO	065168	Aspen Living Center	1795 Monterey Rd.	Colorado Springs
CO	065176	Camellia Healthcare Center	500 Geneva St.	Aurora
CT	075062	Center for Optimum Care-Soundview, The	One Care Ln.	West Haven
CT	075098	Center for Optimum Care-Waterford, The	171 Rope Ferry Rd.	Waterford
CT	075113	Greentree Manor Nursing & Rehab Center	4 Greentree Dr.	Waterford
CT	075158	New London Rehabilitation & Care Center	88 Clark Ln.	Waterford
CT	075186	West Hill Conv Home	60 West St.	Rocky Hill
CT	075209	Hamilton Rehabilitation & Healthcare	50 Palmer St.	Norwich
CT	075223	Center for Optimum Care-Danielson, The	111 Westcott Rd.	Danielson
CT	075237	Kimberly Hall-South Center	1 Emerson Dr.	Windsor
CT	075248	Center for Optimum Care-West Hartford, The	2432 Albany Ave.	West Hartford
CT	075249	Mediplex of Darien	599 Boston Post Rd.	Darien
CT	075261	Regency House of Wallingford Inc	181 E Main St.	Wallingford
CT	075287	Homestead Health Center	160 Glenbrook Rd.	Stamford
CT	075293	Jefferson House	One John H. Stewart Dr.	Newington
CT	075299	Chelsea Place	25 Lorraine St.	Hartford
CT	075314	Olympus HC Center-Manchester Bidwell Bldg	333 Bidwell St.	Manchester
CT	075323	Cambridge Manor	2428 Easton Tnpk.	Fairfield
CT	075338	Harborside Healthcare-Governor's House	38 Firetown Rd.	Simsbury
CT	075345	Coccomo Mem Health Care Center	33 Cone Ave.	Meriden
CT	075360	Wm & Sally Tandet Center for Cont Care	146 Broad St.	Stamford
CT	075397	Clifton House Rehabilitation Center	181 Clifton St.	New Haven

STATE	FACILITY ID NUMBER	NAME OF FACILITY	ADDRESS	CITY
CT	075034	Carolton Chronic & Conv Hosp, Inc	400 Mill Plain Rd.	Fairfield
CT	075329	Ingraham Manor	400 N Main St.	Bristol
CT	075393	Bel Air Manor	256 New Britain Ave.	Newington
CT	075229	Sterling Manor	870 Burnside Ave.	East Hartford
CT	075381	Harbor Hill Care Center, Inc	111 Church St.	Middletown
CT	075246	Whitney Manor Conv Center	2798 Whitney Ave.	Hamden
CT	075404	Maefair Health Care Center	21 Maefair Ct.	Trumbull
CT	075153	Smith House SNF	88 Rockrimmon Rd.	Stamford
CT	075401	Mediplex of Greater Hartford	160 Coventry St.	Bloomfield
CT	075066	St Andrew's Health Center, LLC	2817 N Main St.	Waterbury
CT	075268	Trinity Hill	151 Hillside Ave.	Hartford
DC	095015	Health Care Institute	1380 Southern Ave.	Washington
DC	095031	Rock Creek Manor	2131 O Street NW	Washington
DE	085034	Harbor Healthcare & Rehab Center Inc	301 Ocean View Blvd.	Lewes
DE	085039	Arbors at New Castle Nsg Center	32 Buena Vista Dr.	New Castle
DE	085001	Kentmere Home of Merciful Rest Soc	1900 Lovering Ave.	Wilmington
DE	085032	Westminster Village Health Center	1175 McKee Rd.	Dover
DE	085037	Millsboro Nursing Home	231 S Washington St.	Millsboro
FL	105125	Eason Nursing Home	1711 6th Ave. South	Lake Worth
FL	105178	Heritage Health Care Center	777 9th St. N	Naples
FL	105365	Life Care Center of Altamonte Springs	989 Orienta Ave.	Altamonte Springs
FL	105384	Calusa Harbour Health Center	2525 E First St.	Fort Myers
FL	105407	Harborside Healthcare Sarasota	4602 Northgate Ct.	Sarasota
FL	105408	Treasure Isle Care Center	1735 N Treasure Dr.	North Bay Village
FL	105431	IHS of Central Fl at Orlando	1900 Mercy Dr.	Orlando
FL	105471	IHS at Central Park Village	9311 S Orange Blossom Trail	Orlando
FL	105640	Renova Health Center	750 Bayberry Dr.	Lake Park
FL	105650	Bay to Bay Nursing Center	3405 Bay to Bay Blvd.	Tampa
FL	105730	Mariner Health of Winter Haven	1540 6th St. NW	Winter Haven
FL	105782	Sunbelt Living Center/Apopka	305 E Oak St.	Apopka

STATE	FACILITY ID NUMBER	NAME OF FACILITY	ADDRESS	CITY
FL	105790	NHC Naples	10949 Parnu St.	Naples
FL	105869	Emerald Oaks	1507 S Tuttle Ave.	Sarasota
FL	105884	Arbors at Tampa	2811 Campus Hill Dr.	Tampa
FL	105886	Brighton Gardens of Maitland	1305 W Maitland Blvd.	Maitland
FL	105008	Arch Creek NH	12505 NE 16th Ave.	North Miami
FL	105234	Rehab and Health Care of Tampa	4411 N Habana Ave.	Tampa
FL	105456	Key West Convalescent Center	5860 W Junior College Rd.	Key West
FL	105491	Manhattan Convalescent Center	4610 S Manhattan Ave.	Tampa
FL	105524	Mariner Health of Port Charlotte	25325 Rampart Blvd.	Port Charlotte
FL	105539	Health Care & Rehab of Sandford	950 Mellonville Ave.	Sanford
FL	105565	Halifax Convalescent Center	820 N Clyde Morris Blvd.	Daytona Beach
FL	105622	North Broward Rehab & Nursing Center	401 East Sample Rd.	Pompano Beach
FL	105659	Integrated Hlth Svcs FL-Lake Worth	1201 12th Ave. S	Lake Worth
FL	105783	Sunbelt Living Center-E Orlando	250 South Chickasaw Trail	Orlando
FL	105803	Hialeah Convalescent Home	190 W 28th St.	Hialeah
FL	105897	North Ridge Medical Center TRU	5757 North Dixie Hwy.	Fort Lauderdale
FL	105294	Oak Cove Health Center	210 S Osceola Ave.	Clearwater
FL	105430	Park Lake Nsg and Rehab Center	1700 Monroe Ave.	Maitland
FL	105469	Florida Club Care Center	220 Sierra Dr.	Miami
FL	105555	Jupiter Care Center	17781 Yancy Ave.	Jupiter
FL	105572	Colonial Palms West	51 W Sample Rd.	Pompano Beach
FL	105676	Crown Nursing Center	5351 Gulf Blvd.	Saint Petersburg Bch
FL	105970	Courtyard at the Mill Pond	2600 Forest Glen Tr.	Marianna
FL	105268	Lakeside Health Center	2501 Australian Ave.	West Palm Beach
FL	105382	Integrated Hlth Svcs of FL-Fort Pierce	703 S 29th St.	Fort Pierce
FL	105423	Southlake Nsg & Rehab Center Inc	10680 Old St. Augustine Rd.	Jacksonville
FL	105509	Beverly Hlth & Rehab Center of Pt Salerno	4801 SE Cove Rd.	Port Salerno
FL	105728	Veranda Nursing & Rehab Center, The	830 W 29th St.	Orlando
FL	105841	St Petersburg Health Care Center	1735 Ninth St. S	Saint Petersburg
FL	105078	Jackson Manor NH	1861 NW 8th Ave.	Miami
FL	105183	Coventry Square Health and Rehab	2021 SW 1st Ave.	Ocala

STATE	FACILITY ID NUMBER	NAME OF FACILITY	ADDRESS	CITY
FL	105754	Mariner Health of Conway Lakes	5201 Curry Ford Rd.	Orlando
FL	105052	Fairview Manor	324 Wilder Blvd.	Daytona Beach
FL	105071	Integ Hlth Svcs of St Pete	811 Jackson St. N	Saint Petersburg
FL	105237	IHS of West Broward	7751 W Broward Blvd.	Plantation
FL	105505	Beverly Manor of Margate	5951 Colonial Dr.	Margate
FL	105558	Haverhill Care Center	5065 Wallis Rd.	West Palm Beach
FL	105795	Integrated Hlth Scvs of FL-W Plm Beach	2939 S Haverhill Rd.	West Palm Beach
FL	105155	East Manor Medical Care Center	1524 East Ave. S	Sarasota
FL	105359	Magnolias Nursing Home	600 W Gregory St.	Pensacola
FL	105538	South Port Nursing Center	23013 Westchester Blvd.	Port Charlotte
FL	105669	Wellington Speciality Care & Rehab Center	10049 N Florida Ave.	Tampa
FL	105076	Greenwood Rehabilitation Center	1101 54th St.	West Palm Beach
FL	105345	El Ponce de Leon Convalescent Center	335 SW 12th Ave.	Miami
FL	105367	De Soto Manor Nursing Home	1002 North Brevard Ave.	Arcadia
FL	105851	Stratford Court Health Care Center	6343 Dia de Sonrisa del Sur	Boca Raton
FL	105516	Darcy Hall of Life Care	2170 Palm Beach Lakes Blvd.	West Palm Beach
FL	105306	Atlantis Rehab and Health Care Center	6026 Old Congress Rd.	Lantana
FL	105449	North Shore NH	9380 NW 7th Ave.	Miami
FL	105882	Colonial Oaks Rehab Center-Ft Myers	3250 Winkler Extension	Fort Myers
FL	105336	Colonnade Medical Center	3370 NW 47th Terr.	Lauderdale Lakes
FL	105785	Mary Lee Depugh Nursing Center	550 West Morse Blvd.	Winter Park
FL	105301	Meadowview Life Center	1350 Sleepy Hill Rd.	Lakeland
FL	105495	Washington Manor Nsg and Rehab Center	4200 Washington St.	Hollywood
FL	105263	Newcare Venice Hlth and Rehab Center	200 Field Ave. S	Venice
GA	115327	Windward Nursing Center	Cantrell Rd. Box 640	Flowery Branch
GA	115467	University Nursing & Rehab Center	180 Epps Bridge Rd.	Athens
GA	115482	Decatur Health Care Center Inc	304 5th Ave.	Decatur
GA	115532	Social Circle Nursing and Rehab Center	671 N Cherokee Rd.	Social Circle
GA	115535	Athena Rehab of Clayton	2055 Rex Rd.	Lake City
GA	115582	Brian Center Inn	2255 Frederica Rd.	Saint Simons Island
GA	115635	Clinch Health Care Center	410 Sweat St.	Homerville

STATE	FACILITY ID NUMBER	NAME OF FACILITY	ADDRESS	CITY
GA	115641	Chatham Nursing Home I	6711 Laroche Ave.	Savannah
GA	115771	New London Health Center	2020 McGee Rd.	Snellville
GA	11A561	Heardmont Nursing Home	1043 Longstreet Rd.	Elberton
GA	115304	Lafayette Health Care Inc	205 RoadRunner Blvd.	Lafayette
GA	115469	Starcrest of Conyers	1420 Milstead Rd.	Conyers
GA	115622	Middle Georgia Nursing Home	Chester Rd.	Eastman
GA	115626	Jeff Davis Healthcare	P.O. Box 754 Burketts Ferry Rd.	Hazlehurst
GA	11A508	Smith Medical Nursing Care Center	501 McCarty St.	Sandersville
GA	115115	Specialty Care of Marietta	26 Tower Rd.	Marietta
GA	115246	Manor Care Nursing & Rehab Center	2722 N Decatur Rd.	Decatur
GA	115348	Riverview NH	809 Broad St.	Rome
GA	115464	Old Capital Inn	P.O. Box 32 Hwy. 1	Louisville
GA	115574	Brunswick Health Care Center	2611 Wildwood Dr.	Brunswick
GA	115372	Bel Arbor Health Care	3468 Napier Ave.	Macon
GA	115552	Peachbelt Health Care	801 Elberta Rd.	Warner Robins
GA	115566	Dearfield Nursing Facility	5131 Warm Springs Rd. Box 7068	Columbus
GA	115144	Twelve Oaks Health Care Center	315 Upper Riverdale Rd.	Riverdale
GA	115339	Heritage Park of Savannah	12825 White Bluff Rd.	Savannah
GA	115413	Brian Center Nursing Care/Jeffersonvle	113 Spring Valley Dr. Box 308	Jeffersonville
GA	115580	Community Care of America at Marietta	1480 Sandtown Rd.	Marietta
GA	115539	Arrowhead Nursing Center	239 Arrowhead Blvd.	Jonesboro
GA	115150	Salem Nursing & Rehab Center of Augusta	2021 Scott Rd. Box 5778	Augusta
GA	115411	Pleasant View Nursing Center	303 Anderson St. Box 713	Metter
GA	115569	Springdale Convalescent Center	2850 Springdale Rd. SW	Atlanta
GA	115313	Ashton Woods Rehabilitation Center	3535 Ashton Woods Dr. NE	Atlanta
GA	115375	Riverside Health Care Center	5100 W St.	Covington
HI	125019	Convalescent Center of Honolulu/SNF	1900 Bachelot St.	Honolulu
HI	125035	Keauhou Rehabilitation and Healthcare	78-6957 Kamehameha III Rd.	Kailua Kona
HI	125042	Oahu Care Facility	1808 S Beretania St.	Honolulu
HI	125002	Hilo Medical Center	1190 Waianuenue Ave.	Hilo
HI	125032	Hale Ho'Ola Hamakua	45-547 Plumeria St.	Honokaa

STATE	FACILITY ID NUMBER	NAME OF FACILITY	ADDRESS	CITY
HI	125024	Nuuanu Hale	2900 Pali Hwy.	Honolulu
IA	165019	Chautauqua Guest Home #2	602 Eleventh St.	Charles City
IA	165160	Urbandale Rehabilitation & Care Center	4614 NW 84th St.	Urbandale
IA	165161	Indian Hills Nursing & Rehab Center	1800 Indian Hills Dr.	Sioux City
IA	165172	Greenwood Manor	605 Greenwood Dr.	Iowa City
IA	165185	Vista Gardens Care Center	1600 Summit St.	Red Oak
IA	165188	Integrated Health Services of Winterset	1015 West Summit	Winterset
IA	165197	Cedar Falls Health Care Center	1728 W Eighth St.	Cedar Falls
IA	165227	Fort Madison Health Center	1702 41st St. P.O. Box 327	Fort Madison
IA	165237	Good Samaritan Center	326 Summerset Box 38	Fontanelle
IA	165255	Carlisle Care Center	608 Cole St. P.O. Box N-9	Carlisle
IA	165256	Elmwood Care Centre	222 N 15th St.	Onawa
IA	165291	Friendship Haven	420 S Kenyon Rd.	Fort Dodge
IA	165382	Griffin Nursing Center	606 N Seventh St.	Knoxville
IA	16E034	Eastern Star Masonic Home	715 W Third St.	Boone
IA	16E035	Evangelical Free Church Home	112 W Fourth St.	Boone
IA	16E236	Baxter Health Care Center	407 S East Ave.	Baxter
IA	16E341	Riceville Community Rest Home	915 Woodland Ave.	Riceville
IA	16E370	West Bend Care Center	203 Fourth St. NW	West Bend
IA	16E475	Sunnyslope Care Center	1600 E Steller Rd.	Ottumwa
IA	16E552	Bethany Lutheran Home	7 Elliott St.	Council Bluffs
IA	16E590	Rotary Ann Home	500 S Blaine	Eagle Grove
IA	16E664	Elm Heights Care Center	1203 S Elm St.	Shenandoah
IA	16E673	Oneota Riverview Care Facility	2479 River Rd.	Decorah
IA	165244	Manor of Malvern	905 N Second Ave.	Malvern
IA	16E372	Lakeside Lutheran Home	301 N Lawler St.	Emmetsburg
IA	16E683	Grand Avenue Care Center	3440 Grand Ave.	Ames
IA	165049	Ridgecrest Village	4130 Northwest Blvd.	Davenport
IA	16E091	I O O F Home	1037 19th St. SW	Mason City
IA	165129	Finley Hospital	350 N Grandview Ave.	Dubuque
IA	165202	Integrated Health Services	2348 E Ninth St.	Des Moines

STATE	FACILITY ID NUMBER	NAME OF FACILITY	ADDRESS	CITY
IA	165218	Eagle Point Nursing & Rehab Center	801 28th Ave. N	Clinton
IA	16E040	Ogden Manor	625 E Oak St.	Ogden
IA	16E122	Perry Lutheran Home	2323 Willis Ave.	Perry
IA	16E354	Lutheran Homes Society	2421 Lutheran Dr.	Muscatine
IA	16E705	Akron City Convalescent Center	276 South St.	Akron
IA	165146	Kahl Home for Aged and Infirmed	1101 W Ninth St.	Davenport
IA	165170	Polk City Healthcare Center	1002 W Washington	Polk City
IA	16E576	Marian Home	2400 Sixth Ave. N	Fort Dodge
IA	16E654	Fejervary Health Care Center	800 E Rusholme	Davenport
IA	165149	Rowley Memorial Masonic Home	3000 E Willis Ave.	Perry
IA	165212	River Bend Nursing & Rehab Center	715 Shoquoquon Dr.	Burlington
IA	165306	Parkview Care Center	RR #1 P.O. Box 193	Fairfield
IA	16E069	Manning Regional Healthcare Center	410 Main St.	Manning
IA	16E097	Hilltop Care Center	725 N Second St.	Cherokee
IA	16E545	Pleasant Park Estates	1514 High Ave. W	Oskaloosa
IA	16E453	Riverside Manor	1204 S Fourth St.	Ames
IA	16E686	Risen Son Christian Village	3000 Risen Son Blvd.	Council Bluffs
IA	165194	Valley Junction Nursing & Rehab Center	1211 Vine St.	West Des Moines
IA	16E563	Hallmark Care Center	3800 Indian Hills Dr.	Sioux City
IA	16E124	Perry Manor	2625 Iowa St.	Perry
IA	165175	Heritage Rehab & Healthcare Center	5608 SW Ninth St.	Des Moines
IA	16E103	Country Side Estates	921 Riverview Dr.	Cherokee
IA	16E234	Newton Health Care Center	200 S Eighth Ave. E	Newton
IA	16E688	Southfield Care Center	2416 S Des Moines St.	Webster City
ID	135007	Bingham County Nursing Home	98 Poplar St.	Blackfoot
ID	135064	Minidoka Mem'l Extended Care Facility	1224 Eighth St.	Rupert
ID	135099	Shoshone Med Center Extended Care Unit	Jacobs Gulch	Kellogg
ID	135113	Bridgeview Estates	1828 Bridgeview Blvd.	Twin Falls
ID	135122	Life Care Center of Coeur D'Alene	500 W Aqua Ave.	Coeur D'Alene
ID	135076	Midland Care Center	436 Central Midland Blvd.	Nampa
ID	135079	Integrated Health Services of Boise	8211 Ustick Rd.	Boise

STATE	FACILITY ID NUMBER	NAME OF FACILITY	ADDRESS	CITY
ID	135091	Life Care Center of Idaho Falls	2725 E 17th St.	Idaho Falls
IL	145060	Modern Care Conv & Nursing Home	1500 W Walnut St.	Jacksonville
IL	145147	Sunrise Care & Rehab-Lagrange	339 S 9th Ave.	La Grange
IL	145220	Imperial of Hazel Crest	3300 W 175th St.	Hazel Crest
IL	145309	Mariacare	350 W S First St.	Red Bud
IL	145310	Mercy Health Care & Rehab Center	19000 S Halsted St.	Homewood
IL	145430	Christian Nursing Home	1507 Seventh St.	Lincoln
IL	145517	Jeffersonian Care Center	1700 White St.	Mount Vernon
IL	145536	Our Lady of Victory NH	20 Briarcliff Ln.	Bourbonnais
IL	145564	Trinity Medical Center West	2701 17th St.	Rock Island
IL	145613	River Bluffs Nsg & Rehab Center	3354 Jerome Ln.	Cahokia
IL	145692	Flora Health Care Center	Frontage Rd. W	Flora
IL	145741	Maryhaven Inc	1700 E Lake Ave.	Glenview
IL	145776	Brightview Care Center	4538 N Beacon	Chicago
IL	145809	Lake Cook Terrace Nursing Center	263 Skokie Blvd.	Northbrook
IL	145922	City Care Center of Cobden	430 Front St.	Cobden
IL	145930	Livingston Manor	RR#1	Pontiac
IL	145942	Oak Lawn Pavilion	9525 S Mayfield	Oak Lawn
IL	14A167	Creal Springs Nursing Home	South Line St.	Creal Springs
IL	14A510	Meadows Mennonite Home	Rural Route 1	Chenoa
IL	14E140	Maxwell Manor	4537 S Drexel Blvd.	Chicago
IL	14E197	Eldorado Care Center Inc	3rd and Railroad Sts.	Eldorado
IL	14E264	Litchfield Terrace Ltd	1024 East Tyler	Litchfield
IL	14E333	Basswood Health Care Center	1015 Park Ave E	Princeton
IL	14E357	Villas of Shannon	418 S Ridge St.	Shannon
IL	145058	Heritage Manor-Chillicothe	1028 Hillcrest Dr.	Chillicothe
IL	145476	Oregon Healthcare Center	811 S 10th St.	Oregon
IL	145546	Friendship Manor of Mount Zion	1225 S Woodland Dr.	Mount Zion
IL	145625	California Gardens Nsg & Rehab Center	2829 S California Blvd.	Chicago
IL	145648	Central Nursing Home	2450 N Central Ave.	Chicago
IL	145716	Springfield Health Care Center	2800 West Lawrence Ave.	Springfield

STATE	FACILITY ID NUMBER	NAME OF FACILITY	ADDRESS	CITY
IL	145900	Prairie View Care Center	175 E Sycamore	Lewistown
IL	14A188	City Care Center	315 Brady Mill Rd.	Anna
IL	14E563	Evenglow Lodge	215 E Washington St.	Pontiac
IL	14E807	Altenheim German Home	7824 W Madison St.	Forest Park
IL	145403	Alden Poplar Creek Rehab & Hlth Care	1545 Barrington Rd.	Hoffman Estates
IL	145471	Montebello Health Care Center	16th and Keokuk	Hamilton
IL	145755	Anna-Henry Nursing & Rehab	637 Hillsboro Ave.	Edwardsville
IL	145778	Metropolitan Nursing Center	8540 S Harlem Ave.	Bridgeview
IL	145798	Countryside Healthcare Center	1635 E 154th St.	Dolton
IL	145824	Friendship Manor of Eldorado	1700 Jasper St.	Eldorado
IL	145924	Care Centre of Champaign	1915 S Mattis St.	Champaign
IL	14E618	Bartmann Nursing Home	2282 1275th Ave.	Atlanta
IL	145080	Franklin Hosp SNF	201 Bailey Ln.	Benton
IL	145466	Lynncrest Manor of Paris	310 Eads Ave.	Paris
IL	145639	Fairhaven of Chicago Ridge	10602 Southwest Hwy. Center	Chicago Ridge
IL	145733	Jerseyville Manor	1251 N State St.	Jerseyville
IL	145773	Good Samaritan Home of Quincy	2130 Harrison St.	Quincy
IL	145774	Havana Healthcare Center	609 N Harpham St.	Havana
IL	145926	Vermilion Manor Nursing Home	4792 Catlin-Tilton Rd.	Danville
IL	14E150	Monroe Pavilion Health/Treatment Center	1400 W Monroe St.	Chicago
IL	145394	La Salle Healthcare Center	1445 Chartres	La Salle
IL	145661	Jackson Square Nursing & Rehab Center	5130 W Jackson Blvd.	Chicago
IL	145793	Renaissance Care Center	1675 E Ash St.	Canton
IL	145882	Blossom Hill Nursing Centre	1050 W Jeffrey St.	Kankakee
IL	14E191	Good Samaritan Health Care Center	1910 Springfield Rd.	East Peoria
IL	14E510	Argyle Lake Nsg Center	222 North Hun	Colchester
IL	145144	O'Fallon Health Care Inc	700 Weber Dr.	O Fallon
IL	145726	Timber Point Health Care Center	205 Spring St.	Camp Point
IL	145022	Hopedale Nursing Home	2nd St.	Hopedale
IL	145289	Willow Creek Rehabilitation	40 N 64th St.	Belleville
IL	145581	Cahokia Nursing and Rehab Center	#2 Annabel Ct.	Cahokia

STATE	FACILITY ID NUMBER	NAME OF FACILITY	ADDRESS	CITY
IL	145812	Sunrise Care & Rehab Carlinville	RR #3, Box 81C	Carlinville
IL	14E129	Charleston Healthcare Center	415 18th St.	Charleston
IL	145462	Pinewood Health Care Center	515 E Euclid Ave.	Monmouth
IL	145797	International Nursing Home	207 S Buchanan	Danville
IL	14E253	Good Samaritan NH	407 N Hebard St.	Knoxville
IL	145078	Lindenwood Health Care Center	2308 W Nebraska St.	Peoria
IL	145301	Brighton Pavilion	720 Sycamore Dr.	Quincy
IL	145434	Lake Knoll Health Care Center	700 Jenkisson Ave.	Lake Bluff
IL	145719	Maple Ridge Care Centre	2202 N Kickapoo St.	Lincoln
IL	14E182	Oak Manor Health Care Center	438 W North St.	Decatur
IL	14E773	Galesburg Terrace	1145 Frank St.	Galesburg
IL	145636	Prairie View Care Center-Charleston	716 18th St.	Charleston
IL	145753	Danville Care Center	1701 N Bowman	Danville
IL	145439	Carle Arbours	302 W Burwash	Savoy
IL	145847	Colonial Care Center	3900 Stearns Ave.	Granite City
IL	14A494	Burnside Nursing Home	410 N Second	Marshall
IL	145418	Oakwood Health Care Center	605 E Church St.	Kewanee
IL	14E263	Berkshire Manor of Lexington	301 S Vine	Lexington
IL	14E672	Sullivan Living Center	E View Pl.	Sullivan
IL	145858	Elmwood Nursing & Rehab	152 Wilma Dr.	Maryville
IL	14E190	Parkview Healthcare Center	430 30th Ave.	East Moline
IN	155106	Noblesville HC Center & Alz Spec Care Center	295 Westfield Rd.	Noblesville
IN	155187	Fountainview Place Nursing & Rehab Center	3175 Lancer St.	Portage
IN	155492	Pine Lake Manor	6324 Gardner Rd. P.O. Box 639	Chandler
IN	155523	Richland-Bean Blossom Health Care Center	5911 W State Rd. 46, P.O. Box 537	Ellettsville
IN	155535	Community Care Center of Columbus	3550 Central Ave. P.O. Box 769	Columbus
IN	155565	Sunset Manor	1109 S Indiana St.	Greencastle
IN	155580	Timberview Health Care Center	2350 Taft St.	Gary
IN	15E645	North Lake Nursing & Rehab Center	601 W 61st Ave.	Merrillville
IN	155608	Lutheran Home of Northwest Indiana Inc	1200 E Luther Dr.	Crown Point
IN	15E075	Providence Home Health Care Center	520 W 9th St.	Jasper

STATE	FACILITY ID NUMBER	NAME OF FACILITY	ADDRESS	CITY
IN	155070	Green Valley Care Center	3118 Green Valley Rd.	New Albany
IN	155131	Munster Med Inn	7935 Calumet Ave.	Munster
IN	155226	North Capitol Nursing and Rehab Center	2010 N Capitol Ave.	Indianapolis
IN	155271	Coventry Manor-Miller's Merry Manor	8400 Clearvista Dr.	Indianapolis
IN	155327	University Heights Convalescent Center	1380 E County Line Rd. S	Indianapolis
IN	155393	Broad Ripple Nursing	6127 N College Ave.	Indianapolis
IN	155529	Community Care Center of Seymour	4990 N US 31, P.O. Box 769	Seymour
IN	155601	Sheffield Manor Healthcare	1141 N Sheffield Ave.	Indianapolis
IN	15E172	Colonial Nursing Home	119 N Indiana Ave.	Crown Point
IN	15E502	Englewood Health & Rehabilitation Center	2237 Engle Rd.	Fort Wayne
IN	15E606	Woodcrest Nursing Center	1300 Mercer Ave.	Decatur
IN	155042	Crestview	3801 Old Bruceville Rd., Box 136	Vincennes
IN	155115	Cardinal Nursing and Rehab Center	1121 E Lasalle St.	South Bend
IN	155159	Beverly Rehab & Specialty Care Center	2940 N Clinton St.	Fort Wayne
IN	155165	Willowbrook Healthcare Center	586 Eastern Blvd.	Clarksville
IN	155220	Dyer Nursing and Rehabilitation Center	601 Sheffield Ave.	Dyer
IN	155495	Lakeland Rehab and Healthcare Center	505 West 4th St.	Milford
IN	155499	Windsor Manor Healthcare Center	7465 Madison Ave.	Indianapolis
IN	155552	Capital Care Healthcare Center	2115 N Central Ave.	Indianapolis
IN	155096	Rosewood Terrace	1001 W Hively Ave.	Elkhart
IN	155174	Canterbury Village	5353 E Raymond St.	Indianapolis
IN	155405	Hammond Nursing & Rehab Center	1402 E 173rd St.	Hammond
IN	155603	Flinn Community	614 W 14th St.	Marion
IN	155153	Healthwin Hospital SNF	20531 Darden Rd., P.O. Box 4136	South Bend
IN	155246	Chesterton Healthcare Center	110 Beverly Dr.	Chesterton
IN	155468	Sullivan Convalescent Center	325 W Northwood Dr., P.O. Box 447	Sullivan
IN	155141	Michigan City Health Care Center	1101 E Coolspring Ave.	Michigan City
IN	155218	Regency Place of Dyer	2300 Great Lakes Dr.	Dyer
IN	155497	Saint Francis Hosp Center Trans Care Unit	1600 Albany St.	Beech Grove
IN	155572	Crestmark of Roselawn	10352 N 600 East	Demotte
IN	155278	Fontanbleu Nursing & Rehab Center	3305 South Hwy. 37	Bloomington

STATE	FACILITY ID NUMBER	NAME OF FACILITY	ADDRESS	CITY
IN	15E217	Lockerbie Healthcare Center	1629 N College Ave.	Indianapolis
IN	155095	Willow Ridge Healthcare Center	2001 Hobson Rd.	Fort Wayne
IN	155481	Cherish Nursing Center	1811 S Ninth St.	Richmond
IN	155169	Manorcare Health Services	8350 Naab Rd.	Indianapolis
IN	155191	Westminster Health Care Center	2210 Greentree N	Clarksville
IN	155277	Whispering Pines Health Care Center	3301 N Calumet Ave.	Valparaiso
KS	175146	Hutchinson Hospital SNF	1701 E 23rd Ave.	Hutchinson
KS	175363	Sunset Manor	206 S Dittmann St.	Frontenac
KS	17E029	Park Lane Nursing Home	201 E 13th St.	Scott City
KS	17E330	United Methodist Home	1135 SW College Ave.	Topeka
KS	175126	Valley View Professional Care Center	1417 W Ash St.	Junction City
KS	175184	College Park Village	2925 Florida Ave.	Salina
KS	175193	IHS Highland Park	1821 SE 21st St.	Topeka
KS	175209	Southwinds Rehab & Care Center	1800 W 27th St.	Lawrence
KS	175213	Great Plains Rehab & Nursing Center	400 S Rogers Rd.	Olathe
KS	17E200	St John Rest Home	701 Seventh St.	Victoria
KS	17E206	Lutheran Home-Belleville	500 W 23rd St.	Belleville
KS	17E363	Golden Keys Nursing Home	221 Mill St.	Neodesha
KS	175339	Colwich Health Center	202 S Fifth P.O. Box 367	Colwich
KS	175397	Rossville Valley Manor	600 Perry P.O. Box 787	Rossville
KS	175373	Life Care Center of Burlington	601 Cross St.	Burlington
KS	175078	Integrated Health Services of Wichita	5005 E 21st St. N	Wichita
KS	175176	Indian Creek Nursing Center	6515 W 103rd St.	Overland Park
KS	175179	Horizon Specialty Hospital SNF/NF	8100 E Pawnee St.	Wichita
KS	175240	Specialty Hospital of Mid-America SNF	6509 W 103rd St.	Overland Park
KS	175278	Parkway Health Care Center	2840 S Hillside St.	Wichita
KS	175331	Silver Oak Health & Rehabilitation	2813 S Broadacres Rd.	Hutchinson
KS	175273	Lincoln East Nursing Home	4007 E Lincoln St.	Wichita
KS	175099	Wichita Healthcare & Rehab Center	932 N Topeka St.	Wichita
KS	175332	Village Manor	1100 W 15th St.	Ottawa
KS	17E567	Walnut Hill Nursing Center	2720 E 12th Ave. P.O. Box 845	Winfield

STATE	FACILITY ID NUMBER	NAME OF FACILITY	ADDRESS	CITY
KS	175269	Southgate Village Life Care Center	4101 SW Martin Dr.	Topeka
KS	175321	Heartland Care Center	2075 SW Fillmore St.	Topeka
KS	175324	Beverly Health & Rehab of El Dorado	900 Country Club Ln.	El Dorado
KS	175133	Prestige Rehab & Nursing Center	215 N Lamar Ave.	Haysville
KS	17E572	Terrace Gardens Nursing Center	1315 N West St.	Wichita
KS	17E509	Coffeyville Nursing Home	1203 W 14th St.	Coffeyville
KS	175274	Christ Villa Nursing Center	1555 N Meridian St.	Wichita
KY	185178	Christopher East Health Care Facility	4200 Browns Ln.	Louisville
KY	185198	Sunrise Care & Rehab-Limestone St.	1527 North Limestone St.	Lexington
KY	185233	Shelby Manor Health Center	100 Church View St.	Shelbyville
KY	185356	Annie Walker Nursing Home	Bridgett Dr. Box 639	Mount Sterling
KY	185400	Hearthstone Place	506 Allenville Rd.	Elkton
KY	185402	Medco Center of Henderson	2500 N Elm St.	Henderson
KY	185090	Woodspoint Geriatric Care Center	7300 Woodspoint Dr.	Florence
KY	185103	Berea Hospital	305 Estill St.	Berea
KY	185116	Lexington Centre for Health and Rehab	353 Waller Ave.	Lexington
KY	185120	Hillcrest Health Care Center	3740 Old Hartford Rd.	Owensboro
KY	185230	Mountain View Health Care Center	Highway 197 P.O. Box 650	Elkhorn City
KY	185254	Ridgeway Manor	Ridgeway Dr. P.O. Box 38	Owingsville
KY	185272	Medco Center of Paducah	867 McGuire St.	Paducah
KY	185300	Summerfield Health & Rehab Center	1877 Farnsley Rd.	Louisville
KY	185337	Lee County Constant Care Inc	249 E Main St.	Beattyville
KY	185363	Glasgow State Nursing Facility	State Ave. Box 199	Glasgow
KY	185431	McDowell Appalachian Regional Hospital	9879 KY Route # 122	McDowell
KY	185081	Pavilion Health Care Center	432 E Jefferson St.	Louisville
KY	185336	Medco Center of Springfield	1200 E Grundy Ave.	Springfield
KY	185408	Liberty Care Center	Hwy. 127 S	Liberty
KY	185094	Mountain Manor of Pikeville	182 S Mayo Trail	Pikeville
KY	185219	Sunrise Care & Rehab-Pimlico Parkway	3576 Pimlico Pkwy.	Lexington
KY	185330	Medco Center of Campbellsville	1980 Old Greensburg Rd.	Campbellsville
KY	185005	Murray-Calloway Co Hosp-West View NH	803 Poplar St.	Murray

STATE	NUMBER	NAME OF FACILITY	ADDRESS	CITY
LA	195275	Audubon Guest House	2110 Audubon Ave.	Thibodaux
LA	195364	West Monroe Guest House	1007 Glenwood Dr.	West Monroe
LA	195368	Hillhaven Nursing Center East	4100 North Blvd.	Baton Rouge
LA	195382	Sterling Place	3888 North Blvd.	Baton Rouge
LA	195388	Franklin Healthcare Center	1907 Chinaberry	Franklin
LA	195392	Golden Doors of Franklin	804 Polk St.	Winnsboro
LA	195402	Oakwood Village Nurse Care Center	2500 E Simcoe St.	Lafayette
LA	195416	Pinehaven Nursing Center	19364 Central Ave.	Rosepine
LA	19E122	Mary Anna Nursing Home	125 Turner St.	Wisner
LA	19E234	Crowley Guest House	1400 E Elm St.	Crowley
LA	19E283	Fountain Manor Inc	13001 Chef Menteur Hwy.	New Orleans
LA	195251	St Elizabeths Caring LLC	1020 Manhattan Blvd.	Harvey
LA	195280	Marion Nursing Home	100 W 2nd St. P.O. Box 97	Marion
LA	195414	Resthaven Nursing Center	4532 Sale Ln.	Lake Charles
LA	19E048	Moss Bluff Manor Inc	P.O. Box 12768	Lake Charles
LA	19E063	Convention Street Nursing Center	4660 Convention St.	Baton Rouge
LA	19E186	Care Center, The	11188 Florida Blvd.	Baton Rouge
LA	195321	Maison de Ville	328 Grolee St.	Opelousas
LA	195422	Rosewood Nursing Center	534 15th St.	Lake Charles
LA	19E113	Lady of the Oaks Nursing Home	1005 Eraste Landry Rd.	Lafayette
LA	195435	St Martinville Nursing Home	203 Claire Dr.	Parks
LA	19E121	Martin De Porres NH Inc	200 Teal St.	Lake Charles
LA	195303	Twin Oaks Nursing Home	506 W Fifth St.	La Place
LA	195373	Rayville Guest House	Greer Rd.	Rayville
LA	195412	Autumn Leaves Nursing Home	1400 W Court St.	Winnfield
LA	195421	Oaks Care Center, The	50 Pinecrest Dr.	Pineville
LA	19E028	Community Comfort Cottage Nursing Home	717 Madeline St.	Rayville
LA	19E263	Oaks, The	1000 McKeen Pl.	Monroe
LA	19E344	Concordia Nursing Home Inc	6818 Hwy. 84	Ferriday
LA	195266	Sunrise Care & Rehab for Lake Charles	2717 1st Ave.	Lake Charles
LA	195313	St Agnes Healthcare and Rehab Center	606 Latiolas Rd.	Breaux Bridge
LA	195365	Maison de Lafayette	2707 Kaliste Saloom Rd.	Lafayette

STATE	FACILITY ID NUMBER	NAME OF FACILITY	ADDRESS	CITY
MA	225059	Colonial Nursing and Rehab Center	125 Broad St.	Weymouth
MA	225199	Providence Extended Care Center	119 Providence St.	Worcester
MA	225219	Greenery Extended Care Center	59 Acton St.	Worcester
MA	225233	Brandon Woods Long-Term Care Fac	567 Dartmouth St.	South Dartmouth
MA	225250	Willowood Nsg & Ret Facility	Christian Hill Rd.	Great Barrington
MA	225261	Holyoke Geri and Conv Center	45 Lower Westfield Rd.	Holyoke
MA	225299	Sunrise Care & Rehab for E Longmeadow	135 Benton Dr.	East Longmeadow
MA	225333	Mariner Health Care of Methuen	480 Jackson St.	Methuen
MA	225340	Integrated Hlth Svc Grt Worc-Mill Hill	215 Mill St.	Worcester
MA	225349	Windsor Nursing & Retirement Home	265 N Main St.	South Yarmouth
MA	225357	Winchester Nursing Center, Inc	223 Swanton St.	Winchester
MA	225358	Pilgrim Manor Skilled Nurs & Rehab Center	60 Stafford St.	Plymouth
MA	225392	Ring Nursing Home East	215 Bicentennial Hwy.	Springfield
MA	225399	Governor Winthrop NH	142 Pleasant St.	Winthrop
MA	225425	Emerson Convalescent Home	59 Coolidge Hill Rd.	Watertown
MA	225444	Blue Hills Alzheimer's Care Center	1044 Park St.	Stoughton
MA	225458	Fairhaven Nursing Home	476 Varnum Ave.	Lowell
MA	225464	Greycliff at Cape Ann Conv Center	272 Washington St.	Gloucester
MA	225487	Sunrise Care & Rehab for Quincy	205 Elm St.	Quincy
MA	225499	West Roxbury Manor Nursing Home	5060 Washington St.	Boston
MA	225559	Anchorage Nursing Home	904 Mohawk Tr.	Shelburne
MA	225626	Taunton Nursing Home	350 Norton Ave.	Taunton
MA	225628	Hancock Manor Nursing Home	133 Hancock St.	Dorchester
MA	225642	Country Estates of Agawam	1200 Suffield St.	Agawam
MA	225715	Greenwood Terrace	947 N Main St.	Brockton
MA	22E216	Plymouth Nursing Home	35 Warren Ave.	Plymouth
MA	22E573	Holbrook Nursing Home	45 S Franklin St.	Holbrook
MA	225027	Wayside Center	751 Grove St.	Worcester
MA	225184	Coyne Healthcare Center	56 Webster St.	Rockland
MA	225363	Linda Manor Ext Care Fac	349 Haydenville Rd.	Leeds
MA	225372	Center for Optimum Care-Falmouth, The	359 Jones Rd.	Falmouth
MA	225380	Center for Optimum Care-Westfield, The	60 E Silver St.	Westfield

STATE	NUMBER	NAME OF FACILITY	ADDRESS	CITY
MA	225381	Northampton Nursing Home, Inc	737 Bridge Rd.	Northampton
MA	225491	Shrewsbury Nursing & Rehab Center	66 South St.	Shrewsbury
MA	225525	Cranberry Pointe Rehab & Skilled Nsg Center	111 Headwaters Dr.	Harwich
MA	225039	Mariner Health Care of N Cen Mass	360 Electric Ave.	Fitchburg
MA	225311	Meadowood Nursing Home	573 Granby Rd.	South Hadley
MA	225376	Penacook Place, Inc	150 Water St.	Haverhill
MA	225455	Craneville Place at Dalton	265 Main St.	Dalton
MA	225533	Wachusett Manor Nursing Home	32 Hospital Hill Rd.	Gardner
MA	225666	Life Care Center of Plymouth	94 Obery St.	Plymouth
MA	225565	Olympus Specialty Hosp-Springfield LTCU	1400 State St.	Springfield
MA	225580	Spruce Manor Nursing Home	388 Central St.	Springfield
MA	225291	Chapin Center	200 Kendall St.	Springfield
MA	225300	Woodlawn Manor Nsg and Rehab Center	289 Elm St.	Everett
MA	225316	Mariner Health Care at Longwood	53 Parker Hill Ave.	Boston
MA	225329	Melrose Care Center	40 Martin St.	Melrose
MA	225407	Ashmere Manor Nursing Home	George Schnopp Rd.	Hinsdale
MA	225527	Farren Care Center Inc	340 Montague City Rd.	Turners Falls
MA	22E057	Cliff Manor Nursing Home	431 Rock St.	Fall River
MA	22E202	Summerfield Oak Manor NH	19 Quirk Ave.	Holyoke
MA	225462	Gardner Skilled Nursing Center Inc	155 Green St.	Gardner
MA	225634	Sunrise Care & Rehab for Weymouth	64 Performance Dr.	Weymouth
MA	225203	Franvale Nursing Home	20 Pond St.	Braintree
MA	225262	Riverdale Gardens Rehab and Nsg Center	42 Prospect Ave.	West Springfield
MA	225305	St Mary Health Care Center	39 Queen St.	Worcester
MA	225593	Sunrise Care & Rehab for Brighton	142 Bigelow St.	Brighton
MA	225653	Copley at Stoughton Nursing Care Center	380 Sumner St.	Stoughton
MA	22E002	Acushnet Nursing Home Inc	127 S Main St.	Acushnet
MA	225686	Summerfield Elms Manor Nursing Home	269 Moore St.	Chicopee
MA	225543	Life Care Center of Wilbraham	2399 Boston Rd.	Wilbraham
MA	225377	Resthaven Nursing Home	155 Quincy Ave.	Braintree
MD	215077	Manor Care Health Services Ruxton	7001 N Charles St.	Towson

STATE	FACILITY ID NUMBER	NAME OF FACILITY	ADDRESS	CITY
MD	215104	Manor Care of Largo	600 Largo Rd. Rt 202	Upper Marlboro
MD	215133	Carroll Lutheran Village	200 St Lukes Cir.	Westminster
MD	215145	St Thomas More Nursing & Rehab Center	4922 Lasalle Rd.	Hyattsville
MD	215149	Shore Nursing & Rehab Center	420 Colonial Dr.	Denton
MD	215164	Shady Grove Adventist Nsg & Rehab Center	9701 Medical Center Dr.	Rockville
MD	215167	Church Nursing Center	100 N Broadway	Baltimore
MD	215176	Canton Harbor Healthcare Center	1300 S Ellwood Ave.	Baltimore
MD	215181	Ivy Hall Geri Center	1300 Windlass Dr.	Baltimore
MD	215186	Chesapeake Manor Extended Care Centre	305 College Pkwy.	Arnold
MD	215203	Riverview Nursing Center	1 Eastern Blvd.	Baltimore
MD	215264	Larkin Chase Nursing & Restore Center	15005 Health Center Blvd.	Bowie
MD	215002	Bluepoint Nursing & Rehab Center	2525 W Belvedere Ave.	Baltimore
MD	21E183	Maryland Baptist Aged Home	2801 Rayner Ave.	Baltimore
MD	215009	Greenbelt Nursing and Rehab Center	7010 Greenbelt Rd.	Greenbelt
MD	215020	Regency Nursing & Rehab Center	7420 Marlboro Pike	Forestville
MD	215118	Futurecare-Old Court	5412 Old Court Rd.	Randallstown
MD	215183	Mariner Health of Mount Clare	1217 W Fayette St.	Baltimore
MD	215265	Copper Ridge	710 Obrecht Rd.	Sykesville
MD	215068	Adventist Healthcare-Sligo Creek	7525 Carroll Ave.	Takoma Park
MD	215208	Greenspring Nursing & Rehab Center	4615 Park Heights Ave.	Baltimore
MD	215213	Carematrix	2700 Barker St.	Silver Spring
MD	215271	Sandtown-Winchester Nsg Rehab Centre	1000 N Gilmor St.	Baltimore
MD	215065	Medlantic Manor at Layhill	2601 Bel Pre Rd.	Silver Spring
ME	205086	Varney Crossing Nursing Care Center	45 Elm St.	North Berwick
ME	205089	Dionne Commons	24 Maurice Dr.	Brunswick
ME	205172	Sunrise Residential Care Facility	Ocean St.	Jonesport
ME	205030	York Hospital-Strater Wing	15 Hospital Dr.	York
ME	205071	Woodford Park Center for Hlth & Rehab	68 Devonshire St.	Portland
ME	205082	Greenwood Center	384 Main St.	Sanford
ME	205123	Courtland Living Center	38 Court St.	Ellsworth
ME	205141	Pleasant Heights	30 Mountain Ave.	Fairfield

ME	205162	Evergreen Manor	328 North St.	Saco
ME	205109	Marshall Health Care Facility	High Street Extension	Machias
ME	205167	Trull Nursing Home	15 May St. P.O. Box 1245	Biddeford
MI	235036	Meadowbrook Nursing Center Inc	1480 Walton Blvd.	Rochester Hills
MI	235055	Orchard Hills-A Mercy Living Center AF	532 Orchard Lake Rd.	Pontiac
MI	235249	St Francis Home	915 N River Rd.	Saginaw
MI	235288	Marvin/Betty Danto Family Hlth CC	6800 W Maple	West Bloomfield
MI	235378	Resthaven Care Center at Fountain View	280 W 40th St.	Holland
MI	235447	Harbors Health Facility	243 Wiley Rd P.O. Box 217	Douglas
MI	23E098	Friendship Manor NH	3950 Beaubien Ave.	Detroit
MI	23E768	Heartland Manor at Carriage Town	627 Begole St.	Flint
MI	235196	Belle Woods Continuing Care Center	44401 I94 Service Dr.	Belleville
MI	235360	Arbor Manor Care Center	151 2nd St.	Spring Arbor
MI	235537	Cedar Knoll Care Center	9230 Cedar Knoll Dr.	Grass Lake
MI	235256	St. Lawrence Dimondale Center	4000 N Michigan Rd.	Dimondale
MI	235468	Pembrook Nursing Center	9146 Woodward Ave.	Detroit
MI	235509	Abbey-A Mercy Living Center	12250 E 12 Mile Rd.	Warren
MI	235535	Riverside Nursing Centre	415 Friant St.	Grand Haven
MI	235544	Orchard Grove Extended Care Centre	1385 E Empire Ave.	Benton Harbor
MI	235004	Heartland HCC-Knollview	1061 W Hackley	Muskegon
MI	235022	Tendercare-Clare	600 SE 4th St.	Clare
MI	235170	Woodfield Manor Inc	1211 State Line Rd.	Niles
MI	235416	Greenbriar Nursing Home	500 School Rd.	Sterling
MI	235454	Elmwood Geriatric Village	1881 E Grand Blvd.	Detroit
MI	235508	Charter House of Farmington Hills	21017 Middlebelt Rd.	Farmington Hills
MI	235550	Willowbrook Manor	G-4436 Beecher Rd.	Flint
MI	235050	Harold and Grace Upjohn Community Care	2400 Portage St.	Kalamazoo
MI	235355	Metron of Lamont	13030 Commercial St.	Lamont
MI	235363	Heritage Manor Nursing Care Center	G 3201 Beecher Rd.	Flint
MI	235527	St James Nursing Center	15063 Gratiot Ave.	Detroit
MI	235126	Cambridge West Nursing Care Center	18633 Beech Daly Rd.	Redford

STATE	FACILITY ID NUMBER	NAME OF FACILITY	ADDRESS	CITY
MI	235273	Arnold Home	18520 W Seven Mile Rd.	Detroit
MI	235522	Hillcrest Nursing Centre	695 Mitzi Dr.	North Muskegon
MI	235479	Middlebelt Healthcare Center	14900 Middlebelt Rd.	Livonia
MI	235175	Frankenmuth Conv Center	500 W Genesee	Frankenmuth
MI	235492	Madonna Healthcare Center	15311 Schaefer Rd.	Detroit
MI	23E057	Clara Barton Terrace	1801 E Atherton Rd.	Flint
MI	235272	Heartland Community Care Center	19100 W Seven Mile Rd.	Detroit
MI	235465	Broadstreet Nursing Center	12040 Broadstreet	Detroit
MI	235545	Northfield Place	8633 N Main St.	Whitmore Lake
MI	235206	Hearthland HCC-Whitehall	916 E Lewis St.	Whitehall
MI	235366	Metron of Forest Hills	1095 Medical Park Dr.	Grand Rapids
MN	245045	Community Memorial Hospital C&NC	512 Skyline Blvd.	Cloquet
MN	245089	Roseville Good Samaritan	1415 W County Rd. B	Saint Paul
MN	245102	Sauer Memorial Home	1635 Service Dr.	Winona
MN	245182	Westwood Health Care Center	7500 W 22nd St.	Saint Louis Park
MN	245186	Trevilla of Golden Valley	7505 Country Club Dr.	Golden Valley
MN	245227	Park Point Manor	1601 St. Louis Ave.	Duluth
MN	245286	St Mary's Villa Nursing Home	119 Faust St. SE	Pierz
MN	245328	Margaret S. Parmly Residence	28210 Old Towne Rd.	Chisago City
MN	245428	Deer River Healthcare Center	1002 Comstock Dr.	Deer River
MN	245442	Spring Valley Care Center	800 Memorial Dr.	Spring Valley
MN	245474	Park View Care Center	200 Park Ln.	Buffalo
MN	245495	Leisure Hills Care Center	2801 Pokegama Ave. S	Grand Rapids
MN	245522	Luther Memorial Home	221 Sixth St. SW	Madelia
MN	245530	Samaritan Bethany Home	24 8th St. NW	Rochester
MN	245531	Colonial Place	2401 Chicago Ave. S	Minneapolis
MN	24E515	Pillsbury Board and Care Home	2500 Pillsbury Ave. S	Minneapolis
MN	245271	Nile Health Care Center	3720 23rd Ave. S	Minneapolis
MN	245366	Chris Jensen Health and Rehab Center	2501 Rice Lake Rd.	Duluth
MN	245371	Prairie View Healthcare Center	250 Fifth St. E	Tracy
MN	245414	Viewcrest Health Center	3111 Church St.	Duluth

STATE	FACILITY ID NUMBER	NAME OF FACILITY	ADDRESS	CITY
MN	245508	St Paul's Church Home	484 Ashland Ave.	Saint Paul
MN	245207	Stillwater Good Samaritan Center	1119 Owens St. N	Stillwater
MN	245245	Heritage Manor	321 NE Sixth St.	Chisholm
MN	245258	Franciscan Health Center	3910 Minnesota Ave.	Duluth
MN	245277	Arrowhead Health Care Center	601 Grant Ave.	Eveleth
MN	245318	Falls Good Samaritan Center	1402 Hwy. 71	International Falls
MN	245445	Shakopee Friendship Manor	1340 3rd Ave. W	Shakopee
MN	245506	Samaritan Bethany Heights	1530 Eleventh Ave. NW P.O. Box 5947	Rochester
MN	245370	Green Acres Country Care Center	38315 Harder Ave.	North Branch
MN	245125	Eveleth Health Services Park	227 McKinley Ave.	Eveleth
MN	245138	Ely-Bloomenson Community C&NC	328 W Conan St.	Ely
MN	245152	Crystal Lake Good Samaritan Center	3815 W Broadway Ave.	Robbinsdale
MN	245176	Itasca Medical Center C&NC	126 First Ave. SE	Grand Rapids
MN	245303	Golden Oaks Nursing Home	1025 Ninth Ave. S	South Saint Paul
MN	245308	Osseo Health Care Center	525 Second St. SE	Osseo
MN	245276	Maplewood Care Center	1900 Sherren Ave.	Saint Paul
MN	245476	Whispering Pines Good Samaritan Center	Box 29	Pine River
MN	245586	Mesabi Home	501 Jones Ave. P.O. Box 703	Buhl
MN	245009	Ebenezer Luther Hall	2636 Park Ave.	Minneapolis
MN	245552	Colonial Manor of Balaton	Hwy. 14 E P.O. Box 375	Balaton
MN	245184	Aspen Care and Rehabilitation Center	501 Eighth Ave. SE	Rochester
MO	265007	Colonial Pavilion	894 Leland Ave.	University City
MO	265149	Four Seasons Living Center	2205 Four Seasons Dr.	Sedalia
MO	265194	Troy Nursing & Rehab	200 Thompson Dr.	Troy
MO	265290	Lucy Lee Hospital	2620 N Westwood Blvd.	Poplar Bluff
MO	265294	Carrollton Nursing Center	1502 N Jefferson	Carrollton
MO	265300	Audrain Medical Center	620 E Monroe	Mexico
MO	265346	Caruthersville Nursing Center	500 Truman Blvd.	Caruthersville
MO	265353	Quail Run Health Care Center	1405 West Grand Ave.	Cameron
MO	265397	Sells Rest Home Inc	Railroad St. Rt 1 Box 6A	Matthews
MO	265434	Riverview Nursing Center	10303 State Rd. C	Mokane

STATE	FACILITY ID NUMBER	NAME OF FACILITY	ADDRESS	CITY
MO	265444	Park Place Care Center Inc	11901 Jessica Ln.	Raytown
MO	265487	Heritage Park Skilled Care	1200 McCutchen Dr.	Rolla
MO	265514	Claru Deville Nursing Center	105 Spruce	Fredericktown
MO	265516	Georgian Gardens	#1 Georgian Gardens Dr.	Potosi
MO	265560	Summit, The	3660 Summit	Kansas City
MO	265579	Monterey Park Nursing Center Inc	4600 Selsa Rd.	Blue Springs
MO	265589	St Peters Manor Care Center	230 Spencer Rd.	Saint Peters
MO	265603	St Elizabeth Manor	11400 Mehl Ave.	Florissant
MO	26A396	Woodland Manor	1347 E Valley Water Mill Rd.	Springfield
MO	26E187	Tipton Manor, Inc	601 W Morgan St. P.O. B 599	Tipton
MO	26E290	Gower Convalescent Center	323 S 169 Hwy. P.O. Box 170	Gower
MO	265099	Westview Nursing & Rehabilitation Center	1127 Timber Run Dr.	Creve Coeur
MO	265383	Fountainbleau Lodge	2001 N Kings Highway	Cape Girardeau
MO	265411	Point Lookout Village Health Care Center	1186 State Hwy. V	Hollister
MO	265534	Heritage Care Center	4401 N Hanley Rd.	Saint Louis
MO	265606	Brookside Nursing Center	518 E Marshall	Sweet Springs
MO	26E194	Beverly Manor	1317 N 36th	Saint Joseph
MO	265264	Capital Healthcare Center	1024 Adams St.	Jefferson City
MO	265431	Truman Lake Manor Inc	600 E 7th St. P.O. Box 188	Lowry City
MO	26A364	Fairfield Manor	5303 Bermuda Rd.	Normandy
MO	265261	Woodland Park Healthcare Center	2810 Jackson	Joplin
MO	265391	Milan Community Care	611 W Third St.	Milan
MO	265662	Birchway Healthcare Center	4373 W Pine	Saint Louis
MO	26E074	Lincoln Community Nursing Home	Route 1 Box 302 5 Timberline Dr.	Lincoln
MO	265182	Aurora Nursing Center	1700 S Hudson	Aurora
MO	265251	Columbia Healthcare and Rehab Center	1801 Towne Dr.	Columbia
MO	265371	Hillview Nursing & Rehab	220 O'Rourke Dr.	Platte City
MO	265373	Life Care Center of Waynesville	700 Birch Ln.	Waynesville
MO	265567	Compton Terrace Care Center	3450 Russell	Saint Louis
MO	265334	Grand Manor Nsg & Rehab Center	3645 Cook Ave.	Saint Louis
MO	265577	Marshfield Care Center, Inc	800 S White Oak	Marshfield

STATE	FACILITY ID NUMBER	NAME OF FACILITY	ADDRESS	CITY
MO	265585	Lutheran Skilled Care	1265 McLaran Ave.	Saint Louis
MO	265609	Malden Nursing Center	1209 Strokelan Dr. P.O. Box 525	Malden
MO	265666	Smithview Manor	210 W 8th Terr.	Lawson
MO	265314	Cleveland Health Care Center	7001 Cleveland	Kansas City
MO	265504	Current River Nursing Center	1015 Grand P.O. Box 488	Doniphan
MO	265522	Lakeview Healthcare Rehabilitation Center	1450 Ashley Rd.	Boonville
MO	265663	Fulton Nursing & Rehab	1510 Bluff St.	Fulton
MO	265022	Halls Ferry Nursing & Rehab	2115 Kappell Dr.	Saint Louis
MO	265159	Mary Queen and Mother Center	7601 Watson Rd.	Saint Louis
MO	265523	Forest Haven Care Center	3201 Parkwood Ln.	Maryland Heights
MO	265358	Santa Fe Trail Health Care Center	Hwy 13 S	Lexington
MO	265465	Country Woods Care Facility	Hwy. TT Route 1 Box 12827	Festus
MO	265091	Camdenton Windsor Estates	Hwy. 5 N P.O. Box 812	Camdenton
MO	265526	Chariton Park Health Care Center	902 Manor Dr.	Salisbury
MO	265500	Bernard Care Center	4335 W Pine	Saint Louis
MO	26E040	Daviess Co Care Center	Hwy 6 W	Gallatin
MO	265366	Deerbrook Pavilion	724 NE 79th Terr.	Kansas City
MS	255142	Ocean Springs Nursing Center	1199 Ocean Springs Rd.	Ocean Springs
MS	255156	Grenada Health and Rehab Centre	1966 Hill Dr.	Grenada
MS	255159	Perry County Hospital Nursing Center	P.O. Drawer Y 206 Bay Ave.	Richton
MS	255170	Magnolia Manor Nursing Home	2002 5th St. N	Columbus
MS	25A156	Pearl River Medical Complex	P.O. Box 392	Poplarville
MS	25A365	Riley Nursing Center	3716 Hwy. 39 N	Meridian
MS	25A366	Belhaven Nursing Home	1004 North St.	Jackson
MS	255148	Clinton Health & Rehab Center	101 W Northside Dr.	Clinton
MS	25A190	Tallahatchie General Hosp ECF	P.O. Box 230	Charleston
MS	255207	Plaza Nursing Center	4403 Hospital Rd.	Pascagoula
MS	255232	Corinth Health & Rehab Center	P.O. Box 1417	Corinth
MS	255188	Hillcrest Health Center	1401 First Ave. NE	Magee
MS	25E005	Crawford NH	927 Cooper Rd.	Jackson
MS	255112	Pleasant Hills NH	1600 Raymond Rd.	Jackson

STATE	FACILITY ID NUMBER	NAME OF FACILITY	ADDRESS	CITY
MS	255153	Conva Rest of Newton	1009 S Main St.	Newton
MS	25A174	Yalobusha Co NH	P.O. Box 728	Water Valley
MS	255127	Tishomingo Living Center	1410 W Quitman St.	Iuka
MS	255216	Pemberton Manor Inc	P.O. Box 1958	Greenwood
MS	255229	Holly Springs Health & Rehab Center	960 Salem Ave. Box 640	Holly Springs
MS	255157	Adventist Health Care Center	Hwy. 11 S	Lumberton
MS	25A360	Pinehaven Care Center	1251 Pinehaven Rd.	Clinton
MS	255146	Yazoo City Health & Rehab Center	925 Calhoun Ave.	Yazoo City
MT	275029	Western Manor Health Care Center	2115 Central Ave.	Billings
MT	275035	Evergreen Missoula Health & Rehab Center	3018 Rattlesnake Dr.	Missoula
MT	275115	Evergreen Bozeman Health & Rehab Center	321 N Fifth Ave.	Bozeman
MT	275049	Evergreen Polson Health & Rehab	9 14th Ave. W Box 1419	Polson
MT	275081	Friendship Villa Care Center	2300 Wilson	Miles City
MT	275112	Northern Montana Care Center	30 13th St. P.O. Box 1231	Havre
MT	275140	Aspen Meadows Retirement Community	3155 Ave. C	Billings
MT	275040	Libby Care Center	308 E Third St.	Libby
NC	345131	Meadowbrook Manor of Clemmons	3905 Clemmons Rd. P.O. Box 249	Clemmons
NC	345143	Sunrise Care & Rehab for Siler City	900 W Dolphin St.	Siler City
NC	345175	Smithfield Manor Inc	902 Berkshire Rd.	Smithfield
NC	345217	Britthaven of Jacksonville	225 White St.	Jacksonville
NC	345218	Mary Gran Nursing Center	120 Southwood Dr.	Clinton
NC	345231	Sunrise Care & Rehabilitation-Gastonia	2780 X-Ray Dr.	Gastonia
NC	345238	White Oak Manor-Charlotte	4009 Craig Ave. Box 220130	Charlotte
NC	345252	Sunrise Care & Rehab for Duplin	214 Lanefield Rd.	Warsaw
NC	345260	Guardian Care of Rocky Mount	160 Winstead Ave.	Rocky Mount
NC	345270	Brian Center Health & Retire-Spruce Pine	218 Laurel Creek Ct.	Spruce Pine
NC	345342	Big Elm Nursing Center	1285 W A St.	Kannapolis
NC	345365	Guardian Care of Kinston	907 Cunningham Rd. P.O. Box 1438	Kinston
NC	345385	Cardinal Healthcare and Rehab Center	931 N Aspen St.	Lincolnton
NC	345388	Hunter Woods Nursing and Rehab Center	620 Tom Hunter Rd.	Charlotte

STATE	NUMBER	NAME OF FACILITY	ADDRESS	CITY
NC	345396	Britthaven of Clyde	47 Morgan St. P.O. Box 459	Clyde
NC	345400	Skyland Care Center	193 Asheville Hwy.	Sylva
NC	345449	Scenic View Health and Rehab Center	115 White Rd.	King
NC	345456	Meadowbrook Terrace of Davie	316 NC Hwy. 801 S	Advance
NC	345463	Life Care Center of Hendersonville	400 Thompson St.	Hendersonville
NC	345106	Pellcare Corporation	1125 10th St. Blvd. NW	Hickory
NC	345258	Transitional Health Serv of Kannapolis	1810 Concord Lake Rd.	Kannapolis
NC	345273	Vencor Hospital-Greensboro SNF	2401 Southside Blvd. Drawer 16167	Greensboro
NC	345346	Meadowbrook Manor of Durham	5935 Mount Sinai Rd.	Durham
NC	345421	Laurels of Chatham, The	72 Chatham Business Park	Pittsboro
NC	345448	Britthaven of Greensboro	308 West Meadowview Rd.	Greensboro
NC	345092	Winston Salem Rehab and Healthcare Center	1900 W 1st St.	Winston-Salem
NC	345120	Joseph F. Coble Healthcare Center	2616 Erwin Rd.	Durham
NC	345329	Gateway Nursing Center	2030 Harper Ave. NW	Lenoir
NC	345406	Down East Health and Rehab Center	Rt. 1 Box 224	Gatesville
NC	345441	Grayland Croft	1770 Oak Hollow Rd.	Gastonia
NC	345088	Pellcare Corporation	5350 Old Walkertown Rd.	Winston-Salem
NC	345263	Britthaven of Franklin	3195 Old Murphy Rd.	Franklin
NC	345276	Integrated Hlth Srvces at Crabtree Val	3830 Blue Ridge Rd.	Raleigh
NC	345377	East Carolina Care Center	2575 W 5th St.	Greenville
NC	345387	IHS of Tarboro	911 Western Blvd.	Tarboro
NC	345475	Tsali Care Center	10 Echota Church Rd.	Cherokee
NC	345061	Horizon Rehabilitation Center	3100 Erwin Rd.	Durham
NC	345403	Cary Health and Rehabilitation Center	6590 Tryon Rd.	Cary
NC	345039	Springwood Care Center of Forsyth	5755 Shattalon Dr. Box 11907	Winston-Salem
NC	345133	Avante at Wilkesboro	1000 College St.	Wilkesboro
NC	345293	Britthaven of Hamlet	Hwy. 177 S Box 1489	Hamlet
NC	345322	Laurels of Hendersonville, The	2220 N Main St.	Hendersonville
NC	345227	Maplewood Nursing Center	543 Maple Ave.	Reidsville
NC	345134	Avante at Charlotte	4801 Randolph Rd.	Charlotte
NC	345285	Heritage Health Center	200 Heritage Way	Hendersonville

STATE	FACILITY ID NUMBER	NAME OF FACILITY	ADDRESS	CITY
NC	345389	Laurels of Forest Glenn, The	1101 Hartwell St.	Garner
NC	345130	Avante at Concord	515 Lake Concord Rd. Box 748	Concord
ND	355042	Hillcrest Care Center	E Highway 12	Hettinger
ND	355082	Central Dakota Village	501 19th St. NE	Jamestown
ND	355100	Devils Lake Good Samaritan Center	302 7th Ave.	Devils Lake
ND	355061	Hillsboro Medical Center	320 1st Ave. SE	Hillsboro
ND	355070	Bethel Lutheran Home	1515 Second Ave. W	Williston
ND	355024	Manorcare Health Services	1315 S University Dr.	Fargo
ND	355032	Heart of America Nursing Facility	802 S Main St.	Rugby
NE	285091	Indian Hills Manor	RR 2 Box 35A 1720 North Spruce	Ogallala
NE	285141	IHS at Sutherland	333 Maple St. P.O. Box 307	Sutherland
NE	285159	Plum Creek Care Center	1505 N Adams St. P.O. Box G	Lexington
NE	285182	Alegent Health Midlands Comm Hosp LTC	11111 S 84th St.	Papillion
NE	285203	Beatrice Good Samaritan Center	1306 S 9th St.	Beatrice
NE	285218	Lindenwood Nursing Home	910 S 40th St.	Omaha
NE	285221	Wedgewood Care Center	800 Stoeger Dr.	Grand Island
NE	28A050	Litzenberg Memorial Co Hospital LTC	1715 26th St.	Central City
NE	28E079	Imperial Manor Nursing Home	933 Grant P.O. Box 757	Imperial
NE	28E195	Tri Valley Health System	W Highway 6 and 34, P.O. Box 488	Cambridge
NE	28E223	Saunders Co Community Hospital LTC	805 W 10th St. P.O. Box 185	Wahoo
NE	28E257	Gordon Countryside Care	500 E 10th St.	Gordon
NE	28E275	Jefferson Community Health Center LTC	2200 N H St. P.O. Box 277	Fairbury
NE	285049	Homestead Healthcare and Rehab Center	4735 S 54th St.	Lincoln
NE	285063	Highland Park Care Center	1633 Sweetwater P.O. Box 950	Alliance
NE	285080	Hillcrest Nursing Home	309 W 7th St. P.O. Box 1087	McCook
NE	285104	Plattsmouth Manor	602 S 18th St.	Plattsmouth
NE	28E037	Ponderosa Villa	First and Paddock P.O. Box 526	Crawford
NE	28E180	Garden County Nursing Home	P.O. Box 320, N Hwy. 27	Oshkosh
NE	285095	Scottsbluff Nursing Center	111 W 36th St.	Scottsbluff
NE	285134	Elkhorn Manor Nursing Center	315 Hopper St.	Elkhorn

STATE	FACILITY ID NUMBER	NAME OF FACILITY	ADDRESS	CITY
NE	285147	IHS at Central City	2720 S 17th Ave.	Central City
NE	28A057	Alegent Health-Mem Hospital LTC	104 W 17th St.	Schuyler
NE	285137	Ville de Sante Nursing Center	6032 Ville de Sante Dr.	Omaha
NE	285149	Maple Crest Care Center	2824 N 66th Ave.	Omaha
NE	28A065	Carl T. Curtis Health Education Center	P.O. Box 250	Macy
NE	285150	Crest View Care Center	P.O. Box 861 420 Gordon Ave.	Chadron
NE	285129	Memorial Health Center LTC	645 Osage St.	Sidney
NH	30E016	Morrison Nursing Home	2–6 Terrace St.	Whitefield
NH	30E031	Eventide Home Inc	81 High St.	Exeter
NH	305084	Sunrise Care and Rehab for N Conway	1251 White Mountain Hwy.	North Conway
NH	305052	Ridgewood Center Genesis Eldercare	25 Ridgewood Rd.	Bedford
NH	305087	Mountain View Nursing Home	Route 171	Ossipee
NH	30E062	Merriman House-ECU (Memorial Hospital)	Intervale Rd.	North Conway
NH	305057	Courville at Manchester LLC	44 West Webster St.	Manchester
NH	305081	Sunrise Care & Rehab for Rochester	62 Rochester Hill Rd.	Rochester
NJ	315009	Runnells Spec Hosp of Union Cty	40 Watchung Way	Berkeley Heights
NJ	315064	Ashbrook NH	1610 Raritan Rd.	Scotch Plains
NJ	315182	Bridgeway Care Center	270 Route 28	Bridgewater
NJ	315201	Lutheran Home-Moorestown	255 E Main St.	Moorestown
NJ	315221	Hamilton Plaza Nursing Center	56 Hamilton Ave.	Passaic
NJ	315246	Manor Care Hlth Svcs W Deptford	550 Jessup Rd.	West Deptford
NJ	315247	West Caldwell Care Center	165 Fairfield Ave.	West Caldwell
NJ	315271	Parkview Health Care Center	P.O. Box 391 Fifth & Park Ave.	Carneys Point
NJ	315275	Lakeview Center	963 Ocean Ave.	Lakewood
NJ	315277	King David Care Center	166 S Caroline Ave.	Atlantic City
NJ	315282	Pinebrook Care Center	104 Pension Rd.	Englishtown
NJ	315285	Freehold Rehabilitation & Nursing Center	3419 Hwy. 9	Freehold
NJ	315316	Brakely Park Center	290 Red School Ln.	Phillipsburg
NJ	315344	Castle Hill Health Care Center	615 23rd St.	Union City
NJ	315346	New Jersey Veterans Memorial Home	1 Veterans Dr.	Paramus

STATE	FACILITY ID NUMBER	NAME OF FACILITY	ADDRESS	CITY
NJ	315140	Raritan Health Extended Care Center	633 Route 28	Raritan
NJ	315159	Camden County Health Services Center	Collier Dr. P.O. Box 1639	Lakeland
NJ	315179	Lutheran Home at Ocean View	2721 Route 9	Ocean View
NJ	315233	Nursing Center at Vineland	1640 S Lincoln Ave.	Vineland
NJ	315069	Tower Lodge NH	1506 Gully Rd.	Wall
NJ	315091	Cranford Health Extended Care Center	205 Birchwood Ave.	Cranford
NJ	315096	White Birch NH	59 Birch St.	Paterson
NJ	315134	Harborside Healthcare-Woods Edge	875 Rt. 206 N	Bridgewater
NJ	315258	Lacey Center Genesis Eldercare	916 Lacey Rd.	Forked River
NJ	315328	Maple Glen Center	12–15 Saddle River Rd.	Fairlawn
NJ	315331	Kessler Care Center at Great Falls	77 E 43rd St.	Paterson
NJ	315039	Roosevelt Care Center-Middlesex Cty	1 Roosevelt Dr.	Edison
NJ	315066	Northfield Manor NH	787 Northfield Ave.	West Orange
NJ	315178	Garden State Health Care Center	140 Park Ave.	East Orange
NJ	315202	Lopatcong Center	390 Red School Ln.	Phillipsburg
NJ	315125	Bayview Convalescent Center Inc	395 Lakeside Blvd.	Bayville
NJ	315032	Mt Laurel Convalescent Center	3706 Church Rd.	Mount Laurel
NJ	315290	Heritage at Norwood	100 McClellan St.	Norwood
NJ	31A072	Pineland NH	555 Squankum Rd.	Lakewood
NJ	315255	Liberty House NH	620 Montgomery St.	Jersey City
NJ	315278	Hospitality Care Center	300 Broadway	Newark
NM	325060	Paloma Blanca Health & Rehabilitation	1509 University Blvd. NE	Albuquerque
NM	325061	Betty Dare Good Samaritan	3101 N Florida Ave.	Alamogordo
NM	325070	Red Rocks Care Center	3720 Churchrock Rd.	Gallup
NM	325079	Mimbres Memorial Nursing Home	900 W Ash	Deming
NM	32E048	Laguna Rainbow Elderly Care Center	P.O. Box 490	Casa Blanca
NM	325047	Casa de Oro Care Center	1005 Hill Rd.	Las Cruces
NM	325089	Valle Norte Caring Center	8820 Horizon Blvd. NE	Albuquerque
NM	325036	Las Palomas Nursing & Rehab Center	8100 Palomas Ave. NE	Albuquerque
NM	325039	Las Cruces Nursing Center	2029 Sagecrest Ct.	Las Cruces

STATE	NUMBER	NAME OF FACILITY	ADDRESS	CITY
NV	295017	Desert Lane Care Center	660 Desert Ln.	Las Vegas
NV	295022	Fallon Convalescent Center	365 W A St.	Fallon
NV	295039	Valley Meadows Rehab & Subacute Care	806 Tillman Ln.	Gardnerville
NV	29E036	Cheyenne Residential and Nursing Center	2860 E Cheyenne	North Las Vegas
NY	335048	Williamsbridge Manor NH	1540 Tomilson Ave.	Bronx
NY	335156	South Shore Healthcare	275 W Merrick Rd.	Freeport
NY	335293	Franklin Co NH	Finney Blvd.	Malone
NY	335340	Plaza NH D/B/A Rosewood Heights HC	614 S Crouse Ave.	Syracuse
NY	335383	St Cabrini NH	115 S Broadway	Dobbs Ferry
NY	335428	Lewis Co General Hosp SNF	7785 N State St.	Lowville
NY	335454	United Helpers NH SNF	8101 SH 608	Ogdensburg
NY	335563	Rome Memorial Hospital, Inc RHCF	1500 N James St.	Rome
NY	335608	Ruth Taylor NH	25 Bradhurst Ave.	Hawthorne
NY	335609	Marcus Garvey Manor NH	810-20 St. Marks Ave.	Brooklyn
NY	335768	Cortland Memorial Nursing Facility	134 Homer Ave.	Cortland
NY	335775	St Barnabas Nursing Home	2175 Quarry Rd.	Bronx
NY	335142	Heritage Park Health Care Center	150 Prather Ave.	Jamestown
NY	335165	New Surfside Nursing Home	22-41 New Haven Ave.	Far Rockaway
NY	335323	Victory Lake Nursing Center	101 North Quaker Lane	Hyde Park
NY	335324	Amsterdam Memorial Hospital RHCF	4988 ST HWY. 30	Amsterdam
NY	335333	Hollis Park Manor NH	191-06 Hillside Ave.	Hollis
NY	335337	Howe Ave NH	16 Guion Pl.	New Rochelle
NY	335403	Newark Wayne Community Hosp	P.O. Box 111 Driving Park Ave.	Newark
NY	335406	Wayne Co NH	Rt. 31	Lyons
NY	335425	Albany Co NH	Albany-Shaker Rd.	Albany
NY	335439	Nortonian NH	1335 Portland Ave.	Rochester
NY	335474	United Home for Aged Inc	391 Pelham Rd.	New Rochelle
NY	335565	Barnwell NH	Church St.	Valatie
NY	335586	Van Allen NH	775 E Monroe St.	Little Falls
NY	335657	Campbell Hall Health Care Center	23 Kiernan Rd.	Campbell Hall
NY	335732	HRF NH Co of Rome Inc-Bethany House	800 W Chestnut St.	Rome

STATE	FACILITY ID NUMBER	NAME OF FACILITY	ADDRESS	CITY
NY	335771	Throgs Neck Extended Care Facility	707 Throgs Neck Expressway	Bronx
NY	335780	Casa Promesa	308 E 175th St.	Bronx
NY	335807	Grace Manor Health Care Facility Inc	10 Symphony Cir.	Buffalo
NY	335044	Far Rockaway NH	13-11 Virginia St.	Far Rockaway
NY	335136	Loretto Geriatric Center	700 E Brighton Ave.	Syracuse
NY	335321	Split Rock NH	3525 Baychester Ave.	Bronx
NY	335592	St Regis NH	89 Grove St.	Massena
NY	335658	Groton Community Health Care Center	120 Sykes St.	Groton
NY	335667	Friedman Rehab Institute for Children	Spring Valley Rd.	Ossining
NY	335720	River Manor Care Center	630 E 104th St.	Brooklyn
NY	335205	Dover NH	1919 Cortelyou Rd.	Brooklyn
NY	335409	Sunnyside NH	Bridgeport-Collamer Rd.	East Syracuse
NY	335589	Stonehedge NH	801 N James St.	Rome
NY	335638	Delaware Heights Health Care Center	1014 Delaware Ave.	Buffalo
NY	335706	IRA Davenport Hospital SNF HRF	P.O. Box 350 Rt. 54	Bath
NY	335750	Fishkill Health Related Center, Inc	130 North Rd.	Beacon
NY	335001	Madonna Home of Mercy Hosp SNF	218 Stone St.	Watertown
NY	335017	Reconstruction Home Inc	318 S Albany St.	Ithaca
NY	335303	Mount St Mary's Long-Term Care Fac	2600 Main St.	Niagara Falls
NY	335619	Highland Nursing Home Inc	182 Highland Rd.	Massena
NY	335735	Good Samaritan Lutheran Health Care Center	125 Rockefeller Rd.	Delmar
NY	335794	Loretto Utica Center	1445 Kemble St.	Utica
NY	335253	Vivian Teal Howard RHCF	116 E Castle St.	Syracuse
NY	335382	Mercy Health & Rehab Center NH Co Inc	3 St. Anthony St.	Auburn
NY	335716	Forest Manor Nursing Home	6 Medical Plaza	Glen Cove
NY	335727	Betsy Ross Rehabilitation Center, Inc	Elsie Street-Cedar Brook Ln.	Rome
NY	335260	Summit Park Hosp-Rockland Co Infirmary	Sanitorium Rd.	Pomona
NY	335368	University Heights NH Inc	325 Northern Blvd	Albany
NY	335249	Lakeside NH	1229 Trumansburg Rd.	Ithaca
OH	365283	Hocking Valley Community Hospital	P.O. Box 966 State Rt. 664 N	Logan
OH	365572	Eastland Care Center	2425 Kimberly Pkwy. E	Columbus

STATE	NUMBER	NAME OF FACILITY	ADDRESS	CITY
OH	365626	IHS at Carriage-by-the-Lake	1957 North Lakeman Dr.	Bellbrook
OH	365690	Lebanon Health Care Center	115 Oregonia Rd. P.O. Box 376	Lebanon
OH	365877	Riverside, The	1390 King Tree Dr.	Dayton
OH	365898	Harborside Healthcare-Sylvania R&N Center	5757 Whiteford Rd.	Sylvania
OH	365930	Catalpa Health and Rehabilitation Center	3650 Klepinger Rd.	Dayton
OH	366112	Brown Memorial Home Inc	158 E Mound St.	Circleville
OH	36E071	Sunrise Manor and Convalescent Center Inc	3434 State Rt. 132	Amelia
OH	36E454	Horizon Meadows	1495 Freshley Rd.	Alliance
OH	36F031	Valley View Nursing Home	56143 Colerain Pike	Martins Ferry
OH	365206	Manor Care Health Services	140 County Line Rd.	Westerville
OH	365304	Clifton Care Center	625 Probasco St.	Cincinnati
OH	365315	Heartland-Victorian Village	920 Thurber Dr. W	Columbus
OH	365504	Wesley Glen Inc	5155 N High St.	Columbus
OH	365529	Gardenview Nursing Home	3544 Washington Ave.	Cincinnati
OH	365545	Ashley Place Health Care, Inc	5291 Ashley Cir.	Youngstown
OH	365552	Blanchester Care Center	839 E Cherry St.	Blanchester
OH	366099	I O O F Home of Ohio Inc	404 E McCreight Ave.	Springfield
OH	36E021	Russell Nursing Home	5176 Washington Rd.	Albany
OH	36E421	Hallmark Care Center, Inc	605 Front St.	Portsmouth
OH	365648	Willow Knoll Retirement Community	4400 Vannest Ave.	Middletown
OH	365734	East Galbraith Health Care Center Inc	3889 E Galbraith Rd.	Cincinnati
OH	365795	Carrington South Health Care Center Inc	850 E Midlothian Blvd.	Youngstown
OH	365848	Austin Retirement Village	3071 N Elyria Rd.	Wooster
OH	365918	Hillside Nursing Home	3539 Eden Ave.	Cincinnati
OH	36E209	Christian Care of Cincinnati Inc	1067 Compton Rd.	Cincinnati
OH	36E238	Hillandale Manor	1691 Hillandale Dr.	Euclid
OH	36F011	Butler County Care Facility	1800 Princeton Rd.	Hamilton
OH	365005	Summit Nursing & Convalescent Home Inc	2586 Lafeuille Ave.	Cincinnati
OH	365148	Oak Pavilion Nursing Center	510 Oak St.	Cincinnati
OH	365363	Community Multicare Center	908 Symmes Rd.	Fairfield
OH	365485	Flint Ridge Nsg & Rehab Center of Newark	1450 W Main St.	Newark

STATE	FACILITY ID NUMBER	NAME OF FACILITY	ADDRESS	CITY
OH	365515	Hickory Creek Nursing Center	3421 Pinnacle Rd.	Dayton
OH	365550	Oak Hills Nursing Center	3650 Beavercrest Dr.	Lorain
OH	365644	Winchester Place Nsg & Rehab Center	36 Lehman Dr.	Canal Winchester
OH	365663	Genoa Care Center	300 Cherry St.	Genoa
OH	365815	Country Club Center II	1350 Yauger Rd.	Mount Vernon
OH	365869	Bryden Place, Inc	1169 Bryden Rd.	Columbus
OH	366025	Mount Healthy Christian Home Inc	8097 Hamilton Ave.	Cincinnati
OH	366038	Leigh Lane Care Center	238 S Washington St.	Greenfield
OH	366084	Vancrest Health Care Center of Eaton	1320 Eaton-Gettysburg Rd.	Eaton
OH	366105	Columbia Health Care Center	21 W Columbia Ave.	Cincinnati
OH	366121	Zion Care Center Inc	3610 Washington Ave.	Cincinnati
OH	36F353	Cedars of Lebanon	102 E Silver St.	Lebanon
OH	36F474	Oak Hill Comm Medical Center LTC	350 Charlotte Ave.	Oak Hill
OH	365045	Hillebrand Nursing Center	4320 Bridgetown Rd.	Cincinnati
OH	365065	Harrison House Inc	2171 Harrison Ave.	Cincinnati
OH	365218	Blue Ash Nursing and Conv Home Inc	4900 Cooper Rd.	Cincinnati
OH	365520	Pedone Nursing Center	19900 Clare Ave.	Maple Heights
OH	365708	Rolling Acres Care Center	9625 Market St.	North Lima
OH	365864	Union Manor	18000 State Rt. 4	Marysville
OH	365929	Rosegate Care Center	1850 Crown Park Ct.	Columbus
OH	365296	Ridgewood Place	3558 Ridgewood Rd.	Akron
OH	365423	Mount Washington Care Center	6900 Beechmont Ave.	Cincinnati
OH	365475	Woodlawn Nursing Home	535 Lexingon Ave.	Mansfield
OH	365493	Bethany Lutheran Village	6451 Far Hills Ave.	Dayton
OH	365741	Ashtabula County Nursing Home	5740 Dibble Rd.	Kingsville
OH	366023	Twin Towers	5343 Hamilton Ave.	Cincinnati
OH	365080	Golden Age Retirement Home	3635 Reading Rd.	Cincinnati
OH	365152	Morning View Care Center New Phila Inc	2594 E High Ave.	New Philadelphia
OH	365178	Kenwood Terrace Nursing Center Inc	8440 Montgomery Rd.	Cincinnati
OH	365491	Altercare of Forest Hills	736 Lakeview Rd.	Cleveland
OH	365852	Camargo Manor Nursing Home	7625 Camargo Rd.	Cincinnati

STATE	FACILITY ID NUMBER	NAME OF FACILITY	ADDRESS	CITY
OH	36F123	Golden Years Nursing Home	2436 Old Oxford Rd.	Hamilton
OH	365118	Geriatric Center of Mansfield	50 Blymer Ave.	Mansfield
OH	365721	Overbrook Center	333 Page St.	Middleport
OH	36E631	Riverview Nursing Home	925 N Fourth St.	Steubenville
OH	365716	Grafton Oaks Nursing Center	405 Grafton Ave.	Dayton
OH	36E026	Flushing Hills Nursing Home Inc	1000 E High St.	Flushing
OH	36E281	Lutheran Old Folks Home	131 N Wheeling St.	Toledo
OH	36E379	Ketcham Nursing Home Inc	Rt. 2, 14063 State Rt. 37 E	Crooksville
OH	365415	Pulley Care Center, Inc	Rt. 4 P.O. Box 349A	South Point
OH	365348	Arbors at Gallipolis	170 Pinecrest Dr.	Gallipolis
OH	365490	Victory Park Nursing Home Inc	1578 Sherman Ave.	Norwood
OH	365789	Sanctuary at Whispering Meadows	437 Blackwood Ave.	Dayton
OK	375070	Manorcare Health Services-Norman	1210 W Robinson	Norman
OK	375102	Cimarron Nursing Center	905 Beall Rd.	Kingfisher
OK	375142	Wildewood Manor Health Care Center	1913 NE 50th St.	Oklahoma City
OK	375191	Silver Crest Manor	300 W Washington St.	Anadarko
OK	375230	Leisure Village Health Care Center	2154 S 85th Ave.	Tulsa
OK	375242	B & K Nursing Center	101 S Main St.	Hobart
OK	375280	Sequoyah East Nursing Center	Rt. 1 P.O. Box 393A	Roland
OK	375284	Pleasant Manor Nursing Home	310 W Taft	Sapulpa
OK	375289	Artesian Home	1415 W 15th St.	Sulphur
OK	375293	Skiatook Nursing Home	318 S Cherry	Skiatook
OK	375294	Great Plains Regional Medical Center	1705 W Second St.	Elk City
OK	37E041	Wilson Nursing Center	406 E Main	Wilson
OK	37E185	Callaway Nursing Home	1300 W Lindsay	Sulphur
OK	37E309	Marlow Manor	702 S 9th	Marlow
OK	37E320	Frances Streitel Senior Care Center	2300 W Broadway	Collinsville
OK	37E374	Texoma Manor	Rt. B P.O. Box 83	Kingston
OK	375171	Village Health Care Center, The	1709 S Main	Broken Arrow
OK	375193	Jefferson County Care Center	1100 N Ash St.	Waurika
OK	37E416	Riverside Health Care Center II	711 N Fifth St.	Jenks

STATE	FACILITY ID NUMBER	NAME OF FACILITY	ADDRESS	CITY
OK	375151	Walnut Creek NH	2400 SW 5th St.	Oklahoma City
OK	375154	Tuttle Care Center	104 SE 4th St.	Tuttle
OK	375221	Stratford Nursing Center	131 N Magnolia St.	Stratford
OK	375223	Colonial Living Center	323 W 6th St.	Atoka
OK	375243	Jan Frances Care Center	815 N Country Club Rd.	Ada
OK	37E065	Rosewood Terrace	1200 W Canadian	Vinita
OK	375122	Norman Rehab and Hlth Care Center	201 48th St. SW	Norman
OK	375157	Western Hills Health Care Center	5396 NW Cache Rd.	Lawton
OK	375179	Crest View Life Center	1301 NW Andrews	Lawton
OK	375261	Park Place	3910 Park Rd.	Tulsa
OK	375274	Rest Haven Nursing Home	1944 N Iroquois	Tulsa
OK	375241	Rolling Hills Care Center	801 N 193rd Ave.	Catoosa
OK	375266	Sunset Estates of Watonga	816 N Nash Blvd.	Watonga
OK	375125	Willow Park Health Care Center	7019 NW Cache Rd.	Lawton
OK	375248	Amberwood Nursing Center	5900 N Robinson	Oklahoma City
OK	375291	Cedar Crest Manor	1700 Fort Sill Blvd.	Lawton
OK	375104	Rosewood Manor Nursing Center	501 E Robinson Ave.	Norman
OK	375222	Cedar Creek Living Center	600 24th Ave. SW	Norman
OK	37E436	Mustang Nursing Center	400 N Clear Springs Rd.	Mustang
OK	375187	Grand Place	501 E Grand St.	Sayre
OK	375256	Southern Oaks Manor	301 SW 74th St.	Oklahoma City
OK	37E342	Ross NH No. 1 Inc	205 N Lincoln Ave.	Wagoner
OK	37E510	Morning Star Nursing Home	3804 N Barr St.	Oklahoma City
OK	375271	Quartz Mountain Care Center	702 N Park Lane	Altus
OR	385242	Twin Oaks Care Center	950 Nandina	Sweet Home
OR	385243	St Elizabeth Care Center	3325 Pocahontas Rd.	Baker
OR	385008	Presbyterian Community Care Center	1085 N Oregon St.	Ontario
OR	385172	Evergreen-The Dalles Health & Rehab	1023 W 25th Ave.	The Dalles
OR	385188	Evergreen-Independence Health & Rehab	1525 Monmouth Ave.	Independence
OR	38A025	Sunny Vista Care Center	10435 SE Cora St.	Portland
OR	385024	Medford Rehab & Healthcare Center	625 Stevens St.	Medford

STATE	FACILITY ID NUMBER	NAME OF FACILITY	ADDRESS	CITY
OR	385171	Life Care Center of McMinnville	1309 E 27th St.	McMinnville
OR	38E083	Riverview Convalescent Center	1164 S Water St.	Silverton
OR	385053	Eugene Rehab & Specialty Care	2360 Chambers St.	Eugene
OR	38E030	Ochoco Care Center	950 N Elm St.	Prineville
OR	38E100	Tualatin Valley Health Care Center	33465 SW Tualatin Valley Hwy.	Hillsboro
OR	385220	Albany Care Center	805 19th Ave. SE	Albany
PA	395168	Colonial Manor Nursing Home	970 Colonial Ave.	York
PA	395202	Integrated Hlth Svcs Penna at Marple	43 Church Ln.	Broomall
PA	395231	Nugent Convalescent Home	500 Clarksville Rd.	Hermitage
PA	395248	Autumn Grove Care Center	P.O. Box 387 Main St.	Harrisville
PA	395256	North Penn Convalescent Center	25 W Fifth St.	Lansdale
PA	395278	St Josephs Villa	110 W Wissahickon Ave.	Flourtown
PA	395283	River Woods	One River Rd.	Lewisburg
PA	395286	Broad Mountain Nursing Rehab Center	500 W Laurel St.	Frackville
PA	395288	Stroud Manor	221 E Brown St.	East Stroudsburg
PA	395300	Wexford House	9850 Old Perry Hwy.	Wexford
PA	395371	West Haven Nsg Home	Goodview Dr.	Apollo
PA	395374	Manorcare Health Services-Yeadon	14 Lincoln Ave.	Yeadon
PA	395378	Quincy United Methodist Home	P.O. Box 217	Quincy
PA	395390	Nottingham Village	Strawbridge Rd. P.O. Box 32	Northumberland
PA	395395	Manorcare Health Services-Harrisburg	800 King Russ Rd.	Harrisburg
PA	395449	Chapel Manor Nsg & Convalescent Center	1104 Welsh Rd.	Philadelphia
PA	395458	Clarview Rest Home Inc	RD 1	Sligo
PA	395462	Brookmont Health Care Center Inc	P.O. Box 50 Brookmont Dr.	Effort
PA	395466	Milford Valley Conval Home Inc	HC 77 Box 379	Milford
PA	395484	Butler Valley Manor	RD 1 P.O. Box 1355	Drums
PA	395512	Manorcare Health Services-Sunbury	800 Court St. Circle Dr.	Sunbury
PA	395559	Mennonite Home	1520 Harrisburg Pk.	Lancaster
PA	395561	Reformed Presbyterian Home for the Aged	2344 Perrysville Ave.	Pittsburgh
PA	395602	Wesley Village	209 Roberts Rd.	Pittston
PA	395627	Beverly Manor	21 Fairlane Rd.	Mount Penn

STATE	FACILITY ID NUMBER	NAME OF FACILITY	ADDRESS	CITY
PA	395653	Woodhaven Care Center	2400 McGinley Rd.	Monroeville
PA	395678	Williamsport Home	1900 Ravine Rd.	Williamsport
PA	395683	Highlands Care Center	P.O. Box 10	Laporte
PA	395686	St Ignatius Nsg Hm	4401 Haverford Ave.	Philadelphia
PA	395690	Harlee Manor	463 W Sproul Rd.	Springfield
PA	395706	East Mountain Manor	101 E Mountain Blvd.	Wilkes-Barre
PA	395732	Heritage Shadyside	5701 Phillips Ave.	Pittsburgh
PA	395733	Shepherds Choice of Gettysburg, The	867 York Rd.	Gettysburg
PA	395737	Fairview Retirement Community Inc	780 Woodland Ave.	Lewisberry
PA	395749	Presbyterian Center for Continuing Care	39th and Market Sts.	Philadelphia
PA	395760	Manorcare Health Services-Allentown	1265 S Cedar Crest Blvd.	Allentown
PA	395767	Rose View Center	1201 Rural Ave.	Williamsport
PA	395777	Sugar Creek Sta Skilled Nsg & Rehab	RD #3 P.O. Box 29	Franklin
PA	395845	St Francis Nursing Center-North	5 St. Francis Way	Cranberry Twp
PA	395847	Clara Burke Nursing Home Inc	251 Stenton Ave.	Plymouth Meeting
PA	395858	Montgomery Hospital Skilled Nsg Unit	Powell and Fornance Sts.	Norristown
PA	395860	Loyalhanna Care Center	Ligonier St. Ext. RR 2 P.O. Box 14	Latrobe
PA	395881	Mountain View Care Center	2309 Stafford Ave.	Scranton
PA	395887	Skilled Nsg Unit Greene Co Mem Hosp	Bonar Ave. & Seventh St.	Waynesburg
PA	395888	Progressive Care Center at Hamot, The	201 State St.	Erie
PA	395904	Sanatoga Center	225 Evergreen Rd.	Pottstown
PA	395938	Berkshire Center	5501 Perkiomen Ave.	Reading
PA	395939	Lehigh Center	1718 Spring Creek Rd.	Macungie
PA	395942	Healthsouth Harmarville TU	P.O. Box 11460 Guys Run Rd.	Pittsburgh
PA	395952	Naaman's Creek Country Manor	1194 Naamans Creek Rd.	Boothwyn
PA	395964	Shippensburg Health Care Center	121 Walnut Bottom Rd.	Shippensburg
PA	395988	Continuing Care Nursing & Rehab Corp	Eighth St. at Girard Ave.	Philadelphia
PA	395997	St Francis Central Hospital SNU	1200 Center Ave.	Pittsburgh
PA	396032	Monongahela Valley Hosp Skilled Care	Country Club Rd.	Monongahela
PA	39A412	Friendly Nursing Home-Pitman	RD 1 P.O. Box 118	Pitman
PA	39E150	Zendt Nursing Home	Main St.	Richfield

STATE	FACILITY ID NUMBER	NAME OF FACILITY	ADDRESS	CITY
PA	395075	Personacare at Eastwood	2125 Fairview Ave.	Easton
PA	395083	Willis Nursing Center	1800 West St.	Homestead
PA	395110	Ashton Hall Nsg Rehab Center	2109 Red Lion Rd.	Philadelphia
PA	395252	York Terrace Nursing Center	2401 W Market St.	Pottsville
PA	395367	Oxford Health Center	7 E Locust St.	Oxford
PA	395408	Laurel Center	125 Holly Rd.	Hamburg
PA	395442	Manorcare Health Services-York North	1770 Barley Rd.	York
PA	395666	Skyvue Terrace	2170 Rhine St.	Pittsburgh
PA	396013	Northeastern Hosp Skilled Care Center	2301 E Allegheny Ave.	Philadelphia
PA	395242	Integrated Hlth Services of Hershey	P.O. Box 377 Ruhe Haus Ln.	Hershey
PA	395284	Phoenixville Convalescent Manor	833 S Main St.	Phoenixville
PA	395382	Briarcliff Pavilion Specialized Care	249 Maus Ave.	North Huntingdon
PA	395582	Hazleton Nursing Geriatric Center	1000 W 27th St.	Hazleton
PA	395673	Susquehanna Center	1909 N Front St.	Harrisburg
PA	395822	Bishop Nursing Home	318 S Orange St.	Media
PA	395823	Horizon Senior Care	300 Barr St.	Canonsburg
PA	395825	Kramm Nursing Home Inc	245 E Eighth St.	Watsontown
PA	395879	Countryside Convalescent Home Limited	8221 Lamor Rd.	Mercer
PA	395959	Caring Place, The	103 N 13th St.	Franklin
PA	395066	Jefferson Hills Manor	P.O. Box 10805 Pleasant Hills	Pittsburgh
PA	395080	Phoebe Home Inc	1925 Turner St.	Allentown
PA	395226	Spruce Manor Nursing & Rehab Center	220 S 4th Ave.	West Reading
PA	395251	Shadyside Nsg & Rehab Center	5609 5th Ave.	Pittsburgh
PA	395541	Manorcare Health Svcs-Sinking Springs	3000 Windmill Rd.	Sinking Springs
PA	395855	Hill View Manor-Laurence County Home	2801 Ellwood Rd.	New Castle
PA	395948	Lawson Nursing Home Inc	540 Coal Valley Rd.	Clairton
PA	395164	St John Lutheran Care Center	500 Wittenberg Way P.O. Box 928	Mars
PA	395311	Integrated Hlth Svcs Bryn Mawr Chateau	956 Railroad Ave. & Polo Rd.	Bryn Mawr
PA	395316	Miners Memorial Geriatric Center	360 W Ruddle St. P.O. Box 67	Coaldale
PA	395412	St Joseph Nsg & Hlth Care Center	5324 Penn Ave.	Pittsburgh
PA	395440	Manorcare Health Services-Camp Hill	1700 Market St.	Camp Hill

STATE	FACILITY ID NUMBER	NAME OF FACILITY	ADDRESS	CITY
PA	395708	Praxis Nursing Home	500 Washington St.	Easton
PA	395782	Fairview Care Center of Bethlehem Pike	184 Bethlehem Pike	Philadelphia
PA	395799	Lemington Center	1625 Lincoln Ave.	Pittsburgh
PA	395817	Manorcare Health Services-Yardley	1480 Oxford Valley Rd.	Yardley
PA	395040	Eliza Cathcart Health Center	445 Valley Forge Rd.	Devon
PA	395223	West Shore Health & Rehab Center	770 Poplar Church Rd.	Camp Hill
PA	395353	Heritage Nursing Home Inc	200 S Main St.	Athens
PA	395360	Germantown Home	6950 Germantown Ave.	Philadelphia
PA	395790	St Margaret Seneca Place	5360 Saltsburg Rd.	Verona
PA	395867	Lakeview Senior Care & Living Center	15 W Willow St.	Smethport
PA	396003	Manor Care Health Services-Monroeville	885 Macbeth Dr.	Monroeville
PA	395950	Stephen Smith Home for the Aged	4400 W Girard Ave.	Philadelphia
PA	395399	Mercy Douglas Human Service Center	4508-38 Chestnut St.	Philadelphia
PA	395400	Heatherbank	745 Chiques Hill Rd.	Columbia
PA	395519	Mainline Nsg and Rehab Center	283 E Lancaster Ave.	Malvern
PA	395773	St Francis Nursing Center East	745 N Highland Ave.	Pittsburgh
PA	395345	Dorrance Manor	615 Wyoming Ave.	Kingston
PA	395829	Chester Care Center	15th St. & Shaw Terr.	Chester
PA	395841	Manchester House Nursing & Conv Center	411 Manchester Ave.	Media
RI	415049	Heberts NH	Log Rd.	Esmond
RI	415052	Charlesgate Nsg Center	100 Randall St.	Providence
RI	415097	Mansion, The	104 Clay St.	Central Falls
RI	415043	Carties Health Center	21 Lincoln Ave.	Central Falls
RI	415065	Rose Cottage Hlth Care Center	151 Hunt St.	Central Falls
RI	415038	Bannister Nursing Care Center	135 Dodge St.	Providence
RI	415087	Wildflowers Health Care by the Water	Putnam Pike	Greenville
RI	415104	Roberts Health Center Inc	990 Ten Rod Rd.	North Kingstown
RI	415054	Allens Health Centre Inc	S County Trail	West Kingston
RI	415117	Edmund Place Health Center	350 Taunton Ave.	East Providence
SC	425018	Easley Nursing Center, Inc	200 Anne Dr.	Easley

STATE	FACILITY ID NUMBER	NAME OF FACILITY	ADDRESS	CITY
SC	425341	Lake Moultrie Nursing Facility	1038 McGill St., P.O. Box 1108	Saint Stephen
SC	425023	Jenkins Nursing Center	401 Murray St., P.O. Box 917	Marion
SC	425067	Bay View Nursing Center	11 Todd Dr., P.O. Box 1103	Beaufort
SC	425302	Chesterfield Convalescent Center	1450 State Rd., P.O. Box 1307	Cheraw
SC	425110	Charleston Nursing Center	921 Bowman Rd.	Mount Pleasant
SC	425155	Lancaster Convalescent Center Inc	2044 Pageland Hwy. P.O. Box 1749	Lancaster
SC	425319	Meadow Brook Health Care Center	Jones Bridge Rd. P.O. Box 33	Blackville
SC	425105	Manorcare Health Services-W Columbia	2416 Sunset Blvd.	West Columbia
SC	425326	Hallmark Healthcare Center	255 Midland Pkwy.	Summerville
SC	425143	St George Health Care Center Inc	905 Dukes St. P.O. Box 708	Saint George
SC	425156	Oakbrook Healthcare Center	920 Travelers Blvd.	Summerville
SC	425062	Brookview Healthcare Center	510 Thompson St. P.O. Box 1240	Gaffney
SC	425136	Hermina Traeye Memorial Nsg Home	3627 Maybank Hwy. P.O. Box 689	Johns Island
SC	425295	Prince George Healthcare Center	901 Maple St. P.O. Box 8188	Georgetown
SD	435036	Jenkins Living Center	215 S Maple St.	Watertown
SD	435042	Mother Joseph Manor	1002 N Jay St.	Aberdeen
SD	435062	Morningside Manor Nursing Home	101 Church St. P.O. Box 500	Alcester
SD	435071	Bethesda Home	120 W Hwy. 12	Webster
SD	435072	Castle Manor	209 N 16th St.	Hot Springs
SD	435043	David M Dorsett Health Care Facility	1020 10th St.	Spearfish
SD	435056	Winner Regional Healthcare Center	805 E 8th St.	Winner
SD	435032	Colonial Manor of Custer	1065 Montgomery St.	Custer
SD	435097	Lake Andes Health Care Center	740 E Lake St.	Lake Andes
SD	435065	Prairie Estates Care Center	600 S Franklin P.O. Box 486	Elk Point
SD	435064	Beverly Healthcare-Black Hills	1620 N 7th St.	Rapid City
TN	445111	Hamilton Co NH	2626 Walker Rd.	Chattanooga
TN	445141	Bradley Healthcare & Rehab Center	2910 Peerless Rd.	Cleveland
TN	445151	Allenbrooke Health Care Center	3933 Allenbrooke Cove	Memphis
TN	445155	Manor House of Dover	537 Spring St. P.O. Box 399	Dover
TN	445165	Wesley Highland Manor	3549 Norriswood	Memphis

STATE	FACILITY ID NUMBER	NAME OF FACILITY	ADDRESS	CITY
TN	445260	Briarcliff Health Care Center	100 Elmhurst Dr.	Oak Ridge
TN	445281	Windsor House, The	3425 Knight Rd.	Whites Creek
TN	445287	Sunrise Care & Comm Center for Jackson	131 Cloverdale St.	Jackson
TN	445293	Memphis Jewish Home	36 Bazeberry Rd.	Cordova
TN	445321	Health Care Center of Ardmore	25385 Main St.	Ardmore
TN	445331	Graceland Nursing Center	1250 Farrow Rd.	Memphis
TN	445339	Parkview Manor	2400 Mitchell Ave.	Humboldt
TN	445356	North Side Hospital SNF	401 Princeton Rd.	Johnson City
TN	445363	Standing Stone Health Care Center	410 W Crawford Ave.	Monterey
TN	445366	Tennessee State Veterans Home	2865 Main St.	Humboldt
TN	445369	Royal Care of Cleveland	2750 Executive Park Pl.	Cleveland
TN	445372	Hardin Co NH	2006 Wayne Rd.	Savannah
TN	445383	Coffee Medical Center Nursing Home	1001 McArthur Dr.	Manchester
TN	44A111	Court Manor	1414 Court Ave.	Memphis
TN	44E137	Crestview NH	2030 25th Ave. N	Nashville
TN	445202	Ripley Healthcare and Rehab Center	118 Halliburton	Ripley
TN	445218	Cordova Rehab and Nursing Center	955 Germantown Pkwy.	Cordova
TN	445231	Grand Court I	1005 Mountain Creek Rd.	Chattanooga
TN	445234	Glen Oaks Convalescent Center	1101 Glen Oaks Rd.	Shelbyville
TN	445236	Bel-Air Health Care Inc	105 N Campbell Blvd.	Columbia
TN	445267	Mariner Health Care of Nashville	3939 Hillsboro Cir.	Nashville
TN	445349	Milan Health Care	8060 Stinson St.	Milan
TN	44E436	Ridgetop Haven Inc	2002 Greer Rd. P.O. Box 138	Ridgetop
TN	445033	Nashville Metro Bordeaux Hosp SNF	1414 County Hospital Rd.	Nashville
TN	445184	Palmyra Intermediate Care Center	2727 Palmyra Rd.	Palmyra
TN	445233	Whitehaven Manor	1076 Chambliss Rd.	Memphis
TN	445241	Sunrise Care & Rehab-Sycamore View	1150 Dovecrest Rd.	Memphis
TN	445270	Tennessee Veterans Home	345 Compton Rd.	Murfreesboro
TN	445285	Reelfoot Manor	1034 Reelfoot Dr.	Tiptonville
TN	44E456	Hendersonville Nursing Home	672 W Main St.	Hendersonville
TN	445312	River Park Health Care Center	1306 Katie Ave.	Nashville

STATE	FACILITY ID NUMBER	NAME OF FACILITY	ADDRESS	CITY
TN	445354	Lauderdale Health Care Center	215 Lackey Ln.	Ripley
TN	445125	Oakville Health Care Center	3391 Old Getwell Rd.	Memphis
TN	445146	Harpeth Terrace Convalescent Center	1287 W Main	Franklin
TN	44A112	Mt. Juliet Health Care Center	2650 N Mt. Juliet Rd.	Mount Juliet
TN	445189	Kirby Pines Manor	3535 Kirby Rd.	Memphis
TN	445160	Mayfield Rehab & Special Care Center	200 Mayfield Dr.	Smyrna
TN	445238	Life Care Center of Tullahoma	1715 N. Jackson St.	Tullahoma
TX	455107	River Springs Healthcare and Rehab Center	120 Warden Lane	San Marcos
TX	455460	Fort Worth Nursing and Rehabilitation	1000 6th Ave.	Fort Worth
TX	455463	Mariner Health of North Dallas	8383 Meadow Rd.	Dallas
TX	455500	Jarvis Heights Nursing Center	3601 Hardy St.	Fort Worth
TX	455733	Heritage Place of Grand Prairie	820 Small St.	Grand Prairie
TX	455791	St Mary of the Plains Hospital	4000 24th St.	Lubbock
TX	455940	Lubbock Hospitality House	4710 Slide Rd.	Lubbock
TX	45E800	Winnsboro Nursing Home Inc	402 S Chestnut St.	Winnsboro
TX	45E997	Edgewood Manor Nursing Home	4925 Elizabeth St.	Texarkana
TX	45F064	Tutor Nursing Home, Inc	119 S 33rd St.	Temple
TX	45F366	Crane Skilled Nursing & Rehab Center	100 Campus Dr.	Crane
TX	675149	Rockport Care Center	1004 Young St.	Rockport
TX	675181	Carriage House Manor	210 Pipeline Rd.	Sulphur Springs
TX	675222	Seabreeze Care Center	6602 Memorial Dr.	Texas City
TX	675335	Care Inn of Shamrock	Hwy. 83 S	Shamrock
TX	675349	Texas Choice of Henderson	200 Southwood Dr.	Henderson
TX	675399	Canterbury Villa of Navasota	1405 E Washington	Navasota
TX	675404	Paducah Nursing Center	800 Seventh St.	Paducah
TX	675418	Seago Manor	2416 Elizabeth Ln.	Seagoville
TX	675516	Goldthwaite Senior Health Center	1207 Reynolds St.	Goldthwaite
TX	675519	Pine Haven Nursing Home	1712 N Timberland	Lufkin
TX	675526	Rose Garden Care Center	2901 FM 2767	Tyler
TX	675666	Briarcliff Health Center of Greenville	4400 Walnut St.	Greenville
TX	455413	Professional Care Center	1950 Record Crossing	Dallas

STATE	FACILITY ID NUMBER	NAME OF FACILITY	ADDRESS	CITY
TX	455557	Sunrise Care & Rehab-Corpus Christi	5607 Everhart Rd.	Corpus Christi
TX	455597	Memorial Medical Nursing Center	315 Lewis	San Antonio
TX	455628	Hilltop Village	1400 Hilltop Rd.	Kerrville
TX	455899	Olsen Manor Nursing Home	3350 Olsen Blvd.	Amarillo
TX	455996	Holiday Hills Rehab and Care Center	2428 Bahama Dr.	Dallas
TX	45E392	Kemp Healthcare Center	307 N Adams St.	Kemp
TX	675018	River Oaks Care Center	2416 NW 18th St.	Fort Worth
TX	675134	Whispering Oaks Manor	105 Hospital Dr.	Cuero
TX	675187	Southaven Nursing Center	5300 Houston School Rd.	Dallas
TX	675223	Birchwood Manor	Hwy. 64 W	Cooper
TX	675243	Green Acres Parkdale	11025 Old Voth Rd.	Beaumont
TX	675267	White Dove Nursing Center of Tyler	3526 W Erwin St.	Tyler
TX	675317	Deerings Nursing Home	1020 W County Rd. N	Odessa
TX	675483	Integrated Health Svcs of Iowa Park	1109 N 3rd St.	Iowa Park
TX	675508	Tyler Skilled Nursing and Rehab Center	810 S Porter St.	Tyler
TX	675728	Parkview Convalescent Center	2895 Lewis Ln.	Paris
TX	455514	Forest Hill Nursing Center	4607 California Pkwy. E	Fort Worth
TX	455569	Heritage Manor-Longview	112 Ruthlynn Dr.	Longview
TX	455716	Garden Terrace Health and Rehab Center	1015 W William Cannon Dr.	Austin
TX	45E470	Manor Square	414 N Hackberry St.	San Antonio
TX	675000	Beechnut Manor	12777 Beechnut St.	Houston
TX	675031	South Park Rehabilitation Nursing Center	3115 McArdle	Corpus Christi
TX	675148	Sunrise Care and Rehab for Orange	510 N 3rd St.	Orange
TX	675278	Canterbury Villa of Beaumont	1175 Denton Dr.	Beaumont
TX	675282	Country Club Manor	9 Medical Dr.	Amarillo
TX	675324	Care Inn of Plainview	224 Saint Louis	Plainview
TX	675398	Green Acres Convalescent Center	501 Timpson St.	Center
TX	675460	Park Highland Nursing Center	711 Lucas St.	Athens
TX	675480	Victoria Nursing and Rehab Center	114 Medical Dr.	Victoria
TX	675531	Clark House, The	800 Montague St.	Bandera
TX	675568	Sunset Haven Nursing Center	9001 N Loop	El Paso

STATE	FACILITY ID NUMBER	NAME OF FACILITY	ADDRESS	CITY
TX	675607	Village Creek Nursing Home	3825 Village Creek Rd.	Fort Worth
TX	455467	Alamo Heights Health and Rehab Center	8223 Broadway	San Antonio
TX	455689	San Pedro Manor	515 W Ashby Place	San Antonio
TX	455744	Mulberry Manor	1670 Lingleville Rd.	Stephenville
TX	455831	Paris Healthcare Center	610 Deshong Dr.	Paris
TX	455879	Merritt Plaza Rehab and Living Center	205 W Merritt St.	Marshall
TX	455999	Coastal Healthcare Center	524 Village Rd.	Port Lavaca
TX	45E397	Knight's Nursing Home, Inc	520 Ash Ave.	Littlefield
TX	45E886	Bur Mont Nursing Center	154 Banks Dr.	Livingston
TX	675202	Westridge Manor	611 NW Stallings Dr.	Nacogdoches
TX	675308	Kenwood Nursing Home	2918 Duncanville Rd.	Dallas
TX	675346	Heritage Oaks Nursing & Rehab Center	5301 University Ave.	Lubbock
TX	675395	Retama Manor-Del Rio	100 Hermann Dr.	Del Rio
TX	675501	Rembrandt Center	3200 W 2nd Ave.	Corsicana
TX	455684	Clairmont Longview, The	3201 N Fourth	Longview
TX	45E457	Spur Nursing Home	E State Hwy. 70	Spur
TX	45E891	Silver Haven Nursing Center	1201 Business Hwy. 287 E	Henrietta
TX	45E959	Chandler Estate in Laurel Heights, The	137 W French Pl.	San Antonio
TX	675168	Harvest Care Center of Lumberton	705 N Main	Lumberton
TX	675494	Canterbury Villa of Kingsville	316 General Cavazos Blvd.	Kingsville
TX	455020	Colonial Manor Care Center	821 US Hwy. 81 W	New Braunfels
TX	455429	Colonial Manor Tyler	930 S Baxter	Tyler
TX	455444	Manorcare Health Services	1975 Babcock Rd.	San Antonio
TX	455713	Sunrise Convalescent and Rehab Center	50 Briggs St.	San Antonio
TX	675068	Pine Haven Care Center	4808 Elizabeth St.	Texarkana
TX	675196	Pavilion Nursing Home	1720 N McDonald	McKinney
TX	675205	Fredericksburg Care Center, The	7602 Louis Pasteur Dr.	San Antonio
TX	675253	Azalea Trail	411 Springcreek Rd.	Grand Saline
TX	675272	Willow Bend Care Center	2231 Hwy. 80 E	Mesquite
TX	45E795	Whispering Pines	910 Beech St.	Winnsboro
TX	675133	Highland Pines Nursing Home Ltd	1100 N 4th St.	Longview

STATE	FACILITY ID NUMBER	NAME OF FACILITY	ADDRESS	CITY
TX	675626	Sulphur Springs Nursing Home	301 Oak Ave.	Sulphur Springs
TX	675498	Golden Plains Care Center-Canyon	15 Hospital Dr.	Canyon
TX	675095	Hallettsville Rehabilitation & Nursing	Hwy. 90 A W	Hallettsville
TX	675412	Greenbelt Nursing and Rehabilitation	4301 Hospital Dr.	Vernon
TX	675529	Austin Manor Nursing Home	5413 Guadalupe St.	Austin
TX	455655	University Manor	2400 Quaker Ave.	Lubbock
TX	675409	Mission Oaks Manor	3030 Roosevelt Ave.	San Antonio
TX	455517	Gardendale Rehabilitation and Nsg Center	Hwy. 79 E	Jacksonville
TX	455559	Sun Valley Health Care Center	2204 Pease St.	Harlingen
TX	675617	Canterbury Villa of Eagle Pass	2550 Zacatecas	Eagle Pass
TX	455787	Four States Care Center	8 E Midway	Texarkana
TX	675128	Integrated Hlth Services Wichita Falls	601 Midwestern Pkwy.	Wichita Falls
TX	455598	Colonial Park Nursing Home	509 S Grove St.	Marshall
UT	465132	Bountiful Health & Rehabilitation	523 N Main	Bountiful
UT	465056	Bonneville Health and Rehabilitation	1255 E 3900 S	Salt Lake City
UT	465111	Sandy Regional Health Center	50 E 9000 S	Sandy
UT	46A043	Bear River Valley Care Center	460 W 600 N	Tremonton
UT	465080	Rosewood Terrace	158 N 600 W	Salt Lake City
UT	465086	South Ogden Rehabilitation Center	5865 S Wasatch Dr.	Ogden
UT	465072	Salt Lake Nursing & Rehabilitation Center	165 S 10th E	Salt Lake City
UT	465065	Potomac Healthcare of Ogden LLC	524 E 800 N	Ogden
VA	495068	Harbour Pointe Medical and Rehab Center	1005 Hampton Blvd.	Norfolk
VA	495193	Henrico Hlth Care Center	561 N Airport Dr.	Highland Springs
VA	495210	Norfolk Health Care Center	901 E Princess Anne Rd.	Norfolk
VA	495255	Montvue Nursing Home	30 Montvue Dr.	Luray
VA	495272	Bethany Healthplex	1776 Cambridge Dr.	Richmond
VA	495292	Lovingston Health Care Center	Rt. 29 S Business P.O. Box 398	Lovingston
VA	49A013	Evergreene Nursing Care Center	HCR 33 P.O. Box 200	Standardsville
VA	49E001	Shore Lifecare, Inc	Rt. 1 P.O. Box 185	Parksley
VA	49E078	Augusta Nursing and Rehabilitation Center	35 Crossroads Ln.	Fishersville

STATE	FACILITY ID NUMBER	NAME OF FACILITY	ADDRESS	CITY
VA	49E083	Twin Oaks Conv Home	406 Oak Lane	South Boston
VA	495300	Heritage Hall King George	8443 Kings Hwy. P.O. Box 495	King George
VA	495305	Coliseum Park Nursing Home	305 Marcella Dr.	Hampton
VA	49E111	Mizpah Health Care Center	P.O. Box 70	Locust Hill
VA	495153	Cedars, The	1242 Cedars Ct.	Charlottesville
VA	49E119	Shenandoah Manor-Clifton Forge	Fairview Heights Rt. 1	Clifton Forge
VA	495149	Beverly Manor of Portsmouth	900 London Blvd.	Portsmouth
VA	495190	James Pointe Care Center	5015 Hungtington Ave.	Newport News
VA	495223	Chippenham Manor Nursing Center	7246 Forest Hill Ave.	Richmond
VA	495273	Lafayette Villa Health Care	3900 Llewellyn Ave.	Norfolk
VA	49E030	Highland Manor Nursing Home	Hanks Ave.	Dublin
VA	495239	Jefferson Park Center	1214 Jefferson Park Ave.	Charlottesville
VA	49E194	Brent-Lox Hall Nursing Center	1017 George Washington Hwy.	Chesapeake
VA	495237	VA Beach Healthcare and Rehab Center	1801 Camelot Dr.	Virginia Beach
VA	495047	Park View Nsg and Rehab Center	175 Hatton St.	Portsmouth
VT	475008	Vernon Green Nursing Home	Rt. 142	Vernon
VT	475031	Brookside Nursing Home of Bradford	P.O. Box 729	Bradford
VT	475039	Pleasant Manor Nursing Home	46 Nichols St.	Rutland
VT	475037	Rowan Court Health & Rehab	Upper Prospect St.	Barre
WA	505080	Life Care Center of Kennewick	1508 W Seventh Ave.	Kennewick
WA	505257	Alderwood Manor	E 3600 Hartson Ave.	Spokane
WA	505264	Tacoma Terrace	3625 E B St.	Tacoma
WA	505320	Sunrise Care & Rehab for Moses Lake	1100 E Nelson Rd.	Moses Lake
WA	505503	Sunrise Care & Rehab for Montesano	800 N Metcalf	Montesano
WA	505336	Parkside Care Center	P.O. Box 2986	Wenatchee
WA	505434	Lynnwood Manor Health Care Center	5821 188th SW	Lynnwood
WA	505502	Good Samaritan Center Hlth & Rehab on Mis	12715 E Mission Ave.	Spokane
WA	505324	Valley Terrace Nursing Center	511 10th Ave. SE	Puyallup
WA	505383	Sullivan Park Care Center	14820 E 4th	Spokane
WA	505488	Sunrise Care & Rehab-Richmond Beach	19235 15th Ave. NW	Seattle

STATE	FACILITY ID NUMBER	NAME OF FACILITY	ADDRESS	CITY
WA	505243	Evergreen Nursing & Rehabilitation Center	430 Lilly Road NE	Olympia
WA	505432	Sutton Gardens Health Care	2185 Seamount St. P.O. Box 608	Ferndale
WA	505183	Heritage	7411 Pacific Ave.	Tacoma
WA	505278	Greenwood Park Care Center	13333 Greenwood Ave. N	Seattle
WA	505400	Evergreen Enumclaw Health and Rehab	2323 Jensen St.	Enumclaw
WA	505447	Pinecrest Manor Convalescent Home	601 Power St.	Cle Elum
WA	505128	Port Angeles Care Center	825 E Fifth	Port Angeles
WA	505318	Skagit Valley Convalescent	2019 Hwy. 20	Sedro Woolley
WA	505359	Beverly Enterprises-Monarch Care Center	21428 Pacific Hwy. S	Seattle
WA	505313	Hallmark Manor	32300 First Ave. S	Federal Way
WA	505207	Southcrest Subacute & Specialty CC	W 110 Cliff Dr.	Spokane
WA	505042	Integrated Health Services of Seattle	820 NW 95th St.	Seattle
WI	525040	River Hills West Health Care Center 3058	321 Riverside Dr.	Pewaukee
WI	525230	Mequon Care Center	10911 N Port Washington Rd.	Mequon
WI	525242	Westmoreland Health Center	1810 Kensington Dr.	Waukesha
WI	525344	Mt Carmel Health and Rehab Center	5700 W Layton Ave.	Milwaukee
WI	525371	Silver Spring Health & Rehab Center	1300 W Silver Spring Dr.	Milwaukee
WI	525399	Marian Franciscan Center	9632 W Appleton Ave.	Milwaukee
WI	525460	Fall Creek Valley Nursing Home	344 Lincoln Ave. P.O. Box 398	Fall Creek
WI	525465	Cedar Lake Health Care Center	5595 Hwy. Z	West Bend
WI	525490	Virginia Health and Rehab Center	1451 Cleveland Ave.	Waukesha
WI	525510	Marian Catholic Center 2301	3333 W Highland Blvd.	Milwaukee
WI	525576	Behling Memorial Home Inc 2353	38 N Main St.	Clintonville
WI	525589	Lillian E Kerr Nursing Home 1124	2383 State Hwy. 17	Phelps
WI	525606	Strum Nursing Home	208 Elm St., P.O. Box 217	Strum
WI	525643	Pleasant View Nursing Home	N3150 Hwy. 81, P.O. Box 768	Monroe
WI	52A034	Eagle River Health Care Center 2643	357 River St. P.O. Box 1149	Eagle River
WI	52A045	Fond du Lac Lutheran Home Inc 47	244 N Macy St.	Fond du Lac
WI	52A153	Lincoln Lutheran Home	2015 Prospect St.	Racine
WI	52A431	St Anns Rest Home 245	2020 S Muskego	Milwaukee
WI	525282	Hospitality Nursing/Rehab Center	8633 32nd Ave.	Kenosha

STATE	NUMBER	NAME OF FACILITY	ADDRESS	CITY
WI	525467	Maryhill Manor Inc	501 Madison Ave.	Niagara
WI	525500	Kilbourn Care Center	2125 W Kilbourn Ave.	Milwaukee
WI	525579	Parkside Nursing and Rehab Center Inc	1201 Garfield Ave.	Little Chute
WI	525617	St Paul Home Inc 2988	1211 Oakridge Ave.	Kaukauna
WI	52A204	St Francis Home South	1500 N 34th St.	Superior
WI	525108	Allis Care Center	9047 W Greenfield Ave.	West Allis
WI	525367	Bel Air Health Care Center 2821	9350 W Fond du Lac Ave.	Milwaukee
WI	525417	Heartland of Milwaukee	3216 W Highland Blvd.	Milwaukee
WI	525527	Homme Home for the Aging	604 S Webb St.	Wittenberg
WI	52A418	Lincoln Lutheran Care Center	1600 Ohio St.	Racine
WI	525212	Riverview Manor	921 3rd St. S P.O. Box 8080	Wisconsin Rapids
WI	525475	Rivers Bend Health/Rehab Center 3210	960 S Rapids Rd.	Manitowoc
WI	525429	Family Heritage Medical and Rehab Center	130 Strawberry Ln.	Wisconsin Rapids
WI	52A382	Dallas Health Care Center	104 Dallas St. E P.O. Box 165	Dallas
WI	525328	Court Manor Health & Rehab Services	911 3rd St. W	Ashland
WI	525309	Colonial Manor 3178	1616 W Bender Rd.	Milwaukee
WI	525226	Christopher East Health/Rehab Center 3057	1132 E Knapp St.	Milwaukee
WI	525413	Willowcrest Care Center 2798	3821 S Chicago Ave.	South Milwaukee
WI	525439	St Mary's Nursing Home	3515 W Hadley	Milwaukee
WI	525601	Millway Care Center 3231	8534 W Mill Rd.	Milwaukee
WI	525218	Highland Transitional Care 4047	2308 University Ave.	Madison
WI	525398	St Croix Care Center	1505 Orrin Rd.	Prescott
WI	525300	Shores Health & Rehab Center 2805	6925 N Port Washington Rd.	Glendale
WI	525255	Heartland HCC Marina View	1522 N Prospect Ave.	Milwaukee
WI	525508	Meadow Park Health Care Center	709 Meadow Park Dr.	Clinton
WV	515082	Fairmont General Hospital D/P	1325 Locust Ave.	Fairmont
WV	51A006	Ravenswood Village Health Center	200 Ritchie St.	Ravenswood
WV	515021	Fairhaven Rest Home	302 Adams Ave.	Huntington
WV	51E095	Integrated Health Services of WV	Rt. 9 P.O. Box 220	Charles Town
WV	515035	Riverside Nursing Home	6500 Maccorkle Ave. SW	Saint Albans
WV	515087	Cedar Ridge Health Care Center	302 Cedar Ridge Rd.	Sissonville

STATE	FACILITY ID NUMBER	NAME OF FACILITY	ADDRESS	CITY
WV	515146	Marmet Health Care Center	1 Sutphin Ave.	Marmet
WV	515071	Americare Salem Nsg & Rehab Center	146 Water St.	Salem
WV	515041	Parkview Healthcare Center	1600 27th St.	Parkersburg
WV	515086	Heartland of Beckley	300 Dry Hill Rd.	Beckley
WV	515060	Heritage Manor Nsg & Rehab Genesis Corp	101 13th St.	Huntington
WY	535030	New Horizons Care Center	1111 Lane 12 P.O. Box 518	Lovell
WY	535050	Morning Star Manor	4 North Fork Rd. P.O. Box 859	Fort Washakie
WY	535051	Canyon Hills Manor	1210 Canyon Hills Rd. P.O. Box 1325	Thermopolis
WY	53A016	Niobrara County Nursing Home	921 Ballencee Ave. P.O. Box 780	Lusk
WY	535027	West Park Long-Term Care Center	707 Sheridan Ave.	Cody

APPENDIX N: State Survey Agencies

These agencies can help you find state survey reports on nursing homes you may be considering. They also might help you learn if there are any penalties or violations cited for a particular facility.

STATE	STATE SURVEY AGENCY NAME & ADDRESS	CONTACT NUMBERS
Alabama	Division of Licensure & Certification Alabama Dept. of Public Health P.O. Box 303017 Montgomery, AL 36130-3017	334-206-5075 (Fax) 334-206-5088
Alaska	Medical Assistance Health Facilities Licensing & Certification 4730 Business Park Boulevard, Suite 18, Bldg H Anchorage, AK 99503-7137	907-561-8081 (Fax) 907-561-3011
Arizona	Assurance/Licensure, Health/Child Care Rev Services Arizona Dept. of Health Services 1647 E. Morten Avenue, #220 Phoenix, AZ 85020	602-674-4200 (Fax) 602-861-0645
Arkansas	Health Facilities Services Arkansas Dept. of Health Freeway Medical Twr. 5800 W. 10th Street, #400 Little Rock, AR 72204	501-661-2201 (Fax) 501-661-2165
	Office of Long-Term Care, Medical Services Arkansas Dept. of Human Services P.O. Box 8059, Slot #400 Little Rock, AR 72205	501-682-8486 (Fax) 501-682-6171
California	Licensing & Certification Division California Dept. of Health Services P.O. Box 942732, 1800 3rd Street, #210 Sacramento, CA 94234	916-445-3054 (Fax) 916-445-6979
Colorado	Health Facilities Division, Building A, 2nd Floor Colorado Dept. of Public Health & Environment 4300 Cherry Creek Drive, South Denver, CO 80222-1530	303-692-2819 (Fax) 303-782-4883
Connecticut	Division of Health Systems Regulation Connecticut Dept. of Public Health 410 Capitol Avenue, MS#12HSR Hartford, CT 06134-0308	860-509-7400 (Fax) 860-509-7543
Delaware	Office of Health Facilities Certification & Licensure 3 Mill Road, #308 Wilmington, DE 19806-2114	302-577-6666 (Fax) 302-577-6672

STATE	STATE SURVEY AGENCY NAME & ADDRESS	CONTACT NUMBERS
District of Columbia	Service Facility Regulation Administration Dept. of Consumer and Regulatory Affairs 614 H Street NW, 10th Floor Washington, DC 20001	202-727-7190 (Fax) 202-727-7780
Florida	Division of Health Quality Assurance Agency for Health Care Administration 2727 Mahan Drive, #170 Tallahassee, FL 32308-5403	850-487-2528 (Fax) 850-487-6240
Georgia	Office of Regulatory Services Georgia Dept. of Human Resources 2 Peachtree Street NW, #32-415 Atlanta, GA 30303-3167	404-657-5700 (Fax) 404-657-5708
Hawaii	Hospital & Medical Facilities Branch Hawaii State Dept. of Health 1270 Queen Emma Street, #1100 Honolulu, HI 96813-2307	808-586-4090 (Fax) 808-586-4747
Idaho	Bureau of Facility Standards, Division of Medicaid Idaho Dept. of Health and Welfare 450 W. State Street, 3rd Floor Boise, ID 83720-0036	208-334-6626 (Fax) 208-332-7204
	Laboratory Improvement Section, Division of Health Idaho Dept. of Health and Welfare 2220 Old Penitentiary Road Boise, ID 83712-8299	208-334-2235 x245 (Fax) 208-334-2382
Illinois	Office of Health Care Regulation Illinois Dept. of Public Health 525 W. Jefferson Street, 5th Floor Springfield, IL 62761	217-782-2913 (Fax) 217-524-6292
Indiana	Consumer Health Services Commission Indiana State Dept. of Health 2 North Meridian Street, Section 5A Indianapolis, IN 46204	317-233-7403 (Fax) 317-233-7750
	Health Care Regulatory Services Commission Indiana State Dept. of Health 2 North Meridian Street, Section 3B Indianapolis, IN 46204	317-233-7022

STATE	STATE SURVEY AGENCY NAME & ADDRESS	CONTACT NUMBERS
Iowa	Health Facilities Iowa Dept. of Inspections & Appeals 3rd Floor, Lucas State Office Building Des Moines, IA 50319-0083	515-281-4233 (Fax) 515-242-5022
Kansas	Bureau of Adult & Child Care Services, Division of Health Kansas Dept. of Health & Environment 900 SW Jackson, #1001, Landon State Office Building Topeka, KS 66612-1290	913-296-1240 (Fax) 913-296-1266
Kentucky	Division of Licensing & Regulation Kentucky Cabinet for Human Resources 275 E. Main Street, #4E, 4th Floor Frankfort, KY 40621-0001	502-564-2800 (Fax) 502-562-6546
Louisiana	Health Standards Section Louisiana Dept. of Health & Hospitals P.O. Box 3767 Baton Rouge, LA 70821-3767	504-342-0415 (Fax) 504-342-5292
Maine	Division of Licensing & Certification Maine Dept. of Human Services—BMS 11 State House Station, 35 Anthony Avenue Augusta, ME 04333-0011	207-624-5443 (Fax) 207-624-5378
Maryland	Licensing & Certification Administration Maryland Dept. of Health & Mental Hygiene 4201 Patterson Avenue, 4th Floor Baltimore, MD 21215	410-764-2750 (Fax) 410-358-0750
Massachusetts	Division of Health Care Quality Massachusetts Dept. of Public Health 10 West Street, 5th Floor Boston, MA 02111	617-727-1299 (Fax) 617-727-1414
Michigan	Michigan Dept. of Consumer & Industry Services Bureau of Health Systems Division of Health Facility Licensing & Certification P.O. Box 30664 G. Mennen Williams Building, 525 W. Ottawa, 5th Floor Lansing, MI 48909	517-241-2637 (Fax) 517-241-2635
Minnesota	Facility & Provider Compliance Division Minnesota Dept. of Health P.O. Box 64900 St. Paul, MN 55164-0900	612-643-2171 (Fax) 612-643-2493

STATE	STATE SURVEY AGENCY NAME & ADDRESS	CONTACT NUMBERS
Mississippi	Health Facilities Licensure & Certification Mississippi State Dept. of Health P.O. Box 1700 Jackson, MS 39215-1700	601-354-7300 (Fax) 601-354-7230
Missouri	Bureau of Hospital Licensing & Certification Missouri Dept. of Health P.O. Box 570 Jefferson City, MO 65102-0570	573-751-6302 (Fax) 573-526-3621
	Institutional Services, Division of Aging Missouri Dept. of Social Services P.O. Box 1337 Jefferson City, MO 65102-1337	573-751-3082 (Fax) 573-751-8687
Montana	Quality Assurance, Certification Bureau Montana Dept. of Health and Human Services P.O. Box 202951 Helena, MT 59620	406-444-2037 (Fax) 406-444-1742
Nebraska	Health Facility Licensure & Inspection Nebraska Dept. of Health P.O. Box 95007 Lincoln, NE 68509-5007	402-471-4961 (Fax) 402-471-0555
Nevada	Bureau of Licensure & Certification/EMS Nevada Dept. of Human Resources 1550 E. College Parkway, #158 Carson City, NV 89710	702-687-4475 (Fax) 702-687-6588
	Bureau of Licensure & Certification/EMS Nevada Dept. of Human Resources 4220 South Mary Parkway, #810 Las Vegas, NV 89119	702-486-6815 (Fax) 702-486-6520
New Hampshire	Office of Prog. Support, Licensing & Regulation Services Health Facilities Administration New Hampshire Dept. of Health & Human Services 6 Hazen Drive Concord, NH 03301-6527	603-271-4966 (Fax) 603-271-4968
New Jersey	Division of Health Facilities Evaluation & Licensing New Jersey State Dept. of Health CN 367 Trenton, NJ 08625-0367	609-588-7733 (Fax) 609-588-7823

STATE	STATE SURVEY AGENCY NAME & ADDRESS	CONTACT NUMBERS
New Mexico	Bureau of Health Facility Licensing & Certification New Mexico Dept. of Health 525 Camino de Los Marquez, #2 Santa Fe, NM 87501	505-827-4200 (Fax) 505-827-4203
New York	Bureau of Long-Term Care Services New York State Dept. of Health 99 Washington Avenue Commerce Plaza, #1126 Albany, NY 11210-2808	518-473-1564 (Fax) 518-474-2031
	Health Care Standards and Surveillance New York State Dept. of Health Hedley Park Place, 433 River Street, #303 Troy, NY 12180	518-402-1045 (Fax) 518-402-1042
	Bureau of Home Health Care Service New York State Dept. of Health Freer Building, 2 3rd Street Troy, NY 12180-3298	518-271-2741 (Fax) 518-271-2741
North Carolina	Certification Section, Division of Facility Services North Carolina Dept. of Human Resources P.O. Box 29530 Raleigh, NC 27626-0530	919-733-7461 (Fax) 919-733-8274
North Dakota	Health Resources Section, Division of Health Facilities North Dakota Dept. of Health & Consolidated Labs 600 E. Boulevard Avenue Bismarck, ND 58505-2352	701-328-2352 (Fax) 701-328-4727
Ohio	Division of Health Facilities Regulation Ohio Dept. of Health P.O. Box 118 Columbus, OH 43266-0118	614-466-7857 (Fax) 614-644-0208
Oklahoma	Special Health Services Oklahoma State Dept. of Health 1000 NE 10th Street, #1212 Oklahoma City, OK 73117-1299	405-271-5288 (Fax) 405-271-1402
Oregon	Health Care Licensure & Certification Section Oregon Health Dept. P.O. Box 14450 Portland, OR 97214-0450	503-731-4013 (Fax) 503-731-4080

STATE	STATE SURVEY AGENCY NAME & ADDRESS	CONTACT NUMBERS
	Client Care Monitoring Unit Senior & Disabled Services 500 Summer Street, 2nd Floor Salem, OR 97310-1015	503-945-5833 (Fax) 503-947-5046
Pennsylvania	Bureau of Facility Licensure & Certification Pennsylvania Dept. of Health Health and Welfare Building, #930 Harrisburg, PA 17120	717-787-8015 (Fax) 717-787-1491
Puerto Rico	Regulation & Accreditation of Health Facilities Puerto Rico Dept. of Health Ruiz Soler Former Hospital Bayamon, PR 00959	809-781-1066 (Fax) 809-782-6540
Rhode Island	Division of Facilities Regulation Rhode Island Dept. of Health 3 Capitol Hill Providence, RI 02908-5097	401-222-2566 (Fax) 401-222-3999
South Carolina	Bureau of Certification S.C. Dept. of Health & Environmental Control 2600 Bull Street Columbia, SC 29201-1708	803-737-7205 (Fax) 803-737-7292
South Dakota	Office of Health Care Facilities Licensure & Certification Health Systems Development & Regulation South Dakota Dept. of Health 615 E. 4th Street Pierre, SD 57501-5070	605-773-3356 (Fax) 605-773-6667
Tennessee	Division of Health Care Facilities Tennessee Dept. of Health Cordell Hull Building, 1st Floor 426 5th Avenue North Nashville, TN 37247-0508	615-741-7539 (Fax) 615-741-7051
Texas	Health Facility Compliance Division Texas Dept. of Health 1100 W. 49th Street Austin, TX 78756	512-834-6752 (Fax) 512-834-6653
	Long-Term Care—Regulatory Texas Dept. of Human Services Mail Code E-340, 701 W. 51st Street Austin, TX 78751	512-438-2625 (Fax) 512-438-2726

STATE	STATE SURVEY AGENCY NAME & ADDRESS	CONTACT NUMBERS
Utah	Medicare/Medicaid Prgm. Cert./Resident Assessment Division of Health Systems Improvement P.O. Box 16990 Salt Lake City, UT 84114-2905	801-538-6559 (Fax) 801-538-6163
Vermont	Division of Licensing and Protection Vermont Department of Aging & Disabilities 103 S. Main Street Waterbury, VT 05671-2306	802-241-2345 (Fax) 802-241-2358
Virginia	Center for Quality Health Care Services & Consumer Protection Virginia Dept. of Health 3600 W. Broad Street, #216 Richmond, VA 23230	804-367-2102 (Fax) 804-367-2149
Washington	Facilities & Services Licensing P.O. Box 47852 Olympia, WA 98504-7852	360-705-6651 (Fax) 360-705-6654
	Residential Care Services Washington Dept. of Social & Health Services P.O. Box 45600 Olympia, WA 98504-5600	360-493-2560 (Fax) 360-438-7903
West Virginia	Office of Health Facility Licensure & Certification West Virginia Dept. of Health and Human Resources 1900 Kanawha Boulevard East, Building 3, #550 Charleston, WV 25304	304-558-0050 (Fax) 304-558-2515
Wisconsin	Bureau of Quality Assurance Wisconsin Dept. of Health and Family Services P.O. Box 309 Madison, WI 53701-0309	608-267-7185 (Fax) 608-267-0352
Wyoming	Health Facilities Program Wyoming Dept. of Health First Bank Building, 8th Floor Cheyenne, WY 82002-0480	307-777-7121 (Fax) 307-777-5970

APPENDIX O: State Long-Term-Care Ombudsmen

Under the federal Older Americans Act, every state is required to have an ombudsman program that addresses complaints and advocates for improvements in the long-term-care system. To find the ombudsman nearest you, contact your state ombudsman office.

Alabama
Marie Tomlin
State Long-Term-Care Ombudsman
Commission on Aging
RSA Plaza, #470
770 Washington Avenue
Montgomery, AL 36130
334-242-5743
(Fax) 334-242-5594

Alaska
Suzan Armstrong
State Long-Term-Care Ombudsman
Older Alaskans Commission
3601 C Street, #260
Anchorage, AK 99503-5209
907-563-6393
(Fax) 907-561-3862

Arizona
Catherine Hannen
State Long-Term-Care Ombudsman
Aging and Adult Administration
Department of Economic Security
1789 West Jefferson—950A
Phoenix, AZ 85007
602-542-4446
(Fax) 602-542-6575

Arkansas
Alice Ahart
State Long-Term-Care Ombudsman
Arkansas Division of Aging & Adult Services
P.O. Box 1437, Slot 1412
Little Rock, AR 72201-1437
501-682-2441
(Fax) 501-682-8155

California
Phyllis Heath
State Long-Term-Care Ombudsman
1600 K Street
Sacramento, CA 95814
916-323-6681
(Fax) 916-323-7299

Colorado
Virginia Fraser
State Long-Term-Care Ombudsman
The Legal Center
455 Sherman Street, #130
Denver, CO 80203
303-722-0300
(Fax) 303-722-0720

Connecticut
Teresa Cusano
Acting State Long-Term-Care Ombudsman
Department on Aging
25 Sigourney Street, 10th Floor
Hartford, CT 06106-5033
860-424-5200 ext. 5221
(Fax) 860-424-4966

Delaware
Karen Michel
Acting State Long-Term-Care Ombudsman
Delaware Services for Aging-Disabled
Health & Social Services
Oxford Building
256 Chapman Road, #200
Newark, DE 19702
302-453-3820
(Fax) 302-453-3836

District of Columbia
Deidre Rye
State Long-Term-Care Ombudsman
AARP—Legal Counsel for the Elderly
601 E Street, NW,
4th Floor, Building A
Washington, DC 20049
202-434-2188
(Fax) 202-434-6424

Florida

Steve Rachin, Esquire
State Long-Term-Care Ombudsman
Florida State LTC
Ombudsman Council
600 South Calhoun Street, #270
Tallahassee, FL 32301
850-488-6190
(Fax) 850-488-5657

Georgia

Becky Kurtz, Esquire
State Long-Term-Care Ombudsman
Division of Aging Services
2 Peachtree Street, NW, 36th Floor, #36-385
Atlanta, GA 30303-3176
888-454-5826
(Fax) 404-463-8384

Hawaii

John McDermott
State Long-Term-Care Ombudsman
Executive Office on Aging
Office of the Governor
250 South Hotel Street, #107
Honolulu, HI 96813-2831
808-586-0100
(Fax) 808-586-0185

Idaho

Cathy Hart
State Long-Term-Care Ombudsman
Office on Aging
P.O. Box 83720
3380 American Terrace, #1
Boise, ID 83720-0007
208-334-3833
(Fax) 208-334-3033

Illinois

Beverly Rowley
State Long-Term-Care Ombudsman
Illinois Department on Aging
421 E. Capitol Avenue, #100
Springfield, IL 62701-1789
217-785-3143
(Fax) 217-785-4477

Indiana

Arlene Franklin
State Long-Term-Care Ombudsman
Indiana Division of Aging & Rehab. Services
402 W. Washington Street
Indianapolis, IN 46207-7083
317-232-1750
(Fax) 317-232-7867

Iowa

Debi Meyers
Interim State Long-Term-Care Ombudsman
Department of Elder Affairs
Clemens Building
200 10th Street, 3rd Floor
Des Moines, IA 50309-3609
515-281-8643
(Fax) 515-281-4036

Kansas

Matthew Hickam
State Long-Term-Care Ombudsman
Office of the State Long-Term-Care Ombudsman
610 SW 10th Street, 2nd Floor
Topeka, KS 66612-1616
785-296-3017
(Fax) 785-296-3916

Kentucky

Brenda Rice
State Long-Care-Ombudsman
Division of Family/Children Services
275 E. Main Street, 5th Floor
Frankfort, KY 40621
502-564-6930
(Fax) 502-564-4595

Louisiana

Linda Sadden
State Long-Term-Care Ombudsman
Louisiana Governor's Office of Elderly Affairs
412 N. 4th Street, 3rd Floor
P.O. Box 80374
Baton Rouge, LA 70802
225-342-7100
(Fax) 225-342-7144

Maine

Brenda Gallant
State Long-Term-Care Ombudsman
Maine State Long-Term-Care Ombudsman Program
1 Weston Court
P.O. Box 126
Augusta, ME 04332
207-621-1079
(Fax) 207-621-0509

Maryland

Patricia Bayliss
State Long-Term-Care Ombudsman
Office on Aging
301 West Preston Street, #1007
Baltimore, MD 21201
410-767-1074
(Fax) 410-333-7943

Massachusetts

Mary McKenna
State Long-Term-Care Ombudsman
Executive Office of Elder Affairs
1 Ashburton Place, 5th Floor
Boston, MA 02108-1518
617-727-7750
(Fax) 617-727-9368

Michigan

Nida Donar
State Long-Term-Care Ombudsman
Citizens for Better Care
6105 W. St. Joseph Highway, #211
Lansing, MI 48917-3981
517-886-6797
(Fax) 517-886-6349

Minnesota

Renee Fredricksen
Acting State Long-Term-Care Ombudsman
Office of Ombudsman for Older Minnesotans
121 East 7th Place, #410
St. Paul, MN 55101
651-296-0382
(Fax) 651-297-5654

Mississippi

Anniece McLemore
State Long-Term-Care Ombudsman
Division of Aging & Adult Services
750 North State Street
Jackson, MS 39202
601-359-4929
(Fax) 601-359-4970

Missouri

Carol Scott
State Long-Term-Care Ombudsman
Division on Aging
Department of Social Services
P.O. Box 1337
615 Howerton Court
Jefferson City, MO 65102-1337
573-526-0727
(Fax) 573-751-8687

Montana

Robert Bartholomew
State Long-Term-Care Ombudsman
Office on Aging
Department of Health & Human Services
Senior & LTC Division
P.O. Box 4210
111 Sanders
Helena, MT 59604-4210
406-444-4077
(Fax) 406-444-7743

Nebraska

Cindy Kadavy
State Long-Term-Care Ombudsman
Department on Aging
P.O. Box 95044
301 Centennial Mall South
Lincoln, NE 68509-5044
402-471-2306
(Fax) 402-471-4619

Nevada

Bruce McAnnany
State Long-Term-Care Ombudsman
Division for Aging Services
Department of Human Resources
340 North 11th Street, #203
Las Vegas, NV 89101
702-486-3545
(Fax) 702-486-3572

New Hampshire
Judith Griffin
State Long-Term-Care Ombudsman
Division of Elderly & Adult Services
129 Pleasant Street
Concord, NH 03301-3857
603-271-4375
(Fax) 603-271-4771

New Jersey
Bernadette T. Kelly
State Long-Term-Care Ombudsman for
    Institutionalized Elderly
P.O. Box 807
Trenton, NJ 08625-0807
609-588-3614
(Fax) 609-588-3365

New Mexico
Agapito Silva
State Long-Term-Care Ombudsman
State Agency on Aging
228 East Palace Avenue
Santa Fe, NM 87501
505-827-7640
(Fax) 505-827-7649

New York
Faith Fish
State Long-Term-Care Ombudsman
Office for the Aging
2 Empire State Plaza
Agency Building #2
Albany, NY 12223-0001
518-474-7329
(Fax) 518-474-7761

North Carolina
Wendy Sause
State Long-Term-Care Ombudsman
Division of Aging
693 Palmer Drive
Caller Box #29531
Raleigh, NC 27626-0531
919-733-8395
(Fax) 919-733-0443

North Dakota
Helen Funk
State Long-Term-Care Ombudsman
Aging Services Division
Department of Human Services
600 South 2nd Street, #1C
Bismarck, ND 58504
701-328-8910
(Fax) 701-328-8989

Ohio
Beverley Laubert
State Long-Term-Care Ombudsman
Department of Aging
50 West Broad Street, 9th Floor
Columbus, OH 43215-5928
614-644-7922
(Fax) 614-466-5741

Oklahoma
Esther Houser
State Long-Term-Care Ombudsman
Aging Services Division
Department of Human Services
312 NE 28th Street, #109
Oklahoma City, OK 73105
405-521-6734
(Fax) 405-521-2086

Oregon
Meredith A. Cote, Esquire
State Long-Term-Care Ombudsman
Office of the Long-Term-Care Ombudsman
3855 Wolverine NE, #6
Salem, OR 97310
503-378-6533
(Fax) 503-373-0852

Pennsylvania
Joyce O'Brien
State Long-Term-Care Ombudsman
Department of Aging
555 Walnut Street, 5th Floor
P.O. Box 1089
Harrisburg, PA 17101
717-783-7247
(Fax) 717-783-3382

Puerto Rico
Norma Venegas
State Long-Term-Care Ombudsman
Governor's Office for Elder Affairs
Call Box 50063
Old San Juan Station
San Juan, Puerto Rico 00902
787-725-1515
(Fax) 787-721-6510

Rhode Island
Roberta Hawkins
State Long-Term-Care Ombudsman
Alliance for Better Long-Term Care
422 Post Road, #204
Warwick, RI 02888
401-785-3340
(Fax) 401-785-3391

South Carolina
Jon Cook
State Long-Term-Care Ombudsman
Division on Aging
1801 Main Street
P.O. Box 8206
Columbia, SC 29202-8206
803-253-6177
(Fax) 803-253-4173

South Dakota
Jeff Askew
State Long-Term-Care Ombudsman
Office of Adult Services and Aging
700 Governors Drive
Pierre, SD 57501-2291
605-773-3656
(Fax) 605-773-6834

Tennessee
Adrian D. Wheeler
State Long-Term-Care Ombudsman
Commission on Aging
Andrew Jackson Building
500 Deaderick Street, 9th Floor
Nashville, TN 37243-0860
615-741-2056
(Fax) 615-741-3309

Texas
John Willis
State Long-Term-Care Ombudsman
Department on Aging
4900 North Lamar Boulevard, 4th Floor
P.O. Box 12786
Austin, TX 78751-2316
512-424-6840
(Fax) 512-424-6890

Utah
Chad McNiven
State Long-Term-Care Ombudsman
Division of Aging & Adult Services
Department of Social Services
120 North, 200 West, #401
Salt Lake City, UT 84103
801-538-3924
(Fax) 801-538-4395

Vermont
Jacqueline Majoros, Esquire
State Long-Term-Care Ombudsman
Vermont Legal Aid, Inc.
P.O. Box 1367
Burlington, VT 05402
802-863-5620
(Fax) 802-863-7152

Virginia
Mark Miller
State Long-Term-Care Ombudsman
Virginia Association of Area Agencies on Aging
530 East Main Street, #428
Richmond, VA 23219
804-644-2923
(Fax) 804-644-5640

Washington
Kary Hyre
State Long-Term-Care Ombudsman
South King County Multi-Service Center
1200 South 336th Street
P.O. Box 23699
Federal Way, WA 98093
253-838-6810
(Fax) 253-874-7831

West Virginia
Larry Medley
State Long-Term-Care Ombudsman
Commission on Aging
1900 Kanawha Boulevard
East Charleston, WV 25305-0160
304-558-3317
(Fax) 304-558-0004

Wisconsin
George Potaracke
State Long-Term-Care Ombudsman
Board on Aging and Long-Term Care
214 North Hamilton Street
Madison, WI 53703-2118
608-266-8945 ext. DIR
(Fax) 608-261-6570

Wyoming
Deborah Alden
State Long-Term-Care Ombudsman
Wyoming Senior Citizens, Inc.
756 Gilchrist
P.O. Box 94
Wheatland, WY 82201
307-322-5553
(Fax) 307-322-3283

APPENDIX P: Nursing Home Citizen Advocacy Groups

If you are searching for a nursing home or having difficulty with a facility your relative is already in, these groups can help.

Arkansas

Arkansas Advocates for Nursing Home Residents
9901 Satterfield Drive
Little Rock, AR 72205
Contact: Nancy Johnson
(Home) 501-884-6728
e-mail: gjohnson@artelco.com (Preferred)
e-mail: vacross@juno.com
Contact: Virginia Cross
(Home) 501-225-4082

California

Citizens Serving Long-Term-Care Residents
1212 Broadway, #606
Oakland, CA 94612-1824
Contact: Dorothy Epstein
(Work) 510-465-1065
(Fax) 510-465-1050
e-mail: acombud@sprintmail.com

Foundation Aiding the Elderly
9718 Lincoln Village Drive, #202
Sacramento, CA 95827
Contact: Carole Herman
(Work) 916-481-8558
(Fax) 916-364-0948

California Advocates for Nursing Home Reform
1610 Bush Street
San Francisco, CA 94109
Contact: Pat McGinnis
(Work) 415-474-5171
415-474-2904

Connecticut

Advocates for Loved Ones in Nursing Homes
224 Ledyard Street
New London, CT 06320
Contact: Cathy Wilson
(Work) 860-739-5859
(Home) 860-442-0101

Connecticut Citizens' Coalition for Nursing Home Reform
62 Washington Street
Middletown, CT
Contact: Jane McNichol
860-278-5688 ext. 15
e-mail: cccnhr@hotmail.com

District of Columbia

Washingtonians Improvement of Nursing Homes
4958 Brandywine Street, NW
Washington, DC 20005
Contact: Janet Wells
(Work) 202-966-7760
e-mail: weldon@erols.com

Florida

Florida Advocates for Nursing Home Improvement
P.O. Box 165
Dunedin, FL 34697-0165
Contact:
(Work) 813-734-5765
(Fax) 813-734-5765
1-888-647-3367
e-mail: fanhimg@aol.com

Quality Care Advocates, Inc.
P.O. Box 2213
Port Charlotte, FL 33949-2213
Contact: Linda Pounds
(Work) 941-743-0987
(Fax) 941-625-1964

Nursing Home Hotline Patrol
6429 Gulfport Boulevard South
St. Petersburg, FL 33707-3000
Contact: Fran Sutcliffe
(Work) 813-347-0953
(Fax) 813-347-5683

Coalition to Protect America's Elders
8094 Buck Lake Road
Tallahassee, FL 32311
Contact: Barbara Hengstebeck
(Work) 850-216-2727
(Fax) 850-216-1930
e-mail: bhengstebeck@msn.com

Illinois

Illinois Citizens for Better Care
220 South State Street, #800
Chicago, IL 60604
Contact: Wendy Meltzer
(Work) 312-663-5120

Nursing Home Monitors
6111 Vollmer Lane
Godfrey, IL 62035
Contact: Violette King
(Work) 618-466-3410
(Fax) 618-466-3410

Indiana

V.O.I.C.E.S.
P.O. Box 3208
Evansville, IN 47731
Contact: Judith G. Dockery
(Work) 812-423-2927
(Fax) 812-454-7332

United Senior Action
1920 W. Morris Street, #246
Indianapolis, IN 46221-1540
Contact: Paul Severance
(Work) 317-634-0872
(Fax) 317-687-3661
e-mail: usa.iquest.net

Kansas

Kansas Advocates for Better Care
913 Tennessee, #2
Lawrence, KS 66044-6940
Contact: Deanne Lenhart
(Work) 785-842-3088
(Fax) 785-749-0029
e-mail: dlenhart@kabc.org
website: www.kabc.org

Kentucky

Cease Abuse, Neglect, Dignify Life for the Elderly in Kentucky
16022 Ellington Run
Ashland, KY 41102-9654
Contact: Ann Earl
(Work) 606-928-6237
(Home) 606-928-6237

Louisiana

Citizens for Quality Nursing Home Care
P.O. Box 56041
New Orleans, LA 70156
Contact: Alan Pincus
(Work) 504-586-1627
(Fax) 504-586-1627
e-mail: alanspin@aol.com

Maryland

Advocates for Enhanced Long-Term Care (for Maryland)
6453 Overbrook Street
Falls Church, VA 22043
Contact: Ilene Henshaw
(Work) 703-241-8338
(Fax) 202-293-1094
e-mail: French7225@aol.com
NOTE: This is a MD org. Office is in VA.

Massachusetts

Living is for the Elderly
27 Maple Street
Arlington, MA 02476
Contact: Liane Zeitz
(Work) 781-646-1000 x4733
(Fax) 781-641-4201

Cape United Elderly
P.O. Box 954
Hyannis, MA 02601
Contact: Susan Drinan Bowes
(Work) 508-771-1727
(Fax) 508-775-7488
e-mail: cacci@cape.com

Michigan

Citizens for Better Care
4750 Woodward Avenue, #410
Detroit, MI 48201
Contact: Victor Weipert
(Work) 313-832-6387
(Fax) 313-832-7407

Action! Coalition for Improvement of Nursing Homes
P.O. Box 51463
Livonia, MI 48151-1463
Contact: Catherine Wallace
(24-hour voice mail) 248-988-7139
(Fax) 734-525-3535
e-mail: actioncoalition@ameritech.net

Voices of the Elderly
14170 Mulberry
Southgate, MI 48195
Contact: Raelene Nowak
(Work) 734-285-1507

Minnesota

Advocacy Center for Long-Term Care
2626 East 82nd Street, #220
Bloomington, MN 55425-1381
Contact: Iris C. Freeman
(Work) 612-854-7304
(Fax) 612-854-8535
e-mail: AC4LTC21CF@aol.com

Advocacy Center for Long-Term Care
221 Center Street
Mankato, MN 56001
Contact: Marie Crawford
(Work) 507-387-4234
(Fax) 507-387-4234

Missouri

Missouri Coalition for Quality Care
P.O. Box 7165
Jefferson City, MO 65102
Contact: Joanne Polowy
(Work) 573-634-8717 or 573-896-4866
(Fax) 573-635-1648
e-mail: JoPolowy@aol.com
website: www.mcqc.com

Montana

Montana Coalition for Nursing Home Reform
P.O. Box 7583
Missoula, MT 59807
Contact: Alice Campbell
(Work) 406-543-5761

Nebraska

Nebraska Advocates for Nursing Home Residents
10050 Regency Circle, #525
Omaha, NE 68114
Contact: Bill Seidler
(Work) 402-397-2801
NOTE: Main office

Nebraska Advocates for Nursing Home Residents
5315 North 105th Plaza, #5
Omaha, NE 68134
Contact: Mona G. Phelps
(Work) 402-493-8780
(Fax) 402-397-3801
e-mail: 76153.3703@compuserve.com

Nebraska Advocacy Services Inc.
522 Lincoln Center Building
215 Centennial Mall South
Lincoln, NE 68508
Contact: Eric Evans
(Work) 402-474-3183
e-mail: Nas@navix.net

New Jersey

New Jersey Coalition for Nursing Home Reform
391 Hall Court
South Orange, NJ 07079
Contact: Meyer S. Schreiber
(Work) 973-762-7955

New Mexico

New Mexicans for Quality Long-Term Care
P.O. Box 1712
Belem, NM 87002
Contact: J. C. Beverly, President
(Work) 505-864-7534
(Fax) 505-864-7534

New York

Coalition Institutionalized Aged & Disabled, Inc.
c/o Brookdale Center on Aging
425 East 25th Street, #818
New York, NY 10010
Contact: Geoff Lieberman
(Work) 212-481-4348
(Fax) 212-481-5069

Friends & Relatives of the Institutionalized Aged (FRIA)
11 John Street, #601
New York, NY 10038
Contact: Jean Murphy, Executive Director
(Work) 212-732-4455
(Fax) 212-732-6945

Nursing Home Community Coalition of N.Y. State
11 John Street, #601
New York, NY 10038
Contact: Cynthia Rudder
(Work) 212-385-0355
(Fax) 212-732-6945

North Carolina
Friends of Residents In Long-Term Care
3301 Womans Club Drive, #103
Raleigh, NC 27612
Contact: Marlene Chasson, Executive Director
(Work) 919-782-1530

Ohio
Families for Improved Care, Inc.
3440 Olentangy River Road
Columbus, OH 43202
Contact: Donald Greenberg
(Work) 614-267-0777
e-mail: msmihalov@aol.com
e-mail: LWaldman@juno.com

Oklahoma
Oklahomans for Improvement of Nursing Care Homes
1423 Oakwood Drive
P.O. Box 1551
Norman, OK 73070
Contact: Joanna Deighton
(Work) 405-364-5004
(Fax) 405-364-5004
e-mail: JADCD@aol.com

Pennsylvania
Center for Advocacy for the Rights and Interests of the Elderly
1315 Walnut Street, #1000
Philadelphia, PA 19107
Contact: Diane Menio
(Work) 215-545-5728
(Fax) 215-545-5372
e-mail: carie@libertynet.org
website: www.libertynet.org/~carie

Rhode Island
Alliance for Better Nursing Home Care
422 Post Road, #204
Warwick, RI 02888
Contact: Roberta Hawkins, Executive Director
(Work) 401-785-3340
(Fax) 401-785-3391

South Carolina
Association For Protection of the Elderly
728 A West Main, #127
Lexington, SC 29072
Contact: Judy Murphy
(Work) 803-356-6535
(Fax) 803-356-6212
e-mail: apeapel@aol.com
website: apeape.org

Tennessee
Social Action Group on Aging
P.O. Box 150752
Nashville, TN 37215-0752
Contact: Leonard Hill
615-297-2391
(Fax) 615-385-2157

Tennessee Coalition for Nursing Home Reform
c/o Joe Purcell, Council of Community Services
2012 21st Avenue South
Nashville, TN 37212
Contact: Sharon Shields
Contact: Art Williams
(Sharon) 615-343-2561
(Art) 615-228-8935

Texas
Advocates for Nursing Home Reform
16908 South Ridge Lane
Austin, TX 78734-1235
Contact: Marie B. Wisdom
(Work) 512-266-1961
(Fax) 512-266-3160
e-mail: mbwisdom@swbell.net

Nursing Home Victims Coalition
5010 North Fresco
Austin, TX 78731
Contact: Nancy McCabe
(Work) 512-453-1770
(Fax) 512-453-2499

Texas Advocates for Nursing Home Residents
4033 Congressional
Corpus Christi, TX 78413
Corpus Christi Contact: Gay Nell Harper
(Beth Ferris, Austin, TX, President)
(Work) 512-851-0351
(Fax) 512-851-0515
(Home) 512-851-0351
e-mail: sealbeem@aol.com

Texas Advocates for Nursing Home Residents
P.O. Box 763143
Dallas, TX 75376
Contact: Beth Ferris, President
(972) 572-6330 (Dallas Central Office, phone/fax)
website: www.tanhr.org
Beth Ferris, President—Austin:
500 East Anderson Lane, Apt. 234W
Austin, TX 78752
(Work/Home) 512-719-4757
(Fax) 512-719-5057
e-mail: oferris@aol.com (for Beth Ferris)
Lou O'Reilly, Founder
(Work/Home) 214-371-2942
e-mail: voreilly@swbell.net (for Lou O'Reilly)
Glenda Smelser, Vice President
(Work/Home/Fax) 972-647-2878
e-mail: smelser@swbell.net (for Glenda Smelser)

Texans For the Improvement of Long-Term Care
4545 Cook Road, #303
Houston, TX 77072-1125
Contact: Sam Perlin
(Work) 281-933-4533
(Fax) 281-498-6343
e-mail: sperlin@aol.com

United People for Better Nursing Home Care
P.O. Box 13124
Arlington, TX 76094-0124
Contact: Katherine Bates, Founder
(Work) 1-888-376-HOPE (4673)
e-mail: united@flash.net

United People for Better Nursing Home Care
P.O. Box 61009
Houston, TX 77208-0099
Contact: Robert Lampkin, President
(Work) 1-888-376-HOPE (4673)
(Fax) 817-265-1234
website: www.unitedpeople.com

Virginia
Friends and Relatives of Nursing Home Residents
1347C S. Main Street
Harrisonburg, VA 22801
Contact: Anne See
(Work) 540-433-0313
(Fax) 540-433-2202

Virginia Friends & Relatives of Nursing Home Residents
1426 Claremont Avenue
Richmond, VA 23227
Contact: Joani Latimer
(Work) 804-644-2804
(Fax) 804-644-5640

Citizens Committee to Protect the Elderly
3813 Bonney Road
Virginia Beach, VA 23452
Contact: Bernadette Ambolo
(Work) 757-498-8600
(Fax) 757-498-8774
e-mail: CCFMP@WHRO.org
website: www.communitylink.org/ccpe

Washington
Resident Councils of Washington
East 220 Canyon View Road
Belfair, WA 98528
Contact: Sharon McIntyre
(Work) 360-275-8000
(Fax) 360-275-8000
e-mail: rcwexec@aol.com

Citizens for the Improvement of Nursing Homes
4649 Sunnyside North, #100
Seattle, WA 98103-6900
Contact: Jan Kavadas, Director
(Work) 206-545-7053
(Work) 888-322-2464

Wisconsin
Citizen Advocates for Nursing Home Residents
4565 North 126th Street
P.O. Box 104
Butler, WI 53007-0104
Contact: Robert Snow
(Work) 414-783-7161
(Fax) 414-781-6565

Wyoming
Concerned Citizens for Quality Nursing Home Care
240 South Wolcott Street, #206
Casper, WY 82601
Contact: Beverly Miller
(Work) 307-266-6659

APPENDIX Q: State Hospice Agencies

To help find a hospice in your area, contact the state organization for your state.

Alabama	Alabama Hospice Organization	334-213-7944
Alaska	Hospice of Mat-Su Hospice and Home Health of Juneau	907-352-4800 907-463-3113
Arizona	Arizona Hospice Organization	602-704-0210
Arkansas	Arkansas State Hospice Association, c/o Washington Regional Hospice	501-713-7385
California	California State Hospice Association	916-441-3770
Colorado	Colorado Hospice Organization	303-449-1142
Connecticut	Hospice Council of Connecticut	860-233-2222
Delaware	Delaware Hospice, Inc.	302-478-5707
Florida	Florida Hospice and Palliative Care, Inc.	800-838-9800 850-878-2632
Georgia	Georgia Hospice Organization	770-924-6073
Hawaii	Hawaiian Islands Hospice Organization	808-924-9255
Idaho	Idaho Hospice Organization, c/o Hospice of the Wood Valley	208-726-8464
Illinois	Illinois State Hospice Organization	713-324-8844
Indiana	Indiana Hospice Organization	317-338-4049
Iowa	Iowa Hospice Organization	515-243-1040
Kansas	Association of Kansas Hospices	316-263-6380
Kentucky	Kentucky Association of Hospices	888-322-7317
Louisiana	Louisiana Hospice Organization	504-945-2414
Maine	Maine Hospice Council	207-626-0651

Maryland	Hospice Network of Maryland	410-729-4571
Massachusetts	Hospice Federation of Massachusetts	781-255-7077
Michigan	Michigan Hospice Organization	517-886-6667
Minnesota	Minnesota Hospice Organization	651-659-0423
Mississippi	Mississippi Hospice Organization	601-366-9881
Missouri	Missouri Hospice Organization, c/o Baptist Memorial Hospice	662-232-7891
Montana	Montana Hospice Organization, c/o Big Sky Hospice	406-247-3300
Nebraska	Nebraska Hospice Association	308-687-6065
Nevada	Hospice Association of Nevada	702-796-5531
New Hampshire	New Hampshire Hospice Organization	603-228-9870
New Jersey	New Jersey Hospice & Palliative Care Organization	908-233-0060
New Mexico	New Mexico & Texas Hospice Organization	512-454-1247 800-580-9270
New York	New York State Hospice Association	518-446-1483
North Carolina	Hospice for the Carolinas	919-878-1717
North Dakota	North Dakota Hospice Organization, c/o Mercy Hospice	701-774-7430
Ohio	Ohio Hospice Organization	614-274-9513
Oklahoma	Hospice Association of Oklahoma	918-835-6742 800-356-0622
Oregon	Oregon Hospice Association	503-228-2104
Pennsylvania	Pennsylvania Hospice Network	717-230-9993
Puerto Rico	Puerto Rico Home Health & Hospice Association	787-897-0503
Rhode Island	Rhode Island State Hospice Organization Hospice Care of Rhode Island	401-444-9070

South Carolina	Hospice for the Carolinas	919-878-1717
South Dakota	South Dakota Hospice Organization, c/o Sacred Heart Hospice	605-668-8327
Tennessee	Tennessee Hospice Organization	615-228-1128 800-638-6411
Texas	Texas & New Mexico Hospice Organization	512-454-1247 800-580-9270
Utah	Utah Hospice Organization	801-321-5661
Vermont	Hospice Council of Vermont	802-229-0579
Virginia	Virginia Association for Hospices	540-686-6448
Washington	Washington State Hospice Organization, c/o Hospice of Spokane	509-456-0438
West Virginia	Hospice Council of West Virginia, c/o Hospice of Huntington	304-529-4217
Wisconsin	Hospice Organization of Wisconsin	608-233-7166
Wyoming	Wyoming Hospice Organization	307-362-1990

APPENDIX R: Organ Donor Organizations

If you want to donate your organs, these organizations can tell you how to do that.

Eye Bank for Sight Restoration, Inc.
120 Wall Street
New York, NY 10005
212-742-9000

Kidney Foundation of New York, Inc.
1250 Broadway, #2001
New York, NY 10001
212-629-9770

Living Bank
P.O. Box 6725
Houston, TX 77027
713-528-2971

Massachusetts Eye & Ear Infirmary
243 Charles Street
Boston, MA 02114
617-573-3700

National Kidney Foundation
30 E. 33 Street
New York, NY 10016
212-889-2210

National Temporal Bone Bank Center
University of Minnesota Medical Center
Harvard Street at E. River Road
Minneapolis, MN 55455
612-625-8437

APPENDIX S: Ratings of Long-Term-Care Insurance Policies—Comprehensive Coverage

Listed in alphabetical order; partnership policies follow regular policies.

GUIDE TO THE RATINGS: The individual long-term-care policies with comprehensive coverage and nursing-home-only coverage offered by the companies listed below were rated in the October 1997 issue of CONSUMER REPORTS. The first four columns in the table identify these policies and the Value Index calculated for them.

Since October 1997, many companies have revised their policies and changed their premiums and/or benefits. The **Value Index** from the 1997 analysis may no longer be applicable, but it does suggest which companies may have future rate increases. The Value Index measured the cost of that policy against the average dollar benefits it would provide. Indexes between 0.8 and 1.25 were reasonable in our judgment. Those lower may suggest future price increases; those higher mean relatively high-priced coverage. If you are considering a policy offered by a company with a low value index, ask the company about rate increases in your state and in other states.

The **Replacement Policy** column identifies the policy that the company was selling as of January 1999. If that column shows "still available," the company was still selling the old policy. "No response" means that the company did not provide updated information. Some companies are no longer selling long-term-care insurance. A policy that is **Tax Qualified** meets certain standards; you should determine whether a tax quali-fied policy suits your needs (see Chapter 14).

The remaining columns describe important features of the replacement policy (or the original policy if it is still available). For **Assisted Living** and **Home Care,** the maximum daily benefit describes the maximum benefit a company will sell for those types of care; a value of 100 percent indicates how much you can buy the same daily benefit you could buy for nursing facility care. The percentage of daily charges covered indicates how much of your daily expenses can be reimbursed; 100 percent means the company covers all charges. If a range is shown, it means that the company will pay less if certain conditions are not met, for example, you did not obtain approval for the service. The **Adult Day Care** column indicates whether or not that service is a covered benefit.

Activities of Daily Living (ADLs) summarize features that determine how easy it is to qualify for benefits. See Chapter 14 for detailed expla-nations of these features. **Annual Premiums** show the cost in 1999 of a policy with lifetime coverage, $120 maximum, $120 maximum home-and community-based care benefit (if available), 90- or 100-day elimination period, and 5 percent compound inflation coverage. Those premiums give a flavor of how much you will have to pay for a good policy.

[1] Available only to specific group members
[2] Lifetime coverage not available; premiums are for the maximum benefit period available
[3] Daily benefit = $125/day
[4] Daily benefit = $122/day
[5] 30-day elimination period

Note: Companies that offer group long-term-care insurance coverage, typically through employers include: Aetna U.S. HealthCare, CALPERS (California Retirement System), Continental Casualty, and John Hancock.

The above notes also apply to Appendix T.

From 1997 Consumer Reports Ratings

Replacement Policy as of January, 1999

Company	1997 Policy Number	Tax Quali-fied	Partner-ship	Value Index	Replacement Policy Number	Tax Quali-fied	ASSISTED LIVING		HOME CARE		Adult Day Care	ACTIVITES OF DAILY LIVING (ADLs)			Medical Necessity Included?	ANNUAL PREMIUMS		
							Max Daily Benefit	% Daily Costs Covered	Max Daily Benefit	% Daily Costs Covered		Number of ADLs	Bathing (y or n)	Definition of Assistance		Age 55	Age 65	Age 75
Individual Policies																		
Aid Association for Lutherans[1]	12087 with 12088	yes		1.31	12105	yes	100%	100%	100%	100%	yes	2 of 6	yes	hands-on or standby assistance	no	$2,088	$4,176	$9,288
Allianz Life	N-2721-P	no		.62	N-3000-P(Q)	yes	100%	100%	100%	100%	yes	2 of 6	yes	hands-on or standby assistance	no	$1,580	$2,981	$8,051
Allianz Life	N-2721-P	no		.62	N-3000P(NQ)	no	100%	100%	100%	100%	yes	1 of 6 NH; 2 of 6 other	yes	standby assistance	yes	$1,580	$2,981	$8,051
Allied Life	A-5001-P	no		.70	no longer selling LTC	NA	NA	NA	NA	NA	NA	NA	NA	NA	NA	NA	NA	NA
American Independent Life	LTC-94 with HHCR-94	no		.65	no longer selling LTC	NA	NA	NA	NA	NA	NA	NA	NA	NA	NA	NA	NA	NA
American Independent Network Ins. Of NY	NYPLTC-50-AI	yes	NY	.64	still available	yes	100%	100%	50%	100%–80%	yes	2 of 6	yes	hands-on or supervision	no	$864	$1,757	$3,917
American Travellers	ATL-LTC-6	no		.84	no response	NA	NA	NA	NA	NA	NA	NA	NA	NA	NA	NA	NA	NA
Bankers Life and Casualty	GR-N105	no		.84	still available	no	0%	0%	100%	100%	yes	2 of 5	no	human assistance	yes	$1,843	$3,456	$7,070
Bankers Life and Casualty	GR-N105	no		.84	GR-N165	yes	100%	100%	100%	100%	yes	2 of 6	yes	hands-on or standby	no	$2,114	$3,779	$8,139
Bankers Life and Casualty[2]	GR-N053	no	CA	.97	GR-N090	yes	100%	100%	100%	100%	yes	2 of 6	yes	hands-on or standby	no	$1,465	$2,675	$5,748
Bankers Life and Casualty	GR-N053	no	IN	.91	GR-N090	yes	100%	100%	100%	100%	yes	2 of 6	yes	hands-on or standby	no	$2,114	$3,779	$8,139
Bankers Life and Casualty[2]	GR-N053 w/ home care	no	CT	.96	GR-N053 + 16067-(1) CT	yes	0%	0%	50%	100%	yes	2 of 6	yes	human assist or supervision	no	$1,498	$2,938	$6,192
Continental Casualty	P1-21300-A09	no		.74	P1-N0085 (PS1-NTQ)	no	100%	100%	100%	100%	yes	2 of 6	yes	standby or hands-on	yes	$1,898	$3,433	$7,874

From 1997 Consumer Reports Ratings

Replacement Policy as of January, 1999

Company	1997 Policy Number	Partnership	Tax Qualified	Value Index	Replacement Policy Number	Tax Qualified	ASSISTED LIVING		HOME CARE		Adult Day Care	ACTIVITES OF DAILY LIVING (ADLs)				ANNUAL PREMIUMS		
							Max Daily Benefit	% Daily Costs Covered	Max Daily Benefit	% Daily Costs Covered		Number of ADLs	Bathing (y or n)	Definition of Assistance	Medical Necessity Included?	Age 55	Age 65	Age 75
Continental Casualty	P1-21300-A09		no	.74	P1-N0080 (PS2-NTQ)	no	100%	80%	100%	100%–80%	yes	2 of 6	yes	standby or hands-on	yes	$1,634	$2,956	$6,503
Continental Casualty	P1-N0026-A34		yes	.74	P1-N0100 (PS1-TQ)	yes	100%	100%	100%	100%	yes	2 of 6	yes	standby or hands-on	no	$1,808	$3,270	$7,500
Continental Casualty	P1-N0022-A34		yes	.70	P1-N0100 (PS1-TQ)	yes	100%	100%	100%	100%	yes	2 of 6	yes	standby or hands-on	no	$1,808	$3,270	$7,500
Continental Casualty	P1-N0026-A34		yes	.74	P1-N0095 (PS2-TQ)	yes	100%	80%	100%	100%–80%	yes	2 of 6	yes	standby or hands-on	no	$1,557	$2,815	$6,193
Continental Casualty	P1-N0022-A34		yes	.70	P1-N0095 (PS2-TQ)	yes	100%	80%	100%	100%–80%	yes	2 of 6	yes	standby or hands-on	no	$1,557	$2,815	$6,193
Continental Casualty[2]	P1-18584-A04	CA	no	.84	still available	no	50%	100%	100%	100%–80%	yes	3 of 6 NH, 2 of 6 other	yes	physical assist or constant supervision	yes	$1,339	$2,106	$4,385
Continental Casualty	P1-N0045-A06	CT	yes	.76	still available	yes	100%	100%	100%	100%	yes	2 of 6	yes	substantial assistance	no	$1,610	$2,910	$6,656
Continental Casualty	P1-N0045-A13 (ILTCP)	IN	yes	.76	still available	yes	100%	100%	100%	100%	yes	2 of 5	yes	substantial assistance	no	$1,610	$2,910	$6,656
Continental General	420 with HC/CC	IN	no	.67	still available	no	100%	80%	100%	100%–80%	yes	2 of 5	yes	assistance	yes	$1,350	$2,664	$6,142
Continental General	440 w/ rider		yes	.79	still available	yes	100%	100%	100%	100%–80%	yes	2 of 6	yes	substantial assistance	no	$1,440	$2,753	$6,142
Continental General[3]	414	IN	no	.61	product being updated; still available	no	0%	0%	50%	100%	yes	2 of 5	yes	standby, set up, or perform	yes	$705	$1,692	$4,642
Equitable Life & Casualty	2002+ non Qual		no	.67	still available	no	100%	100%	100%	100%	yes	2 of 6	yes	active assistance	yes	$1,740	$2,149	$4,923
Equitable Life & Casualty	2002+ Tax Qual		yes	.73	still available	yes	100%	100%	100%	100%	yes	2 of 6	yes	substantial assistance	no	$1,740	$2,149	$4,923
Federal Home Life	FQLTC96 + FHHCC96		yes	1.09	no response	NA	NA	NA	NA	NA	NA	NA	NA	NA	NA	NA	NA	NA

Company	Policy Form	State		Ratio	Alt. Form							ADLs		Benefit Trigger		Annual Premium (age 50)	(age 65)	(age 79)
Finger Lakes (BC Rochester)	LTC-CD8		yes	1.14	LTC-CD10	yes	80%	100%	100%	100%	yes	2 of 6	yes	substantial assistance	no	$1,948	$2,938	$6,049
Finger Lakes (BC Rochester)[2]	LTC-RWJ-143-CD6	NY	no	.56	LTC-143-CD6-NY	yes	50%	100%	50%	100%	yes	2 of 6	yes	substantial assistance	no	$900	$1,416	$3,588
Fortis Long-Term Care	4073		no	.59	6073	no	100%	100%	100%	100%	yes	2 of 6	yes	hands-on or standby	yes	$1,620	$2,940	$7,140
Fortis Long-Term Care	4072		no	.49	6072	no	80%	100%	80%	100%	yes	2 of 6	yes	hands-on or standby	yes	$1,452	$2,568	$5,976
Fortis Long-Term Care	4063 (not rated in '97)		yes	NA	6063	yes	100%	100%	100%	100%	yes	2 of 6	yes	hands-on or standby	no	$1,476	$2,676	$6,492
Fortis Long-Term Care	4062		yes	.50	6062	yes	80%	100%	80%	100%	yes	2 of 6	yes	hands-on or standby	no	$1,320	$2,328	$5,436
GE Capital	7020		no	.75	7030	yes	100%	100%	100%	100%—80%	yes	2 of 6	yes	hands-on or standby	no	$1,860	$3,504	$8,172
GE Capital	7020 Tax Qual		yes	.75	7030	yes	100%	100%	100%	100%—80%	yes	2 of 6	yes	hands-on or standby	no	$1,860	$3,504	$8,172
GE Capital	7011	CA	no	.84	7011-A	yes	100%	100%	100%	100%	yes	2 of 6	yes	hands-on or standby	no	$2,088	$3,924	$9,156
GE Capital	5024B with rider	CT	no	1.00	7033	yes	100%	100%	100%	100%—80%	yes	2 of 6	yes	hands-on or standby	no	$1,860	$3,504	$8,172
GE Capital	50024A	IN	no	.70	50024-D-7030AP	yes	100%	100%	100%	100%—80%	yes	2 of 6	yes	hands-on or standby	no	$1,860	$3,504	$8,172
GE Capital[2]	51001	NY	yes	.79	new version pending	yes	NA	NA	NA	NA	NA	NA	NA	NA	NA	NA	NA	NA
Great Republic[2]	UW-IND-100-96		no	1.39	still available	no	100%	100%	100%	100%	yes	3 of 6	yes	hands-on or verbal cuing	no	$2,172	$3,840	$8,004
Harvest Life	HQLTC96 + HHHCC96		yes	1.09	no response	NA	NA	NA	NA	NA	NA	NA	NA	NA	NA	NA	NA	NA
IDS Life	30160A		yes	.73	still available	yes	100%	100%	100%	100%—80%	yes	2 of 5	no	hands-on or standby	no	$1,896	$3,120	$6,768
John Alden	J-5875-P w/ indemnity HCBC		no	.81	J-5875-P(Q) w/J-5875-R2(Q)	yes	100%	100%	100%	100%	yes	2 of 6	yes	substantial assistance	no	$1,663	$3,208	$8,073
John Alden	J-5875-P w/ indemnity HCBC		no	.81	J-5875-P(NQ) w/J-5875-R2	no	100%	100%	100%	100%	yes	2 of 5	yes	supervision or direct assistance	yes	$1,663	$3,208	$8,073

From 1997 Consumer Reports Ratings

Replacement Policy as of January, 1999

Company	1997 Policy Number	Partner-ship	Tax Quali-fied	Value Index	Replacement Policy Number	Tax Quali-fied	ASSISTED LIVING		HOME CARE		Adult Day Care	ACTIVITES OF DAILY LIVING (ADLs)			Medical Necessity Included?	ANNUAL PREMIUMS		
							Max Daily Benefit	% Daily Costs Covered	Max Daily Benefit	% Daily Costs Covered		Number of ADLs	Bathing (y or n)	Definition of Assistance		Age 55	Age 65	Age 75
John Alden	J-5875-P w/ reimbursement HCBC		no	.81	J-5875-P(Q) w/J-5875-R1(Q)	yes	100%	80%	100%	100%–80%	yes	2 of 6	yes	substantial assistance	no	$1,497	$2,887	$7,266
John Alden	J-5875-P w/ reimbursement HCBC		no	.81	J-5875P(NQ) w/J-5875-R1	no	100%	80%	100%	100%–80%	yes	2 of 5	yes	supervision or direct assistance	yes	$1,497	$2,887	$7,266
John Hancock[2]	LTC-CT-91-RWJ 9/94	CT	no	1.37	LTC-96RWJ CT 1/97	yes	80%	100%	80%	100%	yes	2 of 6	yes	hands-on or standby > half time	no	$1,332	$2,316	$5,784
John Hancock[2]	LTC-NY-91-RWJ 3/95	NY	no	1.26	LTC-96RWJ2 NY 9/97	yes	100%	100%	100%	100%	yes	2 of 6	yes	hands-on or standby > half time	no	$1,164	$1,860	$4,116
John Hancock[2]	LTC-NY-91-RWJ 3/95	NY	no	1.26	LTC-96RWJ3 NY 9/97	yes	100%	100%	100%	100%	yes	3 of 6	yes	hands-on or standby > half time	no	$1,092	$1,752	$3,864
John Hancock	LTC96		yes	.91	not replaced, some changes	yes	100%	100%	100%	100%	yes	2 of 6	yes	hands-on or standby > half time	no	$1,716	$3,024	$6,636
John Hancock	LTC-96CL 9/96		yes	1.21	Available in most states, but not actively marketed	NA	NA	NA	NA	NA	NA	NA	NA	NA	NA	NA	NA	NA
John Hancock	NA		NA		LTC-TQ CA 3/98 (not a ptnrshp plan)	yes	100%	100%	100%	100%	yes	2 of 6	yes	hands-on or standby > half time	no	$1,764	$3,216	$7,956
John Hancock	NA		NA		LTC-NTQ CA 3/98 (not a ptnrshp plan)	no	100%	100%	100%	100%	yes	2 of 7	yes	human assist or continual supervision	no	$1,940	$3,538	$8,752
John Hancock	NA	IN	NA		LTC-98RWJ IN 4/98	yes	100%	100%	100%	100%	yes	2 of 6	yes	hands-on or standby majority of time	no	$1,716	$3,024	$6,636

Company	Policy form			State	Status							ADLs		Type of assistance				
Kanawha Insurance	80650 1/97 with 80660	yes	.48		does not want to participate	NA	NA	NA	NA	NA	NA	NA	NA	NA	NA	NA	NA	NA
Lutheran Brotherhood	H3-NC-LTCC-1(97)	yes	.80		still available	yes	100%	80%	100%	100%–80%	yes	2 of 6	yes	hands-on	no	$1,416	$2,844	$5,964
MedAmerica (BC Rochester)	LTC-CD9-MA	yes	.93		still available	yes	80%	100%	100%	100%	yes	2 of 6	yes	substantial assistance	no	$1,948	$2,938	$6,049
MedAmerica (BC Rochester)	NA		NA		LTQ-11-339-MA-XX-998	yes	100%	100%	100%	100%	yes	2 of 6	yes	hands-on or standby	no	$1,919	$3,257	$6,504
MedAmerica (BC Rochester)	NA		NA		LTC-11-339-MA-XX-998	no	100%	100%	100%	100%	yes	2 of 6	yes	hands-on or standby	no	$2,116	$3,582	$7,154
Metropolitan/AARP[5]	Group G.LTC 1497	yes	.85		still available	yes	100%	100%	80%	100%	yes	2 of 6	yes	substantial assistance	no	$2,511	$4,095	$7,612
New York Life	ILTC-4300	yes	1.13		still available	yes	100%	100%	100%	100%	no	2 of 5	yes	substantial assistance	no	$2,163	$3,665	$7,802
New York Life[2]	21156	no	1.12	CA	still available	no	50%	100%	50%	100%	yes	3 of 6 NF, 2 of 6 other	yes	physical assist or constant supervision	yes	$1,878	$2,869	$5,902
New York Life	21126 with 21127	no	1.67	CT	no longer available	NA	NA	NA	NA	NA	NA	NA	NA	NA	NA	NA	NA	NA
New York Life[2]	Long-Term Care 21050RWJ	no	1.37	NY	still available	no	0%	0%	50%	100%	yes	3 of 6	yes	continual one-to-one	no	$1,905	$3,482	$6,981
Penn Treaty Network America	PF2600-P & PF2600-N	no	.58, .49		PF2600-2	no	100%	100%	80%–100%	80%–100%	yes	1 of 7 (or 2 IADLs)	yes	hands-on or standby	yes	$1,728	$3,061	$6,864
Penn Treaty Network America	NA		NA		PF2600-2-TQ	yes	100%	100%	80%–100%	80%–100%	yes	2 of 6	yes	hands-on or standby	no	$1,681	2,978	$6,680
Network America	AP93-(IN)-N	no	1.15	IN	still available	no	0%	0%	50%	100%	yes	2 of 5	yes	continual help or oversight	yes	$1,358	$2,987	$6,675
Physicians Mutual	P124	no	.47		P131	no	100%	100%	100%	100%	yes	1 of 6	yes	human assistance or continual supervision	no	$1,611	$2,934	$7,489
Physicians Mutual	NA		NA		P130	yes	80%	100%	50%	100%	yes	2 of 6	yes	substantial assistance	no	$1,402	$2,551	$6,516
Standard Life and Accident	NA		NA		1272	yes	80%	100%	80%–100%	80%–100%	yes	2 of 6	yes	hands-on	no	$2,232	$3,792	$7,020

From 1997 Consumer Reports Ratings

Replacement Policy as of January, 1999

Company	1997 Policy Number	Partnership	Tax Qualified	Value Index	Replacement Policy Number	Tax Qualified	ASSISTED LIVING		HOME CARE		Adult Day Care	ACTIVITES OF DAILY LIVING (ADLs)				ANNUAL PREMIUMS		
							Max Daily Benefit	% Daily Costs Covered	Max Daily Benefit	% Daily Costs Covered		Number of ADLs	Bathing (y or n)	Definition of Assistance	Medical Necessity Included?	Age 55	Age 65	Age 75
Standard Life and Accident	NA			NA	1271	no	80%	100%	80%-100%	80%-100%	yes	2 of 6	yes	hands-on	yes	$2,316	$3,984	$7,380
The Travelers	H-LTC3JQ2		yes	.68	H-LTC4JQ	yes	100%	100%	100%	100%	yes	2 of 6	yes	hands-on or standby	no	$1,944	3,396	$8,004
The Travelers	H-LC3JQ	CT	yes	.80	H-LC4JQ(CT)	yes	100%	100%	100%	100%	yes	2 of 6	yes	hands-on or standby	no	$1,944	$3,396	$8,004
The Travelers	NA	IN		NA	HLC4JQIN	yes	100%	100%	100%	100%	yes	2 of 6	yes	hands-on or standby	no	$1,944	$3,396	$8,004
The Travelers	H-NYLCJQ	NY	yes	.75	H-LC4JQ	yes	100%	100%	100%	100%	yes	2 of 6	yes	hands-on or standby	no	$1,920	$3,360	$7,920
TIAA[1]	LTC-02 Ed. 11-91		no	1.02	will not be available		NA	NA	NA	NA	NA	NA	NA	NA	NA	NA	NA	NA
TIAA[1,4]	TQ LTC.02 Ed 11-91 with LTC-Q-NY.01		yes	.92	LTC.03	yes	100%	100%	100%	100%	yes	2 of 6	yes	standby	no	$1,728	$2,340	$3,984
TIAA[1,4]	RWJ01.Ed 2-93	NY	no	.94	still available	no	0%	0%	50%	100%	yes	3 of 6 NH, 2 of 6 other	yes	active one-to-one assistance	no	$1,718	$2,457	$4,126
Transamerica Occidental	LTC 124-197		yes	.59	still available	yes	100%	100%	100%	100%	yes	2 of 6	yes	standby	no	$1,546	$3,047	$7,021
Transamerica Occidental	LTC-102-06-194	CA	no	.89	LTC-112-197-CA	yes	100%	100%	100%	100%	yes	2 of 6	yes	hands-on or standby	no	$1,766	$3,323	$7,662
United Security Assurance	LTC-95P w/HHC 95-LTC		no	1.06	TQLTC-97 + LTC-HHC	yes	0%	0%	100%	100%	yes	2 of 6	yes	substantial assistance	no	$1,999	$3,131	$6,824
UNUM	LTC94 + Total Home Care		yes	1.07	still available	yes	100%	100%	100%	100%	yes	2 of 6	yes	standby	no	$3,451	$6,293	$12,077
UNUM	LTC94 + Professional Home Care		yes	.70	still available	yes	100%	100%	100%	100%	yes	2 of 6	yes	standby	no	$1,663	$2,900	$6,394

APPENDIX T: Ratings of Long-Term-Care Insurance Policies—Nursing Home Coverage Only

From 1997 Consumer Reports Ratings

Replacement Policy as of January, 1999

Individual Policies

Company	1997 Policy Number	Partnership	Tax Qualified	Value Index	Replacement Policy Number	Tax Qualified	ASSISTED LIVING Max Daily Benefit	ASSISTED LIVING % Daily Costs Covered	HOME CARE Max Daily Benefit	HOME CARE % Daily Costs Covered	HOME CARE Adult Day Care	Number of ADLs	Bathing (y or n)	Definition of Assistance	Medical Necessity Included?	Age 55	Age 65	Age 75
Aid Association for Lutherans[1]	12087		yes	1.13	12106	yes	100%	100%	NA	NA	no	2 of 6	yes	hands-on or standby	no	$1,464	$2,784	$6,216
Allianz Life	N-2720-P		no	.67	N-3000-P(Q)	yes	100%	100%	NA	NA	no	2 of 6	yes	hands-on or standby assistance	no	$1,053	$1,987	$5,368
Allianz Life	N-2720-P		no	.67	N-3000-P(NQ)	no	100%	100%	NA	NA	no	1 of 6 NH; 2 of 6 other	yes	standby assistance	yes	$1,053	$1,987	$5,368
Allied Life	A-5000-P		no	.83	no longer selling LTC	NA	NA	NA	NA	NA	NA	NA	NA	NA	NA	NA	NA	NA
American Independent Life	LTC-94		no	.66	no longer selling LTC	NA	NA	NA	NA	NA	NA	NA	NA	NA	NA	NA	NA	NA
American Travellers	ATL-LTC-1		no	1.25	no response	NA	NA	NA	NA	NA	NA	NA	NA	NA	NA	NA	NA	NA
Bankers Life and Casualty	GR-N045	CA	no	1.29	GR-N094 w/100% Residential Care	yes	100%	100%	NA	NA	no	2 of 6	yes	standby or hands-on	no	$942	$1,896	$4,502
Bankers Life and Casualty	GR-N045	IN	no	1.02	GR-N094	yes	100%	100%	NA	NA	no	2 of 6	yes	hands-on or standby	no	$1,359	$3,193	$6,434
Bankers Life and Casualty	GR-N100		no	.98	still available	no	0%	0%	NA	NA	no	2 of 5	no	human assistance	yes	$1,238	$2,621	$6,048
Bankers Life and Casualty	GR-N100		no	.98	GR-N160	yes	100%	100%	NA	NA	no	2 of 6	yes	hands-on or standby	no	$1,359	$2,713	$6,434
Bankers Life and Casualty[2]	GR-N053	CT	no	1.14	GRN053 + 16067-(1) CT	yes	0%	0%	NA	NA	no	2 of 6	yes	human assist or supervision	no	$1,080	$2,333	$5,558
Continental Casualty	P1-21305-A09		no	.66	P1-N0075 (PS3-NTQ)	no	100%	80%	NA	NA	no	2 of 6	yes	hands-on or standby	yes	$1,126	$2,196	$4,876

From 1997 Consumer Reports Ratings

Replacement Policy as of January, 1999

Company	1997 Policy Number	Partnership	Tax Qualified	Value Index	Replacement Policy Number	Tax Qualified	ASSISTED LIVING		HOME CARE			Number of ADLs	Bathing (y or n)	Definition of Assistance	Medical Necessity Included?	ANNUAL PREMIUMS		
							Max Daily Benefit	% Daily Costs Covered	Max Daily Benefit	% Daily Costs Covered	Adult Day Care					Age 55	Age 65	Age 75
Continental Casualty	P1-N0030-A34		yes	.84	P1-N0090 (PS3-TQ)	yes	100%	80%	NA	NA	no	2 of 6	yes	hands-on or standby	no	$1,104	$2,153	$4,780
Continental Casualty[2]	P1-20638-A04	CA	no	1.13	still available	no	50%	100%	NA	NA	no	3 of 6	yes	physical assist or constant supervision	yes	$1,080	$1,804	$3,802
Continental Casualty	P1-N0049-A13 (ILTCP)	IN	yes	.95	still available	yes	100%	80%	NA	NA	no	2 of 5	yes	substantial assistance	no	$991	$1,889	$4,242
Continental General	420		no	.79	still available	no	100%	80%	NA	NA	no	2 of 5	yes	assistance	yes	$738	$1,656	$4,193
Continental General	440		yes	.90	still available	yes	100%	100%	NA	NA	no	2 of 6	yes	substantial assistance	no	$787	$1,711	$4,193
Equitable Life & Casualty	2002 non Qual		no	.75	still available	no	100%	100%	NA	NA	no	2 of 6	yes	active assistance	yes	$1,152	$1,490	$3,304
Equitable Life & Casualty	2002 Tax Qual		yes	.84	still available	yes	100%	100%	NA	NA	no	2 of 6	yes	substantial assistance	no	$1,152	$1,490	$3,304
Federal Home Life	FQLTC96		yes	1.35	no response	NA	NA	NA	NA	NA	NA	NA	NA	NA	NA	NA	NA	NA
Finger Lakes (BC Rochester)	LTC-143-LBP8-NY		yes	1.00	LTC-143-LBP10-NY	yes	80%	100%	NA	NA	no	2 of 6	yes	substantial assistance	no	$1,153	$2,203	$4,682
Fortis Long-Term Care	4060		yes	.60	6060	yes	100%	100%	NA	NA	no	2 of 6	yes	hands-on or standby	no	$1,008	$1,896	$4,344
GE Capital	7021		yes	.87	7032	yes	100%	100%	NA	NA	no	2 of 6	yes	hands-on or standby	no	$1,164	$3,144	$6,804
GE Capital	7021		no	.81	7032	yes	100%	100%	NA	NA	no	2 of 6	yes	hands-on or standby	no	$1,164	$3,144	$6,804
GE Capital	7012	CA	no	.96	7012-A	yes	100%	100%	NA	NA	no	3 of 6	yes	hands-on or standby	no	$1,248	$3,372	$7,284
GE Capital	500248B	CT	no	.95	no longer available	NA	NA	NA	NA	NA	NA	NA	NA	NA	NA	NA	NA	NA
GE Capital	NA in 1997	IN		NA	7032 AK	yes	100%	100%	NA	NA	no	2 of 6	yes	hands-on or standby	no	$1,164	$3,144	$6,804

Great Republic[2]	UW-LTC-100-96	no	1.15	still available	no	0%	0%	NA	NA	no	3 of 6	yes	hands-on or verbal cuing	no	NA	$1,248	$3,720
Harvest Life	HQLTC96	yes	1.35	no response	NA	NA	NA	NA	NA	NA	NA	NA	NA	NA	NA	NA	NA
IDS Life	30225	yes	.88	still available	yes	60%	100%	NA	NA	NA	2 of 5	no	substantial assistance	no	$1,224	$2,088	$4,584
John Alden	J-5875-P with ALF rider	no	.93	J-5875-P(Q) w/ ALF rider	yes	100%	100%	NA	NA	no	2 of 6	yes	substantial assistance	no	$948	$1,828	$4,602
John Alden	J-5875-P with ALF rider	no	.93	J-5875-P(NQ) w/ALF rider	no	100%	100%	NA	NA	no	2 of 5	yes	supervision or direct assistance	yes	$948	$1,828	$4,602
John Alden	J-5875-P	no	.86	J-5875-P(Q)	yes	0%	0%	NA	NA	no	2 of 6	yes	substantial assistance	no	$832	$1,604	$4,037
John Alden	J-5875-P	no	.86	J-5875-P(NQ)	no	0%	0%	NA	NA	no	2 of 5	yes	supervision or direct assistance	yes	$832	$1,604	$4,037
John Hancock	NH-CT-91- RWJ 9/94 — CT	no	1.65	LTC-96RWJ CT 1/97 (Comprehensive)	NA	NA	NA	NA	NA	NA	NA	NA	NA	NA	NA	NA	NA
Kanawha Insurance	80650	yes	.67	does not want to participate	NA	NA	NA	NA	NA	NA	NA	NA	NA	NA	NA	NA	NA
Lutheran Brotherhood	H3-NN-LTCN-1(97)	yes	.87	still available	yes	100%	80%	NA	NA	no	2 of 6	yes	hands-on	no	$912	$2,580	$5,676
MedAmerica (BC Rochester)	LTC-LBP9-MA	yes	1.13	still available	yes	80%	100%	NA	NA	no	2 of 6	yes	substantial assistance	no	$1,153	$2,203	$4,682
MedAmerica (BC Rochester)	NA		NA	NTQ11-337- MA-XX-998	yes	100%	100%	NA	NA	no	2 of 6	yes	hands-on or standby	no	$1,437	$2,509	$5,136
MedAmerica (BC Rochester)	NA		NA	NFC11-340- MA-XX-998	no	100%	100%	NA	NA	no	2 of 6	yes	hands-on or standby	no	$1,584	$2,765	$5,648
Metropolitan/AARP[5]	Group G.LTC 1797	yes	1.05	still available	yes	100%	100%	NA	NA	no	2 of 6	yes	substantial assistance	no	$1,472	$2,627	$5,132
New York Life	INH-4300	yes	1.13	still available	yes	100%	100%	NA	NA	no	2 of 5	no	substantial assistance	no	$1,341	$2,312	$4,807
New York Life[2]	21157 — CA	no	1.37	still available	no	50%	100%	NA	NA	no	3 of 6	yes	physical assist or constant supervision	yes	$1,427	$2,242	$4,684

From 1997 Consumer Reports Ratings

Replacement Policy as of January, 1999

Company	1997 Policy Number	Partnership	Tax Qualified	Value Index	Replacement Policy Number	Tax Qualified	ASSISTED LIVING Max Daily Benefit	ASSISTED LIVING % Daily Costs Covered	HOME CARE Max Daily Benefit	HOME CARE % Daily Costs Covered	Adult Day Care	ACTIVITES OF DAILY LIVING (ADLs) Number of ADLs	Bathing (y or n)	Definition of Assistance	Medical Necessity Included?	ANNUAL PREMIUMS Age 55	Age 65	Age 75
New York Life	21126	CT	no	1.47	no longer available	NA	NA	NA	NA	NA	NA	NA	NA	NA	NA	NA	NA	NA
Penn Treaty Network America	P2400 & N2400		no	.77 & .64	ALP	no	100%	100%	NA	NA	yes	2 of 7	yes	hands-on or standby	yes	$1,990	$5,043	$11,388
Penn Treaty Network America	NA		yes	NA	ALP-TQ	yes	100%	100%	NA	NA	yes	2 of 6	yes	hands-on or standby	no	$1,082	$1,901	$4,177
Network America	AP93NF(IN)-N	IN	no	1.14	still available	no	50%	100%	NA	NA	no	2 of 5	yes	continual help or oversight	yes	$834	$1,998	$4,811
Standard Life and Accident	1270-796		no	1.22	still available	no	0%	0%	NA	NA	no	2 of 5	no	hands-on	yes	$1,536	$2,364	$4,884
Standard Life and Accident	1270-796		no	1.22	1270Q-796	yes	50%	100%	NA	NA	no	2 of 6	yes	hands-on	no	$1,536	$2,364	$4,884
The Travelers	H-LTC3JFQ		yes	.77	H-LTC4JFQ	yes	100%	100%	NA	NA	no	2 of 6	yes	hands-on or standby	no	$1,356	$2,376	$5,472
Transamerica Occidental	LTC-124-197		yes	.72	still available	yes	100%	100%	NA	NA	no	2 of 6	yes	standby	no	$1,020	$2,328	$5,196
Transamerica Occidental	LTC-103-06-194	CA	no	1.11	LTC-113-197-CA	yes	100%	100%	NA	NA	no	2 of 6	yes	hands-on or standby	no	$1,080	$2,352	$5,244
United Security Assurance	LTC-95P		no	.82	TQLTC-97	yes	0%	0%	NA	NA	yes	2 of 6	yes	substantial assistance	no	$1,479	$2,081	$4,529
UNUM	LTC94		yes	1.05	still available	yes	60%	100%	NA	NA	no	2 of 6	yes	standby	no	$1,085	$2,256	$5,182

About the Author

TRUDY LIEBERMAN, a journalist for more than thirty years, is director of the Center for Consumer Health Choices at Consumers Union. She is one of the country's leading reporters covering health care and health policy and is an expert on problems faced by the elderly. She has won two National Magazine awards and ten National Press Club awards for her work. She lives in New York City.